THE BEST VERSED MAN IN LAW

Duncan Wellington Perley
and Law's Fate on the Far Western Frontier

Rex Grady

2022
Lilburne & Company, LLC
Santa Rosa

Lilburne & Company, LLC
Santa Rosa, CA
lilburneandcompany@gmail.com

Cover: *What an Unbranded Cow has Cost*, by Frederic Remington, 1895 ([PD-US-expried][PD-Art])

The Best Versed Man in Law: Duncan Wellington Perley and Law's Fate on the Far Western Frontier/Rex Grady—First Edition
ISBN 978-0-578-30052-8

To Becky

Duncan Wellington Perley (1817-1874), c. 1864

TABLE OF CONTENTS

PREFACE

In the writing of the history of American law, the historian tends to concentrate on the great moments that define the law's retreat or advance, the lives of the lawmakers and of the judges who crafted and weighed the meaning of the law, who issued sweeping rulings transforming the nation and setting it along entirely new courses, and so influencing the thoughts and habits of the people that the nation they subsequently inhabit bears little resemblance to its younger incarnation. Much has been written of the principal framers of our higher law, the Constitution and the notable judges of whom a few idolizing authors have been tempted to say defined the nation itself. The work product of historians in this genre appears at times to fall into cliché. The fact that a biography of a lawmaker or judge was written in the past recommends the undertaking of yet another biography of the same personage in the present. For the more significant figures, whose place in history is without dispute, and for whom large caches of organized and curated documentary evidence is extant, revision provides some opportunity for new insights and recovery perhaps of unknown incidents of minor or even major consequence in the life of the subject, bearing in some way on the larger tale of the great man's significance in the story of law and the civilization it governs.

Occasionally, the biography of the previously biographed is a product of intellectual lethargy, or rather more cynically, the knowledge that what is known already will be more readily consumed by readers than what is unknown. The larger the biographer's subject looms in our history, the more likely will be the retreading of their story. John Marshall has generated numerous biographies, some nearly as great as he, but others not so much, and some not worth the reader's time. The most dependable figure for reconsideration is Oliver Wendel Holmes, whose reputation as a progressive—mostly undeserved—adds to the attraction for many writers seeking attention in an academic world dominated and at times distorted by overtly progressive impulses. Anyone seeking to make a name for themselves, to appear important or relevant, is likely tempted to recapitulate the life of that great judge, repeating the oft told stories of his heroics in war and his much-lauded liberal opinions favoring regulation over liberty and the promotion of speech contrary to conservative norms embedded in governing institutions.

Such biographies are of use, particularly the better ones by such luminaries as G. Edward White and R. Kent Newmyer; and even the lesser ones tend to claim some public attention so as to inform new readers of old truths that might otherwise be forgotten. And yet the imbalance of attention paid to the great names in the law distracts readers and scholars alike from a vast body of fact, fascinating in depth and breadth, replete with drama and heroics, dismal expressions of humanity, and triumphs as significant in the lives of reputedly lesser individuals as the great events on the national and world stage are to the fate of nations. Among those neglected in the telling of tales are the lesser known judges at the State level and in the federal district and circuit courts, and the lawyers who brought cases great and small to trial in the far flung reaches of the North American continent, who challenged judges and juries to apply the facts and law to the unique situations presented in particular controversies with all the learning and passion at their disposal.

We know the law to be inherently dramatic. It becomes the measure by which we determine the rightness and wrongness of human action, and the crux on which turn the fortunes of those in dispute over life, liberty and property. From these disputes, in the aggregate, come the currents on which our world floats, influencing our people in ways we cannot clearly track, so complex is the interplay of so many variables and so inadequate our individual minds to grasp it. In ignoring the less known stories beneath the surface of the well-trodden path, the historian of the law ignores law and history both, and perpetuates an inadequate vision of our world.

Our nation is said to be a litigious one. It is, and always has been, and not because of some flaw in our national make up, but because our people have always valued, *or struggled to value,* justice and the rights belonging to every man and woman, and never more so than today. We litigate because justice demands it, because those who are injured must be made whole, and those responsible for injury must be made to do right, whether by yielding up restitution, paying damages, or even bearing the terrible burden of a criminal punishment. And when there is no justice in the cause of those seeking relief, we litigate to defend ourselves from false and misplaced accusations and to vindicate our good names in the view of our neighbors. No society that values freedom discounts the ability of a people to assert their rights in the ordered process of litigation. Any society that would condemn it is unfit to be called free.

The subject of this story, Duncan Wellington Perley, is one of the many men inspired over the course of the past several centuries on the North American continent by the dream of the law, the prestige of the lawyer, and the promise of material success and fame that comes with triumph in so public a forum as the courthouse. If he is known at all today it is only as a footnote in the life of one of the Chief Justices of California, for his role in contributing to a fatal duel fought between that man and a member of the United States Senate. His notoriety in his lifetime, however, was widespread, and his actions often generated controversy and strong opinions. The journalist James O'Meara said he was "a smart, active, able and not very scrupulous attorney" who didn't enjoy "a very reputable name in the community."[1] The attorney George T. Mayre called him "a very good all-around lawyer…who certainly was not wanting in a sufficiently high estimate of his own powers."[2] The first historian of the California Bar, Oscar Shuck, referred to him as "erratic," alluded to the many "ludicrous, pathetic and serio-comedic" events in his life, and described his existence as generally "strange."[3] Nevada Attorney General John R. Kittrell simply said that the man, for all of his faults, was a "genius."[4]

---

[1] James O'Meara, *Broderick and Gwin* (San Francisco: Bacon & Company, 1881), at p. 220.

[2] George Thomas Marye, *From '49 to '83 in California and Nevada* (San Francisco: A.M. Robertson, 1923), pp. 140-141.

[3] Oscar T. Shuck, *History of the Bench and Bar of California* (Los Angeles: The Commercial Printing House, 1901), at p. 384.

[4] John R. Kittrell, "A Sketch From Memory: General John R. Kittrell Gives the Readers of the 'Gazette' a Chapter on the Brainy Men of Nevada in the Long Past," *Reno Gazette-Journal*, March 24, 1896.

Perley never served on the Supreme Court of any State, nor in any legislative body. His true significance was as a lawyer born in the east, but drawn ever westward until he reached the American frontier in the years prior to the Civil War. He was, like many Americans then and now, an immigrant who fled a restrictive society to find liberty in an environment that welcomed and encouraged entrepreneurs of all kinds, including those pursuing the business of law. His remarkable skills and personality allowed him to form friendships with some of the most prominent people on the frontier, indeed in American and Western history, and his personal narrative, to the extent that it is recoverable, is nearly as interesting as his thirty-year long professional practice. His life was adventurous and the proper subject of romance. He crossed the desert with a body of companions, fighting still unvanquished Indians and avoiding death through starvation, thirst and exposure, engaged in duels and fistfights, opposed the lawlessness of the mining camp and boom town by defending those accused of robbery and murder and facing down lynch mobs while doing so. His association with politically prominent men hailing from the American South gave him entry to a world of litigation involving their interests, and for a time he served as legal counsel for a political party that ruled California for two eventful years in the mid-1850s, representing key figures in the government, and even defending the accused successfully in the first impeachment trial ever held in the California Senate. He handled the first death penalty appeal in the State Supreme Court, personally hunted down a notorious criminal, and acted as trustee for the Fremont family and chief counsel in the case that secured the Pathfinder's ownership of the richest portion of the famed Mariposa Estate and more broadly confirmed the trend in American law away from the reservation of public rights in the land toward land ownership almost completely dissevered from public encumbrances. He became one of the most prolific litigators in the Comstock Lode, partnered with some of the most interesting and influential lawyers in the West, and won and lost fascinating and significant court battles, both as a lawyer and a litigant. For thirty years he traversed wide and wild expanses to open new practices, speculate in land and mining claims, and ultimately died while making a go of it in an entirely new territory, yet again in the midst of the Great

American Desert. He was perhaps a living embodiment of what G. Edward White observed was a thoroughly entrepreneurial aspect of the practice of law in the early and mid-Nineteenth Century, or that kind of lawyer identified by Lawrence Friedman who "wandered from town to town, almost like itinerant peddlers, until they found the right opening for their talents."[5] Published accounts of the law in the west and its history occasionally mention him, but never in the company of the great barristers of the era. And yet the record of his practice tells a different story: a man who remained a figure of tremendous public interest, whose cases and controversies both personal and professional sparked frequent and regular comment in the press of his day, and whose doings and sayings appear always to have made good copy. He belongs in the ranking of the great lawyers of the American frontier—a fact evident in this history, as well as in the associations he had with men who are recognized as belonging in that rank: Hall McAllister, A. P. Crittenden, and William M. Stewart, to name but a few.

It is always tempting to say that the subject of a biography is representative of his time, whose life story serves as a kind of metaphor for his era, or a window of insight into it. To some extent that may true of D. W. Perley—he was an adventurer on the frontier in an adventurous time, as rowdy and impulsive as was America during that period—and yet he was a man of tremendous discipline, recognized by his peers as a master of law, who had memorized a vast amount of judicial opinion, statute and regulation and could speak of it fluently and with great power. In an era when high value was placed on eloquence rooted in a study of the classics, Perley suffered no deficiencies. His broad and deep study of law, history and literature, undertaken at a time when institutions of higher learning were relatively few and reserved for the elite, can only be attributed to his own peculiar and insatiable impulse to learn, to master and to excel. In an age of epic building—of cities, roads and railways—creative energy is everywhere manifest, and in Perley the energy exhibited appears at times to have been of heroic proportion. Though mechanisms of travel

[5] See G. Edward White, *Law and American History*, Volume I (Oxford: Oxford University Press, 2012), at pp. 245-247, and Lawrence M. Friedman, *A History of American Law*, Second Edition (New York: Simon & Schuster, 1985), at p. 307.

remained limited to horse or wagon, Perley traversed mountains and deserts to appear in courts in multiple jurisdictions, handling matters in California and Nevada almost simultaneously, and doing so with great competence and skill. He was no homebody, and was never content to remain fixed to the earth, or within a comfortable niche carved out for himself after an initial period of struggle. One struggle for Perley led to another, and regardless of defeat or victory, he was ever ready to move forward to find newer challenges and to try his fortune in an entirely novel environment. His death in 1874 cut short his adventurous life and remarkable law practice, and yet as the size of this book indicates, in the years he occupied the earth, truly he did live. If we today cannot entirely relate to him because of changing times, attitudes and fashions, we can at least admire his remarkable persistence, and his fulfilment of the lawyer's creed to zealously pursue his clients' interests, to advance in litigation with mastery of his case, and to fight the good fight, even if the effort is doomed to failure.

The writing of this story has been many years in the making. D. W. Perley came to my attention when writing the history of the community into which was born my great grandmother. Her family was well acquainted with the Perleys and her husband's family had even migrated with them from Massachusetts to the wilds of mid-Eighteenth-Century New Brunswick. He was a minor character in that earlier tale, and through the researching of it I learned of his quitting of the Province for the far west and the prominence he gained there. So interesting was his story that I followed his trail to Northern California in the mid-1990s and spent the years since that time uncovering the record of his life. The search for evidence of his doings has been rendered difficult by the absence of any collection of papers, including personal correspondence, that would have made the construction of the narrative far easier. The personal papers left behind by Perley in the wake of his death were passed on to his nephew and from there they disappeared. He finds mention occasionally in archival collections here and there, but not often. The richest source of material for his life is found in the repositories of the courts where he practiced, and in the many newspapers of the time, which exhibited a remarkable interest in his often colorful deeds. These surviving sources have proven surprisingly rich and have truly allowed for a meaningful reconstruction of the man's life and law practice.

From the time I was a boy I was intrigued by history. Later I developed an interest in law. A further interest in the writing art has merged with these other interests to give birth to this latest creative effort. The special challenges of writing this history have been compounded by the fact that it is a legal history, entailing the recounting of disputes over principles of law that require much study and practical experience to fully comprehend. My writing of this account might have been possible without legal training, but the legal training I've obtained since commencing my research, as well as my years of legal practice as a trial lawyer, have proven invaluable, if not indispensable. That so few historians actually have practical expertise and formal training in law probably accounts for the dearth, at least until recently, of writing in the genre, and certainly helps to explain the focus on the great judicial and legislative figures, whose lives, because of the vast amount of attention focused on them over the years, are relatively comprehensible. Untrained and unschooled in law, many competent writers and historians have understandably and rightfully shied away from the attempt to reconstruct its past.

I trust this work will be of value to some, and will provide insight into what I have referred to (hopefully not too pretentiously) as the fate of the law on the far western frontier. D. W. Perley may not have been typical, but he was a man thoroughly at home in his time and place, shaped by the great trends of the society in which he lived and the political currents of the day. His courageous commitment to resolving disputes in court rather than through violence, despite his occasional violent outbursts, helped settle the unsettled west, and contributed to the building of a culture committed to law and order that only of late has become threatened by the rejection of principles rooted in logic and reason and a once certain understanding of the contours of human nature. I trust, too, that this work will contribute to a heightening of interest in the study of the historic practice of the law and of the lawyers who engaged in it. It is the lawyers, after all, who often convince the judges, including the great ones, of the justice of a particular outcome. William Pinkney and Daniel Webster had occasion to persuade John Marshall. John J. Crittenden changed the mind of the skeptical Taney from time to time. Many a time did Perley's persuasiveness change the course of litigation and allow for rulings from the pens of the distinguished jurists of the far west: Solomon Heydenfeldt, William Henry Beatty, and the great Stephen Field. Perley shaped the law. Cases he won found their way into citations in future opinions. And yet his true influence we might never know, so intangible is any one person's impact upon events around them, so ineffable the touch of but a single hand on the wheel that ever turns.

July 2022
Santa Rosa, CA

Chapter One

A REMOTE CORNER OF HER MAJESTY'S DOMAIN

To the east of Maine and north of Massachusetts lies the land once known as Acadia, presently called New Brunswick. For a time, it was a district of the Colony of Nova Scotia, presumptively ruled from Halifax, but in truth a master-less place, occupied by the British at the mouth of the St. John River and possessed inland by native peoples and discrete conclaves of descendants of outlawed French colonists. The land was beautiful in some respects, at least from a distance, yet challenging in so many any others. It was buried beneath layers of snow and ice for a good portion of the year, was hot and humid when the snow was absent, and a variety of infernal insects tended to harass and madden both livestock and human in spring, summer and fall. Almost all of the country was covered in forest, comprised of a variety of species both coniferous and deciduous, and harbored moose, bear, deer and packs of wolves whose ranks gradually thinned as the human population expanded. Numerous rivers cut through the mostly rocky terrain, separating lines of low hills one from another and demarcating a series of watersheds, the largest of which emptied exactly where the English constructed their first permanent settlement. One tributary of the great St. John lies approximately in the middle of the Province, in what is now the County of Sunbury, dubbed the Oromocto. It flows northward in quiet isolation toward the larger river from forks comprising its northwest and south branches.

Opposite the mouth of the stream at its northernmost limit lays a large island of the same name, and beyond that the town or settlement of Maugerville. Here was found some of the best, most fertile, soil in the Province, and some of the finest farms in the entire St. John valley. It was, nevertheless, a modest place, where modesty, among its puritan population, was highly valued. It was here that the subject of this book was born, on January 31, 1817—the second of three children of William Perley and Elizabeth Duncan, and named in duel tribute to his maternal grandfather, John Duncan, and the great victor in the recent battle of Waterloo, the Duke of

Wellington. It was a rather inauspicious place of beginning for a man who would later become a leader of the American Bar in the bustling Far West, on the other side of the continent, in an entirely different country.

The remote familial origins of Duncan Wellington Perley lay in Wales, and more recently New England. The first of the Perleys in North America, Allen Perley, arrived with Winthrop's Fleet in 1630, settled in Ipswich in the Massachusetts Bay Colony and there became a freeholder.[6] His neighbors were puritans mostly, dissenters and critics of the reigning Stuart family, and desirous of living apart from England's monarch and church and the many rules imposed by each. The intense commitment to a faith independent of all traditional ties, a certainty that evil was alive and at work in the world, and the vast, dark and unexplored forests that surrounded the nascent colonial settlements oppressed the New England mind and twisted it in some cases so as to allow for the birth of the profoundest conviction that the Tempter's minions were living among them and actively seeking their destruction. Perley's forebears, living in close proximity to one another in the communities of Essex County, Massachusetts, included both accusers and accused. Thomas Perley, Jr.—the grandson of Allen, and son of Thomas, Sr. and Lydia Peabody—married one of the daughters of the Mary Clement who had been accused of witchcraft in 1692, yet escaped execution via an expedient confession of demonic relations of dubious truth. Their son, also named Thomas, married Eunice Putnam, a daughter of the same Joseph Putnam who had so publicly opposed the witchcraft delusion that drew its inspiration from the family of his brother and pursued so cruelly and unapologetically by his wife's uncle, the notorious magistrate John Hathorne. Through Eunice, Duncan Perley could also claim descent from the family of Massachusetts and Connecticut magistrate John Endicott.

Israel Perley, the son of Thomas and Eunice—was born in Boxford, Massachusetts on July 2, 1738, five year prior to the birth of his brother Oliver, and two years ahead of their cousin, Asa.[7] Israel

[6] M.V.B. Perley, *The History and Genealogy of the Perley Family* (Salem: Published by Author, 1906), p. 1.

[7] Id., at p. 117.

married his distant relation, Elizabeth Mooers, the daughter of Peter Mooers and Mary Howe, and a descendant of the Hazen clan, as well as the ill-fated Elizabeth Howe who was executed for witchcraft in the same year that Mary Clement proffered her clemency-winning confession.

As a young man, Israel served in the French and Indian War in the Nova Scotia theatre with other New Englanders, including kinsmen Francis Peabody and the brothers Moses and William Hazen. Moses Hazen took part in the early forays into New Brunswick in 1755 aimed at disrupting the hold on the region by the French Crown. Two years later, he was in Halifax as part of the advance force preparing to attack the French fortress at Louisbourg. A year after that he was commanding the garrison at Ft. Frederick at the mouth of the St. John and raiding the middle reaches of the River, burning Acadian and native villages, and committing what can only be described as atrocities in the name of ridding the place of any remaining French influence.[8] His and Israel's cousins James and Richard Simonds appear to have been among Hazen's armed force.

Having taken note during their service of the lush supply of wood, fish and furs to be found in the region, the Simonds brothers formed a partnership with William Hazen, which they dedicated to pursuing the fishery, the fur trade, and other activities in the St. John River basin.[9] The firm was to be headquartered in New England, with a post at the mouth of the St. John to serve as a kind of gathering point of exports to be shipped back home. In the early 1760s, the partners began quarrying limestone, erected a saw mill and even started building schooners for use in their enterprise.

As the Simonds, Hazen & White Company commenced its activities in New Brunswick, word spread in Essex County among the principals' kinfolk of opportunities to settle in the sparsely populated province. After contemplating the presence of mature farm lands unoccupied following the expulsion of most of the Acadians, and mindful too of the strategic advantage of placing English settlers where the French formerly flourished, Nova Scotia's

---

[8] William Obder Raymond, *The River St. John, Its Physical Features, Legends and history from 1604 to 1784* (St. John: Strathmore Press, 1910), at pp. 242-245.

[9] Id., at pp. 283-289.

Governor issued a proclamation offering favorable terms to any industrious settler who would remove to the St. John River and cultivate the land.[10] A second proclamation articulated a plan to form townships of 100,000 acres each, with the promise that as soon as 50 families were present in any given township, the people would become eligible to enjoy the same rights and protections that the laws of England afforded English colonists elsewhere, including representation in the provincial assembly.[11] In response to these proclamations, men and women gathered at private homes and public houses and drew their plans in conformity with special information provided by Nova Scotia settlement booster, Alexander MacNutt.[12]

Israel Perley was selected by the would-be settlers to lead a surveying team north to the St. John and find a suitable site for a plantation of the kind envisioned by the Governor. With the Simonds brothers and nine other men accompanying him, Perley landed at Machias, then travelled up one of the streams to a portage point in what is now Charlotte County, entered the St. John watershed and discovered Great Oromocto Lake.[13] Travelling downstream to the confluence of the Oromocto and the St. John, the members of the expedition next proceeded up the larger river until confronted at the present-day site of Fredericton by a large assembly of natives, who claimed the abandoned Acadian farms as their own and warned the party to advance no further.[14] After returning downstream, they alighted on the north bank of the St. John opposite the mouth of the Oromocto, where they discovered fine interval soil ideal as a site for a settlement dedicated to purely agrarian pursuits.[15]

Led by Francis Peabody, and with Israel, Oliver and cousin Asa in their ranks, the first set of colonists arrived in 1763 in four vessels and set to work building a community. In the midst of their labors, they were interrupted by representatives from Halifax with the distressing news that the land chosen had previously been reserved

---

[10] Id., at p. 263.
[11] Id., at p. 264.
[12] Id., at 275 and 280-281.
[13] Id., at p. 279; and M.V.B. Perley, op. cit., at p. 117.
[14] Raymond, op. cit., p. 282.
[15] Id., at p. 280.

for military veterans and their families.[16] Francis Peabody, Israel Perley and others composed a memorial to be presented to authorities in England, blaming MacNutt for their error but asking that their settlement be ratified on the basis of their reliance on the word of a Crown agent.[17] Moved by the plight of the settlers, the men from Halifax took up their cause once home and delivered the memorial to Joshua Mauger, who proved successful in convincing the Board of Trade in London to license a settlement that its grateful residents subsequently named Maugerville in the man's honor.[18] Perley's prominence in creating the community and ensuring its legality in the eyes of the Crown garnered him sufficient support amongst the small population to win an early contest for election to the Provincial Assembly, though distance and other concerns likely prevented him from ever actually taking his seat.[19] He did serve as a local Justice of the Peace and became an Elder in the Congregational Church. It was he and several other leaders in the community who procured the services of the New Light-oriented Reverend Seth Noble and encouraged the embrace by the congregation of some of the more flamboyant forms of religious experience current at the time.

When the American Revolution broke out, the people of Maugerville assembled to consider the stance their community would take with respect to that momentous event. Acting as clerk of the meeting, Perley likely played an instrumental role in drafting the resolution asserting the justice of the American cause and calling for the annexation of Nova Scotia to a free and independent Massachusetts.[20] His views were characteristic of his family. Back home in New England, his father was an active revolutionary, while his maternal uncle was none other than General Israel Putnam, a former comrade of Moses Hazen in the French and Indian War and now a leader of New England's militiamen.[21] Perley took a seat on

---

16 Id., at 277.

17 Id., at 275.

18 Id., at pp. 278-279.

19 Stephen Patterson, "Israel Perley," *Dictionary of Canadian Biography*, Vol. V, University of Toronto/Universite Laval, 2003-, http://www.biographi.ca/en/bio/perley_israel_5E.html.

20 Id.

21 Id.

the local Committee of Public Safety and likely endorsed a military expedition eastward to capture Fort Cumberland near modern day Sackville, though it's unclear if he took part in the actual campaign. British forces repulsed the attack, but hesitated to reassert control over Maugerville due to preoccupation with the raids by the planters' allies upon the Hazen, Simonds and White facilities scattered throughout New Brunswick.[22] When the British finally arrived in Maugerville, Perley negotiated a peace, which entailed a pardon for all who would take the oath of allegiance to the Crown.[23] The appearance of his name in the minutes of the meeting where disloyalty was announced nevertheless ensured his arrest and prosecution for sedition, if not treason. The charge was eventually dropped due to lack of evidence that he had taken part in any actual belligerency.[24]

The arrival on the St. John River of the American Loyalists after 1783 posed a threat to the New England Planters and their hold on the territory they had settled two decades earlier. Obliged to repay the futile valor of its faithful subjects from the American States, the Crown surveyed the region and allotted it to soldiers and refugees for post-war settlement. While many of the older settlers lost out, skill as a surveyor brought Perley to the attention of the Provincial Surveyor General, who appointed him as one of his deputies.[25] Over the course of the next several years, he ranged throughout the Province surveying tracts for land-hungry soldiers and their families, and earning a decent living in the process. By the end of his term of service, he'd managed to transition from disloyal Planter to the lower ranks of the British colonial hierarchy. Cousin William Hazen had done slightly better by becoming the agent for the supply of the Loyalists in St. John and taking a seat on the governing Executive Council.[26] Cousin Francis Peabody didn't survive to accept a position in the new colonial administration to which he might have been entitled, but he achieved preeminence

---

[22] Rod Campbell, "William Hazen," *Dictionary of Canadian Biography*, Vol. V, University of Toronto/Universite Laval, 2003-, http://www.biographi.ca/en/bio/hazen_william_5E.html.

[23] Patterson, op. cit.

[24] Id.

[25] Id.

[26] Campbell, op. cit.

through his daughters—who married into families who would become dominant in the administration of provincial affairs—and also through his namesake son, who served as a Justice of the Peace and Judge of the Inferior Court of Common Pleas in Northumberland County on the Miramichi River.[27]

The men responsible for the creation of the post-war provincial regime were men of a mindset considerably different from that of Israel Perley and those who settled Maugerville in the 1760s. In their primitive simplicity, in part forced on them by the scarcity of nature, the latter had created a variation of the frontier that Perley's grandson would find so alluring and liberating in the far West. Elements of the primitive world of the Pre-Loyalists would endure, but it would be heavily overlaid by a thin but rigid hierarchy dominated by men whose loyalty was to innate privilege first, and the monarchy second. Having come of age in the dramatic period of dissent and then war, and harboring some expectation of advancement in the British service, the new provincial elites were eager to establish institutions reflective both of their experience and the attitudes that it engendered. Like many on the more conservative side of the ideological spectrum during in the Age of the Enlightenment, "they regarded man in dour fashion as a greedy, self-exalting, rapacious creature, whose basic instincts inclined him to place his own self-interest above all other considerations."[28] In their view, these innate human tendencies were far more concerning than the oppressive power of the state, and necessitated the government taking steps to refine the baser instincts of man and "broaden men's outlook so as to include some concern for the needs of the community as a whole."[29] Jonathan Sewell, the former Attorney General of Massachusetts, urged the creation in New Brunswick of a system of rules to "encourage individuals to work for the good of the whole and which would make the pursuit of personal gratification subservient to the common welfare."[30] Men

---

[27] W.A. Spray, "Francis Peabody," *Dictionary of Canadian Biography*, Vol. VII, University of Toronto/Universite Laval, 2003-, http://www.biographi.ca/en/bio/peabody_francis_7E.html..

[28] Ann Gorman Condon, *The Envy of the American States: The Loyalist Dream for New Brunswick* (Fredericton: New Ireland Press, 1984), p. 45.

[29] Id.

[30] Id., at p. 46.

such as himself, who possessed a broader perspective due to education, property ownership and the discipline gained from religious instruction, were to "be placed in positions of public leadership and given the predominant voice in directing the affairs of the community."[31] Once in control of officialdom, this cadre would be able to fulfill the great purpose of government, which was "to deliver well-meaning people from themselves, that is to say, to rescue them from the ill consequences of their own actions, which may have been at first, the mere result of honest endeavors."[32] Because Loyalists such as Sewell "felt that the popular, disintegrating forces in American life constituted such a grave danger to orderly, civilized government, their proposals for the internal organization of the remaining colonies revolved around the need to reinforce the aristocratic elements in American society, to strengthen the hierarchical structure of colonial government so that power and prestige would flow from the top of the colonial pyramid."[33]

A crucial element of New Brunswick's post-Revolutionary regime would have to be a strong native aristocracy, closely tied to the colonial executive, whose own authority was to be expanded so as to permit more flexibility than colonial administrators possessed in the days leading up to the American Revolution. Placing greater authority in the hands of the colonial governor and staffing the Executive Council with members of an elite that was to be hereditary were steps in the right direction, as was support for the Established Church in the form of subsidies, the promotion of membership through the evangelizing efforts of the Society for the Propagation of the Gospel and the licensing of pastors lest unauthorized persons spread erroneous and anti-communitarian notions. "In similar fashion," noted the historian A. G. Condon, "it was considered necessary to bind the legal profession and the judiciary to the support of the established government in a firmer, more positive fashion than had ever been known in the former colonies."[34] Salaries of judicial officers were to be ample enough "to induce Gentleman of the first abilities and integrity in the law…to

---

[31] Id.

[32] Id., at p. 47.

[33] Id., at p. 48.

[34] Id., at p. 58.

quit the practice for seats on the bench."[35] The basic aim of the scheme to be imposed in the Province, politically, religiously and legally, was to "habituate men to seek their economic, political, and social well-being within the established imperial order."[36] Dependence for advancement on the state "would naturally incline men to look up to this colonial hierarchy for political favors and to treat the occupants of such powerful offices with appropriate respect. The allegiance of the colonial hierarchy would, in turn, be guaranteed by making the imperial government the source of their appointments, their salaries, and their perquisites."[37]

The Loyalist founders of the Province were fairly successful in establishing a regime along these lines, at least in a very general sense, and of placing themselves and their families in the forefront of provincial affairs. Many of those who had taken refuge in London while hostilities were ongoing had won positions in the new provincial order and accompanied the new Lieutenant Governor to St. John in August of 1784.[38] George Duncan Ludlow and his brother Gabriel, James Putnam, Abijah Willard, Isaac Allen, William Hazen, Jonathan Odell, and Edward Winslow were among the earliest members of the Lieutenant Governor's Executive Council, and were soon joined by Ward Chipman, Daniel Bliss and Joshua Upham.[39] Because of their legal backgrounds and bona fides as Loyalist gentlemen, most of these men secured the highly coveted and well compensated positions in the provincial judiciary, and thereby gave their sons a leg up in the next generation's climb through the lower offices to the top of the colonial establishment. Not being a lawyer, Hazen happily settled for the post of provincial Treasurer, and then witnessed the marriage of his children into the other leading families of the land. Winning the greatest and highest paid award available among the civil offices of the Province, George Duncan Ludlow took the oath as Chief Justice, with James Putnam, Isaac Allen and Joshua Upham assuming seats as his lesser

---

[35] Id.

[36] Id., at p. 66.

[37] Id.

[38] W. Stewart MacNutt, *New Brunswick: A History, 1784-1867* (Toronto: MacMillan of Canada, 1963), at p. 49.

[39] J. W. Lawrence, *The First Courts and Early Judges of New Brunswick: A Paper Read Before the New Brunswick Historical Society* (St. John: J. & A. McMillan, 1875), p. 3.

associates.[40] Ludlow was a New York patrician, learned in the law, who served at the time of the Revolution on his native Colony's Supreme Court.[41] The destruction of his home by New York patriots and attaint by the New York Legislature confirmed him in his commitment to Loyalist independence. Even before coming to New Brunswick he was known for his tyrannical ways and for the favor he showed his friends "with all the influence at his command."[42] He continued on the bench for two decades following his appointment, simultaneously serving as President of the Executive Council. At one point in time he acted as the effective ruler of the Province between the tenures of departing and arriving lieutenant governors.[43]

Ludlow's successor as Chief Justice, Jonathan Bliss, had previously been a leading attorney in pre-revolutionary Massachusetts, served as New Brunswick's Attorney General and member of the Legislative Assembly, and was considered one of the finest lawyers in the Province.[44] His son, William Blowers Bliss, became a Justice of the Supreme Court of Nova Scotia.[45] D. W. Perley's distant relation, James Putnam, who served as one of the first Associate Justices of the Court, was a Harvard graduate, friend and mentor of John Adams, and one of the ablest lawyers in Massachusetts prior to the outbreak of the Revolution.[46] He served only five years on the provincial Supreme Court due to an untimely end.[47] His replacement, John Saunders, originally of Virginia and "bred to the profession of the law," served until 1823 as an Associate and until 1834 as Chief Justice, while simultaneously becoming the largest landowner in the Province.[48] His son, John Simcoe Saunders, served as Master of the Rolls, as a member of the Executive and Legislative Councils, Surveyor General, Provincial

---

[40] Id., at p. 6.

[41] J. W. Lawrence, *The Judges of New Brunswick and Their Times* (1907; reprint, Fredericton: Acadiensis Press, 1985), at p. 19.

[42] MacNutt, *New Brunswick: A History, 1784-1867*, supra, at p. 50.

[43] Lawrence, *The First Courts and Early Judges of New Brunswick*, supra, at p. 10.

[44] Lawrence, *The Judges of New Brunswick and Their Times*, supra, at pp. 155-157.

[45] Id., at p. 165.

[46] Id., at pp. 39-40.

[47] Id., at p. 55.

[48] Id., at p. 113; and MacNutt, *New Brunswick, A History, 1784-1867*, supra, at p. 51.

Secretary, and Clerk of the Circuits.[49] Prior to his appointment to the Court as an Associate Justice, Isaac Allan had been a member of the Supreme Court of New Jersey and an active soldier during the Revolution.[50] His great distinction as a judge was his principled view on the nature of slavery, which he said was "beyond the power of human nature to justify."[51] His son John later served in the Assembly from York County, and his grandson, Sir John Campbell Allen, was the Assembly's Speaker and, later, Chief Justice of the Supreme Court.[52] Allen's successor on the bench was Edward Winslow, a descendant of the Mayflower family of such renown, a Harvard graduate, and a veteran of the British service.[53] His son John later served as High Sheriff of Carlton County.[54] Joshua Upham, like Putnam and Winslow, was a Harvard alum, and a soldier in the British Army.[55] Both he and William Hazen's son William married daughters of the British officer John Murray.[56] He remained on the bench until his death in England in 1808 while lobbying for an increase in salary.[57] His son-in-law, John Wesley Weldon, joined the Court in 1865, while his grandson was elected to a seat in the Dominion Parliament.[58] Yet another Harvard man, the Massachusetts-born Ward Chipman, was perhaps the epitome of the provincial elite, having served before his elevation to the Court as Solicitor General, Attorney General, Advocate General, Clerk of the Circuits, Recorder of St. John County and member of the

---

[49] MacNutt, "John Simcoe Saunders," *Dictionary of Canadian Biography*, Vol. X, University of Toronto/Universite Laval, 2003-, http://www.biographi.ca/en/bio/Saunders_John_Simcoe_10E.html.

[50] Lawrence, *The Judges of New Brunswick and Their Times*, supra, at p. 59.

[51] Id., at p. 71.

[52] Id., at p. 77; and D.G. Bell, "Sir John Campbell Allen," *Dictionary of Canadian Biography*, Vol. XII, University of Toronto/Universite Laval, 2003-, http://www.biographi.ca/en/bio/allan_john_campbell_12E.html.

[53] Lawrence, *The Judges of New Brunswick and Their Times*, supra, at pp. 119-122.

[54] Id., at p. 406.

[55] Id., at pp. 80-81.

[56] Id., at pp. 91 and 222-223.

[57] Id., at pp. 89-90.

[58] Id., at pp. 93-94 and 503; and *The Canadian Biographical Dictionary and Portrait Gallery of Eminent and Self-Made Men* (New York: American Biographical Publishing Company, 1881), pp. 702-703.

Legislative Assembly.[59] Fervently believing that New Brunswick might become "one of the most valuable and important of His Majesty's North American Possessions," he tirelessly worked to advance provincial interests, and achieved perhaps his greatest success in negotiating a partial resolution to the western boundary controversy with the United States. He was also an active mentor to students of the law and young lawyers. He trained a generation of leading attorneys, many of whom attained high positions in the British imperium. It was no small part he played in the creation in New Brunswick of "one of the best qualified bars in British North America."[60]

Another member of the Court in the early years of Perley's life, John Murray Bliss, studied law under Jonathan Sewell and his uncle, Jonathan Bliss. His father Daniel had served in the War, then become a Judge of the Inferior Court of Common Pleas in Sunbury County.[61] His estate at Belmont in Lincoln Parish, between Fredericton and the Oromocto, he bequeathed to his son at his death in 1806. Bliss was one of the small group of lawyers who appeared in Fredericton when the Courts first opened there, and over the years held various offices, including Solicitor General and member of the Legislative Assembly. He took a seat on the bench in 1816 following Winslow's death, and even administered the Province prior to the arrival of Lieutenant Governor Howard Douglas in 1824. His nephew, Lemuel Allan Wilmot, a favorite of the Perleys, became a leader of the radicals in the Assembly, and then settled down into a more conservative posture following his own elevation to the Supreme Court in 1851. He was well known in the Courts of central New Brunswick in his days as a barrister, including at the Courthouse in Burton Parish, where his courtroom histrionics likely drew large crowds of spectators.[62]

Justice Edward Jarvis ascended to the bench in 1822 after service as Clerk of the House of the Assembly. His father Munson had been a loyal subject of the Crown, and after immigrating to St. John

---

[59] Phillip Buckner, "Ward Chipman," *Dictionary of Canadian Biography*, Vol. VI, University of Toronto/Universite Laval, 2003-, http://www.biographi.ca/en/bio/chipman_ward_6E.html.

[60] Id.

[61] Lawrence, *The Judges of New Brunswick and Their Times*, supra, at pp. 231-232.

[62] Id., at p. 430.

became an alderman there and later a member of the Legislative Assembly.[63] His brothers were among the leading merchants in the Province, and his sister married into the Hazen family and became the mother of Robert F. Hazen, protégé of Ward Chipman, Jr. and one-time mayor of the City of St. John.[64] Due to jealousy among his peers on account of his supposed lack of pre-eminence, he was promoted out of the position and eventually won appointment to the Chief Justiceship of New Brunswick's poorer sister colony on Prince Edward Island.[65] His replacement on the New Brunswick bench was William Botsford, son of the Loyalist Amos Botsford, who counseled the first Lieutenant Governor and built up a base of political and economic power in Westmoreland County. The younger Botsford had studied law with Ward Chipman and then replaced Gabriel Ludlow as Judge of the Court of Vice-Admiralty. He then served as Recorder of St. John County, Solicitor General and Speaker of the Assembly.[66] His wife was one of the many daughters of William Hazen, and his children remained prominent in provincial affairs long after his death.[67] When he resigned from the Bench due to the effects of advanced age in 1845, Lieutenant Governor Colebrooke appointed in his place the brilliant attorney, George Frederick Street, a new man, yes, but the son of the famed Sunbury County Assemblymen and barrister, Samuel Denny Street.[68] In time, Botsford was joined on the bench by his nephew, Ward Chipman, Jr., whose career as Advocate General, Clerk of the Circuits, Recorder of St. John County, Solicitor General and Speaker of the Legislative Assembly mirrored that of his distinguished father.[69] When Chief Justice Saunders died in 1834, it was Chipman who replaced him. The tenure on the Court of this learned elitist came to a close in 1851, at a time when the ambitious Duncan W. Perley was making a name for himself in the legal profession far from New Brunswick and its stultifying aristocratic regime.

---

[63] Id., at p. 270.

[64] Id., at p. 272 and p. 275.

[65] J. M. Bumstead & H. T. Holman, "Edward James Jarvis," *Dictionary of Canadian Biography*, Vol. VIII, University of Toronto/Universite Laval, 2003-, http://www.biographi.ca/en/bio/jarvis_edward_james_8E.html.

[66] Lawrence, *The Judges of New Brunswick and Their Times*, supra, at pp. 281-282

[67] Id., at p. 296 and p. 299.

[68] Id., at p. 411.

[69] Lawrence, *The First Courts and Early Judges of New Brunswick*, supra, at p. 27.

The success of the Loyalist order was at times only superficial. As entrenched as the families of Bliss, Ludlow, Chipman, and Hazen became in provincial affairs, tensions remained ever present between them, and between themselves and the British authorities, not to mention between their ranks and those from outside who wished to join or compete with them. Cleavage between the members of the elite, who believed themselves entitled to eternal preference on account of that status and their many sacrifices in the Revolution, and the Crown-appointed executive appeared almost at once and contributed mightily to the first Lieutenant Governor's decision to remove the provincial capital from Loyalist-dominated St. John to the present-day site at Fredericton. Attacks on the privileged position of the Loyalist elite came almost as rapidly as the Lieutenant Governor's departure from St. John, as former soldier and lumber entrepreneur James Glenie entered the political fray as an enemy of the "illiterate, strutting" Chief Justice Ludlow and the rest of his class.[70] Desirous of keeping control of the Crown Lands out of the hands of the elite due to his close relations with the imperial bureaucracy and its willingness to provide him with license to cut timber on behalf of the Royal Navy, Glenie exploited the good will of the settlers of the Oromocto whom he employed in his forest operations from his base in Burton Parish. With their support he won election to the Legislative Assembly, where he became a leader of so-called radicals and the partner in this enterprise with the disaffected Samuel Denny Street.[71] Periodically, the two men brought the Legislature to a standstill, and so enraged their opponents that Glenie was challenged to a duel by John Coffin—a native of Massachusetts, Loyalist veteran of Bunker Hill, Assemblyman and St. John County Justice of the Common Pleas. Shots were exchanged in the woods outside Fredericton and Glenie's thigh was pierced by a bullet, "but his honor was undimmed."[72]

Coffin's challenge to Glenie appears to have inspired the fortitude of the latter's enemies in the Loyalist regime. Taking the helm of the tory faction in the Assembly, Coffin managed to muster

[70] MacNutt, *New Brunswick: A History, 1784 to 1867*, supra, at p. 102.
[71] Id., at pp. 100-117.
[72] Id., at p. 109.

a quorum after Glenie and his supporters abandoned the capitol in a failed ploy to thwart their opponents, and pushed through a much-disputed revenue bill.[73] When the Lieutenant Governor dissolved the Assembly and called for a new election, the tarnished Glenie narrowly held onto his seat, but Street—his Sunbury County colleague—was defeated.[74] Both Glenie and the Lieutenant Governor quit the Province for England in 1803, leaving the radicals without a leader and the administration of the Province in the hands of Chief Justice Ludlow. For the five years of Ludlow's rule, "complete concord between council and assembly appeared to prevail" and constitutional questions ceased to be at issue.[75] MacNutt's tale of the jockeying for position amongst the members of the leading families of the Province during the Imperial interregnum in the wake of Ludlow's death is both humorous and diverting, but hardly distracts from the fact that as jealous as the members of the leadership were of one another, they remained united in their belief that they, and only they, were the rightful heirs of a Revolution lost in the original colonies, but won under their leadership on the soil of New Brunswick.

As competition for the highest judicial offices in the land almost invariably resulted in the appointment of men from the chief families, a similar competition with similar results occurred at the county level. Unable to win the higher rewards available to members of the elite, disappointed office seekers from the best families found some consolation in appointment as Judges of the Inferior Courts of the Common Pleas and as Justices of the Peace. Not so prized as seats on the Supreme Court or the offices of Attorney General and Solicitor General, such positions offered both a steady stream of income as well as opportunities to gain experience that might pay dividends should further promotion ever occur. Though valued less than other positions, these offices were nonetheless of vital interest to the people of New Brunswick, and those who occupied them were responsible for the meting out of most justice in the Province. Both the Inferior Courts and the Justice Courts headed by the Justices of the Peace had their origins in 1785

[73] Id., at pp. 114-115.
[74] Id., at p. 115
[75] Id., at p. 130.

in the Act authorizing the issuance of County Charters. The Act and the Charters that followed vested the County Inferior Courts with authority to hear "all manner of pliants, actions and pleas whatsoever arising from and accruing within the County which shall be brought in the said County and which shall be for more than 40 shillings and shall not exceed 'fifty pounds in value and in which the title to lands shall not come into question.'"[76] In 1841, when Duncan W. Perley made entré into County affairs, Sunbury County's Inferior Court consisted of John Simcoe Sanders, Nathaniel Hubbard, Stephen Peabody, John M. Wilmot and Thomas O. Miles.[77] Saunders, as noted, was the son of the late Chief Justice, still much disappointed in being passed over for elevation to his father's former position. Wilmot was a scion of an important Loyalist family, a former leader in the Legislature, father of Robert Duncan Wilmot and uncle of Lemuel Allan Wilmot. Nathaniel Hubbard's father was the Loyalist William Hubbard, who preceded him on the Inferior Bench, and his first and second wives were members of the Hazen and Street clans respectively.[78] Stephen Peabody, of course, was of the family of Francis Peabody, with whom Perley shared a line of descent. Miles, the least exalted member of the Court, was not without a reputable Loyalist pedigree.

Far more crowded were the ranks of the Justices of the Peace, who were required to hear matters involving debts and any civil action, except for slander and libel, seeking damages not in excess of £5.[79] In 1841, Sunbury's Justices of the Peace were distributed throughout the County's five parishes, and included Miles, Perley's uncle George Hayward, Charles F. Street, Charles Hazen, Henry Thomas Partelow, John Peabody and several others.[80] Street was a son of Samuel Denny Street and a brother of Solicitor General and

---

[76] Ward Chipman, et al, *Report Made to His Excellency the Lieutenant Governor of the Province of New Brunswick by the Commissioners Appointed Into the Judicial Institutions of the Province, 2d January 1833* (Fredericton: John Simpson, Printer to the King's Most Excellent Majesty, 1833), p. 6.

[77] *Merchants' and Farmers' Provincial Almanac, For the Year of Our Lord 1841* (St. John: William L. Avery, 1841), p. 32.

[78] See *New Brunswick Courier*, August 28, 1847; and *New Brunswick Courier*, February 24, 1849.

[79] Chipman, op. cit., pp. 28-29.

[80] *Merchants' and Farmers' Provincial Almanac*, supra, at p. 32.

future Justice George Frederick Street. Hazen was another of the many descendants of William Hazen's brother John. Partelow was an assemblyman of Loyalist heritage and brother of one of the leaders of the Provincial Assembly. The County's legal establishment was rounded out by the Keeper of the Rolls and Clerk of the Inferior Court of Common Pleas, Charles P. Wetmore—a grandson of the late Attorney General—and the commissioners for the taking of affidavits in the Supreme Court: Partelow and Edward Allison Clowes. Serving as the surrogate—or judge in matters involving marriage, divorce and probate—and responsible for the execution of judgments, was the County's High Sheriff, John Hazen: a brother of Charles, son of Judge John, and great nephew of William.

By the 1820s, when Perley was a lad, a formidable and well-defined network of families all but ruled the Province, jealously hording the choicest offices and placing a check on advancement in government service and the legal profession to all but themselves. It was not a particularly friendly or amenable environment for young and ambitious men whose lot in life was to have been born into less privileged, less well-connected families. Locked out of the best positions, they were more or less relegated to fighting for preference for the less exalted ones. In the third decade of the Nineteenth-Century, the center of this ruling network of families was occupied by Justice Bliss. No distant eminence, Bliss resided during the latter part of his life at Belmont in Lincoln Parish, abutting the Oromocto in Sunbury County, a short distance along the Oromocto Road leading to the provincial capital. By the time of his death in 1834, he was said to be "revered and beloved" by the legal profession and that "the dignity of his demeanor and the distinguished urbanity of his manners [had] won...the regard of all who were brought into contact with him."[81] This regard was due more to his rarified status than his abilities as a lawyer or jurist, which the historian Phillip Buckner said was not "above the ordinary."[82] This status he owed mostly to his family and to the prevailing view that only men of the right background were owed advancement. He was a gentleman,

[81] Phillip Buckner, "John Murray Bliss," *Dictionary of Canadian Biography*, Vol. VI, University of Toronto/Universite Laval, 2003-, http://www.biographi.ca/en/bio/bliss_john_murray_6E.html.

[82] Id.

and as a gentleman his honor was ever to be preserved. As a young advocate he once lost his cool when bested by the wily Samuel Denny Street, a rival at the bar who lived across the Oromocto in Burton Parish at an estate called "The Elysian Fields." In one of the great cases in provincial history—involving the issue of the legality of slavery in the Province and pitting the flower of the provincial bar against one another—Street presented arguments in favor of the slave that Bliss believed were rooted in lies.[83] When Bliss loudly complained to Street directly outside the courthouse, Street issued a challenge to settle the matter on the field of honor. Shots were subsequently exchanged, but neither man was injured.

Two decades later, Street's son, George Frederick, made similar forceful arguments that opposing counsel George Wetmore profoundly resented. Wetmore was restrained from committing violence outside the courthouse by his father, the Attorney General, but managed to overcome that restraint a day later when he issued a fateful challenge. He fell on New Maryland Hill not far from Fredericton—the victim of a dispute, said Buckner, arising in part from the intense competition for business among the overcrowded provincial bar, and the two families that dominated it.[84] The younger Street returned voluntarily to the Province after a brief flight to Maine and entrusted his defense to Ward Chipman and Henry Bliss in opposition to a prosecution headed by William Botsford.[85] Chipman and Bliss called a string of witnesses drawn from the Loyalist elite to testify as to Street's "humane character," while those actually present at the duel refused to admit that they had ever seen Street fire the fatal round.[86] Street was exonerated not at the discretion of the jury, but through an order of Chief Justice Saunders directing the jury to acquit him of the charge.

---

[83] Thomas B. Vincent, "Samuel Denny Street," *Dictionary of Canadian Biography*, Vol. VI, University of Toronto/Universite Laval, 2003-, http://www.biographi.ca/en/bio/street_samuel_denny_6E.html.

[84] Phillip Buckner, "George Frederick Street," *Dictionary of Canadian Biography*, Vol. III, University of Toronto/Universite Laval, 2003-, http://www.biographi.ca/en/bio/street_george_frederick_3E.html.

[85] Phillip Buckner, "George Ludlow Wetmore," *Dictionary of Canadian Biography*, Vol. VI, University of Toronto/Universite Laval, 2003-, http://www.biographi.ca/en/bio/wetmore_george_ludlow_6E.html.

[86] Id.

The sense of honor permeating the provincial elite, and particularly the legal class, contributed to Street's proffer of a second challenge to another legal rival, Henry George Clopper—a kinsman of the Winslows. Clopper scornfully refused the challenge after an embittered war of words fought in the local press.[87] The primitive honor of the legal class did not go entirely extinct until 1845, when the future Chief Justice of both New Brunswick and Canada, William Johnstone Ritchie, took to heart the advice of a much older and wiser Street and declined either to apologize or to accept the challenge of Edward L. Jarvis after the latter suffered offense over Ritchie's aggressive cross-examination of his father, the merchant William Jarvis.[88]

Though he only rose so far in the rigid, Loyalist-dominated Provincial hierarchy, Israel Perley was a successful man, whose greatest legacy proved to be his children. Son Israel moved over to Burton in 1786, where he acquired Lot No. 7 on the St. John River. He returned to Maugerville some-time later, and eventually migrated to Upper Canada.[89] Daughter Mehitable Dexter Perley married Isaac Foshay and settled in Kings County, where her daughter Jane came of age prior to her marriage to William Hazen's great nephew, Robert. Daughter Charlotte married George Hayward, a neighbor of John Murray Bliss and a grandson of Maugerville Planters. Son Thomas migrated up-river to Carleton County, where his children proliferated and became prominent in that region. Son Solomon, born in 1779, dabbled in farming, milling, ship building, and lumbering. He married his cousin Eunice Putnam Perley (a daughter of uncle Oliver) and had a large family that included sons James Edwin, Frederick Allen and George Augustus and daughter Frances Elizabeth. He died in Maugerville in 1832.[90] Duncan Perley's father William was born 1781 and was for

---

[87] Id.; and D. M. Young, "Henry George Clopper," *Dictionary of Canadian Biography*, Vol. VII, University of Toronto/Universite Laval, 2003-, http://www.biographi.ca/en/bio/clopper_henry_george_7E.html.

[88] Gordon Bale, *Chief Justice William Johnstone Ritchie: Responsible Government and Judicial Review* (Ottawa: Carlton University Press, 1991), at p. 18; and Gordon Bale & E. Bruce Mellett, "Sir William Johnston Ritchie," *Dictionary of Canadian Biography*, Vol. XII, University of Toronto/Universite Laval, 2003-, http://www.biographi.ca/en/bio/ritchie_william_johnstone_12E.html.

[89] M. V. B. Perley, op. cit., p. 218.

[90] Id., at p. 216.

all of his life quite close with brother Solomon and the latter's family. William married Elizabeth, one of the daughters of John Duncan, a cordwainer who evacuated New York in 1783 and was present in Sheffield as a member of the Congregational Church in 1788. William acquired a number of lots along the River, including one on Oromocto Island used primarily for the pasturing of sheep. He filled a number of minor County offices and operated an inn in Sheffield that became one of the regular meeting places for the Court of the General Sessions.[91] Financial troubles led to the loss of much of his property to cover a judgment debt owed to the prominent St. John merchants and politicians Hugh Johnston and John R. Partelow, but when time came to auction the land, brother Solomon stepped forward with the purchase price.[92] Duncan and his siblings were still quite young when their father died in 1825.[93] Uncle Solomon administered the estate, and Solomon's eldest son James posted the surety bond.

At the time of William's death, his wife's mother still resided in Sheffield, as did at least one of his wife's sisters. The sister, Mary, appears to have moved with her husband, William Nevers, to the South Branch of the Oromocto River prior to 1830, in a Parish soon named for Justice Bliss. In 1830, Elizabeth herself removed to the South Branch, to unite with her second husband John Bailey—a respectable farmer of Loyalist origins. Duncan and his siblings joined their step-father's family of eight children and soon welcomed a new half-sister, baby Matilda Ann.[94] The South Branch community was a rather insular one, surrounded by the forest and poorly connected with the rest of the Province. Its people were mostly of Loyalist origin, making their living cutting timber and tending gardens on the side primarily for their own consumption. The remoteness from the chapels of the Church of England had left the spiritual ground open to itinerant preachers of the rugged, enthusiastic and individualistic brands of Christianity, especially the New Light-influenced Free Will Baptists. It was in this evangelical faith that young Duncan was raised. It was a faith that

[91] Rex Grady, *Oromocto Adieu: Four Decades on the River and the Origins of North Lake Parish* (Santa Rosa: Lilburne & Company, 2019), at pp. 58-59, fn 44.

[92] Sunbury County Registry, PANB, RS 95, K-12/110.

[93] M.V.B. Perley, op. cit., at p. 216

[94] Id., at p. 217

stressed the community of believers yes, but sought also to strengthen the resolve of isolated Christians in both the literal and figurative wilderness, and to instill in them a sense of their personal responsibility for nurturing their faith in God and of their own powers of self-sufficiency in the face of any earthly challenge.

As he grew older, the outgoing and adventurous Duncan wasn't comfortable settling for a life in ponderous Blissville, and looked down stream to the County seat in Burton, where the Court of the General Sessions and the Inferior Court of Common Pleas met, and travelers between St. John and Fredericton stopped amidst their province-wide journeys at the various inns and taverns located at the Oromocto's mouth. In February of 1841, Perley appears to have convinced his mother and two maternal aunts and their husbands to sell him Lot No. 22 in Welch's survey on Long Reach in King's County which they had inherited from their father. He flipped the property for £150 to George Salter of St. John nine months later.[95] The money he probably used to set himself up in "mercantile affairs in Burton," with the aim of becoming a member of the local gentry.[96] To this end, in May, he purchased from his brother and sister-in-law a half lot on Oromocto Island ideal for farming and grazing, in addition to the 100-acre Lot No. 4 near the Oromocto's mouth. It was on the latter parcel that he likely commenced operating as a retailer of foodstuffs and other sundries.[97] That he and his brother were in business together at this time is evident from the lawsuits they jointly brought to recover monies from local farmers—probably for debts arising from purchases made on credit.[98]

If Perley was to advance in the rigidly hierarchical and aristocratic society of New Brunswick, he needed far more than his grandfather's good name and distant kinship with members of the provincial elite. He needed mentors. Obvious candidates were his father's cousin Amos, who had served in the Assembly in the 1820s,

---

[95] Sunbury County Registry, PANB, RS 95, D-2/80.

[96] *Petition of Duncan W. Perley of Burton*, November 9, 1843, Records of Lt. Governor Sir William McBean George Colebrooke, PANB, RS 345, B/4.

[97] Sunbury County Registry, PANB, RS 95, O-16/431; Sunbury County Registry, PANB, RS 95, P-17/17; and Diary of Thomas O. Miles, PANB, MC 451, entry for July 19, 1841

[98] Sunbury County Registry, PANB, RS 95, P-17/122, P-17/123 and P-17/473

and another relation, Moses Henry Perley, an attorney of some note and the Province's resident expert on any topic requiring special study and an official report. Neither man was available to tutor young Perley: Amos died some years before Perley's move to Burton, and Moses Henry, though very much alive, resided in St. John when he wasn't traveling the Province on one of his frequent official errands. Far better prospects for mentorship existed in the persons of the County's two current representatives in the Legislative Assembly: his uncle by marriage, George Hayward, and Thomas Obder Miles. Hayward, as previously noted, had married Perley's aunt, Charlotte Upham Perley, and resided with her in Lincoln Parish, opposite Burton on the Oromocto River, in the rich but somewhat swampy interval characteristic of that part of the County. Hayward's grandparents arrived with the Maugerville Planters in the mid-1760s, hence Hayward was closely tied to Perley's demographic. He won election to the Assembly in 1828 and served continuously in that body until the great political upheaval of the 1840s. He was a man of friendly temperament, reasonable in his thought and noted for his gentle humor. His prestige no doubt was enhanced when he bought the lion's share of the late Justice Bliss's Belmont Estate in 1839 from Bliss's nephew and administrator, Lemuel Allan Wilmot.[99]

Miles, in contrast, was of Loyalist heritage, the son of Elijah Miles, an officer in DeLancey's Brigade. When he settled in Maugerville in 1784, old Elijah at first cut a divisive figure by promoting the supremacy of the Church of England over the native Congregational establishment.[100] Hardly a radical, he entered the Assembly campaign of 1802 in opposition to the incumbents, Glenie and Street. The invalidation of a sufficient number of ballots by the High Sheriff, Gabriel DeVeber, allowed Miles the narrowest margin of victory over Street, who nevertheless took the matter on appeal to the Legislature. When the appeal failed, Street vented his rage by attacking Miles with a staff while screaming obscenities at him inside the Burton Courthouse. Murray Young said of him that "in Sunbury County, he was one of the most active magistrates,

[99] Sunbury County Registry, PANB, RS 95, O-16/223.

[100] D.M. Young, "Elijah Miles," *Dictionary of Canadian Biography*, Vol. VI, University of Toronto/Universite Laval, 2003-, http://www.biographi.ca/en/bio/miles_elijah_6E.html.

performing a variety of administrative tasks, acting as a grammar-school trustee, and carrying out judicial duties as a justice of the Inferior Court of Common Pleas. For many years he also commanded the Sunbury battalion of the Provincial Militia, in which he held the rank of lieutenant colonel."[101] His son Thomas succeeded to his seat in the Assembly and to most of his other posts in the County, and served as Hayward's colleague until his defeat in 1837 by the brother of William Perley's creditor, Henry Thomas Partelow. From his home on the north bank of the St. John, Miles had grain to sell, which young Duncan Perley was eager to buy, and was ever welcoming to the younger man at a dinner table where talk probably ranged from local political concerns to the grand issues of the British Imperium.[102]

Hayward and Miles were both of the same type: reasonable and calming, and ever inclined to be a friend to the world. Perley, in contrast, was prone to excitement, particularly when perceiving a slight or an insult, and was entirely capable of making threats or assaulting those who violated his hypersensitive code of honor. In the stratified world of New Brunswick, such tendencies were hardly conducive to success, hence his need for men who would protect him from himself and guide him along a better course.

Opportunity to play a role in public affairs came early on in his residence at Oromocto, when High Sheriff John Hazen called a public meeting in response to a petition delivered to him in order to discuss the propriety of a formal statement from the County in support of a proposed dissolution of the Assembly for its failure to back Lieutenant Governor Colebrooke's plan to induce fiscal responsibility in the Province and to create semi-autonomous municipal governments. When a meeting opened in Sunbury County to discuss the matter, a former Deputy Surveyor and Justice of the Peace in St. John County, Calvin L. Hatheway, proposed a resolution in support of the Lieutenant Governor's agenda and setting forth popular dissatisfaction with the stance on the issue taken by Miles and Hayward. Aggrieved over the criticism directed at his uncle, young Perley stood up and rather saucily denounced

---

[101] Id.

[102] *Diary of Thomas O. Miles*, PANB, MC451, entries for July 19, 1841 and January 5, 1842.

the measure as premature and the meeting itself as unrepresentative of the County as a whole. A mere thirty-five attendees, he said, "had no right to decide what the opinion of the County was."[103] The fact that so many of the 180 people who had petitioned the Sheriff to call the meeting in the first place had, in the end, declined to actually attend was an indication that they "discountenance the proceedings, and gave as effectual a vote as they could have done in person."[104] Taking the comment as a personal affront to himself, Sheriff Hazen contemptuously told the attendees that it would be best to confine the proceedings to the freeholders of the County—a statement implying that Perley wasn't among them and ought to remain silent.[105] Perley replied to the Sheriff "with great warmth," and proceeded with a "replication to the charges" that had been made against the Assembly. This had the effect of setting off a melee of insults motivated by "private antipathies," which was only halted through the intervention of Miles, who "rose and expressed his disapprobation of the indecorous expressions of Mr. Perley and the hasty sentiments of the High Sheriff, with his deep regret that anything so unpleasant should have occurred."[106] It was a "fair and impartial hearing of both sides of the question" that was desired, not this disgrace of a proceeding. Perley's brother William then declared his support for his sibling and for Hayward's position with respect to the Lieutenant Governor's agenda. When the meeting broke up, the parties retreated to the local pubs where ale appears to have only heightened the level of animosity. At Kehoe's alehouse, Perley ran into Hazen, and in an extension of their earlier dispute, threw a fist or two and possibly "scratched" the Sheriff with a knife.[107]

The consequences of assaulting the representative of the Queen's law in the County were not negligible. The report by Miles of Perley being flogged in June of 1842 likely refers to the punishment meted out to him for his ill-advised attack.[108] Perley's humiliating public reproof, however, was hardly sufficient to cabin

---

[103] *New Brunswick Courier*, July 31, 1841.

[104] Id.; and *New Brunswick Courier*, August 14, 1841.

[105] *New Brunswick Courier*, July 31, 1841.

[106] Id.; and *New Brunswick Courier*, August 14, 1841.

[107] *Diary of Thomas O. Miles*, PANB, MC 451, entry for July 13, 1841.

[108] Id., entry for June 22, 1842.

his ambition to play a significant role in County affairs. In the Fall, he was chosen Secretary of the Sunbury County Emigration Society, the aim of which was to encourage the settlement of the County's wilderness lands by the growing influx of emigrants from the British Isles. That Perley was able to put past differences aside in favor of his larger ambition is evident from Sheriff Hazen's presence as the Society's Treasurer. Any discomfort in this circumstance was likely ameliorated by the presence of Miles as Vice President, and that of the lead officer, John M. Wilmot, a Lincoln Parish neighbor of his uncle, former Mayor of the City of St. John and Judge of the Inferior Court of Common Pleas in St. John County.

During the same season, Perley attended a meeting to nominate candidates for election to the House of Assembly.[109] Miles himself apparently wasn't interested in resuming his former place, but did propose that Whitehead Barker join a ticket with his former colleague George Hayward. Perley seconded the nomination and the motion carried unanimously, with the exception of attendee Calvin Hatheway, who objected on the grounds that it was his understanding that the purpose of the meeting was to nominate a candidate from Maugerville alone. When one of Hatheway's enthusiasts nominated him, he received no support beyond one other man. Hatheway nevertheless stood for election as a member of a slate of candidates whose goal was to unseat Henry Partelow, whose connection with his brother John and the ruling party in Fredericton established a guilt by association for the present chaos of provincial finances. Partelow's withdrawal in favor of his business partner and brother-in-law, William Scoullar, proved an effective dodge, as Scoullar won election in Partelow's place. A far better politician than his rivals, Scoullar garnered so much support on the Oromocto River through his spreading of election-time largess that Hayward slipped to third place in the polls and was excluded from office. A small consolation for the Perley clan was the success to the west, in Carleton County, of first-time candidate Charles Perley—a son of Duncan's uncle Thomas.

The defeat of Hayward came at an ill-opportune moment. Some months before, Perley and his brother had met with their uncle and discussed the prospect of a business venture. Hayward had dabbled

---

[109] Id., entry for September 23, 1842

for several years in the timber business in concert with the Perley brothers' cousin James, but that enterprise was withering due to James' lack of prudence in the operation of his affairs.[110] The brothers no doubt apprised their uncle of the large mass of timber untouched by earlier generations of lumbermen that lay near the headwaters of the South Branch of the Oromocto, at South Branch Lake. With their uncle's backing, the brothers imagined they could succeed in harvesting those pristine stands. Hayward agreed with their proposal and loaned the brothers start-up capital. Reflecting on cousin James' failures in business, Hayward insisted that the loan be secured through the mortgage of William's Blissville farm. With the money in hand, the brothers set to work attempting to secure a large timber berth from which to extract timber to feed a saw mill they hoped to rent, and clearing the furthest reaches of the stream of rocks, downed trees and other obstacles so as to allow navigation of rafts of wood in the coming spring. Hayward's membership in the Assembly would have ensured better access to privilege and preference, and provided the brothers with a lobbyist possessing some clout with the bureaucrats in the Crown Land Office. That Scoullar was there instead was rather disastrous for their enterprise, as he and Partelow harbored the exact same ambition. Scoullar operated mills along the Oromocto River and a small shipyard in the village at the River's mouth, and was soon able to put forward an application for a massive mill reserve around the Lake encompassing the berth the Perley brothers had already obtained. The extensive amount of work the brothers had done in clearing the stream now would inure to the benefit of their competitors unless the aspirations of the latter were thwarted.

Both sides engaged in tremendous lobbying with the Crown Land Office, pleading with the Surveyor General the merits of their respective cases. Simultaneously, a war of words and sometimes more was waged in Sunbury County. Though he was no longer in the Assembly, Partelow remained a local magistrate with power over small suits brought within his jurisdiction. He tended to show disfavor to the Perleys, and even used his official forum as a vehicle for the condemnation of the brothers. The Perleys retaliated by

[110] See *Hayward & Others v. White* (1843) 2 Kerr 304.

attempting to intimidate anyone associated with their rivals. When Scoullar's agent, George F. Wilmot, went to the home of a local Justice of the Peace with Partelow's brother-in-law, Edward Allison Clowes, the Perleys and one of their henchmen menacingly waited outside. After brother William called for a knife to cut the harness of Clowes' team of horses to prevent escape, both brothers launched an assault on Wilmot that left him prostrate and bloodied. While William went into hiding lest he be held to account for his barbarism, Duncan remained unphased by any notion of discretion. He was apprehended in Oromocto by parish constables and placed within the confines of the local gaol, where he was held to answer for his misconduct by Partelow. Remarkably, Partelow's own business-related debts rendered him a probationary inmate at the same time, hence his helming of the proceeding against his fellow detainee was rather indecorous to say the least. Perley was placed on probation, but quickly became the target of further wrath, as Partelow continued, in Perley's words, "to harass and annoy your petitioner with frivolous and vexatious lawsuits" and to engage in activity "utterly reckless of all consequences in the encouragement of unnecessary litigious proceedings to the great detriment and damage not only of your petitioner but of the whole neighborhood in which" Partelow resided.[111] Addressing the Lieutenant Governor directly, Perley demanded Partelow's removal from his position of trust in the County as a Justice of the Peace and member of the Court of the General Sessions.[112]

His troubles with Partelow were not the only legal matters Perley contended with. He and his brother were sued in the Circuit Court by the merchant William Henry Scovil for recovery of an unpaid debt, and subjected after trial to a judgment for £84.[113] His subsequent sale of his Oromocto farm for £50 may have been necessary to cover the debt and avoid further legal complications. That he remained on or near this land as a tenant is evident from the fact that his pastoral activities in the area continued. A frequent source of vexation in Sunbury County, as elsewhere, was the escape of cattle from poorly maintained enclosures. After roaming from

---

[111] *Petition of Duncan W. Perley*, November 9, 1843, Records of Lt. Governor Sir William McBean George Colebrooke, PANB, RS 345, B/4.

[112] Id.

[113] Sunbury County Registry, PANB, RS 95, P-17/192.

their normal pasture on Perley's property, two of Perley's cows were found astray and taken into custody by Edward McNeal. Perley was arrested after seizing the cows back without paying an impound fee and held to answer for the charge at the Burton Courthouse. He apparently managed to convince the Court of the General Sessions that the cows hadn't strayed at all, but had been stolen, and that far more appropriate would be the hauling before its august members of his accuser to explain how it is he came to have possession of another man's livestock.[114] With Charles F. Street, John M. Wilmot and Thomas O. Miles presiding, the Court discharged the accused from custody and dismissed the matter—apparently chalking it up to a misunderstanding.[115] As the proceeding ended, Perley had words with George Nevers, Jr., perhaps over testimony provided in the case. Mere words gave rise to blows, but not significant enough to spawn further litigation.

On the same day that he complained of Partelow, Perley and his brother and uncle petitioned the Crown Land Office for the purpose of informing the Surveyor General of their having "heard with the greatest anxiety and alarm that an application is now before Your Excellency for a mill reserve of the whole country laid open by the industry and capital of your petitioners," and explaining that if the application were granted it would result in "irreparable injury" to their rights.[116] Scoullar, they said, was only tenuously in possession of the mills for which his application related, on account of his debts having recently led to an order of execution and the targeting of his assets for sale to satisfy the demands of his many creditors.[117] Scoullar's personal hostility toward the Perley brothers was also so intense as to raise a complete barrier to their access to the milling facilities still under their rival's control. They insisted on the rather novel concept of free competition on the river amongst Her Majesty's subjects and avoidance of what they predicted would amount to an unjust monopoly if their own request were denied.

---

[114] *Diary of Thomas O. Miles*, PANB, MC 451, entry for July 18, 1843

[115] Id., entry for July 21, 1843

[116] *Petition of George Hayward, William E. Perley and Duncan W. Perley*, November 9, 1843, SU/1845, Timber and Saw Mill Petitions, Timber and Saw Mills, PANB, RS 663a.

[117] Id.

The result of this latest petition was a delay of a decision by the government. Not content to await further action by the Crown, the Perleys opened a new campaign to win the day through the agency of the many people of the river their recent enterprise had employed, and with whom they shared common bonds of kinship and the Free Will Baptist faith. Informing the Lieutenant Governor that they "are in the habit of cutting mill logs on the Oromocto and its branches for the supply of the mills on those streams and elsewhere, and that they have for several years past found themselves much restricted in their operation by the increasing scarcity of good chances," a large group of local resident petitioners praised the efforts of Hayward and the Perleys in investing in the expensive yet highly valuable effort of clearing the South Branch of obstructions so as to make the harvesting of timber around the Lake possible.[118] Conversely, they denounced the attempts "now being made by Mr. William Scoullar to obtain the bounty thus thrown open and to monopolize those advantages under the specious pretense of obtaining a reserve for a mill which he pretends to own on the South Branch." The man's debts were so enormous and the claims of creditors "so numerous that your memorialists scarcely know whom to regard as the proper owners." Scoullar, they said, might well be within his rights under the law to seek such a benefit, but special exceptions in the law were properly applicable under the circumstances. The interests of justice being the most compelling exception, these could not be disregarded lest Scoullar benefit from the industry and investment of others. He was a monopolist, whose desire for a reserve was a "specious pretense" to gain for himself control of a vast region of untapped timber to which he would, in turn, allow entry only to those sublessors able to pay his price.

The petition was effective only in slowing the process of review, but did not achieve the objective of its authors; for Scoullar managed to avail himself of his and Partelow's relationships in Fredericton to taint the claims and reputations of his principal opponents with accusations of poaching in the back woods, even as his own crews raided timber berths belonging to others.[119] In the

[118] *Memorial of the Inhabitants of the Oromocto River*, July 9, 1844, SU/1844, Timber and Saw Mills, 1817-1865, Timber and Saw Mills, PANB, RS 663a.

[119] See Grady, op. cit., at pp. 79-80.

end, Scoullar prevailed, and his opponents were relegated to making futile complaints in the provincial capital, seeking reimbursement for what amounted to public improvements, and plotting to remove their nemesis from his seat in the provincial legislature come the next election.

The relative ease by which well-connected persons could avail themselves of the benefits supposedly open equally to all, even when opposed by a large segment of the population, was a reflection of the reality of the power of patronage in a society formally organized hierarchically in a manner traceable to the Middle Ages, with the toiling orders at the bottom, yet benefitting, it was said, from the superior knowledge and wisdom of the middling and upper tiers, and all enjoying the protection of the Crown. For men such as D. W. Perley, such a regime was intolerably suffocating, and far too constraining on ambition. Some irony existed in the fact of his own descent from the founders of New England and the role of his grandfather and his Peabody and Hazen relations in establishing the Province decades earlier. Close kinsmen such as cousins Amos and Charles Perley and his uncle George Hayward, and more distant relations such as various members of the Hazen clan, might have attained important positions in the colonial hierarchy, but Perley himself was outside the narrow ranks of the most privileged families, and his claims for preference trailed behind a host of elder and younger sons of families of slightly more or equally elevated rank. His interest in pursuing the law as a career, evident in his reading of law either solitarily or with a local barrister, was constrained by the pretensions and interests of the provincial bar, whose members were as jealous of one another as they were hostile to anyone who might breach their ranks.[120] No one could become an attorney without first commencing his study of the law in the Court itself or with an existing member of the bar, sitting for an examination and producing a certificate "testifying to his fitness and capacity," which likely included proper heritage and family relations, possession of knowledge of the law, and, less importantly, exhibition of those civil impulses sufficient to overcome the urge to strangle, beat,

---

[120] M. V. B. Perley, op. cit., at p. 407

shoot or stab one's adversary.[121] A bar association with formal rules for the training and licensing to practice law, and calculated in part to facilitate "a shift 'from family connexion to peer control'" and the "recruitment to the bar from non-elite classes" wasn't formed until 1846, and didn't gain substantial momentum as a force for change in provincial legal culture until some years later.[122] Until the coming of those more progressive times, a handful of men might gain admission to the bar each year, and of these only a few as barristers.[123] The provincial bar throughout the 1840s remained what it always had been: a bastion of convention, native hierarchy and elitist pretension.

The internal obstacles to entry into the legal establishment during this era are exemplified by the reaction to the appointment of a new member of the Supreme Court in the mid-1830s. When Colonial authorities in London deigned to appoint a man unconnected with the leading families of the law, and lacking any relationship with the Province whatsoever, the fury from the

121 Allen Otty Earle, *General Rules and Orders of the Supreme Court* (St. John: George A. Knodell, 1881), at p. 107

122 Philip Girard, *Lawyers and Legal Culture in British North America: Beamish Murdock of Halifax* (Toronto: University of Toronto Press, 2011), at p. 53.

123 In October of 1845, only two men, William J. Gilbert and William B. Chandler, Jr., were admitted as "Barristers," and eight others as "Attorneys." In the following February, Charles A. Hartt, Gabriel and Nelson DeVeber, James Odell, Acalus L. Palmer and James Steadman were promoted to "Barrister" from the thin ranks of the Province's "Attorneys." (See *The Headquarters*, October 29, 1845 and February 7, 1846). The names of these individuals largely confirm the hereditary privilege of membership in the provincial Bar. Chandler was the son and namesake of the legislative leader of the "Compact Government" and a near kinsman of the Botsfords and Uphams. Gabriel DeVeber was the namesake grandson of Sunbury County's first High Sheriff and a great nephew of Sunbury's Chief Justice of the Inferior Court of Common Pleas, William Hubbard. Nelson DeVeber hailed from the same family. James Odell was a child of William Franklin Odell and grandson of Jonathan Odell, who collectively controlled the powerful Provincial Clerkship for 60 years. James Steadman would serve in the Assembly and marry a daughter of Assemblyman John Adolphus Beckwith and Mary Ann Street Berton— herself a daughter of the High Sheriff of York County, granddaughter of Samuel Denny Street, and great niece of Nathaniel Hubbard. Acalus L. Palmer's was the son of a member of the Assembly, and would later serve as a Justice of the New Brunswick Supreme Court. Perley's familial connections were valuable, but not so potent as the connections these men who entered the profession at the same time that Perley was resolving to fly the Province and seek his fortune elsewhere.

disappointed native high-born office seekers revealed the depth of elitist chauvinism. There were, noted the historian MacNutt, "many outbursts in the press against the appearance on the New Brunswick bench of a 29-year-old stranger from England," regardless of his legal pedigree. The condemnation in the newspapers of the day was echoed in the formal remonstrance of the flower of the provincial bar, consisting of men bearing the names Street, Saunders, Putnam, Peters, Wetmore, Robinson, Wilmot and Chandler.[124] The appointee, Sir James Carter, managed to weather the storm of protest. His character, learning and high competence proved "so impressive that the heated reaction against him quickly abated."[125] It is a remarkable commentary on the state of New Brunswick society and a sign of the barriers to entry that instead of becoming a prototype for a new kind of man in the legal establishment, "free of the family connections and alliances that explain New Brunswick politics at the time," Carter was considered a happy exception. Acceptance of Carter by the provincial elite undoubtedly only grew upon his marriage to a granddaughter of the late Justice Winslow.[126]

Carter's independence from the provincial elite allowed the Judge to see clearly the innocence of the charge of libel of two journalists arrested by the House of Assembly in February of 1844 for printing an attack on Lemuel Allan Wilmot for the latter's support for the Lieutenant Governor's call for Responsible Government. When he freed the journalists in response to their Petition for a Writ of Habeas Corpus he effectively "brought to an end the Assembly's old custom of imprisoning those who offended its 'privileges" and established in the Province the principle of "freedom of the press from parliamentary control."[127] Individual members of the Assembly nevertheless retained their right to seek

---

[124] MacNutt, "Sir James Carter," *Dictionary of Canadian Biography*, Vol. X, University of Toronto/Universite Laval, 2003-, http://www.biographi.ca/en/bio/carter_james_10E.html.; and Lawrence, *The Judges of New Brunswick and Their Times*, supra, at p. 343.

[125] MacNutt, "Sir James Carter," supra.

[126] Lawrence, *The Judges of New Brunswick and Their Times*, supra, at p. 359.

[127] MacNutt, "Sir James Carter," supra; and Eric L. Swanick, "Thomas Hill," *Dictionary of Canadian Biography*, Vol. VIII, University of Toronto/Universite Laval, 2003-, http://www.biographi.ca/en/bio/hill_thomas_8E.html.

redress for defamatory comments, so long at least as those comments were unrelated to their official conduct.

Carter's handling of the case brought against those accused of libel proved to be a kind of prelude to a similar action against Perley. The young man's lack of hesitancy in speaking freely of the sins of William Scoullar and the unfair frustration by that man of the Perley family's enterprise ultimately drew a civil suit from Scoullar, and culminated in a trial at the Burton Courthouse over which Judge Carter presided.[128] Conviction of the charge and the award against him of £5 in damages was likely the final blow to Perley's faith in his ability, as a man of merit and energy, to find a place in provincial society commensurate with his sense of his own talents and ambition. If the famously independent judge, once disparaged for his lack of rank in native circles, was prepared to impose punishment on him for his own disparagement of a member of the corrupt native elite, there could for him be no future in New Brunswick.

Where, though, was a man such as Perley to fly? The nearby Provinces of Prince Edward Island and Newfoundland were places dominated by absentee feudal landlords and stone age-like primitivism, and Nova Scotia was as controlled by a native elite as was New Brunswick. Upper Canada had its own Family Compact to contend with, and ancestral New England was utterly foreign to him. Best for an ambitious man to find a blank slate on which to write his future, contending with rivals as free as was he of the advantages acquired from inherited privilege and patronage from well-connected and deep-rooted friends and relations. For a man such as Perley, only the frontier of civilization offered the kind of environment where a free man could prosper, and such could only be found, in the mid-1840s, in the United States, in the American West. It was to the West, then, that Perley went, with little but his experience, his talents and his ambition to aid him along the way. It was a daring and risky decision, but one characteristic of the man, and utterly necessary if he was to achieve the success to which he almost manically aspired.

---

[128] *Diary of Thomas O. Miles*, PANB, RS 451, entry for February 24, 1845.

Chapter Two

FREEDOM ON THE BRAZOS

The country Perley made entry to during the middle of the 1840s was around its perimeter neither impressive nor inspiring. It was said of the place at the time that when approached by sea, low sand beaches, littered with driftwood and "backed by wet and level prairies, offer few inducements to the agricultural settler."[1] From the south across the Rio Grande, "it wears an aspect of aridity," and if approached from the east, through Louisiana and the Red River, "it breaks upon the observer as a poor upland district, overrun with wood, with a weak soil of alternate sand and clay." Setting these aesthetic obstacles aside long enough to penetrate the borders a short distance, it was said that "the scene is entirely changed," and the weary traveler would behold a countryside utterly unlike the initial impression made upon his mind.

As a whole, Texas was still undefined; its political boundaries not entirely resolved. It was a land divided into three regions: a coastal plain in the south; a zone of rolling hills beyond the plain to the north; and, much further north, larger hills and mountains far too remote and in the grasp of the Comanches to inspire any thoughts of settlement or exploitation. The natural orientation of the place runs north to south, parallel with the many rivers that originate in the northern highlands and drain into the Gulf of Mexico. Wherever man might tread, at least in the more inhabited portions of the territory, the foot fell on a verdant ground, adorned with a "multitudinous array of plants and flowers [that] would seem to defy calculation and arrangement"—the dahlia, the trumpet-flower, geranium, heart's-ease, lupin, several varieties of the lily and digitalis, lady's slipper, anemone, jessamine, golden rod, lobelia cardinalis, the passion-flower, various species of the rose,

---

[1] William Kennedy, *Texas: Its Geography, Natural History, and Topography* (New York: Benjamin and Young, John Street, 1844), at p. 10.

primroses, violets and the delicate flower of the ground apple.[2] Grass was everywhere, growing high and green, and top heavy with seed.

Exploring the country in the coastal plain from east to west, following the curve of the coastline for hundreds of miles, the traveler would observe to the north and west of the Sabine River along the border with Louisiana the flat and wooded nature of the land, giving way between Lake Sabine and Galveston Bay to a dull and generally barren prairie, "destitute of trees, except on the margins of the water courses."[3] Beginning at the north-east point of the Bay, the landscape of the coastal plain "improves, and a large extent of gently-sloping prairie, agreeably diversified by skirts of timber, spreads across the wood bottom of the Trinity River, save in the immediate vicinity of Galveston, where the prairie is mostly wet and sterile."[4] Except for some fine rolling lands on the San Jacinto River and Buffalo Bayou, the region extending to the west from Galveston Bay to the Brazos "is one unbroken plain, rather low and sandy," but marked, further inland, "by insulated groves and timbered streams." The greatest of these is the aforementioned Brazos, or Brazos de Dios. Originating in the Guadalupe Mountains in the far north, it flows in a circuitous course a distance of a thousand miles. Like the Red River to the north-east, earthy deposits washed from upstream tinge its waters scarlet, while the flow of one of its tributaries through a large saline reservoir in the interior gives it at times a brackish quality. The slippery red and blue clay banks of the Brazos, for an extent of two hundred miles from its mouth, range from twenty to forty feet in height, making it resistant to overflow, and preventing the drowning of the countryside beneath the seasonal freshet.[5] The mouth of the River is a hundred and seventy yards wide and the River itself remains at a width of between a hundred-and-fifty to two-hundred yards for two-hundred miles upstream, rendering it ideal for navigation were it not for the sand bars and the tangle of accumulated organic debris.

---

[2] Id., at p. 61.
[3] Id., at p. 8.
[4] Id.
[5] Id., at 19

The first steamers had appeared on the lower stretch of the Brazos as early as 1834, and more now were appearing in the middle of the 1840s. Their course upstream from near the mouth was a pleasant journey. As the coast receded behind the passenger, the country rose "in gentle and beautiful undulations above the alluvial region of the Brazos, Colorado, and Guadalupe, extending in a north-westerly direction up those rivers, from a hundred-and-fifty to two-hundred miles, as far as the hilly district," and presenting "a delightful variety of fertile prairie and valuable woodland, enriched with springs, and rivulets of pure and sparkling water."[6] To the east, as one journeyed upstream, lay a partially woody terrain, interspersed with large cane-brakes; to the west, a wide prairie, dissected by "numerous streams and small rivers which discharge their waters into the gulf" and "invite the stranger in search of a fertile settlement to journey inland, where he is certain to obtain the fulfilment of his hopes and wishes."[7] The soil here is rich alluvion, "singularly free from those accumulations of stagnant water, which, combined with a burning sun and exuberant vegetation, render a large proportion of the southern parts of the United States little better than a sickly desert."[8] The porous character of the soil, the gradual elevation of the level lands toward the interior, and the general rise of the banks from the beds of the streams, happily precluded "the formation of swamps to any injurious extent."[9] Called by some the "Italy of America," the region and its climate were saved from excessive heat and humidity by the cool breezes blowing from the Gulf, making it on the whole "favorable to life, and to most of the products which render life agreeable."[10]

Or so it was to a certain class of men, of European heritage, convinced of the superiority of their race over all others, and permitted by the sanction of the law to enslave those supposedly bereft of nature's gifts and set them to work on pain of the lash at the task of transforming the soil watered by the Brazos into a

---

[6] Id., at p. 8.
[7] Id.
[8] Id.
[9] Id., at p. 8.
[10] Id., at p. 40.

garden lush with cotton and sugar to clothe the world and sweeten its palate. It was a country far different from New Brunswick, in climate, terrain and economic and social institutions. A free man might go far there, unrestrained by the hierarchies of the British Empire, but woe to he or she born of Africa and barred from advancement in a society welcoming of the merits of all white men. Their fate was a dolorous one, which only a wrathful destruction wrought by fire and sword could alter.

The Texas seaboard was largely unknown and unvisited by mariners prior to the coming of the Americans.[11] Its treachery, in the form of innumerable sand bars and hidden sandy shoals that shifted so often no navigator could learn and avoid them, counseled an overland transit by Stephen Austin's legendary company in 1820 and 1821. Perley may have come overland twenty-five years later, though it seems more likely, given the advances in seafaring, navigation and harbor facilities, that he came by water, either down the tributaries of the Mississippi and the Mississippi itself, or via sail or steam around Florida's long peninsula from the east coast. One report supplied by his nephew a half century after his death that he went immediately to Philadelphia has been confirmed by no other source.[12] His precise departure date is not even known. His last appearance in the records of New Brunswick before his emigration is in the pages of the diary of Thomas O. Miles, documenting his defamation trial, in an entry dating from February of 1845. That same month, the United States Senate voted 27-25 to admit Texas as a State, setting off a chain of events that would culminate in annexation by year's end. The New Brunswick press covered the happenings on the Texas front, presenting verbatim the words of those favoring annexation, but expressing scorn for what it predicted would be "an immediate occupation of the Territory...by numerous hordes of adventurers" and encouragement by Congress of widescale immigration.[13]

---

[11] Id., at p. 11.

[12] "D. W. Perley," Pioneer Index File: 1906-1934, California History Room, California State Library, Sacramento, California.

[13] *The Headquarters*, December 10, 1845.

The imminent admission of Texas to the American Union certainly portended the organization of Texas society behind the protective shield of American arms, and though slavery was inevitably to find an increasingly safer haven there and contribute to the further divide over the issue of human bondage that America's spread across the continent entailed, the new State appeared nonetheless as an attractive place for an ambitious man, hungry for success and willing to compete for it in rough, egalitarian fashion on a playing field far more level than was found in Great Britain's maritime provinces. That Perley knew few if any people there made his decision all the more daring, and reveals the depth of his independence and the intensity of his confidence in himself.

The commencement of war between the United States and Mexico early in 1846 did not deter Perley's resolve. Energized by the arid climate, so different from New Brunswick, Perley explored the coastal prairie along the lower Brazos, then settled in the Richmond area, near the heart of Stephen Austin's original colony. Ten years earlier, the counties around the mouth of the Brazos had already become extremely prosperous. Fronting the Gulf of Mexico, Brazoria was the most affluent county in the State on account of the rich alluvial bottom lands of the Brazos River, ideal for cotton and sugar cultivation and the establishment of a slave-based plantation system.[14] The river itself had not yet fulfilled its full potential, as it remained filled with oak snags, at least until shortly after Perley's arrival, when the obstructions were being cleared and a steamer worthy of the name was being prepared to service the region.[15] By the time of Perley's settlement, Brazoria was the commercial center of Texas, a cotton clearing house, and the heart of the newly formed First Judicial District, where the sharpest lawyers in the State practiced their profession.

---

[14] Jim L. Bridges, *The History of Fort Bend County, 1822-1861* (M.A. thesis, University of Texas, Austin, 1939), at p. 147; and Roger Allen Griffen, *Connecticut Yankee in Texas: A Biography of Elisha Marshall Pease* (Ph.D diss., University of Texas, Austin, 1973), at p. 49.

[15] "Navigation of the Brazos," *The Democratic Telegraph and Texas Register*, September 13, 1849.

The greatest man of the surrounding region was John Hunter Herndon, a Kentucky native who had migrated overland to Texas in the 1830s via New Orleans, studied law, and received his bar license in 1838.[16] He did legal work for future Texas Governor Elisha M. Pease and the new State's first Attorney General, John Woods Harris, before striking out on his own.[17] His marriage to Barbara Makall Wilkinson Calvitt, the daughter of one of Austin's 300, was his greatest success, as it connected him not only to the enormous Calvitt Estate and sugar plantation, but also to his new bride's aunt, Jane Wilkinson Long. Called "the Mother of Texas" in honor of her service on behalf of the Texas revolutionaries, Long had come to Texas in 1820 with her ill-fated husband, the filibuster Dr. James H. Long. After moving to Brazoria in the 1830s, she ran the boarding house where Austin defied the Mexican Government and where Mirabeau Lamar headquartered his presidential campaign.[18] She received a grant of a league of land in Brazoria in 1828, and occupied it a decade later with Lamar and his family.[19] Herndon stood to inherit something of the Long Estate, thus he was most anxious to safeguard it through application of his legal acumen. As an attorney, he handled its legal affairs from his home at Richmond in neighboring Fort Bend County. His interests in affairs of state prompted him to accept appointment as the Republic's congressional engrossing clerk and to join the ill-fated Summerville Campaign in 1842. It was he and his law partner and kinsman, James S. Sullivan, who drafted Fort Bend County's resolution calling for the annexation of Texas by the United States.[20] By the mid-1840s, he was the largest land holder in the County, and probably its largest slave owner. [21]

Herndon's neighbors along the Brazos were primarily in the cotton business, and, like Herndon himself, held large estates with many men and women in bondage. While they strove ever for

---

[16] Andrew Forest Muir, "John Hunter Herndon," *Handbook of Texas, https://www.tshaonline.org/handbook/entries/herndon-john-hunter.*

[17] Id.

[18] Clarence Wharton, *History of Fort Bend, Texas* (San Antonio, 1939), p. 97.

[19] Id.

[20] Id., at p. 118.

[21] Id., at p. 124.

economic advancement, their mores were traditional, defined by a model of conduct lampooned by its critics as chivalrous, entailing generic good manners, alternating with flashes of mortal passion whenever personal slight was perceived. Duels were an accepted way of life for men in this manly society. Much of the population had migrated across the South from Mississippi, Alabama and Louisiana, fighting the Spanish, the Creek Indians and each other along the way, and they were prepared to fight yet again once they reached their destination. Why the ritualized combat of the duel was so much a part of the culture of Texas and the South is of course open to speculation. Some have suggested that the duel was "a mechanism designed to display macho—to prove honor, fearlessness, implacability in the face of insult," while others have made a connection between the duel and the military-mindedness of Southerners and a "cult of virility," and argue that it was evidence of a disinclination "to use the courts in connection with personal matters."[22] The historian John Hope Franklin has even "worked the whole matter of the duel neatly into his thesis that nineteenth-century upper-class Southerners were violent men, made so by the 'peculiar institution of slavery.'"[23] As true as these theories might be, entirely or in part, the duel was also a fixture of western culture as a whole, evident in that stage of social evolution when legal institutions are weak and compliance with the law is dependent on a personal commitment rooted in honor rather than the police power of the state. The suggestion that a man was less than honest was an attack on his commitment to peace, and rather than deploy one's entire clan in securing vengeance on the slanderer, the accuser and the accused alone accepted the consequence of violence as a means to settle the matter. It is no surprise that military men were prone to dueling. The popularity of the ritual among the legal class both in Texas and New Brunswick, and later in California, is perhaps the best indication that it was the only mechanism by which men living in a primitive state of society could prove that they could be trusted to honestly present the facts in a court of law, preserve the laws on which social order depends,

---

[22] Jack K. Williams, *Dueling in the Old South: Vignettes of Social History* (College Station: Texas A&M University Press, 1980), at p. 5.

[23] Id., at pp. 5-6.

and vindicate the rights of man. Calling a lawyer a liar or a cheat was an attack on the lawyer's commitment to the legal system, and in a much larger sense, on the legal system itself. Any man prepared to make such a charge had best be prepared to defend the charge with his very life.

Herndon's web of acquaintance was large and included such figures as the brothers William and John Austin Wharton: Tennessee-born planters of Brazoria prominent in the Republic's military affairs. The brothers, both lawyers, had come to Texas prior to the Revolution and taken part in many of the great events leading to independence. William led the army in the early stages of the revolt, lost the Presidency to Sam Houston, and was dead from an accidental gunshot wound in 1839.[24] Brother John feuded with the Austins and nearly lost his life in a duel with one of them.[25] He fought valiantly at San Jacinto and served as Representative from Brazoria County in the First Congress.[26] Before his death in 1838, John Austin Wharton had been the original law partner of Herndon's mentor Elisha Pease, and was succeeded in this partnership by his cousin, John Woods Harris. Herndon himself occupied a manor house on land purchased from the Whartons. William Henry's son, named in his uncle John's honor, was in South Carolina during Perley's tenure in Texas, but when he returned, he joined Harris and Pease in a law practice, and then formed a partnership with Frank Terry.

The grandson of a member of the Virginia House of Burgesses and the son of a gambler who chose cards over wife and children, Terry was the chieftain of a rugged Baptist kin-group who migrated across Mississippi, Alabama and Louisiana from Kentucky. When settled for a time in Hinds County, Mississippi, Terry's aunt married Governor Hiram Runnells, thus forging a powerful alliance with a clan that would also settle in the Lone Star State. The Terrys and their kin, the Smiths, had large holdings not only on the Brazos—in Fort Bend and Brazoria Counties—but also in the vicinity of Houston, roughly thirty miles from Richmond. The clan

---

[24] Merle Weir, "William Henry Wharton," *Handbook of Texas*, https://www.tshaonline.org/handbook/entries/wharton-william-henry.

[25] Randolph B. Campbell, "John Austin Wharton," *Handbook of Texas*, https://www.tshaonline.org/handbook/entries/wharton-john-austin.

[26] Id.

was famously proud, and though committed to courtesy, were prepared to fight if honor was denigrated. They were ferociously partisan as well, and committed to the preservation of the southern way of life and its peculiar institution. Uncle Ben Fort Smith had served as a member of the staff of Andrew Jackson at the battle of New Orleans, in the Mississippi Legislature and the Texas House of Representatives, and was a notorious and illicit trader in slaves.[27] Once in Texas, he flaunted Mexican law by bringing slaves from other States and the Caribbean into the rich cotton plains of the Brazos and Colorado Rivers. It's likely that one of his motivations in joining the rebellion against Mexico was to end that government's meddling in his business affairs, including commerce in his fellow man. Harriet Martineau's observation that there was, on the eve of the Revolution, no "more ferocious a company of ruffians than Texas contains at this moment," anxious to "wrench the territory from the hands of the Mexicans," fairly applies to him.[28]

The prominence of Kentuckians in the lower Brazos business and legal communities was quite pronounced. In addition to Herndon, the Smiths and the Terrys, there was James Love, a native of Nelson County, a lawyer, former state legislator and one-time Congressman.[29] He was of the faction of Henry Clay and John Jordan Crittenden, a Whig, hence out of step with most of the men he mixed with in Texas, including Sam Houston, whom he detested.[30] With fellow-Kentuckian Albert Sidney Johnston, he speculated in land and built a significant barony.[31] In 1845, he commenced a single term as Judge in the First District Court of the new State of Texas. Practicing in that Court with distinction was John J. Crittenden's nephew, Alexander Parker Crittenden. The same age as Perley, he entered the legal profession after completing his education at West Point, married young and started a family,

---

[27] May Wilson McBee, "Benjamin Fort Smith," *Handbook of Texas*, https://www.tshaonline.org/handbook/entries/smith-benjamin-fort.

[28] Harriet Martineau, *Society in America*, Volume I (Paris: Baudry's European Library, 1837), at p. 227.

[29] Rose M. Harris, "James Love," *Handbook of Texas*, http://www.tshaonline.org/handbook/entries/love-james.

[30] Margaret Swett Henson & Donald E. Willett, *The Texas That Might Have Been: Sam Houston's Foes Writing to Albert Sidney Johnston* (College Station: Texas A&M University Press, 2009), at pp. 9-10.

[31] Id., at p. 9.

and then moved to Texas in the 1830s, where he worked for a time for Pease and Harris, and later formed a professional partnership with an Alabama-born lawyer, Tod Robinson, who was also his brother-in-law. In time, Robinson would be recognized as "a cogent, logical reasoner, a racy debater," and able to "hurl the shaft of irony with cutting effect."[32] His manner was calm and dignified, and his utterances mellow, earnest in tone, and marked from time to time with quotations from Shakespeare.[33] Crittenden's reputation grew just as prodigiously. At this early date, he surely showed signs of the traits that would make him one of the West's great advocates: a disdain for every tortive approach and an urge to advance "at once to the main idea involved in an inquiry," a "natural quickness and aptitude for reasoning…rendered more acute by training at the Military Academy at West Point," an ability to transform mere inferences into demonstrations, and the "trenchant blade of his logic" that "hewed its way to a conclusion with a force which was irresistible."[34] Together, the two young men were a formidable pair, destined for greatness in the Far West.

The two men most significant in Perley's life, with whom he would form lifelong personal and professional relationships, Perley met in Texas. The first, Volney Erskine Howard, was a rare figure in the Southland—a native of Maine who came south to Mississippi to practice law with an uncle, and grew to prefer the region to his place of nativity. Finding his uncle dead when he arrived, he dedicated himself to his profession, and soon won a place for himself of note among a highly distinguished bar that included Robert J. Walker, S. S. Prentis and John Anthony Quitman.[35] His high degree of energy is evident in the diversity of his endeavors. He served in the State Legislature, purchased, operated and edited a newspaper, and took appointment to the post of Reporter for the Mississippi Supreme Court. He fought a duel against former Governor Runnells after he criticized the Governor for his management of the Union Bank, survived the ordeal and eventually

[32] Oscar T. Shuck, *History of the Bench and Bar of California* (Los Angeles: The Commercial Printing House, 1901), at p. 460.

[33] Id.

[34] Id., at p. 404.

[35] "Death of Volney Howard: A Great Man Passes Quietly Away," *Los Angeles Daily Herald*, May 15, 1889.

made his peace with the man. The intensity of Mississippi politics necessitated his removal to New Orleans, and then to Texas. His eminence as a man of the law won him a seat at the State's Constitutional Convention in the summer of 1845, followed by service as the State's Attorney General and membership in the State Senate. Upon Perley's arrival on the Brazos, Howard was already one of the leaders of the Texas Bar, and a man with whom Perley must surely have become acquainted.

The other man of significance in Perley's life whom Perley met during his years in Texas was David S. Terry, the younger brother of Frank. Terry, whom Perley called "Dave," was a man of singular intelligence and courtesy, yet prone to rage when perceiving an insult. He was a fearless friend and a fearsome enemy. His views on the most controversial subjects were pointed and his faith in God, channeled through the Baptist creed he shared with Perley, was fervent and unquestioning. At the age of 21 he studied law in the Galveston office of his uncle, T. J. B. Hadley, and became an attorney a year later. A more extensive practice of the law was delayed by the Mexican War. He enlisted in Captain Samuel Ballowe's Company of John Coffee Hays' Texas Mounted Rifleman, and fought at the Battle of Monterey and in other armed encounters. Richard Roman recalled seeing him on the frontier, either as a soldier or as one of Hays' Rangers, protecting the homes of outlying settlers from attacks by the Mexican Army, bandits and the Comanches.[36] An interest in politics prompted him to enter the race for the office of District Attorney for Galveston County. Though backed by Hadley, with whom he had formed a law partnership, and endorsed by brother Frank, Hiram Runnells and even former President Lamar, his bid for elective office failed.[37] He and Perley first became acquainted in Houston in 1846 when both were practicing law.[38] "His position at the bar was good," Perley later said of Terry.[39] His character then "was not only unimpeached but

---

[36] *Trial of David S. Terry by the Committee of Vigilance, San Francisco* (San Francisco: R.C. Moore & Co., 1856), at p. 54.

[37] Albert Russell Buchanan, *David S. Terry of California: Dueling Judge* (San Marino: The Huntington Library, 1956), at p. 7, fn. 11.

[38] *Trial of David S. Terry by the Committee of Vigilance, San Francisco*, op. cit., at p. 44.

[39] Id.

unimpeachable...noble, high-minded, magnanimous, and honorable...."[40] He was, however, even then "a man prompt to resent an injury."[41] A. P. Crittenden knew him well from 1841 when Terry was still a teenager, and called him "impulsive, generous and brave, yet not turbulent or quarrelsome."[42] No young man in the community, he said, "occupied a higher position or enjoyed, in a larger degree, the respect and good feeling of the people."[43] There was no question that he had a great future ahead of him, and was a person with whom an alliance, once formed, would prove unshakable.

When Perley settled on the Brazos River, it appears that he made fast acquaintance with all or most of these men. His social impulses were strong and irresistible, though his innate sensitivity, arising perhaps from the loss of his father at a young age and the denial of opportunities by men of greater rank in the class-bound society of the Maritime Provinces, could prove the undoing of friendships so easily made. His sense of personal honor must have been appreciated by these southern men, for whom violence was an acceptable method of resolving disputes over questions about a man's integrity. That some of them were lawyers was decisive for Perley. The lack of any hierarchy so well defined as the one in which he came of age, and the rather libertarian mode of life, at least for white men, made entry into the legal profession relatively easy. Aspirants to the bar were but required to make application and take an exam overseen by a committee of attorneys appointed by a district court judge.

So it was that on October 19, 1846, Perley appeared in the First District Court in Fort Bend presided over by Judge Love and presented his application for a license to practice law in the Courts of the State of Texas in concert with a man named Philemon T. Herbert.[44] Herbert was a native of Alabama and had only recently come to Texas after being expelled from the University for stabbing

40 Id.

41 Id., at p. 53.

42 Id., at p. 58.

43 Id.

44 Fort Bend, Texas, County Court, Minute Books, B/169, entry for October 19, 1846.

a fellow student.[45] He may have followed to Texas a cousin—Henry William Waters—and even studied with him before the latter forsook the legal profession for medicine.[46] The appointment by Judge Love of John Herndon, James S. Sullivan and Porter McGreal to form a committee to examine the two men is indicative of the likely connection already existing between Perley, Herndon and Sullivan, and suggests that these two prominent attorneys were sponsoring him in his study and application to join the profession. Two days after Love's order, the committee reported to the Judge that they found the candidates duly qualified and recommended that they be admitted to the bar. What had been all but impossible in his native New Brunswick, could not have been much easier to accomplish in Texas.

The law that Perley was to practice was essentially the law practiced everywhere in the English-speaking world. Though the United States had thrown off the British yolk, it had retained British law to the extent that it conformed to American republican impulses. "The habits of a lifetime," said Lawrence Friedman, "were not easily thrown over, despite ideology."[47] As American legal sources remained scant, epitomators of the English common law were highly sought after, and American lawyers soon found the greatest epitomator of all in the person of William Blackstone. From the time of Independence through the duration of Perley's lifetime, Blackstone's *Commentaries* "were at once law school and law library," and a veritable "bible of American Lawyers."[48] Those elements of the common law described in the volume exhibiting too great a tone of deference to the state, or were too rooted in an irrelevant feudal social and economic structure, were discarded, leaving a recrudescence that provided the means "to release and harness the energy latent in the commonwealth."[49] The common

---

[45] Martin Hardwick Hall, "Philemon Thomas Herbert," *Handbook of Texas*, https://www.tshaonline.org/handbook/entries/herbert-philemon-thomas.

[46] Philemon Berry Waters, *A Genealogical History of the Waters and Kindred Families* (Atlanta: Foote & Davies Company, 1903), p. 143.

[47] Lawrence M. Friedman, *A History of American Law*, Second Edition (New York: Simon & Schuster, 1985), at p. 112.

[48] Daniel J. Boorstin, *The Mysterious Science of the Law: An Essay on Blackstone's Commentaries* (Chicago: University of Chicago Press, 1941), at p. 4.

[49] Friedman, op. cit., at p. 114.

law, in America, was to serve the demands of consumers, not the government. Texas was no different in this regard than any other jurisdiction in the United States, and yet its law contained variations derived from the long period of Spanish rule and embodied in doctrines originating in ancient Rome and the Germanic invaders of the Iberian Peninsula. Blending the traditions of the common law, as modified during the decades since the Revolution, and the civil law systems of Spain and France, the people of the Lone Star State produced "a unique legal system peculiar to Texas."[50] Instead of jettisoning the civil law infrastructure built by the Spanish and maintained by Mexico, Texans confirmed its enduring hold. The Congress of the Republic formally adopted the English Common Law in 1840, but also directed that the simplified Spanish system of pleading would continue, and directed that courts fashion remedies regardless of the formal division in the English tradition between law and equity.[51] Marital rights were to be governed by the law of the Visigoths, with female spouses enjoying a degree of equality unknown to the Anglo-Saxon milieu, descent and inheritance would look to the canons of the civilians, and land rights would rely on legal precedents going back generations and rest on fluency in the Spanish language for accurate discernment of the truth.[52] For a young lawyer, seeking a thorough education in the law, few places superior to the new State of Texas could there have been to receive it.

Perley's legal apprenticeship began in the employ of Herndon and Sullivan, focused primarily in Richmond, but engaged in matters throughout the lower Brazos--in Fort Bend, Brazoria, Galveston and Harris Counties. There could be, said Roger Griffin, "no better place to practice law in Texas than in Brazoria."[53] It was the richest region of the State, the center of the planation economy and well connected by road and water to the rest of Texas. It was also the principal headquarters of the Court for the First District, and the place where most of the lawyers practicing there

---

[50] J. E. Ericson and Mary P. Winston, "Civil Law and Common Law in Early Texas," 2 East Texas Historical Journal 26 (1964), at p. 26.

[51] See Joseph Webb McKnight, "The Spanish Legacy to Texas Law," 3 Am. J. Legal Hist. 222 (1959).

[52] Ericson & Winston, op. cit., at p. 27.

[53] Griffen, op. cit., at p. 49.

maintained their offices.[54] Hardly glamorous and certainly lacking in courtroom glory, the vocation of the novice attorney entailed the drudgery of drafting legal instruments, pleadings and memoranda, and copying the same for filing with the courts, serving papers on opposing parties and careful insertion of relevant materials into the employer's files. Perley's regular presence in the office accounts for his appearance as a witness to deeds involving Herndon, his family and clients. On April 17, 1847, he formally witnessed the sale by Herndon to Clement Dyer of land situated on the Brazos River in the town of Richmond.[55] On May 14, he witnessed a sale to Herndon of land in Bexar County from Franklin L. Paschal.[56] In October, he witnessed and testified as to a deed on behalf of Jane Wilkinson Long conveying to John Randon a portion of the famed estate she had obtained from the Mexican Government.[57]

Attending to the menial tasks of the law in time gave way to more advanced activities. By the second half of 1847 Perley had joined Herndon in his land speculation efforts. Before the Revolution, the Mexican Government controlled access to the land, but granted it freely and generously once the door opened to immigrants. Speculators in the Southern States long salivated over the prospect of unbounded adventure and enrichment through purchase and resale of the vast empire of Texas real estate. The Revolution might have occurred regardless of the hunger of those wishing to open the province to currency in land, but it was no stretch for Congressman Garland to conclude that "the spirit of land speculation is as strong as the love of constitutional liberty" among those who rallied round the Lone Star flag.[58] The Republic erased the previous legal regime governing the distribution of land, assumed control of a massive public domain and signaled the beginning of a rush on land by those eager to invest a small amount in order to grow it into a larger. Spanish and Mexican titles offered diminished security for owners, who no longer could trust that vast unoccupied tracts would remain inviolable in the eyes of a law that

---

[54] Id., at p. 31.

[55] Fort Bend County Deeds, B/251.

[56] Fort Bend County Deeds, B/334.

[57] Fort Bend County Deeds, B/365.

[58] *Register of Debates in Congress, Comprising the Leading Debates and Incidents of the First Session of the Twenty-Fourth Congress* (Washington, D.C.: Gales & Seaton, 1836), at p. 3533.

now favored the rights of squatters offering at least a pretense of occupation.[59] A land commission came into being charged by the Republic with the task of promoting immigration and filling the treasury with proceeds from sale of public land, and offering certificates easily counterfeited by those eager to turn a profit from the sale of seemingly abandoned older grants.[60] Indian lands and the property of Spanish and Mexican grantees fell subject to the schemes of speculators heading west ahead of the wave of settlers drawn from across the Sabine River and entering the territory through Galveston Bay. It was a pattern originating further east when the frontier began moving toward the Pacific, and Perley would learn its nuances here in Texas before applying his knowledge in the Far West.

Attracted by the opening of a lucrative market in real estate in the vicinity of San Antonio, Herndon and Perley travelled west to Bexar County to make good on a claim to lands that had the appearance of being unoccupied.[61] The land they located was actually part of the Menchaca Estate dating back a hundred years, and was the possession of Don Jose Casiano, a Tejano partisan of the rebels in 1836. Asserting lawful title through purchase of a land certificate issued by the Land Commission, Herndon refused to relent in his reservation of title. Equally stubborn was Casiano, whose attempt to resolve the controversy eventually entailed entering the land with a gang of armed men in October of 1847 and barring Herndon's access. Acting as Herndon's attorney in the matter, Perley filed suit in the District Court in San Antonio, seeking a writ of possession.[62] Though the matter was scheduled for trial in May of 1848, it was continued for several years, and ultimately, after trial in the District Court, resolved in Casiano's favor with the aid of his attorney, Volney Howard.[63]

By the latter half of 1848, Perley had advanced to trial practice and appellate work, which elevated him to membership in the bar of the State's Supreme Court. Organized only in 1846 following the

---

[59] T. R. Fehrenbach, *Lone Star: A History of Texas and the Texans* (New York: Tess Press, 2000), at pp. 282-283.

[60] John Martin Davis, Jr., *Texas Land Grants, 1750-1900: A Documentary History* (Jefferson, North Carolina: McFarland & Company, Inc., 2017), at p. 28.

[61] *Herndon v. Casiano* (1851) 7 Tex. 322.

[62] Petition of John H. Herndon, *John H. Herndon vs. Jose Casiono*, M-64, M Case, Texas Supreme Court Records, Texas State Library Digital Collection, https://tsl.access.preservica.com.

[63] *Herndon v. Casiano*, supra.

entry of Texas into the Union, the High Court consisted of but three members. The Chief Justice, John Hemphill, was a native of South Carolina who immigrated to Texas early in its history and took a position as a judge in the Fourth District, before becoming Chief Justice of the Texas Republic. At the Convention of 1845 he urged annexation by the United States. Once that goal was achieved, he participated in the drafting of the new State Constitution. It was said he possessed "an acute and penetrating discernment, a nice discrimination, a clear perception and a sound judgment."[64] His powers of analysis and amplification "were peculiarly adapted to the elimination and development of the varied issues of law, equity and fact, often presented by the pleadings" in accordance with the unified system of law and equity prevailing in Texas and uncommon in the United States at that time.[65] Associate Justice Abner Lipscomb likewise hailed from South Carolina, but his accomplishments were far more impressive than those of the Chief Justice. After studying law in the office of John C. Calhoun, he moved to Alabama, where he practiced law and served first in the Territorial and State Legislatures, then as Chief Justice of the State's Supreme Court, then again in the Legislature. His move to Texas did not go unnoticed by President Lamar, who vested him with the office of Secretary of State almost as soon as he ventured into the State Capital. He was said to have "loved the law as the grandest edifice ever erected by the mind of man, and as the receptacle into which has flowed the wisdom of ages."[66] His decisions were "neat, plain and lucid," pure without ostentation, forceful without verbosity, and "fixed immovably upon the firm foundations of law."[67]

The third member of the Court, Royall T. Wheeler, wasn't a southerner at all, but a Yankee from Vermont. He practiced first in Ohio, then in Arkansas and Texas. He served as a county prosecutor and then a district court judge and member of the State Supreme Court. On the bench, "he possessed a vigor of intellect, an inquisitiveness of mind, and a practicality of disposition which led

---

[64] James D. Lynch, *The Bench and Bar of Texas* (St. Louis: Nixon-Jones Printing Co., 1885), at p. 70.

[65] Id., at pp. 70-71.

[66] Id., at p. 89

[67] Id.

him to look beyond the existence of the statute to an inquiry into the origin and reason of the law," and was believed by some to have "traced the principles of every branch to their source."[68] Though a man courteous in nature and adverse to controversy, he was a noted dissenter on the bench, whose minority opinions tended to be "rich in legal lore, and even eloquent in the vindication of truth against what he conceived to be the errors of precedent," disclosing on these occasions "beneath his modest and unassuming exterior…an iron will and an inflexible purpose, which nothing could swerve from the path of duty."[69] By nature, he was "inclined to the forebodings of melancholy, which…increased by long and intense mental labor."[70] In later days, as the War between the States turned against the South, his dark and despairing thoughts proved overwhelming and caused him to raise a pistol to his temple and perish by his own hand.[71]

It was before these men that Perley presented his most important arguments during his Texas years. In one of the cases they presided over, Perley represented a plaintiff pursuing a claim against James Walker, the guardian of young Adam Erastus Cloud.[72] The matter was tried in the fall of 1848 in Harris County, and then appealed by Perley early in the new year. Though Perley asked for a copy of the record from the clerk so that he might lodge it with the Supreme Court, it was given to counsel for the Appellee by mistake. Unable to get a second copy in time to meet the filing deadline, Perley instead submitted an affidavit with the Court explaining the reason for his deviation from the rules. The Appellee then lodged the record himself and brought a motion to affirm the lower court's decision on the grounds that Perley had failed to file the record within the allotted time, and because the term of the district court where the appeal originated had already come to a close. Lacking any evidence in the papers that the Harris County Court had adjourned, and observing that the record had nevertheless been filed by one of the parties within the ordinary deadline, Justice Wheeler suggested that the motion was but form

68 Id., at p. 92.
69 Id.
70 Id., at p. 95.
71 Id., at pp. 95-96.
72 *Calvert v. Walker* (1848) 3 Tex. 14.

over substance and denied it. The appeal survived this rather technical challenge, but was continued for so long a time that Perley was no longer in the State when its merits were finally decided.[73]

Also originating in Harris County was the matter of *Portis et al. v. William G. Hill*.[74] The case involved a contested claim to a large land grant originally issued to James Cummings in 1824 by the Mexican Government. On one side was Perley's client, William Hill, the surviving spouse of the late owner, Eliza Westall—a woman who had formerly been married to a member of the Austin clan. Hill's claim was based on a deed of questionable provenance. On the other side was David Portis, the husband of Cummings' sister, and other members of the Cummings family, who occupied a portion of the land and claimed title through the original grantee. William Hill brought the action to partition the grant and distribute his late wife's share to her heirs, who included their four children. Arguing that the action was time barred by the statute of limitations and that quiet possession by himself and his wife had vested him with lawful title, Portis contested the action. Joining the suit in the fall of 1848 was Samuel A. Cummings, who raised defenses based on the fact that the deed on which Hill's claim rested had allegedly been revoked many years before, that one of the mesne title holders had actually been ineligible to contract in Texas due to his status as an alien, and that the time to bring the action had passed.

When the day of trial arrived, Perley took formal exception to the pleading of the limitations defense, as well as to a number of jury instructions whereby Portis and his wife might have been able to establish their right to inherit the Cummings Estate. Portis, he said, was not entitled to claim the land as a whole because he had no actual title and was eligible, at best, to no more of the estate than he actually occupied. If Spanish law were to be relied on, any actual adversity of possession was for far too short a time than was required to perfect ownership. Cummings, he argued, couldn't nullify the Plaintiff's claim because, as a title holder, his claim was no better than the Plaintiff's, and he had not yet accomplished the only thing that would assure him of victory, which was a complete

---

[73] Supreme Court Records, 1840-1980, Subgroup I, Part I, Dockets, 1840-1892, Vol. 1848, p. 67, No. 834, Texas State Library.

[74] *Portis v. Hill* (1848) 3 Tex. 273.

ouster of his adversary from the land. Perley prevailed on all these points, and then won at trial. In reviewing the appeals of Portis and Cummings, Justice Wheeler agreed that the allegations in the Portis Answer were not sufficient to state a defense, but nevertheless held that the Court had improperly denied Portis the opportunity to prove title by virtue of an inheritance from James Cummings through operation of the law of succession. He also found that Samuel Cummings' allegations were proper, if not perfect, hence the defense on limitations grounds should have been allowed. The lower court's decision, thus, was affirmed in part, and partly reversed.

In the matter of *Randon v. Cartwright*, Perley and Herndon took the part of Jesse Cartwright, a native of Mississippi, who possessed a huge estate in Fort Bend, had served as presiding officer of the election of electors for choosing the officials of the State Government in 1846, and sat a term in the Texas House of Representatives. When Perley and Herndon prevailed on a demurrer, counsel for David Randon appealed, but failed to apply sufficient diligence in presenting a statement of the errors to be corrected, or a complete transcript of the record below. "To have authorized a reversal of the judgment it was incumbent on the appellant to have so brought up the record as to show that the entire proceedings in the case sought to be reviewed were before the court below upon his petition, and that they presented a case proper for relief by a bill of review."[75] This, Justice Wheeler concluded, "the appellant has not done." Consequently, he and his colleagues on the High Court could "not undertake to determine that the court erred in sustaining the demurrer."

Perley's relationship with Herndon and his circle naturally brought him into acquaintance with John Woods Harris. Though he served as the State's Attorney General at the time, Harris had continued his law partnership with Elisha Pease on the lower Brazos.[76] When he substituted in as counsel for the Estate of William Walker in place of Herndon & Sullivan, he welcomed Perley's assistance as co-counsel.[77] The subject of their joint

---

[75] *Randon v. Cartwright* (1848) 3 Tex. 267, 269.

[76] Amelia W. Williams, "John Woods Harris," *Handbook of Texas*, https://www.tshaonline.org/handbook/entries/harris-john-woods.

[77] *Swenson v. Administrators of Walker* (1848) 3 Tex. 93.

representation had originated in the 1830s, when William Walker borrowed $1,000 from the firm of McKinney & Williams to cover the overhead of his cotton operation until his crop could be taken to market. The debt remained unpaid after his death in 1840, and became the responsibility of his heirs to resolve. S. M. Swenson purchased the promissory note and pressed for attachment of the Walker Estate when payment was refused. Swenson's suit was contested by Walker's widow, who countered with the claim that it was the Estate that was owed money, not its creditors. With the aid of Perley and Harris, she won judgments against McKinney & Williams and Swenson for $4,000 and $140 respectively, in addition to a restraining order barring further attachment. Swenson's appeal of the judgment addressed the irregularity of the trial court hearing a demurrer to the Estate's complaint after the jury in the case had already been empaneled, and its refusal to issue a particular instruction to the jury. The Defendants had argued that the claim against McKinney & Williams was so belated that it improperly defied the statute of limitations, but the trial judge had rejected the argument because the defense hadn't been earlier pled. They argued, too, that an earlier order of the probate court mandating sale of a portion of the Estate to pay the debt owed to McKinney & Williams was essentially res judicata, hence there could be no escaping the obligation to pay what had already been judicially mandated. The lower court again overruled the Defendants, apparently because it found persuasive the Petitioner's contention to have been sabotaged by the Estate's co-administrator. The rejected jury instruction had to do with the Defendants' claim that the Estate was estopped from denying any legal obligation to pay the debt because of the reliance by Defendant Swenson on assurance that the debt would be honored prior to his acceptance of the debt's assignment.

To defend their victory in the lower Court, Harris and Perley filed "very lengthy and elaborate arguments," without also including a synopses or brief for inclusion in the official published report. In rendering his opinion, Justice Lipscomb disregarded those arguments and concluded that the statute of limitations was not a defense that must be included in an Answer prior to being asserted. The untimely nature of the claim against McKinney & Williams being evident on the face of the Complaint, it was permissible for the Defendants to raise the defense when it did. Justice Lipscomb similarly disparaged the lower court's decision as to the debt owed to the Defendants following a decision in the probate court. If by his conduct the co-administrator had betrayed his trust, "it was in the power of his colleague to have restrained him, either by applying to the probate court or by resorting to the district court." As the administrator did neither, she in effect rejected the remedies available to her and acquiesced in the outcome. As for the rejected jury instruction, Lipscomb thought it ought to have been read to the jury. "If permitted to contradict statements so made, on which the party to whom they were made had acted, such permission might operate to the serious injury of the party who was misled by them."[78] In the wake of so complete a defeat, Perley presented himself to the Court and remitted the sum of $67 in interest payable to Swenson for the judgment money the latter had been forced to pay. The matter, thus, appears to have settled and was never retried.

One additional case Perley and Harris handled was *Morgan Smith vs. James Montgomery*—Smith being a merchant and seller of plantation supplies and owner of the large Waldeck sugar plantation in Brazoria; Montgomery a developer and one-time pre-annexation Texas congressman. Montgomery had acted as a surety for a transaction involving the sale of goods by Smith to a Mr. Tennard for $3,000. When the insolvent Tennard died without paying the debt, Smith sued Montgomery, who argued in response that his obligation was to Smith and his partner, a Mr. Pilgrim, not to Smith alone. His contention appeared to be true on the face of the written promise itself, but doubts were nurtured by the fact that the envelope on which the writing was transmitted was addressed only to Smith. Montgomery managed to prevail at trial in the District Court sitting in Colorado County, prompting Harris and Perley to appeal on Smith's behalf. "The fact that Pilgrim had formerly been a partner of Smith, and that his name was also on the letter," they argued, "cannot affect Smith's right to recover in this action. The letter

---

[78] Id., at 98.

was directed to 'Col. Smith,' and it was proven that Morgan L. Smith, the plaintiff, was that person."[79] Justice Wheeler, however, thought the letter rather than the envelope was the more persuasive evidence, and certainly unambiguous with regard to the identity of the party for whom the obligation to make payment was reserved. A leading English case, as well as the jurisprudence of John Marshall and decisions from various jurisdictions throughout the United States, Wheeler believed were uniform in holding that "the liability of a guarantor or surety cannot be extended by implication, or otherwise, beyond the actual terms of his engagement."[80] A suit seeking satisfaction of a surety's obligation "must be brought strictly within the terms of the guaranty, when reasonably interpreted, or the guarantor will not be liable."[81] Because the promise was expressly made for the benefit of the partnership, a single partner could not enforce it.

With the passing of the Supreme Court's 1848 Session, news from California of stupendous gold discoveries began arriving in Texas, and by the first weeks of 1849, the newspapers were filled with stories of fabulous riches. President Polk's message agitated its readers in December, leading to an outbreak of "California Fever" not merely in Texas but throughout the entire nation. In mid-January, Colonel Hays was exploring possible routes through west Texas and overland companies were beginning to organize. By February, caravans were arriving in Houston from St. Louis, bound for a route rumored to run parallel to the Gila River. The towns of Bexar, Victoria, Austin and Columbus were filled with gathering crowds preparing to venture west. Too impatient to await a group of army surveyors who might lend greater confidence to the path to be taken, some began leaving at once. This haste contributed to privation, misery and the vast cholera epidemic that would soon strike down the lead surveyor, General William Worth.

In the midst of the excitement, Colonel Hays reported on the viability of a route to California starting at Houston and

---

[79] *Smith v. Montgomery* (1848) 3 Tex. 199.
[80] Id., at 209.
[81] Id.

continuing through Fredericksburg, the San Saba River, El Paso and beyond, and expressed confidence that "the emigrant who travels through Texas (as opposed to the sea) may proceed directly to the gold region, carry his own provisions, and his own implements with him, and be ready to commence business the moment he reaches the place of his destination."[82] That same month, an advertisement for an emigrant company appeared in the *Telegraph*.[83] The company was to gather at Austin on the 1st of February and leave that place for California by the 1st of March "by way of the Paseo del Norte on the Rio Grande, and from thence...the most direct route to the Pacific."[84] Judging from all that is known of Perley, his time of arrival in California, his human associations, and the fact that he traveled to California on horseback in the company of David Terry and R. P. Ashe, there can be little doubt that he responded to this ad or one very much like it, and at the appointed time brought with him the recommended two pack mules, a good tent, assorted equipment and a firearm.[85] A new empire, much vaster than Texas, was just opening, and riches were to be had. Still dreaming of glory and wealth and ready for adventure, Perley simply couldn't resist. Others in his circle were prepared to go as well: Terry, Ashe, Philemon Herbert, Alexander Crittenden, Tod Robinson, Thomas Lubbock, Harry Love and Colonel William Jefferson Kyle, to name but a few. Late in April, the *Texas Democrat* reported a party of 20 or 30 departing Austin on the previous Wednesday. Its members were "for the most part residents of the coast counties of this State, and among them some of our most substantial citizens,...well equipped in every respect and had with them five able bodied negro men."[86] They expected "to pursue the route taken by Capt. Haynie and his party who left here some four weeks ago."[87] The group had

---

[82] "Routes to California," *Democratic Telegraph and Texas Register*, January 25, 1849.

[83] "For California!," *Democratic Telegraph and Texas Register*, January 25, 1849.

[84] Id.

[85] Id.; and "D. W. Perley," Pioneer Index File: 1906-1934, California History Room, California State Library, Sacramento, California.

[86] *Texas Democrat*, April 21, 1849.

[87] Id.

made its way to Fredericksburg by April 22, and, amidst a bustle of 50 wagons belonging to numerous companies, David Terry was elected its leader.[88]

The unanimous vote confirmed the tremendous faith in Terry's leadership abilities, his physical courage, and the confidence he instilled, even among such notable figures as seem to have been members of the company. Among them may have been Richard Roman. A native of Kentucky, he came to Texas in 1835 to join Houston's army and distinguished himself at San Jacinto. He served as a Representative in the Texas House and Senate, and later went to Mexico as a soldier, where he fought at Buena Vista and Monterey.[89] Another likely member of the company was Harry Love, a protege of Hays and a skillful and brave scout. Richard Porter Ashe was perhaps the most aristocratic of the group, springing from a noble line of statesmen. His great, great grandfather, John Ashe Jr., of Teffont, Wiltshire County, England, was a second-generation member of the English Parliament and a leader of the Puritan immigration to South Carolina. Ashe's great grandfather was speaker of the South Carolina legislature, his grandfather Governor of North Carolina, and his father a soldier in the Revolution and ardent leader of North Carolina's Federalist Party afterward. Ashe moved to Texas in the early 1840s with his elder brother, Congressman John Baptist Ashe II. A medical man, rather than a man of the law, he was respected and respectable, a good companion, and a man who "loves to give and take a joke equal to any man living."[90] Other men of note travelled overland as well, but in other companies: Alexander Crittenden and Colonel Hays, to name but two. Far too effete to make the trip by land, Tod Robinson opted for a sea route.

Of the journey Perley and his companions were preparing to embark upon, a fellow migrant who departed a month later said afterward that "no sane man will ever travel this route a second

---

[88] Id.; and Testimony of John Hodges, *Trial of David S. Terry*, supra, p. 59.

[89] Hobart Huson, "Richard Roman," *Handbook of Texas*; https://www.tshaonline.org/handbook/entries/roman-richard; and John H. Brown, *Indian Wars and Pioneers of Texas*, Reprint (Austin: State House Press, 1988), at p. 142.

[90] *Stockton Argus*, August 27, 1860.

time."[91] It entailed, he said, transit through "the most disagreeable, uninteresting and mountainous country," replete with "sand, dust and scorching sun."[92] Ignorant of this assessment, the Terry company remained in Fredericksburg for a time, deciding which way to go. Learning from some Comanches that the route to Concho explored by Haynie was good for wagons, and that a trail from the Concho to El Paso was passable despite a series of hills, the men made their decision. In a letter to Judge Love, W. J. Kyle reported that two companies with pack mules were just ahead of them, not to mention the military engineers, thus they expected ample landmarks to guide them on the journey.[93] In the midst of a cold snap, uncomfortable for the "lower county people" who made up the company, the group departed, making slow progress through the west Texas outback along the path scouted by Colonel Hays, dodging hostile Comanches, and entering the territory of the Apaches and Yumas.[94]

According to Terry, the company left Fredericksburg on the 27th of April and "traveled over a poor rolling country without difficulty for a hundred and sixty miles to the Concho."[95] The weather was fine and the party fed itself in part through hunting and fishing. At the Concho they met with a small party of natives, "who professed to be exceedingly friendly, and we, on the strength of it, gave them tobacco and various things, and at night some of the men felt so secure that they left their horses outside the line of sentinels," only to find them missing the next morning.[96] Terry demanded of the natives who remained in camp to select a few of their number to accompany him and a party of his men in a search for the horses, while the others remained behind, apparently as hostages. With some grumbling, they agreed. The natives, however, attempted to break from the ranks further down the trail, setting off a melee, with arrows and bullets flying. Terry bravely rode into a thicket where the Indians lay hidden, firing his gun and coming to a stop amongst

---

91 Mabelle E. Martin, "From Texas to California in 1849: Diary of C.C. Cox," *Southwest Quarterly Review*, Volume XXIX, No. 3 (Jan, 1926), at p. 201.

92 Id.

93 *Galveston Civilian and Gazette*, May 30, 1849.

94 Id.

95 *Democratic Telegraph and Texas Register*, August 30, 1849.

96 Id.

a group of them. More shots were exchanged and an Indian fell dead from a bullet fired by Ladden Byne. An Indian Terry wounded was subsequently tended by the migrants, and then set free with "a pony, his bow and arrows, two gourds of water, a butcher knife and plenty of provisions."[97]

Years later, Perley's nephew recalled the battles Perley and his companions had with the natives.[98] The diarist Benjamin Butler Hayes even reported a death among the company. After Terry's rescue of the mules, Hayes recorded that the Apaches ambushed them at a rocky pass. In advance of the company rode John A. Alexander, whom Harris identified as the former Auditor for the State of Texas. Mounted Indians approached making peace signs and asking for tobacco and then shot him in sight of his companions. Terry reportedly led his men in pursuit of the attackers into a defile, "and amid showers of arrows and bullets for several hours fought the wily scoundrels, but owing to their secure entrenchments and hiding, Terry and his men were obliged to withdraw at the approach of night without administering much punishment to the foe, and with no further serious loss on the part of the whites." The tale was repeated by Wagstaff, and more recently by Leonard L. Richards.[99] And yet the story, though exciting and dramatic, is likely untrue. No such man as John A. Alexander held the office of Auditor in Texas nor has yet been found in records of the day. Terry's own letters to his brother, published in Texas papers in the summer of 1849, omit any reference to Alexander or even a death of a member of the company. Other incidents did occur on the road involving other migrants, and word of them certainly spread eastward. The killing of a dozen Indians by Texian emigrants below El Paso was said to have been the cause of a great stirring among the natives, and the basis for calls for intervention by the government so as to prevent a slaughter "under the tomahawk and scalping knives."[100] Only one

---

[97] Id.

[98] "D. W. Perley," Pioneer Index File: 1906-1934, California History Room, California State Library, Sacramento, California.

[99] A.E. Wagstaff, *Life of David S. Terry* (San Francisco: Continental Publishing Company, 1892), at 52; and Leonard L. Richards, *The California Gold Rush and the Coming of the Civil War* (New York: Vintage Books, 2008).

[100] *Democratic Telegraph and Texas Register*, November 29, 1849.

Indian was killed in Terry's battle, and the other wounded man was cared for and freed. The legend seems to have no truth, and likely arose from the distortions inherent in the propaganda generated during the Vigilance disturbance years later.[101]

With the fight behind them, the company moved east beyond the Concho into a long stretch of countryside bereft of water, which they entered "unwittingly and entirely unprepared."[102] The privations of the journey wore heavily on some, who "lay down by the roadside to die," though they were physically capable of carrying on. Trudging along, they "found packs thrown down by the path, broken-down horses, and even guns and pistols which had been abandoned by the owners."[103] Contemplation of this flotsam created a panic among some members of the company. Careful inspection of the debris led to the fortuitous discovery of a six-gallon keg full of water, which revived many spirits and kept some of the men alive until they found a spring in a hole in a rock, "which enabled us to get through without much difficulty."[104] Reaching the Puereo, they found salty and muddy water, and grass so high and dense that wagons couldn't pass, and too poor even for the horses to eat. They headed next to Presidio, but on information acquired from a trader from Chihuahua, opted to follow an alternative route scouted by Colonel Hays. The route took them "over a mountainous country where water was scarce" and lacking in any good grass for the animals. So horrid were the trails—a mere 18 inches in spots with precipices of 50 to 150 feet on one side—that Terry found one "false step of my mule would certainly have killed both me and himself."[105] Such rigors, he said, were "no joke to one who has lived in a county where a mound was the greatest elevation, and water could not run."[106]

At Presidio the company relieved their horses and mules and then pushed on for El Paso, which they reached on the 25th of June. They found provisions for the next leg of the journey to Monoto Donia Anna in New Mexico, where a body of U.S. Troops was

---

101 *Daily Alta California*, June 29, 1856.

102 *Democratic Telegraph and Texas Register*, August 30, 1849.

103 Id.

104 Id.

105 Id.

106 Id.

stationed. Pausing for a few days, they counted upward of five hundred men along the trail in that vicinity, many of whom were barred from further advance for want of means. From El Paso, Terry expected to be on the Sacramento River within sixty to seventy days. The path he, Perley and the rest of their company took from this point on is not known with certainty, though Kyle's letter to Judge Love and a diarist from that time on the Gila Trail indicates that they followed the Gila River.[107] To reach it from El Paso, the traveler was required to follow a path along a north-west orientation. Several years before, a military expedition approached the Gila directly west from Socoro in New Mexico and found the Gila in a deep ravine, not far from its confluence with the Prieto and San Carlos tributaries. Strolling up the San Carlos, Major W. H. Emory found, "on either side, in the limestone under the basalt…immense cavities, which must have been at times the abodes of Indians and the dens of beasts."[108] Ruins were present, as were the remains of fire and the bones of animals. Along the reaches of the River downstream from the San Carlos, more ruins could be observed, obviously antedating written history, built by unnamed peoples long since vanished and unknown even to the natives of the day. On the table lands around the River, "great quantities of green-barked acacia…and also the chamiza, wild sage and mesquite" was evident, and closer to the River, cotton wood and willow.[109]

High mountains rose at a point downstream, forcing all but solitary and light travelers to detour along a path blazed by Kit Carson, devoid of water, but allowing for passage around the obstruction. From a high point on the trail, 5,724 feet above the sea, could be seen rugged mountains bounding the entire horizon. The way back to the Gila was rough and dry, though evidence of rainfall could be seen nearly everywhere in the form of dry tracks of rushing water. When back in view, the Gila presented an

[107] *Galveston Civilian and Gazette*, May 30, 1849; and Benjamin Butler Harris, *The Gila Trail: The Texas Argonauts and the California Gold Rush* (Norman: University of Oklahoma Press, 1960.

[108] *Notes of Travel in California, Comprising the Prominent Geographical, Agricultural, Geological and Mineralogical Features of the County; Also the Rout from Fort Leavenworth, in Missouri, to San Diego, in California, Including Parts of the Arkansas, Del Norte, and Gila Rivers, From the Official Reports of Col. Fremont and Maj. Emory* (New York: D. Appleton & Company, 1849), p. 38.

[109] Id., at p. 39.

"inhospitable" appearance, "with granite, and red sandstone, in irregular and confused strata," clustering close together and almost choked by the presence of willow, cotton wood and mesquite. A variety of cactus flourished in great luxuriance along the river toward the west, as did pitahaya, usually growing from "the wildest and most unfrequented places."[110] Throughout the region, the Apache roamed, largely stand-offish with migrants, but notoriously savage with the peoples to the south in the Mexican States of Chihuahua, Sonora and Durango, whose numbers of late had been diminishing on account of the uncertainties of life induced by frequent Apache raids.

Near the meeting place of the Gila with the San Pedro, deep dust and sand was everywhere, overgrown with cotton-wood, mesquite, chamiza, willow and black willow, strewn with paving pebbles and piled high with drift wood. "The hills on both side of the River, still high, but now farther off, and covered to the top with soil producing the mesquite and pitahaya" drew closer and lower as the path was followed, until no hills were left to scale. The land became flatter and the mountains were only visible on the far horizon. The residents of the region were the Pimos and Maricopas, markedly unlike the Apaches, whom they considered enemies. Further west there was much desolation, dust and lack of water. The Gila itself in this locale ran dry for part of the year. All around was black basalt, interspersed with agate, chalcedony, vitrified quartz and carbonate of lime, and on many of the boulders there were unknown characters, the work of human hands, indecipherable to the modern Indians and utterly mystifying to the men of the east. Closer to the Colorado River, the mountains rose abruptly from the plains, "resembling in appearance large dykes terminating at top in a sharp ridge which man could, at any part, straddle."[111] Where the Gila finally joined the Colorado, it passed through a canyon, with vertical walls fifty feet high. The ruins of a town built by the Spanish, but sacked by the Apaches a century before, were still visible.

In the vast country already traversed and much of what was left to travel through in California, little existed to detract from the

[110] Id., at p. 43.
[111] Id., at p. 54.

conclusion that it is rightfully classified a desert, unfit for cultivation except in a few watered areas around the major streams. Immediately west of the Colorado was a desert almost destitute of vegetation, with sand so dense that horses and mules and the wagons they pulled made but slow progress. Nevertheless, in time, Terry's company made their destination, perhaps first in San Diego or Los Angeles, but eventually in the north of the State. Once there, the company broke up. Kyle didn't take well to California at all and returned to Texas. He entered a law partnership with Terry's brother Frank, purchased sugar and cotton plantations and opened several mills, eventually operated by an army of slaves.[112] Crittenden remained in Los Angeles for a time, where he won election to the State legislature and became the author of most of the early statutes. Herbert landed in Mariposa, where he later secured a seat in the legislature and rose high in the ranks of the wing of the Democrat Party known as the Chivalry, dedicated to southern norms, faithful to the quasi independence of the States, and ever protective of the institution of slavery, even though it was non-existent in California.

Terry and Perley, along with Ashe, Lubbock and several others made their way to Stockton, the gateway to gold country, looking for opportunities wherever they might arise, beneath the surface of the land in the mines or atop it, but ultimately finding their greatest opportunities in law and the world of politics. Perley refrained from a political career himself, but his closeness to men obsessed with power drew him into their world, and rendered him a member of their bloody faction, less out of ideological solidarity than for the fact that they were his friends. "There are many ways of testing a man's honor, friendship and worth," said Texian migrant to California, C.C. Cox, "but there is no situation in which a man can be placed better calculated to develop his true character, than upon an expedition like ours."[113] As it was for Cox, so it would be for Perley.

---

[112] Stephen L. Hardin, "William Jefferson Kyle," *Handbook of Texas*, https://www.tshaonline.org/handbook/entries/kyle_william_jefferson.

[113] Mabelle E. Martin, op. cit., at p. 209.

Chapter Three

FINDING LAW IN A LAWLESS PLACE

The name San Joaquin "was first given to a rivulet in the foothills of the Sierra Nevada Mountains by Lieutenant Gabriel Moraga, who in 1813 commanded an exploring expedition to the Vale de los Tules."[1] Bestowed first on this minor waterway, the name became affixed to the great river of the Central Valley, and to the County where Duncan W. Perley and his party arrived late in the summer of 1849. The Mokelumne, Stanislaus, and Calaveras tributaries bisect the County and join the great river on its path, divided at one point into a myriad of capillaries, to San Francisco Bay to the west. The San Joaquin is navigable for 350 miles, "and the lower section, from Stockton down, is the highway for a vast trade."[2] The soil is a mix of clay and sandy loam, with much of the western part of the County constituting swamp land that wasn't reclaimed until the 1870s and afterwards. During his 1844 expedition, John C. Fremont described the region as "delightful" and the bottom land as "broad, rich and extremely fertile," with oaks shading much of the uplands, "a showy Lupinus of extraordinary beauty, growing four or five feet in height, and covered with spikes in bloom" along the river's banks, and filling "the air with a light and grateful perfume."[3] Elsewhere were dry gullies, "filled with water in seasons of rain; and perhaps, also by the melting snows," and "an assemblage of green pastures with varied flowers and scattered groves," not quite in the shadow of the distant yet visible "rocky and snowy peaks" where Fremont and his men had lately suffered so much.[4]

The historian Tinkham commented that "in early days grass, clover, filigree and oak grew in a thick matted mass, three or four feet high, and in some localities on the Calaveras they [were] said to

---

[1] *An Illustrated History of San Joaquin County, California* (Chicago: The Lewis Publishing Company, 1890), p. 17.

[2] Id., at p. 18.

[3] Id., at p. 21.

[4] Id.

have grown higher than the head of a man on horseback."[5] The grass in the days before the Gold Rush "was the hiding place of rabbits, squirrels, quail and other small game."[6] Thousands of animals who roamed the prairies—wild horses, cattle, antelope, elk, deer, and bear—fed on the luxuriant flora. The clusters of oak formed "the home of the canary, the blackbird, the blue jay, the dove and many others of the feathered tribes, while ever and anon the eagle from his mountain home" swept down insidiously to snatch its unwitting prey.[7]

Into this idyllic scene intruded the cry of gold, "like the calling of 'cluck-cluck' of the domestic fowl on discovering a little morsel of food," followed by a rush of migrants by the tens of thousands. San Francisco being too far from the mining districts, a secondary hub was needed, where the necessaries of life in the mines could be delivered and then distributed to thousands of miners impatient to start their digging, but mindful of the need for provisions. The confluence of many waters formed a series of sloughs especially advantageous to the throng in need of regular victualling—the greatest being the so-called Stockton Slough, 300 feet wide and deep enough to accommodate vessels weighing 600 tons at all seasons of the year.[8] The fortuity of the geography caused the rather abrupt settlement of the town that came to be known as Stockton. By December of 1849, it was "a city of over 1,000 inhabitants, with many vessels lying in the slough."[9] It sprang up on a portion of a large grant obtained by Charles Maria Weber from the Mexican Government known as the Rancho del Campo de los Franceses, and named in honor of the Commodore of the same name in the hopes that he would use his authority, short lived as it was, to provide material aid to the growing community.[10]

At the time Perley arrived, Stockton appeared "a vast linen city," with the tall masts of barques, brigs and schooners...high-pointed in the blue vault above...as box, bale and barrel were

---

[5] George H. Tinkham, *A History of Stockton* (San Francisco: W.M. Hinton, 1880), at p. 10.

[6] Id.

[7] Id.

[8] Id., at p. 7.

[9] *Illustrated History*, op. cit.

[10] Id., at p. 59.

landed on the banks of the slough."[11] Throughout its thoroughfares, the bustle of life was constant, "the mingled voices of labor around, the click of hammers, the shouts of mule drivers, the jingling of spurs, the jar and jostle of wares in the tents."[12] Every day, reported one eye witness, "launches were arriving and departing…for and from San Francisco, and the number of mule trains, wagons, etc., on their way to the various mines with freight and supplies, kept up a life of activity truly amazing."[13] As a winter station for miners, said the historian H. H. Bancroft, Stockton "displayed itself in varied phases, with drinking and gambling saloons in full blast, and with a criminal admixture that gave the vigilance committee of 1851 no small work."[14] As the tents that housed most of the population gave way to wood-framed buildings, Stockton became the "prettiest little town of California." The streets were wide and shaded by trees, construction proceeded rapidly in every direction (including of "a large building owned by C. M. Weber, occupied by stores, offices and rooms for bachelors, with a theatre attached"), all while "a steady stream of immigration came pouring into the country from across the plains."[15] A fire at the end of the year only slightly impeded the pace of development of this great entrepot of the Central Valley.

An ad hoc government was formed early in 1849 after the military regime recommended reliance on Mexican law and institutions "until the Government of the Territory could be more definitely arranged."[16] A city government was formed following elections in November of 1849, and a former occupation soldier and

---

[11] Id., at p. 67.

[12] Id., at p. 68.

[13] Id.

[14] H. H. Bancroft, *History of California*, Vol. VI (San Francisco: The History Company, Publishers, 1888), at p. 466.

[15] Timothy Coffin Osborne, Journal, BANC MSS C-F 81, entry for June 17, 1850; and *Illustrated History*, op. cit., at p. 62.

[16] Tinkham, op. cit., at p. 131.

Alcalde, George Gordon Belt, was elected municipal judge.[17] The early court was said by Tinkham "to have been more of a farce than the higher courts," where the merits of particular cases paled in significance to the ties of "friendship, bribery and fraud," with the only appeal being the preferences of the mob should it become riled up by particular interests and passions.[18] The Alcaldes and other judges were at the forefront of this corruption. With no training or sense of justice, Belt is said to have "unworthily occupied the bench" and contributed much to "debasing the early jurisprudence of San Joaquin County."[19] The actions of the mobs were often whipped up by Belt himself, and became, at Belt's direction, "the terror of the town, and citizens," and the cause of near constant apprehension over the thought of "offending these lawless men in some way, and thereby bringing vengeance upon their own heads."[20] So arbitrary and irrational was Belt's reign from the bench that he was said even to have sentenced some men to death for mere larceny.[21] His lawlessness only encouraged others to yield to their most anti-social impulses, and greatly contributed to the thwarting of any semblance of law and order. Together, this anarchic fraternity would laugh at creditors, threaten "to shoot the officers of the court that should dare to execute any process thereof," and would actually call "party meetings to intimidate attorneys from taking the claims of honest creditors for collection of the landed clique."[22] Belt's two successors as Alcalde and Judge

---

[17] *Illustrated History*, op. cit., at p. 81. The election, which was held on November 13, 1849, included a vote for the newly drafted State Constitution, as well as for statewide officers. To assist the military authorities in conducting the polling in San Joaquin County was D.W. Perley, who subsequently submitted his account "for certain services rendered…at the recent election in San Joaquin district." See Letter of H.W. Halleck to Hon. G.D. Dickerson, December 1, 1849, in *Index of Executive Documents Printed by Order of the Senate of the United States During the First Session of the Thirty-First Congress, 1849-1850,* Volume 52 (Washington, D.C. Wm. M. Belt, 1850), at p. 29. The federal government declined pay, prompting Perley to seek reimbursement in the amount of $520 from the Legislature once it was seated. (See *Journals of the Legislature of the State of California* (San Jose, Eugene Casserly, 1851), at p. 1645). The legislature voted to postpone the bill "indefinitely." (Id., at p. 1796).

[18] Tinkham, op. cit., p. 131.

[19] Id., at 136-137.

[20] Id., at p. 160.

[21] *Daily Alta California*, April 20, 1850.

[22] Id.

were no better. It was said that when the constable brought a prisoner for trial, Judges James R. Reynolds and Benjamin Williams would invariably ask "whether the culprit had any money."[23] Only if the accused had nothing would the constable release him without charge.

Into this chaotic legal environment Perley gained admission as a lawyer, as did David Terry. They had formed a bond in Texas and on the trail, and now would stick together, in hard times and easy, for the rest of their lives. The thought was to practice law close to the center of the State—the halfway point between the primary port and the mines. The arrival of cousin James E. Perley's gold-hungry son Henry provided the partners with a clerk in the earliest days of their partnership, but even so the field of practice wasn't particularly promising.[24] Terry wrote home that he didn't "think this country is at all likely to prove a good place for making rapid fortunes at the law. There is too great a dread of the expense of litigation and very few people have the means if they had the will to carry on mining suits which are greatly more expensive than any other class of suits."[25] The promise of a decent living, however, was evident enough. "Awash with forty-niners and witnessing the disintegration of the great ranchos, the pioneer bar collected debts, dealt with crime, and transferred property at a feverish pace amid the urban turmoil of the instant cities."[26] With vast freeholds only weakly occupied, lacking written and legal chains of ownership and now invaded by squatters, "lawyers supported the process of quieting title to land through litigation."[27] And in doing so, they conspicuously transferred a portion of the wealth generated by the mines into their own pockets.

The Stockton Bar in these earliest days was small but colorful. Its members originated from throughout the Union and consisted of men of marked ambition, if not legal acumen. Thomas B. Van Buren hailed from the same clan that had produced a President. He arrived in Stockton with the prospectors and quickly won their

---

[23] Tinkham, op. cit., at pp. 131-132.

[24] *Stockton Daily Evening Record*, February 11, 1899.

[25] Gordon Morris Brakken, *Practicing Law in Frontier California* (Lincoln: University of Nebraska Press, 1991), at p. 12.

[26] Id., at p. 41.

[27] Id.

confidence. He bested fellow barrister William D. Fair for a seat in the State Senate, where his friend and ally David Broderick called him the finest debater in that body.[28] Hostility in the Senate to his surname alone among Southern Democrats ruined his chances of enjoying a longer legislative career and advancement to higher office. His rival Mr. Fair, convinced that a hoard of foreigners had tipped the election in Van Buren's favor, pressed a ballot challenge all the way to the body he aspired to join. His accusation of dishonesty on the part of his judges in adjudicating the matter probably foreclosed any prospect of success.[29] Fair's legal practice flagged as the decade proceeded, until one day he was found dead—a "suicide"—with not one but two bullets in the brain.[30] Another member of the early Stockton bar, Henry A. Crabb, was considered a "lawyer of decided talent and excellent character—modest but ambitious and full of life and energy."[31] He was, said one admirer, "true to his friends, magnanimous to his enemies, just and generous to a fault," and the "very soul of honor."[32] In politics he was a Whig, but in loyalty a southerner committed to slavery and Joseph Story's defense of the antebellum status quo in *Prigg v. Pennsylvania*. A fatal duel in Vicksburg with a Democrat following a heated political debate prompted his journey to the far west, and the vibrancy of the mines attracted his professional attention.[33] He won the office of City Attorney in Stockton, and then a seat in the Assembly, where he promoted the mismatched causes of slaveowner rights and feminism. He ended his days a few years later south of the border, tied to a pole, with one hundred Mexican musket balls in his body. His face reportedly peered from a bottle of mescale in commemoration of his failed attempt to filibuster his way to mastery over the State of Sonora. Virginia native Samuel Alfred Booker was another able advocate, nephew of the Municipal Judge in Tuolumne County, and San Joaquin's first District Attorney. He aspired to higher office, failed in a bid for Congress as a Democrat, but won appointment to the post of Major General of

[28] *Stockton Independent*, March 19, 1873.
[29] *Daily Alta California*, January 27, 1851.
[30] *San Joaquin Republican*, December 28, 1861.
[31] *Star*, October 31, 1857.
[32] *Mountain Democrat*, December 19, 1857.
[33] *Los Angeles Star*, October 31, 1857.

the Third Division of the State Militia. His path would cross Perley's for years before he won election to the Bench in the Fifth District. Edward L. B. Brooks, Hairston Amyx, Messers Leak, Slocum and Spofford, in addition to the mysterious Doctor Roberts, rounded out the rest of the local bar in the first years of Statehood.

Before there could be a fair prospect of practicing law, the community would have to be subject to a greater degree of order, "a complete organization of the laws, and the systematizing of a government that would be respected by the incoming population."[34] Society, though lively and highly productive, "had no organization, and men were rough and uncouth in their manners and not very stylish in their appearance." Modes of dress were simple, but the passions of an almost entirely male population, tied closely to success in labor in the mining districts, were not. Blue or red flannel shirts, broad brimmed hats, pants fastened around the waist with a red Mexican sash, were almost universally augmented by arms. "Every one," said Tinkham, "carried arms of some kind, either pistols or knives."[35] In what Tinkham called "this darkest period of Stockton's history," the ultimate authority was the mob of armed men, which citizens good and bad dared not oppose, for "vice was king and virtue a slave." Stockton, he said, "was notably cursed, for here was a side field for action, and gold was the result of crime. Courts were a mockery. Judges and juries were bribed, or threatened with vengeance if they dare oppose the mandates of the ruling power. Knives and pistols were often drawn in open court, and the leader, pistol in hand, and jumping upon a desk, would defy the law" to rule contrary to his will.[36] Perley later commented that he was "generally in the habit of carrying a knife; sometimes a pistol" because he "deemed it necessary to carry arms in Stockton, in court or out of court, for his own protection." The life of an attorney in this lawless time, he said, "was in constant jeopardy."[37] Terry observed that Stockton "had not the most quiet and orderly reputation; and that a Justice's Court, in those days, was not a place of any great sanctity." A lawyer who was zealous in his duty to his

---

[34] *Illustrated History*, op. cit., at p. 62.
[35] Tinkham, op. cit., p. 170.
[36] Id., at pp. 155-156
[37] *Trial of David S. Terry by the Committee of Vigilance* (San Francisco: R.C. Moore & Co., Printers, 1856), at p. 47.

client "was liable at any time to be attacked, for calling things by their proper names." He admitted that he had, "on more than one occasion, been compelled not only to go armed into a Court House, but to have a man stand behind me, whilst arguing a case, to prevent an attack in the rear." Such was necessary for self-defense in a place where almost all men "were armed; and because I had frequently, in the course of my practice, been compelled to speak plainly of desperate characters…I was liable to be called to account by them, at any moment."[38] Once, in Judge Reynold's make-shift court in the newly built Collins House, Perley and Terry were arguing over a debt on behalf of their client. Sensing the amount in controversy wasn't enough to satisfy all the parties, Reynolds swept the money into his hat as payment of his judicial fee, prompting Perley and Terry to demand their share, and Perley to motion to his coat as if to draw a weapon. The result was the bearing down by every man in the room with a cocked pistol.[39]

The tyranny of the community's earliest judicial officers was facilitated by the utter confusion or absence of the law itself. The Mexican regime had abruptly ended, the military government was far removed, and yet most of the legal relations that existed continued to be governed by the defunct regime's laws. California was on the brink of organizing itself as a commonwealth and constituent member of the United States, but even after the proposed Constitution was ratified and the first election held, the State still had no laws. The first Governor took it upon himself to recommend to the Legislature the adoption of a State Code, combining what he said would be the best of the civil and common law traditions.[40] Not quite ready to draft a comprehensive set of statutes combining elements of different sources of law, the Legislature settled for mere reception of the English Common Law, effective April 12, 1850.[41]

Understanding that law alone was not enough, the Legislature provided a more nuanced framework of local and state-wide government wherein what passed for law could be better

[38] Id., at p. 27.

[39] Tinkham, op. cit., at pp. 132-133.

[40] Joseph Clement Bates, *History of the Bench and Bar of California* (San Francisco: Bench and Bar Publishing Company, 1912), at p. 47.

[41] Id., at p. 50.

administered and enforced. San Joaquin was formally organized as a self-governing County via an Act of February 18, 1850, with Stockton as the County seat.[42] The make-shift municipal government that had governed Stockton since the conquest was also replaced by something far superior. Getting ahead of the issue and perhaps hoping to control the end product of the people's discretion, Judge Belt hosted a meeting of the citizenry at his store on the evening of March 15, 1850 "'for the purpose of considering the propriety of recommending the inhabitants to form a town council....'"[43] The end result was a resolution addressed to the Legislature favoring incorporation of Stockton as a City. When the request was granted, a charter was drafted and the first elections for civic office occurred. Beating Terry for the office of mayor was Samuel Purdy, a northern Democrat and future Lieutenant Governor of the State.[44] Terry, likewise was a Democrat, but of the faction known as the Chivalry, whose members were largely from the South and feared the spread of Free Soilism, if not in California, where it had prevailed at the Convention, but elsewhere in the unorganized territories of the United States. Seeing Terry as one of their own, the mob heeded the call of Judge Belt and came to his aid, supposedly seizing the ballot box and running with it toward Belt's store.[45] A more reliable witness recounted "much excitement about the polls, and when the poll was closed, something was said about seizing the ballot-box by some of the other party."[46] R.P. Ashe, Frank Cheatem and Dr. Samuel Langdon suddenly jumped onto a table and "swore they would kill any man who should attempt to seize on or break the ballot-box."[47] Terry himself placed his back to the controverted receptacle "and said that he also would resist any attempt to violate it, and at the same time, did all in his power to pacify Cheatem, who held in his hand a knife."[48]

---

42 *Illustrated History*, op. cit., at p. 80.

43 Id., at p. 69.

44 Id., at p. 88.

45 George H. Tinkham, "Early History of Stockton: The Admission Day City," *The Grizzly Bear*, Volume IX, No. 5 (September 1912), p. 8.

46 *Trial of David S. Terry*, op. cit., at p. 66.

47 Id.

48 Id., at p. 68.

Nearly simultaneously with the organization of the City's government was the organization of the new County's judicial system. By an Act of the Legislature dated February 29, 1850, the old municipal courts were abolished and all jurisdiction formerly exercised by the Court of the First Instance was transferred to the Court for the Twelfth District of California sitting in Stockton—comprehending within its boundaries the Counties of San Joaquin, Calaveras, Tuolumne, Stanislaus and Mariposa—effective on May 13, 1850.[49] Recently elected to the Legislature, Charles M. Creanor was now appointed by his colleagues to the bench and charged with the task of bringing law and order to the disorderly region. He was a native of Pennsylvania who had removed to Texas prior to annexation, and then served with distinction under Generals Taylor and Scott in Mexico. He was a drinker and not the most learned of men, and yet he was regarded highly by the bar who practiced before him as someone who "discharged the difficult and onerous duties of the office...under a present sense of obligation to pursue the right, to do justice, to enforce the law, and subserve and promote the public good," and did so "ably and efficiently, with energy and determination that neither flagged or faltered and distinguished by a spirit of independence and impartiality that took no thought of parties or persons, or of self, save to be (as he was) an upright and incorruptible judge, without fear and without reproach."[50]

For purely local justice, the Legislature provided for municipal courts, or Courts of Sessions, in each County.[51] The Court of Sessions consisted of a primary judge and two associates. It was in essence a police court, with "jurisdiction throughout the County in all cases of assault and battery, breach of the peace, petty larceny, and in all cases of misdemeanor punishable by a fine not exceeding $500, or imprisonment not exceeding three months, or both fine and imprisonment."[52] Having just lost his former job presiding over the Alcalde's Court, Benjamin Williams won the top office in the election held on March 2, 1850, and Hairston Amyx and Oliver

---

[49] Tinkham, *History of Stockton*, supra, at p. 138.
[50] *Mariposa Gazette*, December 23, 1882.
[51] Tinkham, *History of Stockton*, supra, at p. 145.
[52] Id.

Cromwell Emory were chosen to be his junior associates.[53] S. A. Booker won the duty of prosecuting defendants in both Courts, and R. P. Ashe, as County Sheriff, would serve process and ensure all appearances before the County's judicial officers.[54] This Court would soon take up residence in rented quarters on the bottom floor of a building on the corner of Main and Center Street owned by Terry and Perley. It was a most convenient location for the two lawyers, who maintained their offices upstairs.[55]

Many of Perley's early cases were debt recovery actions, or for breach of contract, and many involved disputes over land. He and Terry, for instance, represented Alfred Guthrie in an action against W. B. Stockton. When Stockton's town lot was seized by the Sheriff to cover the debt, Perley purchased the land at auction. He subsequently published a warning to the world that the lot was Guthrie's and could not be occupied by anyone harboring the notion that occupation alone might vest title. He and Terry then purchased the lot from their client for $2,000 and flipped the property to Sheriff Ashe. In April, they brought an action against Andrew Smith for trespass upon the interests of Atherton and Davis, who were operating a ferry on the Calaveras River. Atherton and Davis were upset when Smith started a competing service a mere forty yards from their wharf. With Perley's and Terry's aid, they won damages for tortious interference in the amount of $340 and all but put an end to their nascent competition. Perley next prevailed on behalf of Alexander Todd, Ebenezer Lane, David Douglas and John Baker, but lost in the matter of *Walker v. Hauss*, despite retrial and an appeal.[56]

Occasionally, he and his partner took on adverse parties, guaranteeing the partnership would win, but ensuring it a loss as well. Perley managed to get the best of Terry in the *Lane* matter with

---

[53] Id.; and *Illustrated History*, op. cit., at p. 81.

[54] *Illustrated History*, op. cit., at p. 81.

[55] Minute Book A- Court of Sessions, San Joaquin County, CA 1850-1852," *San Joaquin Historian*, Vol. XV, No. 1 (Jan-March 1979), at p. 188.

[56] See *Alexander Todd v. Carlton Gould and Charles Peck*, San Joaquin Superior Court, Case No. 10; *John Walker v. Fernando Hauss and Francisco Hauss*, San Joaquin Superior Court, Case No. 7; and *Ebenezer Land, David Douglas and John Baker v. George W. Bell*, San Joaquin Superior Court, Case No. 12; and *Walker v. Hauss* (1850) 1 Cal. 183. The appeal in *Walker* was handled by Col. Joseph K. Irving, apparently because Perley had not yet been admitted to practice before the Supreme Court.

an award of $2,276. More memorable was their tête-à-tête in the matter of *Belt v. Davis,* wherein Terry prosecuted an action for damages on behalf of the notorious George Belt, and Perley countersued for the defendant.[57] The matter originated in the February term of Alcalde Reynolds's court and involved a claim by Davis against Belt for division of the profits following the winding down of a business partnership. Having a dislike for his predecessor, and no doubt harboring some animus over Belt's prominence in the mobs that periodically disrupted his courtroom, Reynolds impaneled successive juries until he managed to orchestrate a judgment against Belt for $5,948. Denouncing Reynolds as his "violent personal enemy" and a judge who was "notorious, corrupt and venal," Belt instructed Terry and co-counsel S. A. Booker to appeal the matter, but the appeal was subsequently withdrawn in accordance with an agreement between the parties to stay execution by Davis against Belt's property in San Joaquin and San Francisco Counties—apparently in anticipation of a compromise of the entire action.[58]

Belt may have been pacified, but his following in Stockton wasn't, and its members likely resented Perley's role in crossing their captain and longed for the moment when they might correct the audacious lawyer's independence. That moment came when Perley, "in the faithful discharge of his duty and in vindication of his client's rights before the court," won a judgment against a member of Belt's clique named Marshall. Launching a gross insult at the victorious counsel, Marshall likely expected to prompt a reaction from the excitable Perley.[59] If so, he calculated accurately, as Perley defended his character and his client's rights "on the spot by drawing a pistol on the offender, who cried *peccavi,* and that he was unarmed."[60] Perley "immediately invited his antagonist to step out and settle it by themselves, which was politely declined."[61] The next day, Marshall directed a formal challenge to Perley, which was accepted. "At the time appointed, both parties were on the ground,"

---

[57] *Belt v. Davis,* San Joaquin Superior Court, Case No. 2.

[58] Id.; and *Belt v. Davis,* San Joaquin Superior Court, Case No 64.

[59] *Daily Alta California,* April 20, 1850

[60] Id.

[61] Id.

with Belt himself appearing as Marshall's second.[62] Two shots each were exchanged. Both of Marshall's entered the earth only a short distance in front of himself, though one report had it that a bullet penetrated Perley's coat sleeve and mangled it severely near the shoulder.[63] Perley's first shot whizzed past his adversary's head, causing him to duck evasively, "and the second passed through his hat...within one inch of his cranium."[64] Enthusiasm by both men for a third round was apparently stifled by the seconds, "who insisted that sufficient damage had been done."[65] The duel was considered a victory for law and order, and a defeat for "the principle of silencing by threats and bravado, the manly efforts of an honest attorney in defense of his client's rights, and thereby evade the payment of an honest debt."[66] Hope was expressed that "the minions of the party who swagger and bully, or the chiefs and leaders who wish to trample upon all law, deride justice in her very sanctuary, and, by threats and violence attempt to silence the voice of the fearless and honest advocate, who calls upon them for the payment of their just debts, may learn hence forth that their reign of blustering, bullying, and swindling is over, leaving only the balancing of the past!"[67]

Perley's courage may have stemmed the ambition and the power of the mob, but it hadn't brought it completely to heel, nor convinced its leader that the threat of violence was yet unlikely to yield a reward. A greater deterrent came when Belt ran afoul of Terry. Terry's break with Belt came when the former judge began spreading tales that a fellow member of the Stockton Bar, Dr. Robert Roberts, was actually a notorious gang leader who formerly marauded among the settlements on either side of the Rio Grande in the vicinity of El Paso. The accusation was apparently prompted by Roberts' own statement in the *Alta California* critical of Belt's role in the lawlessness so characteristic of Stockton. Perhaps lacking confidence that a defense of his own honor was plausible, Belt instead launched a very public accusation against Roberts, whom he

---

62 Id.
63 *Daily Alta California*, April 13, 1850.
64 *Daily Alta California*, April 20, 1850.
65 *Daily Alta California*, April 13, 1850.
66 *Daily Alta California*, April 20, 1850.
67 Id.

called Dr. Lemon, alias Captain Bill Snooks, and identified him as the former leader of a band of twenty-five men who lived by plunder in the territory of New Mexico before being slaughtered, with the exception of Lemon, by a group of Mexicans in league with the Apaches.[68] When Belt's tales circulated in the papers, Perley, James R. Maloney, County Treasurer S. R. Alden, Edward L. B. Brooks, James Taber and others publicly expressed their confidence in Roberts, and vouched that "his character and conduct during the whole of that time has not only been irreproachable, but signally honorable and exemplary."[69] Roberts himself posted a notice to the public explaining that Belt's baseless accusation was motivated by the accuser's displeasure with Roberts "for requiring him and some of his friends to pay somewhat of their indebtedness."[70] Terry went further and impulsively declared the story a lie and Belt himself a liar. In response to the charge, Perley's recent adversary Marshall confronted Terry with Belt's challenge to meet on the field of honor.[71] The fearless Terry accepted through the agency of Perley, his designated second, and then tested his co-combatant's metal by insisting that pistols be fired from a mere ten paces apart.[72] Belt balked, even after W. F. Swasey, an expert in such matters, was consulted and ruled that the bantam distance was neither novel nor inappropriate.[73] After efforts to enlist the aid of the police authorities to break up the duel by arresting the parties failed, an unnerved Belt temporarily withdrew his challenge pending the resolution of the technicalities.[74]

The stay in hostilities on the field of honor did not extend to the field of law. The truce between Belt and Davis frayed and finally failed. Execution of the judgment obtained against Belt proceeded and a levy on Belt's property in San Francisco commenced with the aid of Sheriff John Coffee Hays. In response, Belt filed an entirely new action in the District Court, alleging that the judgment had

---

68 *Daily Alta California*, May 2, 1850.

69 Letter to the Editor of the *Alta California*, May 5, 1850, BANC, F 869, S7, R6, phot. x.

70 R. Roberts to the Public, May 9, 1850, BANC, F 869, S77, R6, phot. x.

71 A. E. Wagstaff, *Life of David S. Terry* (San Francisco: Continental Publishing Company, pp. 53-55.

72 Id.

73 Id.

74 R. Roberts to the Public, supra.

been "obtained by means of collusion, venality and corruption."[75] In viewing the pleadings, Judge Creanor thought an injunction restraining execution against Belt was appropriate until a hearing on the merits could be held. When the hearing occurred, only matters of law were addressed. The result was a setting aside of the original Judgment and an order for a new trial. Perley promptly appealed.

Understanding how formidable the task of pursuing justice against the leader of Stockton's mobs would be, Perley procured the assistance of the notable San Francisco attorney, Hall McAllister. A native of Georgia and son of Federal Judge M. H. McAllister, Hall McAllister was said by the historian of the State's early legal profession to have been "the ablest lawyer I ever saw," whose "varied learning, his indomitable industry, his faultless memory, added to a broad minded conception of the right and wrong of each case in which he was employed, together with a magnificent presence, and urbanity of manner in court."[76] Perley and McAllister contended that Judge Creanor had no authority to set aside, modify, or in any way invalidate the judgment rendered by Judge Reynolds, and that even if the authority existed, its exercise here was improper. Opposing them was another of San Francisco's leading attorneys, the Virginia-born Gregory Yale, who months before had done Perley a good turn by moving the Supreme Court to admit him to practice at the Supreme Court Bar.[77] Yale argued that the decision appealed was not technically a final judgment, hence the appeal was barred by Section 258 of the Practice Act of April 22, 1850.

Taking the last issue first, the Court examined the nature of finality in legal matters. Because the matter under appeal originated in a complaint that the defendant answered, proceeded to a hearing of the merits and resulted in an order granting the requested relief, there was no doubt the judgment at issue had "been finally and

---

[75] *Belt v. Davis* (1850) 1 Cal. 135, 136.

[76] Oscar T. Shuck, *History of the Bench and Bar of California* (Los Angeles: The Commercial Printing House, 1901), at p. 391.

[77] Rolls of Certified Attorneys, Volume 1, at pp. 168-169, Inventory of the Supreme Court of California Records, California State Archives.

definitely determined by the District Court, and there is, consequently, no further judgment to be rendered in the suit."[78]

Turning to the issue of whether Judge Creanor was correct in ordering a new trial, the Court considered the power granted to the judiciary by the 29th Section of the Practice Act. That section conferred upon the District Courts jurisdiction over judgments issued by Courts of First Instance when those judgments were transferred into the District Court for enforcement purposes. While the Act granted the District Court power "to hear, try, and determine all suits and proceedings transferred therein, in which judgments shall not have been rendered in the Courts of First Instance,... no portion of the statute gives the District Court, either expressly or by implication, jurisdiction to set aside, modify or impair any judgment already rendered by a Court of First Instance, either upon motion in the same suit founded upon affidavits, or by an original complaint, having for its object the attainment of that end."[79] The District Court was not "in respect to such judgments, a Court of review, and has not, either directly or indirectly, jurisdiction to examine into their propriety or validity, unless, perhaps, where a clear case of fraud should be made out." The proper manner for Belt to have proceeded following his loss in the original case was to appeal, not file an entirely new case in which the relief sought was estopped by the very judgment under attack. Even if the procedure was not improper, no relief should have been granted on account of the fact that the only matter before the court was set forth in the pleadings and contained mutually contradictory facts. As such, there was "no ground upon which the judgment appealed from can be sustained."[80]

Having defeated Belt on appeal, Perley joined Terry and Dr. Roberts in challenging Belt in a case brought by two men whose property had been seized by Belt and his mob, apparently while acting under color of authority. Commencing in the police court, the matter was transferred to Judge Reynolds in the Court of the Sessions. Belt's tension with Terry and Perley eased considerably after proof was forthcoming that Roberts actually was the notorious

---

[78] *Belt v. Davis*, supra, at 139-140.

[79] Id., at 142.

[80] Id., at 143.

thief of the New Mexican bad lands. Belt and Terry resolved their differences, with Terry admitting that he had been wrong. He and Perley, S. A. Booker and Colonel Joseph K. Irving, subsequently represented Belt in an action to recover a debt from the merchants Heath & Emory in the amount of $16,000.[81] A cross-complaint was filed and the matter was continued into the December term. It was then assigned to a panel of referees consisting of Mayor Purdy, E. M. Howison and William T. Shannon. The referees subsequently reported that it was Heath & Emory who were owed money by Belt, not the other way around.[82]

As in many communities in their first days of existence, control over acreage within city limits was the object of an enormous amount of litigation. After surveying a town plat in 1849, Captain Weber transferred title to some of the lots to the surveyor, R. P. Hammond, and kept the rest for himself, which he then sold off in small parcels ideal for the construction of homes and commercial buildings. The land that wasn't immediately conveyed, occupied and developed proved too great a temptation for land and cash poor settlers and outright thieves, who squatted or jumped vacant lots throughout the town. In the Spring of 1850, a large group of squatters occupied some of the land within the town limits claimed by Hammond. Hammond retaliated with armed support to clear the land of the squatters' tents. When the squatters resisted, they were arrested for riot and trespass and prosecuted by Hammond for damages in the Court of the Sessions through the agency of a team of lawyers consisting of W. D. Fair, S. A. Booker, Dr. Roberts and Thomas Van Buren.[83] The squatters countered by retaining Terry and Perley, Edward L. B. Brooks and Hairston Amyx to defend against the charge on the technical grounds that the court in which the case was pending lacked jurisdiction. This was no mere police matter; it involved title to land, thus it was properly heard in either

[81] *The Stockton Times*, December 21, 1850.

[82] *The Stockton Times*, January 8, 1851. Though Perley's relations with Belt were now concluded, the career of the colorful Belt continued for nearly another two decades. After leading a posse to track down outlaws and even plotting to organize Pro-Confederates during the Civil War, he was the victim of a shocking daylight murder in the streets of Stockton in 1869.

[83] Tinkham, *History of Stockton*, supra, at p. 163. Tinkham was incorrect in stating that it was Weber, not Hammond, who initiated the action.

the county or the district court. When the jurisdictional objection was overruled, Perley and co-counsel demurred to the sufficiency of the pleadings. When the demurrer was denied, Perley and his colleagues successfully moved to disqualify the judge due to prejudice arising from his business partnership with one of Hammond's attorneys. Observing Perley's conduct in this case on behalf of the squatters, Earle Williams later said of Perley that he was "definitely on the other side of the fence as far as the ethics of his practice were concerned."[84] More appreciative of the man was Captain Weber, who retained Perley and his partner in the wake of the squatter cases to expel Judge Amyx from a portion of the town square Weber was attempting to sell to the City. The action proceeded in the Court of the Sessions before one of the assistant judges, not Amyx himself, for obvious reasons. Weber ultimately prevailed, but not without a legal bill of $1,000 that he passed on to the County pursuant to an indemnity agreement.[85]

The violence of the mobs was no more pronounced or extreme than when the hue and cry was raised following a murder. The natural urge for justice, combined with a vacuum of entertainment, caused an explosion of blood lust that could only dissipate once the mob's target dangled lifeless from a tree or the gallows. Perley's reputation for courage recommended him as someone to conduct the defense of men unpopular because of their race and the crime they were accused of committing. On the morning of July 20, four Mexicans, three of whom were of Indian stock, were apprehended when discovered in the act of burning the bodies of two Americans. Assuming that the act was that of criminals attempting to dispose of the evidence of their crime, a mob made haste in forcing a summary trial in the town of Sonora. Following the predictable conviction for capital murder, preparation began for a mass execution. Aghast at the lawless scene, a group of local officials, including the municipal judge and the county clerk, temporarily rescued the men and placed them in the Tuolumne County jail. Somehow, they convinced the now two thousand strong mob to take the matter before Judge

---

[84] Earle E. Williams, *Rancho El Pescadero,* Volume One: The Early Years, at p. 62, BANC. MSS 80/58c.

[85] Robert Bonta, "Minute Book A, Court of Sessions (Civil) San Joaquin County, California, 1850-1852," *San Joaquin Historian,* Volume XV, No. 2 (April-June 1979), at p. 194.

Creanor. Viewing the detour to Creanor as a mere formality, representatives of the local vigilance committee went before the Judge and informed him "in unmistakable terms that the trial must go on that day."[86] Creanor bravely replied that their preference was contrary to law and the law would not be discarded, though he thought it best to concede that a trial the following day would be acceptable. It must have been during the night that Creanor contacted Perley and a Mr. Mowe and asked them to stand in defense of the accused, in defiance of the mob and in opposition to prosecutors S. A. Booker and Thomas Van Buren. "Though this was far from being a pleasant task (as the armed men who occupied the place had publicly threatened to hang any lawyer who should dare attempt it), those gentlemen did not shirk from the responsibility."[87] The members of the jury were seated without challenge due to each member's assurance to the court and counsel that they could be impartial. A careless fumbling with a gun during the proceedings caused an accidental discharge, followed by the panicked drawing of numerous weapons, further gunfire and a "struggle to quit the courtroom...indescribably violent."[88] As the witnesses for the prosecution took the stand, "the public was astonished at the weakness of the testimony" against the accused.[89] The evidence "failed entirely on every material point, its stern tone dwindled into insignificance," and "when calmly and dispassionately looked at, it withered into thin air at the first breath of logical analysis."[90] The Defendants themselves testified that they had found the two Americans already dead and were simply disposing of the remains in accordance with their custom. After a short deliberation, the jury acquitted the Defendants and the mob dispersed, satisfied as to the justice of the outcome.

Perley's notoriety as a champion of justice grew with the coming of the District Court's December term. One hundred and twenty-five cases were on the civil calendar in Judge Creanor's court, some of which were of "considerable importance."[91] None were followed

---

[86] *History of Tuolumne County* (San Francisco: B.F. Alley, 1882), at p. 42.
[87] *Sonora Times*, July 27, 1850.
[88] *History of Tuolumne County*, op. cit., at p. 43.
[89] *Sonora Times*, July 27, 1850.
[90] Id.
[91] *The Stockton Times*, December 15, 1850.

with greater public interest than the matter of the allegedly corrupt sessional judge, Hairston Amyx. Acting in the capacity of a justice of the peace, Amyx had arraigned a black man named Millar on the charge of stealing a piece of pie, and then bound him over to the magistrate in the sum of $500, and ordered him to appear before the Court of the Sessions.[92] Bail was granted to the accused upon payment of additional security in the amount of $100, which was deposited with Amyx himself. Amyx then asked Millar what he could pay to "fix" the matter. When Millar produced an additional $50, Amyx declared the case dismissed on the entirely contrived grounds that it had been referred to him frivolously by the Judge of the Court of the Sessions—that is, himself. Appalled by Amyx's overt venality, few nevertheless were willing to take him on, including the District Attorney. In the absence of any properly appointed authority to handle the people's business, Perley stepped forward as a private attorney general and filed a criminal complaint alleging "fraud, taking illegal fees of office, extortion, bribery and corruption, and violating his oath of office as judge of the court of sessions."[93] By his side at trial would be Captain E. C. Marshall, "an able pleader" who stood "unrivaled in severity of sarcasm and ready repartee."[94] In Amyx's defense were the former Governor of Virginia, William "Extra Billy" Smith, and S. A. Booker.[95] Rather than challenge the factual substance of the charge, which apparently was damning, Smith and Booker focused on legal technicalities. Undeterred by the procedural hurdles thrown his way, Perley went forward with the case. He stood, "impetuous, but most astute and logical," his "clear voice" ringing through the court, now in terms of indignation at the offense which had been committed, and then in shrewd and comprehensive argument of the legal questions involved in the case," leaving "a deep and lasting impression upon all present."[96] The jury was persuaded, and after a short deliberation, pronounced a verdict of guilty.

The press lauded Perley for "the position he has taken in this affair," and declared that he had created "a debt of gratitude which

[92] *The Stockton Times*, December 21, 1850.

[93] *The Stockton Times*, December 14, 1850.

[94] *The Stockton Times*, December 21, 1850.

[95] Id.

[96] Id.

cannot be overstated."[97] Conceding that Amyx had been mistaken as to the nature of his official obligations, the paper nevertheless disapproved of "the notion current amongst us—in our city council to-wit—that a man may be wronged with impunity, so that other men obtain advantages therefrom; so that we serve our friends or our own interests—that the effect or motive sanctifies the commission of the deed." This notion, challenged by Mr. Perley, boded well for the institution of justice and of government, and served to dissipate the threat of subversion posed to "all our commercial and social interests."[98] The public approbation of the outcome, however, did nothing to deter an appeal by Amyx and the contention that the presentment filed by Perley was defective in that it failed to allege he had actually taken illegal fees or money in exchange for judicial favor. When the high court finally reviewed the matter two years later, it agreed with the defense and threw out the verdict.[99] By then, Amyx had left office for private practice and few if anyone, Perley included, much cared any more for the controversy.

As the term progressed, Perley and Terry again found themselves on opposite sides of litigation—this time in the matter of *Duchay v. Rand*, involving a partnership contract entered into in Texas but breached in California. The resourceful parties had operated a faro bank as they travelled from Texas, through Mexico, to Mazatlan, and then to San Francisco. The men accumulated $60,000, but instead of splitting it evenly, Rand retained both portions. When first prosecuted a year earlier, Rand successfully demurred on the grounds that the contract was illegal and immoral, hence void and unenforceable, whether in Texas or California. An amended action resulted in a similar outcome. Now, in December, on the third attempt, Rand prevailed on the merits despite the best efforts of Terry and his co-counsel H. A. Crabb to have it dismissed.[100] Having stiffed his partner, Rand now stiffed the victorious Perley, who then brought an action for payment of his

---

[97] Id.

[98] Id.

[99] *The People ex rel. Duncan Perley v. H. Amyx* (1852) 2 Cal. 565.

[100] *The Stockton Times*, December 14, 1850.

fee.[101] Perley and Terry reteamed in the matter of *Joseph D. Hoppe v. John S. Robb*, tried the case, and prevailed.[102] Though they didn't win in *Thomas G. Martin v. Bonsall et al.*, they did the next best thing defense attorneys can do by hanging the jury.[103] Thomas Van Buren had opposed Perley in the latter two cases, and did so again in the matter of *Dodge v. Bell*, wherein he managed to beat the combined talent of Perley and his partner.[104] Far from resenting Van Buren, who was a competent lawyer, Perley next teamed with him and Mr. Brooks in the unsuccessful defense of Aaron Van Camp, whom a member of the public sought to remove from the office of Justice of the Peace due to his being unqualified for the post and having won it via election procedures inconsistent with what the relevant statute prescribed.[105] With "his accustomed ability, force of argument, and strong array of authorities," Perley argued for the absence of any law that allowed a third party or relator to come into court and ask for the kind of relief at issue here, and that the common law, on which the action by default must be based, lacked any analogous procedure. English statutes did exist, but these were not part of the common law of the State, hence they didn't support the Plaintiff's action. Even had the law supplied the basis for a suit, the court possessing jurisdiction was the Court of the Sessions, not the District Court.[106] Judge Creanor disagreed with these arguments and overruled Perley's motion, but was otherwise convinced by Perley that there had been no intentional wrongdoing on Van Camp's part and thus exempted him from payment of the prevailing party's costs.[107] Perley and Terry also unsuccessfully pursued a trespass action in the matter of *David Douglas et al. v. T.J. Kirk et al*—apparently involving a dispute over land.[108] Perley and Terry won a final trial during the term in the matter of *Gavan v. Atherton and Davis* and a very satisfying award in the amount of

---

[101] *D. W. Perley v. Parkman Rand*, San Joaquin County Superior Court, Case No. 170.

[102] *The Stockton Times*, December 14, 1850.

[103] Id.

[104] *The Stockton Times*, December 21, 1850

[105] Id.

[106] *The Stockton Times*, January 1, 1851.

[107] Id.

[108] Id.

$8,300.[109] Of less apparent consequence was the matter of *Henry Russell v. Benjamin Williams, Albert Williams and William Atherton,* involving enforcement of rights arising from a promissory note, in which they took a default against the Justice of the Peace and his associates.[110] The default was subsequently appealed to the Supreme Court, where Chief Justice Murray and his colleagues determined the appeal had been "prosecuted merely for delay."

As the eventful year of 1850 came to a close, the thoughts of many turned to the holidays and celebration. The growth of the community from tent city to full-fledged shire town, containing many tree-lined streets and framed buildings, scores of businesses and a growing population prospering from the output of the mines merited a great deal of gratitude, even if disorder still abounded and the supremacy of the law had yet to be fully accepted by the populace. One of the liveliest events of the season, and perhaps the first such event of its kind in the City's history, was a grand soiree at the home of Mrs. McPherson. Perley, Terry, Ashe, and many others were all present, as were many "respectable women." Yet at nine o'clock, as the merry crowd frolicked to the music, explosions from the direction of the front door caused a stir.[111] The panic dissipated quickly as it became clear that it was merely the resounding of fire crackers, thrown through the temporarily opened door by unknown mischief makers. Perley grabbed a candle-powered lantern and ventured into the darkness outside the home to investigate, followed by Terry, Ashe and T. S. Lubbock. Finding the culprit—a porter employed by Stillman, Prentiss & Evans—Sheriff Ashe attempted to convince the man to desist and depart. When he refused to abide by the request, Terry pummeled the man, and was only stopped from inflicting further pain when Ashe intervened to arrest Terry's victim on the charge of disorderly conduct. Having drank a round or two with other revelers, the porter's employer, M. R. Evans, ran outside upon being informed of the commotion. Observing the porter "so badly cut, beaten and disfigured" that he scarcely recognized him, Evans confronted Ashe and told him he wouldn't allow his man to suffer arrest. Terry

---

109 *The Stockton Times,* January 8, 1851.

110 *Henry Russell v. Benjamin Williams, et al.* (1852) 2 Cal. 158.

111 *Trial of David S. Terry,* op. cit., at p. 48.

warned him not to interfere with the Sheriff, and once satisfied that there would be no compliance, struck Evans "over the head with the butt of a pistol." Perley, Ashe and Lubbock supposedly at once fell upon and beat Evans with pistols and clubs until he became "senseless," all while Terry screamed "Kill the damned son of a bitch!"[112] When asked about the incident several years later, Mrs. McPherson denied that Perley was involved in the assault due to his hands being occupied in holding the lantern. She blamed Evans for the brawl, saying "that he was in the wrong—that he was the aggressor in the fight; that he interfered unlawfully with an officer in the discharge of his duty, and that he tried to uphold and protect a ruffian in his base attempt to break up the first party which had ever been given in Stockton."[113]

Toward the end of the December term of the District Court, sensational news broke of two homicides. The first was that of Nacia Cerdera in the El Dorado Saloon by Joe Morea, known as Little Joe. Arising from a dispute over a debt, and further provoked by alcohol and swagger, the crime elicited an immediate admission of intent by the murderer, followed by his flight from the scene.[114] The youth of both the victim and his assailant amazed those who witnessed the incident, causing them to stand about dumbfounded as Morea escaped in the direction of Mokelumne Hill. A reward of $200 posted by Mayor Purdy incentivized a posse and facilitated the rapid apprehension of the killer. When brought before the magistrate for examination on the charge of murder, Morea presented an appearance of indifference described by observers as extraordinary. Bail was denied and Morea was held in custody until the next session, when his trial would commence and his counsel, Perley and Terry, would present (or so it was said) a defense based on insanity.[115]

The second murder was committed in a drunken haze by the Irishman George Baker, known in town as Mickey. The young man, scarcely passed his teens, "had led a wild and changeful life, was of an erratic turn of mind and could boast of a limited education," yet at the same time possessed a winning way and generous spirit said

---

[112] Id., pp. 20 & 65

[113] Id., at p. 65.

[114] *Daily Alta California*, January 20, 1851.

[115] *The Stockton Times*, January 25, 1851.

to have been "proverbially characteristic of his race." The deed he admitted, but denied any malicious intent. Instead, there was, he said, a perceived threat to his life by men singling him out on account of his Irish origins. As he awaited trial, he joined Morea and others in the county jail, and was present when one of the prisoners broke a leg off of a table and used it as a lever to shatter their chains. When the clanking of the remaining links was heard outside the building, the jailor rushed in with a six shooter and arrested one of the escapees. A Frenchman apprehended Morea, while the rest were taken shortly afterward. The only one of the prisoners foregoing escape was the congenial Mickey.[116]

Little Joe Morea was tried first. On April 12, Perley and his co-counsel entered a plea on his behalf of not guilty.[117] Two days later, as the trial commenced, they sought a continuance for want of a material witness, which was denied.[118] The jury was seated on the 16th and trial proceeded throughout the day. Jury deliberations commenced in the evening and concluded a day later when a verdict of guilty on the charge of manslaughter was handed down, with a sentence of six months imprisonment. The defendant's youth, said the Judge, was the reason for the lenience in punishment.[119] The outcome "created a storm of indignation" and stirred up a public feeling that could only be alleviated by a sacrifice.[120] Mickey being up next for trial, the public's wrath fell upon him, as worthy as he seemed for some measure of mercy. Being perhaps two of the only men in whom the Court had confidence could fearlessly defend the accused amid such a hostile public climate, Perley and Terry again appeared in a capital case, raising at first a number of procedural objections to the trial going forward, including the need for a less biased venue and the absence of material witnesses. Mickey was nevertheless found guilty on April 25 and sentenced shortly afterward by Judge Creanor.[121] Before sentencing could occur, Perley took an appeal to the Supreme Court—the first ever in California in a capital case—

---

116 *The Stockton Times*, March 1, 1851.

117 *The Stockton Times*, April 16, 1851.

118 Id.

119 *The Stockton Times*, April 19, 1851

120 *Illustrated History*, op. cit., at p. 82.

121 *Sacramento Daily Union*, May 3, 1851; and *Sacramento Transcript*, May 6, 1851.

arguing that the locality of the trial and the bias of the community mandated a change of venue, the impropriety of the trial court's refusal to delay the trial to allow the marshalling of necessary exculpatory witnesses, and the jury's lack of impartiality as evidenced by the affidavit of one of the jurors. The Supreme Court rebuffed each argument. While Stockton might be biased, the County as a whole undoubtedly contained many jurors free of any prejudice. If exculpatory witnesses existed, greater diligence by the Defendant's counsel might have secured their presence. And legal authority strongly opposed allowing a single juror to impeach the decision of the Jury as a whole.[122]

The appeal was a hopeless exhibition of valor by an attorney desperate to avoid the worst consequence of the worst crime a man might commit. And that consequence was not long in coming. Looking pale more from confinement than dread of the awful sentence about to be meted out, Mickey was asked by the Clerk if he had any thought as to why a sentence of death ought not to be pronounced.[123] Upon saying that his attorneys had indicated they intended to make another effort on his behalf, he was informed by the Judge that such an effort had indeed been made, but had failed. As the Judge read the fatal sentence, to be carried out on May 3, it was said that there were many who harbored hopes for mercy, if not in this world, then in the next.[124]

On the appointed day, at 3 o'clock, Sheriff Ashe and Deputy Sheriff Blount escorted Mickey out of the jail and led him up the gallows steps to the drop in front of a crowd of about eight hundred people, "all of whom appeared to regard the scene with solemnity, and the fate of the young man with silent respect."[125] After Ashe read the death warrant, Mickey addressed the crowd, taking responsibility for his crime and attesting that others accused of being accomplices were innocent. Once the Rev. James Wood recited a prayer, Mickey, with the noose around his neck and in tremulous accents, thanked Dr. Ashe, Mr. Blount, and the officers of the prison for the kindness they had shown him during his time in custody, and also his attorneys, Terry and Perley, for "it is little else

---

[122] *People v. Baker* (1851) 1 Cal. 403.

[123] *Sacramento Transcript*, May 31, 1851.

[124] *Sacramento Transcript*, May 3, 1851.

[125] *San Joaquin Republican*, May 31, 1851; and *Sacramento Transcript*, May 31, 1851.

that they have received for all they have done for me." As soon as he asked that God bless all in attendance, the signal was given, the trap was sprung, and the unfortunate Mickey was no more.[126]

Perley might have lost, but its significance as the first capital murder case resulting in a lawful execution as opposed to a lynching and his growing reputation as "eminent counsel" were beyond dispute.[127] When the next serious felons were apprehended after committing notorious crimes and public feeling was aroused so extremely as to threaten the exercise of private justice at the expense of due process, it was Perley and Terry to whom the authorities turned. Indeed, rather than prosecute the murderer Frederick Salkmar, known as Flat Foot, and the felon James Boland, the timorous District Attorney deferred to the two partners to handle the matter. They obtained guilty verdicts from the juries empaneled by Judge Emory in the Court of the Sessions in Stockton and sentences of death and 10 years in the penitentiary respectively. The *Stockton Journal* hailed the outcome as a triumphant vindication of justice, while another commentator more soberly assessed the result as "satisfactory to the community and to the law, which has been so often laxly administered."[128]

Perley's eminence was now evident elsewhere. The Legislature's contemplation of a tax to impose on foreign miners operating in California—thought by its members to be an uncontroversial way of raising revenue—generated significant opposition, both from the foreign born and the native. The discovery of gold yielded nothing in the way of wealth without first attracting tens of thousands of men to extract it from earth and stream. While many emigrated from the eastern States, many others came from beyond the nation's borders. The Mexican origin of a majority of the mining class and "the superior and uniform success of these Mexicans in their operations among the gold hills of California" likely encouraged the prejudice of the members of the Legislature and aided in the forging of a majority favoring passage of the law.[129] Being an immigrant himself, Perley took a keen interest in the proposal, and when the population of Stockton assembled at the El Placer Saloon to take

[126] *San Joaquin Republican*, May 31, 1851.
[127] *Marysville Daily Herald*, May 6, 1851.
[128] *Daily Alta California*, October 24, 1851; and *Nevada Journal*, October 25, 1851.
[129] *Daily Alta California*, August 9, 1850.

into consideration the recently enacted law, Perley was in attendance. With Mayor Purdy presiding over the meeting, and Ashe and R. P. Hammond serving as Vice Presidents, a committee was chosen to draft resolutions expressive of the views of the citizenry. While Terry was selected for the committee, it was Perley who was "called upon by the meeting" to speak. "In his usual masterly and clear manner," Perley explained "the iniquitous character of this unjust and unconstitutional law. He dwelt with force and vigor upon the evil of the enactment as even a mere matter of state policy; and during his remarks paid a well-deserved compliment to Captain Fair, who was the only member of our representation in this Legislature, who had the courage to oppose and denounce the iniquity of this tax, before that body."[130] When the applause died down, the committee reported the contents of the draft of the resolution condemning the tax. As Stockton was the center of the mining district of the State, opposition there was not considered irrelevant in the mental calculus of the political class. As opposition grew, the tax was exceeded in unpopularity only by Senator Fremont's proposed federal law to prohibit foreign ownership of mining claims.[131] Heeding the resolutions of the miners and the eloquent denunciation by Perley, the members of the Legislature reflected on just how much the tax had cost the State Treasury "for every trifle it may have put into it... to say nothing of the immense loss which the effect of it has entailed upon the business of the country, in mining, in trade, in commerce." As it was clear that the law lacked popular support, and that the revenue to be gained by its operation was actually outstripped by erosion of the tax base, the law was repealed.[132]

Perley's venture into political activism extended to other matters, though likely his interest in some of these was entirely mercenary. During the meeting of the State's first Legislature, discussion was had of the presence of untold numbers of squatters on land abutting San Francisco Bay. Various San Francisco politicians promoted passage of a law that would solve the uncertainty of ownership by vesting title with a half dozen

130 *The Stockton Times*, March 8, 1851.
131 *Marysville Daily Herald*, May 18, 1850.
132 *Daily Alta California*, March 20, 1851.

speculators who had received dubious and perhaps unscrupulous grants from the City. Approval of the bill would divest the City and County of any right or title to the relevant land, and any revenue to be generated either through sale or lease. So intent were the bill's backers on ensuring passage that it was rumored that up to $60,000 was spent buying the votes of members of the Legislature.[133] Debate over the bill extended into the next legislative session. Supporters (likely including the City of San Francisco, the Firm of Halleck, Peachy & Billings and the financial house of Palmer, Cook & Company) retained the services of Archibald Peachy and Gregory Yale to travel to San Jose, where the Legislature was meeting, and explain the pending bill and aid its passage.[134] Yale took up a room at Taft House, where many of the members of the Legislature were staying. To advance his purpose, he invited members of the relevant committees from both houses to his room "in order that he might explain to them the objects of the bill and to lay before them the laws of other States, particularly of Florida, Mississippi, Louisiana and Arkansas…and of the United States, together with the decisions of the State and Federal Courts upon the subject."[135] Sitting on a box rather inconspicuously in one corner of the room was Perley. He had, it was said, "somehow got wind of the meeting and obtruded himself" for the purpose of dulling the persuasiveness of Yale's presentation, most likely in the service of those opposed to the Bill. After others in attendance expressed their satisfaction with Yale's presentation, Perley questioned Yale about some of the legal authorities he had cited. Assuming his colleague and friend was an invitee sincerely interested in learning about the relevant law, Yale at first made an effort to answer the questions posed. Perley's true purpose, however, became evident when instead of accepting the learned man's response, Perley proceeded to argue a contrary position and even "expressed the opinion that Yale was in error in material instances." It was a rather daring exhibition, both because he was a trespasser on the premises and his opponent was so learned in this area of law that he would in time author the leading treatise on the subject. Momentarily effective in confounding Yale,

[133] *Daily Alta California*, April 13, 1851.

[134] *Daily Alta California*, April 3, 1852, and *Daily Alta California*, December 21, 1884.

[135] *Daily Alta California*, December 21, 1884.

the attack was rejoined and "discussion between the two became a little warm." Not lacking in assurance and impressing observers with his deep reading in the relevant law, Perley retired with the rest of the guests, leaving Yale "nettled and not a little incensed that his adversary had come to the room uninvited."

Aside from the murder trials that occupied Perley and his partner in the spring of 1851, there were the numerous civil cases the two men jointly and severally pursued. They represented Captain Weber in an action against James Lansing for occupying the Captain's land without paying for the privilege.[136] One act of resistance by Lansing emboldened all of Weber's tenants in the town of French Camp to insist that they had every right to possession of the Captain's estate. When Lansing retained W. D. Fair and S. A. Booker his defense became far more sophisticated. Fair and Booker argued that the statute on which Weber's action was based required force in the unprivileged taking and occupation of the property of another, but since Lansing entered peacefully and with the Captain's permission, the statute didn't apply. They argued, too, that as a tenant, Lansing was entitled to a written demand to vacate, and there wasn't one. Finally, they argued that since Weber himself never occupied the premises after he obtained title, California law permitted others to take possession. In the end, the case turned on the last issue: whether Weber had ever occupied the property. On the strength of the evidence presented by Perley and Terry that Captain Weber grazed cattle on the property after obtaining title, the jury awarded Weber $500 in damages plus fair rental value for the period of occupation by Lansing.

Perley and Terry next defended two San Francisco merchants accused of breaching a warranty of the fitness of pork they had sold in Stockton after displaying a sample they claimed to have been representative of the whole. The two lawyers contended that no actual warranty had been extended, though the jury, composed of men who obviously saw the value of implied as well as express guarantees, were unconvinced by the argument.[137] In an interesting turn of events, the partners also took on the defense of two men they had recently obtained a default against in a separate action—

[136] "Important Decision," *Daily Pacific News*, March 4, 1851.

[137] *The Stockton Times*, April 16, 1851.

William Atherton and Justice of the Peace Benjamin Williams. The pair defended the men in an ejectment suit brought by Hairston Amyx on behalf of Francis McNeal. They prevailed after pressing the argument that the form of the action set forth in the complaint was incorrectly based on the English theory, not the American, hence the suit could not go forward.[138] Perley simultaneously handled an appeal by the same two Defendants in another matter involving a default judgment.

Intimacy with Williams appears to have soured Perley's relationship with the man; for it was Perley who supplied the *Stockton Journal* with details of the Judge's career "as the most corrupt official who ever sat on the bench of San Joaquin County."[139] Williams escaped formal impeachment for his "devious, wayward and uncertain" practices through resignation, but not prosecution for bribery, corruption and altering official records of the Court.[140] It was subsequently rumored that the prosecution on those counts ultimately failed through "the intriguing of the district attorney."[141]

Perley also brought an action on his own account against Gallant Dickinson, who had defaulted on a promissory note in the amount of $2,000. To collect on the debt, he foreclosed on the property by which the debt was secured—a building on Center Street operating as a hotel. Though Perley prevailed in the matter and proceeded to enforce his right to take the property, he relented once Dickinson rather belatedly came up with the amount awarded by the Court.[142] Less than a month later, a devastating fire demonstrated how fortuitous the compromise was. Every building on Center Street, including Dickinson's Hotel, was consumed in the blaze, sparked it seems by an incendiary hoping to force the release of persons being held in the local jail.[143] The wind saved the jail, but

---

138 *The Stockton Times*, April 12, 1851.

139 Tinkham, *History of Stockton*, supra, at p. 261; and Albert Russell Buchanan, *David S. Terry of California: Dueling Judge* (San Marino: The Huntington Library, 1956), at p. 9.

140 Tinkham, *History of Stockton*, supra, at p. 147.

141 Id.

142 *D. W. Perley v. Gallant D. Dickinson*, San Joaquin County Superior Court, Case No. 280.

143 "Terrible Conflagration! Stockton Destroyed by Fire!!," *Daily Alta California*, May 8, 1851.

also contributed to the loss of a significant part of the city. Though he had Dickinson's money in hand, he soon learned that his own losses from the fire exceeded that amount by a thousand dollars.[144]

The volume of cases he was handling and the uncertainly of the law at this time in the history of the State all but guaranteed that Perley would find himself presenting arguments before the Supreme Court of the State. The absence of any intermediate courts of appeal at this early date rendered the Supreme Court the sole body charged with the review of objections to decisions reached in the trial courts. Perley had failed to preserve the victory obtained in the Amyx matter, and to secure a new trial in the case of Mickey, but he did manage to finally triumph before the high bench in *Benedict v. Haggin* and win, in the process, a lifelong friend in the person of his client. The case had commenced in the fall of 1851, when C. L. Benedict sued the estate of Sacramento rancher William Taylor for $6,500 that Taylor owed on a cattle sale. The Estate's trustee—the noted land and mining speculator James Ben Ali Haggin—refused to honor the claim for the reason that it was untimely. Though an attorney himself, Haggin possessed the good sense of a doctor who shrewdly refrains from performing surgery on his own body, and retained Perley to pursue the debt. On the brink of trial, Benedict's lawyer, the disgraced Benjamin Williams, skipped town to escape some further consequence of his infamy and thereby forced a delay notwithstanding Perley's strenuous objection. During argument over jury instructions in November of 1851, Perley rather impetuously handed the presiding Judge the statute book to read Section 134 with respect to timely claims. The Judge denied Perley's requested instruction on this point and the jury went on to award $700 in damages. On appeal, Justice Heydenfeldt of the Supreme Court held that Perley's requested instruction—that a claim against an estate must be brought against the administrator "within three months after its rejection, if it is then due, or within three months after it becomes due, otherwise the claim shall be forever barred"—was correct.[145] "I can see no

---

[144] "Another Terrible Conflagration; Stockton in Ashes!; Loss About $1,000,000," *Sacramento Transcript*, May 9, 1851.

[145] *Benedict v. Haggin* (1852) 2 Cal. 385.

reason for its refusal," wrote the Justice, "such is the expressly written law of the land, and obedience to it must be exacted."[146]

In the matter of *Health v. Lent*, Perley successfully appealed a $3,000 verdict for a plaintiff landowner against the surety on an attachment bond, who was now deceased. The plaintiff had sued the administrator of the surety's estate, asking for damages arising from the attachment of his property. In reviewing the record, Chief Justice Hastings observed much of the testimony had been taken by the clerk, "most of which was illegal, and should not have been permitted to go to the jury." The attachment was a mere instrument, never enforced, and not effecting the owner's possession. As such, the damages were excessive, if not utterly unjustified. Moreover, the signature of the surety was improperly introduced without proof. As the surety himself was deceased, the presumption of validity couldn't apply. The surety might confirm or deny his signature via his testimony, but the trustee couldn't. The evidence, too, of the negative impact of the attachment on the property was simply too uncertain to have been considered, and should have been excluded. Other errors abounded, but they only confirmed the propriety of reversal and remand back to the trial court.[147]

In a third appellate matter, Perley challenged a decision by the Court of the Sessions issued in April of 1852 not to forfeit the bail of Benjamin Marshall after he failed to appear at trial for assault with intent to commit murder. The bondsmen, A. B. Lafarge and H. M. Ball, retained Perley in July to pursue recovery of the bond in an equitable proceeding on the grounds that the bond had been posted for Marshall in a separate matter for which an appearance had been made, but had never been exonerated. It was in the refiled matter that Marshall failed to appear, hence the forfeiture was improper. Perley asserted that Marshall's initial appearance was a full compliance with the condition of his release on the recognizance of the bondmen, and that "this extinguished the bond." The second indictment was not merely a new matter, but utterly unknown to the Defendant and his sureties. "The forfeiture of the bond was therefore illegal." They were entitled to a proper hearing, including an opportunity to challenge the pleadings. When the District Court

---

[146] Id.

[147] *Heath v. Lent* (1851) 1 Cal. 410.

granted the Defendants' motion, the District Attorney enlisted the aid of the Attorney General, who appealed to the Supreme Court. Sensing a need for more legal firepower and recognizing that antagonism in the past doesn't preclude a rapprochement at least for professional purposes, Perley reached out to Gregory Yale and convinced him to put their former mis-acquaintance aside and assist him in the matter. Yale's aid may have proved decisive; for Justice Heydenfeldt held that when there was no notice to the parties, the remedy requested "is well recognized in all courts having chancery jurisdiction, and the case made out by the complainants is one which fully entitles them to the interposition of the Court."[148] The trial court's decision was thus affirmed, with costs.

Throughout Perley's residence in Stockton, his desire to advance in the practice of law was rivaled only by his ambition to accumulate wealth through speculation in the State's greatest asset—its land. He had already closely observed what a lawyer might accumulate in Texas, and though he was unwilling to entertain the enlistment of bond labor, he was nevertheless prepared to build a landed empire on free soil when the opportunity arrived. While pursuing victories in court in 1850 and 1851, he bought and sold land with an eye to turning a profit, and at one point even contemplated with Terry and others an effort to obtain a license to build a toll bridge across the Calaveras River to the east of Stockton, near the Atherton Ferry, and thereby control access to an abundance of unsettled and undeveloped real estate for which demand was high.

As emigrants steadily arrived in the State and made their way to the mining districts, a portion of them opted to carve out farms and ranches on the vast and well-watered land of the San Joaquin Valley. Worthless for mining, its value as a generator of wealth in other ways was undoubted. A great barrier to settlement of this enormous territory remained in the form of the claims of reputed owners, tracing their title and possession to governors appointed by Mexico, but often lacking documentation either of the grant or of its actual dimensions. As settlers began locating along the County's primary waterways to the north and east of Stockton, the barrier proved more theoretical than real. By the end of 1851, there was talk

---

[148] *People v. Larfarge* (1853) 3 Cal. 130.

of a contest in the making between "the great body of the emigration" who had settled as squatters within the bounds of various unconfirmed land grants and the reputed grantees.[149] Some miles from Stockton, in San Joaquin and Calaveras Counties, was the Rancho Sanjon de los Moquelumnes, supposedly granted to Anastacio Chabolla by Governor Micheltorena, containing a monstrous eleven square leagues. Overlapping with it to some extent was the equally large grant by Governor Pio Pico to his brother Andrés known as Los Mokelamos.[150] Together these putative Ranchos would become one of the many forums for the contest between alleged grantees and those claiming title by right of actual possession.

One of men competing for land in the region was Myron Hutchinson. Sometime in 1851, Hutchinson, his father and brother arrived in California via steamer and found their way to the Calaveras River. Once there they began asserting ownership of a twenty-thousand-acre tract of land in the putative Ranchos. This caused alarm among nearby settlers, who organized a committee to meet with the Hutchinsons and resolve the confusion. Instead of a calm discussion, an impromptu confrontation turned into a tense affair, with the committeemen telling Hutchinson that they were "going to try to make an honest man of him, but that it would be an uphill business." When told that his family's claim would not be respected, Hutchinson backed off and said he only wanted to keep what had already been fenced in and invited anyone to settle to rest.

Among those who had confronted the Hutchinsons was a Mr. Dubois, who ran into Perley in Stockton the next day, told him about the incident and asked if he wanted to make a claim. When he learned of the land's location, Perley told Dubois that both he and his cousin Frederick were very interested. Frederick had recently arrived in California and settled in San Joaquin County, no doubt after hearing of the prospects from his cousin for success far beyond what the timber-based economy of New Brunswick offered. The following day, Perley, his cousin, Dubois, Joseph Whiting, Christopher Millican and John Oatman rode out on horseback along the Calaveras. "We crossed Wilson's Bridge," said Perley,

[149] *Daily Alta California*, December 27, 1851.
[150] *Illustrated History*, op. cit., at p. 95.

> rode by Hutchinson's house, and along the river up to a place where there were some rails lying. We followed the line right out where the rails lay, then struck across to another corner and then down the river. There was a stake put up by the surveyor at the corner on the river running from the river. We went around the tract, stayed there till the survey was made. At the time this survey was made there was no sign of any occupation, cultivation, improvement, enclosure or possession of any kind that I saw.[151]

Leaving Frederick on the ground to clear the land and make some show of possession, Perley departed for the east coast on January 20, 1852.[152] The vessel on which he traveled made port in Panama.[153] He must have crossed the malarial isthmus on foot, or by wagon; for at Chagres on the Atlantic side he boarded the steamer *United States* and departed for New York City via Kingston, Jamaica. He arrived in New York on February 16, at 11 p.m. Several weeks later he checked into a hotel in Washington, D.C. with Hall McAllister. What business they attended there is unknown.[154] He was next found in Ann Arbor, Michigan, of all places. There, on April 13, 1852, he married a young lady named Louisa Corbett Brigham.[155] How he knew her remains a mystery, though they must have been introduced somewhere by a friend in common. That he went all the way to Michigan to marry her is a compelling indication of his great desire, either for her, or to obtain a respectable wife. California was still very much a man's world, where women were scarce, and women of virtue even more so. In Louisa, he found a woman of a family both respectable and distinguished. Her father was the English-born physician Dr. Phillip Brigham, a pioneer of the Ann Arbor region. Her mother, Sophronia Smith, was the daughter of a gentlemen of the Hudson River Valley, a niece of Congressman Henry Bird Lee and a descendant of New England divine Solomon Stoddard and the family of Governor

---

[151] *Myron Hutchinson v. Frederick Perley*, San Joaquin County Superior Court, Case No. 364.

[152] Id.

[153] *The New York Herald*, February 17, 1852.

[154] *The Washington, D.C. Republic*, March 1, 1852.

[155] *Michigan Argus*, April 14, 1852.

Winthrop. Perley journeyed with her back to California by steamer in July and took up residence with her in Stockton.

Having looked after his interests for him and maintained their law partnership during his absence, his friend Terry departed nearly as soon as Perley returned. Inspired perhaps by Perley's success in love, he recalled the affection he had for the ward and niece of Mississippi Governor Hiram Runnells. With this memory in mind, he journeyed to Galveston to rekindle their acquaintance. Rapid success in doing so led to their marriage. When Terry returned, the two law partners' wives were integrated into a broader friendship and must surely have become leaders in Stockton fashion and society. Nothing in print remains of Louisa, though of Terry's wife Cornelia it has been recalled that "she was one of the sweetest, purest, and noblest of women," and that "her graceful deportment and refined manners attracted the attention of all with whom she came in contact."[156] It was said by one of Terry's biographers that her impact on her husband was so profound that "during the few years following his marriage, he became a very changed man…attentive to business and devoted to his household, and grew largely in the estimation of those with whom he had formerly associated."[157] Any doubt that the two women were of like mind and temperament and that their friendship mirrored the relations between their husbands must be arrested by the knowledge that after Louisa gave birth to a daughter, she named the baby Cornelia Terry Perley.

Following his return to California in July of 1852, Perley checked in on the status of his claim on the Calaveras. He found that his cousin had enclosed part of the land and planted a crop of buckwheat, but not without facing threats from the Hutchinsons. After paying his cousin to haul lumber to the parcel, he employed a carpenter to build a house, then sold a portion of his interest to Samuel Houston Brooks and Thomas Lee. His ranch-building suffered a set-back later in the year when a wild fire ravaged the banks of the Calaveras. According to news accounts from as far off as the City of Boston, Perley was reported to have been among "the principal losers" once the smoke cleared and the damage could be

---

[156] Wagstaff, op. cit., p. 61.
[157] Id.

surveyed.[158] He put these and other cares out of his mind in the summer, when he took part in a clamorous rally of the Democrat Party in Stockton to ratify the State Party's endorsement of Franklin Pierce for President, Milton Latham and James A. McDougall for Congress and Hugh Murray and Alexander Wells for Judges of the Supreme Court. S. A. Booker was chosen President of the rally, with Perley serving as Vice President—a role that appears to have been purely ceremonial, with little in the way of duties to uphold.[159]

As the year neared an end, Perley handled the defense against a suit brought by Judge Williams and his brother Albert against Sheriff Ashe arising from Ashe's refusal to execute a judgment in the Williams' favor due to his concern that the property to be seized was in the possession of a third party. Ashe agreed to perform his duty, but only if the Williams brothers promised to indemnify him. The matter was continued to April of 1853 due to the absence of David Terry, a crucial witness in the matter. Ultimately, it was the Williams brothers who ultimately paid—in the amount of nearly $500.[160] Perley also defended Adelaide Teiriage and Samuel Shirley against the claim by the County of San Joaquin for $4,000. Perley took the matter on contingency, and though he prevailed, he was never paid. He later sued the ungrateful clients for $1,000 and won.[161] In concert with S. A. Booker, he also defended accused murderer William Turner, convinced the court to grant bail prior to trial, and then had to explain to the judge after Turner absconded that he had no prior "knowledge of Turner's intention to forfeit his recognizance."[162]

Continuing his career as a criminal defense lawyer, Perley conducted the defense of Juan Navis, the accused murderer of an Indian, in Calaveras County in February of 1853. During the trial, one of the People's witnesses testified that "the defendant came to him on the evening of the murder with a knife in his hand and

---

[158] *The Courier Journal*, December 17, 1852; *The New England Farmer*, December 18, 1852; and *The Washington Democrat*, December 24, 1852.

[159] *San Joaquin Republican*, August 18, 1852.

[160] *Benjamin Williams and Albert Williams v. David S. Terry and R.P. Ashe*, San Joaquin County Superior Court, Case No. 343.

[161] *Samuel Booker, David Terry & Duncan Perley v. Adelaide Tiriage*, San Joaquin County Superior Court, Case No. 437.

[162] *Daily Alta California*, October 14, 1852.

stated that he had killed an Indian."[163] Attempting to elicit an exculpatory explanation of why his client made such an admission, Perley asked the witness what else Navis had said. The sustaining by the Court of the People's objection was the basis for the subsequent appeal. With the aid again of Gregory Yale, Perley argued that "the confession of a defendant must be taken together," that the entire statement must be introduced, not a mere portion of the same. To this, Justices Heydenfeldt and Wells agreed, saying that "where the admission or confession of a party is resorted to as evidence, it is error to exclude any portion of it made at the same time as the part which is related."[164] Reversal of the conviction and an order for a new trial followed. Whether Perley might have secured an acquittal can't be known since Navis, still jailed pending the appeal, managed to slip his irons and escape. The occurrence was a common one, and highly suspicious to many. "It is utterly impossible," exclaimed one journal, "for a prisoner to take off his irons and escape if the person in charge give any attention to his duty."[165]

As the year 1853 progressed, he and Terry teamed yet again, this time against debtors J. M. Birdsall and Robert Beldon.[166] As the debt was undeniable, the outcome was no mystery. Such victories were now commonplace, hence unworthy of Perley's growing ambitions. He and Terry had conquered mining country, both as attorneys and businessmen. They had gained notoriety in their fearless prosecution and defense of criminals, their bold advocacy against the mob, and their eloquence in politics and matters of public concern. Perley had made a number of appearances before the Supreme Court and acquitted himself well, often in the company of the ablest lawyers in the State, with whom he was becoming friendly. The reports of his professional qualities during this time were highly favorable, as were those of Terry, who was called "a thorough lawyer, a faithful and shrewd attorney and a good pleader, being clear, emphatic and convincing in his statements and eloquent in description, but not ornate."[167] Terry's leadership of the

---

163 *People v. Juan Navis* (1853) 3 Cal. 106.
164 Id.
165 *Calaveras Chronicle*, March 19, 1853.
166 *San Joaquin Republican*, June 16, 1853.
167 *Illustrated History*, op. cit., at p. 92.

Southern wing of the Democrat party in the mining districts had gained for him and Perley acquaintance with many of the important figures in this phase of the State's history, and added to the circle of friends they had brought with them from Texas. Terry was content to remain in Stockton, build his ranch, raise his family and pursue his political options. Perley, however, hungered for a larger stage on which to operate, where the stakes were higher and the opportunities for fame and fortune far greater than was possible in Stockton. The two men would remain partners, working together from a distance, but by the summer of 1853, Perley would be a resident of the State's greatest entrepot, the City of San Francisco.

Chapter Four

A PERFECT INSECURITY OF ALL RIGHTS

Virtually overnight, the Gold Rush transformed the small Spanish Era bayside settlement of San Francisco into perhaps the most dynamic and also one of the largest metropolises in the country. The immediate result was a city with a large population but little in the way of facilities, services or government. As explained by the authors of the *Annals of San Francisco*, "building lots had to be surveyed, and streets graded and planked—hills leveled—hallows, lagoons, and the bay itself piled, capped, filled up and planked—lumber, bricks, and all other building materials, provided at most extraordinarily high prices—houses built, finished and furnished—great warehouses and stores erected—wharves run far out into the sea—numberless tons of goods removed from shipboard, and delivered and shipped anew everywhere—and ten thousand other things...without a moment's unnecessary delay."[1] As these things took time to accomplish, the teeming ranks of the homeless improvised a temporary solution. While the urban planners planned, engineers designed and builders searched out sources of construction materials, "the sand-hills and barren ground around the town were overspread with a multitude of canvas, blanket and bough covered tents."[2] When the plain along the Bay became overly congested, men moved to the more remote hills, and soon there could be made out by observers far below "squatters' eyries perched upon the rugged spurs, and tents nestling in the ravines."[3]

The Bay, says the *Annals*, "was alive with shipping and small craft carrying passengers and goods backwards and forwards—the un-planked, ungraded, unformed streets (at one time moving heaps of dry sand and dust; at another, miry abysses, whose treacherous

---

[1] Frank Soule, John H. Gihon James Nisbet, *The Annals of San Francisco* (New York: D. Appleton & Company, 1855), p. 215.

[2] Id.

[3] H. H. Bancroft, *History of California*, Volume VI (San Francisco: The History Company, 1888), p. 171.

depth sucked in horse and dray, and occasionally man himself) were crowded with human beings from every corner of the universe and of every tongue—all excited and busy, plotting, speaking, working, buying and selling town lots, and beach and water lots, shiploads of every kind of assorted merchandise,...gold dust in hundred weights, ranches square leagues in extent, with their thousands of cattle—allotments in hundreds of contemplated towns, already prettily designed and laid out—on paper—and, in short speculating and gambling in every branch of modern commerce, and in many strange things peculiar to the time and the place."[4] Clay Street above Montgomery, said Bancroft, "became a dry-goods center. Commercial Street was opened and its watery extension, Long Wharf, unfolded into a peddler's avenue and Jew's quarter, where Cheap Johns with sonorous voices and broad wit attracted crowds of idlers."[5] Montgomery Street is where the leading businesses and the lawyers settled, and California Street, "which marked the practical limits of settlement in 1848, began to attract some large importing firms; and thither was transferred in the middle of 1850 the custom-house, round which clustered the express offices and two places of amusement."[6]

The population was one of the most diverse in the world, hailing from the eastern United States, but also the Orient, South America and Europe, with each person seemingly antagonistic to everyone else. "There were victorious warriors braving and flaunting on all sides, while hope swelled the breast of every unwounded soldier [and] unheeded amid the crash and confusion of the strife...the wounded and dying, who had failed or been suddenly struck down in the *mêlée*."[7] Having left their more well-ordered homes, they arrived often shed of all the attitudes of civilization, or had departed simply because they had no use for such things and desired to discover a country where all inhibitions were forbidden. Some of these were openly defiant of all civility, while others were of that species known as secret and "unmanly ruffians, who attacked and plundered all sides alike....a large and fearful class indeed—daily increasing in numbers, boldness and

---

[4] Soule, et al., op. cit., pp. 215-216.
[5] Bancroft, op. cit., p. 172.
[6] Id.
[7] Soule, et al., op. cit., p. 257.

extent of depredation and crime."[8] Casting aside all decorum and thought for the public good, they cooked by fires they let burn after the meal was done, abandoning the open flames to whatever fate nature might direct, causing or contributing, it was thought, "to the extensive conflagrations which so repeatedly laid waste the most valuable portions of the growing town."[9]

Such a population could only be governed by the sword, or by those who lacked any apprehension in drawing it. The proclivities and tendencies of this multitude being hardly a secret even to itself, its members cast ballots during the first municipal election after the American invasion in favor of the bravest of them all. Uncertain still of the outcome, the triumphant candidate for the office of Sheriff "mounted upon a fiery black charger, suddenly appeared, exhibiting some of the finest specimens of horsemanship ever witnessed."[10] The sight of the rider, "as he sat bare-headed and unattended upon his noble animal, took the people by surprise and called forth the admiration and patriotism of the vast multitude of spectators, from every one of whom shout after shout rent the air, deadening the sounds of trumpets and drums, and being heard far and wide over land and sea."[11] If there was any doubt that Texas Ranger John Coffee Hays would be the man to maintain law and order in the lawless and chaotic city, it quickly disappeared as "men crowded around him and on every hand, some seizing the bridle, others clinging to his clothing and stirrups, and each anxious to obtain a grasp of his hand."[12]

The election brought hope of order, but order itself remained elusive, at least for the immediate time being. The former Alcalde refused to yield up his office and with it the rich source of revenue to be had in approving surveys and issuing title to building lots. Jasper O'Farrell nevertheless managed to execute a survey, and every lot was sold by the summer of 1849. A second set of surveys "north of Post Street to Larkin Street, and south of Post to Leavenworth and Eighth Streets" in October nearly sold out immediately, with the remainder offered for sale at a price of $500

---

[8] Id.
[9] Id.
[10] Id., at p. 271.
[11] Id.
[12] Id., at pp. 271-272.

per one hundred vara lot, which appreciated several hundred (and in some cases a thousand) times that value within a period of a few years.[13] The mass of humanity who swelled the town, fighting for place and property, finally obtained a government worthy of the name, but just barely, after the Assembly enacted a bill to issue a charter to a municipal corporation, operating via a bicameral common council, presided over by a mayor.[14] The chaos over land was similarly eased by legislative action when a law was passed confirming all titles issued by the Alcalde. The new civic government quickly proved inept by running up a massive debt, while criminal gangs preyed upon the unsuspecting, robbed them of their gold and goods and excited the more law abiding of the populace to disregard impotent authorities and organize the first of the City's great Vigilance Committees.[15]

Much changed in the City during the several years that followed. By the time Perley took up residence there in the summer of 1853, "the tents and shanties that made up a large part of the City…after the gold discovery, having been cleared away by the great fires, [had been] succeeded by substantial brick buildings."[16] On short notice, "warehouses, wharves, banks, large stocks of merchandise, extensive relations with distant markets, and able newspapers, as well as the social wants of schools, theaters, libraries and churches" were supplied, and quickly made for a functioning "metropolitan center of business."[17] Montgomery Street was paved with cobble stones from the intersection of California all the way to Washington Street. Formal civic facilities had yet to appear, though the town square was enclosed in iron fencing, carpeted with grass and decorated with ornamental trees and shrubs.[18] The town remained rough and unfinished, and its people still had much to learn in the way of manners and refinement, but it was at least losing the sharpest of its sharp edges.

---

[13] John S. Hittell, *A History of the City of San Francisco and Incidentally of the State of California* (San Francisco: A.L. Bancroft & Company, 1878), at p. 150.

[14] Id., at p. 155.

[15] Id., at pp. 156 and 172-174.

[16] Id., at p. 206.

[17] Id.

[18] Id., at p. 209.

The Constitution of 1849 established a State judicial department consisting of a Supreme Court to sit in San Francisco, district courts, county courts, probate courts, justices of the peace, and "other such municipal and inferior courts as the legislature might deem necessary." As authorized by the Constitution, the Legislature chose as members of the Supreme Court S. C. Hastings, Henry A. Lyons and Nathaniel Bennett. The justices would subsequently be elected for terms of six years.[19] The New York-born Hastings drew the short term, and was replaced via election on September 3, 1851 by Solomon Heydenfeldt, who served until his resignation on January 6, 1857. Heydenfeldt hailed from Charleston, South Carolina, and, quite anomalously, was Jewish. He had practiced law in his native State, Alabama and Georgia before removing, in the spring of 1850, to San Francisco, which he represented in the State's First Legislature. "His excellent habits and business assiduity, his generous disposition, broad legal knowledge and dignified presence quickly made him a man of mark in that era of reckless activity."[20] He was a man who "disliked all gloss…glitter, and tinsel and was void of arrogance and affectation," who "kept the mood and habit of a philosopher."[21] Former Governor Peter Burnett served briefly after Heydenfeldt resigned on account of the poor salary the job paid, and was replaced for the brief remainder of Heydenfeldt's term by Stephen Field, who had just been elected to the full term of six years.[22] Field was already a legend in the legal community after service as Alcalde of Marysville, election to the State Legislature, and drafting the State's Practice Act—a feat he completed while fighting a spurious revocation of his law license by a vindictive district court judge.

The second of the original three Justices, Henry A. Lyons, resigned on March 31, 1852 and was replaced by the justifiably unheralded Alexander Anderson for the remainder of the term. Alexander Wells followed Anderson, but died on October 31, 1854, not long after an acrimonious confrontation with Perley. Governor Bigler appointed Charles Bryan to take Wells' seat, which Bryan

---

[19] Oscar T. Shuck, *History of the Bench and Bar of California* (Los Angeles: The Commercial Printing House, 1901), p. 349.

[20] Id., at p. 457.

[21] Id., at p. 459.

[22] Id., at p. 350.

occupied until David Terry was elected on September 5, 1855 to complete Wells' term.

The third of the original justices, Justice Bennett, was a New Yorker who practiced in Buffalo before emigrating to California in 1849. He resigned his seat on October 3, 1851 and was replaced by Hugh C. Murray. Born in St. Louis and raised in Illinois, Murray had only a limited education, but made the most of it by mastering the law within a breathtakingly short period of time. A veteran of the Mexican War who rose to the rank of Lieutenant, he was admitted to the bar on his return home. He arrived in San Francisco via clipper ship in September of 1849 and at once commenced the practice of law. By a fluke, he was named to the Superior Court of the City of San Francisco, where he "displayed so broad a knowledge of law and such superior qualities as a Judge that his appointment to the Supreme bench by Governor McDougal in October, 1851...was a fulfillment of the hearty wish of the bar."[23] Within six months, he was named the State's Chief Justice.

The first session of the Supreme Court opened at a former hotel in San Francisco known as Graham House, on the north-east corner of Kearny Street and Pacific Avenue. The Court would remain there until 1854, when politics disrupted the Court's convenience and transferred it first to San Jose and then to Sacramento. The bar that was to practice in this Court and in the other courts in the City—including the federal court presided over by Matthew McAllister and Ogden Hoffman—was a unique and gifted band, "all young and untried men at home."[24] As "none of them had family alliances here to help them into business success, or to give them fame in this new land, they depended alone on their own resources."[25] Matthew McAllister's son Hall, mentioned earlier, was already a giant among the law men, with a "large, square face, an unusual proportion of it below the eyes; a forehead neither full nor high, and lower than the average of men of ability, with no corrugations to betray the earnest study he concentrated upon his causes, a head...noticeable chiefly for its peculiar and irregular shape; the whole suggesting the seat of a practical mind, highly endowed with the powers of analysis and

---

[23] Id., at p. 436.
[24] Id., at p. 391.
[25] Id.

conclusion."[26] In trial, "he was cautious, but caution never fettered him. He was rapid, but was never carried beyond his object."[27] "No man, it was said, prepared "his cases better than he, and notwithstanding the conceit, roguery, and heartless selfishness exhibited by many of his clients, and the baffling assurance of willing witnesses and perjurers, and the shuffling obstructiveness of those who are unwilling, the stupidity and prejudice of juries, as well as the theories and wayward ignorance of an occasional judge," he was "never thrown from his balance," and appeared "never to be discouraged or made angry."[28] Equal in preeminence at the time was former Congressman E. D. Baker, who arrived in San Francisco in June of 1852, where he "practiced law with distinguished brilliancy and success" until his election to the United States Senate.[29] His moral and physical courage was so great," said the solider turned lawyer Erasmus Keyes, "as almost to entitle him to be called intrepid, and yet in social life he was the easiest and most amiable of men."[30] He was a friend of Lincoln, the defender of those condemned by the Second Vigilance Committee, an ally of Terry and Perley during that terrible time, and one day yet to come, on the battlefield at Ball's Bluff, a hero fallen in the name of liberty and the Union. Recalling his courtroom demeanor, the historian Oscar Shuck said his "delivery was rapid, his voice melodious, his diction polished, his gesture free and full of grace."[31] He possessed "a splendid person, an eye full of fire, a noble forehead; and nose and mouth and chin...finely chiseled," and a manner "marked by perpetual animation."[32] In defense of the murderer Cora, he nobly attested to the greatness of the legal profession, "fearless of public opinion, candid and sympathetic," ever standing up "against the tyranny of monarchs on the one hand, and the tyranny of public opinion on the other."[33]

---

[26] Id., at p. 419.

[27] Id.

[28] Erasmus Darwin Keyes, *Fifty Year's Observation of Men and Events Civil and Military* (New York: Charles Scribner's Sons, 1884), p. 308.

[29] Shuck, op. cit., at p. 432.

[30] Keyes, op. cit., at p. 302.

[31] Shuck, op. cit., at p. 434.

[32] Id.

[33] Id., at p. 433.

The remainder of the roll of distinguished and able counsel practicing in the City was not short. Kinsman of Thomas Jefferson and John Marshall, grandson and namesake of the nation's first Attorney General, Virginia-born Edmund Randolph took a seat in the State Legislature almost as soon as he set foot in the City.[34] He was a perennial favorite for a spot in the U. S. Senate among his fellow members of the Chivalry, wrote the Constitution for the failed Filibuster regime of his friend Walker in Nicaragua, and steered the federal government's case in the matter of the New Almaden Mine. He prevailed in that matter, but at the price of a premature death in 1861 from overwork.[35] Former Whig Congressman from Tennessee, Balie Petyon, was "a man of impassioned eloquence, of kind nature, the friend and champion of the squatters." Partners in time with William Duer, Delos Lake and Julius K. Rose, he would openly oppose the Vigilance Committee while others fled the city, and to this end made common cause with Perley in that controversy.[36] In 1858, he would meet fellow Southerner Gregory Yale on the Field of Honor in Oakland, and only avoided a potentially fatal exchange there because a last minute intervention by Joseph P. Hoge and James D. Thornton successfully resolved the dispute between them.[37] Soldier and military theorist Henry W. Halleck presided over the leading firm in the City, headquartered on Montgomery Street, and handled nearly half of all the claims presented to the Federal Land Commission during the 1850s. One of the founders of the State and the principle author of its Constitution, the husband of a granddaughter of Alexander Hamilton and collector of manuscripts instrumental in the founding of the Bancroft Library, Halleck might have been noteworthy even if he'd never rejoined the Army at the outset of the Civil War, defeated the Confederacy in the West and served as General of the entire Union force. His law partner, Virginia native Archibald C. Peachy, "was a very able man, and a fine looking one—tall, straight, proud, dressing elegantly and tastefully, carrying a cane and wearing large gold-rimmed eye-glasses," who

[34] Id., at p. 452.
[35] Id., at p. 454.
[36] Id., at p. 382.
[37] *Sacramento Daily Union*, June 19, 1858.

served periodically in the State Legislature, in 1852, 1860 and 1862.[38] New York-born Alexander Campbell arrived in the City in 1849 and served for a time as Municipal Court Judge.[39] He would later prosecute David Terry for the killing of Senator Broderick, and after that perform his most notable work as the prosecutor of the killer of A. P. Crittenden. Former District Attorney of Erie County in New York, whom every one called "General," C. H. S. Williams "was a lawyer of the first class" and the idol of Perley in his early years, but "prone to bacchanalian pleasures."[40] Frequently off-kilter and "erratic, he was always conscious of his great powers, and sometimes, after a long 'rest,' he would work up his causes with marvelous application."[41] Finally, among the early bar of San Francisco, none was so remarkable as the brilliant and bizarre Rufus Lockwood—a native of Connecticut, graduate of Yale, whose sense of the strange was first evident in his inexplicable change of name from Jonathan Jessup.[42] His first appearance in San Francisco followed a fitful abandonment of a legal career in Indiana, where a courtroom loss at the hands of a biased jury had prompted a furious pounding of his fist on the counsel table in open court. He clerked for a time while attired in rags, then joined Frank Tilford and Edmund Randolph in what Shuck called "as powerful an alliance as was ever effected at that bar."[43] He took periodic leaves of absence from the law, working as a longshoreman or a shepherd in Australia, but always returned, as counsel for Palmer, Cook & Company, and later as Fremont's chief litigator. When he perished in the wreck of the *Central America* after retiring to his cabin in the midst of doomed efforts to save the vessel, it was said "he died as he had lived, an enigma."[44]

In the Summer of 1853, Perley and his wife moved into quarters on the corner of Dupont and Bush Streets that he purchased from John Paine in April for $4,000.[45] For an office, he found a vacancy in

---

[38] Shuck, op. cit., at p. 411.

[39] Id., at p. 517.

[40] Id., at p. 574; and George Thomas Marye, *From '49 to '83 in California and Nevada* (San Francisco: A.M. Robertson, 1923), pp. 140-141.

[41] Shuck, op. cit., at p. 574.

[42] Id., at p. 577.

[43] Id.

[44] Id., at p. 580.

[45] San Francisco Deeds, Volume 22, page 539.

the "law district" at 23 Montgomery. He retained his Calavaras River Ranch and even vented from afar when vandals stole an expensive gate he had installed. Likely he was already looking for a buyer to take it off his hands.[46] His reputation in San Francisco and prospects for employment were initially good on account of his fine performance in various Supreme Court cases and the relationships he'd forged with such persons as Hall McAllister and Gregory Yale. Yale in fact gave him a leg up in the City by recruiting him in July of 1853 to assist in an admiralty matter in the Federal Court presided over by Judge Ogden Hoffman.[47]

Perley's professional and reputational profile, however, took a slight plunge almost as soon as he landed in the City. In Mid-September, back in Stockton, David Terry had read in an issue of the *Pacific Statesmen* an article "political…in its nature," referencing "a good many names" and alleging "that certain Whigs and Democrats were combining to accomplish a certain political purpose."[48] The letter was said to reflect poorly on "pettifogger" Terry and even alluded to Terry's lack of honesty.[49] Incensed, Terry travelled to San Francisco with John McMullen—a friend from his days as a soldier in the Mexican War. Once there, he met with Perley and informed him of the execrable letter and asked him to join him in confronting the publisher—a certain J. H. Purdy.[50] Perley himself later stated that "I did not know, when I consented to accompany him, that any assault was meditated," though McMullen was slightly more forthcoming when he disclosed that he and Perley were present to ensure fair play and to prevent a crowd from interfering.[51] The three men walked to Purdy's office at 87 Commercial Street and entered the premises. With Perley and McMullen guarding the threshold, Terry strode up to Purdy, who

---

[46] See *San Joaquin Republican*, January 31, 1854, and San Joaquin County Deeds, A/5/197. Perley sold the ranch on March 23, 1854 to James Journey for the sum of $10,000. The sale included four horses, and Spanish mare, some foals, various agricultural implements and two wagons.

[47] *Patrick Ford v. Ship Astrea*, Case No. 494, Admiralty Case Files from the U.S. District Court of the Northern District of California, 1850-1900, Microfilm Role No. 22, Cases 480-521, National Archives and Records Administration (NARA).

[48] *Trial of David S. Terry*, op. cit., at p. 22.

[49] *Sacramento Daily Union*, September 22, 1853.

[50] *Trial of David S. Terry*, op. cit., at p. 45.

[51] Id., at pp. 44-45.

was writing at a desk with his back to the door, introduced himself, held out a paper while asking if Purdy was the editor and pointed "to an extract from a letter…received from Stockton." When Terry demanded the author's name, Purdy refused to comply in consideration of the confidence his sources expected. Though claiming the piece was slanderous and offensive, Terry apparently wasn't able to articulate any particular thing that matched these terms. Not getting anywhere with the man, Terry drew out his cane and aimed for the head. He might have struck the man's crown had Purdy not quickly warded the blow off with his left arm. Grabbing the cane and wresting it from his assailant, he attempted to employ it against Terry in the same way. Screaming "Murder!" and "Police!," he tried to parry a blow from Terry that quickly redirected into a grasping of a knife, which Terry then raised over his head while saying "Now, damn you, give me that name, or I'll take your life!" Terry admitted to striking Purdy on the head with the butt end of his weapon, not to harm the man, but merely to force him to let go of the cane. "If I had desired to slay him, it was in my power to do so," Terry later recalled. [52] Worried that things were getting out of hand, Perley urged Terry not to slice the man as he wrested the knife from his friend's hand.[53] A witness, however, thought Perley's words sounded more like "Kill the damned rascal!"[54]

The two men continued to grapple as Perley returned to the door in a renewed effort to keep a growing crowd from entering.[55] Police managed to break into the room and separate the combatants, but when one of them unceremoniously grabbed Terry by the collar, Terry nearly turned on the officer before thinking better of it and agreeing to accompany him to the marshal's office.[56] As he left, he threw one more punch to Purdy's face, drawing blood and knocking off his wig. Purdy was apparently arrested as well, and the two men were charged with fighting.[57] After some investigation, the charge against Purdy was dropped. Terry alone

---

[52] Id., at p. 27.
[53] Id., at pp. 43 and 46
[54] *Sacramento Daily Union*, September 22, 1853.
[55] *Trial of David S. Terry*, op. cit., p. 43.
[56] *Sacramento Daily Union*, September 22, 1853.
[57] *Daily Alta California*, September 21, 1853.

was accused of assault, with Perley named as an "abettor."[58] On September 19, in a courtroom "filled to overflowing," Terry was prosecuted by Harlow S. Love, with the chivalrous Calhoun Benham handling the defense.[59] He was found guilty, and on the following day sentenced to pay a fine of $300.[60] Though he initially contemplated cowhiding the judge, friend McMullen convinced him to pay the fine and be done with it—advice that he grudgingly heeded.[61]

The incident may have tarnished the reputation of the two lawyers, but it hardly dampened the enthusiasm of a very distinguished third man to join the partnership. Volney E. Howard had known both men in Texas when they were just entering the profession. He did not emigrate with them and other Texans in 1849, but his interest in California was nevertheless significant. As his service representing Texas in the House of Representatives came to a close, he arranged for appointment as law agent attached to the United States Land Commission. His relations with President Pierce were no doubt helpful in this regard, but so too was the fact of his long familiarity "with Spanish and Mexican land titles, having been engaged in many cases in the courts of Texas, and before the Supreme Court at Washington."[62] His appointment was greeted by some with trepidation, as it was feared that his selection was in consequence of his "hostility to the rights of the land proprietors, and that hereafter few or no titles would be confirmed."[63] The more measured opinion was that such pessimistic predictions were "calculated to mislead honest settlers."[64] Howard argued his first California claim in the matter of Valentin Cota in opposition to Henry Halleck, and displayed "great directness, and a clear enunciation of the law and the authorities bearing on the case."[65] Howard undoubtedly harbored a desire to extend the political career that had commenced in Mississippi and continued in Texas,

---

[58] *Sacramento Daily Union*, September 22, 1853.
[59] Id.
[60] *Trial of David S. Terry*, op. cit., at p. 22 and 70.
[61] Id., at pp. 22, 27 and 70.
[62] *Sacramento Daily Union*, July 15, 1853.
[63] *Los Angeles Star*, June 4, 1853.
[64] Id.
[65] *Sacramento Daily Union*, July 15, 1853.

but for the time being the practice of law was his priority. Once he'd established himself in California and developed a network of personal and professional friends, he began looking for an opportunity to earn more than what the federal government provided in the way of a stipend. The temperamental similarities and Texas backgrounds of Perley and Terry, not to mention their success in recent years and association with some of the most prominent politicians in the State, recommended their practice as one he might join. In mid-December of 1853, he resigned his post as the agent of the Land Commission and almost at once returned to its chambers as co-counsel with A. P. Crittenden on behalf of Colonel Sutter.[66] It was at this time, too, that his professional association with Perley and Terry began.[67]

Virtually the first litigation Perley engaged in while residing in San Francisco was in a matter brought by Myron Hutchinson in dispute over the claim his cousin Frederick made in 1851 to land on the north side of the Calaveras River. Representing his cousin, but with Terry's aid, Perley demurred on various grounds: Hutchinson failed to attest to title in the disputed land; his complaint lacked any averment that he had any right of possession; and the absence in the pleadings of any certainty as to the nature of the damages being sought. After Judge Creanor sustained the demurrer, Hutchinson retained A. C. Peachy to file an appeal. Relying on Blackstone and Van Santvoord's treatise on pleading, Peachy argued that the complaint was adequate with regard to the assertion of possession. It was not necessary, he said, "to allege the particular facts from which the legal consequence of the right of possession is deduced."[68] With this assertion, Justice Heydenfeldt agreed. "The allegation that the plaintiff was in possession at the time of the ouster complained of, is a sufficient allegation of title to make the declaration good."[69] As the demurrer had been improperly

---

66 *Sacramento Daily Union*, December 17, 1853; *Sacramento Daily Union*, January 14, 1854; and *Sacramento Daily Union*, July 24, 1854

67 See *LeCourt & Strong's San Francisco City Directory for the Year 1854* (San Francisco: San Francisco Herald, 1854), at p. 191 for evidence that Howard was partnered with Perley in the year 1854 in the City and working out of offices with him at Nos. 21, 22 and 23 on the second floor of the Montgomery Block.

68 *Hutchinson v. Perley* (1854) 4 Cal. 33.

69 Id.

sustained, the matter was returned to Judge Creanor's court for prosecution on the merits.[70]

As the case advanced, Perley's successors-in-interest—Samuel Houston Brooks and Thomas Lee—grew wary that an outcome in Hutchinson's favor would give rise to action against them and ultimately divest them of the thousands of dollars in improvements they had made to the property Perley had conveyed to them. To protect their interests, Judge Creanor granted their request to intervene in the case on July 24, 1855, shortly before the start of trial.[71] Due to Perley being absent on business in Sacramento and in possession of information crucial to the case, Terry requested a continuance of several days, which was granted. When the trial commenced, Hutchinson's witnesses testified to facts supportive of the plaintiff's case in chief: Hutchinson's occupation of the land from November of 1850, the land's partial enclosure, and the planting of crops. They denied the validity of Fred's occupation due to lack of compliance with the relevant law and expressed their conviction that the Perleys were attempting to execute a massive fraud and gain possession of land occupied and improved by others. Perley himself testified at length, as did cousin Fred and others, attesting to the vacancy of the land at issue and the overreaching attempts by Hutchinson to enclose a massive tract he couldn't possibly occupy. Perley explained that he, Fred and others had gone up to view the land back in December of 1851. Finding it unoccupied, they surveyed and staked out 160-acre parcels. He said he recalled the enclosure Fred had built while he was absent from the State and the crop of buckwheat that had been planted, as well as Fred's construction of a house. In the end, the jury found for the Perleys. A motion for a new trial on the grounds of the impropriety of certain instructions to the jury was subsequently denied.

---

[70] The decision was cited frequently afterward—for instance, in *Winans v. Christy* (1854) 4 Cal. 70; *People ex rel. Tallant v. Wood* (1857) 7 Cal. 579; *Nagle v. Macy* (1858) 9 Cal. 426; *Dondero v. O'Hara* (1906) 3 Cal.App. 633, 86 P. 985; *Bond v. Aickley* (1914) 168 Cal. 161, 141 P. 1188; *Fuller v. Fuller* (1917) 176 Cal. 637, 169 P. 369. Judge Matthew Hall McAllister of the Circuit Court spoke of it favorably in *Turner v. Aldridge* (1857) 24 F.Cas. 343. Much later, Justice Samuel Miller of the United States Supreme Court would cite to it in *Burt v. Panjaud* (1879) 99 U.S. 180, 9 Otto 180. The last citation to the case appeared in *People ex rel. Department of Public Works v. Shasta Pipe & Supply Co.* (1968) 264 Cal.App.2d 520, 70 Cal.Rptr. 618.

[71] *Hutchinson v. Perley*, San Joaquin Superior Court, Case No. 364.

Perley's feud with Hutchinson continued on another front and wouldn't be fully resolved until the end of the decade. A business dispute between Hutchinson and Stockton's leading businessman, T. Robinson Bours, gave rise to a lawsuit. Hutchinson had obtained assignment from two farmers of a receipt for the storage of thirty-one tons of grain issued by Montgomery & Company. Later, one of that firm's partners, William Montgomery, borrowed $1,000 from Bours and gave as collateral the very same storage receipt. When Montgomery defaulted on the loan, Bours applied for the wheat pledged in guarantee, which was delivered to him in accordance with the terms of the loan. When Hutchinson attempted to recover the grain himself, he found it gone. He opted to sue Bours, who retained Perley to fight on his behalf. Hutchinson and his lawyer argued that the goods were not Montgomery's to pledge as collateral and that because Montgomery was in the business of consigning the goods of others Bours should have known that the collateral wasn't Montgomery's to pledge. When time came to instruct the jury, Hutchinson's attorneys objected to an instruction "that if Montgomery & Co. were in possession of the property and clothed with the external evidences of ownership, and that it was part of their usual business to buy and sell goods on their own account, that such apparent ownership gave them power to sell or pledge." Relying on case law generated only the year before, Perley defended the proposed instruction with the assertion of its conformity with the law. The Judge sustained the objection and the jury proceeded to award Hutchinson damages. In response to Perley's subsequent appeal, Judge Heydenfeldt noted that the absence of authority by a factor to pledge the goods of their principals only occurred where the party pledging the goods is technically a factor, "where his only business is to sell goods consigned to him for that purpose." In such instances, "on account of his notorious employment, all the world is charged with notice that the goods in his possession are the property of others, and that he has power only to sell them, and no power to pledge them."[72] In the case at bar, however, Montgomery was known as someone in the business of buying and selling goods for himself, hence the

[72] *Hutchinson v. Bours* (1856) 6 Cal. 383.

appropriateness of including a jury instruction on that point. When the matter was retried in January of 1857, Perley prevailed.

Not pleased to lose to Perley nor be deprived of the damages previously secured, Hutchinson moved for a new trial, and then appealed the Judge's decision denying that request. A stipulation among the parties allowed for the filing by Hutchinson of a motion for a new trial during the following session; but when the next session came the Court considered the moving papers and denied the relief sought, in part because of the imperfect nature of the record of the earlier proceedings. The Court simply couldn't recall the details of the matter without the aid of a more substantial record, hence it concluded that the undocumented record must have been sufficient to support the Court's judgment after trial. Speaking two years after the relevant events, Justice Baldwin observed that "the delays and confusion" in the case "suggest the propriety of a speedy settlement of statements and exceptions. They can be better settled soon after the trial than any other time."[73] A delay of nearly five months was simply too long for the trial judge's memory to accurately recall the proceedings at issue. The law favors the vigilant, not those who sleep on their rights, hence Hutchinson's avenue to proceed was barred.

Perley and Terry represented Joseph Cutts and Edwin Colt in Stockton in the Fall of 1853, but were never paid their fee. They received a promissory note, then exchanged it for assignment of a second note to Colt issued by George D. Brush and secured by a mortgage. With Howard now an active member of their partnership, the three men sued in September of 1854 to foreclose on the mortgaged property.[74] After the matter with Brush was settled, they brought an action against Colt and Cutts to recover the remainder of what was owed. Following a trial in Stockton on January 25, 1855, they won a judgment on the debt.[75]

In the Spring of 1854, Perley and Terry handled the case of *Blankenship v. Rutherford and Schell*, yet again in Judge Creanor's Court in Stockton. Referred to in the press as "an action of more

---

[73] *Hutchinson v. Bours* (1859) 13 Cal. 50, 52-53.

[74] *Volney Howard, Duncan Perley and David Terry v. George D. Brush*, San Joaquin County Superior Court, Case No. 619.

[75] *Volney Howard and Duncan Perley of San Francisco and David S. Terry of Stockton v. Joseph Cutts and Edwin Colt*, San Joaquin County Superior Court, Case No. 685.

than usual interest," the case originated in the arrest of the Plaintiff Blankenship near Ragtown in Utah in the Fall of 1853 on the charge of a murder allegedly committed against a Mr. Ball.[76] Blankenship was convicted and sentenced to hang, but then conveyed by the Defendants to El Dorado County and delivered to the authorities there for reasons unknown. Once there, Blankenship was discharged on a writ of habeas corpus "for want of jurisdiction in the courts of this State." Alleging that the Defendants had extorted a bond to secure the "protection and safe delivery of his person" to officials in El Dorado, he sued them to recover damages in the amount of $10,000. Verdict was for the Defendants, though the basis for it is unknown.

The most prestigious aspect of Perley's practice during this time occurred before the State's Supreme Court. Some of the cases brought on appeal he had previously handled at the district or municipal court level, both in Stockton and San Francisco; others he took on when trial counsel failed to obtain the preferred outcome. He handled the matter of William McDermott against David Isbell after Isbell obtained a writ of replevin from a justice of the peace, then seized McDermott's wagon and three yoke of oxen. When the justice of the peace revoked the writ on jurisdictional grounds, Isbell refused to return the property, prompting McDermott's suit for damages. Ironically, Isbell argued that the lack of jurisdiction by the justice of the peace precluded a rescinding of the order. Chief Justice Murray found the argument bogus due to the principle that "a party who sues out a writ of replevin from a justice of the peace having no jurisdiction and obtains the property in an action on the replevin bond cannot set up as a defense the want of jurisdiction of the justice."[77] Perley also championed the cause of James Knowles, who authorized Angus McDonnell to occupy land he claimed, only to have an adverse claimant named Potter sell the land to a third party, who sold it in turn to a fourth. Knowles lost at trial in San Francisco and moved for a new one for the purpose of introducing evidence of actual title. The motion being granted, Perley and Howard appealed, only to be informed by Judge Heydenfeldt in January of 1854 that the lower court was correct in ruling in favor of

[76] *Sacramento Daily Union*, April 29, 1854.
[77] *McDermott v. Isbell* (1854) 4 Cal. 113, 114.

the opposing party due to the fact that his title descended from someone, unlike Knowles, who had actually occupied the land. "Possession is prima facie evidence of ownership; and as between two parties who rely upon possession solely, the presumption is in favor of the first possessor; so that proof of possession by a claimant, however short, will entitle him to recover."[78]

Perley and Terry handled the matter of Azariah Walker, not knowing it would become something of a minor epic. Walker had sold a farm and personal property to a Mr. Sedgwick for $7,200, but failed to memorialize the transaction in a sealed instrument. Sedgwick apparently neglected to pay $2,000 of the purchase price, prompting Walker to sue to recover the value of the promissory notes related to the outstanding debt. After he prevailed in his suit, he sought to enforce his judgment in equity via a statutory "vendor's lien." Citing the fact that the statute relied on applied only in law, not equity, the court ruled against him.[79] On appeal, Justice Heydenfelt confirmed the ruling. Perley and Terry then sought to enforce the matter in equity via the appropriate instrument, whereupon Sedgwick's counsel argued that the Plaintiff lacked a valid title to the land and, in the alternative, that a set off was in order because the land's value had depreciated due to a prior sale of a sizeable harvest to a man named Myers. Sedgewick lost the case, but brought a motion for non-suit on the grounds that the earlier action effectively waived the lien, and because enforcement of the lien was precluded once the notes had been executed. When the Court granted the motion, Perley alone appealed on Walker's behalf due to Terry's ascension to a seat on the Supreme Court. Perley's primary point was that "taking a note for the purchase-money does not affect the vendor's lien, and if part of it be paid, the lien remains for the residue."[80] The crop might have been sold, but the proper remedy was an action for breach of warranty, not an affirmative defense. As for the contention that Walker lacked title to convey in the first place, Perley merely noted that there was no proof on the record of such a fact, and even if there was, Sedgwick's entry onto the land on the strength of the title

---

78 *Potter v. Knowles* (1855) 5 Cal. 87, 88.
79 *Walker v. Sedgwick* (1855) 5 Cal. 192.
80 *Walker v. Sedgwick* (1857) 8 Cal. 398.

conveyed by Walker estopped him from questioning it. With all of these arguments, Justices Burnett and Field agreed. "Under a system where equity and law were administered in different suits, and in different tribunals, it has uniformly been held, that a mortgagee might first sue at law upon the note, and afterwards proceed in equity to foreclose the mortgage." Though Walker might have erred in not combining his legal and equitable claims and remedies, as Field's recent Code modifications permitted, no prejudice was thought to have resulted to the Defendant. Finally, Walker apparently did breach the warranty made to Sedgwick when he sold the crop to Myers, thus Sedgwick was entitled to an offset. The matter, said the Court, was properly remanded for further proceedings in accordance with its ruling, notwithstanding the mixture in the court below of claims in law and defenses in equity. Any confusion, said the Court, that a mixed proceeding of this sort "may become too complex by permitting different questions of law and in equity...though founded in much plausibility and some truth, is not sufficiently strong to overcome the plain provisions of the statute, and the substantial dictates of justice."

With Terry now on the high court, Perley teamed with Howard to defend the outcome of a trial of their clients James Mitchell and A. Wardell, who had prevailed in an action for possession and title to a lot in San Francisco derived from the old municipal government. The Plaintiff in the case successfully enforced a lien against the property of a debtor, and then sought to eject the defendant from the land, only to have the trial court grant a motion for nonsuit on several grounds, including the failure of the Plaintiff to comply with a statute allowing for redemption of the property. On appeal, Perley and Howard argued that the judgment establishing the Plaintiff's title had issued prior to the operative date of the redemption statute, hence the statute didn't apply. They argued, too, against the Defendant's contention that the municipal court that issued the contested decision improperly entertained jurisdiction that belonged instead to the District Court. Justice Heydenfeldt agreed with Perley and Howard, holding both that the statute didn't apply retroactive to the judgment at issue and that the municipal court was one of the inferior courts created by the Legislature and thus was entitled to exercise jurisdiction over any matter unless expressly denied it under the authorizing law.[81] The latter point having been "an adjudicated question...the subject of its correctness is to us a sealed book."[82] Perley and Howard prevailed, too, in an appeal against a San Joaquin District Court decision that had improperly allowed for proof of a mortgage absent presentation of the actual note.[83] Chief Justice Murray ruled that "the mortgage was a mere incident of the debt; and in order to maintain the action, which was founded on the Plaintiff's possession and the mortgage, the debt should have been proved."[84] They didn't win an appeal in a third matter, despite having assistance from attorneys Colonel L. Saunders and E. L. B. Brooks. The action was one to enforce a promissory note.[85] The plaintiff prevailed, prompting Perley and his cohort of attorneys to appeal not the liability of their client, but inaccuracy of the amount of interest awarded. Justice Heydenfelt rejected the appeal, noting that the matter ought to have been brought to the attention of the trial judge and corrected by him. A secondary issue of whether post-judgment interest can be collected on the court's award of pre-judgment interest was decided in the affirmative, contrary to the appellant's position.

Perley alone handled a series of appeals involving pleading issues. In *Angier v. Masterson*, S. N. Angier had brought a suit to foreclose on a mortgaged ranch in San Joaquin County on January 2, 1855.[86] Perley's client Edward Masterson contended that while he was technically in default, the Plaintiff had agreed to allow additional time to repay the debt and had accepted installment payments. Because Masterson's Answer to the Complaint wasn't verified, Angier moved to strike it, which the court denied. Instead, the court allowed Masterson to submit an amended pleading signed under oath, and further allowed introduction of evidence of the subsequent agreement to extend time for payment. Angier appealed the jury's verdict for the defense, which Justice Heydenfeldt rejected because the belated verification hadn't caused Angier any prejudice,

---

81 *Seale v. Mitchell* (1855) 5 Cal. 401.

82 Id.

83 *Bennett v. Taylor* (1855) 5 Cal. 502.

84 Id.

85 *Guy v. Franklin* (1855) 5 Cal. 416.

86 *Angier v. Masterson* (1856) 6 Cal. 61.

and because the evidence of the agreement was for the purpose not of overcoming the original mortgage contract, but in support of the contention that the debt had actually been paid. In *Greenfield v. Steamer Gunnell*, when the losing defendant appealed a decision allowing a complaint to be unverified, Heydenfeldt agreed with Perley that his opponent's "objection to the want of verification to the declaration should have been made before answer or with the answer," and that coming so long afterward, "it comes too late."[87] Perley was less successful in a third matter, involving a debtor against the Sheriff of San Joaquin County for wrongfully seizing his property. In an amended pleading, the plaintiff debtor omitted the sheriff's official title. At trial, Perley showed that his client the Sheriff did, in fact, take possession of the property, but only after his deputy, George Webster, had seized it. Since the controlling pleading failed to indicate that the trespass had been committed by another in the sheriff's official employ, the plaintiff was precluded from introducing evidence of Webster's agency on the sheriff's behalf. The trial judge agreed, the evidence was excluded, and the jury favored the defendant in the end. On appeal, Perley's opponent argued that in combination with the original pleading "the amended complaint was sufficient to charge the defendant with the trespass committed by his authorized agent." Justice Heydenfeldt agreed with the appellant and concluded that "the Judge trying the case should have let in all the evidence."[88]

Perley next prevailed in an appeal in a complex transactional case that had dragged on since the first years of the decade, involving a loan made by D. W. Connelly to Sylvester F. Peck and his associates to finance the building of a commercial structure on property purchased from Captain Weber, and the evasive conveyance of the property by Peck to others following issuance in Connelly's favor of a judgment in the amount of $3,921. Charging fraud by the Defendants via an elaborate scheme to insulate themselves from responsibility for the debt and vest title in friendly third parties, Connelly attempted to obtain a more perfect remedy in equity, only to be denied on pleading grounds without leave to cure the defect via an amendment. Representing Connelly, Perley

[87] *Greenfield v. Steamer Gunnell* (1856) 6 Cal. 67, 68.
[88] *Poinsett v. Taylor* (1856) 6 Cal. 78, 79.

won a reversal of the decision and the right, on his client's behalf, to amend the Complaint.[89] When the case finally resolved, Perley was able to convince the Court that his client was entitled to a judgment against the individual Defendants because the property and promises made were those of the partnership, not its individual members. The losing Defendants appealed, arguing that whether a partnership existed or not did not matter because the partnership was not openly known. "There is nothing," said Justice Heydenfeldt, "to show positively that [the property at issue] ever was…held out to the world as" partnership property.[90] Because the partners and partnership were unknown and the partners dormant, "equity gives no priority to partnership debts." The lower court's judgment was thus reversed and direction was given for the appointment of a master to sell the property and then pay interest and costs to Connelly, with the remainder of the proceeds going to one of the other Defendants.

Perley's representation of a number of Sheriffs of San Joaquin County didn't preclude him from representing a party against a County Sheriff. Sheriff George Webster, who promoted from a deputy position, seized four thousand sacks of grain belonging to Perley's clients, T. Robinson Bours and Sebastian Visher, pursuant to an attachment issued in another action against a man named Hiram Dennis. Visher had been a tenant of Dennis, with whom he conveyed half their joint interest in the land's crop to Bours, but afterward never bothered to deliver it. Webster's counsel insisted that delivery of the grain to Bours and Visher was necessary for title to pass to them, and since the grain was still growing at the time of conveyance, title never changed hands. In contrast, Perley argued that this would be true if grain was a chattel, but as it wasn't, a deed alone was sufficient to pass title in accordance with the State's Statute of Frauds. The Court ruled against Perley and the jury found in the Sheriff's favor. On appeal, Chief Justice Murray, with whom Justices Heydenfeldt and Terry concurred, held in accord with Perley that crops growing on land were neither goods nor chattels,

[89] *Connelly v. Peck* (1853) 3 Cal. 75.
[90] *Connelly v. Peck* (1856) 6 Cal. 348, 354.

hence title could pass by deed and need not be actually delivered for title to vest.[91]

When the matter was retried, Perley attacked the validity of the creditor's debt as a way of invalidating the Sheriff's seizure by attempting to show that the note itself had been altered by the creditor. In contrast, the Sheriff's counsel tried to introduce evidence that Dennis had entered into a fraudulent sale to protect his grain from attachment. Perley won on both points, paving the way to a verdict in his client's favor. Webster appealed the trial judge's decision on the two evidentiary points, and despite Perley's argument that nothing amiss had occurred, Justice Burnett, with the concurrence of Chief Justice Murray, ordered yet another trial.[92]

In the third outing before a jury, Sheriff Webster again argued fraud by Dennis with respect to Visher, but once more Perley prevailed on behalf of his client. In a third appeal, Webster's attorneys argued multiple errors: that the costs of the first trial could not be added to the second; that a written record of the jury instructions was missing, hence a fourth trial should be ordered on the basis of uncertainty; that failure to transfer possession of the grain by Dennis to Visher was fatal to Visher's claim; and that Dennis' declaration denying the sale to the Plaintiff, rendered months afterward, was improperly excluded. Perley was so unimpressed with the arguments that he only bothered to address the last, stating that "the declarations of a vendor made after the sale, cannot be given in evidence to defeat the title derived from him in a suit to which he is a stranger." Justice Baldwin, with the concurrence of Justice Field, agreed with this position and found no merit at all in the Defendant's case.[93]

Perley aided Robinson Bours yet again, but in the rare forum of the Federal District Court presided over by Matthew Hall McAllister. Bours made a purchase of material from a foreign merchant named Dessau. Instead of paying for the purchase on the spot, he issued Dessau a bill of exchange in his own name, modified by the term "agent," accompanied by an entirely verbal explanation that he was acting as the representative of Burgoyne & Company.

[91] *Bours v. Webster* (1856) 6 Cal. 660

[92] *Visher v. Webster* (1857) 8 Cal. 109

[93] *Visher v. Webster* (1859) 13 Cal. 58; and *Sacramento Daily Union*, April 11, 1859

The parties agreed that the law of New York would govern the transaction, rather than the law of California. After Dessau suffered extreme frustration in attempting to cash out the bill, he brought suit against Bours. When Perley answered the suit on behalf of his client, he alleged these very facts, and stated in the context of an affirmative defense that any recovery must be against the principal, not the agent. To this Dessau's attorneys demurred. "The rule," they said, is well settled that where the alleged principal's identity is absent, "the instrument fixes upon the signers an unqualified responsibility."[94] The attempt to establish the existence of an agency relationship with unknown principals being dependent on inadmissible parol evidence, the defense raised was facially defective. Perley apparently cited a number of cases standing for the proposition that where the form of the instrument itself creates some ambiguity as to the agency status of the signatory, parol evidence may be admitted to remove the doubt. Judge McAllister agreed that the exception to the rule barring parol evidence was applicable here, if only because it was supported by the law as it existed in the State of New York.

Perley's estimation in the eyes of his peers, once clouded by his actions with Terry in the Purdy matter, appears to have risen in subsequent years. The occasional brawl, such as one on the street in Sacramento between Perley and another lawyer, W. L. Willis, doesn't seem to have affected the upward trajectory of his reputation.[95] The similarity of temperament of many of his peers hailing from the South blunted the force of any public reproof, as did the power of friendships formed on the trail with men who appreciated Perley's talents. Whether Captain Harry Love accompanied the Terry Company through the Gila Desert isn't confirmed, though he undoubtedly knew Perley from Texas and respected his willingness to fight in defense of his honor. Like Volney Howard, Love left New England for the South and ended up in Texas on the eve of the Mexican War. By virtue of his exploits as a scout for General Taylor, he was already a legend on the frontier when he successfully undertook command of the squad of

---

[94] *Dessau v. Bours* (1855) 7 F.Cas. 540.

[95] *Sacramento Daily Union*, March 28, 1855. The brawl may have been related to Willis' representation of William Roach.

California Rangers charged with hunting down the notorious bandito Joaquin Murietta. In San Francisco, Love married the tempestuous widowed daughter of Vardeman Bennett, who was then in the midst of attempting to handle her late husband's complex affairs. Love got in touch with Perley and Howard and retained them to represent the Estate, with himself acting as administrator. The principle task to be accomplished was confirmation of a claim to property pending before the United States Land Commission.[96] In this task, they were successful, and received an interest in one tenth of the property. A secondary task was the completion of the late Mr. Bennett's probate. To that end, the two lawyers filed a petition in probate in May of 1855 and proceeded to wrap the matter up.[97]

The complexity of the Bennett-Love interests all but guaranteed additional legal work. Prior to Love's appointment as administrator, his wife had entered into lease agreements with tenants with respect to certain property owned by the Estate. Perhaps viewing the lease as invalid due to the incapacity of the widow, or void due to her replacement by an entirely new administrator, the tenants ceased paying rent. Love brought suit against them repeatedly, each time winning a judgment for unpaid obligations. After prevailing in an action for treble rents and restitution of the premises, Love received service of a motion by one of the tenants, a Mr. O'Rourke, asking that the matter be tried anew in the municipal court. When the matter was re-tried, Perley and Howard attempted to present evidence of the chain of administration in the form of the order revoking the widow's status as administrator and the vesting of the office with Love, but the Court rebuffed the attempt and ultimately issued a judgment of nonsuit in the tenant's favor. When Perley and Howard insisted that the issue of Love's capacity to bring the suit had already been established in prior actions, the Court refused to hear it. In appealing the decision, Perley cited to a treatise on the law of evidence supporting his position that Love's right to maintain suit on this lease was res judicata, and argued, too, that "Defendants ought not to be permitted to litigate the same questions forever." The points raised by the tenants, he said, "are

[96] *Love v. Watkins* (1870) 40 Cal. 547, 556.
[97] *Daily Alta California*, May 13, 1855

frivolous and vexatious, and made with the intent to delay, hinder, and defraud the Estate of Bennett out of an honest and just debt." Diverging from his normal tendency to rule against Perley, Justice Burnett actually agreed with him, noting that "so far...as the same issues and facts are directly involved in the two cases, the decision in the former suit is conclusive upon the parties." The questions in the several cases "were substantially the same as those arising in the present case."[98] After the lower court was reversed and an entirely new verdict was directed, Perley set to work collecting Love's damages by forcing a sale of a number of properties owned by the losing parties, including a lot on Bush and Larkin Streets and another on Pacific and Montgomery.[99]

In addition to commercial litigation, Perley engaged in the occasional family law matter. The first such case he handled was the Bingham divorce, which remained largely beneath public notice despite the prominence of the estranged couple. Charles Edward Bingham was a native of Kentucky, who came to California like many others, as a soldier in American arms during the Mexican conflict. Stories abounded of his bravery in the field under the command of General Taylor, and of the gallantry of his wife. A likeable, handsome and persuasive man, he might have made a decent advocate had not the stage so strongly attracted his fascination. Perley must have become acquainted with him in Stockton, for both were living there in 1850 when the Census was taken.[100] Perley even then was a fan of the theatre and likely caught the actor's performances from time-to-time.[101] In those early years of Statehood, Bingham traveled the mining country with his wife and an itinerant company and became quite popular both there and in San Francisco. When his wife and children returned east, Bingham attached himself to various theatrical companies until settling in at the Adelphi in February of 1854 in association with the renowned Thorne Family, headed by the noted actor Charles Thorne. He followed them to the American Theatre in March, where their

---

[98] *Love v Waltz et al.* (1857) 7 Cal. 250.

[99] *Daily Alta California*, January 11, 1858.

[100] United States Census (1850); and George H. Tinkham, *History of Stockton* (San Francisco: W.M. Hinton, 1880), at p. 176.

[101] See Timothy Coffin Osborne, *Journal*, BANC MSS C-F 81, entry dated February 20, 1851 for evidence of Perley's interest in the theater.

success continued. Close proximity with Thornes' daughter Emily proved far too tempting to the lusty Bingham, who romanced the young lady with powers far beyond her ability to resist. Her scruples probably insisted on marriage before any intimacy could transpire, prompting Bingham to procure a minister, who likely was as ignorant of the existence of a wife outside the State as was the young bride. Bingham's preoccupation with romance probably caused significant distraction and accounts for the sudden poor review he received at the time for his portrayal of Othello.[102] Or perhaps it was the fear of discovery of his bigamous marriage to his employer's daughter. In any event, the truth appears to have been discovered no later than March 29, when Bingham vanished from the cast in Thorne's troop and the press reported "unavoidable circumstances" that caused the bill and marquee to abruptly change.[103] In May, Thorne filed an action for divorce in Judge Creanor's Court in Stockton, seeking a termination of the marriage on account of Bingham's fraud, the bride's minor status, and the fact that the couple had never lived together as man and wife.[104] Perley, Howard and Terry represented Bingham, either to contest the action or salvage their client from the total ravaging of his reputation. The action was dismissed soon afterward, perhaps under a belief that the report of Bingham's mortal wounding and death in Panama at the hands of a mob of the actor's fellow travelers headed by Harry Love was actually true.[105] Bingham survived, albeit partially paralyzed, and managed, after providing entertainment on the stage and armed reinforcement for William Walker's doomed legions in Nicaragua, to eke out a living as an actor, playwright, and proprietor of a cigar shop in San Francisco for many years afterward.[106]

A longer term of representation came when Perley accepted employment by John Joyce, a prominent Mormon businessman and

---

102 *Daily Alta California*, March 28, 1854.

103 *Daily Alta California*, March 30, 1854.

104 *Emily Bingham v. Charles E. Bingham*, San Joaquin Superior Court, Case No. 550.

105 *Daily Alta California*, July 3, 1854; *Grass Valley Telegraph*, July 6, 1854; and *Sacramento Daily Union*, August 1, 1854.

106 *Daily Alta California*, March 10, 1857; and *Daily Alta California*, September 19, 1869.

pre-conquest immigrant, in a post-separation matter filed in the District Court in San Francisco involving property held in the name of Joyce's estranged wife. The land had originally belonged to Joyce, but was later conveyed to a relative, E. V. Joyce, on condition that it be re-conveyed to him after certain exigent circumstances had passed. When time came for reconveyance, E. V. Joyce instead conveyed title to the wife as a means to prevent the land from being claimed by Mr. Joyce's creditors. When the couple legally separated, it was agreed that Mrs. Joyce would settle two-thirds of the property on the couple's children, who remained in her custody. Mrs. Joyce subsequently brought an action to annul the agreement and reclaim full title to the property, as well as have a friend, John M. Hosmer, appointed as guardian ad litem for the children. She had her way due to a default judgment, which may have been collusive in nature. When Hosmer mortgaged the property, Joyce filed a bill in Chancery of behalf of his children asking the Court to enjoin further incumbrance of the land and to annul the prior ruling in his wife's favor. The wife demurred on the grounds that her husband's action was precluded by his own unclean hands in arranging the conveyance of the land to Mrs. Joyce to evade creditors, as well as by the prior ruling of the Court appointing Mr. Hosmer, which Mr. Joyce had failed to contest. When the demurrer was sustained, Perley secured the assistance of Howard and presented argument in an appeal on February 19.[107] On March 7, 1855, Justice Heydenfeldt ruled that no evidence of fraud by Mr. Joyce existed, and that it wasn't Mr. Joyce who was seeking to improperly appeal an earlier order, but the children, through his agency, aiming to protect their interests from alleged wrongdoing by their guardian. The lower court's decision, thus, was overruled, and the matter was remanded for resolution on the merits.[108] The Court supplemented its decision in April with the unreported comment that a conclusion of law reached by a referee establishing abandonment of his wife by Mr. Joyce, if based on certain alleged facts, was "quite beyond the comprehension of this Court."[109] When Mrs. Joyce managed to obtain a divorce decree in default, Perley

---

107 *Daily Alta California*, February 22, 1855.

108 *Joyce v. Joyce* (1855) 5 Cal. 161; and *Daily Alta California*, March 8, 1855.

109 *Sacramento Daily Union*, April 14, 1855.

and Howard again appealed, arguing that a proof of service signed by the "under-Sheriff," instead of by the Sheriff, rendered service fatally defective.[110] Justice Heydenfeldt agreed and the matter was remanded to the lower Court for further proceedings.

Before the divorce was final, the two Joyces actually joined forces to contest Hosmer's mortgaging of the property and his default on the obligation to make payment. When Mr. Joyce attempted to intervene in the action to foreclose the mortgage, the creditor demurred. "Mr. Perley," reported the *Alta*, "argued in favor of the right of the husband to be made a party defendant" on the grounds that he was a necessary party pursuant to the relevant statute."[111] Perley's opponent, former Whig Congressman William Duer, countered by asserting that "as the husband and wife were living apart by consent, he had no right to come in and defend as to her separate property." After taking the matter under advisement, the Court ruled in Perley's favor.[112] Perley's efforts ultimately proved of no avail; for the property set aside by the parties was ultimately lost in the foreclosure action, despite rear guard efforts by the couple's children into the middle years of the next decade.[113]

Perley alone represented Stockton publisher John S. Robb in appealing the decision of the District Court granting default judgment in an action brought by his estranged wife Ellen for divorce and determination of property rights. When attempting to set aside the decree on the basis of fraud with respect to material facts presented by his client's ex-wife, Perley argued that Mr. Robb's former attorney had negligently failed to answer the petition, which surely was an instance of malpractice. Chief Justice Murray noted the divergence of opinion on whether the proper course to have followed was to have proceeded legally in accordance with the original case, or to have done what appellant did, which was to bring an entirely new action in equity to set aside the decree, but ultimately held that "it is of but little importance whether we treat the appellant's motion and affidavit as a bill in equity or require him to proceed formally.... [H]aving held in repeated cases that inferior courts cannot grant a new trial, or interfere with their

110 *Joyce v. Joyce* (1855) 5 Cal. 449.
111 *Daily Alta California*, July 17, 1855.
112 Id.
113 See *Joyce v. McAvoy* (1866) 31 Cal. 278.

judgments or decrees, in any material part after the adjournment of the term, we think it best for the sake of uniformity to conform to this rule" and require that the appellant "assert his rights by a proceeding in the nature of a bill to impeach the original decree for fraud." Whether Robb followed this recommendation or not isn't known, though Mrs. Robb subsequently sued Perley for rents from property owed to her, but which Perley paid instead to the Sheriff following enforcement of a lien in accordance with a judgment against Robb in favor of Andrew Randall.[114] Perhaps to resolve the dispute, Perley purchased the Robbs' interest in the lot and then apparently commenced renting it out for profit.[115]

It was owing to a drowning in the Pajaro River on Christmas Eve in 1852 that Perley's tenacity, legal acumen, physical courage and bellicose impulses became perfectly matched with a legal challenge that in time entered the ken of California legend. Jose Maria Sanchez had been the recipient of a large land grant from the Mexican Government in 1835 known as the Rancho Llano de Tesquisquita. He subsequently obtained the Rancho Los Animas and the Rancho Lomerias Muertas as well. At the time of his drowning, his patents for these properties were pending with the Land Commission. Following his death, his widow, Encarnacion Ortega, found a protector for herself, her five children and their vast estate in the person of her attorney, Thomas B. Godden. Godden was killed in the terrible explosion of the steamer *Jenny Lind* in April of 1853, leaving the Sanchez heirs vulnerable to ruthless scavengers eager to lay their hands on the family fortune.[116] Just prior to his death, Godden arranged for the estate to be placed under the administration of a friend, Samuel C. Head, through an action in the Probate Court overseen by Judge Josiah Merritt.[117] Head was reputedly unreliable and corrupt, and was supposedly secreting cash for his own benefit unbeknownst to Widow Sanchez. Her distrust of Head was encouraged by yet a third husband, Dr. Henry Sanford, who soon entertained a recommendation by a friend, Lewis T. Belcher, to pass guardianship of the minor heirs and all

---

[114] *Robb v. Perley*, San Joaquin Superior Court, Case No. 832.

[115] San Joaquin County Registry, A/7/200 and A/7/307.

[116] *Daily Alta California*, April 13, 1853.

[117] Paul R. Parker, "The Roach-Belcher Feud," *California Historical Society Quarterly*, Volume 29, No. 1 (March 1950), at p. 20.

legal responsibility to battle the Estate's administrator on their behalf to a suitably hardened individual: Irish born veteran of the Mexican War and former Monterey County Sheriff, William Roach. Judge Merritt acquiesced in the request to appoint Roach in July, and then approved Roach's petition to force a sale of estate assets to pay the heirs' debts.[118] On September 5, 1853, Merritt ordered Head to give Roach half of the estate's personal property and cash and the other half to Sanford and his wife.[119] Two weeks later, he ordered Roach to sell all the personal property of the estate then in his possession.[120] The proceeds of the subsequent sale totaled $75,604.

It wasn't long after this that the Sanchez heirs became concerned that Roach was converting assets to his own use. His failure to distribute any of the moneys in his custody only fueled doubts about his integrity and motivation. The husband of one of the Sanchez children, Daniel Wilson, asked Roach to turn over his wife's portion to her. Roach not only refused, but also made clear his antagonism toward Wilson and his family by having the priest who officiated at Wilson's marriage arrested, taken before a partisan judge and fined "for marrying a girl under age, without the consent of Roach," the girl's guardian.[121] Consequently, Wilson and Sanford complained to Judge Merritt that Roach was not a suitable guardian and asked that he be removed. Merritt refused to provide any relief, as did the District Court. Insulated from reproach by a friendly local judiciary, Roach reputedly mocked his adversaries by saying that "he could keep the money as long as he pleased, and could defy [them] to get it from him by law for the next five years to come."[122]

For the task of taking on the ruthless Roach and his allies on the bench, only the most fearless counsel would do. The proud, confident and violence-prone trio of Perley, Terry, and Howard possessed all of the necessary qualifications, hence they were eventually retained "to bring Roach to account."[123] After motions filed in Monterey to strip Head and Roach of their responsibilities

---

[118] Minutes and Decrees, Probate Court, County of Monterey, Volume F, at p. 11 and p. 23, http://familysearch.org.

[119] Id., at p. 20.

[120] Id., at 21 and 23.

[121] *Trial of David S. Terry*, op. cit., at p. 28.

[122] Id.

[123] Id.

ended in failure, the three lawyers decided that a change of venue was essential if any relief was to be had. Judge Merritt simply couldn't be relied on to be impartial or to contradict the interests of Roach due to his natural timidity and fear "of assassination at the hands of Roach's hirelings."[124] The residence of Wilson and his wife in Stockton provided a jurisdictional basis for removal of the action to San Joaquin County. While pursuing an ultimately unsuccessful appeal of Monterey Court's refusal to permit removal of the case from Merritt,[125] the lawyers initiated an entirely new action with the filing of a Bill of Equity in Judge Creanor's Court against Roach and Merritt, averring that the Judge had appointed Roach as guardian of the children "fraudulently, and against their own wishes and the wishes of their family and friends," and then had "fraudulently ordered...Roach to sell and convert all their personal property into money."[126] Roach, they said, then engaged in the most obnoxious self-dealing by loaning himself the proceeds of the property sale without any apparent concern for the obvious conflict of interest, and without a dime going to his charges, all with the aid and assistance of the Judge.

In response to the process filed in his court, Judge Creanor appointed Belcher as Receiver and Wilson and his wife as guardians for the other heirs. He also issued an order requiring Roach to surrender $75,000 in cash held in trust. Confident in his power to evade the reach of Creanor's order in far off Monterey, Roach refused to comply. The trio of lawyers then agreed that Perley and Terry would go to Monterey to take Roach into custody and bring him to Stockton to answer a charge of contempt. To ensure service of the order and secure Roach's arrest, Perley obtained appointment by the Court of his friend, the impetuous Samuel Houston Brooks, as agent for service of process. This was a development, Terry later said, that "Roach had not counted on."[127]

Perley finalized the paperwork and then handed it to an ally, Richard Langdon, to deliver via boat, stage and horseback to Monterey.[128] Within several days, Langdon, Terry, Brooks and

---

[124] Id.

[125] *Guadalupe Reyes v. Henry L. Sanford* (1855) 5 Cal. 117.

[126] *The Nevada Journal*, September 8, 1854.

[127] *Trial of David S. Terry*, op. cit., at p. 28.

[128] Id., at p. 49.

Perley rendezvoused. They were joined by Belcher, Dr. Sanford and E. J. Sanders.[129] On August 7, 1854, the men went to Roach's home, where Terry read the defiant guardian the text of Judge Creanor's order and demanded that the money be turned over to Belcher. When Roach mockingly said "you'll have a happy time getting it," an indignant Perley asked him if he meant to refuse to deliver the money. Roach replied "of course I do," and that he "did not mean to give up one cent under any such premise."[130] On that note, Brooks seized the man, piled him into a buggy and commenced the transit back to Stockton in the company of Perley and the others, all armed either with shotguns or revolvers.[131] Before they could cross the divide into the Central Valley, they were overtaken by a party of Roach's friends led by Sheriff Lyons bearing a writ of habeas corpus hastily issued by Judge Merritt.[132] Understanding the writ to be ineffective in superseding Judge Creanor's order, not to mention a possible ruse to bring the party within range of an ambush, Terry advised Brooks and his companions to disregard it. Lyons threatened to take Roach by force, but paused when Brooks unflinchingly informed him "that Roach was his prisoner under an order from the District Judge of San Joaquin County, and he could not recognize the authority of Josiah Merritt...to take Roach out of his custody."[133] If it was truly Lyons' intent to take Roach by force, Brooks informed him it was his duty to resist.[134] Once Lyons backed down in the face of Brooks' persuasion, Perley's company continued on its way.

On August 17, Roach was in Stockton, arguing that Creanor's order was illegal, that the Judge had no authority outside his own County, and no authority over probate courts here or anywhere else. He also said that Brooks couldn't serve process in a county in which he didn't reside. Creanor overruled the arguments and ordered that Roach be "directed to stand committed to the common jail of the County of San Joaquin, there to remain charged with

---

129 Id.

130 *Daniel Wilson et al. v. William Roach and Josiah Merritt*, San Joaquin County Superior Court, Case No. 583.

131 *Trial of David S. Terry*, op. cit., at p. 49.

132 Id., at p. 28.

133 Id., at p. 45.

134 Id., at p. 49.

contempt until he shall have paid over into the hands of said receiver the said sum of $73,000...and also the costs."[135] He also ordered Belcher to render an accounting of money in his possession.

While Roach was in jail, his attorneys submitted a petition to Justice Wells of the Supreme Court for a hearing in the matter of a writ of habeas corpus, which Wells granted. When the matter was heard in San Jose, "all the officials of Monterey were present, aiding and assisting Roach," including Judge Merritt, the Coroner, the Sheriff and Constable, and even the Clerk of the Supreme Court, P.K. Woodside.[136] Perley and his colleagues presented evidence of the existence and the validity of the warrant of commitment, which the Justice concluded was sufficient to justify Roach's confinement. Responding to Roach's protest, Wells informed him "that the existence and validity of the warrant of commitment were the only facts on which issue could be taken; that they might traverse the return, or except it for insufficiency."[137] He could not, he said, reverse the commitment for contempt or set it aside, or "go beyond the colorable authority of the Judge, and it was clear that the District Court was a court of competent jurisdiction over the subject of contempts, and that its judgment was final and conclusive."[138] Some hope was provided Roach in the form of the Justice's acknowledgement of the existence of "some other questions involved in this case, requiring the review by the entire bench when the next session commenced, in October.[139] Shockingly, he released Roach into the custody of Sheriff Lyons. As Lyons was absent at the moment, Wells announced his comfort in appointing an alternate custodian. Perley and his colleagues at once "reminded him of the great importance of the case, that the entire fortune of orphan children was at stake, and that there should be some security against the escape of the prisoner; that if he took him out of the custody of the Sheriff of Stockton, the only person in whose custody he could properly place him was the Sheriff of Santa Clara, who had

---

135 *Daniel Wilson et al. v. William Roach and Josiah Merritt*, San Joaquin County Superior Court, Case No. 583

136 *Nevada Journal*, September 8, 1854.

137 Id.

138 Id.

139 Id.

a jail to keep him in."[140] Perley himself interjected that "there was no color of law for Judge Wells to appoint a deputy; that he had no right to do any such thing; that he must either discharge the prisoner or remand him." Wells appeared to acquiescence in the argument and commit to placing Roach into the custody of someone with facilities to hold him until October, but then changed his mind after Perley and his colleagues left the courtroom and appointed a man named Williamson—the Constable of the City of Monterey—as a special deputy to take charge of the prisoner.

When a dismayed Sheriff of Santa Clara related these happenings to the Sanchez legal team, Perley "thought it absolutely impossible that the Justice could have made a secret order, after giving his judgment in court, and that there must be some mistake about it."[141] Perley and Terry then rushed to the Justice's home "to ascertain the truth." Confronted in his quarters by angry counsel, Wells denied he had dispensed with the Sheriff's services and asked Perley to put his reputed account into writing. As Perley handed Wells a hastily penned statement, he declared "he would swear to it if necessary," which Wells invited him to do. After Perley obliged him by adding a phrase that he made his statement under threat of penalty of perjury, he told Wells that "he had not only written it and sworn to it, but could also prove it."[142] Perhaps intimidated by the ardent counsel's display of resolve, Wells meekly conceded the truth. Terry protested that this "was not the judgment he had given in court, and that they did not understand how he could make such an order; that they would much prefer to have him discharged altogether" on account of Williamson being "a mere tool of Roach" and "his most active partisan and confederate." Perley blurted out that "he thought Judge Creanor would treat all [these] proceedings as illegal and void, and would issue a new attachment, and recommit the prisoner for his misconduct and contempt." Irritated by Perley's impudence and the challenge to his judicial authority, Wells vowed to lock Creanor up in the Supreme Court's very chamber if he dared do such a thing, or even to "make a jail of his private parlor, and lock the prisoner up in it until the meeting of the

[140] Id.

[141] Id.

[142] Id.

Supreme Court." The conversation having become ludicrous, Perley and his colleagues took their leave, "thoroughly disgusted at the exhibition we had just witnessed, without any definite idea of the course his Honor meant to pursue, after numerous and conflicting statements he had made on the subject."[143]

So appalled were Perley and his colleagues over Wells' conduct that they penned and published a public denunciation of a "decision…of so extraordinary and startling a character," and accused Wells "of a gross violation of law, and of his official duty." In ordering one thing in open court, then vitiating it during what amounted to an ex parte session through issuance of an entirely contrary order, Wells had effectively discharged Roach "from the imprisonment for the contempt," and allowed him "to go to Monterey, where he will have full opportunity to gather up the money belonging to these heirs, and place it not only beyond their reach, but beyond the process of Court."[144] Reviewing the charge, the editors of the *Sacramento Daily Union* noted that the accusers "are men of high character, and make out a strong case against Judge Wells as a Judicial Officer."[145] The *Times and Transcript* rather cryptically commented on "the outside influences producing the wonderful revolution in the mind of the Judge," and attributed these ultimately to "the great San Francisco political Trading League," of which Roach was reputedly an agent. The paper suggested that Roach's incarceration would have impaired the man's ability to win an upcoming election to the Legislature where even greater service to his masters might be provided.[146] To corruptly develop in the Judge an understanding of "the importance of reversing his first decision and letting loose on straw bail this tender guardian of infant children," a State Senator belonging to the faction with which Roach was affiliated had supposedly been "dispatched in real poste hast speed."[147] Roach himself answered the public allegation, denying everything, declaring "himself able to account for every dollar of the property," and accusing the children's mother of impropriety—of marrying

[143] Id.
[144] Id.
[145] *Sacramento Daily Union*, September 4, 1854.
[146] Id.
[147] Id.

twice in four months, of essentially forcing her minor daughter into marriage with a stranger who couldn't speak Spanish or, despite his sudden conversion to Catholicism by a priest, even "explain in English the mysteries of his faith," and whose own motives were not love for a girl with whom he could barely communicate, but a naked "thirst for money."[148] He condemned Perley and his colleagues for their incredible "appeal to the public," their misplaced faith in the client—"a man who apostatized and married, for the purpose of obtaining the fortune of an unsuspecting California girl"—and their unfair campaign "to awaken odium against the action of the Judge and myself."[149]

Wells' action ultimately proved to have been legally unjustified. When the Supreme Court met en banc in October, Judge Creanor's original order was upheld.[150] Chief Justice Murray said the matter was allocated by the Constitution to the jurisdiction of the chancery aspect of the District Courts. "The claim of exclusive jurisdiction in the Courts of Probate over this subject is unfounded. Chancery may at any time interfere, and remove the proceedings before it. All the proceedings in this case are entirely consistent with the power and jurisdiction of the Chancellor." As for the various other arguments raised by Roach's attorney, they were easily disposed of. "Many objections and assignments of error have been made," said Murray, "which cannot be taken advantage of on this appeal, but are properly the subject of demurrer or answer."

With his past actions now ratified, Judge Creanor soon issued a new order for Roach's arrest, directing the Sheriff of Santa Clara County to apprehend Roach and return him to Stockton. On January 25, 1855, Roach was back in Creanor's Court asking for a continuance in order to find counsel. Perley and Howard pointed out that Roach already possessed abundant counsel—Ord and Gregory from Monterey, Scott in Los Angeles, Wallis and Ryland in San Jose, and Hall and Huggins here in Stockton—hence his request was specious and obviously calculated to cause delay. Doubting the complete sincerity of the plea, but not utterly insensible to the due process rights of the Defendant, Creanor granted Roach's request

---

148 *Sacramento Daily Union*, September 14, 1854.
149 Id.
150 *Wilson v. Roach* (1854) 4 Cal. 362.

and gave him until the afternoon to secure the services of an attorney.

On the following day, Roach changed course and informed Judge Creanor that he would indeed comply with the order to produce the estate's assets if he could, but wasn't able to since the money was no longer in his possession. His witness, John Hart, testified at a hearing on February 1, that less than a month before, Roach employed him to go to his Carmel Ranch and procure from a safe $20,000 and bring it to him in Stockton. When he and the District Attorney of Monterey County inspected the safe, they found it empty. Another witness, Andrew Randall, testified of his acquaintance with Roach since 1849, his opinion of the man's untrustworthiness, and his belief that Roach "has now in his possession or under his control a large amount of the money belonging to the complainants in this action." Daniel Wilson's attorney, Andrew J. Yates, also said Roach still had the money. For his own part, Roach testified that the money had been in his safe, but the key was left in a coat pocket when the Sheriff seized him. There was a "Mexican man" living at his ranch whom he suggested was the most likely suspect in the money's disappearance. Both Belcher and Sanford objected to the testimony, declaring it to be a lie, that the money was hidden, and that some of it had been converted into real estate. Weary of the evasions, Creanor held Roach in contempt yet again and denied any further continuances.[151]

On February 5, Judge Creanor issued a permanent injunction against Judge Merritt and ordered Roach to pay Wilson $70,600, plus interest. As unreliable as he was, Sheriff Lyons was directed to make seizure of Roach's property, which Lyons actually did, though the mere $390 in proceeds from the subsequent sale suggested a collusive arrangement among the bidders. When Roach suddenly expressed contrition and asked the Court to grant him liberty in order that he might locate the money secreted at his Carmel Ranch, Perley scoffed, saying that "Roach is not worthy of being believed under oath," and that the tale "about the money being left at Carmel Valley [was] a poor fabrication and made with the fraudulent intent of deceiving this court and to enable himself to get out of prison

---

[151] *San Joaquin Daily Republican,* January 27, 1855.

without complying with the order of court, and without paying over any money."[152] Nevertheless, Judge Creanor granted him leave to go to Monterey in a special deputy's custody to retrieve the money owed.

Perley's objections were soon vindicated. Once in Monterrey, Roach "succeeded in evading his keeper and made his escape."[153] Aided by Terry and Perley, a San Joaquin Deputy Sheriff tracked down and arrested the fugitive at the Mission of Buena Ventura, near Santa Barbara.[154] By the end of the month, Roach was back in custody in the San Joaquin County jail.[155]

Meanwhile, the acrimony among the partisans of either side in the dispute escalated. In March, on the same day that judgment was issued in the still-ongoing proceedings in the District Court in Monterey against the Sanchez heirs, a chance meeting in town between Roach's brother-in-law, Jeremiah McMahon, and Dr. Sanford led to gunfire and the mutual assassination of the two men.[156] "The two met," it was reported, "at McMillan's United States Hotel, and after some high words, they drew their revolvers and fired. The shots took effect in vital parts, and both of the combatants fell dead."[157] The death of Sanford undermined an appeal by his attorneys pending in the Supreme Court of the latest decisions from the Courts in Monterey refusing the request to dismiss the probate proceedings in that County. Roach's attorney, D. S. Gregory, filed a motion to dismiss the appeal "on the ground of the death of Sanford, guardian of plaintiff."[158] Noting that the affidavit of Roach's counsel was not contravened, Chief Justice Murray stated that "there was…no authority for prosecuting the cause in the name of the deceased; but all proceedings ought to

---

[152] *Daniel Wilson et al. v. William Roach and Josiah Merritt*, San Joaquin County Superior Court, Case No. 583.

[153] *San Joaquin Daily Republican*, March 25, 1855.

[154] *Daily Alta California*, March 25, 1855; Trial of David S. Terry, op. cit., at p. 45.

[155] *Sacramento Daily Union*, March 26, 1855; and *Daily Alta California*, March 29, 1855.

[156] *Daily Alta California*, March 18, 1855.

[157] *Daily Alta California*, March 19, 1855; and *San Joaquin Daily Republican*, March 20, 1855.

[158] *Sacramento Daily Union*, July 11, 1855.

have been stayed until, by suggestion, his executor or administrator was made a party."[159] Consequently, the appeal was dismissed.[160]

Perley and his colleagues fared better in the appeal of the Monterey Court's dismissal of their action in Chancery to set aside Judge Merritt's probate rulings. Relying on Story's treatise on Equity, his own brief in the matter of *People v LaFarge & Ball* and several decisions from other jurisdictions, Perley argued that "the District Courts of this State have jurisdiction to vacate and annul a decree of a probate court when obtained by fraud." Appeal of such a decision was not required since the Chancery Court afforded an alternative route of obtaining relief. Justice Bryan and the Supreme Court agreed, noting the "familiar maxim of law, that fraud vitiates everything."[161] The State's District Courts, Bryan observed, "are clothed with original jurisdiction in law and equity where the amount in controversy exceeds two hundred dollars, exclusive of interest." Such a Court can, "in a case in equity, where fraud and collusion are charged against the Judge, in entering an order or decree, review the same, and annul it, if the facts justify such a conclusion."[162] The Judge in the lower court, who Bryan noted was the very man charged with collusion with the administrator in the misappropriation of the funds of the estate, had quite improperly sustained the demurrer.

After lingering in jail for a month, Roach again escaped confinement on September 27.[163] Reports trickled in on his whereabouts: one that "this notorious scoundrel...is supposed to have gone to Sonora by way of the Tejon Pass" in the possession of a large amount of money; another that he was accompanied by a man leading a gray horse. A posse was reportedly in pursuit of Roach and only three hours behind him.[164] Another source alleged Roach's presence near Pacheco's Pass and that he was preparing to leave for the eastern States as soon as possible. He had taken "the road through French Camp, and from there to the mouth of the Stanislaus River, where he forded the San Joaquin. He then crossed

---

159 *Sanchez v. Roach* (1855) 5 Cal. 248.

160 *Sacramento Daily Union*, August 3, 1855.

161 *Sanford et al v. Head et al.* (1855) 5 Cal. 297.

162 Id.

163 *San Diego Herald*, October 6, 1855.

164 Id., and *Stockton Weekly Republican*, September 30, 1855.

the plains to the coast range, and up along the foothills until he reached the Ranch." He was said to have bragged that "he had plenty of horses along the road, also plenty of men who were his friends, and would stand by him to the last."[165]

Even with Roach on the loose, the Sanchez matter moved forward. In the summer, prior to Roach's escape, the Probate Court in Stockton reviewed Roach's accounting of the Sanchez Estate. Finding his accounts short, the judge ordered him to pay the difference directly to the Court. Instead of paying it, Roach resigned his position and, when the opportunity provided itself, took flight. Perley and Howard brought an action in the District Court against his bond and the guarantees of his sureties. Judge Creanor considered Perley's argument that Roach should have tendered payment directly to the court and concluded that the proper procedure in probate would have been the appointment of a new administrator who could then have tendered payment. With Howard's assistance, Perley appealed, citing to authorities exclusively from other jurisdictions to the effect that an heir's right of action against the bond and its sureties accrues as soon as a failure to render an account occurs. When the matter reached the Supreme Court, Justice Heydenfeldt issued a curt opinion explaining the absence of any rule derived "either from the ecclesiastical law or our statute of estates, which makes the Judge of Probate a fiscal agent, either to keep or disburse the money of an estate."[166] As the law did not permit payment of money to the Court, Roach's refusal to do so was no breach of the condition of the bond. Though Perley's request for a rehearing of the matter was denied, it really was of no import since the affairs of the Estate were nearly resolved.[167] In October, Belcher compromised with the sureties in the Probate Court in Monterey by accepting from them a total of $9,000.[168] This and other moneys recovered for the heirs were a far cry from what was owed, but at least it was something.

Less than a year after the case concluded, Perley appeared before the Vigilance Committee to debunk the charge that Terry had colluded with Roach to allow him to go free. "Terry and myself," he

[165] *Stockton Weekly Republican*, October 4, 1855.
[166] *Willson v. Hernandez* (1855) 5 Cal. 437.
[167] *Sacramento Daily Union*, October 10, 1855.
[168] *Daily Alta California*, October 9, 1855.

recalled, "risked everything in behalf of the Sanchez heirs—life, fortune, and success at the bar. We had to confront and defy Alexander Wells, Judge of the Supreme Court, in his lawless attempt to liberate Roach contrary to law," and month-after-month braved "assassination at the hands of the aiders of Roach."[169] Though Roach remained free, as an outlaw in the backcountry, Perley and his colleagues were able to salvage a total of about $40,000 for the heirs. It wasn't everything they were entitled to, but had it not been for the courageous actions of the lawyers, a complete rather than merely a partial injustice would have been the result.

The experience was an edifying one, both for Perley and for everyone engaged in the practice of law in the State, reaffirming the hard truth that law and order in California was still an unattained ideal, and that the very process of obtaining justice through orderly proceedings in accordance with rules and a Constitution remained subject to the violence endemic to the state of nature, and the "perfect insecurity of all personal rights and life in our midst."[170] Perley and Terry braved threats. S. H. Brooks stared down a posse. Their client Dr. Sanford died in a gun fight with a partisan of the party opponent, and Belcher, in July of 1856, was assassinated outside a hotel in Monterey.[171] His dying words attributed the deed to the outlawed Roach, Sheriff Lyons and their associates. Roach himself remained in hiding for some time, but finally did reemerge and was able to resume his life unmolested by the law. Like so many of the figures prominently featured in the accounting of Perley's life, he died violently, from a fall into a well a year after the loss of all but one of his children during a local diphtheria epidemic.[172] Whether his final plunge was accidental or by design—a homicide or a suicide—no one can say.

---

[169] *Trial of David S. Terry*, op. cit., at p. 45.

[170] *Sacramento Daily Union*, June 27, 1856.

[171] Id.

[172] *Santa Cruz Weekly Sentinel*, September 30, 1865; and *Sacramento Daily Union*, September 6, 1866.

Chapter Five

KNOW NOTHING

Though Perley was close to the southern wing of the Democrat Party, his political involvement was minimal during his first years in California. Likely he handled a larger share of the partnership's business due to Terry's leadership of the Party in San Joaquin. The preoccupation by his partner with politics may well have prompted the addition to the legal team of Volney Howard. As Perley expanded the sphere of his practice, both in Stockton and his new home in the City of San Francisco, the Chivalry's struggle against the northern wing of the Party intensified, as did the ambitions of members of the Chivalry for the advancement of their cause at the State level, nationally, and beyond. Among other initiatives, the Chivalry heavily backed William Walker's invasion of Mexico. Pro-Walker rallies occurred in Democrat-friendly Stockton in January of 1854 while Walker's force was maneuvering in Sonora, and Walker's agents actively recruited there for men to replace those fallen in the field or absent due to desertion.[1] An even more aggressive recruitment drive was undertaken in support of Walker's subsequent Nicaraguan adventure by southern fire-breather E. J. C. Kewen, a Mississippi native and California's first Attorney General. Kewen's success in the endeavor made possible the transport of shiploads of men from Stockton to Central America in January of 1856.[2] Anticipating the expedition's complete success and his own appointment to a key post in Walker's regime, a ridiculously uniformed Kewen boarded a ship bound for Nicaragua that same month—his wife and children by his side.[3]

At home, the prospects of the Chivalry were less optimistic. Governor Bigler had caused a schism among the Democrats through his opposition to Stephen Douglas's Kansas-Nebraska Act. In need of some special glamour to enhance their faltering appeal,

---

[1] *Daily Alta California*, January 11, 1854; and *Daily Alta California*, January 26, 1854.
[2] *Daily Alta California*, January 6, 1856.
[3] *Daily Alta California*, January 22, 1856.

the Chivalry turned to Benjamin Franklin Washington—a great nephew of President Washington—as the standard bearer of their cause heading into the 1855 General Election. David Broderick's mastery of partisan intrigue and his employ of the methods of Tammany Hall impeded these electoral plans and caused many in the pro-southern faction to look elsewhere for a solution. And they found it in the form of the nascent Know Nothing movement. "Just what it was, its principles, its nature and its design—beyond the single fact that it was opposed to each of the old parties, Whig and Democrat, but mainly to the latter—none or very few seemed able to explain."[4] Most inquiries, especially in the early days, were met with silence, or with a general criticism of political corruption and the threat posed by Catholics and the foreign-born if allowed easy naturalization as citizens. In California, where diversity may well have diluted the nativist element of the Know Nothings' motivation and appeal, concern over corruption in politics, particularly in San Francisco, propelled the Party's initial momentum. "Good citizens were in despair over the fraud and vice with which elections were manipulated, and were ready to revolt against the corrupt politicians who dominated their city government."[5] The hopelessly divided nature of the Democrat Party, arising from the dueling ambitions of David Broderick and William Gwin to attain a seat in the U.S. Senate, also demoralized many voters and prompted them to seek a viable alternative.

The nascent Party's first successes came in the municipal elections in San Francisco in May of 1854. In the campaign in that year, the local Party exploited the desire for honesty and reform, and announced that "they were interested in 'placing good men in office…for the best interests of the city,' and that they were not going to select mere politicians but men who would 'administer the government with economy and a desire to the welfare of the people.'"[6] Once the Broderick-controlled State Democrat Convention locked the Chivalry out of the top positions on the Democrat ticket, "a large number of anti-Broderick Democrats who

---

[4] James O'Meara, *Broderick and Gwin* (San Francisco: Bacon & Company, 1881), at p. 111.

[5] Peyton Hurt, "The Rise and Fall of the 'Know Nothings' in California," *California Historical Society Quarterly*, Volume 9, No. 1 (March, 1930), at p. 25.

[6] Id., at p. 27.

had set their faces resolutely against the re-election of John Bigler as Governor, adopted this means to compass their purpose."[7] When the Know Nothings commenced their State-wide campaign in June of 1855, southern Democrats hailing from Stockton and thereabouts were prominent on the stump. At the opening rally on June 24 in Sacramento, David Terry, ex-Governor Foote of Mississippi, Balie Peyton and E. C. Marshall took their turn in succession to stir the enthusiasm of the crowd.[8] The Chivalry's influence in the Party was evident from the platform fashioned at the State-wide convention in August—a watering down of the national Party's commitment to nativism, and an utter disavowal of any agitation on the issue of slavery.[9] Samuel Houston Brooks was selected by the Party to attend the national conventions in the eastern States and received careful instruction to avoid the slavery issue and support only those candidates who maintained a strict and uncompromising commitment to the status quo. When the State convention was over, the inoffensive Joseph Neely Johnson was the Party's candidate for Governor, Terry and the incumbent Chief Justice Hugh Murray were slotted for seats on the Supreme Court, Richard Roman's nephew William T. Wallace would vie for the Attorney Generalship, George W. Whitman of Tuolumne got the nod for State Controller, and Henry Bates was presented as candidate to oversee the State Treasury.[10]

Know Nothings swept the State in September, took both houses of the Legislature and won every executive and judicial office, including the governorship.[11] From the outset, the Party's hybrid nature, its members' variant and often contradictory objectives, seemed hardly conducive to effective governance. In the wake of electoral celebrations, it likely dawned on many in the Party that those who had aided them most to achieve such dazzling success were among those against whom they had struggled so contentiously in the past. Honest reformers, die-hard nativists, anti-Catholic bigots, Chivalrous zealots, and doughty Whigs simply couldn't manage to produce a coherent agenda, hence the record of

[7] O'Meara, op. cit., at 117.
[8] Hurt, op. cit., p. 39, and *Daily Alta California*, June 30, 1855
[9] Hurt, op. cit., at p. 41-42; and *Daily Alta California*, January 22, 1856.
[10] Hurt, op. cit., at p. 42.
[11] Id., at pp. 45-46.

achievement by the legislative session's end was paltry. The surest sign of legislative inertia was the failure of the majority even to select a candidate to fill the highly prized vacant Senate seat. A four-way battle between Governor Foote, E. C. Marshall, H. A. Crabb, and W. I. Ferguson ended inconclusively, much to the pleasure of David Broderick, whose control of the northern Democracy played a crucial obstructionist role, and of William Gwin, who, like Broderick, remained anxious to occupy the seat himself. Failure to proscribe the foreigner and the Catholic alienated the nativists, and the inability to enact any other meaningful legislation alienated just about everyone else. When over a hundred thousand dollars disappeared from the State Treasury, the good government reform element of the party balked and blamed the circumstance on the collusion of the Know Nothing Controller and Treasurer with the banking house of Palmer, Cook & Company. While no luck was had in filling the empty Senate seat, the Know-Nothing majority did manage, in self-condemnatory style, to enact a law designed to check their own Party's suspected thievery by requiring a Board of Examiners staffed by the Governor, Lieutenant Governor and Attorney General to personally inspect the books and physically count the money in the Treasury on a monthly basis, and for the Board to approve each and every expenditure explicitly.[12] The law constituted what James O'Meara called "a statutory declaration that the Know Nothing Government could not be trusted in handling or keeping the public moneys by the votes of the members of the very Party which was thus popularly impeached."[13]

As the dismal legislative session reached its conclusion, the support of the voters for the majority Party reached a nadir. Recently a center of Know Nothing strength, Stockton rejected the Party in the spring municipal elections.[14] The sufficient cause of the revolution was said by some to have been the Know Nothing Governor's shoddy removal of the respected Resident and Visiting Physicians from their positions at the State Lunatic Asylum, located in Stockton. Some doubts also existed as to whether the Governor

---

12 O'Meara, op. cit., p. 134.

13 Id.

14 *Daily Alta California*, May 6, 1856.

had any power to appoint successors, even when the Legislature failed to make a selection when the officials' terms ended. In the absence of a legislative nomination, and after the session ended, Governor Johnson appointed the highly qualified and administration-friendly Samuel Langdon to replace the incumbent Resident physician. Hostility by the Asylum Trustees, who were holdovers from the previous Democrat administration, led to instruction to Langdon's predecessor to remain at his post.[15] The Know Nothing Attorney General quickly instituted a suit in the Fifth District Court to remove the incumbent, but Judge Creanor denied relief on the grounds that "the appointment of Dr. Langdon is void and…there was no vacancy in the office of Resident Physician…authorizing the Governor to commission Langdon."[16]

Having established a certain expertise before the High Court and found some success as an advocate there, D. W. Perley wasn't an odd choice to handle Langdon's appeal, though it cannot be doubted that his close proximity to leading figures in the Know-Nothing Party and his friendship with Langdon, not to mention with one of the Justices who would decide the matter, were factors that led to his selection by Attorney General Wallace as the man who would persuade the Court to reconsider Judge Creanor's decision and overrule it. As the matter was one touching on the powers of the Governor and entailed construction of provisions of the State's Constitution implicating the separation of powers, the Chief Justice himself opted, after the presentation of briefs and the arguments of counsel, to speak for the Court. As far as he was concerned, the true issue before him and his brethren was "whether the governor has power to appoint a resident physician, in case of the failure of the Legislature to elect."[17] To his mind, "the answer is so obvious, that we cannot but wonder there should be more than one opinion on the subject."[18] He noted that the statute creating the post provided that the term is limited to two years. "Having fixed the term, upon its expiration the office de jure becomes vacant, and can be filled in two ways; either by election in the manner which may be provided by law, or by appointment by the Governor,

[15] *Daily Alta California*, May 5, 1856

[16] *Daily Alta California*, May 28, 1856.

[17] *People ex rel. Langdon v. Reid* (1856) 6 Cal. 288, 289.

[18] Id.

under the eighth section of the Fifth Article of the Constitution."[19] It made no sense to him that in the event the Legislature failed to elect a successor that the incumbent should be permitted to remain in office indefinitely by default, or that the Governor is without power to make a temporary appointment in the interim. He saw a proper construction of the statute as necessary to fulfill the intent of the People, and to preserve for them the right to select officials, as opposed to having them foisted on them by mere operation of law. On the strength of Perley's advocacy, Judge Creanor's decision was reversed.

Greater trouble loomed in San Francisco, where many who had longed for real reform and the end of the compelling vestiges of lawlessness remaining in the saloons, gambling houses, brothels, and the headquarters of the various political organizations, felt little but exasperation due to the failures of the majority party to make good on its promises to purge the social and political order of disease. A string of high profile infamies, capped off by the assassination of the reformist newspaper editor James King of William by one of the targets of his searing editorials sparked fiery public meetings well-fueled by the pent up frustrations of honest men and women over the apparent ratification of corruption by officials who had so recently promised the inauguration of good government and the establishment of law and order. Recalling the days only a few years ago when citizens organized a counter government to sweep away the criminal refuse that terrorized the City, a large gathering of townsmen organized what is now known as the Second Vigilance Committee, and committed itself to bringing the worst offenders to justice, cowing the lesser offenders into compliance with the law, and warning elected officials to obstruct their reformist agenda at their peril. King's murderer was apprehended and other high-profile criminals placed under arrest, tried and even executed, while others were merely loaded onto outbound vessels for exile abroad. Fearing for its own safety, the political class, including David Broderick, abandoned the City. Though leaving the field to the vigilantes, they spread word throughout the land of the revolution unfolding at the Golden Gate and fears that once the power of the insurgents was consolidated in

---

[19] Id., at 289-290.

San Francisco, they would pursue a similar course throughout the rest of the State.

As the political status quo in San Francisco disintegrated, Perley himself faced daunting personal challenges. His life two years before had reached a milestone: growing fame and professional success, establishment of a burgeoning law business in the State's hub, and a young wife and beautiful son bearing the name of his esteemed uncle, George Hayward. His wife's retreat to Michigan and their son's death at age 14 months while there ended this short era when the Perley dynasty's California branch seemed to be in promising early bud. His wife's return and a second pregnancy may have nurtured hopes that the family might recover from its loss, but not long after daughter Cornelia's birth, Perley's wife suffered an attack of consumption. She expired at the end of March, only 23 years of age, leaving behind a bewildered husband and a child too young, in subsequent years, even to remember her.[20]

Still mourning the loss, Perley nevertheless was surely aware of the Governor's declaration that the City was in a state of insurrection, that many of the prominent political leaders had made themselves scarce and that the venue for the practice of his profession—the courts—had been shuttered for the foreseeable future. Though hardly a man experienced in war or violence, the Governor at first had repaired to the center of the commotion, met with the Committee leaders and attempted to broker a peace.[21] When the peace effort failed and the Committee expressed no intention to relinquish power, the Governor naturally deferred to those more schooled in the ways of force. As head of the militia serving the San Francisco District, William T. Sherman reported a shortage of arms, but said he was prepared to take action against the Vigilantes if Federal authorities in the harbor would rectify the deficit.[22] The reluctance of General Wool and Admiral Farragut to lend federal aid without authorization from the President or

---

20 *Daily Alta California*, March 31, 1856. The event was reported two months later in New York, where Louisa's family connections on the maternal side remained strong. See *New York Daily Herald*, May 1, 1856.

21 William T. Sherman, *Memoirs of General William T. Sherman*, Volume 1 (New York: D. Appleton and Company, 1875), at pp. 121-122.

22 Id., at 125.

Congress created a vacuum that men of greater belligerence were prepared to fill.

At a hotel in Benicia, the Governor set up an ad hoc headquarters, flanked closely by David Terry and Volney Howard, both of whom spoke "furiously against Wool, denouncing him as a d—d liar, and not sparing the severest terms."[23] Terry sneeringly declared the Vigilantes to be "a set of damned pork merchants; that they were getting scared and that General Wool was in collusion with them to bring the State into contempt."[24] More conciliatory or cautious solutions to the situation Terry venomously rejected, calling those who took the more lenient position to be "no better than 'Vigilantes.'"[25] When a committee of neutral residents of the City, composed of A. P. Crittenden's cousin James D. Thornton, J. B. Crockett and G. W. P. Bissell and others, appeared at the hotel in Benicia, Howard and Terry both interposed themselves and informed the men that any communication with the Governor must be in writing.[26] After submitting a statement for the Governor's review, they were admitted, only to find the place teeming with the State Militia's high command, along with Mr. Jones of Palmer, Cook & Company, from whom the Governor still hoped to obtain funding for an armed assault on the City. Surrounded by such a belligerent crew, the Governor listened politely, and then issued a written response to the effect that it was his great desire that the difficulties could be terminated without bloodshed, but that this could only happen if the terms of his proclamation were complied with.

Sensing that a more prudent approach was hopeless "and that violent counsels would prevail under the influence of Terry," Sherman resigned his military office and was replaced, even before he left the room, by Howard.[27] Vowing to whip the entire committee with 500 men, Terry wrote out a writ under his own authority as a member of the Supreme Court to secure the release of captured law and order men, including William Mulligan and his and Perley's friend from Stockton, James R. Maloney. To ensure service of process, Terry resolved to deliver it himself with the aid

---

[23] Id., at p. 129.

[24] Id., at p. 130.

[25] Id.

[26] *Sacramento Daily Union*, June 11, 1856.

[27] Sherman, op. cit., p. 130.

of a band of like-minded men, ready to fight and shed blood if necessary. While Terry was so occupied, the Governor would raise an army in the interior, turn it over to Howard's command, and overawe anyone still possessing the impulse to resist lawful authority.[28] As these plans were underway, Terry told a compliant Chief Justice to take refuge in the mountains and then announced to the public at large that so long as he was on the Court no lawyer who gave aid and comfort to the Vigilantes would ever cross its threshold with the intention of presenting an appeal, or responding to one.[29] Thousands of miles away, in Washington, D.C., while charges of murder were pending in the wake of his murderous rampage in a Capital City hotel, Congressman Philemon Herbert introduced a Resolution authorizing the intervention in San Francisco of the Army and Navy to suppress the insurrection.[30] In this time of crises, Perley's law partners and closest friends and associates had coopted any energy in the executive, and were pushing the Governor upon the most confrontational of paths.

Volney Howard, no true soldier, had played at being one by virtue of appointment some time before to high rank in the militia operating in the Sacramento District.[31] With his commission as a General still very fresh, Howard proceeded immediately to the City, but once there found that "without money, and with only a few arms" he was incapable of mounting any operation with the exception of one geared toward self-defense.[32] "We had not the necessary means to form even an efficient encampment; and I therefore thought it advisable to let the companies continue their drills in the various armories, without making any demonstration on the streets."[33] As the drilling under the commands of Lieutenants Calhoun Benham, John Coffee Hays and others proceeded, Judge Terry arrived with his writ, found Maloney still free after a run-in with the Vigilantes at sea while attempting to deliver weapons to Howard's forces, and decided that prudence compelled retreat to R.P. Ashe's naval agency office on the second floor of the Palmer,

[28] *Daily Alta California*, June 6, 1856; and June 22, 1856.
[29] *Daily Alta California*, June 15, 1856.
[30] *Nevada Democrat*, September 3, 1856.
[31] *Daily Alta California*, June 9, 1856.
[32] *Daily Alta California*, June 26, 1856.
[33] Id.

Cook & Company building at the corner of Washington and Kearny. With Perley present for the occasion, an earnest discussion ensued over the course the party should take. One man—attorney James G. Baldwin—attempted to persuade Terry "that he had done everything that the most scrupulous or punctilious sense of official duty could require of him, and that there was no use to continue here any longer."[34] Impressed by the power and nature of the Committee's organization and the error of his own initial estimation of the same, Terry seemed at first moved by this presentation. Any inclination to leave town without achieving his purpose, however, was quickly corrected by an "ill-timed and intemperate appeal by Dr. Ashe" to stay the course lest Terry suffer the disgrace of failure.[35]

In any event, retreat at this point would have been futile. Learning of Maloney's presence and aiming to arrest him, the Committee's deputy, Sterling Hopkins, and three other men arrived at the scene, entered the building, ascended the stairs and found their mark, along with Terry, Ashe and others, all of whom "drew and cocked their pistols" and took aim. Hopkins repaired to Committee headquarters for further orders, and was directed to surveille the building and await reinforcements. Upon return, he found Terry, Ashe, Maloney and others, "all armed with double barreled shot-guns...turning the corner of the bank building from Washington Street into Kearney." On Jackson Street, near the intersection with Dupont, Hopkins made his move, rushing past Terry and Ash for the purpose of seizing Maloney, but then grasping Terry's gun in an apparent attempt either to disarm him or deflect what he thought was an imminent discharge. As the melee commenced, Ashe raised his weapon, only to have it struck away. Another man excitedly shot his firearm in Terry's direction. Terry drew his notorious bowie-knife "and plunged it into the left side of Hopkins' neck, to the depth of about six inches." Terry and his company then fled as the severely wounded Hopkins cried out to rally his men. They took refuge in a near-by armory on Dupont Street, not far from Perley's home, and slammed the doors shut.

---

[34] *Trial of David S. Terry*, op. cit., at p. 51.
[35] Id.

Howard heard the report of the incident while on Montgomery Street and immediately rushed to the armory, only to find that the Committee had surrounded the building with a multitude of armed citizens and heavy ordinance. Howard bellowed a demand for an interview with the Committee's leader, William Coleman, and then insisted that Terry's continued detention could only result in "an immediate collision of arms, which would involve the peace of the whole State, the consequences of which no one could foresee." Coleman declined to conclusively consent to or reject the demand. Instead, as Howard impatiently waited—threatening to shoot anyone who laid a hand on him and to lay the City in ruins—he quietly directed Vigilance forces around the City to swarm the State Militia's armories, compel each in turn to surrender, and march the entire law and order force, some two hundred prisoners in all, to a make-shift prison. Such decisive and effective action convinced Howard of the utter extremism of the Vigilantes, that they intended not merely the overthrow of law and order in the City, but the inducement of a revolution throughout the State. "They have," he told the Governor, "committed treason, murder, piracy and the felony of kidnapping. They have violently, and with force of arms, trodden down the authority of the Executive and the Judiciary. They have at the point of the bayonet, resisted the execution of the writ of habeas corpus—for ages justly considered the bulwark of personal liberty. They have assembled around the jail for the County of San Francisco large numbers of armed men, and planted a cannon against the front, and thus compelled the surrender of two persons therein detained in the custody of the law, whom they have since put to death, without legal trial, or the form of judicial proceedings," broken in the doors of innocent citizens, forcibly searched their homes in the dead of night, "outraging families and terrifying defenseless females," and for now nearly six weeks trampled through armed military despotism "every constitutional right secured...by Magna Charta and the Bill of Rights."[36]

Having been exposed as utterly impotent in San Francisco, Howard retreated to Sacramento, where he held a rally for law and order, and on the stump there condemned the revolutionaries and pled for support in an effort to free Judge Terry, whom he lionized

---

[36] *Daily Alta California*, June 24, 1856; and *Daily Alta California*, June 26, 1856.

as "one of the most illustrious citizens of the State...a man of unimpeachable and unblemished character—one whom the people delighted to honor," a man now sitting in "a loathsome, dark dungeon." Howard's melodramatic presentation proved to be too much for the crowd, whose members hooted, laughed, yelled, interrupted with impertinent questions and mocked until the General couldn't be heard over the din. "Fools and cowards may laugh at it, but honest men... You may laugh...." Each time he resumed in the wake of derisive commotion, the noise became greater and the taunts more cutting. "Where is your army?," one voice screamed; "go on with the lecture" yelled another. The rally finally degenerated into a heckler's paradise, with Howard abandoning any semblance of dignity to spar with his detractors. That the rally was a failure became evident even to Howard when the crowd started chanting in support of the Committee.[37] Bancroft said of Howard that "he did have a reputation as a man of talents before he made that speech; he did succeed in convincing those who heard him, that he was not half equal to his reputation."[38] More general in its condemnation was the comment of a journalist impugning the entire cadre of "Texas Men" who appeared at the outset of the vigilance disturbance "to think that the free men of this State can be driven like Indians on the western border of that State, at the point of a few hundred bayonets," but must surely have "changed their minds since one was captured by the Committee and the other had his little army and their arms taken away before his very eyes."[39]

With Terry in custody, the great concern of the day became the life or death of Hopkins. The man's death would surely prompt a crisis even greater than the one at hand; for the Committee, having charged itself with meting out justice to those long-immune to the law's impartial application, would be faced with the task of applying it to a murderer whose deed was committed while under color of authority, and not any modest authority, but the highest in the State. As Hopkins' demise or recovery was awaited, Terry himself fared well in detention. His wife was soon on scene and

---

[37] *Daily Alta California*, June 25, 1856.

[38] H. H. Bancroft, *Popular Tribunals*, Volume II (San Francisco: The History Company, Publishers, 1887), at p. 449.

[39] Id., at 449-450.

lodged at the home of Perley and his daughter on Dupont Street. The Committee humanely granted her leave to daily attend her husband in the place of his captivity. Meanwhile, much rumour and speculation appeared in the columns of the press, both for and against the doings of the Vigilantes. Far more discreet was the operation of an effort to use legal devices to free the Judge. Sensing that the Vigilantes were far too powerful to overcome with the scant martial resources at his disposal, Howard rightly thought it more prudent to encourage a collision between the jurisdiction of the Committee and the power of the United States. He instructed the Virginia-born attorney Benjamin Watkins Leigh, Jr. to seek Perley's guidance in these matters and discuss with him the drafting of a process to file in the federal court with the hope of obtaining an order for Terry's release which the Committee could only resist on pain of enforcement by the full weight of the power of an armed federal authority that was as yet uninvolved in the commotion. [40]

Perley at first appeared reluctant to involve himself too greatly in the forefront of the law and order movement. The initial public effort to negotiate with the Committee was handled by Balie Peyton, Frederick A. Woodworth, H. M. Naglee and Andrew J. Randall.[41] They succeeded in winning from the Committee the concession that a legal team consisting of Perley, James D. Thornton, Henry P. Lubbock, and A. P. Crittenden be allowed to "interview and consult with Terry, but only and strictly on the subject proposed and on their pledge of honor not to agitate any other question."[42] As they visited "the bastille to negotiate terms with a mob about the disposal" of Terry, Perley and his team were also active behind the scenes in efforts to influence the community in Terry's favor.[43] One high ranking committeeman, Charles Dempster, later commented that he had "never known or heard of a case where a man's friends worked so hard on his behalf." Presented daily with informal advocates for Terry's release, Dempster became "wearied by the increasing efforts to argue the

---

[40] *Daily Alta California*, June 29, 1856.

[41] Theodore H. Hittell, *History of California*, Volume III (San Francisco: N.J. Stone & Company, 1898), at p. 585-586.

[42] Id., at p. 586.

[43] *Tri-Weekly Times*, August 13, 1856.

matter out of court."[44] Coleman noted how "every effort, every device, artifice, pretext, persuasion, and power of [Terry's] friends, old and new, was brought to bear at once on every separate individual member of the Committee, on every part of its organization that they thought could be reached by influence social, moral, religious, political, public, private, sectional, general, and every other kind; and when they found the Executive firm and unwavering...the leaders in this movement then tried to sow dissension and to create divisions in every part of the organization that they could, and it may well be conceived how much trouble could thus be given to us by strong, zealous, numerous influential people who under the circumstances deemed any expedient, any policy, any tactics or efforts justifiable."[45]

With Hopkins still in peril, it was decided that Terry would stand trial, not for murder, but for assault on the Committee's agent and a host of other alleged crimes dating back to 1850, including attacks on a Mr. Evans in Stockton, on Joseph Roadhouse in the San Joaquin County Courthouse, on a Mr. King during the Stockton City Charter election, and on J. H. Purdy in San Francisco. Rather improbably, he would also face justice for aiding and abetting the defrauding of his own clients, the Sanchez heirs, by allowing the notorious Roach to escape.[46] The days leading up to the trial and during its pendency were marked by reports in the press of Terry's actual and alleged enormities over the years, occasionally in Perley's company, and always involving violence. The publication of the rather indecorous details of an assault by the two law partners on a pair of merchants in Stockton years before prompted from Perley a forceful denial of any violence and his further complaint, after his denial was published, that the editor's omission in the printed version of a crucial comma, probably by design, wrongly turned the denial into an admission.[47] Further public embarrassment occurred when men purporting to have the Governor's authority to negotiate Terry's release appeared in the City, conferred with Perley, then met with the Committee. The upshot of the meeting was the Committee's agreement to allow a

---

[44] Bancroft, *Popular Tribunals*, supra, at 440

[45] Id., at pp. 440-441.

[46] Id., at pp. 436-437.

[47] *Daily Alta California*, July 18, 1856; and *Daily Alta California*, July 19, 1856.

single member of Terry's legal team—A. P. Crittenden—to communicate directly with the imprisoned man. During their conference, Terry presented Crittenden with a letter explaining his willingness to be tried by the regular civil authorities and his promise to resign his office if convicted. Crittenden then passed the letter on to Perley, who in turn, in pursuance of Terry's explicit instructions, transmitted it to the *San Francisco Herald* and the *Sun* for publication. Not knowing of Terry's instructions, the Governor's emissaries charged Crittenden with breach of confidence, both with respect to the Judge and themselves. In explaining the facts, including Perley's involvement, Crittenden complained in the press that had his critics "proceeded with that caution which becomes men in questions involving character, and made inquiry as to the truth before parading their imaginary grievances before the public, they would have spared themselves and me what is always disagreeable—a newspaper discussion of personal matters."[48]

For Terry's trial, the Vigilance Committee rejected any thought of Terry retaining the counsel of his choice, but did afford him the legal services of the respectable Miers F. Truett. Confident of his power before any tribunal, Terry tolerated Truett's presence, while opting to conduct a preponderant share of his own defense.[49] In his support, he mustered a series of witnesses, chief of whom was Perley, whose primary task was to defend his friend's character and address the charges antedating the unrest in San Francisco. In his lengthy testimony, Perley confirmed many of the facts about the incident with Purdy, but explained the situation as one involving gross insult and surliness on Purdy's part. He denied that his friend had ever been associated with "all that class known as shoulder-strikers and ballot box stuffers," and had actually opposed such characters. He knew nothing of any fights, quarrels, street brawls, private difficulties or public encounters in which Terry had allegedly engaged since coming to California, with the exception of the situation with Evans, though he hedged his statement with the suggestion that the term "private difficulties" was "too indefinite a phrase" to permit a more precise answer.[50] He knew of Roadhouse,

---

48 *Marysville Daily Herald*, July 13, 1856.

49 Bancroft, *Popular Tribunals*, supra, pp. 435-436.

50 *Trial of David S. Terry*, op. cit., at p. 46.

and instead of denying any of the facts of the conflict between that man and Terry, dismissed the fellow as "a bully and shoulder striker," "quarrelsome and turbulent—fond of fighting, drinking and carousing." He didn't have personal knowledge of Terry's use of a cane against George Ryer, though he was aware of some incident involving that man, as well as a conflict with someone by the name of Jackson. As for a Mr. Snick or Sink and a jeweler on Eldorado Street in Stockton, he knew nothing. It was also true, he said, that Terry was in the habit of carrying arms, usually a knife, sometimes a pistol, for his own protection, while defending or prosecuting criminals. "The life of an attorney was in constant jeopardy," he said, "and I would state further, that up to the time I left Stockton, it was the usage and custom for a majority of the people to carry arms."[51] What he found most astonishing of all was "the utter falsity of the charge of aiding Roach in defrauding the Sanchez heirs," and the "utter ignorance [of] those who have trumped up this vile slander." The truth of the matter, he explained, was that Terry, himself and others had braved threats of violence and assassination, and in fact "risked everything in behalf of the Sanchez heirs," and had even taken on numerous judicial officers, including Justice Wells of the Supreme Court, who astoundingly, in the face of Terry's strident opposition, had ordered Roach's release.[52] "No counsel ever in this State, nor I believe in any other, encountered and overcame difficulties we had to contend against, on behalf of these heirs."[53] The David Terry he had known since his days in Texas, he concluded, was a man of "the most unblemished character…of perfect sobriety," who had "never been addicted to gambling," or been "a rowdy, street-fighter, or bully."[54]

Others came forward with similar testimony. Judge Shattuck said he'd "never met in this country a more upright and courteous gentleman," and that "so far from his being a bully, I consider him a magnanimous man."[55] He was "utterly amazed and confounded at hearing imputations and aspersions against the fidelity and kindness of Judge Terry as a husband," and "equally astonished or

---

[51] Id., at p. 47.
[52] Id., at pp. 44-45.
[53] Id., at p. 45.
[54] Id., at p. 44.
[55] Id., at p. 52.

astounded to hear that Judge Terry's position in the Roach or Sanchez case has been exactly reversed by a falsification of the relation he stood toward it."[56] Judge Creanor testified that he'd known Terry since 1849 and had been an intimate friend of his since the Spring of 1850. "I know of no man whose character is better than his." Terry, he said, was "high minded, honorable," and a man who abstained from common vices of the sort associated with "grog shops, gambling houses and houses of ill fame."[57] He was aware of Terry's "having some kind of a fight in Stockton, but never heard of his shooting any one," was unaware of his alleged assault on a Mr. H. N. Gage or on a Mr. Jackson with a chair, and knew nothing of the attack on the jeweler on El Dorado Street.[58] Samuel Houston Brooks testified that Terry, though "a man of ardent temperament," who "would be quick and prompt to resent anything like a personal insult," was "entirely free from harboring sentiments of malice or revenge." He was unimpeachable for perfect sobriety, for incorruptible honesty, was a man of "generous and noble impulse, and has never been known to commit a mean or dishonorable action."[59] Captain Hays said he'd known Terry from long-ago in Texas and that "his reputation was most excellent, and he was looked upon as a man of the highest reputation, as an upright and honorable gentleman."[60] Richard Roman stated that he knew Terry from when he was a boy, and had "frequently met him on the frontier of Texas, when we were engaged in repelling the Mexican and Indian incursions from our border settlements." Terry, he said, was free of any addiction "to any disreputable vices, such as gaming and drinking," and that "his character was always of an opposite kind."[61] A. P. Crittenden recalled their acquaintance from many years before in Brazoria and said Terry was "a high minded, honorable and correct young man—impulsive, generous and brave; yet not turbulent or quarrelsome."[62] Even political foes, such as R.W. Heath, who was defeated in a race for San Joaquin County

[56] Id.

[57] Id., at pp. 52-53.

[58] Id., at p. 53.

[59] Id., at p. 50.

[60] Id., at p. 53.

[61] Id., at p. 54.

[62] Id., at p. 58.

Sherriff through Terry's influence, came to his defense. Despite their difficulties in politics, Heath attested that Terry "has acted with great manliness, candor, and honesty of purpose—so much so, that I have never since entertained for him other feelings than those of the highest respect and admiration."[63] Likewise, A. C. Bradford, whom Terry campaigned against in a race for an assembly seat during the fall elections in 1855, testified that while Terry had "spoke against me," he had "never heard him say anything or do any act against me or his opponents not admissible in political contests or unbecoming of a man of honor and a high-toned gentleman."[64]

Other witnesses came forward to testify to the events of June 21 and the altercation with Hopkins, as did Terry himself. In his own defense before the Committee, he contended that he was acting under immunity as an officer of the law when defending Maloney; that his attack on Hopkins was in justifiable self-defense and defense of another against a man whose own authority was without legal sanction. Knowing the temperament of juries and of this one in particular, he conceded that "the evils you arose to repress were glaring and palpable," that the men "who most warmly oppose your organization, were associates and sympathizers with ballot-box stuffers and other disreputable characters," and that he, like the Committee, was an opponent of this class, and had even broken with the Democrat Party because "I uniformly refused to support for office candidates whose nomination had, as I believed, been procured by fraudulent practices."[65] Not once did he ever resist the Committee, as he was charged with doing. Hopkins hadn't produced a warrant, and none had ever been issued. As there was no warrant, there was no probable cause for Hopkins to act and no resistance to lawful authority when Hopkins was opposed. Absence of a warrant precluded his knowing of Hopkins' capacity, and all but mandated that he resist this "stranger, whose name I did not know, without producing any warrant or authority from any man or body of men, and having no authority to arrest me so far as I yet know," who had "committed a fierce and violent assault on me,

---

63 Id., at p. 56.
64 Id., at p. 57.
65 Id., at p. 24.

attempted to wrest a gun from my hands, with the...evident intention of taking my life."[66]

He contended he took a more moderate law and order role than reported by others, said he saw the hopelessness of opposing the Vigilance Committee, and expressed his commitment to obtaining intervention by the federal government. His role, in fact, had been a reluctant one. "I was urgently requested by gentlemen of undoubtful character and standing to take a prominent position, for the reason, as they stated, that it would be useful in keeping the organization alive under the very unfavorable aspect of the contest."[67] He admitted to underestimating the power of the Committee, and to feeling dispirited over the neutrality of the federal military officials, but that "fidelity to my friends who were in like circumstances with myself—pride, obstinacy, or what you will—prevented my relaxing my efforts as long as a hope remained." Skirting over the fact that he came to San Francisco for the express purpose of injecting himself into the controversy and forcing a confrontation by serving a writ on the Committee, he contended that he "thought it my duty to resist any infractions of the law attempted in my presence, however little prospect I may have had of ultimately succeeding."[68] To this end, he managed to prevent the arrest of Maloney and nearly made it to the armory, "where we expected to receive and obey the orders of General Howard."[69] He decried the media for publishing sensationalized billingsgate, especially the *Evening Journal*, to which he attributed especially sinister motives. "Being ultra-abolitionists, their constant aim has been to establish a sectional party in our midst, and to introduce into California the bitter war of sections which now agitates our brethren in the Atlantic States, and in which California should have no part. The greatest of my crimes, in their eyes, is having been born in the South, except daring to establish a reputation as to obtain the support of the people of a State in which the merits of this same journal to urge upon the Committee actions having a tendency to forward those objects heretofore alluded to."[70]

---

[66] Id.
[67] Id., at p. 25.
[68] Id., at p. 25.
[69] Id.
[70] Id., at p. 26.

The other charges, involving incidents dating back to 1850, appeared to be based on the desire of certain persons, "anxiously striving to furnish some sort of plausible pretext, and, by reviving and falsifying transactions long past, excite, as far as possible, the mind of the community."[71]

With the trial concluded, doubt exercised the minds of both the members of the Committee and Terry's friends. The former agonized over a capital sentence and what wrath it might bring down upon the City and themselves; the latter feared for Terry's life. In this uncertain twilight between trial and the rendering of a verdict, Perley finally took action to ensure Terry's safety from execution or exile. Having contemplated the matter for weeks and likely struggled to find a jurisdictional basis for relief in a federal judicial forum, he discovered a solution in the very paralytic condition of California's courts that Terry's confinement had caused. To his attention had come the plight of a Monsieur Des Rochers, whose action for recovery of $16,000 was now stalled in the Supreme Court after having been argued in January. The temporary absence of Judge Heydenfeldt from the State and the unlawful incarceration of Terry rendered a quorum impossible, hence his ability to obtain justice had become impaired. That Des Rochers was a citizen of France provided the essential diversity of citizenship to extend the man standing to address his plea in federal court. Assisted by A. P. Crittenden, Perley drafted a petition for *ex parte* relief for the ultimate purpose of securing Terry's release so that Des Rochers' case in Sacramento might be resolved.

Upon reading Perley's brief, Judge Matthew Hall McAllister commenced his opinion with a recounting of the history of the writ in the common law tradition. Observing that its potency in the United States and California was attributable to the fact that it was grafted onto both the State and Federal Constitutions, McAllister noted that "whenever a person has been deprived of going when and where he pleases, and restrained of his liberty, he has a right to inquire if that restraint be legal, whether it be by a jailor, constable, or private individual."[72] The great challenge for the court, however,

---

[71] Id.

[72] *Ex Parte Des Rochers*, 1 McAll. 68, in *Reports of Cases Argued and Determined in the Circuit Court of the United States for the Districts of California*, Volume I (New York: John S. Voorhees, 1859), at p. 70.

centered on the question of jurisdiction. "If the proceeding shows a want of jurisdiction, it is the duty of the court to take notice of it, without waiting for an objection from either party."[73] The jurisdiction of the court was defined and limited by the statutes of Congress and their authoritative interpretation by the Supreme Court. On first glance, the crucial fourteenth section of the Judiciary Act of 1789 didn't appear particularly helpful to the applicant. That section of the Act provided "that writs of habeas corpus shall in no case extend to prisoners in jail, unless they are in custody under or by color of the authority of the United States, or are committed for trial before some court of the same, or are necessary to be brought into court to testify."[74] The provision was obviously designed to bar use of the power of the federal judiciary to interfere with State judicial process and thereby invade the sovereignty of the States. Those seeking liberty from State authorities were required to go directly to State court. Terry himself would have been thwarted by this provision had he, not Des Rochers, sought the writ, but Des Rochers was not himself a prisoner of those acting under color of State law. He was, however, nevertheless subject to a restraint on his ability to enforce his rights in court. He was a prisoner, yes, not of State authorities, but of his circumstances, that only the liberation of Justice Terry could remedy. It was a rather creative argument, and a creative use of the writ, but it was one that Judge McAllister found compelling enough to issue the order to Terry's captors to appear in court to explain the justness of Terry's continuing captivity.

Judge McAllister's integrity likely would not permit a corrupt outcome, even when he who asked for relief was numbered among his friends, or was the some-time colleague of his son. Nevertheless, it undoubtedly dawned on the Committee's leadership that McAllister would, at the very least, issue the writ and require their presence before the tribunal. The collision between the interests of the Committee and that of the federal government, stayed momentarily by the caution of General Wool and Admiral Farragut, might yet occur in the event the Judge issued the writ. A rapid decision, thus was called for, and a moderate one, well removed

[73] Id., at p. 71.
[74] Id., at p. 75.

from the extreme punishments the more sanguine Vigilantes preferred. Terry was pronounced guilty of offenses against Hopkins and the City of San Francisco, but innocent of the charges of conduct occurring years before. Since Hopkins had passed from danger and was sure to recover, the Committee's sentence was for Terry to be released with the admonition that he "should resign his position as judge of the supreme court."[75] Word of McAllister's order having likely been received, the Committee opted to release the Judge at once and had him escorted from their headquarters in the dead of night and taken to Perley's home, both to rejoin his wife and to convince his attorney that service the following morning of the writ was no longer necessary.[76]

Threats against Terry remained and a large group of Vigilantes, disgruntled by Terry's release, was soon rumored to be roaming the City seeking to impose a more fitting punishment, hence the Committee opted to send word to Perley's residence to warn the Judge that he best leave town at once.[77] Finding the Judge asleep amidst a boisterous and rum soaked celebration of his liberation, the Committee's representatives conveyed the message.[78] After the Judge was awakened, it was decided to evacuate to the U.S. sloop of war *John Adams*. There Terry remained until the steamer *Helen Hensley* departed inland with Terry aboard, along with his wife and "a large number of law and murder bloods, many of whom were drunk or still drinking."[79] Upon his arrival in Stockton, a large group of his friends and supporters greeted him with cheers and the discharge of a mighty cannon.[80] Terry was free, but his Know-Nothings, through his antics and those of his Party, were now facing disaster as both a viable political movement and a safe harbor for the southern wing of the Democracy.

With Terry at liberty and the interior country held by the Law and Order forces of the Governor, the affairs of the Supreme Court in the State Capital were able to resume by August 26.[81] One of the

---

75 Bancroft, *Popular Tribunals*, supra, pp. 468-469.

76 Id., at p. 473.

77 Id., at p. 474.

78 *San Francisco Bulletin*, August 8, 1856

79 Id.

80 *San Joaquin Republican*, August 17, 1856.

81 *Daily Alta California*, August 26, 1856.

cases that appeared on the docket at this time was the appeal in a matter involving a trust established for the benefit of the wife of Senator Gwin. The matter had originated in the Superior Court in San Francisco some years before. In April of 1853, George Pendleton Johnston, as the trustee for Senator Gwin's wife, leased to Benjamin C. Barney a ranch at a monthly rent of $500 for the period of five years, and also sold to Barney personal property on the ranch for $31,000, to be paid in five annual installments. Barney became insolvent and his surety, former Congressman and current principal at Palmer, Cook & Company, George W. Wright, refused to pay, hence the filing of suit for recovery of $14,000 on the contract. Wright's obligation was subsequently discharged by his partners at Palmer, Cook & Company via a release, conveniently executed in accordance with a power of attorney supposedly issued by Trustee Johnston and his agents at the bank. Perley and Hall McAllister were retained to represent the Trust, and in that capacity they moved the District Court to exclude the release on the grounds that its relationship to the power of attorney by which it had been executed was fatally flawed. Their motion was sustained, and the jury ultimately awarded their client $14,000, plus costs.[82]

For the August arguments in the inevitable appeal to the Supreme Court, Volney Howard somehow managed to calm the state of agitation that had possessed him on account of the Vigilance disturbance and join Perley at the bar in McAllister's place, accompanied by Joseph P. Hoge. A former Ohio Congressman and perennial Senate hopeful, Hoge possessed a rare ability to "present his side with a clearness and privity unequalled by any of his colleagues.[83] He was, said Erasmus Keyes, second only to McAllister in his power before a jury.[84] In their brief, Perley and his two colleagues argued that the power of attorney at issue in the case extended only to settling and adjusting partnership debts, accounts and demands, and that the release given to Wright fell outside this scope. Consequently, the debt owed by the surety (Mr. Wright) remained payable. With this, Justice Heydenfeldt agreed. "The debt sued on is not a partnership debt, but is a covenant to which the

[82] *Daily Alta California*, May 24, 1855.

[83] Erasmus Darwin Keyes, *Fifty Year's Observation of Men and Events Civil and Military* (New York: Charles Scribner's Sons, 1884), at p. 305.

[84] Id., at p. 308.

grantor of the power is a joint covenantee with two others.... The rule laid down by the authorities," including Joseph Story's treatise on agency, "for the construction of these instruments, requires them to be confined to the simple meaning of the terms expressed, and not to be extended by implication in any case except where the implication is absolutely necessary to carry out the expressly granted power."[85] The language of the instrument here "must in interpretation be confined to such debts and demands whereof the principal had a several and sole interest, and cannot be made to include a covenant which he jointly held with others." As the power of attorney related only to the concerns of one of the Bank's partners, and not the Bank as a whole, its scope could not extend to exonerating or settling debts owed to the Bank or its clients. Perley prevailed, as did the Chivalry's undisputed leader, Mr. Gwin.

William Gwin, like most others in the State, had been surprised by the sudden appearance and success of the Know Nothings, and may well have been dismayed as he witnessed many of his allies in the Chivalry defecting to its ranks to transform the nascent party into a Trojan Horse of southern Democracy from which its members schemed to spring once safely within the walls of power. Like his great rival, David Broderick, Gwin appears to have waited the revolution out, perhaps imagining that this odd permutation in the State's political history would quickly pass and the traditional institutional adversaries would reassume their complicated rivalry for control of government and the spoils that come with it. By the fall of 1856, Gwin's patience was being rewarded, as the Know Nothings, having accomplished little other than scandal and the humiliation of its leaders both politically and militarily at the hands of San Francisco's "pork merchants," withered in the days leading up to the General Election. When the great day came and went, the news was that the Know Nothings had lost control of both houses of the Legislature and that the Democrats, now in the majority, were out for blood and vengeance. Almost at once, they announced their intention to investigate those in charge of tracking and safeguarding the State's money, and within a short time produced a committee report detailing the woes afflicting the public fisc and identifying those at fault. None were surprised over the role of Palmer, Cook &

---

[85] *Johnston et al. v. Wright* (1856) 6 Cal. 373.

Company in the scandal. Once the banker of choice for the Treasury Department, the banking house suffered in the general economic downturn of 1854. Default by its own borrowers deprived it of the moneys given it by the State to make payment on the State's debt to financial interests in New York. Henry Bates, the Know Nothing Treasurer, opted to place the State's money in the hands of Lloyd Tevis and James Ben Ali Haggin of Wells Fargo. But before he did so, he made one last payment to Palmer, Cook & Company pursuant to an existing contract, resulting in further losses to the State. Failing to obtain the Governor's approval of his bond, the liability became his own. The worst was yet to come, in the form of the placement into the hands of a former treasury clerk, Edwin A. Rowe, now the head of an express company, of over $120,000 intended to meet yet another interest payment, but actually destined for the pockets of Mr. Rowe and his co-conspirators, or so the Assembly's investigators surmised. The makings of a grander scheme was soon in view with the discovery of the deposit into the Treasury of promissory notes authorized by the State Controller in place of actual money owed to the State by the Counties, the placement of the actual money into the coffers of Wells Fargo and other financial institutions. and then the compromise of County debts at a discount, with a kind of brokerage fee going to Rowe and others connected with the Treasury and the office of the State Controller.[86] It wasn't long before Articles of Impeachment against Bates and Controller G. W. Whitman were in the works.

With the coming of the new year, it appeared that everywhere in California it was open season on the Know Nothings. In the saloon of the Steamer *Golden Gate,* San Joaquin's long-time Treasurer and Know Nothing stalwart Samuel Houston Brooks was recognized by a former Vigilante named Dodge. When Dodge used an "opprobrious epithet" calculated to instigate a fight, the hardly reticent nor physically retiring Brooks struck him in the face and then pulled a knife with the intention of striking Dodge with its handle. Instead, a degree of artlessness no doubt related to his business in the saloon resulted in a minor cut to Dodge's cheek. Brooks was arrested for the offense and hauled before Judge Coon

---

[86] See *Journal of Eighth Session of the Assembly of the State of California* (Sacramento: James Allen, 1857), pp. 255-261.

in the Police Court in San Francisco.[87] The matter was referred to a Grand Jury and Brooks, after Dr. Ashe pledged his surety, was released on bail.[88] An indictment soon followed, as did Brooks' retention of Perley as defense counsel. Mindful of the enormous hostility with which many of the City's potential jurors held his friend, Perley wisely moved for a change of venue.[89] The motion apparently was soon mooted due to the resolution of the case, no doubt on the grounds that Brooks' alleged victim was as much to blame for the fray as Brooks himself.

Animus toward the Know Nothings, and the latter's current propensity to react poorly when feeling its heat, was evident, too, in the conflict that erupted between Perley's client, Dr. Langdon, and a medical colleague, Dr. Ryer, following some public comments on the affairs of the Insane Asylum.[90] Though initial reports were that the two men quarreled over a woman, with many others expressing utter "ignorance as to the cause of the misunderstanding," there can be little doubt that the matter was inspired and propelled by the political rivalries of the day, Langdon's recent success in thwarting the Democrats' attempt to bar him from office through litigation, and perhaps a rekindling of anger on Ryer's part following the publicity generated in the press during Terry's trial about how Brooks' friend Langdon had served on Ryer the indignity of a slap across the face.[91] After several attempts to meet on the field of honor and the circulation of false rumors that the mutual expression of willingness to duel had resulted in an amical adjustment of the difficulty, the men at last were able to rendezvous by steamer some miles from Stockton on private property. There, with their seconds in place, they set themselves apart by a distance of ten paces and opened fire on one another with pistols.[92] Langdon's slug followed a trajectory wide of its mark. Ryer's was not much better in its aim, but did manage to strike Langdon in the knee. The wound, it was said, was "painful, but not dangerous," though it proved serious

[87] *Weekly Butte Record*, January 31, 1857.

[88] *Daily Alta California*, January 23, 1857.

[89] *Daily Alta California*, April 10, 1857.

[90] *Sacramento Daily Union*, February 26, 1857.

[91] *Daily Alta California*, February 25, 1857; and *Marysville Daily Herald*, February 26, 1857.

[92] *Daily Alta California*, February 25, 1856.

enough even after healing to cause a limp in the doctor's walk evident throughout the remainder of his life.

The precise context of the controversy out of which Langdon's duel arose was the investigation by a joint committee of the Legislature into complaints about Dr. Langdon's handling of affairs at the Lunatic Asylum and, more ominously, the committee's consideration of whether or not to replace Langdon with another candidate. Confusion over whether Langdon's term was two years from the date of appointment or, as an interim appointee, it terminated once the Legislature selected a permanent incumbent, stalled any action on the matter. The hesitation proved only momentary following Senator Coffroth's insistence that because an appointment represented a constitutional issue, the matter could not be put off any longer. After expressing his opinion that the Supreme Court's ruling in *People ex rel. Langdon v. Reid* had established the interim nature of the doctor's appointment, Coffroth allowed introduction of a declaration by a former employee of the Asylum attesting that Dr. Langdon improperly employed maniacs in the performance of labor, suppressed news of the unusual number of deaths of patients during his tenure and failed even to pay wages.[93] Within two days, Langdon denounced the allegations against him as "malicious, false and unfounded," said they amounted to "an unmitigated calumny," and arose from "a vile conspiracy to rob me of my character and reputation."[94] His accuser he called an "ignorant but plaint tool" and a "puppet in the hands of others," whose own motivation was "to get his revenge on me for having discharged him, being compelled to act thus on account of his habitual drunkenness."[95] He asked that the "election of Physicians to the Insane Asylum may be deferred until these charges are properly examined, that he "may not be condemned though an ex parte statement without a full and fair chance of justification."[96] Others, including the Trustees of the institution, vouched for Langdon's competence and integrity and even confirmed the malicious and perjurious nature of the accusations and the habitual inebriation of the accuser, but it was of no matter

[93] *Sacramento Daily Union*, March 11, 1857.
[94] *Sacramento Daily Union*, March 14, 1857.
[95] Id.
[96] Id.

to a Legislature dominated by opponents of the sitting Governor, his Party and anyone who happened to have benefited from Know Nothing largess.[97] That the matter was one that "still continues to excite a great deal of animosity" all but ensured, in these highly charged times, that Langdon's removal from office would hardly set the seal of finality upon it.

Most certainly aware of the undoing of his effort from a year earlier to preserve Dr. Langdon's tenure at the Lunatic Asylum, Perley was unable to devote more time or energy to any legal response despite his presence in Sacramento. The dual impeachments of Bates and Whiteman having been sent to the State Senate, the two implicated officials lawyered up. Bates secured the services of the redoubtable E. D. Baker, who appeared briefly at the outset of the Senate trial to argue the mootness of the proceeding due to his client's resignation from office several months before. A short debate on the issue concluded with the finding that impeachment remained necessary as a formal declaration of political guilt and the only means available to disqualify the disgraced Treasurer from ever again holding public office. With Bates insisting on the Senate's lack of jurisdiction and refusing even to contest the matter, let alone appear, the Senate proceeded to a voice vote and an easy conviction.[98]

The rapid disposal of the Bates impeachment freed the Senate to consider the merits of the charges against the Controller, G. W. Whitman. When the matter was called, Perley appeared on Whitman's behalf, with the estimable Colonel Philip Legget Edwards as co-counsel. The charges were several in number: that Bates instructed his subordinates not to provide the Board of Examiners with data in the Comptroller's possession; that he failed to provide such data himself; that he paid expenses presented to him by the lessee of the State Prison without approval from the Board of Examiners; that he conspired with his subordinates to defraud the Treasury; and that he caused a loss to the Treasury due to his negligence.[99] To all of this Perley proffered a formal written denial. It would be shown, he stated, through the presentation of

---

[97] *Sacramento Daily Union*, March 16, 1857.

[98] *Sacramento Daily Union*, March 13, 1857.

[99] *Journal of the Eighth Session of the Senate of the State of California* (Sacramento: James Allen, State Printer, 1857), at pp. 340-346.

evidence that Whitman's instruction to his subordinate to withhold information was consistent with the scope of his Department's duty under the law—a duty that entailed opening the books to the Examiners only, not digesting and abstracting the information for their benefit—; that Whitman's withholding of information was due to the failure of the State Treasurer to convey the same to him; that his payment of the Prison Lessee's warrants without prior approval of the Examiners was in keeping with an obligation pursuant to a contract between the State and the Prison authority and thus could not be subject to interference by any mere legislative act; and that he neither defrauded the Treasury nor was responsible through negligence for any loss. In response to Whitman's formal denial, one of the managers of the impeachment trial—Assemblyman Swezy—attempted to refute the various defenses, prompting Perley to reply that he and co-counsel had no reasonable opportunity to address the same because its substance had only been handed to them moments before. He thought a short continuance to the next day was appropriate to allow for a proper reply, as well as to give time for numerous Senators and the Lieutenant Governor to complete their journeys to the State Capital and form the requisite quorum the Constitution in such matters demanded. Perley's argument prevailed and a short continuance was granted, but it was further resolved that the Senate was free under the Constitution to elect a presiding officer, and that a simple majority was all that was needed for the trial to proceed. A small concession was granted in the form of a rule that no Senator who didn't hear all of the evidence presented could cast a final vote, yeah or nay.[100]

The witnesses to be called by the managers were a who's who of California's legal and political elite: Governor Johnson, Secretary of State David F. Douglas, State Prison Lessee James M. Estill, former Chief Justice S. C. Hastings, and the jailed E. A. Rowe, not to mention a handful of minor functionaries. The Secretary of State was the first to take the stand. The primary goal of the managers in calling him was to adduce evidence of obstruction by the Controller. Douglas, who served on the Board of Examiners, testified that Whitman expressed outrage over the law requiring Board approval for any public expenditure, that he considered it a personal affront,

---

100 *Sacramento Daily Union*, March 24, 1857.

and that indeed, when Douglas and the Governor appeared at the Controller's office, they were denied any active assistance in reviewing the books by Whitman's staff. On cross examination, however, Perley elicited the Secretary's admission that no actual obstruction to the Examiners' review of the books occurred. They were given access, but nothing more, which was consistent with Whitman's own view of his obligation under the law.[101] Whitman's subordinate, Mr. Vaughan, confirmed that the books had been opened to the Examiners and that they were free to spend the day reviewing the numbers and reaching any conclusions their review justified.[102] Perley had the books brought into the Senate chamber "to show, from the manner in which they were kept, that any member of the Board could get the information they sought in ten minutes." Under Perley's cross-examination, Vaughan further admitted that the Treasurer had failed for the previous eight to ten months to transmit his monthly reports to the Controller, hence the information relevant to the inquiry transmitted by the Treasury Department was incomplete and out-of-date. "It would have been an utter impossibility to tell how much money there should have been in the Treasury, because our books varied from the State Treasurer's books about $100,000.... We depend upon those returns to balance the Controller's books with the State Treasurer's."[103] Whitman, thus, could hardly be held responsible for a failure to produce information he never possessed.

On the following day, after a delay due to the absence of the Governor and the Attorney General, the proceedings resumed with the belated appearance of Governor Johnson. Taking the stand, he recounted his march on the Controller's office to examine the Controller's books in order to perform his statutory duty to determine the Treasury's current balance. He recalled that Whitman's clerks brought the books out for him to view, but provided no other assistance. Not being able to make heads nor tails out of the figures, he departed no more in the know than when he arrived, and after a few days, repaired to the Treasury itself—this time alone due to the Attorney General's absence from town and a

---

101 *Sacramento Daily Union*, March 25, 1857.
102 Id.
103 Id.

momentary fit of apoplexy suffered by the Secretary of State. It was while physically counting the money that had been brought out to him in bags that he received word of the Vigilance excitement in San Francisco and apprehended a need for his presence there to pacify the commotion.[104] When his turn came to cross examine the Governor, Perley asked the man what the law required with respect to the books, and why he didn't have his own clerk attend to the matter, rather than himself. When Perley wondered if the reason had to do with the clerk's incompetence, the Governor refused to answer so "impertinent" a question and was relieved of any obligation to do so when the Senate ruled that Perley was out of order.[105]

Perceiving a need to establish at least an implied obligation by the Controller to render assistance beyond merely making the books available for inspection, the managers asked an accountant who had examined the Treasurer's books how long it would take a non-expert to comprehend the accounts kept in the Controller's office. Perley objected on the grounds that knowledge of how long it would take a non-expert to examine one set of books was irrelevant to the issue of how long it would take a non-expert to examine an entirely different set, and characterized the question as "frivolous and not to be tolerated." Though the objection was overruled, the subsequent testimony proved more helpful to the defense than the prosecution; for the witness testified that it took no more than a week to evaluate the books, but that such would have been utterly fruitless in light of the absence of any current data from the Treasury Department.[106]

Having failed to make a case on the first two articles of impeachment, the mangers moved on to the charge that Whitman had conspired to defraud the Treasury, or at least had negligently performed his duties to the great loss of the State. A key figure in this charge was E.A. Rowe. His presence, however, was complicated both by his incarceration pending criminal trial for his various alleged misdeeds and an ongoing neuralgic illness that "confined him to his bed" and rendered him in no "condition to be

---

[104] *Sacramento Daily Union*, March 26, 1857.
[105] Id.
[106] *Sacramento Daily Union*, March 27, 1857.

removed."[107] After some discussion about forcing the man to attend regardless of the state of his health, or sending a delegation of Senators to evaluate his condition personally, the Senate declined to call him and moved on to the examination of a number of County Treasurers who allegedly had been instructed by Whitman to deposit only promissory notes into the Treasury, and to make actual cash deposits with Wells Fargo and Palmer, Cook & Company. The County Treasurers largely confirmed that this was the case, except that Whitman had nothing to do with it. Instead, it was his subordinate, Mr. Hughson, who instructed them, often doing so while Whitman was absent from the office.[108] The only role Whitman appears to have played in any of this was in subsequently authorizing settlement of the amounts owed and payment on the various Counties' behalf by the financial institutions where the money had been deposited.[109]

The calling of Deputy Treasurer Maddux of Sacramento County marked the most dangerous moment of the trial for the defense. The Deputy Treasurer had entered into a deal with A. B. McNeil of Wells Fargo and Whitman's subordinate Mr. Hughson to make all payments to the Treasury in promissory notes or warrants issued by Mr. Whitman, and to deposit the actual money with the bank. The managers asked the Deputy if he was actually required to pay in cash or bullion. Knowing an affirmative answer might establish that the law had been openly flaunted with the consent of his client's office, Perley launched a series of objections designed either to bar or circumscribe the testimony. When the matter went to a vote, the Senators split down the middle, prompting the Know Nothing Lieutenant Governor to cast the deciding vote in favor of sustaining Perley's objection.[110] The result was an inability of the Managers to establish that any of the Deputy Treasurers knew that payment via promissory note was unlawful or otherwise irregular and thus had engaged in any conspiracy with the Controller's office for which Whitman might be held at least vicariously accountable. The outcome also had the effect of shifting any blame from Whitman, who appears largely to have been unaware of the scheme, to his

---

[107] Id.

[108] Id.

[109] *Sacramento Daily Union*, March 28, 1857.

[110] Id.

subordinate, Mr. Hughson. By day's end, it was difficult not to dispute the conclusion that Hughson's responsibility for the fraud had been "established beyond the shadow of a doubt."[111]

Two of the last witnesses called by the Managers were the barely recovered and incarcerated Rowe, and A. B. McNeil. Already facing criminal jeopardy, there was some concern that Rowe might plead the Fifth, hence the insistence by the Managers that a recent statute barring invocation of the right to remain silent by public employees should apply to his testimony. Perley and Edwards argued that any appearance by the witness must be consistent with the State's version of the Bill of Rights rather than a dubious statute of recent vintage, and that the witness should at the very least be afforded the opportunity "to have the advice of his counsel, as to what questions would be proper and what improper to answer."[112] Once the objection was sustained, Rowe was examined, but to no positive end since he denied memory of just about everything. He didn't recall much about warrants being substituted for cash, or who gave him a particular warrant, or if Whitman benefitted from it in any way. The few things he was asked that he might have possessed knowledge of, Perley and Edwards were able to keep off the record, including any inquiry into the whereabouts of over a hundred thousand dollars in State monies that should have been accounted for by the Comptroller's Office. Introduction of such matter no doubt would have only served the highly prejudicial purpose of imputing the fault of others for its disappearance to Whitman, who had as yet been un-implicated in that crime. Mr. McNeil, for his part, acknowledged his involvement in the scheme to substitute promissory notes issued by the Controller's office in place of cash payments to the Treasury, but insisted that it was entirely in keeping with a recent opinion by the Know Nothing Attorney General. While the point of the scheme was to run a profit, it wasn't intended to be at the State's expense. His practice had been to obtain a warrant on behalf of various Counties from the Controller's Office, and then turn the warrant over to the Treasury in fulfillment of the Counties' depository obligations. He would then issue his own script as a form of security, sell them to

---

[111] Id.

[112] *Sacramento Daily Union*, March 31, 1857.

investors, and split any profits with Mr. Hughson. That the Controller himself was even aware of the scheme he denied. So helpful was the testimony that Perley and his co-counsel declined to ask a single question on cross.[113]

Realizing that neither Rowe nor McNeil had advanced the case against the Controller, the managers asked leave to recall Rowe to further answer regarding the missing treasury moneys, to which Perley rightly objected on the grounds that the managers proposed "to go entirely beyond the ordinary rules of order and the articles of impeachment, and to bring a matter which they have not charged in any part of the articles of impeachment." The issue the managers wished to explore was

> entirely the same question which this court here decided against on yesterday—that they shall call upon Mr. Rowe and go into an examination of what he knows about that \$190,000. It was rejected by a very large vote in this Court yesterday, and...was entirely foreign to the case. It should not be allowed in here. If new matter of impeachment is discovered, the managers have a right to file new articles, and the defense to reply. But to endeavor to bring in new matter in this way, which the court has eight times decided was not pertinent was a most extraordinary proceeding. It was an insult to the dignity of the Court.

On behalf of the managers, Mr. Hall took umbrage at Perley's peroration. "I think our conduct does not merit the severe criticism passed upon it by the gentleman who has just taken his seat." Perley and his co-counsel had "endeavored, as attorneys and lawyers, and always in a pettifogging manner, to conduct this grave and solemn trial as if they were sitting in a common criminal court." But this wasn't a criminal court, bound by strict statutory and constitutional provisions designed to protect the accused and ensure the integrity of a system of justice operating for the benefit of a State whose citizens were sovereign and free. No, this was an entirely different sort of proceeding subject to very different standards. It was, he said,

---

[113] Id.

> the only high and solemn tribunal where the right or trial by jury is taken from the citizen, and because it is a Court constituted by the Constitution itself to try offences unknown in the criminal calendar. We do not sit here by virtue of any law, either civil or criminal, but we sit here as a most extraordinary court. We sit here as a court of impeachment—not to impeach an officer for the violation of any law known to our criminal code, but he is examined here for a political offense, and if found guilty, his punishment will be a deprivation of political privileges.

The Court of impeachment, as "guardians of the State against corruption of its officers, constituted by the Constitution itself," sitting as "a Political Court, with the highest, broadest, and firmest and equitable powers," was not limited by the Bill of Rights or by any mere rules of procedures, nor bound or trammeled "within the limits of a Court of ordinary jurisdiction."[114] Hall's was a passionate argument, albeit an unconvincing and unsuccessful one.

The prosecution's case encountered further obstacles when two of its witnesses—William Willis and Attorney General William T. Wallace—failed to appear, causing a gap in the proceedings. Wondering if the witnesses could possibly advance the case for removal, the Senate asked the Managers to explain what they hoped the witnesses might prove. Manager Hall was far more interested in the cause of the non-appearances, which was, to his mind, the failure of the Senate to make a public pronouncement ordering witnesses to attend. That would have been far preferable than explaining now the prosecution's case and revealing its strategy to their adversaries. All they needed was some time: Wallace, he assured the Senate, would be present tomorrow; Willis, however, was actively evading service of a subpoena. Perley scoffed at the excuses. "Mr. Willis was here after the Court was in session for several days. If he was here for several days on the subpoena of this Court, and these gentlemen gave their consent to Willis to go away, and are not now able to have him attached..., I think the fault is theirs." He chaffed at the Managers' desire for secrecy. "Is there," he asked, "any difference between the conducting of this prosecution and an ordinary criminal trial? If a man was indicted for murder,

---

114 *Sacramento Daily Union*, April 1, 1857.

and the attorney wished a continuance, wouldn't he be compelled to set out by affidavit what he expected to prove by absent witnesses?" There was, in his view, nothing "more proper than...if these witnesses are not here, that the learned Managers should be compelled to say by affidavit what they expect to prove by them. If they make affidavit to what they want to prove...perhaps we would admit it." Perley's own witnesses were ready to take the stand, and this delay, if unjustified by those who requested it, would only prejudice the Defendant's case by compelling the Defendant's lawyers to keep their witnesses at the ready.[115] The Senate didn't exactly grant the Managers' request, but did adjourn for the day, with the intention of resuming in the morning whether the missing witnesses were present or not.

When the high court of impeachment reconvened, Attorney General Wallace took the stand and told of Whitman's apparent hostility toward the law mandating oversight of the Controller's office by a Board of Examiners. Perley objected, saying "we do not object to any facts coming within the knowledge of the witness, but we do object to his giving his opinions, or his impressions. That is not evidence." After the objection was sustained, Wallace noted that he was contacted by Mr. McNeil, who asked that he suppress his letter endorsing the legality of the use of warrants in place of payments into the Treasury, saying its publication would depress the value of his securities. When the Attorney General expressed a willingness to report the contents of the letter, Perley objected on the grounds of hearsay, but the Senate as a whole voted to allow his testimony to come in.[116]

With Willis still evading service of a subpoena, the Managers invited the defense to commence its case.[117] Perley informed the Court that "there is one witness here on the part of the defense who is exceedingly anxious to go home, and we are willing to examine him now. He is the County Treasurer of Tuolumne County," Mr. W.W. Taylor. When Taylor was called, Perley questioned him about the settlement he made with Whitman, hoping no doubt to elicit testimony that there was nothing amiss in Whitman crediting

[115] *Sacramento Daily Union*, April 2, 1857.
[116] *Sacramento Daily Union*, April 3, 1857.
[117] *Sacramento Daily Union*, April 6, 1857.

Tuolumne for its obligations. Manager Hall objected, saying that there was nothing in the impeachment articles about settlements with Tuolumne County's Treasurer. Perley had previously denied the right of the Managers to exceed the scope of the charges, but now wished to exercise the right himself. "It will be remembered," Hall declared, "how very rigidly the Managers were confined to the examination of settlements made within the months specified in the Articles of Impeachment. Before the Managers can allow an examination now contrary to the ruling of the Court upon that occasion, and allowing the counsel for the defense to extend their examinations entirely beyond the limits of the specifications in the Articles of Impeachment—allowing them to extend to settlements made by other County Treasurers—we must interpose our objections."[118]

The subsequent testimony provided nothing particularly meaningful, and when Taylor left the stand, the Managers announced their final witness was still at large, last seen on Montgomery Street in San Francisco. The papers reported that "after the usual lawyer sparring," the court of impeachment adjourned for five days to allow for Willis' apprehension.[119] Continued evasion by Willis compelled the Managers to rest their case and yield the rest of the proceeding to the defense, though they expressed their desire to amend the Articles to include the entirely novel charge of collusion between Mr. Whitman and other parties and to recommence their case on this new charge after the defense rested. Colonel Edwards rose to declare this request an impermissible irregularity.[120] Perley called it "a monstrosity unheard of before in the annals of criminal jurisprudence."[121] The Senate denied the request, but did rule that should Willis eventually make an appearance, the managers would be allowed to call him to the stand in support of the existing Articles.[122]

Having managed to deprecate the evidence of Whitman's guilt, the gist of the defense's case-in-chief was to counter the possible prejudice that might accrue in connection with the allegation of any

---

[118] *Sacramento Daily Union*, April 6, 1857.
[119] *Sacramento Daily Union*, April 11, 1857.
[120] *Sacramento Daily Union*, April 16, 1857
[121] *Daily Alta California*, April 16, 1857
[122] *Sacramento Daily Union*, April 16, 1857.

effort by speculators in government warrants to suppress the contents of the Attorney General's letter. Perley did this by calling General James Allen, the Editor of the *State Tribune*, who published the letter even as Whitman was alleged to have been striving to spike it as a way of maximizing the private profit he and his clerks were supposedly reaping. Perley's further attempt to introduce the published contents of correspondence between Mr. Maddux and the Attorney General were objected to as irrelevant. Perley explained that his intent was to address the Managers' attempt to implicate by inference the Controller in the scheme to speculate in government promissory notes. "I want to show," he said, "that the substance of that letter was not concealed, but published in the month of May, 1856." The Managers replied that they were entitled to establish a connection between the Controller and McNiel and others in relation to the suppression of this letter, that they had "endeavored to show this by establishing collusion between Whitman and McNiel in the suppression.... We wished to show that he had it in his possession long anterior to its publication, that it was in his possession and that these speculations were going on at the same time. All of these facts we have endeavored to bring up as circumstantial evidence to show the collusion between the defendant and those other parties, McNiel and Hughson, in the substitution of scrip for cash in the State Treasury." The evidence proffered by Perley, they said, had "nothing to do with the case, and we object to it as entirely irrelevant and inadmissible." Perley rejoined with an extended argument.

> It will be recollected that one of the charges against Whitman is that he made money by the suppression of this letter, although not a charge made in the Articles of Impeachment. It is a charge made outside and upon the floor of this House, that he, at a certain time, in the month of July, received information from the Attorney General of this State that State warrants could be received in payment for taxes, and that he, in order to make money out of that, very willingly suppressed it, in order that he and his clerks might have the whole advantage of keeping that matter secret, and thereby making of the money themselves. We wish these letters read for a two-fold object. In the first place, to show that McNiel did not get his information from Whitman or

> from anybody else, but that it was a matter of public record—was talked upon the public streets, and that the information was derived from the same source, and was of the same character, embodying the same facts published two months before the date of the letter of the Attorney General to Col. Whitman, in a letter to the County Treasurer of this County. If Mr. Wallace wrote a letter to Mr. Maddux two months before he wrote to Whitman, containing the same facts in substance, and that letter was published, Whitman would have no motive to suppress the same facts widely known. We offer this fact to show that it was published in the papers and known by everybody; therefore, that it was not incumbent upon Whitman to published his letter at all, because the facts were well known before.... In the next place, we show that Whitman did not conceal the information from the public, by proving this as evidence before the Court. In this point of view, it is relevant, and it is material, that it may be read.

After winning the point, Perley called Mr. Estill, who was both the Lessee of the State Prison and a member of the very body that was judging his client. Estill was said by the Managers to have received payment authorization from the Controller in violation of the law. Perley's defense against the charge was not a denial, but the affirmative statement that the payment was mandated by the Contract Clause of the Constitution of the United States. "Do you recollect," he asked Mr. Estill, "sometime after the first payments were made to you, under your contract as State Prison Lessee, about the month of May, 1856, of calling upon the Controller for your second month's salary?"[123] After he answered in the affirmative, Estell further explained that Mr. Whitman at first hesitated because of some doubt about the application of the Act and a concern that payment might require Board approval. When Estill later informed him that the Governor's opinion was that Board approval wasn't necessary for this particular transaction, Whitman authorized payment. Perley then called the Governor to confirm the conversation with Estill. The Governor stated he couldn't recall it, but didn't rule out that it had actually transpired.

---

[123] *Sacramento Daily Union*, April 18, 1857

The closing arguments were rather anti-climactic. For the Managers, Mr. Swezy wasn't quite up to the task and asked for a short continuance. He needed time to collect his thoughts and organize his points. No doubt anxious for the prolonged matter to come to a close, the Senate insisted that the ill-prepared Swezy proceed. Some mercy was granted before he concluded on the grounds of his obvious fatigue, hence he was allowed to return in the morning to complete his argument.[124] Perley then rose and displayed "a thorough acquaintance with all the minutiae of the case, and as a consequence made a very sensible argument in favor of his client." He declaimed "for upwards of two hours, reviewing the evidence adduced upon…the Articles of Impeachment." It was, said the *Alta*, "an elaborate, eloquent and able speech."[125] He was followed by the "argumentative and truly eloquent effort" of Colonel Edwards, and then by Mr. Hall, who appeared cognizant of "the want of a sufficient foundation in the shape of testimony, to base his argument upon," but in the course of two hours did the best he could with "the material at hand."[126]

After so monotonous a trial, the matter ended rather abruptly. Declining a public debate over the sufficiency of the evidence, the Senate went into closed session and after merely an hour of discussion recalled the Defendant and his attorneys to announce its verdict. "Resolved by the Senate, sitting as a High Court of Impeachment, that George W. Whitman be declared acquitted of the charges preferred against him by the Assembly on the 25th of February, 1857." Perley had saved his client and defended the Know Nothings from the further disgrace that would have come had the first impeachment trial in the State's history resulted in a conviction. His satisfaction, however, was lost in the rush of Senators and others to the well of the Senate to congratulate the Controller, who was now free to resume his official duties. The anti-climactic nature of the conclusion was noted by the *Union*. The entire proceeding "from beginning to end has presented none of those imposing features which we should naturally look for, in a case of such an unusual character."[127] Perley's efforts were so

124 *Sacramento Daily Union*, April 18, 1857.
125 *Daily Alta California*, April 20, 1857.
126 *Daily Alta California*, April 23, 1857; and *Sacramento Daily Union*, April 22, 1857.
127 *Sacramento Daily Union*, April 22, 1857.

effective that it was evident to even the most casual observer "that no testimony had been elicited which justified such a prosecution, or which even excused it." That it originated as a political initiative by the dominant party against its rival was undeniable. The Controller had been "made to walk upon the heated plowshare of a political prosecution, and he has passed the fiery ordeal untouched in character and reputation. He has come out of the furnace purified, not degraded." Though Perley wasn't credited with the result, his thorough presentation of the defense and the successful outcome he secured must surely have been a substantial factor in the emergent consensus that impeachment is no trifling matter, and that mere political opposition should never be a motive in undoing what the free voters in a sovereign state had done, which was to entrust high office to a person of their own choosing.

With the conclusion of the Whitman impeachment, Perley was able to resume his focus on the matter of Dr. Langdon. Though the Legislature had corrected its omission from the previous year and voted in an incumbent, Langdon refused to yield his office on the grounds that his appointment had been for the remainder of the prior incumbent's term, not merely until the Legislature acted to fill the office through the normal procedures. A judicial hearing was held in Stockton before Judge Creanor on May 25 and resulted in a victory for his presumptive successor, Dr. Aylett.[128] On appeal, Perley argued that "adherence to the doctrines mentioned in" the previous Langdon case "is all that is required to enable the defendant to maintain his present title and right of possession to the office."[129] He contended that construing the operative law with the Constitution mandated a decision in Langdon's favor. The Constitution provided that "All officers, whose election or appointment is not provided for by the State Constitution, and all officers whose offices may hereafter be created by law, shall be elected by the People, or appointed, as the Legislature may direct."[130] The office at issue having been created by an Act of the Legislature must therefore be one that is filled by the People through a general election, or appointment. The law at issue

[128] *Daily Alta California*, June 1, 1857.
[129] *People ex rel. Aylett v. Langdon* (1857) 8 Cal. 1, 3.
[130] Id., at 5.

provided for the election of a candidate by the Legislature, who would then hold office until his successor was appointed. Perley's construction of the language was that the office was one that the Legislature would fill at its creation, but that afterward the Governor would make appointments for two-year terms. He thought that the language of the law made clear that "it was never intended by the Framers of the Constitution to allow the Legislature to create the office, and then to fill it by an election by themselves."[131] Such a procedure would violate the Appointment Clause, as well as the commitment of the Constitution to the separation of powers. As the term of office was for two years, and the law itself was silent as to a particular date on which a term would begin, it was logical to infer that the term began from the time the Governor made the appointment. As such, Langdon's term had yet to expire.

Chief Justice Murray didn't quite see it the same way. He distinguished the *Reid* case by noting that it involved the appointment by the Governor to fill a vacancy. It did not involve the Legislature's power to select an incumbent. The Governor only appoints when both a vacancy occurs *and* the Legislature fails to act, and his appointment lasts either until the unexpired term ends, or the Legislature opts to properly elect a candidate. Once the Legislature makes a selection, its candidate assumes his office for the full two-year term, commencing at the time of appointment. As for Perley's argument that the exercise of the power to appoint is a violation of the separation of powers, Murray said the power was one exercised by every State's legislature and cannot be erroneous here. Langdon wasn't entitled to remain in office and must give way to the duly appointed successor.

Perley's service to the Know Nothings wasn't quite concluded. In the fall of 1855, W. S. White ran for the office of Sacramento County Sheriff on the Know Nothing ticket. Like nearly every candidate running on the slate, he prevailed and assumed office. When his term expired in the fall of 1857, he refused to yield up to his successor the tax monies collected while in office, and expressed his intention to continue collecting the tax and passing it on to the Treasury. No one denied that a law enacted in 1853 had vested the

---

131 Id., at 6.

duty of completing the execution of all unfinished business, including the collection of taxes, with the outgoing sheriff, nor that Section 33 of the Revenue Act of April 29, 1857 transferred the duty to the incoming incumbent. An amendment passed the next day, however, exempted Sacramento and several other counties from the change in law. The new Sheriff, Dr. William Stark Manlove, elected as a Democrat and no doubt committed to ending the Know Nothing insurgency, sued to strip White of his continuing control of County monies. He lost in Judge Charles H. Botts' courtroom in Sacramento, then appealed to the Supreme Court.[132] At the High Court's bar, Perley's adversary, future Governor Milton Latham, argued that "the fifty-fifth section of the Act of Twenty-Ninth April, 1857, repealed the thirty-ninth section of the Act of Twenty-Ninth April, 1851, and that the Supplementary Act of April 30th, 1857, did not revive it, and could not do so, under the provisions of the Act of March 14th, 1853, which provides that the repeal of a repealing act does not revive the act repealed without express words."[133] Finding this almost incomprehensibly complex argument to possess "a great deal of force," Justice Burnett nevertheless noted that such a construction of the relevant statutes here would lead to the conclusion "that neither the old or the new sheriff would be authorized to collect the unpaid taxes," that "the former sheriff would not be compelled to deliver over the assessment-roll to the new sheriff, and the latter would have no means, and no authority, to make the collections." Not possessing a clear statement of the legislative intent behind the act preserving the former sheriff's power to complete the collection of taxes, Justice Burnett inferred that with respect to incumbents holding office at the time the Act took effect, the Legislature must have considered the completion of unfinished business to be "in the nature of a contract, binding in good conscience upon the State." The law, thus, was simply a means to avoid prejudicing the rights of incumbents operating under the earlier legislative scheme. Once they had passed from the scene, the law would become superfluous. Sheriff White, then, did indeed have the right to complete the unfinished work of his term.

---

[132] *Sacramento Daily Union*, October 22, 1857.
[133] *Manlove v. White* (1857) 8 Cal. 376, 378.

So it was that in his last bid on behalf of the Know Nothings, Perley prevailed. It was indeed a remarkable occasion that this son of New Brunswick, not even an American Citizen, had in the course of a mere year and half become perhaps the preeminent attorney in political cases, infused with prodigious energy, fearless in the face of equal or even superior legal ability, and perhaps more likely to prevail than not in situations where most would shrink from controversy and seek a more placid circumstance. Perley had saved Judge Terry, successfully defended Samuel H. Brooks, championed the cause of the State Controller and thereby thwarted a retaliatory impeachment, protected the post-incumbency rights of Sacramento's Sheriff and had even preserved the Know-Nothing's resident physician in office for a year longer than many thought he was entitled. As a legal operator in a violent and unpredictable world, Perley was indeed a man to be reckoned with. As new challenges faced members of the political elite of California, it was to Perley they often would come seeking aid.

Chapter Six

THE MARIPOSAS

For many in the mid-Nineteenth Century and beyond, John Charles Fremont fitted the description of a man of destiny. Despite his troubled and unconventional childhood, entailing movement from place-to-place with a scoundrel of a father who masqueraded as a continental Frenchman and a mother still married to another man, Fremont somehow managed to obtain a recommendation to West Point, graduate from that institution, serve in the surveying corps and then lead a series of famed expeditions into the West, exploring, documenting and later publicizing through his detailed reports his findings, including the best paths to the Pacific Coast. Along the way, he fought and befriended Indians, overcame enormous hardships in the wilderness, led men fearlessly and with great resourcefulness and even claimed the provisional governorship of California after a fortuitous appearance in the territory at the moment rebellion and war caused a rupture with Mexico. Charges of insubordination resulted in his arrest by General Kearney and his transportation back east to stand trial before a court martial. A last-minute conveyance to Thomas O. Larkin of a power of attorney to seek out and purchase Mexican lands for investment and profit proved initially irksome to the explorer following his return. After prevailing before the military tribunal and returning west with his wife and children, he found his agent had carelessly purchased a large tract of land from Californio grandee Juan Bautista Alvarado far from the primary centers of the Territory's rapidly growing population, and described by the historian Nevins as "a wild tract in the Sierra foothills, more than a hundred miles from the ocean and nearly that far from any settlement," where "hostile Indians of the sturdy Cauchile tribe roamed…in such numbers that it was impossible to reside there, or to pasture cattle, which would have been quickly destroyed."[1] The

---

[1] Allan Nevins, Fremont: *Pathmarker of the West* (New York: Longmans, Green and Co., 1955), at p. 371.

land, said Nevins, "was apparently almost worthless," much to the outrage of Fremont, who impulsively threatened Larkin with litigation.[2]

Fremont's disappointment, however, proved premature. The rapid increase of the population following the discovery of gold and the formation of a Republic eagerly agitating for statehood rendered inevitable the necessity of selecting representatives to fill offices in the Nation's capital. Fremont's fame, apparent moderation with respect to the contentious slavery issue, and his relations with the rich and powerful back east, including his influential father-in-law Thomas Hart Benton, placed him at the forefront of candidates, and all but guaranteed his election to one of two new Senate seats. Drawing the short straw, his term was unnaturally brief, though he did manage while in power to sponsor numerous pieces of legislation helpful to the State. Illness and absence on the Atlantic Coast barred the dedication of his energies to re-election in 1850, but failure in that regard opened new vistas as the sovereign of what he later would refer to as a mighty principality, far from San Francisco, but flush with natural beauty and enormous subterranean riches. It would try his patience and his resources, too, as men the world over swamped the land armed with pick and pan, indifferent or even contemptuous of his claims, prepared to fight, often in confederation, against his prior possession, and convinced that he lacked any title to anything below the earth's surface between boundaries as yet unfixed and unconfirmed by the powers that be.

The massive estate was actually two: Las Mariposas and El Pescadero, in Mariposa and San Joaquin Counties respectively, but it was the former that offered the most promise due to the discovery of numerous veins flush with quartz and gold. For the next fifteen years of his life, Fremont would dedicate his prodigious energies to financing and developing what he anticipated would be an endless source of wealth. Its remoteness from water and rail transport posed enormous challenges and mandated the raising of capital to funnel into the Sierra foothills the resources necessary to fully exploit the property. His estate's history, noted Nevins "is a thorny and profitless maze… a perfect Pandora's box of complications."[3] Its

---

[2] Id.

[3] Id., at p. 394.

boundaries were undetermined, and there was great difficulty in obtaining an American title, "for Congress in 1851 passed an Act refusing confirmation to any California titles without absolute written proof, and the papers of the Mexican administration were nailed up in various repositories."[4] After the surface ore was exhausted, much of it by men he deemed trespassers, Fremont remained convinced that heavy investment in machinery to plumb the earth's unexplored depths would lead to the bountiful flow of treasure. But before investors could be coaxed into lending him the needed capital, assurance that he even owned the land was demanded.

One of the bills he sponsored while serving as California's Senator was an Act to facilitate the confirmation of California land titles. The Act was heavily modified by his colleagues and gave way in time to a version signed by the President in 1851 that not only provided a process for confirmation, but also created the formal commission that Volney Howard would serve as chief counsel during the latter half of 1853.[5] As his agents sought investors in England and elsewhere, Fremont moved to perfect his title with federal authorities in accordance with the law he sponsored. He filed his claim with the Commission early in 1852, and by the autumn of 1853 it was being contested by the Attorney General of the United States.[6] His fortunes received a mighty boost when the Commission confirmed to him the Rancho las Mariposas, "containing 10 square leagues, bounded on the north by the Sierra Nevada, on the east by the River Choachilles, on the south by the San Joaquin, and west by the Merced."[7]

Fremont's sense of relief following confirmation was short lived due to the Attorney General almost immediately appealing the matter to the U. S. District Court. Despite Fremont's retention of Volney Howard, Rufus Lockwood and other luminaries of the California Bar to steer the case in favorable fashion past Judge Ogden Hoffman, the Land Commission's decision was reversed,

---

[4] Id.

[5] W. W. Robinson, *Land in California* (Berkeley: University of California Press, 1948), at pp. 99-100; *Sacramento Daily Union*, April 20, 1853; and *Sacramento Daily Union*, December 17, 1853.

[6] Nevins, op. cit., at pp. 395-396.

[7] *Daily Alta California*, January 1, 1853.

prompting Fremont's own appeal to the Supreme Court of the United States.[8] There, the issue was not merely Fremont's title, but the protection, or devastation, of "rights originating under grants from the foreign government with which the United States had concluded a treaty."[9] In time, Fremont's attorneys, Senator John J. Crittenden and his own brother-in-law, William Cary Jones, memorably battled Attorney General Caleb Cushing "and charmed a large and brilliant audience...by a discourse of unusual interest and strength, a good portion historical, and having the attractiveness of romance, and all of it, such as to engross the attention of the Court, the Bar and all hearers."[10] Crittenden, it is said, "brought into the argument, not only legal acumen and research, but all the impassioned eloquence that has distinguished his most powerful efforts, whether in the Senate or before judicial forums, and was listened to with marked attention by a crowded audience of the beauty and intellect, at present congregated in the city."[11] By the time it was over, Chief Justice Taney was convinced of the merits of Fremont's case and he and his brethren on the Court confirmed the Land Commission's original decision on the grounds that Mexico's grant to Alvarado was valid, that any conditions of the grant were excused, and that the decade old conveyance vested title in the property to Fremont.[12]

Victory in the Supreme Court signaled both to Fremont and potential investors the prudence of any action to develop the Estate. His first endeavor to do so was "a shadowy arrangement with the banking house of Palmer, Cook & Company," facilitated by transfer of an ownership interest in the property, "though not fully reflected in legal instruments."[13] The banking house advanced Fremont money "to carry on the suit for the recovery of the Mariposas estate, for a certain portion of it, if successful."[14] As the bank's interests became one with Fremont's, its lawyers, Rufus Lockwood, Hall

---

[8] *United States v. Fremont* (1853) Hoff. Land Cas. 20; and *Daily Alta California*, January 8, 1854.

[9] Charles Warren, *The Supreme Court in United States History*, Volume II (Boston: Little, Brown, and Company, 1926), at p. 350.

[10] Id.

[11] Id.

[12] *Fremont v. United States* (1854) 17 How. 542.

[13] Nevins, op. cit., at p. 396.

[14] *San Francisco Morning Globe*, August 19, 1856.

McAllister and Colonel Charles James, formed Fremont's very formidable legal team.[15] The bankers were interested in preserving the estate and profiting from it, but also in politicking to protect any investment and enhance it through advantageous legislation. As the Whig Party disintegrated on the national level and the Democracy split asunder in California over the issue of slavery, Fremont entertained thoughts of seeking the Presidency himself. Chief among those piquing a renewal of his political ambitions were the principals of Palmer, Cook & Company, especially Joseph Palmer, who met with leaders of the nascent Republican Party in Washington, D.C. in November of 1855 "to persuade them that Fremont was their best candidate."[16] Within a month, Frank Blair, Nathanial Banks, Preston King, Salmon P. Chase and Charles Sumner were in agreement that Fremont was the most suitable person to advance their Party's fortunes: an opponent of the expansion of slavery possessing Southern roots and a Western base of support.[17] A less flattering report held that Palmer and his colleagues, far from persuading Party elders of Fremont's superior merits, spent $50,000 to purchase the nomination.[18] By March of 1856, Fremont was officially a candidate, and a memorable, bruising campaign epoch commenced.[19] Inevitably, his relationship with his primary financial backers became an issue, and soon all the unsavory attributes and actions of the banking house were imputed to the candidate. One California paper, "in a long and venomous article, reviewed these business affairs and also accused Fremont of complicity with Palmer, Cook & Co., in trying to swindle the public in exploiting the Mariposa mines."[20] The reform-minded James King of William defended Fremont, but not without acknowledging that "'this disreputable firm has lost thousands of votes for Fremont in this State,' and that it had injured him more than any other factor.'"[21]

---

15 Edward Bosqui, *Memoirs* (San Francisco: Edward Bosqui, 1904), at pp. 72, 84, and 94-95.

16 Nevins, op. cit., at p. 426.

17 Id., at p. 427.

18 *San Francisco Morning Globe*, August 19, 1856

19 *Daily Alta California*, March 20, 1856.

20 Nevins, op. cit., at p. 447

21 Id.

After his defeat in the Fall canvas, Fremont and his family returned to California, arriving in San Francisco early in 1857, and then made their way to Mariposa with the intent of residing there permanently. In the wake of his victory in the Supreme Court of the United States, he was intent on establishing the concrete bounds of his estate. On the basis of his federal patent, he had already applied to State authorities for the measuring off in an irregular pattern seventy square miles along both banks of the Merced River. The State balked at the request on the grounds that compactness was more in keeping with the interests of the public, members of whom had already established themselves within the bounds Fremont requested. The whole tract, surveyed by John Coffee Hays, containing twenty-nine different gold-bearing veins, "had been overrun by prospectors who had cut up its fields, chopped down its timber, and used its grass at will," but not without severing from him the privilege of paying the taxes, now assessed at sixteen thousand dollars a year.[22] Overcoming the opposition of State officials, Fremont obtained the requested bounds, only to face legal opposition by the most powerful of the interests prejudiced by the outcome, the Merced Mining Company, which was rumored to be behind the emergent armed hostility of the individual miners operating in the area.[23]

The Merced Mining Company had snatched possession of the richest veins in the estate, including the Josephine, during Fremont's preoccupation with the Presidency and had invested a large sum of money in mining infrastructure. Its proprietors were of the view that lack of actual possession by Fremont, not to mention the uncertainty of his boundaries, justified their presence on the land. Independent miners viewed the matter similarly, and appeared prepared to ally themselves with the Merced interests on the principal of the enemy of my enemy is my friend. General hostility soon gave way to organized resistance and the formation of what came to be known as the Hornitas League.[24] Fremont's careless finances contributed to the general dissatisfaction and caused his own workers to revolt, seize control of one of the veins in

---

[22] Id., at p. 463.
[23] Id., at pp. 463-464.
[24] *Daily Alta California*, January 28, 1857.

his possession, and vow not to relinquish it until they'd been compensated for their work. To quell the riot, estate counsel Rufus Lockwood hurried to San Francisco, obtained up to $18,000 from Palmer, Cook & Company and returned to settle up with the disgruntled employees.[25] The resolution of this in-house disturbance hardly assuaged the concerns of those settlers and miners aligned with Merced, and it was they who invited Merced's new corporate counsel—who formerly represented the United States against Fremont in the matter that was ultimately decided by Chief Justice Taney—to address a meeting and give his views as to "the present location of the Fremont grant."[26] Initiation of a lawsuit by Fremont's lessee, Biddle Boggs, to eject Merced and obtain damages for Fremont's exclusion from the land, generated intense agitation throughout Mariposa and captivated attention all over California.[27] Trial in Judge Burke's court in Mariposa in time commenced, leading to a ruling that while Fremont had title to the surface, the mineral rights were another matter, and as Merced had possession for the purpose of extracting ore, an injunction protecting their interests from interference by Fremont was certainly in order. A post-trial motion to dissolve the injunction failed, but posting of heavy bond caused a suspension of the order pending the outcome of an appeal to the State Supreme Court.

Fremont was absent from the State when Judge Burke issued his ruling. He didn't return to California via the steamer *Sonora* until August.[28] Within a short time he was back in Mariposa, where his arrival had been anxiously awaited, and where he was soon reported to be "attending to disputes about his great claim there."[29] Fremont's affairs were said to have "become sadly confused by want of a proper management in mining operations," and wobbled on the edge of disaster as the dispute with Merced, "waged with so much legal acumen between the Merced Mining Co. and the agents of Col. Fremont," came closer to the brink of resolution by the Supreme Court.[30] A man of remarkable energy and a need for

---

[25] *Daily Alta California*, May 24, 1857.
[26] *Daily Alta California*, June 23, 1857.
[27] *Daily Alta California*, May 15, 1857.
[28] *Daily Alta California*, August, 14, 1857.
[29] *Daily Alta California*, September 13, 1857.
[30] *Daily Alta California*, September 14, 1857.

constant movement, he was soon abroad again, on the East Coast, on a mission to find money, likely to service the interest on a loan used to purchase, for the sum of $250,000, a mining ditch from a private operator.[31] There was too much at stake to remain still.

While the case against Merced was pending in the Supreme Court, Fremont's cause suffered a horrendous blow with the loss at sea of his chief counsel, Mr. Lockwood. It was in the terrible sinking of the steamer *Central America* whereby he met his end, but not before playing the hero by ensuring the entry of innumerable passengers, including his wife and children, onto lifeboats from which they were later rescued.[32] Lockwood's genius was uncontroverted, as was the high regard in which the legal community of Northern California held the man. For days, the Courts of the State were closed and the entire City of San Francisco took on a subdued and sullen character. Nevertheless, the litigation had to go on. Fremont's massive tax liability was to be tested in Court in February of the new year, even as his agent, H.G. Worthington, filed up to a hundred ejectment suits on the threshold of the lapse of the statute of limitations.[33] But far more vital to Fremont's interests was the Biddle Boggs case against Merced, which now would have to be argued without the participation of the charismatic Lockwood. Though attorneys of far more than mere passing competence, co-counsel Heydenfeldt and Botts were hardly up to the task of replacing the brilliant chief counsel, hence it was hardly a surprise that the Court found in Merced's favor in March.[34] Bowing to the argument of the formidable S. W. Inge, Judge Burnett concluded that when Juan Alvarado obtained the Mariposas from the Mexican Government, the mineral rights were reserved to the state, and that when the United States assumed sovereignty over the territory, all that was reserved was assumed along with it.[35] The confirmation of Fremont's patent only vested what Fremont himself had obtained via purchase from Alvarado during the period of

---

[31] *Daily Alta California*, October 17, 1857; and *Daily Alta California*, October 19, 1857.

[32] *Daily Alta California*, October 23, 1857.

[33] *Daily Alta California*, February 8, 1858; and *Daily Alta California*, February 14, 1858

[34] *Daily Alta California*, March 17, 1858; and *Daily Alta California*, March 19, 1858.

[35] *Merced Mining Company et al. v. Fremont et al.* (1857) 7 Cal. 130.

direct federal control, hence the mineral rights remained with the United States until their implicit conveyance to California upon the advent of Statehood.

Appalled over the Court's disregard for what he believed was controlling precedent, Heydenfeldt quickly filed a request for reconsideration.[36] Prior authority, he contended, held that while mineral rights may or may not have reposed with the government, "to authorize an invasion of private property, in order to enjoy a public franchise, would require more specific legislation than any yet resorted to."[37] Other legal authority, he noted, supported the right of any man to prospect on public lands, but not on private property such as Fremont's Mariposas. The Court's odd decision, he said, threatened to upend innumerable prior transactions involving "thousands of acres of land containing the precious metals" and entered into by purchasers harboring utter "confidence that they would hold them in good faith forever."[38] For the Supreme Court to now say "that the law is different leads to a result which shocks the sense of justice of all mankind; ignores the very basis of the social compact; leaves society without safety, without law; and subject merely to the arbitrary edicts of each man's will who happens to sit as judge."[39] Only chaos and inconsistency would now ensue, he predicted, with the engrafting onto California's common law system principles of foreign law that the State's legislature had expressly repealed.

Fremont returned to California in April, in the company of financial agent A. A. Selover, attorney Colonel James and the historian H. H. Bancroft, and was back in Mariposa soon afterward.[40] Fremont had earlier brought several cases against Merced in the federal District Court in the Court's diversity jurisdiction, no doubt hoping for a ruling better than the one obtained from Judge Burnett. These he dismissed, only to file within days a suit helmed by Hall McAllister, praying that the Court "restrain the defendants from cutting down and wasting the oak timbers on his ranch in Mariposa County," and averring "that the

---

[36] *Daily Alta California*, March 30, 1858.

[37] Id.

[38] Id.

[39] Id.

[40] *Daily Alta California*, April 13, 1858; and *Daily Alta California*, April 27, 1858.

defendants have cut down hundreds of his best trees, and are now engaged in cutting down more, thus doing great injury to his property."[41] The Merced had barely answered this latest suit when conflict in the disputed ground erupted, prompted in part by the frustration of those opposed to Fremont over the "manifest injustice…such a maze of quibbles and fictions" characterizing the entire Mariposa litigation. There was suspicion, too, that Judge Burke, who once had seemed such a proponent of the settlers, had been corrupted in some way by the wiles of Fremont and his financial backers.[42] Agents of Merced reputedly bribed a watchman of Fremont's Black Drift Mine to leave his shaft open to them and had at once entered and fortified it with the ruffians at their command. Six of Fremont's men held out in two other shafts, "entrenched themselves behind rocks, machinery, and powder kegs," besieged by the members of the Hornitas League. Fremont himself rallied those loyal to him and confronted the besiegers.[43] The stand-off was only relieved when Fremont's kinsman, Governor Weller, activated and deployed the State Militia.[44]

With the siege lifted, Fremont's action for possession of the Josephine vein could proceed. In late July, a jury in Judge Burke's court returned a verdict in Fremont's favor with respect to two individuals in possession of the vein, Messrs. Clark and Vandewater, but not the Company. The circumscribed scope of the verdict was of no matter since the result was an order entitling Fremont to possession regardless of who stood in the way. However, when an unsympathetic Sheriff, Joshua D. Crippen, attempted to serve a writ of ejectment, he found persons other than those named in the writ in actual possession. When held to account for failing to act on the mandate entrusted to him, the Sheriff brazenly refused to execute the "writ against any other person or persons because by said writ I was only 'commanded to remove'" Clark and Vandewater.[45] He further explained that since the shaft had been made much longer and deeper by the trespassers, it was

---

[41] *Daily Alta California*, May 11, 1858.

[42] John Boling's Response to Governor Weller, *Daily Alta California*, August 2, 1858.

[43] *Daily Alta California*, July 16, 1858; and *Daily Alta California*, July 21, 1858.

[44] Nevins, op. cit., at p. 464.

[45] *Daily Alta California*, September 3, 1858

no longer possible to put Fremont in possession of what he was entitled to, which was, said the Sheriff, whatever possession he had at the time of the ouster. He was not required by the command of the writ "to restore to John C. Fremont the possession of the increased size and depth" of the mine.[46]

When Judge Burke ordered the Sheriff to jettison his rather esoteric concerns and serve the writ, the Sheriff appealed. It was at this point that D. W. Perley finally entered the case. Lockwood's absence from the litigation as a whole had remained obvious. A new addition to the legal team was necessary, and if Lockwood's charisma and brilliance couldn't be replaced, perhaps supreme confidence and an ability to fight in the face of the greatest threats would serve as an adequate substitute. Volney Howard apparently was neither available nor entirely suitable given his defeat in Judge Hoffman's court several years before. However, he remained of good reputation in the legal community, as well as on good terms with Fremont's backers, Palmer, Cook & Company. There can be little doubt that both he and Hall McAllister were friendly to the idea of the pugnacious Perley standing in the place that Lockwood once had occupied. Thus it was on September 4, 1858, that Perley presented his argument in the Supreme Court defending Judge Burke's ruling ordering Crippen to serve the writ.[47] Of the reasons given by the Sheriff for non-action, Perley said "the first affords no legal excuse or justification, and the second is frivolous, nonsensical, and absurd." The Sheriff, he explained, was ordered to do two things, eject Clark and Vandewater, and to give the Plaintiff peaceable restitution of the property. Though Crippen said he couldn't eject the two men because they weren't there, he still could have put Fremont in possession, but refused. Of the Sheriff's response as a whole, Perley characterized it as "inveigling, uncertain, inferential, and argumentative." He had, in essence, constituted himself an appellate court and determined the legal force and effect of the jury's verdict, and replaced that verdict with one of his own: that is, that the Merced Mining Company was in peaceable and quiet possession of the property, and that it was entitled to the possession as against Fremont and all the world. The

---

[46] Id.

[47] *Fremont v. Crippen* (1858) 10 Cal. 211.

Sheriff's action was not only procedurally invalid, but factually unfounded. The jury may well have failed to find that Merced had unlawful possession, but this was hardly the equivalent of a finding that its possession was lawful, or that its entry wasn't forced. The better position truly was that a "writ of restitution puts everybody out of possession holding adversely to the plaintiff," whether their identity is expressly stated in the instrument or not. The Sheriff had a duty to execute the writ, not question it.

It was hardly a disadvantage for Fremont that of the three Justices on the Court, one was an intimate friend of his new attorney. Nor was it unwelcome when Judge Terry was assigned the writing of the opinion. Terry was off-put by the Sheriff's apparent view that the jury found that Merced was in lawful possession of the premises, rather than Fremont. Such a view, in his mind, was untenable. "The peaceable and actual possession of the plaintiff is incompatible with the lawful possession of another."[48] The verdict for Fremont that he was entitled to possession, he said, was "conclusive against the possession of the Merced Mining Company."[49] The more difficult issue, he thought, was whether the Sheriff could dispossess parties who were strangers to the proceedings and who were not named in the writ. Terry concluded that he could. The object of the relevant statute concerning forcible entries, he explained, "would be entirely defeated if a defendant, after judgment, could, by transferring the possession to a stranger, prevent the execution of the writ."[50]

Shortly after Terry and the Court found for Fremont, Crippen appealed again, this time citing lack of opportunity to be heard before the decision of the Court was rendered. Little weight did the Court give to this rather desperate measure, hence it was easily rejected.[51]

The victory in the matter was of tremendous import: it put the Pathfinder "in possession of the whole of the Great Johnian Vein, the largest and richest in California and…the world, which 500 men

---

[48] Id., at 214.
[49] Id.
[50] Id.
[51] *Daily Alta California*, October 2, 1858; and *Daily Alta California*, October 12, 1858

could not exhaust in 500 years."[52] In his first outing, Perley had proven his value to Fremont's cause.

No sooner had the Crippen matter resolved than Perley was back in Judge Burke's Court addressing the matter of Fremont's long-delinquent taxes.[53] Fremont had been assessed $8,000 in taxes as owner of the Mariposas, but for a variety of reasons, including his forcible exclusion from the land by trespassers, he hadn't paid. In January of 1858, Sheriff Boling had brought an action for sale of the Estate for settlement of the delinquent tax debt. Perley countered the action with a request for an injunction on the grounds that Boling was in fact no longer Sheriff, hence his suit lacked any foundation in the official status necessary for him to act against the Estate. Perley prevailed at the local level and then beat back an appeal in the Supreme Court. As if sensing a change in momentum following the addition of Perley to the legal team, one of Fremont's financial backers now expressed optimism as to the outcome of the Biddle Boggs matter. Reinforcing this optimism was the fact that Peter Burnett was no longer on the Court and had been replaced by Joseph G. Baldwin, whose views appeared to be more friendly to Fremont's interests—largely because he had formerly been one of Fremont's attorneys. Fremont, this particular backer opined, "can rely with confidence on having all vexed questions settled in his favor."[54]

Fremont's prospects were to worsen apparently, before they improved. In November of 1858, Judge J. M. Bondurant issued an injunction restraining the Sheriff from execution of Fremont's writ of possession and preventing the restoration of the disputed premises, with the exception of the upper shaft of the Josephine Vein.[55] Meanwhile, Fremont's debt to the County, though stayed by Perley's defensive maneuver, had yet to either be reduced or resolved. Fremont's property taxes remained in arrears and the County was eager to collect.[56] As various legal actions were launched against him, Fremont sold a portion of the Mariposas to C.

---

[52] John T. Howard to John James Dixwell et al., October 1858, Papers Relating to the Sale of a Portion of Fremont's Mariposa Estate, 1858-1859, BANC MSS 85/128c.

[53] *Fremont v. Boling* (1858) 11 Cal. 381.

[54] John T. Howard to John James Dixwell, supra.

[55] *Daily Alta California*, November 12, 1858.

[56] *Daily Alta California*, November 27, 1858.

K. Garrison and planned for the development of a quartz mill.[57] With the Sheriff supposedly on the hunt for him and Fremont actively evading service of process, Fremont arranged for the settlement of his tax debt and readied, with Perley's aid, for a return to the Supreme Court.[58]

Taking momentary leave of the Fremont matter, Perley attended to the request of the County of San Francisco to assist in the prosecution of a sensitive case during the absence of the District Attorney. The case was the prosecution of the lawyer Richard F. Ryan and his client, R. C. Brooks, along with the latter's brothers. The case originated in a business deal gone wrong, between Brooks and steam boat commodore William M. Lubbock. Desiring to build a steam powered vessel and operate a commercial transit business, but lacking the capital to do so, Brooks agreed with Lubbock to borrow $30,000 to build the vessel and then operate as partners for a year, with Lubbock owning half the boat until the debt was paid off. The boat was built and put into operation. Though the enterprise yielded revenue, Brooks grew dissatisfied. He accused his partner of fraud and sued him in Stockton for breach of contract and deceit.[59] A judgment hardly concluded the controversy between the men, as litigation commenced for proprietorship of the vessel itself.[60] The original contract and title documents from the previous case, on file in the San Joaquin County Court, having disappeared, Captain Lubbock's ability to prove his claim faded. Based on information provided by a clerk formerly employed by one of Brooks' attorneys, police learned that the missing documents were secreted in Ryan's office in San Francisco. A search was conducted on January 31 and discovery was made of the missing and obviously purloined material out of reach and out of sight behind a piece of furniture.[61] No doubt aware of Perley's occasional service as a public prosecutor, City officials contacted the busy man to

---

[57] *Daily Alta California*, December 8, 1858; and *Daily Alta California*, December 18, 1858.

[58] *Daily Alta California*, December 24, 1858; and *Daily Alta California*, December 29, 1858.

[59] *Sacramento Daily Union*, February 25, 1858.

[60] *Sacramento Daily Union*, February 2, 1859.

[61] *Daily Alta California*, February 1, 1859; *Daily Alta California*, February 5, 1859; and *Daily Alta California*, February 8, 1859.

inquire into his availability. When Perley appeared at the opening of the matter in Judge Coon's Police Court ready to prosecute Brooks, Ryan and others, he and opposing counsel proceeded to spend most of the time arguing arcane points of law in utter disregard for any of the evidence or witnesses in the case.[62] When the prosecution's star witness took the stand, Perley elicited what appeared to be damning testimony, utterly contradicting Brooks' former attestation that he had no knowledge of the whereabouts of the missing documents.[63] Nevertheless, Ryan's attorney sought a discharge of his client, which Perley opposed for lack of any rebutting testimony. As the matter had become overshadowed by the operation of a grand jury, the attorneys stipulated to a continuance that ultimately morphed into a dismissal when Ryan was indicted.[64] Continuing to act in the District Attorney's stead, Perley prosecuted the case in the Court of the Sessions, opposed by Alexander Campbell. The tension between the two men intensified as the trial unfolding. An incident was triggered finally when, during Perley's examination of a witness, Campbell "intimated that Perley was suggesting the answers he wanted to the witness." Typically offended at even the slightest impugning of his integrity, Perley exclaimed "Don't you dare to say so; don't you dare to say so!" Campbell dismissively said that he "would say what he thought," and if Perley had any doubt of his readiness to answer on the field of honor, he volunteered that he "was responsible for it."[65] After the men paused in open court in the midst of the trial to insist to one another how responsible they were and ready to take action to prove it, the case resumed its plodding course without, said the *Union*, "a duel growing out of the affair."[66] In the end, the jury could not convict, the defendants went free, and suits for malicious prosecution commenced. Perley's role in the affair, however, was at an end, just as his duties to Fremont were returning to focus.[67]

---

[62] *Daily Alta California*, February 4, 1859.

[63] *Daily Alta California*, February 8, 1859.

[64] *Daily Alta California*, February 22, 1859, and *Sacramento Daily Union*, February 23, 1859.

[65] *Sacramento Daily Union*, May 2, 1859.

[66] Id.

[67] *Sacramento Daily Union*, May 23, 1859.

Fremont and his family removed to San Francisco in the Spring of 1859.[68] In May, he was explaining to his financial backers that efforts to obtain loans in Boston for the development of the Mariposas had not as yet born fruit and he was now unable to service his existing debts.[69] The building projects that had been underway were now on hold due to further difficulties with Trenor Park, who was asserting an interest in the property "on account of moneys advanced, or said to have been advanced, to Mr. Palmer," of Palmer, Cook & Company. Disappointed in his desire for a formal partnership with Fremont, Park brought several lawsuits "which produced embarrassment, only temporary, but which obligates me," said Fremont, "to put the property in a state of defense and which obliges me to ask [for] aid and interference in furtherance of the objects of the trust mortgage."[70] What he needed was help with the delinquent interest payments, a stay preferably, so that he could complete the construction projects and start generating revenue. He proposed transferring title to a representative to act in his creditors' stead, and thought that an appropriate candidate for this position was either Major Keyes or Hall McAllister, whom he noted was serving with Perley as counsel for the Estate. No doubt it was Perley who urged on him the selection of David Terry, who was still on the bench but whose term was coming to an end. With Terry, Fremont said he had "no personal acquaintance," but harbored "the utmost confidence in his honor and integrity, and considering the magnitude of the case, he may possibly be induced to act."[71]

In the end, it wasn't Keyes or even McAllister, let alone David Terry, with whom Fremont entrusted the property. Instead, it was Perley himself. On June 20, Fremont and his wife conveyed to Perley for a mere $1.00 a large share of the El Pescadero Estate.[72] A similar conveyance of an eighth interest in the Mariposas occurred around the same time, as well as half of the distant Rancho San

---

[68] Nevins, op. cit., at p. 467.

[69] John C. Fremont to John James Dixwell, May 18, 1859, John C. Fremont Collection, BANC, C-B 397 (Part 1), Box, Folder 2.

[70] Id.; and *Trenor W. Park v. J.C. Fremont et al*, District Court of the United States, Equity Case Files, 1855-1863, NARA, RS 21, Box 9, Case No. 73.

[71] John C. Fremont to John James Dixwell, supra.

[72] San Joaquin County Deeds, A/9/556-557

Emigdio in the southern reaches of the great Central Valley.[73] Perley was now the owner of a substantial portion of Fremont's empire, charged with its careful management for the benefit of the Fremonts and their children. The responsibility, of course, was monumental. Three massive estates, separated from one another by many miles, each too large to suffer enclosure, and for too long entered unmolested by strangers intent on exploiting the ground for grazing and mining without a thought as to who might actually possess title. The well-known chaos of the Mariposas was nearly equaled by the condition of El Pescadero. In 1856, Fremont's agent Edward Bosqui discovered stock raiser L. R. Bradley and others in actual possession of much of the property.[74] Efforts to collect rents from the unsanctioned occupants produced revenue insufficient even to pay the State and County taxes owed on the land.[75] Portions of the land subsequently seized by the Sheriff for uncleared tax debts were put up for sale at public auction, only to be purchased by the squatter Bradley. On the eve of his being vested with the office of trustee, Perley confronted Bradley and negotiated a transfer of the tax certificate back to Fremont in exchange for $510.[76] Far more action was necessary to set the estate into order, but it was a start.

Unlike Rufus Lockwood, his predecessor as counsel for the Estate, who actually lived on the Mariposas, Perley apparently remained a resident of San Francisco, occupying a home in town with his daughter. His business was primarily in the Courts of the City, where he pursued an active law practice apart from his duties to the Fremonts. For some purpose, probably to speak with Fremont's confidant and financial supporter A.A. Selover, Perley was at the breakfast table of the International Hotel in San Francisco on the morning of June 26. Also present were Selover's wife, the lawyer Colonel James and his wife, and David Broderick, the leader of the Free Soil Democrats and the great foe of the Chivalry, but who was nonetheless close to both Selover and Fremont. Broderick was preoccupied with the ongoing political campaigns and was

---

[73] Mariposa County Deeds, G:239, and G:417; and Paul R. Spitzzeri, "Getting the Shaft: F. P. F. Temple and the Rancho San Emigdio, 1864-1876," https://homesteadmuseum.blog.com.

[74] Bosqui, op. cit., at p. 137.

[75] Id.

[76] Earle Williams, *Rancho El Pescadero*, Volume 1, at pp. 11-12, BANC MSS 80/58c.

much distressed by an account in one of the papers reporting the details of a speech delivered by David Terry concerning Broderick himself, little of which was particularly flattering. Leaning across the table toward Perley, he muttered "I see your friend Terry has been abusing me in Sacramento." Referring to Terry as a wretch who'd been expelled from the recent Democrat Convention, he noted the man should still be grateful for the clandestine support Broderick had provided him during the Vigilance disturbance, but obviously wasn't. "I have hitherto spoken of him as an honest man—as the only honest man on the bench of a miserable, corrupt Supreme Court; and now I find I was mistaken. I take it all back. He is just as bad as the others."[77] Not knowing of whom Broderick was speaking, Perley asked for clarification. When the Senator indicated that it was Terry of whom he spoke, Perley impulsively reacted, saying that were Terry in the room Broderick wouldn't dare use such language to the terrifying Judge's face. Broderick said otherwise and then appeared to mock Perley after the latter said he would inform his friend of the Senator's disrespect. Though rumors later spread that the two men had screamed profanities at one another, and that Broderick had even grabbed Perley by the nose and tweaked it, the conversation seems to have occurred in low tones, no doubt out of respect for the two women at the table.[78] Nevertheless, declaring that he would hold the Senator personally responsible for the language of insult and menace that had been used, Perley left the Hotel in a state of agitation. An uncomfortable Selover expressed "regret at what had occurred," to which Broderick replied that he had been "provoked into it by the attack of Judge Terry."[79]

After the incident's fatal consequences came to pass, many defenders of the Senator imagined that Perley's action had been instigated by Perley himself on behalf of a larger conspiracy of the Senator's political enemies in the Gwin faction of the Democrat Party. The historian Hittell speculated that Perley seized the moment as it presented the "opportunity of placing himself in a

---

[77] Theodore H. Hittell, *History of California*, Volume IV (San Francisco: N.J. Stone & Company, 1898), at p. 222-223.

[78] *Daily Alta California*, June 28, 1859; and *Sacramento Daily Union*, September 19, 1859.

[79] *Sacramento Daily Union*, September 19, 1859.

position of great prominence by taking up the Terry and especially the Chivalry fight against Broderick, professing to be highly incensed with Broderick's sneer."[80] Such talk of conspiracy likely wasn't well founded. Rather, the incident reflected Perley's impulsive nature and his reflexive defense of a friend with whom he'd enjoyed a strong bond since his time in Texas. Senator William M. Stewart was probably closer to the truth years later when he noted that Perley "was not happy unless he could start some personal difficulty."[81] Perley himself said he had "never been either a political or personal enemy of Mr. Broderick," nor harbored much interest "in the success of any ticket," and denied that he commenced any attack at all. Rather, it was Broderick's comments that provoked the excitable man to such a state of mind as to be capable, even willing, to kill his momentary adversary. Perley's preoccupation with the Fremont Estate litigation and his law practice generally leaves little support for any theory other than Perley's personal vexation over Broderick's lack of decorum being the moving factor in the lawyer's subsequent conduct.

An increasingly irritated Perley apparently left the scene of the disagreement and went about finding a second to deliver a formal challenge to the Senator to a duel. Reports, whether accurate or not, were that up to 30 different individuals declined any involvement. Finally, he was able to convince Samuel H. Brooks to act temporarily until the arrival of E. J. C. Kewen, who reportedly was willing to play the role on Perley's behalf.[82] Early in the morning of June 27, Brooks went to the International Hotel and delivered to the Senator's servant Perley's card, which read, "Sir: for the unjustifiable and unprovoked insult I received from you this morning at a public table, and in the presence of ladies, I demand satisfaction due from one gentleman to another."[83] Believing Perley's "mode of procedure"—of having one man deliver the message with a reply to be sent to another—was "so unprecedented," Broderick felt that he "had no recourse but to decline the recognition of any note coming under the circumstances

[80] Hittell, op. cit., at p. 222.

[81] William M. Stewart, *Reminiscences* (New York: The Neale Publishing Company, 1908), at p. 120.

[82] Hittell, op. cit., p. 222.

[83] *Stockton Weekly Democrat*, July 10, 1859.

by the hand of a servant." Brooks and Kewen then appeared personally and spoke to the Senator, explained the discrepancy in the procedure, apparently to the Senator's satisfaction. The rapid spread of word of the pending challenge and the appearance of the matter in the press supposedly offended the Senator, who insisted such affairs were of tradition to be prosecuted in utter confidence. Blaming Perley for the indiscretion, he informed his challenger that such rumor mongering had "placed it out of my power to" meet him on the field. In a letter to Perley sent via a "negro" servant, he chided Perley for making a challenge he knew the Senator could never actually accept. "Your own sense of propriety should have taught you that the positions we relatively occupy are so different as to forbid my acceptance of your challenge." Perley had reputedly highlighted this disparity in their conditions only days before when attesting under oath of his status as a subject of Queen Victoria in federal court in an effort to remove one of Fremont's cases from State to federal jurisdiction. "The giving or accepting a challenge could not, therefore, affect your political rights, as you are not a citizen of the United States." Ending the communication as condescendingly as he could, he explained that he could only accept a challenge from "a gentleman holding a position equally elevated and responsible," but even if the two men had been similarly situated, he wouldn't have accepted anyways during the present electoral season due to the fact that it was well known that his enemies were striving to force him into difficulties. "I cannot afford at the present time to descend to a violation of the Constitution and the State laws to subserve either their or your purposes."[84]

Perley no doubt went into a rage upon receipt of the communication, partly because of the insult embedded in the Senator's rebuff of his challenge on the basis of Perley's inferior position—something no doubt reminding him of the reasons he left his native land—and partly because it was delivered by the hand of a mere servant, rather than the Senator's second, Joseph C. McKibben. He instructed Kewen to contact McKibben and express his utter inability to recognize how "the fact of foreign birth should subject him to willful insult and deprive him of the ordinary means

[84] David Broderick to D. W. Perley, June 29, 1859, as reported in the *Stockton Weekly Democrat*, July 10, 1859. See also *Sacramento Daily Union*, August 3, 1859.

of redress." He could apprehend "no distinction of official position or otherwise, which enables one man with impunity to trample upon the feelings or outrage the sensibilities of another." Such unreasonableness, he reported, did have the singular benefit of freeing him to publicize the matter fully "and allow a candid public to determine the merits of this unexpected controversy."[85]

Rumors continued to spread, some of them no doubt utterly fanciful, such as the tale that Terry himself was preparing to intervene at once and "settle the difficulty between Mr. Broderick and Mr. Perley" by issuing a challenge of his own.[86] More accurate was the *Alta's* report that the "misunderstanding" between Broderick and Perley "has ended without bloodshed, or a violation of the laws of the State." The paper's condemnation of dueling as unchristian, and praise for Broderick in resisting indulgence in the same, could hardly have assuaged Perley's outrage, nor could the hint that Perley was but an instrument in a conspiracy to do away with the Senator. "The belief is quite general that there are certain political opponents of his who long for a chance to shoot him, either in a fair or unfair fight, and that efforts would be made sooner or later to involve him in a personal difficulty. It is wisdom on his part to avoid the traps set for him, and thus defeat all the plans of those in whose path he happens just now to stand."[87] Perley's response was to further justify his conduct and emphasize Broderick's insult of him "in the grossest manner," and "in the presence of ladies" no less, "without the slightest excuse or provocation of any kind." Broderick was a scoundrel and utterly disingenuous and quite likely a coward, who now attempted "to shield himself from personal responsibility for the outrage he has committed." The Senator's explanation of his declination to duel was "a tissue of falsehoods from beginning to end, and was a mean quibbling and dastardly evasion of the whole difficulty in which his misconduct has placed him." Broderick, he thought, seemed to believe "he could browbeat, insult and bully me as he has done other men with impunity. In this he found himself mistaken." Attempting to goad the Senator into casting aside his prior objections, he referred to the

[85] *Stockton Weekly Democrat*, July 10, 1859.
[86] *Daily Alta California*, July 1, 1859.
[87] *Daily Alta California*, July 6, 1859.

refusal "either to fight or apologize," as well as to Broderick's effort to shelter "himself behind the senatorial honors which he did not fairly win, but basely stole through a long systematic course of fraud, bribery and corruption."[88] The Senator, he concluded, was "as devoid of courage as he is of principle, and that he has no longer any right to call himself a gentleman."[89]

Perley's taunts did not go unanswered. The *Sacramento Register* declared that Broderick had every right to style himself a gentleman because he "has sufficient manliness and sense of duty to refuse Mr. Perley the distinguished honor of firing at him." It mocked the "consummate bravery this valorous knight exhibited to issue his challenge, when he knew it would not be accepted," and said any courage attributable to the man, in light of this knowledge, was undeserved, and could only have been presented as a cheap means "to manufacture chivalry capital," and to "enable this Knight of the Garter to swell himself into the proportions of a modern giant."[90] The *Stockton Weekly Democrat* said that Perley had "made himself notorious," and must be an ignoramus for recently declaring himself a foreigner and thus disqualifying himself from practicing law, which the commentator incorrectly stated is a privilege reserved exclusively to citizens.[91] Everywhere, the reports flew: to Buffalo, Nashville, Louisville, Augusta, Dayton, and even the great capital of Perley's native British Empire.[92] When word of the Broderick incident reached Perley's native province, he was acknowledged to be a son of Sunbury County, though judgment on his conduct was withheld.[93] Journals as far off as St. Louis castigated Perley as an "obscure lawyer," prompting at least one person to point out that he was actually "one of the shrewdest attorneys in California," and both "high tempered" and "fearless."[94] Presently

---

[88] *Stockton Weekly Democrat*, July 10, 1859.

[89] Id.

[90] *Stockton Weekly Democrat*, July 10, 1859.

[91] Id.

[92] See *Buffalo Daily Republic*, July 25, 1859; *Nashville Union & American*, July 26, 1859; *Reading Times*, July 26, 1859; *Louisville Daily Courier*, July 26, 1859; *Baltimore Sun*, July 26, 1859; *The Daily Exchange*, July 26, 1859; *The Daily Empire*, July 28, 1859; *Daily Constitutionalist & Republic*, August 2, 1859; *The Valley Spirit*, August 3, 1859; *The Morning Post*, August 8, 1859; and *The Morning Chronicle*, August 8, 1859.

[93] *The Head Quarters*, October 19, 1859.

[94] *Sacramento Daily Union*, November 7, 1859.

running for the office of State Treasurer, Perley's second, Mr. Brooks, was attacked for his involvement, and declared by some to be legally disqualified due to his part in the matter.[95] Broderick himself did not refrain from making a campaign issue of the dispute. In a speech at Weaverville, he accused Perley of being an instrument of the Chivalry, who had been "put forward by designing men, who desired to get rid of me." Perley was but a "little wretch" sent by his masters "to insult me, and, if possible, to involve me in a difficulty." Broderick denied the account of pro-Chivalry papers that he had "grossly insulted Perley at the public table of a hotel." He had, in truth, been with his friends—two ladies and two gentlemen—and the ladies never heard a word that passed between himself and Perley, "so quiet was the whole affair."[96]

Campaigning against Broderick's slate of candidates, Senator Gwin took up Perley's defense, accusing Broderick of "going through the State attacking private characters, and at the same time [announcing] that he will not be responsible, as in the San Francisco difficulty with Perley." Such a worthless person as Broderick, he said, was best ignored. "If we club him it will do no good; if we kill him it will only make him a martyr."[97] Reports of escalation of the war of words between Broderick and Gwin spread, including Gwin's reference to a willingness to "'settle their private griefs in a private manner,' coupled with sneers, insults and personal affronts on every occasion on which the elder Senator has alluded particularly to his younger rival." The Chivalry press was reported to have cast off any disguise of "the wish to force Broderick into a private encounter." The many "imputations upon the personal courage and honor of Broderick have been carried on since the Perley affair, and seem fully to corroborate his view of that matter, and that it was arranged by his enemies to provoke a hostile collision." The treatment of Broderick, it said, was consistent with the Chivalry's *modus operandi* in the State. "It has been reserved for this State to set an example of political rewards as the price of service under the 'bloody code' instead of the laws of the country. It has been reserved for our own people in our own day to endure the

---

[95] *Stockton Weekly Democrat*, July 10, 1859.
[96] *Sacramento Daily Union*, August 3, 1859
[97] *Sacramento Daily Union*, August 4, 1859.

humiliation and disgrace of an election contest conducted on the part of their United States representatives with a degree of vituperation and personal abuse that would shame a ward meeting in the City of New York."[98]

When election day came, on September 7, the Chivalry completely routed Broderick's faction.[99] Virtually the only loser on the Gwin side was Terry himself, whose own allies apparently had grown weary of his controversial adventures and nominated W. W. Cope in his stead. The following day, Terry abruptly resigned his lame duck position on the bench.[100] The report soon circulated throughout the State that Terry had left Sacramento by steamer in the company of Perley and was intending once in San Francisco to call Broderick's bluff that the Senator couldn't accept any challenges during the pendency of the election.[101] Terry soon sent a note to Broderick demanding retraction of the offensive statement about his honesty, or lack of it, and when Broderick temporized, followed the note with a challenge delivered by his second, Calhoun Benham. Within a short time, it was said all of San Francisco was caught in "a fever of excitement…in regard to the rumored duel," with every tongue inquiring where it was to come off and whether the combatants were to fight with pistols or rifles.[102] When report came that the matter was to be resolved the following morning, "some twenty carriage loads of persons, anxious to witness the blood scene," flew from town to be sure not to miss the exchange of fire, only to find that the report was false. Police intervention and a short appearance of the parties before a judge delayed matters, but a meeting finally occurred on the morning of September 13, on the shores of Lake Merced in San Mateo County.[103] Accompanying Terry in his carriage were Benham, Samuel H. Brooks, a brother of John Coffee Hays, and his physician, Dr. Aylett, who was also the supplier of the pistols—the same set he had used in his own duel

---

[98] *Sacramento Daily Union*, August 6, 1859

[99] H. H. Bancroft, *History of California*, Volume VI (San Francisco: The History Company, 1888), at pp. 730-731.

[100] Id., at p. 731.

[101] *Stockton Weekly Democrat*, September 18, 1859, reporting from *Sacramento Bee.*

[102] *Daily Alta California*, September 12, 1859.

[103] Benjamin Cummings Truman, *The Field of Honor: Being a Complete and Comprehensive History of Dueling* (New York: Fords, Howard & Hulbert, 1884), at p. 396.

with Dr. Langdon a few years earlier. With Brooks handling the requisite rituals of the code duello, the two duelists inspected their weapons, took their places a murderously short distance apart and fired. Broderick's weapon discharged well short of the mark. Terry's fired a second later and sunk its slug into its target's chest. Thinking the bullet too wide to have wounded the Senator mortally, Terry quietly departed the field.[104] Among those in the rather large crowd that had journeyed in a fleet of buggies was Duncan Perley, and he was one of those in attendance, no doubt, who watched idly as Broderick's friends on the field struggled to lift him into a litter and carry him away.[105] It was, said the *San Francisco Call*, "in very bad taste for Perley, the originator of Tuesday's difficulty, to be on the ground." Though he had every right to be present, "good taste would have dictated that he should not have been present where he might have an opportunity of exulting over a fallen foe."[106]

The outcome of the duel caused a sensation. It was in some ways the culmination of years of acrimonious political combat between two wings of the Democrat Party. Whether the duel was a result of a plot or not, the inflamed state of the passions of the politically involved in the few short years before the outbreak of the Civil War rendered bloodshed all but inevitable. One commentator of the day, forgetting Broderick's operation of a Tammany-inspired urban racket, lamented the loss of a "fearless champion of principle, the relentless opponent of political corruption, the persistent antagonist of political combinations dangerous to the interests of the public."[107] Another said the Senator was the victim of the violence of an enemy, sacrificed "to satisfy the malignity of a polluted partyism."[108] Broderick's own words, reported by Senator E. D. Baker, were that he had been killed because of his opposition to human bondage. Others toasted his commitment to the fight for "the great, grand principle of human liberty and against the

---

[104] *Sacramento Daily Union*, September 19, 1859.

[105] *Sacramento Daily Union*, September 27, 1859, citing the *San Francisco Spirit of the Times*.

[106] *Sacramento Daily Union*, September 17, 1859.

[107] *Sacramento Daily Union*, September 27, 1859, quoting the *San Francisco Telegram*.

[108] Id., quoting the *San Francisco Call*.

extension of the blighting curse of slavery."[109] Later commentators such as Allan Nevins regarded the duel as but one of the many birth pangs preceding the calamity that would be the Civil War.[110] Rather more speculative in his thinking, Kevin Starr saw Broderick's demise as neatly fitting into a fable Californians were writing of themselves.[111] Arthur Quinn viewed it as the collapse of a center that simply couldn't hold.[112] For the participants it was a landmark—for Broderick, a monument figuratively identifying his grave site; for Terry a fork in the road that led him first to Nevada and then to the Confederate States of America. For Perley, it was but one of the many "ludicrous, pathetic and serio-comedic" incidents that constituted his life, and which would accumulate with the passage of the years.

The immediate fall-out for Perley of the duel was generally negative. Correspondents from Los Angeles reported the deep censure of Perley in those parts, and the general view that "the British Government ought to send for him and make him a member of Parliament for his valuable services" in slaying so great a defender of American principles.[113] A fire that consumed a stable he owned in Stockton exhibited all the telltale signs of an incendiary, but any nexus between the criminal act and resentment over Perley's role in Broderick's fall remained as unknown as the identity of the arsonist.[114] His principle employer, John C. Fremont, could not have been comfortable with Perley's role in inciting the incident, nor in Broderick's death. He was friendly with the Senator, and his primary investors also backed Broderick. Indeed, the man seated next to Broderick at the breakfast table when the entire chain of events commenced was Fremont's principle broker, and Colonel James (also present) had served as one of his attorneys. Not surprisingly, prominent at Broderick's funeral were Joseph Palmer,

---

[109] Id., quoting the *San Francisco Times.*

[110] Allan Nevins, *The Emergence of Lincoln: Prologue to the Civil War, 1859-1861* (New York: Charles Scribner's Sons, 1950), at p. 68.

[111] Kevin Starr, *Americans and the California Dream: 1850-1915* (New York: Oxford University Press, 1973), at pp. 122-123.

[112] Arthur Quinn, *The Rivals: William Gwin, David Broderick, and the Birth of California* (New York: Crown Publishers, Inc.: 1994).

[113] *Daily Alta California*, September 27, 1859.

[114] *Daily National Democrat*, November 2, 1859.

Charles W. Cook and A. A. Selover.[115] When subscriptions were sought for a monument to honor the late Senator atop Lone Mountain, not far from the resting place of Perley's late wife, Fremont was conspicuous in the generosity of his donation.[116]

Fremont's personal feelings about the circumstances and outcome of the duel appear not to have upset his confidence in Perley's adequacy as counsel for the Estate. Shortly after the duel, Perley, Fremont and Selover sought and obtained an injunction from Judge Burke in the Thirteenth District Court, restraining the Merced Mining Company and its agents and employees working at the Pine Tree or Josephine Veins from any further operations. A further request was made "for possession of the Black Drift, and also damages to the amount of $60,000 for waste and injury...by the defendant."[117] These efforts were no doubt in anticipation of what the moving parties hoped would be a successful outcome of the arguments scheduled to occur on November 8 in the Supreme Court.[118] Leading the effort in that matter would be Perley, whose brief was perhaps his finest to date.

Perley was not the only counsel appearing before the supreme bench in the matter. Heading into the courtroom with him were Solomon Heydenfeldt and several others, but Perley was the chief, and his argument was the one designed to overcome the concerns expressed by the Court back in 1858. A most helpful change in the Court's personnel since that earlier decision boded well for his effort. The dissenting Field was thankfully still on the bench, joined recently by Fremont's former counsel, Joseph Baldwin and the Kentuckian Warner Walton Cope, who replaced Terry. Opposing him was S. W. Inge, in addition to Perley's erstwhile collaborator Gregory Yale and the entire firm of Halleck, Peachy & Billings, who brought new arguments rooted in equity and fraud to reinforce those that had prevailed over a year before.

Perley's argument was divided into several parts. He argued first that the prior ruling of the Court ran counter to the long-

---

115 Alexander E. Wagstaff, *Life of David S. Terry: Presenting an Authentic, Impartial and Vivid History* (San Francisco: Continental Publishing Company, 1892), at pp. 208-209.

116 *Daily Alta California*, October 27, 1859.

117 *Daily Alta California*, September 25, 1859; and *Los Angeles Star*, October 8, 1859.

118 *Daily Alta California*, November 8, 1859.

established view in the United States that when the Nation assumed control over foreign territory and incorporated it into the Federal Union, any foreign law reserving mineral rights to the government terminated in favor of a presumption that such rights were retained by those seeking confirmation of their foreign titles. It was Robert J. Walker, Perley noted, who made the argument in the matter of *Walker v. Eldridge*, showing that every time the United States had been ceded territory from 1781 onward—whether by New York, Virginia, Massachusetts, Connecticut, North and South Carolina in the 1780s, by Georgia in 1802, or France in 1803—it never pretended to claim any mine on the grant to an individual pursuant to the law of the pre-cession jurisdiction, including grants made by France and Spain.[119] He argued, second, that while Mexico did indeed assert ownership over all mineral rights, this assertion was the result of despotic seizure during the imperial Spanish era, and was a principle that was "inconsistent with the public policy of the United States and with the rights of its citizens," hence they were implicitly annulled by the American conquest.[120] The United States took up possession of the conquered territory "as proprietor, and not as sovereign," meaning that when the land passed into private possession, all aspects of ownership passed with it, including ownership of the minerals beneath the soil.[121] That California could have succeeded to the sovereign prerogatives of Spain and Mexico when it entered the Union was impossible, since those prerogatives vanished with the governments of those nations over the territory in question. Those prerogatives could not have been inherited from the United States either, since the United States never possessed them. "If the United States could not acquire it, it is too clear from controversy that they could not hold it in trust for the State of California, or for any other purpose whatever."[122]

It had been suggested by counsel for the Merced Mining Company and by Justice Burnett that California also possessed the powers of the English Crown via the Common Law, including the power over the mineral wealth of the earth. Perley denied this contention as well. "The whole sovereignty of the State of California

[119] *Biddle Boggs v. Merced Mining Co.* (1859) 14 Cal. 279, 333-335.

[120] Id., at 337.

[121] Id.

[122] Id., at 338.

is vested in the People, and all the powers of the government are derived from the Constitution, which is the fundamental law."[123] All power not granted, he said, is necessarily withheld. The State's Constitution did not adopt the Common Law, either implicitly or explicitly. Instead, that body of legal principles had been received by an overt Act of the Legislature dated April 13, 1850, but only in so far "as it was not repugnant to, or inconsistent with, the Constitution of the United States, or the Constitution or laws of the State of California."[124] Even had the Legislature mandated the rule insisted on by Merced, it would have been void. If the State actually could adopt principles of sovereignty nowhere evident in the State's or the nation's constitutional scheme, "it might assume royal and kingly powers, and overthrow the Constitution altogether."[125] More significantly, there was no valid comparison between the Crown and the States of the federal union because the latter "are totally destitute of all the higher attributes of sovereignty."[126] The great powers, he observed, "of war and negotiation, or regulating commerce with foreign nations and among the several States, of coining money, of fixing the standard of weights and measures, of establishing rules of naturalization, of establishing post-offices and post-roads, of granting letters of marquee and reprisal, and patents for useful inventions, of punishing piracies on the high seas and offenses against the law of nations, are not possessed by the States."[127] Nor, he said, could the States enter "into alliance or confederation," nor "coin money, emit bills of credit, pass any bill of attainder, or make any law impairing the obligation of contracts."[128] In fact, "the States possess scarcely any sovereign powers whatever, and the idea put forth by the learned Judge [Burnett]...that the States possessed all the *jura regalia* of the King of England, has no foundation."[129] The fact that the King claimed the land's minerals was largely due his need to use them to support his fleets and armies, and as an incident to his prerogatives regarding coinage. As

---

[123] Id.
[124] Id.
[125] Id.
[126] Id., at 340.
[127] Id.
[128] Id.
[129] Id.

the State possessed no power in these areas, and was denied it by the federal Constitution, the maxim that the law ceases when the reason for it expires must surely apply.

Perley next argued that when California entered the Union, it did so in accordance with a federal statute, dated September 9, 1850, that included the condition that the new State should enact no law "whereby the title of the United States to the public lands should be impaired or questioned." This relinquishment of any title to the public lands in favor the United States was acknowledged by the State in Article 9 of its own Constitution, and via statute.[130] By yielding up any claim to the public lands within its boundaries, the State "relinquished all right to the mines on those lands, and every right of property appendant or appurtenant thereto."[131] This was so because the term "public land" had long been understood to include mines. Even if this were not so, California's claim would be untenable due to the fact that the land at issue, Fremont's Mariposas, wasn't public land at all, but private property. The power of Congress to dispose of mines on the public lands "gives Congress no right to dispose of private lands, nor to regulate the use that shall be made of such lands, nor the products thereof."[132] The Constitution grants Congress no such power, and none can "fairly be deduced."[133] Indeed, "if the lands were never public lands, the power of Congress never could attach to them in any matter whatever; neither can Congress prohibit the owners from using the mines on their own lands, in any manner they may think proper."[134]

Perley's final argument, based on various provisions of the Constitution of the United States was perhaps the strongest. The claim of the State to the mining rights on private property was contradicted by the Contract, Treaty and Takings Clauses.[135] The conveyance to Fremont by Alvarado and then the United States was an executed contract, which cannot be impaired by any law of a State. Even in the absence of the prohibition on the impairment of

---

[130] Id., at 341.
[131] Id.
[132] Id.
[133] Id.
[134] Id.
[135] Id., at 342.

contractual rights, the Treaty between the United States and Mexico, confirmed the interests of those holding property granted by Mexico prior to the end of Mexican jurisdiction over the State, hence it preempted any mere Act of the State's legislature. And any assertion of sovereign rights over minerals on private property would amount to a Taking, which required just compensation lest the Taking be rendered void.

When the Court took the matter under submission, Justice Baldwin opted to recuse himself due to his prior relationship with Fremont. Baldwin's recusal might have led to a split among the two remaining justices had Field and Cope been of different minds in the matter. Likely they did differ on the rationale, as indicated by Cope's silent concurrence. For reasons that might relate to a desire by Field to bar an appeal to the Supreme Court of the United States, Field took a less ambitious position than the one offered by Perley by avoiding Perley's constitutional arguments and rationale and finding less appealable State law grounds on which to rest his decision. Perley argued that Fremont owned the minerals along with the land above it. Field was rather more circumspect. The defendant's right against Fremont "as to the possession and use of the land must be based on the ground that the mineral does not pass with the soil as an incident to it, but belongs either to the United States or the State of California and that the defendant has an effectual license to enter upon the premises and extract the same."[136] Such a right, if it originates in federal jurisdiction, can only be one authorized by Congress. But here, "Congress has adopted no specific action on the subject and has left the matter to be controlled by its previous general legislation respecting the public domain."[137] Any inference of a right to enter Fremont's land based on the continuing sovereignty of the federal government over buried minerals even on private property is itself highly problematic from the standpoint of the State's competing sovereignty over rules governing such property. But this, said Field, didn't permit the State to authorize either explicitly or by implication the invasion of the private domain by those laying claim to a portion of the public estate in minerals. "The premises in controversy in the present case,

[136] Id., at 373.
[137] Id., at 374.

being private property, it follows that there is no pretense for the justification of the defense of a license from either the General or State governments."[138] Whether the minerals belonged to either one government or the other, "there must be more specific legislation than any yet resorted to, before the invasion of private property can be permitted in search of it for extraction."[139] Field agreed with Heydenfeldt's argument from over a year before, that Merced's position, if upheld, "must lead to the spoliation of landed estates, under the pretense of mining, without possibility of protection or redress on the part of the owner."[140] Were it to have its way, "where the land is held in private proprietorship…the whole might be invaded and for all useful purposes destroyed, no matter how little remuneration the product of mining."[141] He found it shocking to the notion of private property that "one man may invade the possessions of another, dig up his fields, cut down his timber and occupy his lands, under the pretense that he has reasons to believe there is gold under the surface, or if existing, that he wishes to extract and remove it."[142] Field hardly concluded that Fremont owned the minerals. Instead, he merely said that no one but Fremont had a right to access them even if they were part of the public domain. Perley might have been disappointed that Field resisted the force of his argument, but he couldn't have been unhappy with the outcome as a whole.

When the decision was published in late November of 1859, word spread rapidly. The *Alta* declared the obvious, that "by the decision not only is the Merced Mining Company entirely disposed and stripped of all their claims, locations, improvements, etc., but the rights of Col. Fremont in and to the tract Las Mariposas are indisputably and forever settled to be co-extensive with and equal to the rights of the holders of real estate in any portion of the Union; or in other words, he owns the land, woods, water privileges and everything else pertaining to real estate that has not by him been disposed of."[143] The *Star* reported that review by the U.S. Supreme

---

138 Id., at 378.
139 Id., at 379.
140 Id.
141 Id.
142 Id.
143 *Daily Alta California*, November 26, 1859

Court was to be sought, but morosely admitted that "our Constitution and laws do not provide for any appeal from our Supreme Court, so we fear this application will fail."[144] Complaints were made that the interior press, largely Democrat in orientation, was remarkably silent, despite the fact that the decision was "by far the most important one that has ever been presented for public consideration" — a response attributed to a partisan unwillingness to criticize a Court comprised entirely by Democrats.[145] At least one commentator praised the conduct of the case "with surpassing ability to a just conclusion by the Hon. Solomon Heydenfeldt, Hon. Charles T. Botts, and Duncan W. Perley."[146] Such praise, while welcome, appears to have been Perley's only compensation due to the cash shortage of his client. No doubt insisting that his enterprise would soon bear fruit now that title to the land was settled, Fremont handed Perley a promissory note fated never to be redeemed.[147]

In the wake of the Court's decision, Fremont's legal team, still headed by Perley, set about the "very delicate piece of business...to recover possession." Despite the ever-present threat of violence and blood "almost amounting to a civil war," the effort soon resulted in the recovery from squatters of most of the Estate's lands.[148] Meanwhile, the actual work on the land proceeded apace. The solid rock into which the Josephine and Pine Tree Mines delved made possible the forsaking of timber to shore up the shafts and facilitated use of powder to blast deeper along the ore rich veins. Massive quartz mills had risen on the banks of the Merced, in Bear Valley and elsewhere, and a road was leveled from the mines to the mills to allow for a steady conveyance of raw ore for processing, and was soon to be augmented by construction of a permanent

---

144 Id.

145 *Daily Alta California*, November 27, 1859

146 *The Newsletter*, November 21, 1859, as cited in Lona Ingham Robinson, *The Black Art of Our Land Tenure* (Hermosa Beach, 1914), at p. 45; and "John C. Fremont Victorious in his Claim to the Mariposa Estate," *The Cleveland Plain Dealer*, December 16, 1859.

147 According to a story appearing in *The San Francisco Chronicle* on November 28, 1920, Perley made a prudent sale of the note to William Sharon. When Fremont failed to honor it, Sharon filed suit to collect the debt on August 4, 1863. Despite retaining the services of Hall McAllister, Sharon never lived to see the resolution of the case. It was finally dismissed from the court's docket in 1920.

148 *Daily Alta California*, August 7, 1860.

railroad through the mountains and the chartering of a steamboat from Stockton all the way to the Merced River.[149] After Perley's tremendously effective representation, Fremont's enterprise, long held hostage to confused and competing claims as to the meaning of the law, appeared to be on its way to a degree of success equal to Fremont's most wild expectations.

The settling of the *Merced* matter in Fremont's favor presaged an end to litigation and a focus, instead, on development of the Estate. Perley's role, thus, was no longer necessary, though for the time being, he remained a co-owner of the Mariposas and trustee of the El Pescadero, charged with the selling or leasing of land to settlers, negotiating the quiet departure of squatters, and even instigating suits when necessary. Even before the *Merced* case was decided, he, Fremont and Selover had initiated a suit as plaintiffs against George Crenshaw and others in Mariposa for possession of a number of smaller mines in the Josephine Vein. The action was demurred to, but Perley, Charles Botts and Delos Lake convinced the Court of the demurrer's lack of merit and of the failure of the defendants to raise any legal defense, resulting in entry of judgment on December 1. In March, the three men commenced another suit to eject E. B. Holcroft and others and enjoin further waste of property within the bounds of Fremont's premises. A settlement seems to have been reached, hence the case was dismissed on March 13. This marked the final service of Perley to Fremont as trustee and lead counsel, for in a matter of days, Fremont appears to have released Perley from his duties and paid him $10,000 in exchange for the re-conveyance of his interest in the Mariposas. Hall McAllister continued to represent Fremont, including in a further case before the Supreme Court that wasn't decided until January of 1861. With a court fully in line with his views as to the supremacy of property rights, Chief Justice Field finally embraced the core of Perley's argument and concluded that long historical tradition supported the contention that in no instance had the United States asserted any right to the mines as being reserved from the operation of the patents. Instead, it had "uniformly regarded the patent as transferring all interests which they could possess in the soil, and everything imbedded in or

149 *Daily Alta California*, May 9, 1860; and *Daily Alta California*, December 12, 1859.

connected therewith."[150] Perley was no longer Fremont's counsel, but his work on Fremont's behalf had finally been consecrated in California's binding legal authorities.

As Perley's involvement with Fremont came to a close, so did his involvement with the consequences of his trouble with Senator Broderick. After the duel, Terry had retreated inland to Stockton with Colonel Thomas Hays, Calhoun Benham and County Sheriff John O'Neal. When lawmen came in search of him at Terry's home, they were confronted with four shotguns and the promise by Terry that he would remand himself over to law enforcement in Oakland.[151] Instead, Terry opted to appear for arraignment in the Court of the Sessions in San Francisco with his friend, Sheriff O'Neal. On application, bail was granted, and Stockton friends B. W. Bours and G. W. Trahorn, and his attorney in the Vigilance matter, Miers Truett, pledged themselves as sureties.[152] The hostility of the people of San Francisco toward him all but guaranteed a change of venue. Yet when his attorney A. P. Crittenden asked that the clerk be ordered to transfer the case to a more neutral location, the Judge refused.[153]

The issue of a change of venue was renewed in the Spring by new counsel Joseph P. Hoge, who presented a thorough declaration bearing Terry's signature detailing the former judge's experiences as a victim of intense animus due largely to his role as a leading figure in the law and order movement in 1856 and the rumored ongoing yet clandestine activity of the Vigilance Committee in the City, and that this animus was alive and well in every adjacent County save perhaps Contra Costa and Marin.[154] Though Perley wasn't acting as counsel of record, he did offer his support by submitting an affidavit attesting to the hostility against his friend in the City from the time of the Vigilance Committee until the present.[155] Judge Hager doubted that the officials employed in the courts were as biased as Terry claimed, but concluded none the less

---

[150] *Moore v. Smaw & Fremont v. Flower* (1861) 17 Cal. 199.

[151] William B. Secrest, *Dark and Tangled Threads of Crime: San Francisco's Famous Police Detective, Isaiah W. Lees* (Sanger: Quill Driver Books, 2004), at p. 86.

[152] *Daily Alta California*, September 25, 1859.

[153] *Daily Alta California*, December 13, 1859.

[154] *Daily Alta California*, June 8, 1860.

[155] Id.

that the man was entitled to a proceeding free of any suspicion of prejudice by those who would be charged with determining his fate.[156] The Judge's order indicated that a change of venue was mandated on account of his belief that there was not "an intelligent person in this community who has not formed an impression, which it would require evidence to remove, that the defendant fought a duel, and that his antagonist fell."[157] In accordance with the rulings of the Supreme Court, "unless such men, when examined, misrepresented the true state of their feelings, they would not be competent to serve as jurors."[158]

Once the case was removed to Marin County, visiting Judge James Hardy of Calaveras, an Ohio born member of the Chivalry and a close friend of Terry's, proved highly partial to the Defendant. When some delay was had in the arrival of the prosecution's witnesses, Mr. Hoge rose and said to the Judge "that if the prosecution had no testimony to offer, he should move that a verdict be rendered immediately."[159] Judge Hardy agreed and explained to the jurors that "under the statute, where no testimony was offered on behalf of the prosecution, it became his duty to instruct them to bring in a verdict of not guilty, and this verdict they could bring in without leaving their seats." In this rather questionable manner, Terry was acquitted, but his life in California, for the time being, was in ruins. He therefore took the proceeds of a sale by Perley of a mining claim and made for Washoe and the Comstock Lode to place the money in a joint account and exercise his discretion in the prosecution of investments for their mutual benefit.[160]

Perley's would-be Second in the duel that was never consummated, Samuel H. Brooks, also encountered trouble in the wake of Broderick's death. Unlike Terry, Brooks had managed to prevail in his quest for higher office in the September of 1859 General Election—in his case, the office of State Controller. Some doubts, of course, were expressed that he was disqualified from

---

[156] *Daily Alta California*, June 9, 1860.

[157] *Daily Alta California*, June 12, 1860.

[158] Id.

[159] *Sacramento Daily Union*, July 7, 1860.

[160] A. Russell Buchanan, *David S. Terry of California: Dueling Judge* (San Marino: The Huntington Library, 1956), at p. 113.

serving due to his involvement in Perley's attempted duel and Terry's successful one. When the time came to take office, he received his commission from the Governor, took the oath administered by Justice Baldwin, submitted his bond and then asked the current incumbent to make way. That incumbent, A. R. Meloney, refused. His reason was that the Governor had appointed him in September of 1858 when a vacancy occurred, and now, using an argument nearly identical to Perley's own on behalf of Dr. Langdon, insisted that he was not merely entitled to complete the unfinished term of his predecessor, but to an entire two-year term the Controller was ordinarily elected to fill. The parties first appeared in the District Court in Sacramento in February, with Perley and Attorney General Thomas H. Williams as counsel for Brooks, and Frank Hereford and Mr. Long for Meloney.[161] As the matter remained pending, some consideration was entertained in the Legislature for a law freezing Meloney's pay until the litigation was resolved, though it seems to have died in committee due to concerns over the constitutionality of depriving an acting officer of his compensation.[162] When Brooks managed to take physical control of the office in March or April, he commenced drawing his salary, but as the Court had not yet reached a decision in the case, Meloney continued to receive a paycheck as well.[163] After some delay, the Supreme Court resolved the dispute by ruling that Meloney's appointment had been for the purpose of filling a vacancy and was intended to endure for the remainder of the former incumbent's unfinished term of office.[164] Brooks, with Perley's help, was thus confirmed as the rightful Controller of the State of California—a fitting compensation perhaps for his willingness to stand by Perley's side in the contest with Senator Broderick.

Though he had long been closely associated with the Chivalry branch of the Democrat Party, Perley does not appear to have been actively involved in party politics. He defended the Chivs in Court, but only because the client in question was a friend who reached out for aid in a time of need. He may have harbored some sympathy for the predominant ideology of the South, which embraced a

161 *Sacramento Daily Union*, February 24, 1860.
162 *Daily Alta California*, February 9, 1860.
163 *Sacramento Daily Union*, May 8, 1861.
164 *People ex rel. Brooks v. Meloney* (1860) 15 Cal. 58.

suspicion of federal authority that may well have dovetailed with the pride his native New Brunswick exuded when contemplating its separation from the United States. He was unlikely a supporter of slavery, though the indignity he felt when Broderick's black servant delivered a message to him may reflect a racial bias that transcended party lines. The extreme animosity the Republican and anti-Lecompton Democrats levelled at him for his role in the death of Broderick, however, may have motivated him to take more interest in the defeat of those factions as the next election approached. For that reason then, it may be that Perley was reported to have joined Volney Howard, Solomon Heydenfeldt, John Weller, James Ben Ali Haggin, Lloyd Tevis, James D. Thornton, J. W. Mandeville, B. F. Washington, and Hall McAllister in signing a resolution of Chivalry Democrats endorsing Breckinridge for President and to have joined a committee with Terry, Benham and Tom Hays to canvas the State on behalf of the so-called "bolters.[165] His presence at the Lecomptonite Convention and support for the southern Democrats in the fateful election of 1860, though, was quite distinct from formal endorsement of a candidate, particularly in the wake of Broderick's exposure of his ineligibility to take part in American elections on account of his alienage. Consequently, Perley publicly denied he had signed the Breckinridge document and then quietly proceeded to check any further attacks on his right either to show an interest in the outcome of any balloting in the State or his status as a member of the American polity.[166] On August 8, in Judge Hoffman's District Court, he formally swore allegiance to the United States and became a naturalized American citizen.[167]

After more than a decade in the State, Perley had indeed become a man of some prominence in his profession and great notoriety personally. Having come to California in the company of many violent and ambitious men, he aggressively pursued success as an advocate in court and an investor in property. He moved from Stockton to the City, associated personally and professionally with

---

[165] *Sacramento Daily Union*, July 28, 1860; and *Daily National Democrat*, August 24, 1860.

[166] *Sacramento Daily Union*, August 3, 1860.

[167] *Daily Alta California*, August 9, 1860; and *New York Daily Herald*, September 3, 1860.

the best lawyers in the State, litigated numerous cases successfully on behalf of prominent men and women, including elected officials, and in time took the helm in litigation on behalf of the State's most celebrated resident, where his success was greater even than that achieved by the greats who preceded him. The Broderick affair elevated his profile substantially, but not entirely for the good; for instead of being known for his obvious and unquestioned talents in the courtroom, he was now tainted by a controversy made all the more poignant by the election of Abraham Lincoln and the crises of Secession and Civil War. Broderick became a martyr to the cause of Liberty and Union, and all those who opposed him were enemies of the state. Some of the latter ilk faded into obscurity, such as Senator Gwin, while others fled the State and joined the Confederacy, including Terry, Brooks, Benham, Lubbock, B. W. Leigh, Philemon Herbert, two sons of A. P. Crittenden and the latter's cousin Harry Innis Thornton, Jr. Perley remained behind, but in time, as the new decade advanced, he opted to leave California for the Washoe. Until then, the mixed bag of his prominence, and the oddity that was his life, would be on public display in San Francisco, Stockton and Sacramento.

Chapter Seven

NOT A LARGE PRACTICE

By the end of the 1850s, Perley's reputation as a brilliant practitioner, albeit an odd, erratic and hot-tempered man, was solidified. His eccentricities, combined with his association with a controversial group of politicians, may have repelled some from the thought of retaining him professionally, but when faced with a legal challenge, many others brooked no qualms about Perley filing or defending a suit on their behalf, answering a criminal charge or pursuing enforcement actions to recover outstanding debts and judgments. If the valiant champion of the Republicans in the campaign of 1856 had enlisted the man's services, others couldn't have been so apprehensive. During the late 1850s and early 1860s, Perley represented a fascinating range of small and large businessmen, prominent figures on both sides of the political aisle and members of the Chivalry who hadn't quite yet followed their hearts South. His moorings never tightly secure, and his venue unfixed to a particular courthouse, he would appear during this time throughout Northern California—in San Francisco, Stockton, Marin County, Sonora and elsewhere. He had, said attorney Edward J. Pringle, "not a large practice, but he had some important cases."[1] In truth, Pringle's assessment was only half right.

With the end of the Gold Rush, it was on the land itself, not beneath it, that wealth, or the dreams of it, were to be found. Though never a miner, Perley had almost at once upon his arrival in California become a speculator in property, buying up lots in Stockton and San Francisco, holding onto them and then turning them over to tenants in exchange for rents, or flipping them for a profit. He and Volney Howard became quite active in gaining control of lots on the outskirts of the growing city—in the districts known as the Western Extension and the Mission Dolores—but as the competition was fierce and the competitors cut throat, Perley's own impulsive and violent tendencies surfaced from time-to-time.

---

[1] *Pout v. Perley*, California State Archives, Supreme Court Records, Supreme Court Civil Case Files, San Francisco Office, 1850-1960, Case No. 3278.

In his actual law practice, he seems to have labored largely alone, with the aid only of a series of clerks: Samuel Neil, Blair Laurie, John P. Bell, and the English-born attorney turned saloon keeper, Frederick Pout, who later sued him for unpaid wages. Periodic collaboration short of actual partnership marked his relations with Howard, Hoge and even Gregory Yale, A. P. Crittenden and Judge Heydenfeldt. For a short time, from July of 1860 until sometime in 1861, he engaged in a formal partnership with Mansfield Compton and occupied offices with him at 110 Montgomery Street.[2]

It might have been normal, following a sufficient time to mourn the loss of wife and a child, for a man of Perley's age to establish a new emotional attachment to a woman and begin again the process of building a family. For whatever reasons, Perley resisted this norm. His family nevertheless continued to grow. Cousin Frederick, of course, was well established in the Stockton area as a farmer. Joining him now in the West was Frederick's older brother, James Edwin Perley, along with wife and children. James had followed somewhat in his own father's footsteps as a lumberman-farmer in central New Brunswick, but instead of remaining in Sunbury County, he tried his fortune in the provincial capital, at Fredericton. His business initially flourished. He cut and transported timber to St. John for export, operated a general store with the aid of one of his brothers and won appointment to a number of offices, including public auctioneer and constable under the charge of the High Sheriff of York County. In 1841, legal troubles brought on a collapse of his business. Defeat in the Circuit Court in Saint John compelled him to enter into a collusive arrangement with his uncle George Hayward. He conveyed title to certain claims to disputed timber to Hayward, then declared bankruptcy. At a public auction of his belongings he opportunely served as the auctioneer, and in that capacity declared his uncle the highest bidder. After a jury found James' actions culpable, attorney George Frederick Street tepidly defended the jury's verdict, while Street's brother John and Lemuel Allen Wilmot insisted (successfully) on the propriety of a new trial.[3] Street certainly bore no animus toward James, and relied on his

[2] *Langly's San Francisco Directory for the Year Commencing July, 1860*, p. 251.

[3] *Hayward & Others v. White* (1843) 2 Kerr 304.

strong arm when serving as a Justice of the Supreme Court to aid him in his personal effort to suppress the rioting of the Irish in 1847.[4] When called to the stand to testify against the rioters, James insisted under cross-examination by Wilmot on his lack of malice toward the Catholic defendants and his embrace of the Savior's admonition to love one's neighbor.

In 1849, with his business largely a failure, he returned to Sunbury County, where he settled down not in his native Maugerville, but on a 175-acre portion of the Belmont Estate in Lincoln Parish purchased from Hayward.[5] Here he must have learned of cousin Duncan's adventures in California, perhaps from his son Henry who had travelled west and served for a time as Duncan's law clerk. In 1851, the sense of intrigue having become too powerful to resist, he travelled West by steamer to view the place himself and determine whether it was a suitable land wherein to resettle his family.[6] Concluding that it was, he journeyed back to New Brunswick, resolved his affairs and prepared to move his household to the Far West. He cut his ties with his homeland on October 19, 1854 when he signed his Belmont property over to Duncan's brother William for £600.[7] He and his wife and four of their children arrived in San Francisco on November 20 aboard the steamer *Sierra Nevada,* with over 400 other passengers.[8] Undoubtedly, they met with cousin Duncan in the City, perhaps staying with him for a short interval, before making their way through the Sacramento Delta to Stockton—there to assert a claim to a homestead in the Rancho Moquelumnes. Son Henry had already staked out a lot on the Moquelumnes River dominated by a large white oak tree. Henry sold whatever interest he had in it to his father for $500, but actual title remained elusive.[9]

As his kin-folk deepened their roots in the Central Valley, and the whirlwind of Know Nothingism and the Vigilance uprising upended conventions in and around San Francisco and preoccupied

---

[4] *The New Brunswick Reporter & Fredericton Advertiser*, November 19, 1847.

[5] Sunbury County Registry Office, R/19/126

[6] Louis J. Rasmussen, *San Francisco Ship Passenger Lists*, Volume II (Baltimore: Genealogical Publishing Co., 2002), at p. 232.

[7] Sunbury County Registry Office, S/20/338

[8] *Sacramento Daily Union*, November 21, 1854.

[9] San Joaquin County Deeds, A/5/62.

a significant amount of Perley's time, his penchant for accumulating high profile clients remained in evidence. Besides Fremont, among the clients he served in the middle and late 1850s was one of the largest landowners in California, William Richardson. An advantageous marital alliance and good relations with Mexican authorities before the American conquest facilitated Richardson's acquisition of most of southern Marin County through the title he gained over the Rancho Sausalito. Ambitions to expand his business enterprise to include a fleet of cargo ships met with disaster when all of his ships sank with full loads in the space of six months, plunging his financial affairs into chaos.[10] Richardson borrowed heavily in an effort to accumulate the capital needed to stave off bankruptcy, and offered the Estate itself as security to creditors. In short time, the debt became staggering and the likelihood of escaping foreclosure appeared dim. An earlier retention of Volney Howard to aid in the confirmation of his Mexican title before the Land Commission prompted his resort to Howard's door, where he begged for help in saving the Estate from dissolution. Howard thought that selection of an appropriate person to act as a trustee for the Estate and extricate it from ruin was the best option. His inquiries led him to San Francisco attorney Samuel Reading Throckmorton. He and Perley subsequently "acted rather as the friends of both parties than as the attorney of Richardson," doing what they could to stall impatient creditors while Throckmorton attempted to raise capital in the East.[11] As payment for their services, the two attorneys each received an interest in the massive Estate that promised to grow in value as the years passed and demand for pasture and building lots in the ever-expanding demographic of California similarly ballooned.

But payment for services rendered might never come if the bulwark against creditors failed. In 1856, the host of note holders would wait no longer. Representing chief creditor Barton Ricketson, the attorneys Gregory Yale and Calhoun Benham demanded

---

10 Anna Coxe Toogood, *A Civil History of Golden Gate National Recreation Area and Point Reyes National Seashore*, Volume I (Denver: National Park Service, 1980), at p. 96.

11 *Howard & Perley v. Throckmorton*, California State Archives, Supreme Court Records, Supreme Court Civil Case Files, San Francisco Office, 1850-1960, Case No. 3637.

payment of both principle and interest in the amount of tens of thousands of dollars. When this first of many cases against the Estate hit the docket of the Superior Court in Marin County in the summer of 1856, Perley handled the matter with Howard in the early stages, but at some point, he grew ill and was disabled for a time from doing much of anything. So bad was his condition that E.L. Goold, who occupied an adjacent office, recalled that "I never thought I would see him alive for three months, or longer than that."[12] In the fall of 1857, Goold agreed to assume a role in the matter in exchange for half of Howard's and Perley's share in the Rancho Sausalito.[13] It proved a fortuitous decision. Of "stalwart frame, handsome face and pleasing manners," the Brooklyn native had come to California in June of 1855 after reading law between shifts at a saw mill in New Orleans and learning the basics from his mentors Judah P. Benjamin, Pierre Soulé and Henry Janin.[14] Very quickly he gained admission to the bar in San Francisco and was recognized as "a lawyer more conspicuous in the higher departments of the profession—the construction of constitutional law, and the litigation of important land case."[15]

Entering the fray on behalf of the Richardson Estate, Goold took command of the defense in the litigation brought by Ricketson and others, even as negotiations proceeded with the federal government to sell the 2,300-acre Lime Point portion of the Estate to serve as a lighthouse and military fortification. Howard's connections in Washington, D.C. and his and Perley's good relations with Senator Gwin undoubtedly smoothed a path that benefitted the Estate and led to the inking of a deal for the purchase of Lime Point for the monumental sum of $300,000. When the matter was brought to the floor of the Senate for approval, Senator Gwin "spoke very feelingly of the necessity of the Government procuring the site for military

---

[12] Id.

[13] This wasn't the only stake he passed on to Goold at this time. On August 29, 1857, Perley assigned to Goold all of his interest in the Juan C. Galindo Grant in Santa Clara County. Perley and Howard had contracted with Galindo to represent his interests on June 20, 1855 in exchange for half of all that portion of the grant they were able to confirm. See *Western Land-Owner*, April 1874 (Vol. 1, No. 1), at pp. 6-7.

[14] "An Eminent Lawyer Gone," *Daily Alta California*, January 29, 1880.

[15] Id.

purposes" and expressed his support for the appropriation.[16] Senator Broderick, however, seized on the matter in debate, pronounced the deal a swindle, and would later accuse Gwin of taking a bribe in exchange for his endorsement.[17] The outrage aroused by Broderick and the press prevented confirmation of the sale, and prompted instead the exercise by the government of its power of eminent domain.

With Howard's and even Perley's occasional assistance, Goold fended off Ricketson and the other creditors and sought to defeat the federal government's attempt to condemn the property. The Ricketson matter went to trial in July of 1858, and was then retried in August of 1859, with both results favoring the plaintiff.[18] Before enforcement of the judgment could occur, the federal government's condemnation action threatened to preempt all rights save those entitled to just compensation for a governmental taking. At a hearing of the matter in Marin County, Goold asserted that the reliance by the government on a statutory delegation of the State's power of eminent domain to the federal government was actually repugnant to the State Constitution. Judge McKinstry agreed, but was later overruled by Justice Baldwin and the State Supreme Court.[19] When a jury later settled on $125,000 as just compensation for the land, Goold appealed, supported this time by all of the mortgage creditors, each of whom viewed the higher sale price rejected by the Congress as more likely to lead to satisfaction of all of their outstanding claims. When Justice Baldwin and the Court reviewed the jury's award, they held the condemnation proceeding to be invalid due to the fact that a contract for sale had already been formed.[20] The good news for the Estate only got better when the Supreme Court reversed Judge McKinstry's foreclosure decree.[21] When encountering Perley on the street, Throckmorton "expressed himself perfectly satisfied" with Goold's exploits, particularly in

---

[16] "The Lime Point Swindle," *Nevada Democrat*, June 23, 1858.

[17] John Shertzer Hittell, *A History of the City of San Francisco, and Incidentally of the State of California* (San Francisco: A.L. Bancroft & Company, 1878), at p. 305.

[18] *Sacramento Daily Union*, July 13, 1858; and *Sacramento Daily Union*, August 8, 1859.

[19] *Gilmer v. A Certain Tract of Land* (1861) 18 Cal. 229.

[20] *Gilmer v. Lime Point* (1861) 19 Cal. 47.

[21] *Ricketson v. Richardson* (1861) 19 Cal. 330.

defeating Mr. Gregory Yale," and just "lauding him to the very skies."[22] Clearly, the Estate's interests, and Perley's, were in excellent hands.

While Throckmorton relied on Perley and Howard for counsel in Estate matters, he came to rely on them for aid in his personal affairs as well. One such affair involved a land purchase contract between himself and the heirs of Francisco Haro, San Francisco's first Alcalde. Well before the coming of American arms to the Pacific Coast, Haro had obtained from Governor Alvarado a large grant of land in the Mission Dolores, on what became the corner of Center and Dolores Streets and extending westward, and a second grant known as "Protrero." Neither Haro before his death in 1848, nor any of his eight children, were able to obtain a deed prior to the American occupation. Justice John McLean and the Supreme Court of the United States eventually upheld a Land Commission decision confirming the Haros' ownership of the Mission Dolores property, but Protrero was a more difficult matter.[23] To dispose of the headache and turn a profit, Haro's widow, Natividad Tissot, conveyed the property to the attorney Julius Rose, who subsequently transferred it to Throckmorton. Rather than peaceably enjoy his new property, Throckmorton received from Mrs. Tissot and her second husband the unsettling news that Rose had defrauded them and never paid the promised consideration. They brought suit in the District Court, but rather than contest the matter, Throckmorton sagely agreed to save time and litigation fees by entry into a compromise. He issued a note for $1,250 in exchange for a new deed. Confidence in the settlement faded when Rose returned to town and informed Throckmorton that the Tissots were lying; that he had indeed made good on the purchase price. Throckmorton returned to Court to undo the settlement and sought a continuance to prepare his case based on the new evidence, but was denied. An appeal was filed, and with it the posting of a bond equal to the contested amount.

In both his written brief and oral presentation before the Supreme Court, Perley argued in favor of a rescinding of his client's

---

[22] *Howard & Perley v. Throckmorton*, California State Archives, Supreme Court Records, Supreme Court Civil Case Files, San Francisco Office, 1850-1960, Case No. 3637.

[23] See *United States v. the Heirs of Francisco de Haro* (1860) 63 U.S. 293.

promise to honor the note on the grounds that the compromised action initiated by the Tissots was technically flawed. Mrs. Tissot was married at the time the note was received, hence had no authority to buy, borrow or sell given the legal incapacity of married women at that time. The relevant case law established that promissory notes were personal property, or chattels, and were deemed the possession of the husband, not the wife. It was true that no demurrer was raised by Throckmorton at the outset of the action, but this ought to be excused, Perley said, because the operative statute "reserves the right to make the objection at any time that the complaint does not state facts sufficient to constitute a cause of action." As the note belonged to the husband, the action belonged to him as well, and the joinder of the wife in the pleadings constituted a fatal defect demanding reversal.

Judge Heydenfeldt thought his friend Perley's reliance on procedural technicalities was outweighed by the interests of justice. "The objection that the wife is improperly joined comes too late; it should have been taken advantage of by demurrer." Mr. Throckmorton's only option, if he couldn't or wouldn't pay the debt, was to return the deed, or at least offer to return it.[24] For the time being, Throckmorton was obligated to honor the note. When Throckmorton refused to do so after the Supreme Court issued its opinion, the Tissots sued the men who signed Throckmorton's appellate bond as his sureties, including William A. Darling.

Following loss of a demurrer and then being nonsuited, Darling appealed to the State Supreme Court, with Perley as his attorney. Perley argued that in order to enforce the bond against the sureties, the judgment creditor "must exercise ordinary diligence…to collect the judgment from the principal before he has a right of action against the sureties." The undertaking itself, Perley said, was unsigned. While California had no rule on this point, many other jurisdictions required a signature, and this was certainly the better rule. Finally, there was the issue of the improper joinder of the wife in the action—a point Perley had already lost in the previous appeal. The wife only had a right to proceed if the property was her own. The principle he traced to the matter of *Snyder v. Webb*. It was a remarkable fortuity that the lawyer who had persuaded the court

[24] *Paul Tissot v. S.R. Throckmorton* (1856) 6 Cal. 471

of the soundness of the principle was the Tissots' own attorney, Mr. B. S. Brooks. Perley referred the Court to Brooks' excellent "argument in the case, showing that he then maintained the same grounds now contended for by appellants, and these grounds were fully sustained by the Court."

With the concurrence of Justices Terry and Field, Justice Burnett held that the terms of the undertaking lacked any statement of the obligation of those who would enforce it against the sureties to first seek out payment from the principal judgment debtor.[25] The lack of a signature by the sureties also was not material since the Court had the previous January decided that very point. The issue of the misjoinder of Mrs. Tissot received no credit either. No objection was made as to the inclusion of Mrs. Tissot earlier in the case, and Throckmorton himself admitted along the way that she did indeed possess an interest in the suit. So unmerited was the appeal that Burnett concluded that it appeared "to have been taken for purposes of delay."

Another of the prominent people Perley represented during this time was Andrés Pico, the brother of the last Mexican governor of California and a prominent Southern California landowner and politician. Pico claimed estates in the north, too—notably Los Mokelamos. The lingering ambiguity of title and the lack of any specificity as to the actual bounds of the tract probably contributed to a failure on his part to pay his annual property tax. Pico was also apparently alienating portions of the Rancho to settlers, hence argument was possible that the specific ground subject to the tax belonged to someone else. The uncertainties as to ownership hardly deterred the County from assessing the land for the tax and sending the bill to the most prominent of the claimants. Observing Pico's agent in Stockton receiving money for the purchase of some portion of the Rancho, Sheriff George Webster concluded that it was fair game to seize it in order to cover Pico's delinquent tax debt. The Sheriff approached the ongoing transaction and literally raked the gold coin "from the table into his hat and carried [it] away to his office."[26] In time, the Sheriff was charged with robbery and tried in Justice of Peace Walthall's Court, where it was determined that

[25] *Paul Tissot and Wife v. Darling et al.* (1858) 9 Cal. 279.
[26] *Daily Alta California*, July 30, 1857

Webster had "no right to attach moneys in the hands of a third party to satisfy [Pico's tax], much less to forcibly seize it without legal process; and that the transaction was robbery."[27] The agent, John Brodie, then sued to recover the money and for damages in Judge Creanor's District Court, but was unsuccessful due to the finding that the money he sought to recover belonged to Pico, not to him.[28] Pico then instituted a suit of his own and won restitution in the amount of $2,083, plus interest and a single dollar in damages.[29] The Defendant appealed on the grounds that the Plaintiff was estopped by the conclusion of the previous trial, but the Court held that "it would present a strange anomaly if a suit were brought by one and defeated on the ground that the property belonged to another, and then the other sued, if the last suit were defeated, on the ground that the first concluded the last plaintiff."[30]

Unable to recover against the Sheriff, Pico sought legal counsel to assist in the effort to claim against the sureties who guaranteed the Sheriff's bond. Perley's interest in Rancho real estate and the presence of his family on farms in the area hint that Pico knew Perley from earlier negotiations to secure Pico's acquiescence in settlement within his ill-defined domain. The Pico family's friendly relations with Fremont, from whom the latter obtained half of El Pescadero, may also have played a role in Perley's retention to recover against the sureties. In any event, once retained, Perley initiated a lawsuit. In response to the suit, the sureties attempted to introduce testimonial evidence that the Sheriff's underlying conduct didn't constitute a trespass and the property seized didn't belong to the Plaintiff. Sustaining Perley's objection, the trial court refused to admit the testimony. The judgment against the Sheriff, it ruled, "was conclusive of all the facts passed upon and decided by the record." Pico won a second judgment equal to the first, plus interest.[31] The sureties appealed, arguing that since they didn't have notice of the original suit, they were not bound by the earlier findings of fact. With the accord of Justices Field and Cope, Justice Baldwin agreed, noting that while "a judgment is always admissible

---

[27] Id.

[28] *Sacramento Daily Union*, August 22, 1857.

[29] *Sacramento Daily Union*, May 3, 1858.

[30] *Pico v. Webster* (1859) 12 Cal. 140, 142

[31] *Los Angeles Star*, May 21, 1859.

as proof of its rendition when that fact is important or relevant," it couldn't be charged to a stranger to the action.[32] The matter was retried in Judge Hager's Court in April of 1860 and apparently resulted yet again in judgment for Pico.[33] Yet another appeal was argued in the Supreme Court on September 7, 1860, and this time yielded an affirmance of the lower court's decision.[34]

Pico's legal troubles over taxes apparently did not provide any powerful incentive for him to comply with his obligations under the revenue laws. His debt grew when he failed to pay the assessments for the years 1859 and 1860. Rather than pay the $2,671.66 debt for these two years when suit was brought by the Attorney General under a special law enacted in May of 1861, Pico again retained Perley to oppose the government's action. Perley sought to dismiss the suit via a demurrer, alleging that the complaint was deficient because it failed to establish the court's jurisdiction by averring that the action was only brought after "the tax collector had failed to collect the taxes, by reason of his inability to find, seize or sell the property."[35] Such "vital and material" allegations could not be omitted from a pleading, he said, without fatal results. He noted, too, that the description of the property subject to the delinquent tax was "fatally defective." The Supreme Court agreed with respect to the first point. While it is true that the complaint stated that the action was brought "in pursuance of the act," it also omitted "altogether to state the fact that the failure of the Tax Collector to collect the delinquent tax for the reason above specified, or for any reason. Without such an averment the complaint shows no cause of action under that act."[36] The court agreed on the second point as well, and even ventured to opine that the defect in the description of the land subject to the tax might have been the result of the assessor's vagueness when describing the tract to be taxed.

Pico's troubles over taxation would not end here, despite the positive outcome. The government would persist in its effort to

---

32 *Pico v. Webster* (1859) 14 Cal. 202, 204

33 *San Joaquin Republican*, April 7, 1860.

34 *Sacramento Daily Union*, August 30, 1860; and *Sacramento Daily Union*, December 25, 1860.

35 *People v. Pico* (1862) 20 Cal. 595.

36 Id., at 597.

collect what it claimed was owed, and Pico would continue his resistance, though Perley himself would no longer be involved.[37]

Perley represented the less famous as well. In *Brotherton v. Hart*, the parties disputed ownership of an original town lot in the Court for the Twelfth District. At the trial of the matter the Court admitted secondary evidence of a deed to the Plaintiff, apparently without a prior determination that the deed itself was unavailable. The Plaintiff then proved the missing deed had actually been recorded with the Alcalde, but was subsequently mislaid.[38] After the Plaintiff prevailed, Perley moved for a new trial on the grounds that the secondary evidence should never have been allowed, and then appealed when the motion was overruled. The matter was argued in the Supreme Court on October 30, 1856 before a full bench.[39] The Court agreed with Perley that the introduction of the evidence of the deed was improper. "Parol evidence of the contents of a deed which has been recorded and lost, is not admissible unless the failure to produce the record is accounted for."[40] The parties apparently were displeased with the scope of the Court's opinion and agreed that all issues ought to be clarified before the matter was retried. The parties thus stipulated to an outcome and that Perley's subsequent motion for a new trial could be denied and then appealed. The matter was back in the Supreme Court on July 22, 1858 when it was argued, and again on the 27th, when the Court granted an additional ten days for the parties to submit their written briefs.[41] In an opinion published in August, Justice Terry couldn't comprehend the irregularity of adverse parties stipulating to defeat of a motion as a prelude to an appeal. He succinctly affirmed the dismissal with the words: "Having consented to the order, they cannot now question its correctness."[42] When one's closest friend couldn't assent to one's clever maneuvers, it would seem that legal trickery had found its true limit.

---

[37] *Daily Alta California*, June 29, 1864. Pico would win his private tax war against the County in the end, but only because the Supreme Court of the United States ruled that his putative grant was fraudulent.

[38] *Brotherton v. Hart* (1856) 6 Cal. 488.

[39] *Sacramento Daily Union*, October 31, 1856.

[40] *Sacramento Daily Union*, November 22, 1856.

[41] *Sacramento Daily Union*, July 23, 1858, and July 28, 1858.

[42] *Brotherton v. Hart* (1858) 11 Cal. 45; and *Sacramento Daily Union*, August 19, 1858

In 1857, Perley handled the defense against an action for ejectment from a half of a one-hundred vara lot (Number 110) in the City of San Francisco.[43] The lot was originally granted by Alcalde Leavenworth to a man named Harrison, who in turn deeded it to the Plaintiff, Squire P. Dewey and a joint tenant, Aristides Welch. To defeat the action, Perley argued that the Plaintiff's interest was incurably tainted by the fact that no law federal or state authorized Leavenworth's power to issue land grants. Leavenworth's authority was based on Mexican law, which no longer applied once the military assumed control of the State. Perley's argument was to no avail, hence he appealed to the Supreme Court. Chief Justice Murray thought the argument unsound for the same reason the Supreme Court had in the earlier matter of *Cohas v. Raisin*—that is, that at the time of the American occupation, the City of San Francisco owned the ungranted lands within the municipality's bounds, and its chief executive was authorized to dispose of the same, at least until the American authorities imposed new regulations. More persuasive was Perley's argument that the Plaintiff's action was invalid due to failure to join the joint tenant, Mr. Welch. Opposing counsel countered that a statute of 1855 had the effect of splitting the tenancy between the joint tenants, thereby making them functionally independent of one another, but the Chief Justice observed that the statute's application was entirely prospective. It didn't apply to tenancies already in existence when the statute took effect.

Perley came to the aid of the rising attorney Elisha Cook in the spring of the same year in a matter tried in the Superior Court in San Francisco. The case involved the assignment of a mechanics lien. When the assignee attempted to enforce the lien by foreclosing on the servient property, the property owner objected that the lien could only be enforced by the mechanic himself. The Court disregarded the objection, allowing the assignee to prevail, but also giving rise to an appeal helmed by new co-counsel. On appeal, Perley and Cook argued that while a mechanic's lien was assignable, the necessity of a writing invalidated the assignment at issue. The writing submitted to prove the lien at trial had not, in fact, ever been delivered, hence it was ineffective to transfer the

[43] *Dewey v. Lambier* (1857) 7 Cal. 347.

right. The underlying account hadn't been conveyed either, which was a necessity when a mechanic's lien was assigned. With this contention Chief Justice Murray agreed. The writing having never been transferred, and the account itself never assigned, the evidence of the writing should never have been admitted. The Chief Justice concluded that what was before the court was less an assignment than "an agreement to pay the plaintiff's debt out of a particular judgment."[44] After reversal and remand, the matter was again tried, and this time the property owner prevailed. When, at the instigation of the assignee, the case was reviewed a second time by the Supreme Court—this time without Perley's involvement—Chief Justice Terry observed that it had "been heretofore decided by this Court upon the same statement, and that decision has become the law of the case."[45]

In addition to controversies involving land, Perley represented parties whose property had been subjected to post-judgment levies by county sheriffs. The matter of *Perlberg v. Gorham* commenced after Sheriff William Gorham of San Francisco seized a stock of goods in Perlberg's possession, believing they were owned by judgment debtors, Makouski and Eisenburge. Perlberg claimed the goods as his own on the basis of a bill of sale from Makouski and Eisenberge, wherein the latter owed over $3,000. Perlberg prevailed at trial, and the Sheriff appealed. Perley's efforts proved unsuccessful in thwarting reversal and remand.[46] In *Gregory v. Higgins & Mann*, Perley represented a plaintiff in the Thirteenth District, in Mariposa County. The matter arose from a June 23, 1856 judgment against a man named Marshall for $952. In enforcing the judgment, the Sheriff issued a notice of garnishment. Marshall responded by producing a note indicating a debt to Higgins for $1,250, but not actually payable until January of 1857. When the date came, Higgins' partner Mann retained Perley's impeachment co-counsel, Philip L. Edwards, and brought another suit to recover a second debt from Marshall. Marshall responded with a memorandum stating he possessed the money, but was obligated to pay Higgins first. Higgins then intervened in the matter and

---

[44] *Ritter v. Stevenson* (1857) 7 Cal. 388.

[45] *Ritter v. Stevenson* (1858) 11 Cal. 27.

[46] *Perlberg et al. v. Gorham* (1858) 10 Cal. 120.

asserted the priority of his rights. When the Court found in Higgins' favor, Mann retained Perley, who filed an appeal. In the end, Justice Field concluded that Mann's attachment, having occurred prior to the maturity of the note, was incapable of binding the debtor.[47]

Sheriff Gorham figured in another of Perley's cases during this period. *Meyer v. Gorham* involved an effort to recover the value of personal property worth $4,000 seized by Sheriff Gorham pursuant to a post-judgment levy. Siegmund T. Meyer had previously issued a chattel mortgage to secure a debt owed by the firm of Mitchell & Nunes. Meyer later moved to foreclose on the property, but never actually dispossessed the debtors. The Sheriff then executed a post-judgment levy in an entirely unrelated matter against the indebted partners and seized the property via a lien. With Whig luminary Harlow S. Love as his counsel, Meyer sued the Sheriff on the basis of the priority of his instrument. When Meyer won, the Sheriff appealed on the grounds that the mortgage didn't bind parties other than the principles, and that since Meyer never actually took possession of the property, the property remained available for seizure by other creditors. On the strength of this argument, the judgment was reversed and the matter retried.[48] Again, Meyer prevailed, prompting another appeal by Sheriff Gorham. In this second appeal, Love enlisted Perley's aid, perhaps to avoid a repeat of the disappointing outcome of the previous appellate proceeding. Bringing Perley into the case certainly didn't make matters worse, but didn't help much either. In a decision issued on November 10, 1858, Justice Baldwin, with Terry's concurrence, held that "the plea of former conviction is not supported by the evidence, and was properly overruled. The objection that the evidence did not warrant the judgment is equally unsupported by the record."[49] As such, the judgment was affirmed.

The years 1858 and 1859 were among Perley's most active. How he managed his case load is difficult to fathom. In addition to the Fremont litigation, he was handling dozens of other matters, many of which went up on appeal. *Tissot v. Darling*, *Pico v. Webster*, *Brotherton v. Hart*, *Ritter v. Stevenson*, *Greggory v. Higgins & Mann*,

---

[47] *Gregory v. Higgins & Mann* (1858) 10 Cal. 339.

[48] *Meyer v. Gorham* (1855) 5 Cal. 322.

[49] *Meyer v. Gorham* (1858) 11 Cal. 392; and *Sacramento Daily Union*, November 11, 1858.

and *Meyer v. Gorham* certainly did, but they were not the only ones. In addition, there was *Phelps v. Owens*, arising from a deputy sheriff's seizure in Stockton of the Plaintiff's goods from the premises of a third-party debtor laboring under a court judgment. After the sheriff sold the property to satisfy the debt, the Plaintiff, Phelps, sued for the market value of the items. At trial, the Defendant asked for a jury instruction limiting damages, but Judge Creanor refused. The jury subsequently awarded not only the pre-market value of the property, but the lost profits and apparently exemplary damages as well. Not content to accept the jury's verdict as the final word in the matter, Owens added Perley to his legal team and pressed forward with an appeal. Speaking through Justice Baldwin, the Supreme Court held that because the seizure of goods by a public officer did not constitute a "willful and wanton trespass, or trespass marked by some circumstance of malice, oppression or fraud" neither the lost profits from the sale nor any exemplary damages were proper. Creanor shouldn't have rejected the proposed instruction. Because he did, the case would have to be retried.[50]

Phelps was followed closely by *Lawrence v. Knight*. The case originated back in 1853, when the Defendant Mr. Knight leased a lot to a Mr. Allen for seven years. In return, Allen would pay $350 per month and erect a number of buildings, the value of which would be reimbursed by the landlord. When Allen defaulted on his obligation, Knight entered the property, as the contract allowed, but only after waiting several months in vain for Allen to make good on the arrears. The Plaintiff Lawrence had an interest in the improvements as Allen's assignee and sued for the value of the same when Knight took possession. Knight demurred to the complaint and prevailed, hence Lawrence appealed. On Lawrence's behalf, Perley and Judge Heydenfeldt argued that equity demanded Lawrence be paid for the improvements. In an opinion issued on December 30, 1858, Justice Baldwin disagreed.[51] He explained that Allen and his assignee could not breach the agreement and then, by resort to claims in equity, come out ahead of where they would have been had the contract been performed. If Plaintiff was correct,

[50] *Phelps v. Owens* (1858) 11 Cal. 22, 25.
[51] *Daily Alta California*, December 31, 1858.

then "all a lessee would have to do, under a contract of this sort, to rid himself, at any time, of a bad bargain, would be to refuse to pay his rent, and claim at once payment for his improvements."[52]

In two of Perley's appellate cases during these years, the Supreme Court acted in rather summary fashion. Justice Baldwin curtly rejected Perley's appeal in *Magruder v. Melvin*. The appellant's case, he said "is supported by neither law, justice, or fact" and was "evidently intended for delay."[53] For the apparent waste of the Court's time, Baldwin added another five percent to the jury's award. Perley's former law partner, Justice Terry, was kinder in the matter of *Fee v. Starr*. There Leander Quint and James W. Coffroth had appealed the outcome of a trial, but shockingly failed to submit a properly authenticated appellate statement or bill of exceptions, in addition to a copy of the record signed by the trial judge or agreed to by the parties.[54] Without a reliable record, the Court opted to review the judgment roll, where no irregularities were disclosed.

Terry was similarly kind to Perley in the complicated matter of *Smith v. Dall*, originating in the Twelfth District.[55] The case arose from a dispute over land and entailed the attempt by one party to eject the other. Both parties derived their title from a grant issued to Charles Richardson by Alcalde Leavenworth in the twilight period immediately before the formal establishment of American control of San Francisco. The Plaintiff traced his title to parties who had received title from Richardson. The Defendant traced his title to Richardson through Malachi Fallon. With Perley's aid, the Plaintiff contended that Defendant's title was defective due to the failure of Fallon to record his deed. Defendant claimed Plaintiff's title was invalid because the seal the deed supposedly was under wasn't recorded in the recorder's book, and that the Defendant's own defective title was cured by the fact that occupation of the property by tenants who had no relationship with the Plaintiff gave constructive notice to the world of Defendant's interest in the land. The matter was assigned to a referee, who ultimately recommended that title be vested with the Plaintiff. Judge Norton set the

52 *Lawrence v. Knight* (1858) 11 Cal. 298.
53 *Magruder v. Melvin* (1859) 12 Cal. 559.
54 *Fee v. Starr* (1859) 13 Cal. 170.
55 *Smith v. Dall* (1859) 13 Cal. 150

recommendation aside due to what he perceived to be defects in fact and law and calendared the matter for trial. Arguing that the referee's recommendation was correct, Perley appealed. Once the matter was before the Supreme Court, Chief Justice Terry concluded that (1) the presence of tenants was not notice of Defendant's interest in the land, (2) the law did not require the recording of the actual seal, just a statement that the filing occurred under seal, and (3) the title of Plaintiff, as a bonafide purchaser for value, took precedence over anyone claiming through an unrecorded deed.

Terry again favored Perley in a matter arising from the Twelfth District. In *Steinbach v. Leese*, Perley represented the Defendant, Jacob P. Leese, the former Alcalde of Sonoma and a brother-in-law of General Vallejo. Leese and another brother-in-law, Salvadore Vallejo, had obtained a large land grant from Governor Alvarado, encompassing much of the embarcadero. After the American conquest, their title was contested. Vallejo tired of the conflict and conveyed his interest in some or all of the land to Leese, in exchange for a $20,000 mortgage payable if and when Leese was able to confirm his title. When Leese conveyed half of the property to Gregory Yale along with a promise to pay him $30,000 at a future date, Vallejo sued, alleging that payment of the long-deferred $20,000 was proper in light of the apparent benefit Leese had obtained from the breached agreement. Perley unsuccessfully demurred on the grounds that the complaint didn't allege that the conditions precedent for payment had occurred. He argued, too, that the transaction with Yale was essentially an employment contract. Yale was deferring payment for work to be done litigating Leese's title against the adverse claimants. If and when Yale won, he would be paid, and Vallejo's own rights would become ripe. After Vallejo prevailed against the demurrer and won at trial, Perley appealed. Upon reviewing the briefs and hearing arguments, Terry found that Perley was indeed correct that the complaint was deficient in relevant facts. "It is not alleged," he wrote, "that Leese has 'succeeded in the litigation which was pending at the time of the contract,' that he has 'entered into possession of the premises by virtue of the judgment of any Court,' or that he has 'consummated any compromise with the opposing claimants for the relinquishment of his or their claim.'"[56] As for the contention that conveyance to Yale was a breach for which damages were owed, Terry observed that "it is difficult to understand how the conveyance...could be construed into a breach of the covenant to Vallejo. It seems to have been made in furtherance of the very object of the contract.... The employment of counsel was absolutely necessary to the conduct of the litigation, and certainly the adoption of a mode of compensation which was calculated to stimulate the zeal of counsel, by making his compensation depend upon the success of his efforts, could not injuriously affect Vallejo."[57]

Terry wasn't as helpful to his old friend in a final case brought by Perley to the Supreme Court during the 1858-1859 period.[58] The matter had originated in the Thirteenth District, in Stanislaus County. The Plaintiff had issued a promissory note to the Defendant pursuant to a settlement. The note, however, was for an amount larger than was agreed. When the Plaintiff discovered the error he requested that the note be amended. When Plaintiff ultimately paid off the note, the Defendant refused to relinquish it, and even intimated that he might bring an action to enforce it for the stated amount. With Perley's aid, the Plaintiff sued for an order requiring Defendant to return the note. Defendant's demurrer failed, but his plea in abatement did not. Understanding that the Defendant had filed an earlier suit in the Twelfth District to enforce the note, the Judge dismissed the case. On appeal, Perley argued that while the Twelfth District case had indeed been filed earlier, the summons and complaint hadn't yet been served. Since service had been effected in his client's case in the Thirteenth District, that Court's jurisdiction over both subject matter and the parties was complete. Justice Baldwin didn't dispute this fact. Instead, he pointed out that Perley's case, though based on law, sought equitable relief in the form of an order to relinquish the note. Law and equity had been merged in a single court, but equitable remedies still required foundation on equitable theories. It was best, he said, for Perley and his client to pursue the purely legal action in the Twelfth District and resolve the matter there.

---

[56] *Steinbach v. Leese* (1859) 13 Cal. 363, 367.

[57] Id., at 368.

[58] *Smith v. Sparrow* (1859) 13 Cal. 596.

During this period, Perley did not use his skills as a litigator and advocate exclusively for others. At times, he sued on his own behalf, or was sued personally for offenses he committed, either actually or as alleged. He sued George T. Mayre in San Francisco when the latter failed to pay Perley for his legal services. After the action concluded in a judgment for Perley, Mayre happened to run into Perley's attorney at the County Clerk's office. Incensed over "harsh allusions to the character of Mayre" made at trial, Mayre tackled the man, and had to be pulled away by bystanders in the room.[59]

More significant was his defense of his family's continuing effort to retain possession of farmland in the 35,000-acre tract straddling San Joaquin and Sacramento Counties comprising the Rancho Sanjon de los Moquelumnes. The Rancho had been granted to Anastacio Chabolla by Governor Micheltorena prior to the American occupation, but no title ever passed in Chabolla's lifetime. Upon his death, his widow sold much of her interest in the grant to William Govers, who in turn transferred it to William Hicks.[60] The Land Commission rejected the claim, and Chabolla's heirs appealed to the District Court with the aid of A. P. Crittenden. After reviewing the record, and hearing testimony that Chabolla had constructed a home on the property, employed a steward, grazed cattle there and grew wheat, barley and other crops, Judge Ogden Hoffman reversed the decision.[61] U.S. Attorney Inge somewhat reflexively appealed the decision, as he did with many such cases heard in Hoffman's Court, but the appeal was dropped on the recommendation of Attorney General Jeremiah Black.[62] In the meantime, the uncertainty of title and the attractiveness of the largely unsettled land encouraged an invasion by a host of squatters. Hostility by Hicks and the Chabolla heirs led to efforts to repel the invaders, as well as push-back from the latter in response.

---

59 *Sacramento Daily Union*, July 14, 1859.

60 *McCauley v. Harvey* (1875) 49 Cal. 497, at 497-499.

61 *Heirs of Anastasio Chabolla v. United States, Reports of Land Cases Determined in the United States District Court for the Northern District of California, June term, 1855 to June Term 1858*, Volume I (San Francisco: Numa Hubert, Publisher, 1862), at p. 131.

62 William Thomas Carroll, Clerk of the Supreme Court of the United States, to President James Buchanan, August 17, 1858, in Sanjon de los Moquelumnes, Hiers of Anastasio Chabolla, Docket No. 306, California Private Land Claims, Records Group 49, National Archives.

The prosecution of James E. Perley and his sons Solomon and Charles for "malicious mischief" likely arose out of the Perleys' efforts to assert ownership of the homestead they had staked out in the disputed territory earlier in the decade.[63]

The Perleys' commitment to maintaining possession and acquiring formal title meshed well with the interest of other squatters in the area, and led, in October of 1858, to a meeting at Woods Ferry near Woodbridge and the organization of a Settlers' League similar to the ones operating in the Mission Dolores and elsewhere in the State. After winning election as Chairman of the League, James stated that "the object of the meeting was to devise some means to defeat or remove the survey of the grant recently made, or that portion of it lying on the south side of the Mokelumne River, and to deliberate on the best means of defending the just rights of the settlers."[64] When one of the participants noted that the Surveyor General had not yet either seen or approved the survey, a committee was formed "to consult, and if necessary, employ a competent attorney, to investigate the above matter."[65] A week later, the Committee reported that "legal gentlemen in Stockton...believed that the grant had not been surveyed where it belonged and there would be but little difficulty in getting the same removed."[66] The "legal gentlemen" surely must have included D. W. Perley himself; for it was he who drafted a remonstrance to the government that fifty-four of the squatters signed, asking the Surveyor General to assent to their contention that the land was part of the public domain on account of the Mexican grant being void.[67] Dissatisfied over the lack of response from the Surveyor General, Perley then wrote to Thomas A. Hendricks, Commissioner of the United States Land Office, to contest the survey being forwarded to Washington, D.C. for final approval. Without a formal hearing to confirm the accuracy of the survey, Perley said his clients would be deprived of their "legal rights and...property and suffer

[63] *San Joaquin Republican*, October 7, 1857.
[64] *San Joaquin Republican*, November 12, 1858.
[65] Id.
[66] Id.
[67] *Sacramento Bee*, November 11, 1858.

irreparable injury."[68] The correspondence proved effective in raising doubts about the precision of the boundaries. Though the grant itself was confirmed, the matter was returned to Judge Hoffman's Court for resolution of the uncertainty over the precise metes and bounds.

It appears that Hoffman never made a ruling on the merits of the case. Instead, it would be the State courts where the issue would be decided. The path to a decision commenced with the bringing by putative grantee William Hicks of suits to win damages and eject the Perleys and other members of the League from what Hicks contended was an illegal occupation.[69] As counsel for the defense, Perley lost the matter of *Hicks v. McMullin*, entailing an effort by Hicks to obtain a writ of replevin to gain possession of cord wood cut within the alleged boundaries of the grant.[70] In Hicks' separate effort to eject McMullin and the majority of other settlers, Perley prevailed, but only temporarily through a continuance.[71] Hicks' action against Matthew Borland to partition the land was similarly delayed.[72]

The ejectment suit against McMullin came to trial in April of 1861, with Henry Oscar Beatty and Henry T. Higgins representing Hicks, and James D. Thornton joining Perley on behalf of the settlers.[73] Beatty attempted to delay the matter via a motion to continue without success, forcing his client to finally play his hand and prove his right to exclusive possession.[74] The press excitedly reported the keen interest with which the public viewed the case due to the great consequence it had with respect to "the titles to the homes of hundreds of settlers," and the likelihood of a trial lasting several days, comprising "a vast amount of testimony, some of it very ancient," and likely to shed light on "some of the early history

---

[68] D. W. Perley to Thomas A. Hendricks, December 4, 1858, in Sanjon de los Moquelumnes, Hiers of Anastasio Chabolla, Docket No. 306, California Private Land Claims, Records Group 49, National Archives.

[69] *Hicks et al. v. Josiah Johnson et al*; and *Sacramento Daily Union* March 20, 1860.

[70] *Stockton Argus*, August 15, 1860.

[71] Id.

[72] Id.

[73] "The Hicks Land Case," *San Joaquin Republican*, April 10, 1861.

[74] "Overruled," *San Joaquin Republican*, April 10, 1861.

of San Joaquin."[75] A jury of twelve men was empaneled and the first witness was called.[76] This proved to be Mr. Von Schmidt, a deputy land surveyor appointed by James Mandeville, the United States Surveyor for California. To a packed courtroom the man occasionally was able to answer a question without being interrupted by objections from Perley and Thornton, who "contested every point inch by inch."[77] Von Schmidt was followed by Dr. Mathewson, C. Ashley, P. Wheeler, F. Turner, and John Sanford.[78] A running battle to rule out an array of documents punctuated the proceedings, followed by the concession of Plaintiff's counsel that any claim for damages arising from trespass was less likely to prevail than a claim merely for possession and confirmation of title.[79] Rumors of a non-suit proved bogus, but gave way to more concrete predictions that the jury would ultimately side with the settlers.[80] That prediction appeared more likely as Perley and Thornton presented the testimony of their witnesses and were successful in excluding a sizeable amount of evidence harmful to their case.[81] With the close of the evidentiary phase of the trial, Mr. Beatty addressed the jury for little more than an hour. He was followed by Perley, and then by Thornton, who was cut short for lack of time.[82] Thornton concluded the following day, and Beatty provided rebuttal argument.[83] After Judge Creanor gave the jury "instruction of a general character regarding their being required to designate the location" of the original Chabolla grant, the jury retreated from the courtroom to deliberate.[84] At half past 10 p.m. that same day, the Judge received a sealed envelope. When opened

---

[75] "The Land Case," *San Joaquin Republican*, April 11, 1861; and "The Hicks Land Case," *San Joaquin Republican*, April 10, 1861.

[76] "The Hicks Case," *San Joaquin Republican*, April 13, 1861.

[77] "The Land Case," *San Joaquin Republican*, April 11, 1861.

[78] "The Hicks Case," *San Joaquin Republican*, April 13, 1861.

[79] Id.

[80] "Non-Suit," *San Joaquin Republican*, April 11, 1861; "A Mistake," *San Joaquin Republican*, April 12, 1861; and "The Hicks Case," *San Joaquin Republican*, April 14, 1861.

[81] "The Hicks Case," *San Joaquin Republican*, April 13, 1861.

[82] "The Hicks Case," *San Joaquin Republican*, April 14, 1861.

[83] *San Joaquin Republican*, April 16, 1861.

[84] Id.

the following morning, the predictions in the press of a settler victory were vindicated.[85]

The conclusion of the case all but pre-ordained the outcome of the many additional cases brought by Hicks to eject other settlers on the southern bank of the Mokelumne, including those against Perley's cousins. When those cases finally came to trial on December 19, 1861, the Perleys prevailed. They won a defense verdict, as well as costs of suit, in the amount of $18.[86]

The Moquelumnes cases highlight the continuing presence of Perley as a litigator in the District Court in San Joaquin County. Among his cases there was *Bridges & Hall v. Paige*, for recovery of $1,500 in attorney fees. Perley represented Defendant, and General Booker the Plaintiffs.[87] After a continuance of several months, the case was tried. The witnesses being all "legal gentlemen...pretty well posted in forensic dodges," the contest was said to have been "a sharp one."[88] Perley didn't win, but he managed to whittle the sum owed by his client down to $1,097.[89] He also represented a shooting victim, James Allen, in a civil action for $5,000 after a grand jury declined to indict because it concluded the act was justifiable.[90] Allen, it seems had threatened to kill Mitchell after

---

85 *San Joaquin Republican*, April 17, 1861.

86 *Hicks et al. v. Josiah Johnson*, San Joaquin County Superior Court, Case No. 1552. The judgments in *Hicks* would not be the end of the controversy for the settlers. Andrés Pico's separate claim to the overlapping Rancho Los Mokelamos was confirmed by Judge Ogden Hoffman in the U.S. Court for the Northern District at around the same time *Hicks* was decided. The Supreme Court subsequently overturned that decision for want of evidence after noting the "suspicious character of the grant." (*United States v. Pico* (1860) 63 U.S. 406). Pico attempted to better prove the claim on remand to the District Court, but failed, and then fell short again in 1864 when Justice Field and the Supreme Court held that a new document attesting to the grant prior to the American conquest had clearly been "introduced among the archives subsequently to the acquisition of the country." (*Pico v. United States* (1864) 69 U.S. 279). A final challenge to the settlers was posed by the Western Pacific Railroad, which had obtained a grant of land already occupied by hundreds of farms. Though it took years, the settlers finally prevailed when the Supreme Court decided that the territory at issue in *Pico* was ineligible to be granted to railroads. ("Los Moquelemos," *Sacramento Daily Union*, May 20, 1876; and *Newhall v. Sanger* (1875) 92 U.S. 761).

87 "District Court," *San Joaquin Republican*, December 14, 1858.

88 Id.

89 "District Court," *San Joaquin Republican*, December 16, 1858.

90 "Damages for Shooting," *San Joaquin Republican*, December 6, 1859.

learning the latter had accused him of overcharging for services as a school teacher. He borrowed a revolver from General Booker, who thought Allen simply wanted to go target shooting. A confrontation with Mitchell led to Mitchell striking Allen in the face, Allen attempting to fire at Mitchell, and Mitchell firing in response and hitting Allen in the stomach and leg.[91] The matter was continued twice, and probably eventually settled.[92]

In *Powell v. Oullahan*, Perley represented the Plaintiff Powell, who had received a patent to 160 acres of swamp or overflow land in San Joaquin County in accordance with the Act of April 28, 1855. His case at trial consisted solely of Perley reading the contents of the Patent into the record and submitting the allegations of the verified Complaint. Oullahan moved for a non-suit on the grounds that Plaintiff had failed to prove what he contended were essential elements of the case: the State's ownership of the land when it conveyed the property to the Plaintiff, and Defendant's possession of the parcel at the outset of the lawsuit. After the motion was granted, Perley appealed. His opponents contended that reading the Patent in Court was not sufficient to establish ownership, and the reading of the allegations wasn't an appropriate means of supplementing the deficiencies in the evidence. On October, 8, 1859, Justice Field opined that "under the pleadings in this case, no evidence was necessary on either of the points specified in the motion as a ground of nonsuit." It was only necessary for the Plaintiff to aver that title originally rested with the State to establish the fact of the State's power to convey the property. The court below, Field concluded, "erred in nonsuiting the Plaintiff on the grounds stated in the motion of the Defendant."[93] When the case was retried, Perley obtained a judgment for $230 and possession of the property. The incongruity of this award being not even half of Perley's fee prompted payment by Powell of but $80 to his attorney. Perley brought an action for debt against his client on January 12, 1860 in San Joaquin, but lack of resolution at trial indicates the matter was dismissed in the wake of a settlement.[94]

---

[91] "Another Shooting Affray," *San Joaquin Republican*, June 19, 1858.

[92] "Suit for Damages," *San Joaquin Republican*, August 4, 1859; and "District Court," *San Joaquin Republican*, December 22, 1859.

[93] *Powell v. Oullahan* (1859) 14 Cal. 114; and *Daily Alta California*, October 11, 1859.

[94] *Perley v. Oullahan*, San Joaquin Superior Court, Case No. 1530.

Another Stockton area matter handled by Perley was *McCloud v. O'Neal*—an action against his and Terry's friend, Sheriff O'Neal. McCloud claimed ownership of barley purchased via a writing under seal from Kelty and Reynolds. Sheriff O'Neal seized the goods in execution of a judgment against the two men in favor of a Mr. Fisher. With Perley as counsel, McCloud sued the Sheriff for trespass, and further alleged fraud in the sale by Kelty and Reynolds. At trial, when Kelty and Reynolds appeared as witnesses on behalf of the Sheriff, Perley objected due to the incongruity of the two men impeaching their own misdeed. The objection was overruled, yet Perley still managed to prevail. After a short continuance, the Court considered O'Neal's motion for a new trial.[95] Though he opposed the motion, Perley argued that in the event a new trial occurred, the testimony of Kelty and Reynolds ought to be excluded. His argument was disregarded and a new trial was granted.

On appeal of the decision granting a new trial, Perley was joined as co-counsel by his friend A. P. Crittenden. In arguments presented on September 7, 1860, he and Crittenden maintained that Kelty and Reynolds were not competent defense witnesses, that the Court should have excluded their testimony at the hearing of the Defendant's motion, and not relied upon it in granting the Defendant's request.[96] In an opinion in the matter published in late October, Justice Cope, with Field concurring, cast shade upon Perley's assessment of the case. "The court, in passing upon the motion for a new trial, could not properly have disregarded any portion of the evidence upon which the jury acted, in making up their verdict."[97] The question for the Court was "whether upon this evidence, they had arrived at a correct conclusion."[98] The verdict might be set aside when obtained upon incompetent evidence, "but this cannot be done where the evidence was admitted without objection; nor can it be done even where the evidence was objected to, upon the ground that effect was given to it by the jury."[99]

---

95 *San Joaquin Republican*, April 10, 1860.

96 *Sacramento Daily Union*, September 8, 1860; and *McCloud v. O'Neill* (1860) 16 Cal. 392.

97 *McCloud v. O'Neill*, supra, at 397.

98 Id.

99 Id.

Perley's disagreement with the evidence alone wasn't sufficient to keep it out; and once admitted into the record, the judge and jury possessed every right to weigh it as they saw fit.

Not every San Joaquin case handled by Perley proceeded to the Supreme Court. In one such matter, Perley brought suit against Hodges & Shafer to enforce a promissory note he obtained from B.F. Landford. Landford had taken assignment of the note from George Drew, who in turn had received it from Hodges in lieu of payment for a 5,000-pound shipment of flour.[100] When his attempt to collect on the note was rebuffed, Perley sued both Hodges and the latter's surety, a Mr. Shafer. The matter was in the District Court in Stockton in December of 1860, where it was continued all the way until August of 1861.[101] During the long-delayed trial, Hodges raised a series of technical objections, but on August 23, 1861, Perley won $726 in damages, plus costs and interest calculated at a rate of 3% per month.[102] Perley was less successful at trial during the same session in the matter of *Pierson v. McCahill*, involving the question of whether a payment of part of a $4,000 debt constituted a compromise in full or a mere installment followed by an extension of time to pay the remainder.[103] He and Mansfield Compton argued the former position, but failed to impress either the judge or the jury.

Early in 1860, Perley entered into another matter arising in the Fifth District involving the Tuolomne Redemption Company's insistence on its superior right to redeem a water ditch subject to a judicial foreclosure against the ditch's owner, the Columbia and Stanislaus River Water Company. Columbia had incurred heavy debt, apparently in connection with its effort to construct a drainage and irrigation ditch to be used in the reclamation of land to be sold for agricultural purposes. Default followed the company's failure to service the debt. Numerous creditors brought actions both for recovery of damages and to foreclose on the property. One of the

---

[100] *D. W. Perley v. John Hodges & J. K. Shafer*, San Joaquin Superior Court, Case No. 1860.

[101] *Stockton Daily Independent*, December 13, 1860; *San Joaquin Republican*, January 12, 1861; and *Stockton Daily Independent*, August 6, 1861.

[102] *San Joaquin Republican*, August 22, 1861; and *Stockton Daily Independent*, August 23, 1861.

[103] *San Joaquin Republican*, August 15, 1861.

creditors was Evan Davis, who recovered a judgment against Columbia in March of 1859. Two months later, the ditch was sold to Davis pursuant to an execution of Davis' judgment.

Though alarmed by this development, mortgage creditors opted to assign their interests in the ditch to Toulomne in lieu of litigation. With access to capital, Tuolumne now redeemed the ditch from Davis. Davis accepted the money and handed it to the Sheriff for an accounting. The complexity of the situation grew as the assignees of the interests of the defunct Columbia also attempted to redeem the property. The money they tendered was accepted and a certificate to that effect was issued by the Sheriff. Sensing a threat to his ability to recover the monies he'd previously handed to the Sheriff, Davis attempted to reclaim the property himself as assignee of two unrelated judgments against Columbia from July of 1859. Contending that it had priority as the assignee of an earlier judgment and that Davis couldn't redeem because he hadn't first paid the underlying judgment debts as required by the governing statute, Tuolumne refused to honor the attempted redemption. Though recently amended, Tuolumne said the older provisions of the law still applied. Imagining it could now take title to the ditch, Tuolumne found its efforts stymied by the Sheriff, who, in a marked show of support for Davis, refused to issue a deed. Unable to gain formal title to what it believed it now owned, Tuolumne sought a mandamus to force the Sheriff to do his duty. Denied relief by the District Court, Tuolumne appealed.

Argument in the Supreme Court occurred on February 7, 1860.[104] The Tuolumne legal team consisted of the formidable trio of Perley, Joseph P. Hoge and Leander Quint. Together, they took the position that absent any express statement on this point, the amendments to the redemption statute relied on by Davis didn't apply retroactively. The older statute, therefore, must necessarily govern the circumstances of the case. Retroactivity was doubly erroneous given the unconstitutional effect it would have on existing contractual obligations. Application of the new terms to existing contracts, altering pre-existing rights and duties, would run afoul of the Contract Clause in Article I, Section 9 of the federal Constitution. Much impressed with opposing counsel Solomon

---

104 *Sacramento Daily Union*, February 8, 1860.

Heydenfeldt's construction of the statute, the Court nevertheless found the equities of the Tuolumne's case overwhelming. The amendment of the statute might have destroyed Tuolumne's legal rights, but the Company retained its rights in equity. Heydenfeldt's remarks haunted the majority, however, and when a motion for reconsideration was presented, the Court granted it.[105]

The decision of the Court following re-argument involved, said the *Sacramento Daily Union*, a constitutional question, a synopsis of which "would do injustice to the views of the Court."[106] Crafted by Perley, the argument on that question was ignored by Justice Baldwin, who commenced his analysis with the redemption statute itself. "The correctness of the decision below," he opined, "depends upon the construction and effect of the redemption laws."[107] The relevant statute provided "that a subsequent redemptioner may redeem from a prior one by tendering 'the sum paid in the last previous redemption with six per cent thereon in addition, and the amount of any assessment of taxes which the said last previous redemptioner paid after the redemption by him with interest thereon, and the amount of any liens held by the said last redemptioner previous to his own interest." The law was the source of any rights the redeemer had, and to avail himself of those rights, he was required to follow it closely. The Tuolomne Redemption Company argued that the earlier Act controlled because the judgments of which it was the assignee were issued prior to the enactment of the amendment. Justice Baldwin said that what mattered was when the effort to redeem occurred, not the date of the judgments assigned. In this case, redemption occurred after the amendment took effect. The Plaintiff complained that such application was in effect a retrospective law and represented an impairment of an obligation on a contract, and thus was fundamentally unfair. "The effect of the Act of 1859," countered Baldwin, "is not retrospective when applied to this case, for…the contracts contemplated by the Act of 1859 were future redemptions, and not the less in the future because they might grow out of sales by the officers, under judgments already in existence before the

[105] *Sacramento Daily Union*, February 10, 1860; *Sacramento Daily Union*, February 24, 1860; and *Sacramento Daily Union*, March 9, 1860.

[106] *Sacramento Daily Union*, May 7, 1860.

[107] *Tuolumne Redemption Company v. Sedgwick* (1860) 15 Cal. 515.

passage of the Act of 1859." The law, too, didn't alter substantive rights; it merely affected the remedy, or the mechanism whereby the rights secured by the contract were to be enforced. As such, the District Court was correct in refusing Tuolumne's attempt to enforce its rights in accordance with the provisions of the older law. Davis had every right to redeem and Tuolumne should have honored it.

In April of 1860, Perley tried the matter of *Blockley v. Fowler* in Judge Creanor's court.[108] The case arose from competing claims to ownership of two lots in the City of Stockton originally part of Captain Weber's grant. Weber had conveyed the lots to A.M. Jackson, who confused matters by mortgaging the properties to M.B. McKinney and later selling them off to Perley's client, John Blockley. Perley brought an action to eject the defendant Richard Fowler, who claimed the land by virtue of a deed derived from a foreclosure on Jackson's mortgage. The foreclosed land had been sold at auction to W. H. Fairchild. Fairchild in turn conveyed the properties back to McKinney, who then transferred title to Fowler. Fowler's attorneys, John B. Hall and Henry T. Huggins, argued that Fairchild's ignorance of the cloud created by Jackson's conduct rendered him a bona fide purchaser possessing the power to convey good title to others. Scrutinizing Fowler's chain of title closely, Perley identified a defect. At trial, he elicited testimony that Fairchild was no disinterested purchaser; he was McKinney's agent, and had paid the purchase price with his principal's cash, not his own. Without payment for value, he wasn't a bona fide purchaser, and the title he conveyed to others was void. The argument persuaded the judge, who instructed the jury that if it was believed "from the evidence that M. B. McKinney…employed W. H. Fairchild…to attend said sale as his agent, and to buy…the property specified in said mortgage…for the benefit of said McKinney himself…that said Fairchild was not a bona fide purchaser but purchased said property for said McKinney, and that no consideration was passed between said Fairchild and said McKinney," thereby making the sale void.[109] An overruled Motion for a new trial prompted an appeal by Hall and Huggins that wasn't

---

[108] *San Joaquin Republican*, April 10, 1860.
[109] *Blockley v. Fowler* (1863) 21 Cal. 326, 329.

actually argued and decided until 1863. Perley's preoccupation with litigation in Nevada mandated enlistment of the services of E. L. Goold to assist with the matter in California. This renewed collaboration proved unavailing. In reviewing the case, Justice Edward Norton commented that "a mortgagee who sells under a power contained in the mortgage and becomes himself the purchaser indirectly by having the mortgaged premises bid in for himself, cannot hold it against the mortgagor if the latter chooses to file his bill to set aside the sale or to redeem, provided this be done within a reasonable time after being apprised of the sale."[110] Such a sale, he concluded, was voidable at the option of the mortgagor or his successor-in-interest, not void, hence the judge's instruction to jury was erroneous.

Continuing his run in the Fifth District, Perley took on the City of Sonora after the latter refused to honor the claim of a municipal bondholder. Perley filed a Complaint on the bondholder's behalf. The City demurred due to Perley's failure to identify the specific ordinance referred to in the bonds, the names of the City's agents, and the date of the expiration of the statute of limitations. When the District Court sustained the demurrer, Perley appealed.[111] Relying in part on the common law of the States of Michigan, Connecticut and Minnesota, Perley contended that no need existed to identify the ordinance and the City's agents, and that the bonds themselves were sufficiently identified. The particular statute of limitations referred to by the Defendant, he noted, had been amended, therefore it wasn't material to the case. Justice Baldwin and the rest of the Court agreed with Perley on the sufficiency of the allegations. With regard to the statute of limitations, Baldwin acknowledged that the "bonds upon their face are payable at dates which show a bar under the General Statute."[112] He nevertheless agreed that this seemingly dispositive fact was immaterial due to enactment by the Legislature of several laws that addressed the repayment of municipal debt. The laws in question had the effect of freeing the Plaintiff from the fatal close of the limitations period. Though the ultimate merits of the case were yet to be determined, Baldwin

---

[110] Id.

[111] *Underhill v. Trustees* (1860) 17 Cal. 172.

[112] Id., at 177.

opined that "the plea of the statute, if successful, would, under these circumstances, be nothing less than an act of unqualified repudiation of a just and honest obligation, to the payment of which the faith and honor of the defendant are pledged."[113] Such an unconscionable outcome he and the Court could not condone.

In the months preceding Secession and the outbreak of the Civil War, the Chivalry's presence in State affairs remained pronounced. Occasionally in need of legal assistance, the ranks of the Chivalry called on Perley, as had the Know Nothings in former times, and Perley generally obliged, less as a contribution to the cause of the Southern wing of the Democracy than as the payment of tribute to friends in need. One such friend—Austin E. Smith, an attorney and son of former Virginia Governor William Smith—had played a prominent role in Chivalry-inspired controversies and brawls from the time of his arrival in the State. His election-day assault back in 1854 on Edmund Gallagher with a cane to the head had the singular virtue of being the only disturbance during a contest most expected would be riotous.[114] Within a year's time, a duel resulting from a disagreement with H. B. Truett left the twenty-four-year-old Smith shot through the leg.[115] A hundred spectators observed with fascination as the gallant Smith, fashionably arrayed in "navy cap and dress coat," stylishly fired his pistol at his adversary until, with a pallor overtaking the normal appearance of his face, he threw his weapon to the ground to signal his inability to continue. Unable to walk, Smith relied on his seconds, Volney Howard and E.J.C. Kewen, to load him into the genial Truett's rockaway for transport to an infirmary.[116] Smith landed in the police court early in 1856 after setting a ship adrift that had encroached upon a wharf under his control.[117] Later the same year, Smith and another young Chiv named Harry Logan accompanied William H. Werth in an attack on a journalist employed by the *Evening Journal* whose printed words

---

[113] Id., at 178.

[114] *Daily Alta California*, September 6, 1854.

[115] *Sacramento Daily Union*, October 22, 1855; and *Empire County Argus*, October 27, 1855.

[116] Also injured on the field was James D. Thornton, whose attempt to negotiate an end to the dispute was interrupted by a stray, rampaging bull.

[117] *Daily Alta California*, February 10, 1856.

had impugned the Chivalry's honor.[118] His brother Caleb fought a duel with Broderick, but Austin respected the Senator, was personally friendly with him and even joined him in a mission to spy on the doings of the Vigilance Committee inside its headquarters. His antipathy for efforts to end slavery was nearly matched by a similar, well-publicized personal disregard for Gwin; hence when Smith was nominated to succeed R. P. Ashe as federal naval agent in San Francisco, Gwin vainly voiced his opposition.[119] He was loud, boisterous, headstrong and apt to act before thinking. His friend Harry I. Thornton called him the "bravest of the brave," with a "daring, restless spirit," a man of great worth and loved by his friends.[120] In some ways he resembled Perley, who became acquainted with his father in the Courts of Stockton in his early days in California. In time, he and young Smith became so friendly that they ventured jointly into land investment and acquisition in the wilds to the west of downtown San Francisco.

Perley served several times as the conflict-prone Smith's counsel. The first occasion came in the context of Smith's problem relations with some of his tenants. In November of 1858, Smith's tenant Ogg Shaw refused to pay rent on a parcel of land to which he held a month-to-month lease. On January 8, 1859, Smith posted notice that Shaw was to quit the premises, which Shaw refused to do. A suit was brought in the Court for the Twelfth District to eject the defaulter, but Judge Norton ruled that Shaw could remain on the land. After being retained by Smith, Perley appealed on the grounds that breach of the terms of the lease by Shaw justified his eviction. In a decision issued on July 7, 1860, the Supreme Court agreed and remanded the matter for a new hearing.[121] In Judge Norton's hands for a second time, the case resulted in a judgment for Smith in the form of an order of possession.[122]

---

118 *Sacramento Daily Union*, March 26, 1856; and *Empire County Argus*, May 24, 1856.

119 *Sacramento Daily Union*, December 2, 1857.

120 H. I. Thornton, Jr., "Recollections of the War by a Confederate Officer From California," *Southern California Quarterly*, Volume 45 (Sept. 1963), at p. 205

121 *Austin E. Smith v. Thomas Ogg Shaw* (1860) 16 Cal. 93; and *Daily Alta California*, July 8, 1860

122 *Daily Alta California*, July 22, 1860.

As Perley did business with Smith, so too did he do business with Smith's friend, Harry Logan. Though the charge of being a Chivalry rowdy was fair, Logan's role as a founder of the San Francisco Stock Exchange and investor in mining ventures reflected his more serious side.[123] A tepid friendship existed between himself and Perley, resulting perhaps more from common associations than from true affinity. In any event, Perley came to the aid of Logan after William Hillegass obtained a default judgment against him. With Perley's help, Logan brought an action to set the judgment aside due to failure to serve the Complaint in accordance with the Practice Act. Hillegass demurred and prevailed, prompting an appeal. Appearing in concert with co-counsel George Cadwalader, Perley argued that the setting aside of the default was the proper outcome below because the complaint lacked a seal, hence was void and could not support a judgment by default. Moreover, service was defective in that the language in the proof explaining how service occurred was impermissibly vague.[124] Justice Field found Perley's argument rather strained. An utterly void judgment, he said, can be defeated via a motion to quash when enforcement is attempted. A voidable judgment can be overcome via a post-judgment motion or on appeal of the merits of the case. Perley had avoided both these approaches in favor of impugning the formalities of the pleadings and service of the same. Such an irregular attack on the judgment the law did not support.[125]

Logan's activity in the State's financial circles all but guaranteed a foothold in legal disputes, and a role for Perley in Logan's life. Logan only narrowly missed further involvement with Perley when he paid $400 for an assignment from General Vallejo of a bank certificate worth $1,800 issued to the General by the banker Joseph Palmer. Desiring the cash, Logan demanded payment from Palmer, but was denied. Though he submitted a notice of protest as if he intended to litigate, he cashed out by selling the certificate to H.L. Coye. When Coye in turn attempted to collect the money, Palmer again refused, thereby inspiring Coye to file suit in the Court for the Twelfth District. After Coye prevailed, Palmer appealed. Trial

---

[123] Joseph L. King, *History of the San Francisco Stock and Exchange Board* (San Francisco: Jos. L. King, 1910), at p. 74.

[124] See *Sacramento Daily Union*, September 13, 1860.

[125] *Logan v. Hillegass et al* (1860) 16 Cal. 200.

counsel Solomon Heydenfeldt being indisposed or otherwise unavailable, Coye retained Perley to argue the mater in July.[126] In rendering his opinion, Justice Cope explained that "the plaintiff holds the certificate subject to all the equities existing between the endorser and Logan."[127] He took it after maturity, and in the wake of a formal protest over non-payment, and must therefore be deemed to have assumed ownership "with full knowledge of these equities."[128] Citing Joseph Story, he said that "there is no principle of law better settled than that a person who purchases negotiable paper after it has been dishonored or is overdue, takes it subject to all the equities which properly attach thereto between the antecedent parties."[129] As no authorities supported Perley's and Coye's position, "the judgment of the Court below must be reversed, and the cause remanded for a new trial." After remand, retrial was scheduled for September 24.[130] The trial yielded the same outcome and another appeal followed. Seemingly bored with the issue, Justice Cope succinctly stated that "we adhere to our former opinion in this case, and do not consider it necessary to give any additional reasons for our decision."[131] Knowing of Palmer's interests in the Pescadero, Perley then exercised an option to enforce the $2,362 judgment against a portion of that estate. When the land was put up for sale at auction, Perley bid $1,000 and won the prize.[132]

The pace of Perley's practice in 1860 necessitated either a leveling off of his case load, or the addition of a partner. Why he formed a professional association at this time specifically with Mansfield Compton isn't known. A recent migrant to the State, his status as an attorney was of recent vintage, and barely post-dated his release from the State Prison at Auburn, New York following a pardon by Governor Seymour in 1854 after serving less than two years of an eight-year sentence. His crime was the intentional ignition of a fire to his own store in Jamestown, New York on New

---

126 *Sacramento Daily Union*, March 6, 1860.

127 *H.L. Coye v. Joseph C. Palmer et al* (1860) 16 Cal. 158, 159.

128 Id.

129 Id., at 159-160.

130 *Daily Alta California*, July 7, 1860; and *Daily Alta California*, August 31, 1860.

131 *Sacramento Daily Union*, December 11, 1860.

132 Earle Williams, *Rancho El Pescadero*, Volume I, at p. 20, BANC MSS 80/58c.

Year's Day, 1852. The "perfect stampede of men, women and children" filling the streets on that terrible day gave cover to a wave of pilfering and crime, and nearly paralyzed efforts to extinguish the flames.[133] The pardon outraged the New York public, who turned on the Governor in favor of his opponent in the General Election of 1854, and likely compelled Compton to leave the State, at least for the time being, to avoid the withering hostility.[134] His own controversial history perhaps rendering Compton sympathetic in his eyes, Perley brought the man into his practice, and by the summer of 1860, Compton was appearing in Court on Perley's behalf. On August 30, Compton initiated a suit in Perley's name against Hiram Pearson for $400 in unpaid fees for "professional services."[135] As noted earlier, they tried the matter of *Pierson v. McCahill* in August of 1861, but lost. The two of them later joined forces in an action against David M. Elder on behalf of the merchant L. B. Benchly. Alleging fraud in the application of the Insolvency Act, they convinced the Court that Elder had both used and broken the law to evade his creditors. Their joint action in Benchly's cause ultimately proved futile, as the jury found in favor of the Defendant. Bereft of payment for a debt and facing a bill from his attorneys despite losing in court, Benchly refused to pay Perley's portion of the fee on the grounds that he had only authorized Compton to act, not Perley. As the case approached trial, the parties waived a jury and proceeded to present the case directly to the Judge in the Twelfth District.[136] After presenting evidence that Benchly was aware of Perley's engagement as one of his attorneys despite the absence of a written contract, the Judge paid tribute to equity by awarding Perley $300.[137]

Perley and Compton also defended Tuolumne County Sheriff John Sedgwick in Court against a Mr. Kuhland, who had claimed title to goods the Sheriff had seized in the course of enforcing a judgment for debt. When a vital witness was out of State and

---

133 *Daily Journal*, May 31, 1902.

134 *Buffalo Daily Courier*, June 8, 1854; and *Horneville Weekly Tribune*, December 21, 1854.

135 *Daily Alta California*, August 31, 1860.

136 *Daily Alta California*, January 15, 1862; and *Daily Alta California*, October 10, 1862.

137 *California Law Journal*, Volume 1 (1862), No. 15, p. 239.

unavailable for deposition or trial, Perley sought a continuance. Concluding that Perley ought to have pursued a commission to take testimony out-of-State, the Court denied the motion. After losing at trial, Perley brought an appeal addressing the issue of the continuance, as well as the failure of the Plaintiff to establish the value of the goods at issue, and the fact, heretofore unnoticed, that the Complaint hadn't been verified. In a decision issued on December 17, 1860, Justice Cope rejected Perley's arguments.[138] He thought the motion for a continuance had been properly denied due to the absence of any showing that diligence had been employed. He also noted that the Complaint's verification was adequate and that the Answer didn't sufficiently deny the alleged value of the goods at issue. As such, the trial court was correct in instructing the jury as to the value of the goods, and that no real denial by the Defendant had occurred. Cope was apparently becoming tired of Perley's attempts to introduce issues never raised in proceedings below. "We cannot," he complained, "tolerate the practice of raising such objections for the first time in this court."[139]

When Perley was next before the Justices of the Supreme Court, Cope didn't sign on to the Court's opinion, though he didn't dissent either. In the matter of *Stone v. Stone*, it was Chief Justice Field who undertook the task of declining Perley's latest invitation to overturn a lower court outcome with which the litigious counsel disagreed. The case involved a divorce and division of community property arising again from the Fifth District Court in Stockton. At issue were a series of motions—for change of venue, an injunction on alienating property during pendency of the matter, a continuance and a dismissal that Perley and his client were on the losing side of. Having brought the case seeking alimony and a property division on behalf of his female client, Perley found himself seeking restoration of the case to the docket after the entire action was dismissed, apparently due to failure of the petitioner to qualify for a divorce in the first place. When Justice Field reviewed the record, he found it bereft of the original affidavits on which the motions were based. "Orders," he said, "cannot be brought up for review on appeal from a final judgment in this way. A regular statement must

---

[138] *Sacramento Daily Union*, January 1, 1861.
[139] *Kulhland v. Sedgwick* (1860) 17 Cal. 123, 128.

be prepared in the manner pointed out by the statute, in which so much of the affidavits or evidence upon which the rulings were had must be inserted as to explain and point the exceptions taken."[140] More devastating to Perley's case was the fact that while Perley was appealing a final judgment, none of the orders at issue in the appeal were themselves appealable. Instead, they could only be reviewed via a Bill of Exceptions, which Perley neglected to prepare.

Field was even more harsh in the matter of *Wright v. Solomon*—rejecting Perley's arguments, as well as overturning a precedent Perley had been instrumental in establishing several years earlier. In *Wright*, Perley represented a Plaintiff who had a security interest in goods seized by a U.S. Marshall enforcing a judgment against a warehouseman obtained by the goods' owner. The goods had been shipped from the east coast by Elias E. Davison to a consignee in San Francisco—Perley's former client William A. Darling. Darling was in the business of buying and selling on his own account, but also bought and sold on behalf of others. As a buyer for the Davison goods was being sought, Darling placed the items in storage with Isaac Swain. Needing an infusion of capital to keep his business going, Darling obtained a loan from the Plaintiff, Mr. Wright, and pledged Davison's goods as collateral. Unhappy that his property remained unsold in Swain's warehouse, Davison brought an action for claim and delivery in federal court. After he prevailed, he employed the U.S. Marshall to effect a seizure. Under the law of the State, anyone claiming an interest in personal property seized in accordance with a court judgment was required to demand the property's return within five days, but neither Wright nor Swain did so. Instead, Wright employed Perley to bring suit against the U.S. Marshall. To defend himself from Wright's action, the Marshall employed future Senator Eugene Casserly. Casserly objected to the suit on the grounds that Darling had no right to encumber the property held in trust, hence Wright's claim was null. In response, Perley raised the rule he helped establish in the matter of *Hutchinson v. Bours*. Since Darling was not employed merely as a factor for others but was also engaged in buying and selling on his own account, Darling had every right to put property in his possession up as security for a loan. In engaging with a versatile merchant like

[140] *Stone v. Stone* (1861) 17 Cal. 513, 514.

Darling, Davison acted at his own peril and should have expected Darling to use the goods in his possession to advance his own interests. Casserly retorted that the doctrine of *Hutchinson v. Bours* was "without support in the common law."[141] Maybe so, but the case was controlling precedent, thus the court permitted the matter to go to trial. When it was over, Perley obtained a judgment in the amount of $3,325.

At the subsequent hearing of Casserly's appeal held on February 19 and 20 of 1861, Casserly boldly demanded that the Court revisit *Hutchinson* and overturn it.[142] After considering the arguments and briefs, Chief Justice Field made his view clear from the outset of his written opinion. "That a factor cannot pledge, as security for the payment of his individual debt, the goods of his principal consigned to him for sale has been the established doctrine of the common law for more than a century."[143] A factor is but an agent, he said, who has power only to bind his principal when his acts are within the scope of his authority. "A power to sell for the benefit of his principal, can in no way be stretched into a power to pledge for his own benefit."[144] It is true that the Supreme Court had adopted Perley's exception in the *Hutchinson* case, but no citation to authority was made in Perley's arguments, and none appeared in the Court's opinion in that case. The authorities, in fact, were opposed to it. Field expressed concern that since so many factors buy and sell for others as well as on their own account the *Hutchinson* exception would ultimately become an exception that swallowed the rule. In light of the weight of precedent, history, and reasonable public policy, the *Hutchinson* exception simply "cannot be maintained."[145] *Hutchinson* was "anomalous in [its] character, and in conflict with the law upon the authority of factors, as it is recognized by the United States Courts and the Courts of every State of the Union, where the Legislature has not interfered to make a change." As *Hutchinson* and its now rejected principle was the primary basis on which the lower court reached its decision in favor

---

141 *Wright v. Solomon* (1861) 19 Cal. 64, 69
142 See *Sacramento Daily Union*, February 20, 1861, for the date of oral arguments.
143 *Wright v. Solomon*, supra, at 72
144 Id.
145 Id., at 77

of the Plaintiff, the decision was overturned, and the lower court was "directed to enter judgment for the defendant."

Nearly as dismal for Perley was the outcome of *Terrill v. Groves*. In that matter, Perley sued a defendant in Stockton on behalf of a client who claimed title to four parcels obtained via a tax collector's deed. In response, the Defendant claimed the tax had been paid and that the sale itself didn't adhere to the requirements of the governing Revenue Act. Specifically, rather than being assessed, valued and sold as a block to cover the tax debt, the lots should have been disposed of separately. An appeal followed Perley's victory at trial. Countering the Defendant's procedural argument, Perley contended that formalities shouldn't defeat substance, that "the lots constituted one piece of property, owned by one individual, and could therefore be assessed and sold in gross, just as a whole block, if owned by one person, could be so assessed and sold."[146] Justice Baldwin and the Court were not convinced. In reviewing the case, Justice Baldwin observed that the Revenue Act provided that "the Assessor shall set down in his assessment book: 1, the names of all taxable inhabitants; 2, all real estate and improvements on public lands taxable to each, giving the metes and bounds, or describing by lots or fractions of lots; [and] 3, the cash value of the all improvements on real estate, etc."[147] He concluded that because the rationale of the law appeared to ensure that each lot and its owner bore the precise burden of the tax owed and to avoid inexact assessments that collective valuations might cause, "the true meaning of the provision is to require a separate assessment and valuation of each lot in cases like this of city property."

A belated echo of Perley's exploits as Fremont's attorney in Mariposa County came in the matter of an appeal in *Johnson v. Van Dyke*—one of the last cases taken by Perley to the Supreme Court during this period. While serving as Fremont's counsel, he had participated in the selling of individual lots to squatters. Rather than eject bona fide settlers, Perley and Fremont simply had the settlers purchase the right to remain with their improvements. Johnson, however, had competition for possession and control of the

[146] *Terrill v. Groves* (1861) 18 Cal. 149, 150.
[147] Id., at 151.

property he occupied. When Johnson, with Perley's aid, sought to eject the competitor, a Mr. Van Dyke, the latter contended that the applicable limitations period for pursuing legal action had lapsed. "No action for the recovery of real property, or for the recovery of the possession thereof, shall be maintained, unless it appears that the plaintiff, his ancestor, predecessor or grantor, was seized or possessed of the premises in question, within five years before the commencement of such action; provided, however, that an action may be maintained by a party claiming such real estate, or the possession thereof, under title derived from the Spanish or Mexican Governments, or the authorities thereof, if such action be commenced within five years from the time of the final confirmation of such title by the Government of the United States or its legally constituted authorities."[148] The trial court concluded that the action hadn't been brought in time, and dismissed the suit. On appeal, Perley argued that "the question of the limitation is disposed of by the ruling of this Court in the case of *Fremont v. Seals* (18 Cal. 434). The patent was issued February 19, 1856. The action was commenced on the twelfth day of November, 1860. Five years had not run; and within that time the Plaintiff had a legal seizing by virtue of his patent."[149]

The matter came before the Supreme Court in April. Rather than dispute with one another unnecessarily, the parties stipulated that the cause would be submitted on the briefs alone when the case was called, with the respondent submitting his opposition memorandum within the subsequent ten days.[150] On July 1, the Court issued its decision.[151] Justice Field accepted that the action was brought on November 12, 1860, but nevertheless asked whether this date "was within five years from the time of the final confirmation of the title to the premises in controversy 'by the Government of the United States or its legally constituted authorities.'"[152] Field noted that while the grant was confirmed on June 27, 1855, the grant didn't become certain until the survey was complete. "Such being our construction of the Act of 1855, the

[148] *Johnson v. Van Dyke* (1862) 20 Cal. 225, 227.
[149] Id., at 226.
[150] *Sacramento Daily Union*, April 19, 1862.
[151] *Sacramento Daily Union*, July 2, 1862.
[152] *Johnson v. Van Dyke*, supra, at 228.

conclusion follows that the Act only began to run against the Plaintiff from the issuance of the patent, and that being within five years previous to the commencement of the action, the Plaintiff was entitled to judgment in his favor upon the facts found by the Court."[153] Field, thus, reversed the lower tribunal and directed it to enter judgment in favor of Perley's client.

Field wasn't always so kind to Perley and his clients. *Wright v. Solomon* and *Stone v. Stone* are but two examples of Field's rejection of Perley's claims and arguments. There was no animus, of course. Field's vision of the law tended to overcome personal feelings regarding the parties or their counsel. Where corruption ate away at the heart of civil institutions, or property ownership rested on foundations of sand, Field tended to act with indifference to those who might take offense. It was one of the traits that rendered his ambition for the highest office in the land an unfulfilled fantasy.

After *Wright* and *Stone*, another of Field's rulings against Perley in this era arose in a case in which Perley was not even representing a litigant. The case was *Phelan v. County of San Francisco*. It had been brought in the City's Superior Court by purchasers of warrants issued by the County in recognition of a debt owed to those from whom the County Court of Sessions had purchased land for construction of a courthouse and other municipal buildings. When the County failed to pay the debt for lack of funds, the holders of the warrants sold them to third parties, who then took to the courts to enforce their rights. Among those who purchased the unredeemed warrants was Francois Pioche, one of the richest men in the West. Hired by Pioche to enforce the warrants in his possession, Perley filed suit in the Superior Court along with other litigants, including the banker James Phelan.[154] Phelan's case prevailed early due to the County's failure to answer the complaint after an unsuccessful demurrer. An appeal proceeded all the way to the Supreme Court in 1856. Chief Justice Murray, with Justice Heydenfeldt's concurrence, reversed the decision of the lower court on the grounds that the State Constitution vested no power with the judiciary to enter into contracts of the kind at issue in the case, or to

---

153 Id., at 229.

154 "Report of the City and County Attorney," *San Francisco Municipal Report for the Fiscal Year 1861-1862* (San Francisco: Eastman & Godfrey, 1862), at p. 108.

offer scrip as payment for debts.[155] After being remanded to the Court for the Fourth District for further proceedings, the matter was transferred to the Court for the Twelfth District, where the Plaintiff retained A. P. Crittenden as counsel and recast the principle theory of the case from law to equity, wherein what was a void contract was rendered enforceable on account of the supposed ratification by the County Supervisors. With litigation of Pioche's matter and related cases stayed pending resolution of what had become a sort of bell-weather, Crittenden took *Phelan* back to the Supreme Court. It was there that Justice Field entered the fray, opining with the support of Justice Cope that the earlier precedent remained in place, and that the new ratification theory possessed no merit due to the principle that there could be no ratification of an act for which the Constitution provided no authority.[156] Having won the case, the District Attorney reported to the County Supervisors that the actions to enforce the warrants that had been long abated, including the Pioche matter, "should now be placed upon the trial calendar and disposed of with as little delay as possible."[157] That appears to be exactly what happened, for Perley appealed the dismissal of the case to the Supreme Court and even drafted a brief in support of his client's position. The matter, however, was never decided by the Court; for it either settled or was dismissed unilaterally once Perley realized the hopelessness of obtaining a positive outcome.

The loss of Perley's wife several years before left a vacuum in his life that he was inclined by nature to attempt to fill. Matrimony wasn't a particular priority for him, even though he had a young daughter who would have appreciated a loving mother figure and perhaps siblings. Perley's spouse seemed to be his work, but he never ceased falling prey to the distractions posed by women in a still largely male world. When he wasn't thinking of a woman with whom to pass the time, he was speaking of them—gossiping really—and articulating his thoughts about the quality or status of their chastity. His famous confrontation with Broderick was one wherein he had attempted to portray himself as the defender of the honor of offended women—ironic really given his notoriety for

---

155 *Phelan v. County of San Francisco* (1856) 6 Cal. 531.
156 *Phelan v. City and County of San Francisco* (1862) 20 Cal. 39.
157 "Report of the City and County Attorney," supra, at p. 113.

being "very liberal with his lip," prepared to "talk about most everybody," and even to "speak disrespectfully of many ladies" reputed to be virtuous, or about whom nothing scandalous was known.[158] Such talk, said John W. Gashiler, "was his general scheme."[159]

Perley's salacious conversational tendencies and his boldness in the matter of women made it unsurprising to many when the newspapers became flush with stories of Perley's affair with a Mrs. Fall, lately from Cincinnati. "Without fear of the Seventh Commandment before his eyes, he went into his neighbor's house, and took himself his neighbor's wife."[160] Another account had it that Perley had actually had the discretion to arrange a meeting at "an assignation house on Stockton Street," and it was there, after the suspicious husband tracked the amorous pair down, that the cuckold staged a confrontation, derringer in hand, without first the courtesy of a knock on the door.[161] The far-off *New York Times* reported Perley's production of a pistol as his paramour interceded on his behalf, followed by a physical struggle between Perley and the husband's friend, and resulting in the knocking of the weapon free.[162] Still another report described Perley narrowly avoiding assassination at the hands of the enraged husband by jumping "out a window undressed," and then running through the street as "his shirt tails rustled and whistled in the wind."[163] He took his flight, said the unsympathetic editor of the *Sacramento Bee*, "and like Joseph, left his garments behind!"[164] A more reliable account described how Perley, alarmed over the sudden intrusion, and in a state of near undress, "sprang to the door, and descended the stairs by rapid strides."[165] A confused resident of the building attempted to stop him by grabbing his garment, which stripped away what was left of Perley's modesty. Rushing down the street "to the great astonishment and scandal of the neighborhood," he was nearly

---

158 *Official Report of the Trial of Laura D. Fair for the Murder of Alex. P. Crittenden* (San Francisco: San Francisco Co-Operative Printing Co., 1871), at p. 193.

159 Id.

160 "Scandalous Affair—A Lawyer in Limbo," *Stockton Argus*, August 18, 1860.

161 *Trinity Journal*, August 25, 1860.

162 *New York Times*, September 13, 1860.

163 "A Bad Scraps," *Shasta Courier*, August 25, 1860.

164 *Sacramento Bee*, August 16, 1860.

165 "Scandalous Affair— A Lawyer in Limbo," *Stockton Argus*, August 18, 1860.

tackled by a group of laborers who had mistaken him for a lunatic.[166] Evading them, Perley took shelter in a livery stable, donned a buffalo robe, procured a buggy and "left post-haste for parts unknown," or, said another account, "to San Mateo or some other point from which it is believed he will never return."[167] The dishonored husband deposited Perley's clothing, pistol, knives and $200 in gold with the police, apparently made a complaint, and then declared he would initiate a lawsuit demanding $50,000.[168] Recalling the details of Perley's earlier disgrace in the Broderick matter, sarcastic rumors spread that Perley had dispatched Brooks to offer satisfaction on the field of honor, only to be refused yet again.[169]

There was some suspicion that Perley had been entrapped in a scheme in which the Falls were each complicit; for within days of the incident, they were reported to be on a steamer heading out of the Bay after having pawned jewelry "to get away."[170] Another report was that the Falls were not actually married, but instead were on a long assignation from Cincinnati, where Fall's wife remained ignorantly behind to tend the family home, while her place at her husband's side was assumed by a Miss Spangler for the duration of a long jaunt to the west coast—at least until press reports circulated in New York and elsewhere that "Perley had broken up their Arcadian bliss in a big row."[171] The final word in the matter appeared to be that Perley was set up and was "the victim in every way."[172]

This rather lenient view of the barrister's role in the scandal didn't put a halt to tithers in drawing rooms and public houses where high and low society met to discuss the events of the day, nor jokes being made at Perley's expense, sometimes in his presence. A challenge that might have issued had a man passed the insult to Perley directly was avoided not long after the affair, when a woman

[166] *Trinity Journal*, August 25, 1860.

[167] Id., and "Scandalous Affair—Lawyer in Limbo," *Stockton Argus*, August 18, 1860.

[168] Id.

[169] *Sacramento Daily Union*, August 18, 1860.

[170] *Sacramento Daily Union*, August 23, 1860.

[171] *Red Bluff Independent*, August 24, 1860.

[172] *Detroit Free Press*, September 19, 1860.

feigned commiseration with the temperamental lawyer over the recent "loss of his suit." When asked by Perley to which of his suits she was referring, she nonchalantly "returned on her heal and replied, 'Your suit of Clothes."[173]

As prominent a place in his life as his law practice held, Perley's greater obsession was with the accumulation of landed wealth. He had grown up downstream from the country estates of Samuel Denny Street, John Murray Bliss and John McNeil Wilmot. He had worked in the employ of the great plantations of the Brazos and tried but failed to build a plantation of his own in the Central Valley. Once situated in the City, his ambition to accumulate land and establish a manorial estate only intensified. At first, he may have had an eye toward establishing a legacy for his heirs—his daughter Mina, as well as other children he might have once the press of his profession quieted and he remarried. In time, his efforts to build a landed empire took on a life of its own, and any thoughts in his head of the end or goal of laying the foundation for a dynasty was extinguished by an obsession strictly with the means to that end.

The opening of the so-called Western Extension and the spread of the geographic scope of the squatter-friendly Van Ness Ordinance prompted a rush on Perley's part to lay claim to the valuable lots to the west and south of the City. He did not, however, confine his acquisitiveness to the newly opened municipal terrain. Any part of the City was fair game for he and his joint venturers: Volney Howard, James Ben Ali Haggin, Lloyd Tevis, Austin Smith, and others. An early target of their efforts was the property at Clark's Point that comprised the 1839 grant issued by Governor Alvarado to J. P. Leese and Salvadore Vallejo, and bounded by Broadway, Battery and Vallejo Streets and San Francisco Bay. The land was the same property subject to the contract dispute in which Perley had represented Leese in 1858 and 1859. As noted, Leese had obtained Vallejo's share, then conveyed an interest to Gregory Yale as Yale pushed forward to confirm the grant by Alvarado before the United States Land Commission and the federal courts. During the course of that litigation, Yale distributed pieces of his share to his

---

173 *Sacramento Daily Union*, August 27, 1860; and *Sonoma County Journal*, September 7, 1860.

friends Howard, Perley, Haggin, Smith, Tevis, Tully R. Wise, and E. L. Goold.[174] After Leese failed early in 1860 in Judge Hager's Fourth District Court to eject William S. Clark and up to fifty others holding over on the property under the authority of an Alcalde's deed, Perley, Howard and their cohort filed their own action to eject Clark and the rest of the occupiers.[175] They also appear to have taken control of Leese's case and steered it toward the Supreme Court. Because the much older Leese action would settle the issue for both cases, it was *Leese v. Clark* that would form the tip of the spear vindicating Perley's interest in the extremely valuable Clark's Point property.

Howard took the preeminent place among the advocates for Leese, Perley and the rest of the plaintiffs, while Orville Pratt litigated on behalf of the defense. Howard initially contended that the Mexican Grant, once confirmed by federal authorities, preempted any state or local title. Pratt argued that this was only true for grants falling outside the limits of "the Pueblo." Because the property was inside those limits, "the Board of Land Commissioners had no jurisdiction" under the federal Act "to pass upon the claims of the grantees; and that the subsequent action of the United States District Court…and of the authorities in Washington issuing the patent, were without authority and void…." Alternatively, he argued that the Defendants were "third persons" whose interests the federal Act expressly stated were unaffected by the Commissioner's decisions. As such, they were free to question the grant, including its specific location. On appeal, Howard, with the aid of Haggin, H. P. Irving, and Edmund Randolph, modified the Plaintiffs' argument by focusing on Spanish and Mexican law that surely vested the right to make grants within the limits of Pueblos to municipal authorities, but nevertheless recognized the continuing power of the Crown, acting through the Governor, to grant any ungranted Pueblo lands. Ungranted municipal lands could be granted by the Governor, and these grants in turn were subject to protection under federal law following the

---

174 San Francisco Deeds, Volume 171, Page 46 and Volume 187, Page 49.

175 *Daily National Democrat*, December 16, 1859; *Sacramento Bee*, December 23, 1859; *Daily National Democrat*, December 24, 1859; *Daily Alta California*, March 3, 1860; *San Joaquin Republican*, March 4, 1860; and *Sacramento Daily Union*, March 5, 1860.

American conquest. This argument convinced Justice Field, who noted that while the federal Act was a bit ambiguous, it was clear that Congress intended that any grantees receiving grants from former Mexican Governors be able to confirm their claims with federal authorities.[176] Because the Land Commission had jurisdiction, its decision, un-appealed by the Attorney General, was final. As for the claim that the Defendants were "third persons" not bound by the Commission's decision, Field said such "third persons" were not entitled to dispute the lawful authority of superior authorities, such as the Governor. When the Alcalde issued the grant to Clark, the land had already been granted. Once the grant by the Governor to Leese and Vallejo occurred, "all granting power of the subordinate officers of the pueblo with respect to the property ceased."[177] Judge Hagar and the jury had got it wrong.

Field and his colleagues remanded the case for retrial. In conducting the new trial Field said the Defendants "were obliged…to make their defense within [the Supreme Court's] decision—that is to say, without calling in question its principles."[178] They might, he instructed, attempt their defense "by tracing title from the patentees, or showing outstanding title in grantees from them, and perhaps in other ways."[179] However, "they could not retry the case in disregard of the decision, nor was it permissible…to refuse to follow it on the retrial."[180] Field described a very narrow gap through which the Defendants might enter. To their delight, the new trial judge, Samuel F. Reynolds, widened it considerably to their benefit. When Field reviewed the handiwork of the lower court a second time, he was dismayed to find that the court had "disregarded and overruled [the Supreme Court's decision] in almost every particular. It disregarded the decision as to the operation of the patent as a record of the Government with respect to the title of the patentees at the date of the cession, and declared that the patent had no greater effect or operation than a simple deed of the United States…. It disregarded the decision that even if the grant of the Mexican Governor passed only an equitable

---

176 *Leese v. Clark* (1861) 18 Cal. 535, 568-569.
177 Id., at 574.
178 *Leese v. Clark* (1862) 20 Cal. 387, 415.
179 Id.
180 Id.

title, the Alcaldes had no authority to make a subsequent grant of the property; and decided that as the grant passed only an equitable title, and was subject to conditions, it was liable to be denounced, and the land to be regranted by the Alcalde, and that the subsequent grant, followed by location and settlement, constituted such denouncement."[181] Judge Reynolds and the jury also "overruled the decision that the defendants, claiming under the Alcalde grants of 1847, were third persons within the meaning…of the Act of Congress, who could contest the patent as evidence of the location of the grant, and ruled that the defendants, by their Alcalde grants, had a perfect and legal title to the premises—one paramount to the title derived from the Mexican grant confirmed by the patent of the United States."[182] Field concluded that because the result of the retrial "conflicts with our own previous decision, the verdict and judgment cannot stand."[183] The lower court's decision was therefore reversed and the trial judge "directed to enter judgment for the plaintiff…."[184] Perley and his friends had prevailed, but by the time the matter was conclusively resolved, following numerous post-trial proceedings that led to two more visits to the Supreme Court, Perley appears to have divested himself of his interest in the property.

While the *Leese* case proceeded, Perley, Howard, Smith and Goold also defended their interests in the property against the City of San Francisco. Lyman Mowrey was apparently one of the persons claiming title under Clark. To finance his purchase, Mowrey obtained a $20,000 mortgage from the City in a deal arranged by then City Treasurer William T. Sherman. The terms of the mortgage included the promise that Mowrey repay portions of the debt with interest on the 22nd of each month, and that should he fail to pay the installments, the entire principle would suddenly come due. In time, Mowrey quit-claimed the land to Leander Sawyer. When approached by Perley, Howard and a Mr. Thorne, Sawyer was threatened with litigation. Rather than fight, Sawyer took a settlement and quit-claimed his stake in the property to his would be assailants. Thorne subsequently sold his interest to E. L. Goold

---

181 Id., at 416

182 Id.

183 Id.

184 Id., at 426.

and Austin Smith. Perley, Howard, Goold and Smith then commenced leasing out the property for profit. When the mortgage payments to the City ceased, the City took notice and imposed a lien. The City then sued Perley and his partners, as well as Mowrey's Estate, to foreclose on the mortgage and recover damages.[185]

The matter came to trial in June of 1860, again in Judge Hager's Court.[186] Perley presented evidence of the Mexican grant and the patent issued by the Government of the United States. It wasn't, however, until September that the Court issued its ruling: a decree of foreclosure in the City's favor, to which was later added an award of damages in the amount of $46,000.[187] Perley (with Howard's assistance) took the case to the Supreme Court and argued it himself in July of 1861.[188] He again referenced the evidence of his and fellow Defendants' title in the form of "a grant from the sovereign power, regularly confirmed, and upon which a patent had been issued."[189] This evidence, he insisted, was conclusive against the Government "and all parties claiming under the Government, and against all parties claiming no higher title than mere possession."[190] The City's contention that Perley and his fellow Defendants were estopped by the equities in the City's favor was unconvincing. The City's claim against the property arising from Sawyer's default came through operation of a quit-claim by Mowrey. This might be effective against heirs, or parties holding title in some other form, but not against the claims of the Defendants, whose title was paramount to any deed, including the quit-claim. Once the Defendants produced their title, the entire matter should have been dismissed. There might have been a legitimate dispute about the validity and priority of title, but a foreclosure suit was not the appropriate venue for its resolution.

In his opinion, Justice Field agreed with Perley that a foreclosure suit was an improper vehicle to determine actual interests in the property. "Adverse titles to the premises held by parties claiming

---

185 *Daily Alta California*, September 9, 1860

186 *Daily Alta California*, June 28, 1860.

187 *Daily Alta California*, September 9, 1860 and October 5, 1860.

188 *Sacramento Daily Union*, July 31, 1861.

189 *San Francisco v. Lawton, et al.* (1861) 18 Cal. 465, 469.

190 Id.

by conveyance from the mortgagor prior to the mortgage, or from third parties prior or subsequent to the mortgage, are not the proper subjects of determination in the suit. Such titles must be settled in a different action, giving rise, as they generally do, to questions of purely legal cognizance."[191] In the case at bar, Perley and the other Defendants "set up in their Answer title to a portion of the mortgaged premises, under a grant from the former Mexican Government, bearing date in May, 1839, and a patent of the United States, issued upon its confirmation, in March, 1858, and also under a deed executed by the Tax Collector of the City and County of San Francisco, upon a sale for unpaid taxes for State and County purposes, for the fiscal year ending in June, 1856."[192] Certainly, to the extent that the Defendants succeeded to Mowrey's Estate through Sawyer's quit-claim, they were subject to the foreclosure action, but the separate source of their own title immunized them from a loss of their rights following the Court's decree. Various other arguments Field addressed, but in the end, he thought it unnecessary to rest on any issue other than the Defendants' adverse title. He believed the record of the trial was a sufficient basis for the lower court to correct its decision. If not, the parties could still "use that already embodied in the transcript, and add such further testimony as they may deem essential to the proper presentation of the case."[193]

The matter was thus remanded back to the Court for the Fourth District, where it lingered for a time. Incredibly, as happened in the *Leese* matter, the new trial judge, Samuel F. Reynolds, and the jury reconfirmed the original decree. They also increased the damages owed, along with litigation costs, to $58,700, and ordered "that the defendants, and all persons claiming...and all persons having liens subsequent to said mortgage by judgment or decree upon the lots of land described in said mortgage, and his or their personal representatives, and all persons having any lien or claim by or under said subsequent judgment or decree, and their heirs or personal representatives, and all persons claiming under them, be forever barred and foreclosed of and from all equity of redemption

[191] Id., at 474.
[192] Id.
[193] Id., at 478.

and claim of, in, and to said mortgaged premises, and every part and parcel thereof, from and after the delivery of said Sheriff's deed."[194] Though the Court reserved the rights Perley, Howard, Goold and Smith had derived from the United States to a small portion of the property they claimed at the south-west corner of Battery and Vallejo Streets, the sweeping nature of the Court's decree, allowing for conveyance of the property to the City, prompted them to request that an injunction be put in place pending final determination of the parties' rights pursuant to a second appeal to the Supreme Court.[195]

Even before the injunction was granted, Perley's case suffered the enormous embarrassment of his co-Defendant Smith's arrest and imprisonment for disloyalty following the utterance of comments highly favorable to the Confederacy while en route to the Nation's Capital to render an accounting of his late service as United States Naval Agent for the port of San Francisco. Smith would be released from federal custody after refusing to take an oath of loyalty even as he demanded he be allowed to return to California to attend "an important legal case," but only on condition that he enter the Confederate lines and never return to Union territory.[196] Perley would labor on in Court on his and his co-Defendants' behalf, but the matter would remain unresolved for several more years notwithstanding a successful appeal decided in 1863—by which time Perley had disposed of his interest and was no longer even in the State.[197]

Perley's fight for control of valuable City land proceeded on other fronts. During the 1850s, as the City grew more crowded, interest in the low lands surrounding the Mission Dolores west of the town plat intensified. By 1856, the City authorized the formation of a committee to oversee the surveying of the undeveloped western territory within the Charter limits, including the so-called "Mission Additions." What the committee failed to survey, private parties undertook themselves. Settlement remained deterred, however, by the lingering claims of Peter Smith, Peter Sherreback

---

[194] *San Francisco v. Lawton* (1863) 21 Cal. 589, 591.

[195] *Sacramento Daily Union*, October 1, 1861.

[196] *The War of the Rebellion: A Compilation of the Official Records of the Union and Confederate Armies* (Washington: Government Printing Office, 1902), at p. 424.

[197] *San Francisco v. Lawton* (1863) 21 Cal. 589.

and the dubious successors of Prudencio Santillan, but in 1860, when these claims were either revealed to be fraudulent or otherwise worthless, a flood of claimants scrambled to stake out homesteads.[198] In the Mission District, a toll road made of planks was supplemented by a steam railroad operating on Market Street and Valencia, giving "cheap and convenient access to the Mission and to Hayes Valley," and added much to the value of the land.[199] It provided, too, a more convenient route to the undeveloped lots strewn about the heights to the north and west of the Mission itself.

Perley likely took notice of the Mission Heights while travelling the Presidio road to visit his late wife's grave atop Lone Mountain. Volney Howard, Thomas H. Holt and others Perley knew had already obtained title to Mission properties from the successors of Santillan. After inquiring with them regarding prospects for settlement, Perley made no less than ten trips into the heights for the purpose of evaluating its adequacy as the site of a homestead. The lots he selected lay on the sand hills rising above the western most part of the Mission District, and were bounded on the west by the Charter Line separating the City of San Francisco from the vast un-incorporated and largely uninhabited region between the highlands and the coast. Situated on a flat section of the hillside just below the peak now comprising Buena Vista Park, was the parcel previously occupied by William Pierson. To him belongs the credit for dubbing it the Bird's Nest Ranch. Perley described the property as a "dense wilderness," dominated by "a hill that rises to an elevation of five hundred feet above the level of the sea, and then begins to slope" beyond a fence he built on its western boundary.[200] Timber and brush abounded throughout the property and was quite dense in places. For a man walking the ground, the going was rough, but posed "not the slightest difficulty to a man on horseback." Cows, too, had no difficulty navigating the property from adjacent farms, though the green-thumbed Perley tried mightily to bar them access through installation of hedges and wooden fences.

---

198 John S. Hittell, *The History of the City of San Francisco,* at p. 319-320.

199 Id.

200 *Davis & Sharp v. Perley et al,* Transcript on Appeal, Making of the Modern Law Print Editions, Trials, 1600-1926, at p. 401.

When Perley's fencing came to the attention of the property's adverse claimants, George F. Sharp and Isaac Davis, they sent a crew of workers to install a fence of their own to mark what they believed was the true boundary. The foreman found Perley on the premises inspecting the progress of a project to level the sand hills, plant trees and gardens, and build a homestead. From horseback he arrogantly informed Perley, "you have got some of my land enclosed," and that he and his men were going to install a boundary fence. "You perceive," said Perley, "there is a fence there already."[201] If the foreman intended to go forward with his plan, Perley informed him that it "would be an act of lawless violence and might lead to a breach of the public peace."[202] The man on horseback apparently knew of Perley's reputation, but said he wasn't afraid and would carry out his task. "I warned him against doing it," Perley recalled, and said that if he made the attempt "I would resist by force." When later he discovered a fence indeed had been erected, he sent a note to Sharp "requesting him to remove it."[203] Sharp met Perley at his office, declined to remove the fence but expressed a willingness to submit the matter to court for determination of the parties' rights. Feeling that he "could not permit any one to go inside of my property and claim possession, and then ask me to litigate with him," Perley told Sharp he would take it down himself.[204] Leaving the meeting in a state of annoyance, Perley later marched his men up the hill, tore out the fence, made eight piles of debris, and put them all to the torch.[205]

Conflict arose with other neighbors as well. In September, when men in Perley's employ demolished a fence abutting Frank Hassey's property, Hassey sent a group of his men led by Andy Thompson to address this act of vandalism. The result, said Perley rather euphemistically, was "a difficulty," but which others called "the Mission Squatter War."[206] Weapons were drawn and men in Perley's employ were arrested—George Flint and James Rogers—but not, as the press reported, Perley himself. With charges of

---

201 Id., at p. 398.
202 Id., at p. 399.
203 Id.
204 Id.
205 Id., at p. 400.
206 Id., at p. 415; and *Sacramento Daily Union*, September 28, 1860.

"malicious mischief" pending in the Police Court, Perley apparently disavowed any connection with the men. Instead, he introduced various titles, including one in his own and Volney Howard's names, as evidence that the ruined fence constituted a trespass that was rightfully repelled. The matter became so confused that Judge Coon felt the only solution to the dilemma was to dismiss the case. "Some trouble may be expected" in the future, reported the *Alta*, "as each party assert a determination to maintain their rights at all hazards."[207]

The *Alta's* prediction wasn't long in coming true, as Hassey soon filed suit against Perley, Howard, Holt, James Tobin, Edward Jones, and George Flint to eject them from 85 acres of land northwest from the Mission, immediately in the rear of "the Hermitage," and known as the Hollingshead and Johnson claims.[208] Hassey and his co-plaintiffs "claimed by possession held since 1851," while Perley and the Defendants asserted "title under the Santillan Grant, a school warrant laid in 1853, and possession" from the same year.[209] The case proceeded for a week before it was turned over to the jury for determination of the verdict. "When the case was called..., all the jurymen were present, and when asked whether they had agreed upon a verdict, the foreman said they had" and presented a sealed verdict agreed upon the previous evening. The verdict, when opened, "bore the signature of every member of the jury and was in favor of the plaintiff."[210] Perley then asked that the members of the jury be polled. When the names of the jurors were called, two of the jurors, perhaps uncomfortable with public exposure, sheepishly disavowed their handiwork.[211] Perley then moved that the jury be sent out again for further deliberation. In denying the motion, the Judge stated that "he was disposed to recognize the sealed verdict as final and not to be repudiated." After the jury was discharged, Perley's aggressive litigation practice continued in the form of a request for an order staying for ten days entry of judgment and that he be given opportunity to argue against entry. While the matter

207 *Daily Alta California*, September 28, 1860.

208 *Daily Alta California*, September 29, 1860; and "Jurymen Repudiating their Verdict," *Daily Alta California*, October 3, 1861.

209 Id.

210 "Jurymen Repudiating their Verdict," *Daily Alta California*, October 3, 1861.

211 Id.

was pending, unknown vandals committed "wanton depredations ...upon his garden" at the Bird's Nest. Enraged, Perley offered a $100 reward "for discovery and conviction of the plundering thieves who have during the past and present month been in the habit of sneaking into my grounds at the Mission Dolores, and cutting and destroying the camelia and other valuable shrubbery."[212]

Combative and perhaps a bit paranoid, Perley became especially sensitive at this time to affronts to his honor and integrity, and only the slightest indignity or perceived slight might spark an explosion that was, in these post-Broderick days, guaranteed to come to light in the media. When a man named McNab and two associates attempted to seize a property claimed by Perley, Perley rounded up nine men, "arrived on the spot, and with force of arms endeavored to gain possession."[213] Shots were fired, apparently by Perley's men, but none were returned. Fists seem to have flown freely, and Perley's men, though greater in number, were repelled. Apparently the aggressor, Perley nevertheless was not long in obtaining a warrant "for the arrest of McNab & Co., on a charge of riot."[214] Discerning the true culprit through the fog of litigation, the court dismissed the case, but slapped a $30 fine on the plaintiff "for his assault and battery."[215] A short time later, when crossing on the Contra Costa Ferry, apparently on his way between Stockton and San Francisco, the barring of a narrow passageway by a ship's steward to allow a nearby clerk to finish collecting fares set Perley off on a violent outburst, during which he drew a knife and threatened to stab the perceived offender.[216] Perley's earnestness convinced other passengers of the imminence of bloodshed and some were moved to restrain the inflamed lawyer, or at least to interpose themselves amidst the drama. Noting that Perley had yet "again turned up," one commentator said that through such antics, Perley "is bound to gain to himself an unenviable notoriety."[217]

---

212 *San Joaquin Republican*, December 18, 1861.

213 *Sacramento Daily Union*, November 22, 1860.

214 Id.

215 "Perley Fined," *Sacramento Bee*, November 24, 1860.

216 *Nevada Democrat*, January 17, 1861.

217 *Red Bluff Independent*, January 22, 1861.

Perhaps unprepared to respond to Perley's act of self-help in kind and further enrage the volatile counsel—yet mindful, too, of not surrendering the conflict over highly valuable land both they and Perley claimed—Sharp and Davis resorted to more passive aggressive strategies. The cows of their tenant, H. W. Zimmerman, suddenly developed an irrepressible propensity to wander through Perley's fences, often aided by Zimmerman himself, who helpfully pried the slats apart to open a passage wide enough to accommodate his animals' girth. When Perley's men re-installed or repaired the slats, Zimmerman repeated his earlier maneuver. Finding the cows in his pasture one too many times, Perley ordered that the fence be temporarily removed so that the cattle could be driven back to where they originated. Spying one day both Zimmerman and his cattle on the property, Perley ordered his men to drive them out. Zimmerman resisted the effort by force, and when it was clear he had the better of Perley's men, Perley whipped his horse into a gallop, overtook Zimmerman and proceeded to ferociously flog the man with his riding crop. After crying out for mercy, Zimmerman fled, possibly with Perley's mastiff or bull dogs on his tail, until he ran headlong into an open pit that proved to be an unmarked well.[218] In pursuit, Perley and his horse barely managed to avoid a similar fate. Displeased with the mistreatment of their tenant and convinced that Perley's bothersome claim had persisted long enough, Sharp and Davis filed a complaint in the Justice Court, which James D. Thornton subsequently prosecuted.[219] The matter dragged on for some time, and was finally tried in November of 1862.[220] Of the outcome, Perley later said, "I paid for that once."[221] Perley was apparently more successful in combatting Zimmerman's suit to quiet title to the property, orchestrated from behind the scenes by Sharp, if for no reason other than the fact that

---

[218] *Davis & Sharp v. Perley et al.*, Transcript on Appeal, op. cit., at p. 410.

[219] Id., at p. 103 & p. 405.

[220] *Daily Alta California*, September 16, 1862. Perley often seemed to have dogs around him. In addition to the mastiffs he owned in San Francisco, he had owned a greyhound back in Stockton. Named *Loufra*, the dog went missing in January of 1853, prompting Perley to post an offer of reward for its return. See *San Joaquin Republican*, January 15, 1853.

[221] *Davis & Sharp v. Perley et al*, Transcript of Appeal, op. cit., at p. 75.

Zimmerman was but a cypher at this point, with not a care to the merits of claim to land on which he no longer lived.

The end result of Perley's struggle for control of the Bird's Nest hinged in part on the rights of claimants to land within the boundaries set by the Van Ness Ordinance. Perley derived his title through a chain of mesne title holders traceable to the original Mexican grantee, while his competitors depended for their rights on actual possession regardless of title status. The Van Ness Ordinance granted significant preference to the latter, hence in Perley's mind it was a law needing revision if not obliteration. To achieve either outcome, Perley pursued the matter of *Abram Wolf et al. v. E.J. Baldwin* all the way to the Supreme Court. Wolf and his fellow Plaintiffs had sued to eject the Defendant from a fifth vara lot, No. 1353, on Turk Street, between Hyde and Larkin, not far from what is now the Tenderloin District. Wolf and company claimed actual possession of the lot from August of 1860. Baldwin ejected them without first making an averment of title. Wolf presented proof of possession in the form of a fence erected in December of 1853, which he contended was sufficient, in accordance with the Van Ness Ordinance, to prove his claim. With Perley representing Baldwin, the Court ruled in Wolf's favor in August of 1861, prompting Perley to appeal to the Supreme Court, where the matter was argued in November.[222]

Opening his argument, Perley declared that "the only material facts of the case were whether the Plaintiffs had actual possession at the date alleged, and whether they were ousted or expelled by Defendant. Upon these two facts the Plaintiffs must recover, or they cannot recover at all."[223] The Plaintiffs here based their claim exclusively on actual possession, though they did also possess a title derived from the discredited Peter Smith. The defense was within its rights to introduce this title, show it to be without validity, and thus set the Plaintiffs up for defeat through introduction of Defendants' actual legal title. Even if credence were given to the notion of ownership by possession, the possession here was *de minimus* at best: "a two-board fence, with two by three posts set ten

---

[222] *Daily Alta California*, August 15, 1861; *Daily Alta California*, November 2, 1861; and *Sacramento Daily Union*, November 19, 1861.

[223] *Abram Wolf et al. v. E. J. Baldwin* (1861) 19 Cal. 306.

feet apart." No house had ever been built, let alone occupied, nor improved in any way. No proof was even submitted that the fence, built in 1853, was even in existence following enactment of the Van Ness Ordinance. As the Plaintiffs weren't in actual possession of the land when the Defendants entered, no ouster could have occurred.

In deciding the case, Justice Field relied on the terms of the Ordinance, by which the City "relinquished and granted all her right and claim to the lands within her corporate limits, as defined by the charter of 1851...to the parties in actual possession thereof, by themselves or tenants, on or before the first of January, 1855...."[224] Actual possession was meant to be "the possession which follows the subjection of the property to the will and dominion of the claimant to the exclusion of others," and evidenced "by occupation or cultivation, or other appropriate use, according to the locality and character of the particular premises." He agreed with Perley that "an enclosure, by an ordinary fence, of the premises without residence thereon, or improvements or cultivation, or other acts of ownership, is of itself insufficient."[225] As the fence was the only indicia of occupation, and no evidence of its presence on the land after the Ordinance took effect was adduced at trial, "the Plaintiffs entirely failed to establish any actual possession of the premises in controversy." Field couldn't contemplate allowing the Plaintiffs' claim to prevail "upon such flimsy evidence." The court that would allow it would soon "teem with cases brought by squatters" making only temporary locations on the land, and the purpose of the Ordinance—"to protect actual possessors—parties who were seeking by settlement to build up homes within the city limits, and not migratory squatters or mere land speculators"—would be thwarted. In light of this logic, Justice Field ordered a reversal of the decision of the lower court, and remanded it for a new trial.[226]

The *Alta* opined that "the decision is undoubtedly an important one" due to the fact that "it will affect the title to a large portion of the property outside of Larkin and Johnston Streets and will even effect some titles inside of those Streets."[227] The hope that the Van

---

[224] Id., at 313.

[225] Id.

[226] *Daily Alta California*, December 27, 1861.

[227] *Daily Alta California*, December 31, 1861.

Ness Ordinance would resolve most of the uncertainty arising from the conflicting titles of the Spanish and Mexican and early Occupation Eras was long gone, as were the days favoring squatters and an assurance of title through construction of a fence. Perley must have been pleased with the outcome, and not merely because it marked another victory for him in the Supreme Court. The decision was precedent, and appeared to support his claim as an actual possessor and someone who could prove title traceable to a much earlier age. It would hardly reduce the conflict over the land, or put an end to the veritable squatters' war raging to the west of the City and would likely prompt a crazed rush to erect more persuasive fences and other structures under the false pretense that the land was occupied by actual settlers. San Francisco was growing in population, and if the City was to accommodate the new residents, the empty lands in the interior of the peninsula offered space on which to build. Fortunes stood to be made, hence conflict brewed among squatters. He who most boldly wielded the shotgun and most confidently and persistently argued in court was destined now to prevail.

Perley's unflinching desire for land, and his lack of hesitation in fighting others for it, sprang from that self-same acquisitiveness and urge for preeminence that had motivated his earliest enterprise as a nascent timber baron on the Oromocto. He wanted success and the fortune that came with it, and was jealous of those who would compete against him. Those who succeed in business and life often exhibit generous impulses, arising either from nature or the realization that the friends one makes in life through small gestures and middling favors are often hungry to reciprocate and give far more than they received. Perley may well have been capable of this kind of altruism, but his cheapness was evident too, bordering on ingratitude, even greed. He could be friendly enough, and didn't shrink from a conversation or a casual friendship, and he was capable of profound affection and a kind turn. In the streets of the City, he met all kinds, and one of those he became acquainted with was a down-on-his-luck English lawyer named Frederick Pout, recently arrived from Sacramento and harboring "a view of procuring some employment."[228] They had met on the corner of Clay and Montgomery Streets, not far from Perley's office. Pout told Perley that "he was destitute and suffering a condition that he had not a dollar left, wherewith to buy a meal of victuals, or to pay for a night's lodging." For several weeks he would "importune Perley at his office and on the street to hire him, often "with tears in his eyes." Perley wasn't prepared to partner with the man, but he needed a skilled clerk. Pout claimed the offer of compensation was commensurate with his status as a learned professional, but after laboring in Perley's busy practice for just over a year, he'd only been paid $256 for all of his efforts. He contended that he "rendered work, labor and services as clerk to him…in and about his business as an attorney and counsellor at law for the space of eight months for which…defendant…promised to put him…so much as such services should be reasonably worth." He had been paid $256, but actually earned a thousand dollars more than that. Instead of conceding a single point, Perley audaciously denied Pout worked for him at all, or that he had earned $1,250, or had even been paid a dime for his labor. Pout had solicited work, but Perley already had a clerk. Instead, he made Pout "a donation as an act of charity in the street of all the money he happened to have with him, amounting to several dollars, for which at the time [Pout] expressed his gratitude."

In a trial in the Court for the Fourth District in San Francisco on August 20, 1862, Perley's now former law partner, Mansfield Compton, testified that he knew both Perley and Pout quite well. He had seen Pout in Perley's office "writing there as a clerk…frequently." Pout was present at times when Perley was absent, including at night. Hall McAllister also observed Pout working in Perley's office, and was aware he had labored on the case against Hassey. That case, McAllister said, was an important one, and "Pout was diligently employed…and did much more service than a mere errand boy. He drew pleadings for Perley under Perley's directions." He often was in McAllister's office on Perley's business as well. He thought the work Pout did was worth $100 to $150 per month, to which Perley's counsel objected. City Attorney

---

[228] See *Pout v. Perley*, California State Archives, Supreme Court Records, Supreme Court Civil Case Files, San Francisco Office, 1850-1960, Case No. 3278.

John McHenry recalled Pout appearing in matters in court and had even argued motions.

When finally questioned on the stand, Perley did admit that Pout worked for him from July of 1861 to March of 1862, but not as an employee, but as a kind of intern. Pout had offered to work for whatever Perley would give him in charity. Seeing the advantage to himself, Perley discharged his existing clerk, John P. Bell, and allowed Pout to work, not for a salary, but for "what I chose to allow him." Pout had claimed to be an experienced English attorney, but wasn't competent at all, even as a copyist. He was ignorant of the Practice Act, was incapable of drafting an affidavit or a pleading, and suffered from violent cramps of the hand so frequently as to disable him from service as a bare copyist. Perley's previous clerks had tended to housekeeping matters, but Pout wouldn't even put wood on the stove. The tolerance Perley had for the frequent arguments with the man suggests he relished the verbal sparring and thrived on it, and enjoyed contesting Pout's frequent complaints about his need for more money. He admitted that Pout appeared for him in Court against Mr. McHenry and had even argued a motion for leave to file a supplemental Answer, but the matter was so simple "a fifteen-year-old boy could have done all I required him to do." When the arrangement with Pout ended, Perley said he gave him $20 to purchase shirts and shook hands with the man. He said Pout acknowledged the harsh words that had passed between them but vowed that his "lips should forever be a sealed book" with regard to these things. Apparently, the mind that conceived those words was a fickle one; for the very next day Perley was contacted by Pout's lawyer with a demand for payment of what was owed.

The jury wasn't entirely convinced of Pout's claims, but it apparently believed Perley hadn't been fair to the man. Pout had claimed a wage of $150 a month, but the best his witnesses could attest to was a $50 to $75 per month wage for service as a competent clerk. The jury relied on the higher of the two figures and awarded the man a total of $325.[229] Annoyed, Perley filed a motion for a new trial within four days, but the motion was denied. Calling on Gregory Yale to represent him in post-trial proceedings, Perley

[229] *Sacramento Daily Union*, August 21, 1862.

launched an appeal and went so far as to lodge the record for review by the High Court, but the case was dismissed before the Court ever addressed the merits.[230] Perley's anger over the situation had probably dissipated, and his wisdom, liberated from the passion of the moment, counseled a compromise.

Had Perley remained in San Francisco he might have been more inclined to litigate the matter. Familiarity with the environment and immersion in the experiences of the moment, not to mention the lack of brighter prospects, might well have overcome his better judgment and plunged him further into a controversy that had every potential to tarnish his reputation in the field and add to his notoriety. When the Pout trial occurred, Perley was actually no longer a resident of San Francisco, nor even of California. In the wake of Terry's disgrace, Perley and the former Chief Justice had spoken of the possibility of a joint venture in the Washoe, which was then showing promise as a mining and litigation frontier. With financial backing from Perley, Terry had actually gone there and won renewed fame, if not ultimate success, in the contest over the Comstock Lode.[231] Just after the election of 1860, at the time engineers had succeeded in creating a sophisticated system of mines to reach the underground ore, Perley purchased interest in a mining claim of his own, and continued thereafter to add to his portfolio. By that time, San Francisco had become a hub of mining speculation. Mining companies were organized there and stock was sold, and much talk was in the air about the future prospects of silver in the great desert east of the State. The certainty of the presence of wealth and the perfection of the arts of men in extracting it assured the advent of conflict over control of the earth, requiring audacity, physical courage and legal skill if any particular claimant was to prevail. The ongoing dispute between the great Ophir Company, the Gould & Curry, the Chollar and everyone else guaranteed that "the best talent of California and Nevada" would be in mining litigation for the next several years, "during which questions of law, of geology, and of veracity were about equally

[230] *Sacramento Daily Union*, July 9, 1863.

[231] Russell Albert Buchanan, *David S. Terry of California, Dueling Judge* (San Marino: Huntington Library, 1956), at p. 113.

contested."[232] Terry no doubt had a line on work available for his old friend, and now that Perley was prepared to emigrate and join him, he could return Perley's favor of two years earlier. On June 19, 1862, Terry reimbursed the advance Perley had made by purchasing for an identical amount part of one of Perley's existing mining claims.[233] On the same day, in the very deed issued to Terry memorializing a related transaction, Perley identified himself as a resident of Nevada Territory.[234] Perley was a man of the Washoe, and the next great epic of his career was just beginning.

---

[232] Bancroft, *History of Nevada, Colorado, and Wyoming: 1540-1888* (San Francisco: The History Company, Publishers, 1890), at p. 124.

[233] Storey County Deeds, H:38.

[234] Storey County Deeds, K:47.

Chapter Eight

WASHOE

"One used to the climate of California for a number of years, whose appreciation of its evenness and healthfulness has become dim from long enjoyment, has only to cross the Sierra Nevada, to feel revived within him, with doubled force; a higher appreciation of its pleasant temperature and balmy atmosphere."[1] The general character of the country on the eastern side of the divide, said the cartographer Henry Degroot, "is one of wildness and sterility. Three-fourths of the Great Basin lying between the Sierra Nevada and the Rocky Mountains, stretching away to Oregon on the one hand and Mexico on the other, is nothing but a desert; and, with only the natural agencies at work, or the fertilizing means now known to science, must remain such, if not forever, at least for many ages to come."[2] Most travelers entering it from California in the early 1860s came across on a wagon road connected to Sacramento by way of Placerville in the Sierra foothills. The route, made at first on mules, wound a course through the mountains, with occasional roadside hotels along the way. It was to some "a most delightful" passage, replete with "magnificent trees in the midst of snows, with deep ravines, towering mountains, beetling cliffs, roaring torrents, and beautiful streams leaping down rocky canyons, and coursing through valleys."[3] In time, the southern-most portion of the Washoe was reached—the Carson Valley—a mere fraction of the great desert, thirty miles long and six wide, most of which being bare of pasturage and largely useless for agricultural purposes. It is bounded on the west by the pine covered eastern slope of the Sierras, out of which flow numerous streams, including the Carson River, and on the other sides by "barren ridges, composed of rocks, sand and mountain drift...bare of vegetation, except the artemisia

---

[1] *Daily Alta California*, February 1, 1860. See also Henry DeGroot, *Sketches of the Washoe Silver Mines, With a Description of the Soil, Climate and Mineral Resources of the Country East of the Sierra* (San Francisco: Hutchings & Rosenfield, 1860).

[2] *Daily Alta California*, February 26, 1860.

[3] *Daily Alta California*, March 7, 1860.

and an occasional tuft of grass."[4] Tucked into the western side of the valley is Genoa, the earliest settlement in the region, and the original territorial capital, replaced after a time by Carson City. In 1860, the latter place was "regularly laid out with straight wide streets," and a number of handsome squares had been reserved for public use.[5] It had the advantage of water, as well as timber for building, hence it grew in importance as the surrounding population swelled.

From the Carson Valley, heading north, ran the old emigrant road, until it merged with a toll road leading up to Gold Canyon, and continued on past Silver City, Gold Hill, all the way to Virginia City. Further north and a bit to the west is the actual Washoe Valley, after which the entire country took its name. To the south, separating it from the Carson and other valleys, lay "a chain of rugged hills, termed the Silver Range." From these hills runs a ridge between them and that portion of the Sierra Nevada known as the Washoe Mountains.[6] On the eastern margin of the valley is a lake, five miles long and two wide, shallow and shrinking in the dry season, surrounded by alkali, lending the water a brackish quality, without impeding its fitness to drink.[7] The presence of water makes the land here somewhat arable and suitable for pasturage. Other valleys are found nearby—the Eagle, the Pleasant, and Steamboat—all relatively isolated from the larger settlements due to an absence of good roads. North lies the Truckee Meadows and the Truckee River, flowing north-easterly to Pyramid Lake. Farther to the east is the great entrepot of the Washoe, the heart of Nevada mining country and site of the richest mines, Virginia City. In 1860 it was an isolated mining camp surrounded by barren hills containing some fifty houses and a population of approximately 200 souls, many of whom lived in tents, others in holes in the ground and a few in the mouths of tunnels.[8] The Ophir Company, the Mexican and several others were busy at work on the great bed of underground silver-bearing ore known as the Comstock Lode. It was a miserable country, not easily entered, "lonely, inhospitable, and unfruitful…,

---

[4] *Daily Alta California*, February 28, 1860.
[5] *Daily Alta California*, February 29, 1860
[6] *Daily Alta California*, March 1, 1860.
[7] Id.
[8] *Daily Alta California*, March 7, 1860.

of savage aspect and dubious wealth—a land abounding with bitter waters and blistering rocks; a basin filled with mephitic pools and ponds of lye, thickly strewn with lava, basalt slag, and cinders, the apparent vestiges of a pre-existent system—a primitive wilderness so scorified, saline, and sulphurous that it would seem to have been rained upon with fire and brimstone, and afterwards sown with salt."[9] But for the presence of mineral wealth, the condition of the land here was "not one calculated to encourage a rapid increase of permanent settlers."[10]

During the winter of 1859 and 1860, news spread west to San Francisco of the discovery of massive numbers of quartz veins, the broad dimensions of which suggested a depth that was for all practical purposes bottomless. Sixty tons of ore from the Ophir and the Central Mines reaching San Francisco in the late fall "dispelled all doubts as to the riches of Washoe and created unparalleled excitement throughout California."[11] Men and pack animals started crossing the mountains even before the February thaw. Though blizzards and rumors of Piute atrocities chilled enthusiasm during the spring, ten thousand Californians made their way to the Comstock by the end of the summer.[12] The towns of Virginia City, Gold Hill and Silver City appeared almost instantly.[13] During the spring of 1862, the Ophir Company's mill went into operation on high-grade ore; the Gould & Curry was engaged in the construction of an enormous mill; new discoveries in Aurora, Austin and the Humboldt region were announced, and stocks began to climb in value.[14] A stock boom commenced, culminating, at least in part, in the organization in San Francisco of a Stock Exchange on September 11, 1862.[15] Virginia City's population ballooned to 15,000 and became a city in more than just name. "Homes, business buildings and office blocks were built, many of them of brick; gas and sewer pipes were laid in the principal streets;" the International Hotel was

[9] *Daily Alta California*, March 17, 1860.

[10] *Daily Alta California*, March 8, 1860

[11] Grant H. Smith, *The History of the Comstock Lode, 1850-1997, With New Material by Joseph V. Tingley* (Reno: Nevada Bureau of Mines and Geology, 1998), at p. 20.

[12] Id., at p. 21.

[13] Id.

[14] Id., at p. 26.

[15] Id.

enlarged to contain a hundred well-furnished rooms—with an elevator from the 'C' Street entrance; "daily stages brought in all of the luxuries of the Bay region; the restaurants vied with those of San Francisco; [and] three theatres played to crowded houses."[16] Most important of all, the ore being extracted surpassed all expectations. The great mines—the Ophir, the Gould & Curry, the Savage, the Little Gold Hill, the Mexican, the Chollar, the Potosi, the Yellow Jacket, Belcher and Sierra Nevada—were booming, and by year's end the value of the yield of the mines had doubled from the previous annum and was in excess of a staggering $12,000,000.[17] "The mineral wealth hidden beneath Nevada's rock-ribbed hills," said one historian, "even exceeded the dreams of fiction writers in their wildest flights of imagination."[18]

Not one to ignore opportunities for profit, Perley began purchasing timber land and mining claims in the Washoe in the Fall of 1860.[19] His enthusiasm for investment picked up considerably beginning in January of 1862, when he made a string of purchases, including 25 feet in the Irving Ledge in the Virginia Mining District, various claims in the Silver City District, 50 feet in the Virginia Company claim in Ophir, or Spanish Ravine, where the Ophir Company's flume was situated, and various claims in the Gold Hill District.[20] He purchased a 10-acre town lot on the road between Virginia City and Gold Hill for $1,000, and made further parcel and mining claim purchases in the months to come.[21] At the beginning of 1863, he launched his career as a mining company operator. He and four other men incorporated the Kansas Gold & Silver Mining Company with the intention of operating in the Devil's Gate District

---

[16] Id., at p. 28.

[17] Id., at p. 32.

[18] J. P. O'Brien, *History of the Bench and Bar of Nevada* (San Francisco: Bench and Bar Publishing Company, 1913), at p. 6.

[19] Deed from E.E. Edson to D.W. Perley for one-sixth of an undivided interest in 954.36 acres in Carson County, Utah, dated October 5, 1860, Russell McDonald Papers, NSA [Nevada State Archives]; Deed from C.H. Brown to D.W. Perley for half an undivided interest in 309.91 acres of timber land in Carson County, Utah, dated October 5, 1860, Russell McDonald Papers, NSA; and Storey County Deeds, K:41.

[20] Storey County Deeds, E:319, E:320 and C:226.

[21] Id., at E:322, C:260, D:639, E:438, E:456, F:257, H:1, H:41, H:39, K:45, K:48, A:12:448.

in Lyon County, with capital stock valued at $510,000 in the aggregate, to sell at $100 per share.[22] On March 18, 1863, he and four partners incorporated the Bailey Gold & Silver Mining Company, with capital stock valued at $1,100,000.[23] Laying claim to 2,200 feet of ground, the Bailey "attracted considerable attention and now bids fair to become one of the favorite stocks in the market."[24] With future Nevada and Alaska Governor John H. Kinkead and three others, Perley next organized the Bennett Gold & Silver Mining Company.[25] He also became a shareholder of the Cherokee, Warsaw, Aylesworth, Colorado, Colusa, Ontario, Gentle Annie, Consolidated Yucatan & Mary Annie, and the Pioneer Gold & Silver Mining Companies.[26] Among his fellow investors in the Aylesworth was Laura Fair, soon to file bankruptcy in Sacramento, and very much a source of gossip for Perley himself when in the company of just about anyone who would listen.[27] Those privy to the colorful commentary would later refuse to repeat it in mixed company, so apparently vulgar did it appear.[28] The company he kept in these endeavors was reflective of the circles in which he moved. Assemblyman Charles E. Delong was a fellow shareholder in one enterprise, while R. P. Ashe, Richard Roman and Sierra County Judge W. S. Sherwood were co-owners with him of a number of lots in Virginia City, which they subsequently flipped.[29]

Though it was not noted in the press until the beginning of the new year, it was in August of 1862 that his practice commenced "in several courts of the Nevada Territory and the Supreme Court of the United States," from offices at the corner of C and Taylor Streets in Virginia City, in partnership with C. H. S. Williams and George D. Keeney.[30] The partners represented plaintiffs in suits against the Burning Moscow Gold & Silver Mining Company and Patrick

[22] Nevada Territorial Records, 0080:66, NSA.

[23] Id., at 0075:42.

[24] *Virginia Evening Bulletin*, December 21, 1863.

[25] Nevada Territorial Records, 0074:36, NSA.

[26] Id., at 0068:33, 0073:39, 0076:60, 0076:64, 0076:73, 0078:70, 0085:20, 0091:30, 0091:71, NSA.

[27] See *Gold Hill Daily News*, November 10, 1863; *Sacramento Daily Union*, June 11, 1863; and *Sacramento Daily Union*, April 13, 1871.

[28] *Sacramento Daily Union*, April 13, 1871.

[29] Storey County Deeds, N:381, N:617, S:30, and S:37.

[30] *Territorial Enterprise*, January 10, 1863.

O'Toner, and defended others in the second half of the year: the Burning Moscow against the Madison Gold & Silver Mining Company, and George W. Frink against James Morgan and others.[31] The firm was brought in to assist Stewart, Kirkpatrick and Rising in a complex matter involving two claimants to the proceeds of a sale compelled by two different judgments against the same debtor, the noted surveyor Jasper O'Farrell. When the Court reduced the amount subject to the judgment, Perley and his partners appealed to the Territorial Supreme Court. Responding to the rather anemic brief, Justice Turner affirmed the original decision.[32] When the brief partnership came to an end for reasons unknown, Perley invited Judge Joseph Baldwin's nephew, John Garber, to join him at the Taylor and C Street office in a collaboration that lasted an even shorter length of time.[33]

For the first five months of 1863, Perley worked alone, filing complaints in two cases, including one on behalf of W. H. Howard, who had sold nearly 56,000 pounds of quartz-bearing rock to the operators of the Rodgers Gold & Silver Mining Company in November of 1862, but hadn't been paid. Perley's opponents argued no payment was due on account of the ore being fourth class, hence not of sufficient value to justify hauling away and sifting.[34] During the same period of time, he answered on behalf of three parties. One was his own Bennett Gold & Silver Mining Company, which was

---

[31] See the following records from the Nevada State Archives [NSA]: *Marston v. the Burning Moscow Gold & Silver Mining Company*, Storey County District Court, Register of Actions, Books A-C, Register No. 267; *James Morgan et al. v. George W. Frink*, Storey County District Court, Register of Actions, Books A-C, Register No. 272; *Ed. Ruhling et al. v. Jasper O'Farrell et al*, Storey County District Court, Register of Actions, Books A-C, Register No. 295; *The Burning Moscow Gold & Silver Mining Company v. The Madison Gold & Silver Mining Company*, Storey County District Court, Register of Actions, Books A-C, Register No. 299; and *William Barron v. Patrick O'Toner*, Storey County District Court, Register of Actions, Books A-C, Register No. 332.

[32] See *Ruhling v. O'Farrell*, Case No. 27, Nevada Territorial Supreme Court Records, NSA.

[33] J. Wells Kelly, *Second Directory of Nevada Territory* (San Francisco: Valant & Co., 1863), at p. 270.

[34] *W. H. Howard v. Rodgers Gold and Silver Mining Company*, Story County District Court, Register of Actions, Books A-C, Register No. 515, NSA.

being sued by Stewart, Baldwin and Rising on behalf of a rival company, the Imperial.[35]

The unmistakably light weight of Perley's litigation in the early months of 1863 can be attributed to any number of factors, but lack of opportunity to take on clients likely wasn't one of them. Public enthusiasm for mining spread in the first days of the year eastward into the more forbidding rock deserts of the Territory. Discovery of promising mining ground in the Nevada badlands along the Reese River in the very center of the modern State "gave extraordinary impetus to prospecting, and soon a very large area of country was run over and new districts formed."[36] Desiring to take advantage of this newest bonanza and banking that it could prove richer than even the Comstock, Perley repeatedly wrote his cousin James and relations back in New Brunswick, urging them to join him in Nevada in exploring investment opportunities along the Reese River. Convinced that their fortunes awaited, Walter Perley, son of cousin Charles, and Perley's sister Frances's son Theodore Clowes Miles, prepared to leave the Atlantic Provinces for central Nevada. Knowing his cousin Duncan all too well, James approached the opportunity rather more circumspectly. When his neighbors opined as to the soundness of the endeavor, James and sons Solomon and Charles bought a wagon for $215, in addition to clothing and other items, and embarked on "a journey over the mountains into a new country."[37] While his sons drove the wagon, James rode on horseback, following the route described by Duncan in his letters. Once in Virginia City, the cousins discussed the situation and agreed that James "was to go to Reese River and to look for chances to speculate, for good town lots and town plats and look out for good ranches." As James recalled, "I was also to prospect around for mines and in all cases where I saw a good chance or good chances look out for him in common with myself in locating lands and mines."[38] Duncan would pay his expenses if there was no

---

[35] *Imperial Silver Mining Co. v. Bennett Gold & Silver Mining Company*, Story County District Court, Register of Actions, Books A-C, Register No. 540, NSA.

[36] *History of Nevada, With Illustrations and Biographical Sketches of its Prominent Men and Pioneers* (Oakland: Thompson & West, 1881), at p. 425.

[37] *Duncan W. Perley v. James E. Perley*, San Joaquin Superior Court, Case No. 2179-80.

[38] Id.

success, but if success came their way, James would get half of the profits. With such incentives compelling him forward, he left his horse with his cousin and journeyed to the Reese River by stage. He explored Jacobville, Penny Canyon, Clifton and Austin, but found nothing but high prices for food and lodging. He finally settled upon the purchase of six lots in Austin on Main Street, four of which he put down in his cousin's name. After he apprised Duncan by letter of his success, Duncan joined him in the town, and together they went "round the country prospecting for vineyards, mines, and gardens."[39] They found one spot that Duncan thought had great promise for a quartz mill, but by day's end, his outlook became rather morose. "This place," he opined, "is going to hell. It is not worth a damn. The mines went bust no time at all." After insisting for months on the unparalleled opportunity to be found on the Reese River, Duncan now explained that "I have invested very largely here and I mean to get out of it as soon as I can." He told James he'd keep James' horse as consideration for $200 of the $350 James had collected, and James could send him the balance later. With that, Duncan abruptly "turned and left." James had spent $800 getting out to Nevada at his cousin's urging and spent considerable time exploring for chances, only to have his cousin suddenly abandon the venture in the most casual of ways. Duncan, of course, kept the four lots and then sold them in October of 1863 for $2,000 in gold coin, but didn't share a dime with James. James returned to California, displeased with his cousin, but utterly distracted once home by the great developments in the politics of the nation and his own growing eagerness to enter the fray and participate in moving the State more solidly behind the Union effort.

Perley's stint as a solo practitioner in the hectic Comstock country would be short lived. A relatively new attorney, with limited experience in court but enormous enthusiasm for the work, Charles E. DeLong possessed a resume that included service in the California Senate representing Marysville, in addition to broad connections with the more moderate elements of the Democrat Party. He supported the Party generally, but opposed the expansion of slavery. He joined the Law and Order League during the Vigilance uprising, but measured his emotional response far better

---

[39] Id.

than David Terry. His entry into Party politics resulted in regular contact with Party leaders, with whom he grew friendly. During the election of 1859, he met with Broderick frequently, and spoke often on his behalf. The news of Broderick's wound and subsequent death caused him "great indignation" and "immense sensation."[40] Leaving office after two terms, he took up the practice of law in partnership with George Rowe. Disappointed in his hopes for a political comeback, he headed east for Washoe.[41] Soon after his arrival there reports circulated back home in Marysville that Delong had "formed a co-partnership with a resident attorney."[42] By June, the news was that it was Perley, "an able practitioner," with whom DeLong had partnered, and that his plan was to split time between Marysville and the Comstock Lode.[43]

Not so jaded to life as was his new partner, DeLong remained slacked jawed over the conditions in Virginia City and Nevada as a whole, describing "this country" as "a lawyer's paradise...the wildest for law that you ever heard of," and "much more extravagant in its proportions than California ever was."[44] The two men proved to be a good fit both professionally and personally, though Perley might have suffered shock, at least at first, reading of his law partner's elevated enthusiasm for the Union when addressing his friends at home during his regular trips over the Sierras to Marysville.[45] DeLong settled into the Taylor & C Street office, got to work on what would be a large portfolio of cases, often with the aid of the firm's law clerk, W. E. F. Deal, who would briefly join the practice as a third partner in 1865, just prior to Perley's

---

[40] Carl I. Wheat, "'California's Bantam Cock,': the Journals of Charles E. DeLong, 1854-1863," *California Historical Society Quarterly*, Volume 10, No. 2 (June 1931), at p. 174.

[41] Carl I. Wheat, "'California's Bantam Cock,': The Journals of Charles E. DeLong, 1854-1863, Appendix: Outline of DeLong's Career After December 11, 1862," *California Historical Society Quarterly*, Volume 11, No. 1 (March, 1932), at p. 47.

[42] *Marysville Daily Appeal*, May 23, 1863.

[43] *Marysville Daily Appeal*, June 16, 1863.

[44] Charles E. DeLong to James R. DeLong, September 2, 1863, in Carl I. Wheat, "'California's Bantam Cock,': The Journals of Charles E. DeLong, 1854-1863, Appendix: Outline of DeLong's Career After December 11, 1862," *California Historical Society Quarterly*, Volume 11, No. 1 (March, 1932), at p. 60.

[45] *Marysville Daily Appeal*, July 19, 1863.

return west.[46] By September of 1863, when the Fall Session of the District Court convened, the partners had 18 cases on file, with 7 already scheduled for jury trials, and opposed in them by Williams & Keeney, Stewart, Baldwin & Rising, Clayton & Hardy and other luminaries of the Comstock bar.

As active as Perley was as an investor, speculator and attorney with interests and ambitions unique to himself, it cannot be doubted too vigorously that a primary objective of Perley in coming to the Washoe was to assist his closest and oldest friend, David Terry. He had provided Terry with $5,000 to invest in a joint account after the Broderick debacle, and Terry seems to have acted on the entrustment following his acquittal in Judge Hardy's Court by heading to Nevada.[47] Along the way, he was joined by Hardy's former law partner, Joseph P. Vaughn, recently the Clerk for both Solano County and the Secretary of State (and a witness in the Whitman impeachment trial). They were quickly retained by Hart and Scott, the adverse claimants in the Comstock Lode, and opposed by the superior might of the Gould & Curry Company and their intimidating counsel, William M. Stewart, formerly the Acting Attorney General of California. A suit was filed in Carson City in August of 1860 and the first great legal battle of the Washoe was on. In August of that year, Scott conveyed his interest to Terry and Vaughn, while Hart, perhaps thinking the cause lost, made a conveyance to their opponent.[48] A motion was brought to dismiss the case, which was answered with the contention that Terry and Vaughn had succeeded to at least half of the claim. Soon the *Alta* predicted the worst regarding the former Chief Justice. "Terry, it is understood, feeling the untenable position he occupies, and probably not relishing his client's getting the cash, and his case gone, has expressed himself as going to take by violence and mob law that portion of the mine claimed by him, even if the courts decide he has no rights."[49] The litigation was as trying as any Terry had been involved with in Texas or California, due in part to his opposing counsel, a man as fierce and unyielding as Terry himself.

---

[46] O'Brien, op. cit., p. 288.

[47] Russell Albert Buchanan, *David S. Terry of California, Dueling Judge* (San Marino: Huntington Library, 1956), at p. 113.

[48] *Daily Alta California*, September 17, 1861.

[49] Id.

Though opponents, Terry and Stewart respected one another, and were able to reach an accord on the issue of which of the two competing federal judges would be acknowledged as legitimate. When Terry opted out of the agreement and then left for a visit to San Francisco, Stewart seized the opportunity to gain a crucial strategic advantage. Having forced an unfriendly judge to resign in favor of the one who was more amenable to his interests, Stewart (and everyone else) supposed that Terry "would be very indignant and that something sensational might occur."[50] Instead, Terry conceded Stewart's superior organization and resolve, and blamed the loss on himself and his ill-timed absence in San Francisco.[51]

It could not have been a coincidence that Perley's relocation to Virginia City in the summer of 1862 corresponded with the opening of the Supreme Court and the other courts organized under the Territorial Government. Almost immediately on taking up residence in Nevada, Perley purchased Terry's interest for $5,000. He sat on the claim for a year before filing an entirely new suit against the Gould & Curry Company, asking for $1,000,000.[52] Stewart answered Perley's Complaint on July 10, denying Hart and Scott had possession, or that they had ever owned or even worked it, hence they could never have conveyed a legitimate interest to Perley. Further bolstering his clients' claim, said Stewart, was the half million dollars in improvements made in the preceding year, not to mention the conveyance by Hart of the entire interest to the Gould & Curry. Not denying the conveyance had occurred, Perley scoffed that it was received with full knowledge that the grantee had no capacity to convey what his cohort, Scott, had previously transferred to Perley's predecessor-in-interest, David Terry. Declared by the press to constitute "an important suit," the case was but one of the seventeen or so filed by Perley and DeLong that were scheduled for further action in the fall session of the District Court.[53]

---

[50] Davis, op. cit., at p. 281.

[51] Id.

[52] Storey County Deeds, H:38; *D. W. Perley v. Gould & Curry Co.*, Superior Court of Storey County, Register of Actions, Books A-C, Register No. 610, Suit No. 167, Judgment No. 579, NSA; and *Sacramento Daily Union*, June 23, 1863.

[53] *Sacramento Daily Union*, June 23, 1863; *Marysville Daily Appeal*, June 24, 1863; and *Santa Cruz Weekly*, June 27, 1863.

The slow pace of legal proceedings, delaying outcomes for years, owed to the oppressive congestion of the courts arising from the spontaneous flooding of a very primitive system of justice serving a largely uninhabited country. A vast desert that the Spanish and Mexicans had overlooked, the Washoe had no settlements of note and no legal history or institutions prior to 1850. The first tribunal was a probate court venued in Carson City and staffed by Orson Hyde, an Apostle of the Mormon Church and an official of the Territorial Government situated in far off Salt Lake City.[54] Following the dictates of the Mormon Prophet, Hyde "expressly renounced the common law as a judicial imperative" in the Territory for fear it would be used against the faithful.[55] The unsettled mixture of Mormon colonists, gentile homesteaders and godless miners created a clash of cultures reflected in differing expectations regarding the law and legal system that were to govern disputes, while the at best only temporary presence of judicial officers in the area rendered even the semblance of legal authority the most fantastic of chimeras. By the summer of 1856, a group of non-Mormon citizens of the Carson Valley declared that "they will no longer be governed or tried by Mormon law," and forswore any intention or obligation to pay taxes "levied on them from that source."[56] A District Court of the United States was created to address the vacuum, and the first Judge took his seat in 1856 in a venue doubling as a barn with a known prostitute by his side. Dismayed by the desiccated and lonely Nevada landscape, the Judge soon resigned and moved on to California.[57] His successor, Judge John Cradlebaugh, made a more lasting impression. He convened the first real session of the Court in an old building, repaired and furnished with a $750 allocation from the Congress, thirty by sixty feet in dimension and one and a half stories tall, with so large a gap between the ground and the doorway that a ladder

---

[54] Thomas Wren, *A History of the State of Nevada, Its Resources and People* (New York: The Lewis Publishing Company, 1904), at p. 232.

[55] David A. Hardy, *The Nevada Territorial Supreme Court: A Transitional Influence From Frontier Lawlessness to Statehood*, Ph.D. diss., University of Nevada, Reno, 2015, at p. 9.

[56] Id., at p. 17.

[57] Id.; and Wren, op. cit., at p. 232.

was needed in order to reach the court room.[58] His efforts complicated by continuing confusion about the control over law and justice by the distant Mormons, and the miners themselves having taken matters into their own hands by forming a self-governing mining district subject to laws of their own devising, Cradlebaugh lost the confidence of most of the population. As predictions of "scenes of anarchy of bloodshed, fearful to behold" circulated amidst the chaos of competing mine locations, the Judge was removed by President Buchanan and replaced by R.B. Flennicken on May 11, 1860.[59] When Flennicken arrived in October, Judge Cradlebaugh asserted that the President had no Constitutional power to remove a member of the judiciary and that he was still a lawful judge.[60] He possessed the singular advantage of the support of both Terry and Stewart, who had reached an agreement that they both would recognize Cradlebaugh as the legitimate incumbent.[61] This soon changed when Terry announced he would henceforth only try cases before Flennicken. The controversy over the judges came to a close early in 1861 when Stewart terrified Flennicken into conceding the post to his rival.[62] In time, Judge Cradlebaugh was displaced by a new Territorial judicial establishment, including three district court judges who would also serve as the Territory's Supreme Court. They would hold office a mere two and a half years and would lose their posts with the coming of Statehood.

The judges who presided over the great mining litigation of the Comstock, and Perley himself, were surrounded by a remarkable class of lawyers, "some of which were cleavers and battle axes, some Damascus blades, and in the wielding of those weapons they were all trained until they had become real gladiators." In the many trials over the bizarrely tangled and conflicting claims over mining ground, "a spectator saw only flashings of great lights; there were arguments which Burke would have listened to enchanted; there were bursts of legal eloquence which would have charmed Clay or

---

[58] Wren, op. cit., at p. 62.

[59] Hardy, op. cit., at pp. 33-39; and Sam Post Davis, *The History of Nevada*, Volume I (Reno: The Elms Publishing Co., 1913), at p. 277.

[60] Davis, op. cit., at p. 278.

[61] Id.

[62] Id., at pp. 280-281.

Prentiss." It was, said one historian of the State's early bar, "an arena where giants contested."[63] As early as September of 1860, doubts were expressed "whether any Court in California can show as brilliant an array of talent as is now engaged in the trial of different cases before the U.S. District Court, in Genoa."[64] Because of the riches at stake and the unbridled impulse of men to locate claims regardless of the prior rights of others, "disputes arose which eventually developed into an almost endless chain of litigation that taxed the litigants to the extent of many millions of dollars.[65] In such an environment, with so much to be won and lost, it was inevitable that the Comstock "became the Mecca of the legal fraternity," where attorneys "earned princely fees for their work."[66]

The call, said O'Brien, "was heard and heeded by the very flower of the legal profession in many adjoining, even distant States. It brought men of mature years well versed in every precedent of jurisprudence, together with the beardless embryo, proud possessor of a crackling, shiny sheepskin and a legal library of two volumes labeled respectively: Blackstone and Kent."[67] The unsettled nature of the jurisdiction, the absence of any accepted legal authorities therein, and the novel problems of law never dreamed of in the more settled places of the nation turned the conflicts from those involving the application of settled principle to a free-for-all, not unlike in the early days of California over a decade before, in which he who proved the most physically courageous, psychologically impervious to intimidation and persuasive in the eyes of those rough, vulgar and jealous men who constituted most juries in that time and place, emerged as the preeminent members of the bar. When anything approaching doctrines of law gained currency, they resembled the barest of those first principles of common sense and reason, and contributed to what one of the pioneer lawyers of the day referred to as "a sort of common law, customary in mining districts."[68]

---

63 O'Brien, op. cit., at p. 77.
64 *Marysville Daily Appeal*, September 20, 1860.
65 O'Brien, op. cit., at p. 6.
66 Davis, op. cit., at p. 391.
67 O'Brien, op. cit., at p. 6.
68 Wren, op. cit., at p. 233.

When the Territorial Supreme Court took office on June 2, 1862, its justices moved immediately to organize the bar and establish rules more fixed and certain than existed in the earliest days of the Washoe. Virtually the first order of business was the admission to practice of the small group of distinguished counsel who had already become engaged in Comstock litigation. The group included former California Justice Joseph G. Baldwin, future Territorial District Court Judge John Wesley North, William M. Stewart, Jonas Seely, Thomas B. Reardan, California's former Know Nothing Governor John Neely Johnson, and C. H. S. Williams. Of these men, Baldwin, Reardan and Williams were ordered to form "a committee to draft and report rules for the government of proceedings in this Court."[69] They and several others at this early time provided leadership for the profession and commanded the highest respect among the lawyers, judges and litigants in the many, many cases that moved through the Nevada courts. No mean judge of legal talent, Judge Rising said of Williams that he was by far the most able he ever saw, possessing "in a fuller measure perhaps than any other the qualities which go to make up a great lawyer." Called "the Nestor of them all," he emitted charisma and bon vivant, in addition to a degree of erudition that would prompt Perley—as often opposed to his one-time law partner as aligned—to exclaim "why, the damned old fool knows everything!"[70] Not only did Williams obtain a large share of the mining litigation and even draft a code of procedure for the first regular court in the Territory; he also became the moving force in the organization of the local Bar Association.[71] When Perley sought admission to the bar of the Territorial Supreme Court in April of 1864, it was Williams who vouched for and formally sponsored him.[72] Baldwin, of course, was a former critic of Perley's on the California Supreme Court, lately resigned in order to pursue the lucrative employment to be found on the eastern side of the Sierras. His talented son Alexander was also in the Washoe and would serve for a time as a Federal District Judge until his premature death in a train wreck in Oakland later in

---

[69] Davis, op. cit., at p. 283.

[70] See O'Brien, op. cit., at p. 76; and George Thomas Marye, *From '49 to '83 in California and Nevada* (San Francisco: A.M. Robertson, 1923), at pp. 140-141.

[71] *Virginia City Daily Union*, May 20, 1864.

[72] Minutes of the Supreme Court of Nevada Territory, NSA, at p. 86.

the decade.[73] Ex-Governor Johnson would soon play a leading role in organizing Nevada as a State as a member of the State's Constitutional Convention and would eventually take a seat on the State's Supreme Court. North was a pioneer in the founding of the Republican Party, a former member of the Minnesota Legislature, and President Lincoln's appointee to the office of Surveyor General of the Nevada Territory. A native of Maryland and former Judge in Sutter County, he joined the migration to the Washoe, served briefly as District Court Judge for Virginia City and a member of the three-man Territorial Supreme Court, and would later return to the Bench in California, in Nevada County.[74]

The most dominant man of the Washoe Bar was Stewart. Six feet two inches tall, with "a great wealth of reddish-brown hair, with immense whiskers and mustache of the same hue; his eyes...were gray, but under any light except sunlight, they seemed to be black.... He had, too, a bearing like that of a lion when he stalks up and down his cage and dreams of his days in the jungle when he was lord of all."[75] He was a native New Yorker, a prospector, ox team driver, and then lawyer in the Sierras, who managed to marry the daughter of ex-Senator Foote of Mississippi. "He was not sensitive, neither was he sentimental, and his nature all his life was to conquer any difficulty that he met."[76] In the lawless Comstock, he could defeat any lawyer greater than himself. It was said that he "was never fazed; he could appeal to juries and to those chumps of judges successfully, when his case had been torn to shreds, and in a thousand adroit ways baffle all legitimate conclusions."[77] More brilliant and polished than Stewart but no less effective was Tod Robinson, already recognized as one of the best lawyers of the past decade practicing in California, "a fine scholar, an eminent lawyer, an orator most careful in his selection of language, always in a public address to adjust himself to his audience...most intense in his sectional prejudices, but veiling them all in his dealings with

---

[73] "Death of A. W. Baldwin," *Sacramento Daily Union*, November 15, 1869.

[74] J. M. Guinn, *History of the State of California and Biographical Record of the Sacramento Valley, California* (Chicago: The Chapman Publishing Company, 1904), p. 892.

[75] O'Brien, op. cit., p. 65.

[76] Id., at p. 66.

[77] Id., at p. 67.

men."[78] "He depended," said O'Brien, "upon the cold logic of truth to point his argument and the perfect logical rhythm of his thoughts to kindle men's admiration. Naturally he was most effective in the court-room, one of the class that judges lean upon, for he never juggled with a legal principle and never misstated a legal proposition."[79]

There were other notable lawyers, too. "On the stump and at the bar," Former California Supreme Court Justice Charles H. Bryan "was equally effective and his companionship was courted by all classes of people."[80] Like many of the lawyers of the age, he indulged often in drink, and it was said of him that he did so "until his mind lost its balance, and then became a monomaniac on the subject of electricity," convinced that this particular force of nature, harnessed by man for the benefit of civilization, "was destroying him."[81] He was later arrested and charged with malicious mischief after cutting down a mile or more of telegraph poles between Carson City and another town.[82] Fresh from his impeachment and removal from the bench for disloyalty, but in reality for dismissing the Terry prosecution, Judge James Hardy was soon in the ranks of the Washoe Bar, briefly joining Terry and Vaughn in a partnership, and doing quite well until returning to California, where he resumed a prominent place in society. When Terry and Vaughn departed east to join the doomed Confederacy, Hardy teamed with another great Washoe advocate, Leander Quint, a native of Vermont, former Judge in Tuolomne County, of "tall and commanding figure, and of manly address," ever able to inspire affection "by thorough good nature and accessibility."[83] C. J. Hilyer, Thomas H. Williams, Jonas Seely, John R. McConnell, Jesse Pitzer, W.W. Bishop, William Clagget, Henry H. Highton, William Campbell, Thomas Sunderland and even for a brief time A.P. Crittenden rounded out the leading attorneys of the Washoe: peers, allies and competitors of Perley, friends as well as adversaries, who

---

[78] Id., at p. 62.

[79] Id.

[80] *San Francisco Call*, January 28, 1894.

[81] Id.

[82] Id.

[83] *Sketches of Leading and Representative Men of San Francisco* (London: London and New York Publishing Company, 1875), at p. 884.

played roles of varying significance throughout the remainder of his life. Together they would facilitate the orgy of litigation characterized by "tampered juries, fixed judges, manufactured evidence, false witnesses available for hire, and questionable lawsuits to cloud title" that defined the Comstock Lode and succeeded in consuming twenty percent of all mining revenues through the year 1865.[84]

Terry may have stayed for a brief time to practice law with Perley in 1862 and 1863, but any joint venture of this kind did not endure. Terry's heart lay with his people in Texas and with the political movement that had inspired the wing of the Democrat Party to which he belonged. Subject to questions about his loyalty, hardly quelled even after he swore allegiance to the United States, Terry watched with profound displeasure the unfolding of Lincoln's war policy. Having decried the prosecution of the war while on the stump in 1861 and 1862 on behalf of Copperhead candidates and become convinced of the duty "to pursue the warfare against this unconstitutional power which has arisen among us," he finally reached a decision to abandon California and return east to serve his State and the putative nation which Texas had opted to join.[85] Possessing now a uniform made for him in San Francisco, his commission as an officer in the Confederate service and a horse costing his admirers $2,000, Terry was joined in his decision to journey east by his law partner, Joseph P. Vaughn, who would later secure a major's commission in a Missouri division under General Price.[86] Conflicting reports had Terry in Nevada Territory and Mazatlan in February of 1863. In Mexico, he and T.T. Bouldin, Duncan Beaumont, Isaac Hewitt, Jonathan Loveless, Edward Grayson and Tod Robinson's two boys boarded the steamer *Oregon* for the East.[87] As the ship steamed southward toward Panama wonder was expressed in the media over what "branch of service to which Davis will assign Gen. David S.

[84] Hardy, op. cit., at p. 53.

[85] *Red Bluff Independent*, September 23, 1862; and *Sacramento Daily Union*, July 24, 1863.

[86] *Marysville Daily Appeal*, March 13, 1863; and *Los Angeles Star*, November 29, 1862.

[87] *Marysville Daily Appeal*, March 10, 1863.

Terry."[88] By late April the company with which he traveled was now referred to as his "staff," and had grown to number 68 souls.[89] Sometime in the spring, Terry's party arrived at the sugar plantation in Oakland, Texas jointly owned by his brother Frank and W. J. Kyle.[90] In a letter published in the press, one of Robinson's sons noted that "Judge Terry leaves in about a week direct for Richmond, on important business with the government," to report on various theories of how to win California for the South, or even to use Mexico as a base of operations. The Confederate Government, however, was far less interested in Terry's strategic thoughts than it was in his service in the field. In time, he assumed his late brother's position in command of Terry's Texas Rangers for the duration of the war, fighting in some of the awful battles preceding the collapse of the South—Chickamagua, Knoxville, and the hopeless harrying of Sherman during the relentless March to the Sea. Alongside him were Judge James Love, one of Terry's nephews and John Austin Wharton—the latter of whom fell not in battle but in a brawl in camp with a comrade. Periodically, Terry's alleged deeds were reported in the California press: his presence on various battlefields, his supposed execution of an abolitionist preacher, and his escape and exile to Mexico at war's end to avoid arrest and imprisonment.

The departure of his closest friend since his days in Texas was but a larger process of transhumance by the members of the circle with which Perley most closely associated. Some of these associates chose willingly to take their leave of loyalty and the Union; others were pronounced guilty either by association or by what they said or didn't say, and suffered summary exile as a result. A principal leader of the Chivalry, a confidante of Andrew Jackson and, until recently, an esteemed member of the United States Senate, William Gwin was arrested in Panama with Calhoun Benham in October of 1861 on suspicion of being on his way to join the Confederacy and

---

[88] *Marysville Daily Appeal*, March 5, 1863.

[89] *Marysville Daily Appeal*, April 28, 1863; and *Marysville Daily Appeal*, May 1, 1863.

[90] *Marysville Daily Appeal*, July 17, 1863.

lend what aid he could to its cause.[91] Gwin soon retired to Mississippi with his family, and then found refuge in Mexico as a grower of cotton. Benham was later rumored to have found a place on the staff of Albert Sidney Johnston and taken part in the Battles of Pittsburg Landing and Shiloh.[92] Crittenden's kinsman, Harry I. Thornton, Jr., resigned his seat in the State Assembly and gave up his law practice in order to return to his native Alabama, where he enlisted in the 58th Regiment of the Alabama Infantry and fought at Fishing Creek, Shiloh and Baton Rouge.[93] Two of A. P. Crittenden's sons departed east and joined the Confederacy, while Crittenden himself, after failing to lead his party to victory in California in 1862, was rumored to have followed suit and taken the rank of General in a South Carolina regiment.[94] In truth, he departed California with R. P. Ashe, Richard Roman, Judge Heydenfeldt and others for Nevada, where the oath of allegiance to the Union wasn't required. Gregory Yale actively resisted the oath, claiming in a matter before the California Supreme Court that the power to impose it on lawyers was outside the scope of any authority vested in the Legislature by the Constitution.[95] His claim rejected, he submitted to the oath, though many doubted his sincerity in doing so.[96]

George Pendleton Johnston found refuge in Mazatlan for much of the war, growing cotton on a large plantation. His use of free labor provided northern critics with all the proof they needed of the fallacy of slavery and the hypocrisy of its defenders.[97] Samuel H. Brooks resigned his post as State Treasurer before the expiration of his term after defeat in a bid for re-election and took a steamer to Panama and another to Texas. He lived quietly for a time in Montgomery, Alabama, but eventually accepted a commission in a cavalry unit under General Benjamin F. Cheatem and fought at

---

[91] *The War of the Rebellion: A Compilation of the Official Records of the Union and Confederate Armies*, Additions and Corrections to Series II, Volume II (Washington: Government Printing Office, 1902), at p. 1009.

[92] *Sacramento Daily Union*, July 27, 1862; and *Los Angeles Star*, November 29, 1862.

[93] *Los Angles Star*, November 29, 1862.

[94] *Sacramento Daily Union*, July 27, 1862; and *Los Angeles Star*, November 29, 1862.

[95] *Ex parte Yale* (1864) 24 Cal. 241.

[96] Robert J. Chandler, "California's 1863 Loyalty Oaths: Another Look," *Arizona and the West*, Vol. 21, No. 3 (Autumn 1979), at p. 227

[97] *Marysville Appeal*, July 17, 1863 and *Daily Alta California*, September 24, 1863.

Murfreesboro and Chickamauga.[98] He later transferred to the Trans-Mississippi Department and commanded the Thirty-First Texas Cavalry Regiment before ending his war service as a Lieutenant Colonel under David Terry.[99] Former congressman Philemon Herbert, who had entered the legal profession with Perley back in 1846 and later attempted from the floor of Congress to rally federal support for the armed suppression of the Vigilantes, returned to Texas in 1859, but when the War commenced, he obtained a commission to raise three companies for service in Arizona.[100] He died of wounds received at Mansfield in 1864 during the Red River campaign.[101] Also killed in battle was Tom Lubbock, who fought side-by-side with Terry's brother at Manassas and then assisted Frank Terry in organizing Terry's Texas Rangers. He succeeded Frank from a sick-bed to command following Frank's death, but expired the following day from typhoid fever.[102] E.J.C. Kewen remained loyal, but only barely in the eyes of some, who commented on "that lamblike apostle of peace" who waxed "eloquent in his late speech of the horrors of war invoked by pro-slavery fanatics for the destruction of our free government."[103] It was hardly forgotten by minds stirred with the passions of a great war how "he went with the filibuster Walker to impose foreign rule and a slave constitution upon the inoffensive people of Nicaragua," and attempted to spread the curse of slavery in that place.[104] Harry Logan also refrained from disloyalty and the urge to defend with arms his native South Carolina, but nevertheless failed to escape suspicion during a visit to Washington, D.C. that his true purpose was to slip through enemy lines and join his secessionist friends.[105]

---

[98] *Red Bluff Beacon*, November 28, 1861; and *Los Angeles Star*, November 29, 1862.

[99] Brett J. Derbes, "Samuel Houston Brooks," *Handbook of Texas*, https://www.tshaonline.org/handbook/entries/brooks-samuel-houston.

[100] Martin Hardwick Hall, "Philemon Thomas Herbert," *Handbook of Texas*, https://www.tshaonline.org/handbook/entries/herbert-philemon-thomas.

[101] Id.

[102] See Francis Richard Lubbock, *Six Decades in Texas* (Austin: Ben C. Jones & Co., 1900), at pp. 314-316 and p. 377; and Thomas W. Cutrer, "Thomas Saltus Lubbock," *Handbook of Texas*, https://www.tshaonline.org/handbook/entries/lubbock-thomas-saltus.

[103] *Marysville Appeal*, May 24, 1863.

[104] Id.

[105] *Sacramento Daily Union*, February 17, 1863.

The loss of Terry was undoubtedly painful to Perley on a personal and professional level. The fate of his friend, client and business partner Austin Smith, while not as affecting as Terry's journey east, must have made an impact as well. As noted earlier, Smith had gone east at the end of his term as Naval Agent, and while in New York was arrested and charged "with being a defaulter to the government and having the books and papers of the Naval Agency in his possession and with being a secessionist and rebel."[106] He apparently had been en route to Washington, D.C. to settle his accounts in the Nation's Capital. By order of Secretary of State Seward, he was consigned to Fort Lafayette as a political prisoner. Witnesses discretely came forward and confirmed that Smith possessed "disloyal and rebellious sentiments and purposes…that he was a rabid and fiery rebel and that he had openly declared on board ship that had he had in his possession any considerable amount of Government funds he would have retained it for the use of the army South." A Federal examiner found him "in all respects…a disloyal man—energetic, active and determined."[107] Initially he refused to pledge his loyalty to the United States, or even to promise not to consort with the Nation's enemies. After four months confinement, he proposed to "pledge and bind myself upon my honor if set at liberty by the President of the United States to proceed without unnecessary delay to Washington to settle my accounts and thence if required by the President to return immediately to California."[108] It wasn't until the Government became aware of a valuable Union prisoner in Confederate custody that it negotiated the release of Smith in exchange for the other man, but only on condition that he go south, not west. He was set loose in May of 1862 and rendezvoused with his father, now a Confederate General stationed in Virginia. He received a major's commission in the Confederate Army, served on General Whiting's staff in Stonewall Jackson's corps and fell severely wounded in battle on

[106] *The War of the Rebellion: A Compilation of the Official Records of the Union and Confederate Armies* (Washington: Government Printing Office, 1902), at p. 424.
[107] Id., at p. 427.
[108] Id.

June 27, 1862.[109] An arm was amputated in an effort to save him, but to no avail. He expired mere hours afterward.[110]

The summer doldrums in Nevada allowed Perley an opportunity to respond to those outside the State in need of his legal services. Far to the east, his former client General Fremont weathered controversy after controversy, first during his famed 100 days as the savior of the west in Missouri, and then in the Mountain Department, suffering slings and arrows more political in nature than military. Resignation from his command in Virginia prompted a self-imposed exile to New York, which had the singular advantage of placing him amongst a host of money men from whom either to borrow funds or at last unload the anchor that had become the Mariposas. Lawsuits in California continued, but without his direct involvement. To address a civil action brought against him by a disgruntled former occupant of the Estate, as well as other maters requiring prosecution, Fremont arranged for a message to go out to his erstwhile attorney. With time on his hands waiting for the opening of the courts in Nevada, Perley accepted the assignment and took up the appeal of a $1,000 judgment against Fremont arising from the physical removal of the prevailing plaintiff from property Fremont's agents had acquired within the Rancho's bounds. The property was "an old dilapidated building, of little or no value," occupied by tenants of the agent of a man who claimed ownership. A negotiated resolution fell apart when a second tenant—the Plaintiff—entered the premises and refused to depart. A less than dignified ejection from the property caused the Plaintiff to sue. Rather than address the merits of the case, Perley focused on the technicalities. An unsuccessful demurrer brought at the outset of the matter correctly identified numerous violations of the Practice Act. The Plaintiff, said Perley, had wrongly "united several causes of action in his complaint, to wit: injuries to personal property with injuries to real property, [and]... also united injuries to his person with injuries to both real and personal property. He has also united with the aforesaid actions, an action for a false

[109] *Sacramento Daily Union*, July 27, 1862; and John W. Bell, *Memoirs of Governor William Smith of Virginia: His Political, Military, and Personal History* (New York: The Moss Engraving Company, 1891), at p. 89 and p. 120.

[110] *Marin Journal*, August 23, 1862.

imprisonment; which could not be done under the statute."[111] It might be true that the Practice Act itself contained some ambiguity on the relevant points, but doubts were easily resolved by reference to the reliance by the Act's author, Stephen Field, to the handiwork of his brother David. As California's law derived from New York's Code of Procedure, New York decisional law was relevant to clarifying its meaning. The Court need only consult New York judicial construction of New York law to realize that Fremont's demurrer should have been sustained.

The Supreme Court of California agreed with Perley, noting that while it is permissible for a plaintiff to unite various causes of action in the same complaint, it can only be done "when they all arise out of certain classes of contracts or injuries."[112] The Plaintiff erred in bringing classes of action that were incompatible and including them all in a single count, in "clear violation of the provisions of the Practice Act." Though the court need not have gone further in its analysis, it gratuitously offered that the damages awarded by the jury were plainly excessive. The damages were in part for harm to property that the Plaintiff didn't own and had no authority to occupy. He was merely a trespasser attempting to obtain and maintain possession of property that wasn't his. The alleged injuries he suffered to his person when removed from the land by force were trivial, and the removal itself was no more forceful than necessary for that purpose. The excessive amount awarded, in the view of the more Republican oriented Supreme Court, appeared to have been "given under the influence of passion and prejudice."[113]

Perley also initiated two suits in Justice Field's federal court sounding in common law against two defendants previous sued in State court, but withdrew in favor of B. S. Brooks and Hall McAllister.[114] These matters would be Perley' final service to the Pathfinder, proving to be naught but useless valor in a cause that was doomed on account of the latter's profligacy and overreaching. Fremont sold the Mariposas that year to a consortium of

---

[111] *McCarty v. Fremont* (1863) 23 Cal. 196.

[112] Id., at 197.

[113] Id., at 198.

[114] Minutes, United States Circuit Court, District of California, Volume 3, June 1, 8163 to January 3, 1865, at p. 180, http://familysearch.org. The matters were *Fremont v. John Van DeWater* and *Fremont v. S.B. Allison*.

millionaires in New York City, ending a misery that had only grown with the passage of time.[115] For Perley, the outcome was at least beneficial financially, and brought him to the attention of law observers around the country. Writing some time later, one commentator noted that the new statute governing pleadings owed much to the contribution of California courts, which had construed the derivative Practice Act in a helpful way, notably in *McCarty v. Fremont*, where it was held that "causes of action must be separately stated and that it is improper to unite in one complaint damages for injury to both person and property."[116]

With the opening of the Fall Term of the District Court presided over by newly appointed Judge North, Perley and DeLong engaged in an entirely different kind of war. In *Grass Valley Company v. Bajazet & Golden Era*, they fended off the effort of Stewart, Baldwin and Rising to bar the Bajazet from mining a rich vein two rival mining outfits disputed.[117] On the eve of the Term, the men of the Bajazet had tunneled into the Grass Valley's shaft, driven the latter's employees out, and started working the shaft as if it were their own.[118] A second front was opened when William Stewart and his partners filed suit on behalf of the mighty Hale & Norcross Company seeking the Bajazet's ejectment from 40 contested feet of ground.[119] In the former case, Perley and DeLong demurred to the complaint, but soon agreed to withdraw the demurrer and simply file an answer.[120] Even before that answer was received by the Court, Perley was seeking issuance of a commission for service out-of-State to obtain the deposition of a vital witness.[121] The parties agreed to continue the matter, apparently for the purpose of

---

115 Allan Nevins, *Fremont: Pathmarker of the West* (New York: Longmans, Green and Co., 1955), at pp. 585-586

116 George Rossman, "Joinder of Causes of Action," 57 Am. Law Rev. 532 (1923), at 546

117 *Grass Valley Silver Mining Company v. Bajazet & Gold Era Company*, Storey County District Court, Register of Actions, Books A-C, Register No. 560, NSA.

118 *Virginia Evening Bulletin*, August 11, 1863.

119 *Virginia Evening Bulletin*, July 7, 1863; and *Hale & Norcross Silver Mining Co. v. the Bajazet & Golden Era Consolidated Gold & Silver Mining Co.* Storey County District Court, Register of Actions, Books A-C, Register No. 637, NSA.

120 *Virginia Evening Bulletin*, September 16, 1863; and *Virginia Evening Bulletin*, September 17, 1863.

121 *Virginia Evening Bulletin*, September 18, 1863.

working toward a resolution of the dispute. Perley and DeLong similarly withdrew demurrers in the *Cerro Paseo* case; while in *Rohr v. Young* they stipulated to a judgment on the papers.[122] They agreed with plaintiff's counsel to submit the matter of *Noyes v. Lyford* to a special master for a determination of the facts and the issuance of a judgment, and with defense counsel to do the same thing in the matter of *Shelton v. Baxter*.[123] They demurred in *Harrison v. Madison*, but soon agreed to withdraw the motion and submit an answer within 30 days. With the partners so occupied in litigation, only DeLong was able to appear to argue against a demurrer filed in the matter of *Peter Rice v. North American Company*.[124] Coordinating with six or seven other lawyers, Perley and DeLong also made common cause against a group of claimants adverse to the Potosi Company, alleging trespass in the digging of a shaft known as the Junction Tunnel and liability for damages in the amount of $10,000.[125] In their greatest suit of all, against the Gould & Curry Company, nothing of note occurred, as the matter was continued into the Court's subsequent term.

As the Fall Term of the Court proceeded, Perley and DeLong didn't merely concentrate on cases already filed. Perley continued his effort to develop mining claims by incorporating new mining enterprises. Great promise appeared with respect to the Baily Gold & Silver Mining Company with its emergence as "one of the favorite stocks in the market."[126] Perley and his partners in that venture managed to dig a tunnel running 175 feet and open a ledge 20 feet in width.[127] The extraction and crushing of ore-bearing rock

---

[122] *Virginia Evening Bulletin*, September 17, 1863; *Cerro Paseo Gold & Silver Mining Co. v. The Insurance Co.*, Storey County District Court, Register of Actions, Books A-C, Register No. 614, NSA; and *Rohr v. Young*, Storey County District Court, Register of Actions, Books A-C, Register No. 695, NSA.

[123] *Virginia Evening Bulletin*, September 16, 1863; and *Virginia Evening Bulletin*, September 24, 1863.

[124] *Virginia Evening Bulletin*, September 18, 1863.

[125] See *Potosi Gold & Silver Mining Company v. M. Emerson et al.*, Storey County District Court, Register of Actions, Books A-C, Register No. 664, NSA; and Charles E. DeLong to James R. DeLong, September 2, 1863, in Carl I. Wheat, "'California's Bantam Cock,': The Journals of Charles E. DeLong, 1854-1863, Appendix: Outline of DeLong's Career After December 11, 1862," *California Historical Society Quarterly*, Volume 11, No. 1 (March, 1932), at p. 60.

[126] *Virginia Evening Bulletin*, December 21, 1863.

[127] Id.

proceeded to the jubilation of the stockholders, who hoped for the "turning out [of] silver bricks before too long."[128] He and DeLong also continued to sign up new clients and file appropriate pleadings on their behalf, either in the form of complaints seeking damages or equitable relief, responsive pleadings, and motions seeking termination of any further litigation. From the beginning of September through the end of the year, they took legal action on behalf of Plaintiffs F. S. Malone, James Woods, E. M. Earl, Ferdinand Scherr, Solomon Jewett, the Harrington Company, Eli McDaniel, the Potosi Company (against L. E. Horton, represented by Mesick, Stewart, Baldwin and Tod Robinson in one case, and the Belvedere and Bonanza Companies in another), A. K. Cowger, Mrs. L. E. Frinke, Peter Rice, the Fairview Company, the Double Eagle (against the Burning Moscow), John Dickey, W. H. Sarles, John McCausland, and Bouth & Prescott.[129] They filed suit against the Pioneer Stage Company on behalf of Judge Heydenfeldt for $50,000 to compensate him for injuries when a stage he was riding in overturned, and also eight individual actions on behalf of individual claimants against the Uncle Sam Gold & Silver Mining

---

128 Id.

129 See the following records from the NSA: F.S. Malone v. E.A. Probois, Register No. 721; *James Woods v. William Hartnell et al.*, Storey County District Court, Register of Actions, Books A-C Register No. 767, *E.M. Earl v. Grove Adams*, Storey County District Court, Register of Actions, Books A-C Register No. 797; *Ferdinand Scherr v. John Denniger*, Storey County District Court, Register of Actions, Books A-C, Register No. 806; *Solomon Jewett v. E.L. Henry et al.*, Storey County District Court, Register of Actions, Books A-C, Register No. 807; *Harrington Co. v. John Doe and Richard Roe*, Storey County District Court, Register of Actions, Books A-C, Register No. 852; *Potasi Co. v. L.E. Horton*, Storey County District Court, Register of Actions, Books A-C, Register No. 878; *Potasi Co. v. Belvidere Co.*, Bonaza *Co. and Youuve Co.*, Storey County District Court, Register of Actions, Books A-C, Register No. 891; *A.K. Cowger v. Mary Annie Co.*, Storey County District Court, Register of Actions, Books A-C, Register No. 949; *Mrs. L.E. Frinke v. Kenosha Co.*, Storey County District Court, Register of Actions, Books A-C, Register No. 950; *Fairview Co. v. Maria Bell et al.*, Storey County District Court, Register of Actions, Books A-C, Register No. 952; *Double Eagle Co. v. Burning Moscow Co.*, Storey County District Court, Register of Actions, Books A-C, Register No. 953; *John Dickey v. A. Newman et al.*, Storey County District Court, Register of Actions, Books A-C, Register No. 1025; *W.H. Sarles v. Oliver Hyder*, Storey County District Court, Register of Actions, Books A-C, Register No. 1062; *John McCausland v. Maria Bell et al.*, Storey County District Court, Register of Actions, Books A-C, Register No. 1064; and *Bouth & Prescott v. Cobbon*, Storey County District Court, Register of Actions, Books A-C, Register No. 1066.

Company after it was disclosed that there were "more claimants for ground…than the Company actually possesses."[130] The Uncle Sam apparently sold claims to purchasers to 3,000 feet of ground, despite owning 600 feet less than that.[131] Two suits were brought by Perley himself as a plaintiff: one against the Iowa Gold & Silver Mining Company, in which he apparently owned shares; another against a Mr. Chandler, about whom Perley alleged a taking of $26 through misrepresentation.[132] He and DeLong also defended others against suits brought by numerous individuals and mining companies: Jesus and Florentine Alvarez, H. A. Shelton, the Laboring Gold & Silver Mining Company (against the Yellow Jacket, represented by Stewart, Baldwin & Rising), Charles Levy, J. R. Hardenburg, a Mr. Jackson, the Potosi Company (against the Chollar, represented by Stewart), the Original Hawkeye Gold & Silver Mining Company (against the Lafayette and Uncle Sam Companies, represented by A.P. Crittenden, James Hardy and Thomas Sunderland), the Fairview Company (against Grass Valley), and the Fairview, Croesus, Bullion, Minerva, Superior, Alpha and Four Twenty Companies in a suit brought by Stewart and Baldwin on behalf of

---

130 See the following records from the NSA: *Heydenfeldt v. Pioneer Stage Co.*, Storey County District Court, Register of Actions, Books A-C, Register No. 1067; *Gold Hill Daily News*, December 16, 1863; *David Nattine v. Uncle Sam Co. and Baltic Co.*, Storey County District Court, Register of Actions, Books A-C, Register No. 890; *Joseph Dellapiane v. Uncle Sam Co.*, Storey County District Court, Register of Actions, Books A-C, Register No. 893; *Peter Larkin v. Uncle Sam Co. and Baltic Co.*, Storey County District Court, Register of Actions, Books A-C, Register No. 943; *McCloskey v. Uncle Sam Co.*, Storey County District Court, Register of Actions, Books A-C, Register No. 955; *Piccoli v. Uncle Sam Co. and Baltic Co.*, Storey County District Court, Register of Actions, Books A-C, Register No. 994; *Anisin v. Uncle Sam Co. and Baltic Co.*, Storey County District Court, Register of Actions, Books A-C, Register No. 995; *Ellis v. Uncle Sam Co. and Baltic Co.*, Storey County District Court, Register of Actions, Books A-C, Register No. 1030; *Keenan v. Uncle Sam Co.*, Storey County District Court, Register of Actions, Books A-C, Register No. 1235.

131 "Lots of Claimants," *Virginia Evening Bulletin*, November 21, 1863.

132 *D.W. Perley v. Iowa Mining Co.*, Storey County District Court, Register of Actions, Books A-C, Register No. 100, NSA; *Gold Hill Daily News*, December 24, 1863; and *Virginia Evening Bulletin*, December 24, 1863.

Theodore Winters.[133] In the flux of all of this litigation, Perley somehow managed to return to San Francisco in mid-November and file suit in the Twelfth District Court to quiet title to two parcels at the northeast corner of the so-called "College Lot" near the Mission Dolores. He was back in Virginia City via the Pioneer Stage on December 7.[134]

With the coming of the January Term in 1864, most of the above-mentioned cases appeared on the docket of Judge North's Court, along with others filed in previous terms that had not yet resolved. The term, like the one following it in March, was likely a "long and tedious one."[135] Perley was absent from Virginia City for the first part of the month of January, attending the first of several trials in San Francisco in the notorious "Bird's Nest Case," but returned via stage on January 23.[136] Perhaps it was mere coincidence that he departed and returned with a Miss Caldwell, the daughter of one of his business associates. His mining speculation continued with the

---

[133] See the following records from the NSA: *Nelson Brobank v. Jesus and Florentine Alvarez*, Storey County District Court, Register of Actions, Books A-C, Register No. 746; *Marie A. Bell v. H.A. Shelton*, Storey County District Court, Register of Actions, Books A-C , Register No. 766; *Yellow Jackett Silver Mining Co. v. Laboring Gold & Silver Mining Co.*, Storey County District Court, Register of Actions, Books A-C, Register No. 786; *Mary Young v. Charles Levy*, Storey County District Court, Register of Actions, Books A-C, Register No. 795; *C.L. Ross v. J.R. Hardenburg*, Storey County District Court, Register of Actions, Books A-C, Register No. 825; *Lee McGowan v. Jackson, Roe, Doe, et al.*, Storey County District Court, Register of Actions, Books A-C, Register No. 832; *Chollar Silver Mining Co. v. Potasi Co.*, Storey County District Court, Register of Actions, Books A-C, Register No. 865; *E.A. Hyde v. Potasi Co.*, Storey County District Court, Register of Actions, Books A-C, Register No. 882; *Lafayette Co. v. Original Hawkey Co.*, Storey County District Court, Register of Actions, Books A-C, Register No. 896; *Uncle Sam Co. v. Original Hawkeye Co.*, Storey County District Court, Register of Actions, Books A-C, Register No. 904; *Baltic Co. v. Gentle Annie Co.*, Storey County District Court, Register of Actions, Books A-C, Register No. 908; *Chollar Silver Mining Co. v. Potasi Co.*, Storey County District Court, Register of Actions, Books A-C, Register No. 924; *Grass Valley Co. v. Faireview Co. & Bellvedere Co.*, Storey County District Court, Register of Actions, Books A-C, Register No. 925 & 926; *Theodore Winters et al. v. Fairview, Croesus, Bullion, Minerva, Superior, Alpha and Four Twenty Companies*, Storey County District Court, Register of Actions, Books A-C, Register No. 966.

[134] See *Daily Alta California*, November 21, 1863; and *Gold Hill Daily News*, December 7, 1863.

[135] *Virginia City Daily Union*, March 6, 1864.

[136] See *Daily Alta California*, January 13, 1864; and *The Mountain Democrat*, January 23, 1863.

purchase from a Mr. Thompson of an interest in the Kitch & Baker and Dorra Mining Company claims and his involvement as an incorporator of the Columbia Gold & Silver Mining Company with DeLong and others.[137] A set-back occurred with the Colorado Company, incorporated the previous year, as conflict with the Uncle Sam complicated extraction efforts and the belligerency of the Piutes halted them completely.[138] Encroachment on the Company's tunnel by a competing concern quickly convinced the operators of the need to overcome their fear of Indian attacks and resume work. The Colorado's workers managed to sink the shaft 75 feet and plank it to a depth of 30 feet. Their intention was to work "night and day till they are down 200 feet and then drift to the west of the ledge."[139] A general downturn in the mining economy was the likely cause of Perley's decision not to pay assessments on stock owned in the Sunrise Gold & Silver Mining Company, hence he probably shed no tears when the stock was sold at public auction.[140] He and other counsel involved were undoubtedly behind the streamlining of the litigation surrounding the Bajazet Company, for which the stockholders were publicly praised.[141] He reached an agreement with the Imperial to settle the case brought on behalf of the Bennett Company, and the case was dismissed.[142] Litigation on behalf of the Fairview Company bogged down in pleading motions against various parties, which Perley soon dismissed in order to focus on the merits.[143]

By far the biggest development of the first quarter of the year was Judge North's decision to deny Stewart and the Chollar Company an injunction to prevent the Potosi and others from occupying mining ground in accordance with the dubious theory that all ledges were in fact outcroppings of a single ledge belonging to the first locator, the Chollar.[144] The decision effected every single

137 Storey County Deeds, W:65.

138 *Virginia City Daily Union*, March 27, 1864.

139 *Virginia City Daily Union*, April 26, 1864.

140 See *Gold Hill Daily News*, February 25, 1864; and *Gold Hill Daily News*, May 26, 1864.

141 *Virginia City Daily Union*, April 5, 1864.

142 *Virginia City Daily Union*, April 7, 1864.

143 *Virginia City Daily Union*, March 29, 1864.

144 See *Virginia Evening Bulletin*, April 1, 1864; and *Virginia City Daily Union*, April 1, 1864.

mine operating in the Comstock and directly impacted Perley's cases on behalf of the Potosi, Bajazet and himself against the Chollar, Grass Valley and Gould & Curry Companies. The decision partially reversed Stewart's victory against David Terry several years before. Appeal to the Territorial Supreme Court offered some hope for the vanquished. Though North was not likely to change his view in conference with his two brethren, the Chief Justice appeared favorable to the single ledge theory, perhaps because of a $20,000 bribe.[145] A race, thus, commenced to win the allegiance of the third member of the tribunal, Justice Locke, who was soon seen drinking to excess first with one set of mining interests and then another.[146] When the Court's 2-1 decision to sustain North's injunction was published, it undoubtedly convinced Stewart that the Court was stacked against him. If he could not be rid of the vexing North through a subsequent campaign of public vilification, he might obtain a similar result through successful agitation for the replacement of the territorial regime with a State government—one that Stewart himself aspired to control.[147]

Perley's return to San Francisco at the start of 1864 and stay there over the course of several weeks certainly allowed him to reconnect with his daughter Mina, who was living with a family named Ford, as well as catch a glimpse of a young lady he must have been at least vaguely familiar with years before in Stockton. The young lady, Josie Mansfield, was said to be "of full, dashing figure, not at all gross," with eyes that were "large, deep and bright," and hair black with a hint of purple, "worn in massive coils over a well-shaped head" that was "a wonder in its luxuriance and native gloss," not to mention "her well-cut lips…her magnificent teeth, her clear pearl complexion suffused at times with a soft pink flesh."[148] She was the daughter of the late Joseph Mansfield, the proprietor of *The San Joaquin Republican*, gunned down on the street by rival newspaperman John Tabor in 1854. Tabor was convicted by a jury and sentenced to hang by Judge Creanor, notwithstanding

[145] Hardy, op. cit., at p. 67.

[146] Id., at p. 68.

[147] *Gold Hill Daily News*, July 26, 1864.

[148] R.W. McAlpine, *The Life and Times of Col. James Fisk, Jr., Being a Full and Impartial Account of the Remarkable Man* (New York: The New York Book Company).

the efforts of David Terry and S. A. Booker on his behalf.[149] Perley may have been acquainted with the girl and her mother after they removed to San Francisco two years later and remained in touch while the widow Mansfield sojourned in Stockton with the gambler, Richard Warren, to whom she eventually wed. What is known for certain is that by early 1864 Perley had reconnected with Josie and become "her preferred admirer above all others." The not entirely innocent nature of the relations became evident one day at the home of Josie's mother, when Warren burst into Josie's locked bed chamber, pistol in hand, ready to fire into the temple of Perley, as Josie herself fainted from shock and fright.[150] Josie later recalled the incident, confirming that "the pistol was pointed at D. W. Perley" by Warren "in the parlor of my mother," though she claimed, rather unconvincingly, not to "know why the quarrel happened," to have "no recollection of any circumstances which caused it to happen," and denied any intimacy with Perley whatsoever.[151]

Accusing Perley of criminal intercourse, Warren coerced him into signing a check for $5,000, ordered him out of the house at gun point, and threatened that "if he ever spoke of the affair he would shoot him on the spot."[152] A less authoritative, albeit more contemporary account had it that Perley was "compelled...to sign a check for $1,000 by a lady border at the Lick House, who accused him of having seduced her daughter, a young lady not long a resident of this city."[153] Where the reports conformed is in the fact that once the source of coercion disappeared, Perley's prudence overcame his panic and he rushed to the bank to stop payment on the check.[154] Hardly a surprise, the story almost at once became the subject "of an immense amount of street and parlor gossip" and added to Perley's legend as a rather inept disciple of the notorious Seducer of Seville.[155] Contemplating the damage the tale might do to his personal and professional profiles, it may well be that it was

---

149 George H. Tinkham, *History of Stockton* (San Francisco: H.M. Hinton, 1880), at pp. 139-140.

150 See *San Francisco Call*, December 1, 1901.

151 *Sacramento Daily Union*, December 7, 1871.

152 *San Francisco Call*, December 1, 1901, check.

153 *Red Bluff Independent*, April 21, 1864.

154 Id.

155 *Red Bluff Independent*, April 25, 1864.

Perley himself who went to the press, described it as a black-mail operation between the flirtatious Josie and her pandering step-father, and boasted of how he "boxed the ears of the man who drew the pistol…and then kicked him down the stairs into the street."[156] Josie herself insisted that the affront to Perley was no conspiracy, but a result of duress by Warren and her own mother, from whom she sought protection from another admirer, the actor Frank Lawlor.[157] Her account is doubtful in light of the fact that within a matter of a month, she and Lawlor exchanged vows and departed for the east coast. The motive behind the hasty flight from the City was not, as one paper reported, Perley ordering Lawlor out of the State within thirty days "on penalty of death," but for entirely personal reasons.[158] Lawlor and Josie would soon divorce due to Lawlor's suspicions about her faithfulness. In time, she would become the mistress of the financier Jay Fisk and the impetus for Fisk's sensational murder at the hands of a rival paramour, Ed Stokes.

Back in Nevada, Perley pursued various suits on his own behalf against E. P. Spiller and a Mr. Struss in Judge Ferris' Probate Court.[159] His suit on behalf of Judge Heydenfeldt settled, as did his case against the Iowa Gold and Silver Mining Company.[160] He and DeLong took on the causes of J. E. Colburn in an appeal from the Probate Court, Isaac Summer, a Mr. Farrington, the Original Hawkeye Company, Frederick Sawyer, the Virginia Company, James Keenen, a Mr. Drake, John A. Canbray, and a series of cases

---

[156] Id.

[157] *Sacramento Daily Union*, March 6, 1872.

[158] Id.

[159] *Virginia City Daily Union*, May 3, 1864; and *Virginia City Daily Union*, May 10, 1864.

[160] *Virginia City Daily Union*, May 3, 1864.

against Gould & Bernstein.[161] Perley re-teamed with C.H.S. Williams to defend the Twin Company against the Pride of the West, which Perley was also suing in a separate suit.[162] He and DeLong defended numerous individual parties as well: Ignacio Franco, a Mr. Alvarez, C. Lintoll, and two former clients, Henry Sheldon and W. H. Howard.[163]

Perley's ambitions in the Comstock, as before at the Bar in San Francisco, tended to push all else save perhaps his interest in women to the side. Though it is lost sight of in the flux of Perley's adventures in California and Nevada, it cannot be ignored that Perley was a father to a young child, whose loss of a mother when still an infant could only have created a void that a doleful spirit filled in the frequent absences of the only parent she had left. Little remains behind of the girl save her name, inferences to be drawn from her mother's death and father's preoccupation with work, and

---

161 See the following records from the NSA: *S.E. Colburn v. J.E. Colburn*, Storey County District Court, Register of Actions, Books A-C, Register No. 1097; *Isaac Summer v. J.J. Brundage*, Storey County District Court, Register of Actions, Books A-C, Register No. 1104; *Farrington v. Saunders*, Storey County District Court, Register of Actions, Books A-C, Register No. 1126; *Fred Sawyer v. S.M. Cook*, Storey County District Court, Register of Actions, Books A-C, Register No. 1183; *Virginia Co. v. Alban Co.*, Storey County District Court, Register of Actions, Books A-C, Register No. 1187; *James Keenan v. Uncle Sam Co.*, Storey County District Court, Register of Actions, Books A-C, Register No. 1235; *William Meyer & Co. v. Gould & Bernstein*, Register No. 1338; *David Feris v. Gould & Bernstein*, Storey County District Court, Register of Actions, Books A-C, Register No. 1339; *Scholl & Brothers v. Gould & Bernstein*, Storey County District Court, Register of Actions, Books A-C, Register No. 1340; *Drake et al. v. Thomas Delany*, Storey County District Court, Register of Actions, Books A-C, Register No. 1348; and *John A. Canbray v. Inhabitants of Gold Hill*, Storey County District Court, Register of Actions, Books A-C, Register No. 1353.

162 Pride of the West Mining Co. v. Twin Co. No. 2, Storey County District Court, Register of Actions, Books A-C, Register No. 1113, NSA; and *Twin Co. v. Comstock Combination Co. and Pride of the West Co.*, Storey County District Court, Register of Actions, Books A-C, Register No. 1112, NSA.

163 See the following records from the NSA: *Thomas Manifee v. Ignacio Franco et al.*, Storey County District Court, Register of Actions, Books A-C, Register No. 1155; *S.W. Hearst v. Alvarez*, Storey County District Court, Register of Actions, Books A-C, Register No. 1239; *W.W. Knox v. Henry Seldon*, Storey County District Court, Register of Actions, Books A-C, Register No. 1256; *Gould & Curry Company v. C. Lintoll et al.*, Storey County District Court, Register of Actions, Books A-C Register No. 1314; and *L. King v. W.H. Howard*, Storey County District Court, Register of Actions, Books A-C, Register No. 1351.

a blurred copy of a daguerreotype placed into an edition of the published genealogy of the Perley family. Its origin is lost in the oblivion of most of our world's history, though a few statements from he who appears to have produced the image indicate that she was a sweet and gentle child. Since his removal to Virginia City—a place her father aptly concluded was unfit for a girl of tender years—she remained in the care of Mrs. Ford, residing in San Francisco at 615 Pine Street. Mina apparently grew ill early in the summer of 1864 and did not improve. The end must have been expected; for when the poor girl expired, on Thursday, June 23, at 8 p.m., her funeral was already prepared. The following day, some of the papers printed an invitation to "her friends, the friends of her father, and those of Mrs. Ford's family" to attend a service at the Ford home at 4 p.m. the very same day.[164] Referred to as the "only child of D. W. Perley," she was reported to have been aged "8 years and 8 months."[165] She was buried near her mother atop Lone Mountain, windy as ever, with a hint of salt in the air, but surrounded now by the creeping suburbs of the City.

Perley's relations with his family had become quite strained. Little contact was there with cousin Fred, who busied himself in the San Joaquin countryside pioneering the science of viniculture. Relations with cousin James undoubtedly remained chilly in the wake of the debacle on the Reese River. James' growing prominence in the State as an advocate of President Lincoln and the Union movement may have further contributed to the drift between the men. In the summer of the preceding year, James won the nomination of his Party for a seat representing San Joaquin County in the State Assembly, and then went on to win the General Election so convincingly against his Democrat opponent that it was announced that "Secession and Copper-headism is whipped out effectively and forever in San Joaquin County."[166] Sworn into office early in December of 1863, he received an assignment to the Commerce and Navigation Committee and set to work drafting a Bill to authorize the establishment of a public pound in the County for wayward livestock. He defended the funding of an effort to

---

[164] *Daily Alta California*, June 24, 1864.

[165] Id.; and *The Daily Bee*, June 25, 1864.

[166] *Stockton Daily Independent*, June 15, 1863; and *Stockton Daily Independent*, September 2, 1863.

renovate the Insane Asylum, was instrumental in the defeat of a bill to permit theatrical performances on the sabbath, and lent his support to a proposal to construct a wagon road up to the Nevada border, to connect with another highway from the border all the way to the Reese River.[167] A resurgence of mining activity there and reports in Stockton papers of the riches being discovered on a daily basis, no doubt irked the Assemblyman, and may have contributed to his oration during the session condemning the State's exemption of mining claims from a property tax imposed exclusively on farmland.[168] Though hardly a leader in the legislature, he was considered to have been "among the most attentive of members and the hardest of workers."[169]

James' legislative prominence did not extend to him any general immunities, including against his cousin. In the lull between legislative sessions, and less than two months after Mina's death, Perley arranged for service on James of a complaint seeking damages for breach of contract to repay loans made in 1857 and 1861 totaling $3,400, in addition to interest.[170] The loans were secured by a mortgage on James' 320-acre homestead on the Mokelumne River, sixteen miles from Stockton—the very same property the cousins had wrested from adverse claimants a decade before. With the aid of counsel, George W. Tyler, James denied the allegations, and insisted that the debts had been paid in full, in part by the proceeds of the sale of a portion of his land in 1862. He also sought offsets for all the expenses Duncan forced him to incur on his fool's dream of riches in the Nevada desert, and the loss of his horse. When the matter came to trial in December, James attempted to explain how his cousin had stiffed him. After listening to the many minute details of James' ordeal, Perley disregarded his own attorney's admonition and burst out with an objection, demanding that the testimony be stricken from the record on the grounds that "no contract of any kind...had been proved with regard to his going

[167] *Stockton Daily Independent*, February 1, 1864; *Stockton Daily Independent*, February 6, 1864; and *Stockton Daily Independent*, February 15, 1864.

[168] *Stockton Daily Independent*, February 12, 1864; and *Stockton Daily Independent* February 20, 1864.

[169] *Stockton Daily Independent*, January 20, 1864.

[170] *Duncan W. Perley v. James E. Perley*, San Joaquin County Superior Court, Case Nos. 2179-2180.

to the Reese River and his actings and doings there." Piping in on his client's cue, Perley's counsel denounced the testimony as "wholly sham and frivolous, because it is utterly false in point of fact; because it is interposed for delay only, and was not pleaded in good faith!" Cowed by these screaming advocates, James' counsel offered that had he known the statement was going to be made, he would have advised against it because of its dubious sufficiency as an answer to the Plaintiff's affidavit. Ultimately, the Court sustained the objection. On December 14, the Parties rested and the case was given over to the jury for a verdict.[171] The jury found for Perley on both debts and awarded nearly $5,000 in damages, plus costs, minus the value of the horse. An order was issued to the Sheriff to seize a portion of James' property for sale at auction. Perley himself placed the winning bid. On June 13, 1867, when the last dime of the jury award was paid and the final traces of resentment had likely faded, Perley conveyed the property back to his cousin in exchange for a dollar in payment.[172]

As Perley's case against his cousin approached the date of trial, the people of Nevada entertained the call for Statehood. Unionists in Washington, D.C. were seeking to consolidate support for the War effort and perhaps enhance enthusiasm for the ratification of amendments designed to render permanent the fruits of the great sacrifices made to obtain what was hoped would be victory over the Confederacy. Others, like William Stewart, saw Statehood as a means of gaining control over the region so that his interests and those of his clients might prevail. Stewart had promoted Statehood in late 1863, taken part in the first Constitutional Convention, but then suffered defeat when the voters rejected the proposed Constitution, in part over concerns that Stewart's influence in the new State would lead to the imposition of oppressive taxes and the replacement of Judge North with a magistrate more amenable to the single ledge theory.[173] Perley and DeLong likely resented Stewart's intrigue to overthrow Judge North's decision in the Chollar case, and now to overthrow Judge North himself. The emotional distress of Stewart's campaign following defeat of the Constitution to vilify

---

171 *Stockton Daily Independent*, December 16, 1864.

172 San Joaquin County Deeds, A/17/213.

173 Hardy, op. cit., at pp. 59-62.

North as an agent of corruption had forced the Judge temporarily from the bench, placing all litigation on the Washoe on hold. In August, Perley, DeLong and other members of the bar signed a public address to the Judge, expressing regret over his "continued ill health which has heretofore delayed you in discharge of the duties of your office," and assuring him "that we have undiminished confidence in the purity and integrity of your public and private life," and that he had, in their view, "given the highest evidence of prompt attention, patient industry, energetic dispatch, commendable legal ability, official courtesy, and the more crowning quality of a judge—stern, unflinching integrity of purpose."[174]

Nevertheless, many of the same men, including Perley and DeLong, understood the benefits of Statehood in breaking the log jam in territorial courts that appeared in the view of many to be generally incompetent and corruptible. In June, DeLong won election to a second State Constitutional Convention, to attempt with his fellow delegates to formulate yet again an organic instrument to govern the State. With legislative experience behind him, DeLong took a leadership role at the Convention, pointing out the reality of California as a source of most of the Territory's population and proposing from the start that the delegates "adopt the amended Constitution of California as the basis of the one which they were to form for submission to the people of Nevada."[175] Nevadans, he said, were a people "that have lived and acquired property there for years past—who have lived under and are acquainted with the Constitution of that State as it has been construed from time to time by the Supreme Court of that State."[176] The California Constitution, and the interpretations of it by learned and able men such as Stephen Field, set forth in the Reports that nearly every lawyer in the Washoe had on a shelf for reference, provided a short cut to a mature system of law, with which the people of the new State would be entirely at home. He lost the point, but fought his colleagues issue-by-issue to conform the provisions of the State Constitution as closely to that of California as possible, citing detailed facts off the top of his head, tossing out

---

[174] *Virginia City Daily Union*, August 25, 1864.

[175] *Official Report of the Debates and Proceedings in the Constitutional Convention of the State of Nevada* (San Francisco: Frank Eastman, Printer, 1866), at p. 14.

[176] Id.

witticisms and bringing the entire convention to laughter, making eloquent appeals on particular matters, and if not dominating the assembly, then contributing significantly to its handiwork. There can be little doubt as he left the Convention behind and contemplated the Constitution's ratification that his prominence in the organization of the State might well be parlayed into a seat in the United States Senate.

That Stewart was a lock for one of the two Senate seats no one doubted. Aiming to check the influence in the new State of his and Perley's rival at the bar, DeLong opted to throw himself into the fray, politicking wherever he could on behalf of his interests, speaking with a tone of boyish ebullience of the waxing fortunes of the Union and his and the Territory's commitment to the success of the nation in war and peace. As the day for public endorsement or rejection of the Constitution approached, the Storey County Bar—Perley and DeLong included—issued a public statement of support for Statehood, and their intention to "use all honorable means in our power to favor the same."[177] Once the Constitution received popular approval, election of officials to fill the various branches of government delimited within the document occurred. Upon taking their seats, the new members of the two houses of the Legislature set themselves to the task of convening into a joint session for the purpose of selecting two representatives to enter the United States Senate. Stewart remained the front runner, and DeLong was certainly a favorite for the other seat, but the competition was steep. Territorial Governor Nye aimed to go to Washington, D.C., as did former Judge Cradlebaugh. The candidates and their supporters in the Legislature busied themselves lobbying behind the scenes, except for Stewart, or so it seemed, as he relaxed in the parlor he maintained at the Ormsby House, holding court with supplicants and favor seekers before his all but inevitable election. On the first vote, he won more than the required minimum, with DeLong coming in second, tied with Governor Nye. A second vote was held, with Nye pulling ahead 23 to 17, but four short of the votes needed to be confirmed. Six further rounds of voting occurred without a change in the result. On the seventh vote, DeLong's support defected to Nye and the latter was confirmed for the second seat to

[177] *Virginia City Daily Union*, August 25, 1864.

the sound of enormous applause. With haste, both Senators-elect addressed the Legislature, followed by a flourish of a band in their honor. Respecting the good fight fought by DeLong, it played a separate tune afterward especially for him.

The Constitution of the new State provided for an elected judiciary. In accordance with the will of the People expressed late in 1864, James F. Lewis, Henry Oscar Beatty, and Cornelius M. Brosnan prevailed in the canvas and took their places on Nevada's high bench in December of the same year.[178] Taking the chief position was the 30-year old Lewis, who wasn't especially distinguished by any qualities remarkable for a competent practitioner of the law to possess. His success as both attorney and judge was said to be "attributable to his well-applied industry rather than to reliance upon readiness of thought or language at the argument."[179] A marked disinterest in politics accounts for his defeat for re-nomination by his own party in 1872, but he remained afterward in practice and was much appreciated for his "purity of character, and his many deeds of unostentatious charity."[180] Associate Justice Henry Beatty's predominant characteristic was a ravenous hunger to sit on the bench. The previous decade of the Kentucky native's life was strewn with failed efforts to win judicial positions in California and Nevada.[181] A prudish unwillingness to raise a glass with his constituents may have inhibited his electoral chances, but not indefinitely. When he left the bench in 1868, a friendly critic noted that while "no judge makes infallible judgments, and Beatty may have sometimes been in error...he wrought with rare industry, he decided fearlessly and promptly and in accordance with a conscientious understanding of the law."[182] His greatest legacy was his son, William Henry Beatty, who would serve as Judge of the Eighth Judicial District, a member of

---

178 Id., at p. 233; Davis, op. cit., at pp. 300-302; and *Reports of Cases Determined in the Supreme Court of the State of Nevada, Reported by the Judges of the Court During the Year 1865*, Vol. I (Sacramento: James Anthony & Co., 1866), at p. 8.

179 "Proceedings in the Supreme Court," *Reports of Cases Determined in the Supreme Court of the State of Nevada, During 1885, 1886 and 1887*, Vol. XIX (San Francisco: Bancroft-Whitney Company, 1888), at p. 452.

180 Id.

181 "Henry O. Beatty," Online Nevada Encyclopedia, https://www.onlinenevada.org.

182 *Carson Daily Appeal*, November 10, 1868.

the State's Supreme Court and its Chief Justice, and for twenty-eight years, Chief Justice of California. The last of these first members of Nevada's Supreme Court, Cornelius Brosnan, hailed from Ireland. Having immigrated to the United States in 1831 and later commenced a legal practice in California, he became known for "his genial manners, his eloquence, learning and integrity," in addition to "a fine taste, a classical education," and the ardency of his feelings. That he didn't make a fortune as a Washoe lawyer was later attributed to the fact that "the practice of the law had to some extent degenerated into the practice of villainy."[183] While "chicanery won more suits than eloquence and learning, and bribery and corruption more than solid merit," Brosnan "honored his profession, and scorned these practices."[184] Justice Beatty's son said of him that while on the bench Brosnan exhibited a firmness of character "which enabled him to pursue the straightforward course of an upright Judge, seeking only to ascertain the law and decide the right regardless of personal consequences to himself," and in utter disregard of the many "temptations which were attempted to be brought to bear on his judicial decisions."[185]

Nine judicial districts were also provided for in the new Constitution. The First, based in Virginia City, was the largest and certainly the most significant. Because of the high volume of litigation anticipated, it was comprised of three separate divisions, each presided over by a different judge: R. S. Mesick, Richard Rising and Caleb Burbank.[186] An exceptionally able lawyer, Mesick is said to have accepted the job out of frustration at the process of "trying to get a little information through the brains of those incompetent judges" who preceded him.[187] A Yale graduate and Argonaut of 1849, he had practiced in Marysville and, while there, came to know Stephen Field (and probably DeLong) quite well. One historian of the Nevada Bar opined of him that "he was about the greatest man that ever gave the best years of his life to the Golden Coast." He was

---

[183] "Proceedings of the Court Had Upon the Death of Justice Brosnan," *Reports of Cases Determined in the Supreme Court of the State of Nevada, During the Year 1867*, Vol. III (San Francisco: Towne & Bacon, 1868), at p. 16.

[184] Id.

[185] Id., at p. 19.

[186] Id.

[187] O'Brien, op. cit., at p. 77.

"not only as great a lawyer as Field, but...possessed elements of statesmanship which were denied" that illustrious man.[188] A native of Philadelphia, Richard Rising was a relatively young man when he came to the Comstock, where he had the good fortune of making a good impression upon William Stewart, who accepted him into a law partnership that became legendary in Silver country. When Rising took the bench, it wasn't contemplated by anyone that he would successively beat back periodic electoral challenges, win the support of both political parties, and preside over the District for three decades.[189] He grew so venerable as to become "a household word in the judicial and social history of Nevada...as familiar as the croppings of the old Comstock Lode" itself.[190] Though not considered on par with a John Marshall or a Joseph Story, it was believed by many that he "stood highest of any in judicial correctness of his decisions, including many cases where valuable property interests as well as life and death were at stake."[191] Completing the trio of judicial officers in the First District was Maine native, Caleb Burbank. His distinguished years of practice in New England and California, his service as Judge of the Fourth District in San Francisco and member of the California Legislature prior to coming to the Comstock certainly raised him in the esteem of the Nevada electorate. Despite the confidence the people placed in him, he wouldn't long serve on the bench. He suffered periodic bouts of nervous prostration that impaired his ability to perform his work. After attempting suicide with the aid of opiates and a hatchet, he was declared incurably insane and ended his days in the State Lunatic Asylum.[192]

It might at first glance seem curious that the calendar for the December term in Virginia City was enormous. The boom time of 1864 was relenting and the economy as a whole sliding into the doldrums. "Assessments and expenditures," said the historian Grant, "exceeded the dividends. High costs of operation, wasteful

---

[188] Id.

[189] *San Francisco Call*, November 7, 1897.

[190] *Pioche Weekly Record*, November 17, 1897.

[191] Id.

[192] *Marin Journal*, January 23, 1873; *Sonoma Democrat*, May 31, 1873; and Oscar T. Shuck, *History and the Bench and Bar of California* (Los Angeles: The Commercial Printing House, 1901), at p. 381.

and extravagant management, and 'millions uselessly and foolishly expended in exploration work,' together with vexatious and costly litigation, had consumed that splendid output."[193] Production at the leading mines declined, while fifty of the lesser ones suffered extinction.[194] So long, however, as any ore was extracted, the Lode emitted the promise of a turning of the wheel and a restoration of the great fortunes of the Washoe. It would remain, therefore, a fertile battleground for speculators and their attorneys.

In Judge Mesick's Court, the Twin matter, Original Hawkeye and other suits aimed at the Uncle Sam Gold & Silver Mining Company, *Booth v. Colton & Wade*, various suits targeting the Iowa Company, *Lafayette v. Original Hawkeye*, and Perley's own case against Gould & Curry, among others, were all scheduled for trial.[195] Also on calendar for trial was *A.B. Harvey v. Sides Co.*, wherein Perley's client, A.B. Harvey, sought damages for the obliteration of structures on his property caused by the Defendant dumping fifteen hundred tons of earth and rock whilst mining on adjacent ground. Scheduled for trial in Judge Burbank's Court were *Yellow Jacket v. Laboring Company*, the case of the Alpha verses Perley's own Bennett Company, three cases against the Uncle Sam Mining Company brought by Joseph Ellis, Peter Larkin and David Nattine, *John McCausland v. Maria Bell et al.*, *Theodore Winters v. Fairview*, *Peter Rice v. North American Company*, and others.[196] And in Judge Rising's Court, there were *Otis Manchester v. John Roberts et al.*, *Bennett v. Imperial*, *Noyes v. Lyford*, *R.S. Farrington v. N.H. Sanders*, and *Double Eagle v. the Burning Moscow*.[197]

DeLong handled matters for much of December, until Perley returned from another of his Western journeys via stage.[198] Perley was too late to participate in the trial of *Noyes v. Lyford*, which the Judge had already taken under advisement.[199] Pleading matters were addressed in *Fairview v. Maria Bell* by Judge Mesick, who

---

[193] Grant, op. cit., at p. 59.
[194] Id., at pp. 58-59.
[195] *Virginia City Daily Union*, December 23, 1864.
[196] Id.
[197] Id.
[198] *Daily Alta California*, December 31, 1864.
[199] *Virginia City Daily Union*, December 31, 1864.

pointed out errors on the part of both parties.[200] *Jewett v. Jewett* and *Henry & Bell v. Shelton* were continued into the next term.[201] So time consuming were the larger mining company cases that many matters suffered further delay: *Earle v. Adams & Mitchell, Baltic v. Mary Ann, Original Hawkeye v. Uncle Sam, Lafayette v. Original Hawkeye, Harvey v. Sides, Gould & Curry v. Lintott, Fairview v. Maria Bell*, and the various Twin Company lawsuits.[202] The trial calendar was reformed in March, with many of Perley's matters scheduled to go before a jury within 30 days, including a new case, *Gray v. Harrison*, involving title to a lot on which a large livery stable was located. That case was argued and submitted to the jury on March 19, 1865, but lack of agreement among the jurors caused a mistrial.[203] Perley had better fortune in *Rice v. North American*, in which he overcame a demurrer and won a judgment on the pleadings alone.[204] Equally satisfying was a jury verdict in the amount of $3,800 in *Harvey v. Sides*, at least until the Judge granted a new trial due to an error in instructing the jury on the issue of damages.[205] *Gray v. Harrison* was retried, and the jury this time found for the plaintiff.[206]

By far the most gratifying outcome during the first half of the year was in Perley's action against the Gould & Curry. Rather than take it to trial, Perley and Stewart negotiated a dismissal of the case and $8,000 in cash in exchange for conveyance to the Gould & Curry of the title Perley obtained from David Terry.[207] Perley made his peace with the representative of the preeminent mining interests in the State, and any trouble the two men might have had otherwise was stayed, but this accord would hardly stop Stewart from forever recalling Perley as a "pugnacious little Canadian."[208]

---

200 *Virginia Daily Union*, January 1, 1865.

201 *Virginia Daily Union*, January 23, 1865.

202 *Virginia Daily Union*, February 13, 1865; *Virginia Daily Union*, February 14, 1865; and *Virginia Daily Union*, February 21, 1865.

203 *Virginia Daily Union*, March 19, 1865; and *Virginia Daily Union*, March 21, 1865.

204 *Virginia Daily Union*, April 15, 1865.

205 *Virginia Daily Union*, April 29, 1865.

206 *Virginia Daily Union*, May 14, 1865.

207 *Virginia Daily Union*, February 11, 1865; and Storey County Deeds, Y:451, NSA.

208 William M. Stewart, *Reminiscences of William M. Stewart of Nevada* (New York: The Neale Publishing Company, 1908), p. 120.

The year 1865 marked the opening of Nevada's Supreme Court and the hearing of the very first appeals. As it was in California, so it would be for Perley in Nevada, with numerous appeals to address, initiated either by himself or his opposing counsel. The first appeal in which he appeared, *Davis v. Thompson*, arose not in the First Judicial District, but in Lander County.[209] Perley and DeLong represented the Defendant during the trial, against whom a judgment was entered. Perley's history as an attorney for office holders and role as defender of the impeached recommended him for the job. His client's adversary, the current Recorder of Lander County, had accepted payment to cover the cost of recording deeds and other legal instruments, but never got around to actually performing the service. Nor did he transfer the money collected to his successor. Feeling duty bound to record the documents entrusted with his office, the successor then demanded payment from his predecessor, who refused. A successful motion for a non-suit on the grounds that the relevant statute imposed no duty on the successor to record any documents his predecessor neglected, rendered the victory at trial short lived. On appeal, Perley insisted that the logical and rational practice was for the incoming recorder to record any documents entrusted to the office, and that if money had already been proffered to the predecessor and pocketed by him, equity demanded that he turn it over to he who actually performed the work. While the Court acknowledged that the statute was silent on the obligation of an in-coming Recorder in the situation confronting the parties here, there was a need to maintain a "proper and orderly arrangement of business" in the office. In such a situation, the law is not truly silent, but implies both a request for payment of the monies tendered by the beneficiaries of the official acts, and an obligation by the recipient of the moneys to turn them over to whomever eventually undertook the action. The non-suit, thus, was granted in error and the case as a whole would have to be retried.

In *Geller v. Huffaker*, Perley argued on behalf of a Defendant who had prevailed in Judge North's Territorial Court and thereby defeated the Plaintiff's request for damages arising from the diversion of a stream that formerly had flowed through the

[209] *Davis v. Thompson* (1865) 1 Nev. 17.

Plaintiff's land.[210] At trial, the Plaintiff argued two theories: the older common law theory of entitlement to some measure of the natural flow of a stream; and the theory born recently in the arid and under-populated West of prior appropriation. The primary point of contention on appeal was actually neither theory, but instead the appropriateness of the use of a neighbor, Mr. Langley, as a general witness to establish the fact that the stream's natural flow, prior to the Defendant's intervention, would have been through the Plaintiff's property. Perley successfully moved to exclude the witness on the grounds that as a potential user of the water, he had an interest in the outcome of the case, and thus could not be relied upon to provide unbiased testimony. Chief Justice Lewis and the Supreme Court disagreed. It might be true at some time in the future that Langley might rely on the evidence as to the natural channel of the stream in a case of his own, but he would not be able to cite *Geller v. Huffaker* as conclusive on that point, for the form of the verdict was general, not special. There being more than one theory at issue, and only one to which Langley's testimony was relevant, it could never be certain afterward on what basis the jury reached it decision. Was the case decided in accordance with the older theory or the new? As no one would ever know, the case and all the evidence therein meant nothing to any case save itself. The exclusion of Langley, on the basis of Perley's objection, was therefore erroneous.

Early in Perley's residence in Virginia City, the International Hotel provided accommodations for traveler and resident alike. The Hotel was the property of mining pioneer Andrew B. Paul. Rather than operate it himself, he leased it to M. L. Winn. When Winn defaulted on payment, Paul sued in the Court of the Justice of the Peace for possession and damages. The litigation appeared simple on its face, but eventually turned into what some referred to as Virginia City's version of the interminable chancery controversy of *Jarndyce v. Jarndyce* of which Dickens had written so drearily.[211] In time, Paul prevailed, regained possession and immediately entered into a new lease with a Mr. Armstrong. To avoid the frustration and cost recently experienced in litigation, Paul insisted on a right to re-

---

210 *Geller v. Huffaker* (1865) 1 Nev. 23.

211 *Virginia Evening Bulletin*, January 5, 1864.

enter the premises in the event of any deviation in the payment provision, without any notice or right to object, and with express consent, from the outset of the lease, to allow the owner's attorney, Tod Robinson, to confess judgment in the owner's favor. When Armstrong paid the monthly rent in greenbacks rather than the contractually required bullion, Paul and his partner, Mr. Bateman, called Robinson and Robinson's associate, J. C. Foster, to take action. While Robinson filed suit, Foster submitted a confession of judgment against Armstrong, which was duly granted the same day by a justice of the peace. Armstrong retained Perley and DeLong to salvage his interest and defend against Paul's action.[212] The lawyers gave notice of an appeal, but then withdrew it in lieu of a motion for a new trial in the Justice Court. Robinson countered by moving to dismiss the motion on the grounds that the filing of the appeal had stripped the Justice Court of any jurisdiction. Perley won the argument. At the subsequent rehearing of the original matter, Perley prevailed again and won an order of restitution that reinstated his client's possession of the Hotel.

Paul and Bateman insisted on an appeal. In argument before the Supreme Court, Robinson contended that the only remedy available to the tenant was the one they aborted: an appeal to the Probate Court. In presenting their positions before the bench, both sides impressed the justices with "the earnestness and ability with which this cause has been argued by counsel of acknowledged candor and learning."[213] With Robinson's argument as to an appeal being the exclusive remedy available to the tenants, however, the Court did not agree. The relevant statute governing appeals in similar situations did not mandate only an appeal once the landowners obtained a judgment. "Such a construction," said Justice Brosnan, "would...defeat the ends of justice."[214] An appeal via a writ of certiorari to the probate court was certainly appropriate "where an inferior tribunal exercising judicial functions has exceeded its jurisdiction, and there is no appeal or other plain, speedy and adequate remedy."[215] In this case, an appeal to the probate court was not proper due to the fact that the judgment to be appealed was

---

212 *Paul v. Armstrong* (1865) 1 Nev. 92; and *Armstrong v. Paul* (1865) 1 Nev. 134.

213 *Paul v. Armstrong*, supra, at 104.

214 Id., at 95.

215 Id.

essentially a judgment in default, where only one party had appeared. Such judgments are not by nature appealable. As an appeal in this case would have entailed a new trial, the default nature of the lower court proceeding rendered such a thing impossible. Consequently, the appeal was properly withdrawn and a motion for a new trial properly granted.

Robinson and his clients were hardly in a position to argue against the Court's conclusion given the highly irregular nature of the procedure: a broad right to reenter the premises, even when payment was received, a waiver by the tenant of any right to notice or a hearing in a timely fashion, and an agreement to allow a judgment to be read into the record by the landlord's own attorney. Confessions of judgment, said Brosnan, were authorized by law, but they were supposed to adhere to particular formalities. As they were confined to money judgments, not equitable relief, there was no propriety here in allowing it, even with the consent of the tenant, who remained ever powerless to expand the statutory scope of the Justice Court's jurisdiction.

Another defect in the procedure was the Justice Court's failure to abide even by the terms of the waiver of a right to contest the matter, which extended only to notice, not to time. The statute required ten days' time from filing the judgment, and this the tenant never waived. Moreover, the statute didn't permit confession of court costs, and Foster himself never actually averred that he was an attorney employed by the firm of Robinson & Foster, who the tenants had specifically authorized to confess the judgment on their behalf. Finally, while no statute authorized the Justice Court to issue a writ of restitution, the power to annul, clearly granted by the law, "would be barren and inefficient, unless the defendant could be restored to that of which he had been illegally deprived."[216] The Justice Court, thus, was right to act as it did in overturning its own decision. If the owners desired a return of their property, they would have to conform more closely to the terms of the waiver, if the waiver in fact was even legal.

In the wake of the Justice Court's initial decision approving the confession of judgment, and before the Supreme Court opined on the merits of that decision, Armstrong filed a suit of his own,

[216] Id., at 104.

seeking recovery of the premises and damages. A demurrer was brought by Robinson, objecting to the Complaint due to technical defects in the timing of service and the form of a required revenue stamp, in addition to the Court's lack of jurisdiction. The demurrer was overruled and the matter proceeded forward until a judgment for the Plaintiff in the amount of $4,459 was entered. On appeal to the Probate Court, the jurisdictional issue was reviewed, with the result that the Court agreed with Robinson, vacated the outcome and dismissed the case. Perley then appealed to the Supreme Court, arguing that while it was true that the State's new Constitution vested authority in cases such as this one in the District Courts, those Courts had not yet been created by an Act of the Legislature, and the Legislature itself hadn't even been seated. By default, then, jurisdiction remained where it was prior to ratification: in the Justice Courts of the Territory of Nevada. Justice Brosnan agreed. The purpose of the Constitution, he said, "was not to suspend the operation of any portion of the laws of the Territory," including the courts of law in operation at the time of ratification.[217] "The former judiciary system...continued in existence until the new one should be in a condition to exercise its functions. It follows, therefore, that the justice [court] did not lose jurisdiction during the interval...."[218] Losing on that argument, the resourceful Robinson nevertheless found a way to win the case by focusing on the Territorial law's limitation of the Justice Court's jurisdiction to claims not in excess of $100. As Armstrong's claim was far in excess of that amount, a reversal was in order.

Because of the shifting of judicial power from one set of courts to another, jurisdictional disputes continued to plague Nevada litigants during the first months of Statehood. In another case involving A.B. Paul, Paul's attorneys claimed that the State Constitution's limitation of the jurisdiction of the District Courts to disputes involving claims of no less than $300 implied that all disputes involving lesser amounts were within the jurisdiction of the Justice Courts.[219] Arguing that jurisdiction must be expressly allocated rather than implied, Perley successfully disputed Paul's

---

217 *Armstrong v. Paul*, supra, at 139.

218 Id.

219 *A.B. Paul & Co. v. W.H. Beegan & Co.* (1865) 1 Nev. 328.

contention. Perley and DeLong also turned back an appeal to an order by Judge Burbank setting aside a default.[220] Perley contended that the appeal was improper due to the requirements of the Nevada Practice Act, which limited appeals to special orders made after a final judgment. He argued, too, that default itself was improper, hence, the order setting it aside was erroneous. Chief Justice Lewis had no issue with the second argument, but disagreed with the first, thereby affirming the setting aside of the judgment against Perley's client.

Tried in March, the case of *George A. Gray v. L.A. Harrison* pitted Perley and DeLong in the defense against Perley's friends, James Hardy and Leander Quint.[221] After the trial, Perley located several witnesses with what he believed was highly material testimony that wasn't known beforehand. When his motion for a new trial was denied, Perley filed an appeal. Pointing out the fact that the appellant's papers lacked a statement on appeal or assignment of errors, Quint and Hardy clearly rested more on form than substance. In response, Perley appears to have argued that such a statement wasn't necessary due to the error being in the denial of the motion for a new trial and the evidence to be introduced, not on the record of the trial itself. In a decision published at the beginning of December, Chief Justice Lewis agreed.[222] "Where an appeal is taken from an order made on affidavits, no statement is required, and those sections of the Practice Act making it the duty of the appellant to prepare a statement containing the grounds upon which he intends to rely on appeal, have no application to an appeal from such an order." The deeper issue revolved around the relevance of the new matter. Quint and Hardy said it was material, but entirely cumulative, hence of no special merit. The Chief Justice disagreed, hence the lower court's judgment was reversed.

A sixth appeal in the year 1865 was heard in October in the familiar matter of *Harvey v. Sides Silver Mining Company*. Tried in April, the case involved the destruction of a fence and stone wall and the flooding of a cellar resulting from a trespass in the form of a massive deposit of mined earth and rock. When at trial Judge Rising

---

[220] *Ballard v. Purcell* (1865) 1 Nev. 342.

[221] *Gray v. Harrison* (1865) 1 Nev. 502.

[222] *Virginia City Daily Union*, December 1, 1865.

instructed the jury that "the true measure of damages was the sum of money it would require to remove the dirt from the Plaintiff's lot, with a reasonable compensation for injury to buildings and fencing, together with the amount of rent which was lost by reason of the unlawful acts of the defendant," the defense objected.[223] When the instruction was read anyways and the jury found for Perley and the Plaintiff, the defense successfully moved for a new trial. On behalf of his client, Perley appealed, insisting on the propriety of the original outcome. With this, in a decision issued in December, the Supreme Court differed.[224] While Judge Rising was correct generally, the rule he cited wasn't always true, especially when the cost of repair exceeded the value of the property destroyed. Consequently, Judge Rising ought to have given a more complete instruction—a fact he seems to have acknowledged when he granted the Defendant's motion for a new trial.

Several other appeals were neither heard nor decided until the end of the year and early in 1866. *Chase v. Savage Silver Mining Company* involved the claims of a mine locator that emerged only after massive amounts of labor and treasure were expended to make the mine profitable. In 1859, L. C. Savage and five others, including C. C. Chase, located a ledge containing silver ore. After the claim was recorded, a contract between the principals and a group of six other men was drawn up wherein the latter agreed to prospect the ground "until they struck pay dirt in exchange for conveyance of half the entire claim." The prospectors ultimately conveyed their interests to others, who in turn conveyed to the Savage Silver Mining Company. The latter then developed the mine at vast expense to itself. With remarkable timing, Chase emerged from the desert to make claim to the half share that was conveyed to the prospectors, now possessed by the Savage. He sued on the theory that he never authorized the other locators to enter into the contract to convey an interest in the ledge, and therefore wasn't bound by it. When the Plaintiff's case was lost, Perley and DeLong joined with attorneys James F. Hubbard and J. M. Nougues to take on the triumphant counsel, A. P. Crittenden and Thomas Sunderland. Perley apparently argued that any valid right to act on

223 *Harvey v. Sides Silver Mining Company* (1865) 1 Nev. 539.
224 *Virginia City Daily Union*, December 9, 1865.

behalf of Chase had to be expressly granted, yet nowhere was there any evidence that such a grant occurred. Nor was there any indication, outside of the contract among the parties, that Plaintiff understood the terms of the contract and consented without rancor to the Defendant or the Defendant's predecessors-in-interest working the claim. There having been no actual or apparent authority by Savage and others to contract on Chase's part, the conveyance of interest in the location was limited only to those who signed the instrument. Reluctantly, the Supreme Court agreed with the argument; for it viewed Chase as a mere opportunist—one of those "who shirk the burden and the labor, and emerge only from obscurity to claim the fruit produced by the industry and perseverance of others."[225] The Court felt obliged to mechanically apply the law and order a new trial, but called on the Legislature "to protect her mining interests by such wholesome and just legislation as will, in the future, relieve it from the evils which have beset it in the past."[226] It was a victory for Perley, but not without shame.

The final appellate matter Perley handled during his Virginia City days was in the matter of *Mitchell v. Bromberger*. Attorney H. K. Mitchell had represented Mr. Bromberger in a legal matter, only to have Bromberger renege on the fee after the work was performed. Perley defended Bromberger in Mitchell's suit and attempted to demonstrate at trial the lack of any express contract between the parties, or any promise by his client to pay for whatever services were rendered. He reiterated this argument on appeal of a $600 judgment by the trial court. On reviewing the papers and hearing argument by counsel, Chief Justice Lewis agreed with Perley. The person for whom services were actually rendered were creditors of Mitchell's client, who authorized Mitchell to take a confession of judgment in their favor. As the work at issue appeared to be on behalf of persons other than the Defendant, Mitchell could only seek a fee from them. That, said the Court, was not a fatal defect in the Plaintiff's claim—he was entitled to make a showing of who the true client was, even if the creditors were the ones for whom actual

---

[225] *Chase v. Savage Silver Mining Co.* (1866) 2 Nev. 9

[226] Id.

representation in Court was performed.[227] The fatal defect was actually in the contract itself, which rendered the outcome at trial null and void.

A contract-based action being now impossible, Mitchell refiled the case as one in equity, or *quantum meruit*. When Mitchell once again prevailed at trial, Perley appealed a second time on Bromberger's behalf and argued that certain evidence improperly admitted presented his client in a false light before the jury. Specifically, Perley complained of an inference of dishonesty arising from the testimony that Bromberger agreed to confess judgment in favor of one of his creditors to the exclusion of all others.[228] Moreover, because the evidence at issue was based on a statement Bromberger made to Mitchell while the latter was acting in his capacity as Bromberger's attorney, its introduction at trial violated a privilege existing between the parties that could not be breached. Seemingly weary of the case, the Court found no prejudice in the testimony, nor in an act by Mitchell that was entirely legal; for while it was true that the duty of confidentiality with respect to client confidences was a high one, no rigid prohibition on their introduction at trial exists when it would deprive the attorney "of the means of obtaining or defending his own rights." Pleased, no doubt, that it had seen the last of these litigants, the Court affirmed the outcome of the trial.

As the various appeals moved forward and were decided, Perley continued doing daily battle in the district courts. *Bell v. Shelton* went to trial, with Perley for the defense in Judge Mesick's Court. It was continued the next day and then taken under advisement by the Judge.[229] Perley and DeLong won a $200 judgment in *Howard v. Rogers Gold & Silver Mining Company*, after which Perley headed west to San Francisco, from whence he returned on June 13.[230] Also in Judge Mesick's Court, the matter of *Hale & Norcross v. Bajazet* was placed at the head of the June

---

[227] *Mitchell v. Bromberger* (1865) 1 Nev. 604

[228] *Mitchell v. Bromberger* (1866) 2 Nev. 346.

[229] *Virginia City Daily Union*, May 10, 1865; and *Virginia City Daily Union*, May 12, 1865.

[230] *Virginia City Daily Union*, May 17, 1865; and *Virginia City Daily Union*, June 14, 1865.

calendar.[231] Further attempts to delay the matter were rejected and the jury was empaneled.[232] The trial extended over the course of several days and ended when the jury came in unanimously against the Bajazet.[233] The first of Perley's cases against the Uncle Sam Company proceeded to trial in May. A jury was empaneled, "trial proceeded and after due argument by counsel and charge of Court, the jury retired and brought in a verdict for defendant."[234] Perley's defeat in the case was followed by continuances ordered in the other cases against the now victorious defendant: David Nattini, Delaphine, and Piccoli.[235] Piccoli's case, however, was sent to trial despite the continuance, with a verdict yet again for Uncle Sam.[236] The Peter Larkin case came up next, with an outcome this time in the Plaintiff's favor in the form of an order granting him "170.5 feet in the claim of the above company."[237] The McCluskey, Nattini, Anisini and Original Hawkeye actions against the Uncle Sam were all then dismissed.[238] A final action against the Uncle Sam was that of Judge Joseph F. Atwill of the Justice Court. It was continued into the Fall, when it likely was dismissed as well.

The ferocity of the pace of litigation continued. Perley's frequent errands outside of Nevada, either on business, or with women—the most recent being a Mrs. Gass—shifted the burden of daily cares onto his partner and perhaps even created a rift between the two men.[239] The unabating depression of material fortunes and the mixed results of litigation no doubt contributed to a growing alienation. Pistol shots through the law office in the dead of night, shattering two windows reminded the men that one of them was not the most popular of people on either side of the Sierras.[240] Mining stocks, rather than bearing dividends, continued to be assessed, and when Perley failed to make payment, his stocks were

[231] *Virginia City Daily Union*, June 16, 1865.
[232] *Virginia City Daily Union*, June 21, 1865.
[233] *Virginia City Daily Union*, June 24, 1865.
[234] *Virginia City Daily Union*, May 3, 1865.
[235] *Virginia City Daily Union*, May 6, 1865.
[236] *Virginia City Daily Union*, May 8, 1865.
[237] *Virginia City Daily Union*, May 12, 1865.
[238] *Virginia City Daily Union*, October 28, 1865; *Virginia City Daily Union*, November 3, 1865; and *Virginia City Daily Union*, November 15, 1865.
[239] *Virginia City Daily Union*, November 14, 1865.
[240] *Virginia City Daily Union*, November 15, 1865.

sold.[241] Worthlessness of land as sources of ore-bearing rock rendered property tax payments a waste, hence Perley allowed an 8-acre parcel on the Virginia and Gold Hill Tunnel Toll Road to be sold at auction to pay his delinquent tax.[242] The two partners continued in actions together into December. They fought to prevent a matter from being reinstated on the calendar in Judge Rising's Court and joined with Leander Quint before Judge Mesick in a suit to recover real estate. They won the trial, but were nonsuited, and were now contemplating an appeal.[243] They defended against a suit brought by Jesse Pitzer to recover possession of property in Virginia City, and after stipulating to a court trial, prevailed in the action.[244]

Their victory against Pitzer was the last they enjoyed together. No further cases were filed by the partners. DeLong operated alone for a time, but by January had formed a new partnership with Judge Lewis Aldrich.[245] Perley's attorney, W. E. F. Deal, filed a solo action against Judge Atwill for enforcement of an $800 promissory note assigned to Perley by one of Atwill's creditors. Then, without a word, Perley was gone.[246] A report circulated in April of 1866 that he was returning to Virginia City to form a new partnership with John R. McConnell.[247] The location of the enterprise was later changed to Nevada City, but then faded entirely without ever really materializing.[248] He returned to Virginia City once in June, but afterward appears to have proceeded west again and remained whither he had gone.[249]

---

241 *Virginia City Daily Union*, November 26, 1865.

242 *Virginia City Daily Union*, November 30, 1865; and *Gold Hill Daily News*, December 26, 1865.

243 *Virginia City Daily Union*, December 3, 1865.

244 *Virginia City Daily Union*, December 12, 1865.

245 Carl I. Wheat, "'California's Bantam Cock,' The Journals of Charles E. DeLong, 1854-1863, Appendix, *California Historical Society Quarterly*, Volume II (1932), at p. 47.

246 *D. W. Perley v. Joseph F. Atwill*, Storey County District Court, Register of Actions, Books A-C, Register No. 2215, NSA.

247 *Marysville Daily Appeal*, March 30, 1866; and *Gold Hill Daily News*, April 7, 1866.

248 *Marysville Daily Appeal*, July 13, 1866.

249 *Gold Hill Daily News*, June 29, 1866.

Chapter Nine

THE BIRD'S NEST

Perley's return to San Francisco might have been a result of necessity rather than preference. Once so fruitful, his partnership with DeLong was at an end for reasons we may never know. The economy fueled by silver had slowed, the stock prices Perley depended on for some measure of income fell, and his remaining landed interests in the City were under threat. Title to a forty-acre portion of the home he had staked out back in 1860 on a tract known as the Bird's Nest Ranch on the heights overlooking the City between the mountain where lay his wife and daughter in perpetual rest and the steadily developing Mission District remained under a cloud. The fate of the Bird's Nest continually perplexed and distracted him, even as he and DeLong made headway through the Courts of Nevada and pursued riches in the mines. In November of 1862, Perley's competitors for the land brought suit in the Court for the Twelfth District, seeking ejectment of the interloping Perley. He denied every single allegation and asserted his own claim of right, traceable through a long chain of title to the discredited Santillan, but bolstered by an actual possession sufficient, he contended, to defeat any competing claim through the ancient principle of adversity, not to mention the running of the statute of limitations. As the case slowly proceeded through the Courts with Hall McAllister at the helm, Perley readied his own contrary action to quiet title to the land.[1]

Much had changed in the City's judicial landscape since 1860. Having presided over the Court for the Fourth District until 1861, John S. Hager resumed private practice, and there he remained until taking a seat in the State Senate and, for a short time thereafter, in the Senate of the United States. It was he who presided over the notorious Broderick will case and declared the instrument an utter forgery.[2] Even before that memorable event, Hager had labored

---

1 *Daily Alta California*, November 21, 1863.

2 *Sacramento Daily Union*, January 3, 1862.

under some uncertainty when the voters selected Caleb Burbank to fill his seat on the assumption that he had only been selected to serve out his predecessor's remaining term. A rather comical scene transpired at the opening of the January session in 1859, when both Hager and Burbank arrived to preside over the docket and each addressed a courtroom packed with curious and bemused attorneys with a statement of confidence that their opponent was not the rightful incumbent.[3] Ultimately, Justices Terry and Baldwin determined that Hager's appointment was not merely for the purpose of filling an unexpired term, but for the full six-year tenure of a district court judge.[4] Succeeding him in 1862 was Samuel F. Reynolds, followed, in 1864, by Ebenezer D. Sawyer. The latter fellow was a mining country lawyer from Calaveras and former State Senator, who served on the bench until the end of the decade. In the City's other Court, serving the Twelfth District, Edward Norton held the seat until 1860 with the blessing of both the Know Nothings and Democrats, but poor health led him to retire. An offer to ascend to the Supreme Court in 1862 appeared to affect a miraculous cure of his ailing body. Succeeding him in the Twelfth District for a brief stint was Alexander Campbell, followed just as briefly by Lorenzo Sawyer and, finally, for a longer duration, Orville Pratt—a former member of the Supreme Court of Oregon and Campbell's law partner, and the author of the decision striking a blow against racial segregation in the matter of *Charlotte Brown v. Omnibus Railroad.*

The profile of the judges filling the local bench in the aftermath of Sumter and Manassas was perhaps one of the more remarkable developments in California's legal environment. Unlike so many of the judicial officers of the previous decade, southern born or southern in their sympathies, the judges of the 1860s tended to be from the north, of Whig, Know Nothing and even Republican proclivities, committed to the Union cause and even hostile to slavery and racial inequality. The trend among the members of the judiciary was no more apparent than when considering the men who served on the Supreme Court from approximately 1860 onward. Terry's defeat for reelection and premature resignation in

[3] *Sacramento Daily Union*, January 11, 1859.

[4] *People ex rel. Attorney Gen. v. Burbank* (1859) 12 Cal. 378.

1859 yielded the interim appointment by Governor Weller of the victorious candidate, W.W. Cope. Lincoln's appointment of Stephen Field to the United States Supreme Court and the commencement of that epic career on the nation's high bench paved the way for Governor Stanford's selection of the abolitionist Edwin B. Crocker to fill the vacancy. Cope and Crocker, along with Edward Norton, served until the beginning of 1864, when all five members of the Union Party slate won seats on the newly expanded and entirely elected supreme bench. Of the five new justices, Augustus Rhodes would serve the longest, until 1880. Born in upstate New York and arriving in California in the mid-50s, he won election as District Attorney of Santa Clara County and then to the State Senate, where he served with Perley's cousin James. A New Yorker like Rhodes, John Currey came to California as a 49er and eventually emerged as one of the leading land title attorneys in the West.[5] He affiliated with the Broderick Wing of the Democrat Party, and even ran as its nominee for Governor in the election of 1859 that saw the last triumph of the Chivalry before the awful denouement of Secession. Distaste for slavery and love of Union prompted his enlistment in the Republican Party, where he came to the attention of both leadership and rank-and-file as an ideal candidate for a seat on the high court. Vermont native Silas Sanderson practiced first in Florida and then in Gold Country. He served in the legislature as a staunch Republican and found his way onto the Supreme Court because of his pro-Union bona fides. Lorenzo Sawyer hailed from Jefferson County, New York, but entered the bar in Ohio, where he practiced in the office of Noah Swayne, a future member of the Supreme Court of the United States.[6] Raised in the traditions of the Whig Party, he idolized Webster and Clay, but discovered to his dismay the lack of currency such partisanship had in California in the 1850s. When silver fever struck, he went east with C. H. S. Williams and formed a partnership with that great advocate, only to abandon it when notified by Governor Stanford that he'd been appointed to the position of Judge of the Court for the Twelfth District.[7] It was his departure from the partnership with Williams that opened a

[5] *Sacramento Daily Union*, December 19, 1912.

[6] Shuck, *Bench and Bar in California: History, Anecdotes, Reminiscences* (San Francisco: The Occident Printing House, 1887), at p. 67.

[7] Id., at p. 73.

vacancy for Perley and facilitated his immigration to the Washoe. At the bar and on the bench, Sawyer was known as "a man of business, richly endowed with common sense, practical, prudent." Guided by the watch words truth and duty, ever prepared to plumb the depth of a subject, he was, early in his career, a rare victor in a courtroom duel with the great Lockwood, who surrendered in open court and graciously extended his hand in admiration.[8] Born in Vermont, and educated at Harvard, the fifth of the justices of 1864, Oscar Shafter, practiced in Wilmington for a time, then immigrated to California in 1854. He worked at the Firm of Halleck, Peachy, Billings and Park, then joined a partnership with Park and C. H. S. Williams. With the latter firm, he enjoyed the dubious distinction of representing both the execrable Adams & Company and the equally distasteful Palmer, Cook & Company.[9] Various incarnations of the firm included his brother James, as well as Solomon Heydenfeldt. He was, recalled Shuck, "wise in council, and impressive in the forum, a man of erudition, a thorough lawyer, massive in intellect as in physical build; in habits maintaining regularity, frugal, abstaining from drink, but a hearty eater, and a firm chewer of tobacco."[10] Politically, the chief principle that motivated him was an intense distaste for slavery.

It was in Judge Pratt's Court that the Bird's Nest case was to be tried, but it wasn't until January of 1864 that trial finally commenced.[11] At issue, said the press, was "about forty acres of land adjoining the Hart Tract, and but a short distance back of the Orphan Asylum in this City and County…generally known as the Birds' Nest tract."[12] Both parties claimed right from title and from actual possession, but, as the press noted, "the great conflict in this case is as to who has the real possessory title."[13] Possession turned on the Van Ness Ordinance, and whether Davis and Sharp perfected title under that law through exclusive enjoyment and control of the land during the nearly six-month period from January 1, 1855 to June 20 of the same year. Perley, of course, denied his

---

[8] Id.
[9] Id., p. 193.
[10] Id., at p. 194.
[11] *Daily Alta California*, January 13, 1864.
[12] Id.
[13] Id.

opponents' rights, denied either they or their grantors ever had possession sufficient to satisfy the Ordinance, and if they had, contended that the premises had either been abandoned before title could vest, or hadn't been secured through an action to eject Perley and his fellow plaintiffs within the five year statute of limitations.[14] To prove his case, Perley was prepared to call witnesses whose testimony could establish the lack of fencing and cultivation prior to his own occupation of the land.

Being an attorney, George Sharp led the prosecution, aided by Perley's erstwhile collaborator Elisha Cook. The pair would hardly be a pushover. Yale graduate Sharp had come to the City from his native Manhattan in 1849 and quietly established a practice with his lawyer brother William. Though they were unaffiliated with the political factions that battled for control of City and State during the 1850s, they built a reputation for competence, particularly in the area of City land titles.[15] More formidable still was Cook, known as "a burning and a shining light" at the San Francisco Bar, who was presently in the midst of a career "crowded with masterly performances, so rewarded by success, so marked by exhibitions of unbending will and sense of duty."[16] The man had learned the law from his brother Eli in Buffalo and followed mentor Nathaniel Bennett to California. He died prematurely in 1871, but not before the completion of his most celebrated case: the defense of Laura Fair for the sensational murder of A. P. Crittenden aboard the Oakland Ferry in November of 1870. No negligible legal talent himself, Perley was joined at the counsel table by Hall McAllister, and together they pursued the matter "with great determination and earnestness."[17]

Davis and Sharp presented their case-in-chief first. Their witnesses included the original occupant of the Ranch—William Pierson—John Center, James B. Johnson, the attorney Harlow S. Love, Stephen Otis, F. A. Upton, Samuel Daniels, Horatio Fox, W.H. Farnum, C. Potter, J.D. Stevenson, and the two Plaintiffs themselves. Taking the witness stand first, Pierson recalled his original

---

[14] Answer of D.W. Perley, *Davis et al. v. Perley et al.*, Transcript on Appeal, Makers of the Modern Law Print Editions, pp. 6-10.

[15] "Death of George F. Sharp," *Daily Alta California*, October 18, 1882.

[16] Shuck, *History of the Bench and Bar of California*, op. cit., at p. 442.

[17] *Daily Alta California*, January 13, 1864.

occupation of the land, that he had settled upon it after purchase from the Guerreros, that it had already been under cultivation by two men named Stack and Wilson, but that he expanded upon their enterprise, introduced livestock, built a house and erected fences.[18] John Center confirmed Pierson's occupation and cultivation, as well as the fact that certain sand hills were the proper boundary between the Bird's Nest and the Roundtree Ranch to the north. Stephen Otis testified to his own ownership and occupation of the lot after Pierson, how he let the property out to a series of tenants and remained there as superintendent after he sold his interest to Sharp.[19] He recalled Zimmerman being there in the late 1850s, as well as Perley's first appearance. Perley's fence, he said, was exactly where earlier fences lay, which confirmed both the boundary of the property and the earlier occupation by the Plaintiffs' predecessors-in-interest.[20] On cross, McAllister attempted to introduce Otis' testimony from the earlier *Zimmerman* matter as to the location of the property for the purpose of impeaching the present account.[21] The effort was stymied by Otis' inability to recall precisely what his testimony had been. The actual written lease to Zimmerman he did say might have burned, which McAllister found intriguing given the alleged reference in the missing document of the extent of the fee placed into Zimmerman's possession.[22]

The next witness, F. A. Upton, didn't help the Plaintiffs' case when he testified that back in 1853 the property "appeared to be filled up very much with shrubbery and undergrowth" and "did not have the appearance of having ever been cultivated."[23] The willows in certain places were thick, and though a building was seen on the Presidio Road that ran through the property, it was "very much dilapidated."[24] His testimony that he renovated the property, fixed up the house, installed his family there and built a hennery proved far more helpful.[25] Samuel Daniels recalled coming

---

[18] *Isaac E. Davis and George F. Sharp v. D.W. Perley at al.*, Statement on Motion for a New Trial, Transcript on Appeal, supra, at pp. 1-25.

[19] Id., at pp. 41-48.

[20] Id., at pp. 75-78.

[21] Id., at pp. 103-107.

[22] Id., at pp. 112-114.

[23] Id., at p. 115.

[24] Id., at p. 116.

[25] Id., at pp. 117-118.

to the property in 1855 and agreeing to maintain the existing fences.[26] When a carpenter hired by Davis to install fences in 1860 testified, Perley's impatience overflowed in the form of interruptions of opposing counsel and the witness. A surveyor confirmed that the property appeared to lay within the Charter lines, thus was subject to the Van Ness Ordinance. Sharp himself testified as to his understanding that the western boundary of the property was contiguous with the Charter line, that the land, as of 1854, was entirely enclosed by fences, and that it had been occupied by his grantor's tenants prior to his own ownership, and by his own tenants afterwards. When on direct examination he recounted Perley's construction of an entirely novel fence on the disputed property, Perley again interrupted—this time pointedly asking Sharp if he knew "of your own personal knowledge that I built a fence there?"[27] When recalling his attempts to discuss the matter with Perley, his primary recollection was the man's violent tone.[28] McAllister handled the cross-examination, challenging every miniscule fact at Sharp's disposal. Sharp handled the interrogation coolly, without any hint of distress or irritation, until McAllister pressed him on the details of Zimmerman's ejectment suit, which Sharp admitted had been instituted after Zimmerman left the State for Nevada.[29] He denied quite clearly, though, that Perley had ever been in actual possession of the disputed land.[30]

With the closing of the Plaintffs' case, Perley took the offensive by calling Thomas H. Holt, Milo Hoadley, Titus Wackenruder, George Flint, James J. Garner, Charles Brown, Thomas Dolan, James D. Thornton, Michael Fennell, Arthur Quinn, Isaac N. Benniston, Russell K. Rogers, L. Valencia, D. P. Barstow, Isaac N. Thorne, C.J. Hutchinson, J. R. Wilkinson, Otis, Upton, Sharp, Gardner, and finally, himself. First up for the defense, Holt testified that he had been the owner of the adjoining Holt Ranch since 1853. He recalled a lack of fencing on the western side of the Bird's Nest property during the mid-1850s, which suggested the land was unclaimed. George Flint was asked about the presence or absence of fencing,

[26] Id., at p. 130.
[27] Id., at p. 169.
[28] Id., at p. 171.
[29] Id., at p. 182.
[30] Id., at p. 188.

but his recollection was vague, and though he was familiar with the property, he was surprised to learn that Holt—Perley's predecessor-in-interest—had ever claimed it as his own. Perley's surveyor, James A. Gardner, was more certain about the absence of any fencing, though he claimed to be unaware of the presence of survey notes that might confirm his recollection.[31] Charles Brown and Thomas Dolan were both ignorant of any fencing prior to Perley's occupation, though the two men managed to contradict one another on the ability of teams of oxen or horses to crest the steep incline of the western most-portion—a contradiction that hinted at a lack of actual knowledge of the condition of the property at the time at issue. Brown recalled going over the crest, but Dolan said it couldn't have been done due to lack of an adequate trail.[32] Arthur Quinn remembered working for Holt and selling milk to his men, driving his wagon up from the Mission along the Presidio Road through the Bird's Nest tract. He didn't recall many fences, though he had memory of the trouble with Zimmerman. Contrary to the Court's initial sua sponte objection that the Zimmerman matter was inadmissible, he managed to testify about Zimmerman's presence on the land and the dispute over cows on the property. D.P. Barstow didn't recall any fences on the western line, nor did Isaac Thorne.

The climax of the case came with the testimony of Perley himself, commencing on January 20. He testified that he first became aware of the property in August of 1860 through Volney Howard, and inspected the premises at that time with Howard and the putative owner, Thomas Holt.[33] Upon purchase of title from Holt, he immediately put up a fence on the west side of the tract, employed men to clear the land, made permanent improvements for a homestead, leveled one of the large sand hills, planted trees and made regular inspections of the property to review the progress of the work.[34] Any cultivation or improvement of the land not sponsored by him was done after the commencement of his occupation, not before.[35] On cross, Sharp spent much time inquiring

---

31 Id., at p. 321.
32 Id., at pp. 327, 334 and 432.
33 Id., at p. 394.
34 Id., at pp. 396-397 & p. 404.
35 Id., at p. 403.

about Perley's disputes with his neighbors, apparently attempting to highlight Perley's unsympathetic qualities, but also to demonstrate the earlier proximity on the land of others in adversity. In rebuttal, Sharp called the Judge who had presided over the Zimmerman trial, apparently to confirm that Otis' testimony on that occasion was consistent with his testimony at trial here, but also, again, to revisit Perley's questionable treatment of Zimmerman. Finding an account in his notes of Perley's admission that he whipped Zimmerman over the cows, Judge Blake read from the document to augment his testimony, Perley's objection notwithstanding.[36]

After the testimony concluded, the jury took a tour of the premises at issue, led by Sharp and Perley, then returned for the hearing of the arguments of counsel and a reading of the Judge's charge to the jury. A significant war of words erupted over the instructions that would guide the jury in its deliberations. Perley insisted that the jury be informed that abandonment need not rest on intention, that a claim under Van Ness could not exceed in scope a single city block, that a plaintiff who seeks title via possession who also holds under a deed describing particular premises is not necessarily entitled to possessory title conforming to the description in the deed, and, finally, that the statute of limitations defense he raised could only be defeated upon a showing that an action had been commenced no later than five years after the plaintiff had possession of the land. The judge disregarded Perley's concerns, instructed the jury in accordance with his understanding of the law, and released the jurors to deliberate.

When the jury returned, the verdict was for the Plaintiffs. Not one to accept defeat, particularly in a matter of such importance to himself personally, Perley moved for a new trial.[37] Judge Pratt, he argued, had improperly excluded certain material witnesses, refused to consider the effect of his victory against Zimmerman in the matter of *Zimmerman v. Perley*, and issued a number of erroneous instructions to the jury. Unremarkably, Judge Pratt denied the motion and Perley signaled his intent to seek review by the Supreme Court. As a condition of staying further proceedings

---

[36] Id., at pp. 437-438.

[37] *Daily Alta California*, October 12, 1864.

and thus permit a timely appeal, the Judge ordered the payment of an undertaking in the amount of $3,202.60.[38]

With the appeal pending, Perley proceeded in actions for control of other Mission properties. In one transpiring in the Court for the Fourth District against the City and County of San Francisco, a continuance was granted for the remainder of the term.[39] In the other, against F. A. Hassey in the Court for the Twelfth District, a dismissal was granted, but then vacated upon Perley's motion and restored to the docket.[40] What ultimately happened with these two cases is unknown, but likely they settled without decisions ever being reached on the merits.

When the *Davis* appeal came before the Supreme Court, there was a question of when it would be heard. The parties stipulated that it be placed at the foot of the Supreme Court's calendar.[41] The parties then further stipulated to a briefing schedule, with Perley's brief coming due within twenty days, an additional twenty passing until the response would be due, and another ten for Perley's reply.[42] When this stipulation proved unsatisfactory and the parties couldn't agree to a change, McAllister brought two successive motions for further time to file the brief, both of which were granted.[43] The term appears to have ended before further action could occur; for at the beginning of August, Davis and Sharp had yet to file their opposition and were granted another ten days to do so.[44] The Court, accordingly, extended another ten days to Perley to file his reply.[45]

During this prolonged period of briefing and delay, Perley stepped back from the litigation and allowed McAllister to handle matters in concert with a new member of the appellate team, George Cadwalader—a professional acquaintance of Perley, and a vast imposing figure of a man whose "conduct of a case was in

---

[38] *Daily Alta California*, October 22, 1864.

[39] *Daily Alta California*, December 9, 1864.

[40] *Daily Alta California*, December 11, 1864.

[41] *Sacramento Daily Union*, January 4, 1865.

[42] *Sacramento Daily Union*, January 11, 1865

[43] *Sacramento Daily Union*, February 20, 1865; and *Sacramento Daily Union*, March 13, 1865.

[44] *Sacramento Daily Union*, August 4, 1865.

[45] *Sacramento Daily Union*, August 29, 1865.

keeping with his giant stature."[46] He created, said Shuck, "the impression of immense strength, and lawyers who had not thoroughly equipped themselves to meet him felt like getting out of the way."[47] He was a farm boy from Ohio, of undistinguished stock, mentored by Perley's former associate Colonel Edwards, and a quick study who after reading a lawyer's entire law library took the oath and commenced a practice that happily took him all over the State and led him to become perhaps the most prolific Supreme Court advocate of his day.

When the parties at last came before the bench, McAllister, accompanied by his brother Cutler, proceeded on a wide front. They argued that *Zimmerman v. Perley* should have been admitted into evidence. Since Zimmerman was the plaintiffs' tenant and the latter had actually conducted the litigation and paid for it, it was properly applicable in this case. Perley's victory in that matter, they said, stood for the proposition that Perley had the superior claim; for he could not have prevailed otherwise. And if this was true in that matter, it should have been accepted by the Court in this one. Perley's payment of real estate taxes since 1860 was improperly excluded as well, as it showed both possession and claim of title—a legal position unfortunately supported only in the case law of the State of New Hampshire. They contended, too, that the Court committed error in concluding that one might abandon land only when intending to do so, and that the Van Ness Ordinance allowed for claims of land no larger than a single city block. Finally, they argued that the instruction as to the statute of limitations was invalid—that if the Plaintiffs had once acquired the legal title to the entire tract of land, there could be no adverse possession of any one part so as to set the statute of limitations in motion so long as they retained possession of another part. The opposite, said the McAllisters, was the correct statement of the law, at least in other jurisdictions.[48] Cadwalader added that the Court erred in excluding the instruction that "the mere fact that plaintiffs held under deed describing the tract in controversy, did not in any degree extend their actual possession, because the Van Ness Ordinance did not

---

[46] Oscar T. Shuck, *History of the Bench and Bar of California*, op. cit., p. 463.
[47] Id.
[48] *Isaac E. Davis & George F. Sharp v. D.W. Perley et al.* (1866) 30 Cal. 630.

apply to any other but an actual possession, and did not extend the actual possession or recognize the constructive possession of one who entered under color of title by deed and took actual possession of only a part of the land."[49]

On April 12, 1866, the Court issued its holding, and two weeks later released its actual opinion, which the *Union* published in its entirety.[50] Justice Rhodes' tone from the outset of the Court's opinion struck a dismissive note as to Perley's contentions. Little of what Perley argued to support his position—that his grantors had prior possession of the disputed land and that he had actual possession in satisfaction of the Van Ness Ordinance—found merit in his eyes. The exclusion of the record in *Zimmerman* was hardly improper. That action, being one for forcible entry and detainer, differed materially from the action at bar, which sought remedy for ejectment. Had *Zimmerman* been an action of the same sort, the record would have been admissible; for the tenant's rights are subject in such a matter to that of the landlord, and in that case, the landlord was merely using the tenant as a cypher to confirm his own rights. "But in forcible entry, no right or title of the landlord is an issue, and it cannot therefore be said in any legal sense that the action is prosecuted for the benefit of the landlord."[51] The tenant in such an action has rights flowing from the contract with the landlord and it was those rights that were at issue, not the landlord's. Moreover, it was unclear on what grounds Perley prevailed in the former action. Were his triumph the result merely of a finding that no forcible entry or any entry at all ever occurred, it would surely be of no relevance to the case at bar.

The exclusion of evidence of Perley's payment of taxes owed on the disputed land wasn't improper, either. Under the relevant law, any claimant to land, including one disputing another's adverse claim, is required to pay the tax. Payment of tax on land, therefore, hardly establishes one's ultimate right of possession; instead, it only establishes one's as yet unadjudicated claim. Also, limiting the claims of the Plaintiffs to a single city block, as Perley insisted upon "with great earnestness," was a misreading of the statute and the

---

[49] Id.

[50] *Sacramento Daily Union*, April 13, 1866; and *Sacramento Daily Union*, April 24, 1866.

[51] *Isaac E. Davis & George F. Sharp v. D.W. Perley et al.*, supra, at 635.

law. Perley's argument on this point clearly was aimed at curtailing the scope of his adversaries' victory and preserving some measure of his own claim to the land, but the Court was having none of it. The point, said Justice Rhodes, was "decided against the defendant in *San Francisco v. Beideman*, 17 Cal. 462, in which it is said: 'when the act says 'the city of San Francisco relinquishes and grants all the right and claim of the City to the lands within the corporate limits, to the parties in the actual possession thereof, by themselves or their tenants, on or before the first day of January, 1855, and to their heirs and assigns forever,' and no limitation of the quantity of the land so possessed is made, we cannot add such limitations, unless we had the power to make the ordinance conform to our own views and notions, instead of determining what the City and the Legislature have done.'"[52] Pouring salt into the wound, the Court then recalled Justice Field's words in a case argued and won by Perley himself, *Wolf v. Baldwin*, which were "to the same effect."[53] The large portion of Perley's argument "devoted to the support of the ground that the evidence is insufficient to establish the actual possession of the premises in dispute, by the plaintiffs or their grantors as required by the Van Ness Ordinance, in order to entitle them to its benefits," the Court disregarded due to an inability to ascertain from the general verdict whether the jury found for the Plaintiffs "on the ground of title or prior possession.[54]

The trend of the Court's decision, however, changed radically toward the end. Justice Rhodes agreed that the trial court's rejection of Perley's requested instruction distinguishing actual from constructive possession was in error—that is, that "the mere fact that the Plaintiffs hold under deeds describing the tract in controversy does not in any degree extend their actual possession."[55] Instead, it would appear from the law at issue—both *Wolf v. Baldwin* and the Ordinance itself—that a claim to actual possession is limited merely to those portions of the land that a claimant has made improvements to, is occupying and has developed. "To hold that entry under color of title by deed extends the actual possession to the limits of the entire tract, would be to

[52] Id., at 637-638.
[53] Id., at 638.
[54] Id., at 642-643.
[55] Id., at 638.

assign to him a better position, in some respects, as the claimant of lands, of which he has in fact no title than the owner in fee has, who is deemed to be in constructive possession, because of his title."[56] To allow this principle to prevail, would defeat "the beneficial and equitable results intended by the ordinance…, and the ordinance, instead of passing the title to those who had occupied and improved lands, would give preference to those who had been so fortunate as to have acquired the constructive possession of immense tracts, under deeds that were barely sufficient to give color of title."[57] Also improperly denied was Perley's requested instruction as to the statute of limitations applicable to claims seeking to confirm actual possession under the Ordinance. Instead, the trial court compounded its erroneous failure to distinguish in the earlier instruction between the relationship of actual to constructive possession in the context of the Ordinance, and instructed the jury that "if the plaintiffs obtained a title to the whole under the Van Ness Ordinance, and entered under a deed embracing by its boundaries the whole, and since acquiring title under the Ordinance have been in possession of a part, claiming under their deed the whole, within five years before suit was commenced, the Statute of Limitations does not apply."[58] The instruction, confusing as it was, suggested that once the Plaintiffs had acquired the legal title to the entire tract of land, there could be no adverse holding of any one part so as to set the statute of limitations in motion, so long as Plaintiffs retained possession of another part. In other words, if Perley only occupied part of the disputed property, the Plaintiffs had no obligation to bring an action within five years of their own possession. This was an incorrect take on the law and had the effect, said Justice Rhodes, of placing "the person acquiring the constructive possession by his entry under color of title, in a stronger and better position to resist the adverse possessor than on entering into the actual possession of the whole, under a deed conveying the true title."[59]

With Perley prevailing on two points, Davis and Sharp brought a motion for a rehearing by the Supreme Court and additional time

[56] Id., at 639.
[57] Id., at 640.
[58] Id., at 641.
[59] Id., at 642.

to file their motion.[60] The continuance of the matter pushed the hearing onto the October calendar. When October came, the Plaintiffs' motion was denied, thus sending the case back to Judge Pratt's court for a new trial.[61] In the interim between the Supreme Court's two decisions, Perley found time for more notoriety. Late in the summer, news spread of a fist fight between Perley and Michael Heverin on Montgomery Street in front of the Stevenson House over "an affair of gallantry."[62] The impulsive Perley made a move on Heverin, but was utterly embarrassed when the powerful marble cutter got Perley's "head into chancery."[63] Restrained in a vice-like hold, he reached for his pistol, but couldn't quite grasp it. When at last released, he came out "badly damaged, while Heverin was unmarked."[64] A complaint was made in the Police Court, and though the evidence was "clear and proven," the jury waxed unsympathetic to the injured Perley and issued a verdict of not guilty after virtually no deliberation.[65]

Other physical conflicts were avoided, but just barely. His fortune in real estate and stocks having eroded considerably, his sensitivity to expenses joined his sensitivity to slights to his honor and dignity. His erstwhile friend Harry Logan was the focus of his ire as a result of some business differences, and rather than fight, they agreed to mediate. With the banker Lloyd Tevis serving as mediator, the men convened at the Russ House in San Francisco. "We were seated at a table, Perley on the side where the drawer was opened," recalled Tevis.[66] "Logan was his vis-à-vis, and I sat at one end." The mediation went badly from the beginning, as only it could between the hypersensitive Perley and the "hot-blooded and impetuous" Logan. In the heat of the dispute, as Perley recited a particular set of alleged facts, Logan impulsively accused Perley of being a liar. "Perley sat with bloodless face and quivering limbs as though praying that the floor would open to let him through." The

---

[60] *Sacramento Daily Union*, May 23, 1866.

[61] *Daily Alta California*, October 4, 1866.

[62] *Sacramento Daily Union*, August 24, 1866; and *Gold Hill Daily News*, August 27, 1866; *Red Bluff Independent*, August 29, 1866.

[63] Id.

[64] Id.

[65] *Sacramento Daily Union*, August 30, 1866.

[66] Oscar T. Shuck, *History of the Bench and Bar of California*, op. cit., at p. 385.

extreme discomfort and desire to flee, however, yielded to an overwhelming impulse to fight. "Quickly pulling open the drawer of the table and catching up a brace of revolvers, he thrust them in the face of his astonished adversary, and, with terrible emphasis, bade him take his choice...as he leaped from his chair, his face more crimson with rage and flashing fury." While Perley savagely declared they would "settle this matter instantly," Logan sensed his adversary's earnestness and relented "with as much grace as could be expected under the circumstances."

Re-trial of the Bird's Nest suit commenced in the Court for the Twelfth District, again before Judge Pratt.[67] Preliminary proceedings continued for several days, then opening statements were made and the first witnesses called.[68] Proceedings continued through February 7, when the case was given over to the jury. When making his charge to the jury, Judge Pratt acknowledged the frequency of controversies about land in the City and the tediousness of the facts presented in such matters. "The proper determination of alleged rights when brought before Courts and juries, connected with lands lying within the City, involving, as is often the case, long and tedious inquiry into facts, many of which there is too often much of conflicting testimony," demands "patience, great care, and more than ordinary scrutiny and diligence."[69] This case, he said, was "no exception, and it must be determined by a careful consideration and application of the rules respecting possessory rights."[70] At issue, he noted, was possession under the Van Ness Ordinance. The Ordinance vested title with he in whom real and effectual enjoyment of the property exists, between January 1, 1855 and June 20 of the same year. "It is the possession which follows the subjection of it to the will and dominion of the claimant, to the exclusion of others; and this possession must be evidenced by occupation or cultivation, or other appropriate use, according to the locality and character of the particular premises."[71] An enclosure of the premises by an ordinary fence, he noted, "without residence thereon, or improvements, or cultivation, or use, or other acts of

---

[67] *Daily Alta California*, January 31, 1867.

[68] *Daily Alta California*, February 1; and *Daily Alta California*, February 2, 1867.

[69] *Daily Alta California*, February 8, 1867.

[70] Id.

[71] Id.

ownership, is of itself insufficient." The jurors were told that should they find the appropriate indicia of "possession of the tract in any of the plaintiffs' grantors, and during the whole time prescribed by the ordinance, then the title of the City became vested in such possessor; and subsequently to the vesting of title, the owner stood in the same position, with reference to the land, as though he or she had received an actual grant."[72] Once such title vested, he was no longer required to keep up the appearances of occupation, either through the maintenance of fences, or habitation, or cultivation. "To such a title, perfected, the doctrine of abandonment would not apply."[73] Entry afterward, no matter how seemingly compliant with the ordinance, would do nothing to disturb the earlier vesting of title, and would be illegal.

As it was in the first trial, so it was in the second: the verdict came back in favor of the Plaintiffs.[74] If Perley considered an appeal, he must soon have thought better of it; for no record of one has been found. He did at least fight to reduce the costs claimed by the victorious parties in a motion filed in Judge Dwinelle's Court. His success in reducing the Plaintiffs' award certainly assuaged the sting of losing a valuable property, but hardly removed it.[75] Indeed, the sting was actually compounded through the fee owing to his own attorneys. Though it is possible there was collusion between the two men, the appearance is that Hall McAllister sued Perley for his unpaid fee in the Justice Court, and when he prevailed, enforced the judgment though an order mandating the sale at auction of Block Numbers 100, 101, 118, 119, 120, and 121 in the Mission District that appear to have been situated on the hillside leading up to what is now Buena Vista Park and adjacent to the property at issue in the late trial.[76] A fraction of his Mission Estate seems to have survived the sale, including a portion of Block 101 that was later sold pursuant to an order following a suit against Perley by John Austin, as well as a fine garden and nursery on the northern boundary of Mission Blocks 117 and 118 purchased in time by the Hillside Homestead Association for the purpose of selling shares,

---

[72] Id.
[73] Id.
[74] Id.
[75] *Daily Alta California*, February 25, 1867.
[76] *Daily Alta California*, May 28, 1867.

grading lots and promoting construction.[77] San Francisco was growing, and it was growing at Perley's expense.

It was not all for naught. The work they had done together in the *Davis* matter perhaps convinced George Cadwalader to recruit Perley to assist him in preserving the outcome in the matter of *Desormaux v. Meader* on behalf of the prevailing plaintiff, who was now facing an appeal. C. T. Meader operated a copper smelting facility in Copperopolis. The first batch of copper ever smelted in California left Meader's works in March of 1867. A contemporary press account glowingly exclaimed that "it is cheering to know that the works which have produced it, erected at great cost, and in successful operation, are not merely an experiment but a permanent feature of the utmost economical importance in the development of the mineral wealth and mining progress of the country."[78] The facility itself was "constructed upon the most approved scientific principles," with nothing left undone which skill and capital could accomplish in subserving the end in view. They are the offspring of earnest and well-matured business consideration and not of rash adventure. Not only those interested in copper mining, but every person having the prosperity of the country at heart will not fail in congratulating the enterprising proprietor upon his success in achieving a purpose so advantageous to the interests of labor and efficient in adding to the general wealth from a source which would otherwise be in a measure altogether valueless."[79]

Employed by Meader as superintendent of the copper works was Pedro Desormaux, "a gentleman of large experience and scientific acquirements."[80] To induce his best efforts, Meader agreed to pay him an annual salary of $6,000, plus fifty cents for every ton of ore smelted. The imperfection of the machinery and the complexity of the processes employed unfortunately contributed to periodic stalls in the operation of the works, and caused the superintendent a good deal of frustration over the loss of his premium pay. When Desormaux sued to recoup what he insisted was his due, Meader retained Cadwalader to defend him. Instead of

---

[77] *Daily Alta California*, October 22, 1867; and *San Francisco Examiner*, June 25, 1869.

[78] *Sacramento Daily Union*, March 28, 1867

[79] Id.

[80] Id.

fighting the matter on the merits, Cadwalader demurred, then demurred again, and ultimately won a dismissal of the action. When notice of an appeal was submitted by former Senator James W. Coffroth on Desormaux's behalf, Cadwalader moved that the Clerk of the trial court deliver to the Supreme Court copies of the original complaint, the two demurrers, and the court's several orders.[81] Shortly afterward, Coffroth submitted his brief, to be followed thirty days later by Meader's response.[82] To ensure the accuracy of the record, Cadwalader obtained leave to file an amendment to the transcript.[83]

Perley came into the case in May, replacing Cadwalader as lead appellate counsel. Perley successfully moved the Court to allow his client ten extra days to file a brief.[84] When the case was finally decided, on November 30, 1867, the outcome favored Meader.[85] The decision was never formally published, though it was printed in the pages of the *Sacramento Daily Union*. Justice Sawyer opined that "clearly under the terms of the contract in suit the Defendant was not bound to run the 'copper-smelting establishment,' to be erected under it, to the full extent of its capacity for a period of five years or for any other time." Defendant was to pay the Plaintiff $6,000 per year plus fifty cents for each and every ton of ore smelted in the establishment during the period, whether it was superintended by him or not. Meader, however, wasn't obligated to consistently run the facility. It was, said Sawyer, an "enterprise…of great hazard. If profitable, the profits were doubtless supposed to be sufficient inducement to Defendant to carry on the business after going to the expense of erecting the necessary furnaces and machinery. If Defendant was willing to risk his capital, it may well be supposed that Plaintiff might risk the chance of further profits, after getting a certain and liberal salary of six thousand dollars per annum for his services, without requiring Defendant to obligate himself to work the establishment for the sole purpose of giving Plaintiff fifty cents

[81] *Sacramento Daily Union*, April 3, 1867.
[82] *Sacramento Daily Union*, April 5, 1867.
[83] *Sacramento Daily Union*, April 6, 1867.
[84] *Daily Alta California*, May 28, 1867; and *Marysville Daily Appeal*, May 11, 1867.
[85] *Daily Sacramento Union*, December 2, 1867.

per ton for the rock smelted, whether he obtained any profit or not." No such bargain as this was in the contract, nor could be inferred.[86]

Perley was equally successful in an action of unknown nature on his own behalf against Alex McPherson.[87] The matter was one of many he likely handled in what appears to have been a growing caseload in the City. No surprise is it then that his practice now had need of an additional practitioner. His actual choice of a partner, however, must surely have drawn gasps. An "odd mixture" is how one paper described it. "Tom Fitch, the eloquent eulogist of Broderick, has formed a law corporation with D. W. (Shirtail) Perley, the fellow who entrapped Broderick into his fatal duel with Terry."[88] Though renowned for his oratorical skills, Fitch had only become a lawyer a few years earlier after a long career in journalism. He and Perley must have met in the Washoe, if not earlier in the decade when Fitch served in the California Assembly representing El Dorado County. He took part as a Delegate in the Nevada Constitutional Convention alongside C. E. DeLong, served as District Attorney for Washoe County and made a dark horse run for a vacant senate seat to represent the State of Nevada in Washington, D.C. Back now in California, he and Perley, once so incompatible politically, set up an office in the City at the corner of Sacramento and Kearney Streets.[89] Fitch commenced practice with Perley in San Francisco toward the end of September after he was admitted to the California bar on the motion of K. D. Wheeler in the Court for the Fifteenth District.[90] One of their earliest cases was on behalf of Plaintiff William E. Barron against John Parrott and others.[91]

The partnership didn't last long. Apparently it was intended to be temporary to begin with. No sooner had he formed it than Fitch authorized the *Virginia Enterprise* to inform the public that he remained a resident of Belmont in the State of Nevada, and that his

---

[86] *Sacramento Daily Union*, December 13, 1867; and *Desormaux v. Meader* (1867) 1 Cal. Unrep. 400.

[87] *Daily Alta California*, September 13, 1867.

[88] *Weekly Trinity Journal*, October 12, 1867.

[89] The professional card of the two men appeared in the *Daily Alta California* from September 19, 1867 until October 20, 1867.

[90] *Daily Alta California*, September 24, 1867.

[91] *Daily Alta California*, September 29, 1867.

law practice in San Francisco was out of necessity during the Fall and Winter so long as an illness in his family compelled his presence there. By December, as Perley commenced the prosecution of Swaney in Mariposa, and Fitch was engaged with the District Attorney in the prosecution of the alleged murderer of Richard P. Ryan at Ophir Canyon, the temporary partnership was obviously over.[92] Back in Nevada, Fitch continued his law practice, lectured to the public on a variety of issues, and plunged back into Union Party politics in concert with DeLong and John Neely Johnson. Following nomination by his Party for a seat in Congress, he went on to win the seat in the Fall.[93]

Perley's association with Fitch, brief though it was, marked a gradual move by Perley to the Republican side of the political spectrum that had actually commenced with the departure for the Confederacy of David Terry and many other of Perley's closest friends and associates. His affinity and admiration for the Chivalry was not so strong as to lead him either to arms against the Union or involvement in copperhead fantasies. In Nevada, he formed a close working relationship and friendship with DeLong, a former devotee of Broderick, a founding member of the Union Party and upbeat apologist for Lincoln and the Republican cause. When required by law as attorneys to submit an oath of allegiance to the National Government, A. P. Crittenden, Solomon Heydenfeldt and Gregory Yale balked. Perley, however, expressed no scruple in filing one in Judge Cowles Municipal Court in San Francisco.[94] By September of 1868, Perley made news when he—"another old Democrat"—announced his support for Grant and Colfax in the upcoming Presidential election.[95] The announcement prompted some surprise, in addition to cynicism. Scoffing at Perley's turn from the dark side of Secession, one commentator quipped that he bore "no very exalted name for morality or honesty" and had made himself notorious for "a shirt-tail race up Montgomery Street, San Francisco, with an enraged husband and loaded pistol after him."[96] In a similar

[92] *Sacramento Daily Union*, November 5, 1867.

[93] *Sonoma Democrat*, September 26, 1868; and *Daily Alta California*, November 14, 1868.

[94] *Daily Alta California*, August 14, 1866.

[95] *Weekly Trinity Journal*, September 12, 1868.

[96] *Napa County Reporter*, October 10, 1868.

vein, others would continue the mockery more generally by guffawing at the recommendation that travelers heading east into the desert equip themselves with light and entertaining reading, including Fox's *Book of Martyrs,* Crabb's *Synonyms,* Shepart's *Touchstone,* the *Tribune Almanac* and something referred to as *Diversions of Perley.*[97]

The move toward the Republicans was a trend evident within his family as well. His estranged cousin James had made the move with far less hesitation at the outbreak of the War. He rose in prominence in Republican circles, was nominated for a seat in the Assembly representing San Joaquin County, campaigned extensively throughout the summer and fall of 1863, and prevailed in the general election.[98] Despite the energy he exhibited in office and the success his son Solomon had in winning a position as Assistant Secretary of the County Convention, support for him lagged when time came for re-nomination; and though he failed in the bid, he demonstrated his loyalty to the cause by campaigning vigorously for the Union Ticket.[99] When the Democrats experienced a resurgence of fortune following the close of the War and the advent of the Johnson Administration, James returned as a candidate, this time for the State Senate. The strength of his appeal proved sufficient to counter the Democrat tide that swept nearly everything else away. In the Senate, he formed part of the narrow majority in opposition to the Democrat controlled Assembly and a Governor who defiantly denounced Reconstruction and the Republican policy of putting white Americans under "the domination of a mass of ignorant negroes just freed from slavery" and encouraging "an additional influx of Chinese to compete with white laboring men in all industrial departments."[100] He secured for himself the position as Chairman of the Agriculture Committee, and no doubt assisted his son Allen to win the post of Senate Clerk.

---

[97] "Rules for the Watering-Places," *Sacramento Bee,* July 23, 1869.

[98] *Stockton Daily Independent,* June 12, 1863; *Stockton Daily Independent,* June 15, 1863; *Stockton Daily Independent,* August 8, 1863; *Stockton Daily Independent,* August 25, 1863; and *Stockton Daily Independent,* September 2, 1863.

[99] *Stockton Daily Independent,* August 7, 1864; and *Stockton Daily Independent,* September 1, 1864.

[100] Inaugural Address of H. H. Haight, *The Journal of the Assembly During the Seventeenth Session of the Legislature of the State of California, 1867-1868* (Sacramento: D.W. Gelwicks, 1868), at p. 97 and p. 100).

At the end of the 1868 session, entailing a productive and energetic performance on behalf of the agricultural interests of the Central Valley, James and his daughter "took their departure…on a visit to their former home in Canada."[101] Expecting to be absent from the State for several months, he "expressed his determination to be back to his home in time to vote for General Grant for President."[102] In June, the New Brunswick press reported "the pleasure of a visit from James E. Perley, formerly citizen of Fredericton, now a resident of California."[103] Enjoying his return to the land of his birth, he attached himself to an expedition up the St. John River as far as Tobique, consumed freely of ice water and ice cream, and soon afterward suffered fever and the chills.[104] On the return journey downstream, at Woodstock, he found refuge and care at the home of his sister and her husband, Abner Bull, but soon developed full-blown pneumonia.[105] He expired there on June 17. Mourned by his many kinsmen in the region, and by the daughter who accompanied him, his body was taken to the home of his brother George in Fredericton, where services were held two days after his death.[106] Of his passing, the Democrat Lieutenant Governor William Holden later acknowledged the "sadness in the hearts of those who held seats in the Senate two years ago" and the loss of "the beloved and kindly expression of a venerable Senator whose voice then mingled with yours" because he had "passed to that country from whose bourn no traveler returns."[107]

Despite their differences following the ill-fated venture on the Reese River, Perley likely regretted the passing of his cousin. Blood, they say, is thicker than water, and of all his relations, James was the one with whom he had been closest since his departure from New Brunswick. Even after their memorable dispute in Court, Perley retained possession of James' ranch and ultimately deeded it back to him. The time for mourning, however, was short, as the

---

[101] *Stockton Daily Independent*, May 2, 1868.
[102] Id.
[103] *New Brunswick Reporter and Fredericton Advertiser*, June 5, 1868.
[104] *Morning Freeman*, June 23, 1868.
[105] *Morning Telegraph*, June 23, 1868.
[106] *New Brunswick Reporter and Fredericton Advertiser*, June 19, 1868.
[107] *Sacramento Daily Union*, December 7, 1869.

press of business quickly overtook him, and the call of duty from the People of Mariposa drowned out the sound of the dirge.

On September 30, 1867, "an old and prominent citizen of that place," James W. Seale, dropped dead from some form of paralysis. The screams of Mrs. Seale alerted venerable Sheriff Crippen and others, who came running to the scene of her husband's collapse.[108] Dr. T. J. Turner was called, only to find the man *"in articulo mortis,"* flat on his back with his head up, eyes looking particularly bright, his extremities cold, feeble of pulse, his breath labored and wrecking of vomit, pupils dilated, with only flashes of the appearance of conscious intelligence.[109] A hasty burial occurred absent a post mortem examination, though not without thoughts among the public that something was amiss. Five days later, a suspicious coroner exhumed the body, removed the stomach and applied various chemical agents obtained from San Francisco in order to discover whether poison was to blame for Seale's demise. With the aid of two other physicians, the coroner analyzed the contents of the stomach and found traces of prussic acid. Three additional tests confirmed the shocking discovery and strongly reinforced the suspicion that a toxin had been administered deliberately. Warrants were issued for the arrest of the widow—a voluptuous 19-year-old, recognized as "the belle of Mariposa County—and Andrew M. Swaney, the editor and publisher of the *Mariposa Gazette*. Evidence was procured that the widow attempted several times to poison her elderly spouse using Hamberg Tea, causing vomiting due to over exposure, until a small dose did the trick. A partially empty bottle of prussic acid was found among her effects, and a receipt for its purchase was uncovered in Swaney's home. The purchase, Swaney explained, was for himself, though no disease it might cure could be conjured up by the befuddled suspect. It was a different bottle, too, than the one in the belle's possession, yet his bottle's whereabouts remained elusive.[110] The circumstances appearing so damning, and an improper intimacy between Swaney and Mrs. Seale having long been suspected, a

---

[108] *Sacramento Daily Union*, December 27, 1867.

[109] *Sacramento Daily Union*, December 26, 1867.

[110] See *Russian River Flag*, November 7, 1867.

grand jury indicted the pair. Bail was denied and they awaited trial for their very lives in the local jail.[111]

From his jail cell, Swaney appealed to the public in an effort to counter the "unjust and cruel, not to say malicious fabrication and exaggerations that have obtained circulation and are busily being circulated to the hindrance of justice, the destruction of my character and blasting of all hopes for that impartial investigation of the charges made against me, that is guaranteed by the laws of the land to every citizen of the realm."[112] Asking not for sympathy but for justice, he reminded the public of the presumption of innocence, and the propriety of a "suspension of your judgment until I have had an opportunity of being heard before that tribunal whose adjudication may of right be regarded as legitimate and conclusive, when, I trust, I shall be able to vindicate my innocence."[113] Whether acquitted or condemned, he insisted, "I shall still know that I am not guilty."[114] The animus directed at him locally led to a request for a change of venue, but the Court was unimpressed by the degree of prejudice against him and his fellow defendant, and denied the motion.[115] Appearing for him was a veritable army of lawyers: S. A. Booker, William L. Dudley, J. B. Campbell, and retired Judges L. F. Jones and A. L. Collins. To counter this array of legal talent, an outmatched public prosecutor reached out to experienced murder trial counsel and netted the assistance of Perley and Jeremiah Burckhalter—the latter a former Judge, whose greater notoriety was as the builder of the local toll road.[116] On December 16, proceedings commenced. Separate trials for the Defendants were requested and granted, with Swaney to be tried first. A pool of fifty jurors was drawn, voir dire was completed and a full jury took its seat, all on the trial's first day.[117]

The medical examiner, Dr. Turner, took the stand first. He testified as to what he knew of the dead man, how he found him

---

111 *Marin Journal*, November 2, 1867.

112 *Sacramento Daily Union*, November 6, 1867.

113 Id.

114 Id.

115 *Mariposa Gazette*, December 7, 1867.

116 *Sacramento Daily Union*, December 23, 1867; and *Sacramento Daily Union*, December 26, 1867.

117 Id.

shortly before his demise, and the conduct of the autopsy. After the Court was satisfied with his qualifications, he was allowed to opine as an expert.[118] The doctor was followed the next day by the druggist, John R. Williams, of Stockton. He produced Swaney's written order, dated September 23, 1867, calling for three ounces of prussic acid, and recalled that Swaney explained to him that the compound was unavailable in Mariposa.[119] He wasn't certain that a broken vial found in Swaney's privy was the same he filled with the offending compound at his apothecary shop, but speculated that it might be.[120] Another man spoke of how he found Swaney's bill discarded in the street and had passed it around among his acquaintances before it was confiscated by the authorities.[121] Other witnesses spoke of seeing Swaney at the Seale home with Mrs. Seale while Seale himself was away.[122]

On December 20, the prosecution resumed. Dr. Bedford testified about the conduct of the post mortem examination and gave his opinion that prussic acid was the cause of the odd coloring of the interior of Seale's stomach.[123] More fascinating to those in attendance no doubt was further testimony about the frequent interaction between Swaney and Mrs. Seale on the street—speaking for a few minutes, walking for a short time together, and regularly appearing to be "intimate."[124] Sheriff Crippen thought the relations between the man and woman so questionable that he even brought the issue up with Swaney, "who denied being guilty of anything wrong."[125] Some, however, didn't notice anything notorious in the contact, nor any conduct by Swaney that was ungentlemanly.[126] Finally, there was the matter of the Hamburg Tea that was served to Seale shortly before his death. One witness reported to have sold it to Mrs. Seale the day of her husband's demise.[127]

---

[118] *Sacramento Daily Union*, December 26, 1867.
[119] *Sacramento Daily Union*, December 27, 1867.
[120] Id.
[121] Id.
[122] Id.
[123] *Mariposa Gazette*, December 28, 1867.
[124] Id.
[125] Id.
[126] Id.
[127] Id.

After the prosecution's case closed, Perley's colleague, District Attorney Corcoran, asked to introduce another witness. Once approved by the Court, the witness took the stand and told a tale of Swaney's attempt to hire some "cut-throat Mexicans" to kill Seale. Obviously a hard man himself, the witness confessed that he had no interest in the contract, but recommended that the best approach would have been to pick a fight with the man and take his chances in a duel.[128] Perhaps suggesting that a bond of confidence existed between them, he said both he and Swaney were Oddfellows, and gave each other that fraternity's handshake as they parted.[129] Suspiciously, he admitted he hadn't informed the prosecutors about the conversation or the handshake until the morning of his testimony.

When the time came for the defense to begin, Mr. Collins delivered the opening statement for the Defendant. He then called Dr. Smilie, a dentist and physician who was present at the autopsy. Smilie testified that he hadn't been convinced that the test conducted on the liver showed any trace of prussic acid at all. He admitted that while he never prescribed prussic acid to Swaney as a cure for a health complaint involving the liver, Mr. Swaney did suffer from a disease of that organ and that prussic acid is used to cure it. Various witnesses spoke of the privy in which had been found the broken bottle that might have contained the toxin, but noted that it was a public place frequented by many people—the inference being that anyone could have left the shards there. Other witnesses spoke of the close and innocent relationship of the Seales and Swaneys. Mrs. Seale herself testified that she and her husband breakfasted with Swaney and three of his children the very morning of Seale's death. She described her husband's behavior that day, and how he complained of ill health from the morning until his collapse. The Hamburg Tea she did indeed purchase. It was intended to sooth Mr. Seale's unsettled stomach, but he refused to take it.

Upon the conclusion of her testimony, Perley rose to conduct the cross-examination. He asked her if she had ever spoken to anyone about the nature of prussic acid and the manner of detecting

---

[128] Id.

[129] Id.

it. She said no. He asked if anyone saw her obtain any of the fruit she said she served her husband that day. She again said no. Perley then questioned her "minutely as to the meals eaten during the day of the death of Mr. Seale, and as to his condition." In a whirlwind of testimony, Mrs. Seale again recounted the day's events, denied she had ever done or said certain things, including barring a witness from assisting her dying husband, and stated that she had no knowledge of who opened the package of Hamberg Tea. When her testimony was completed, the Court admonished Perley and the prosecution to keep any argument "strictly confined to the cross-examination and to draw no new matter" unless it derived from the testimony of Mrs. Seale elicited on their own direct examination.

Swaney then was called in his own defense. He explained how he came to obtain the prussic acid and why he ranged so far from home in getting it. He explained, too, how he came to lose the receipt, and how one or more of the bottles fell out of the box and broke. He had the acid, he said, to treat a long-term malady, and had used the substance before to effect a similar cure. As for the man who accused him of wanting to hire cut-throats to assassinate Seale, he said the man recounted a conversation that never took place. Mexicans had come up in another conversation, but only in connection with the recent election. The thought that he would consider having Seale murdered he found absurd, for the man, he said, was his friend. When cross-examination came, likely by Perley, whose role appears to have been to break the Defendants on the stand, Swaney further explained his experience with the ailment for which prussic acid was applied. A medical book was produced and he showed the page he consulted regarding the dosage to take. He admitted he didn't consult a physician, but suggested his experience with the ailment was so broad that he knew how to treat it himself.

The defense's case came to a close on Christmas Eve. The parties and the jury, not to mention the spectators, returned two days later and for the next three days listened to the various arguments of counsel. The case went to the jury on Saturday evening, December 28.[130] Speculation abounded as to the outcome of the trial. The *Alta* reported a conviction was certain due to the "formidable chain of

130 Id.

evidence," and was especially impressed by the testimony that Swaney attempted to hire a murderer.[131] The *Marysville Appeal* was quite convinced the evidence proved "the intimacy existing between the prisoners on trial for murder."[132] In truth, though, the evidence was weak. An older man had died after complaining of stomach discomfort and other problems. His wife and he were friendly with Mr. Swaney, whose own wife had recently passed away following childbirth. Swaney himself had an internal ailment and took prussic acid for it, which some evidence, hardly uncontested, indicated was present in the body of the deceased. The inferences of guilt of the most heinous of crimes being so tenuous, it isn't surprising that Perley and his colleagues couldn't convince the jury to convict. The jury hung, with nine for conviction and three for acquittal. A new trial was scheduled, but due to the concern of defense counsel that "the public bias was too strong for trial at home," the venue was changed to Stockton.[133]

With that, the prosecutors and the defense team decamped from Mariposa, and together made their way north toward Stockton. Leaving on December the 30th, Booker and Dudley slogged their way over bad roads until they arrived at Merced Falls, procured a stage and made it six miles to Snelling. The worsening condition of the roads, no doubt due to rain and mud, barred their departure for two days.[134] Joined now by Perley, Judge Deering and others, they made their way to the Tuolumne River, crossed it in a small boat and took up quarters for the night with a Mr. Salter. The next day, conveyance in a wagon lacking elliptical springs proved both uncomfortable and unsettling, and slowed their progress so much that they missed the stage bound for Stockton at Dry Creek. Further travel by wagon prolonged the journey so that by the time they reached Stockton, five days had passed.

Retrial of the case by the same prosecution team wasn't a foregone conclusion. The Mariposa County Supervisors considered the matter, and with some dissent, approved of a $500 appropriation to pay Perley and Burckhalter, provided that they

---

[131] *Daily Alta California*, January 1, 1868.

[132] *Marysville Appeal*, January 5, 1868.

[133] *Weekly Calaveras Chronicle*, January 11, 1868; and *Sacramento Daily Union*, May 8, 1868.

[134] *Sacramento Daily Union*, January 9, 1868.

tried the case to a final termination.[135] Swaney himself arrived in town on January 10 in the company of Sheriff Crippen.[136] Rather than proceed immediately with jury selection, Judge Cavis consulted his calendar and set the matter for May 6.[137] When the day of trial finally came, Swaney was present, along with his defense team of Booker, Dudley and Jones, as were the prosecutors, Perley, Burckhalter and San Joaquin District Attorney, Evans S. Pillsbury.[138] With forty spectators filling the small courtroom, a jury was selected and, as the proceedings terminated for the first day, the prediction was offered that the case would "no doubt occupy the great part of the present session of the Court."[139]

As the trial progressed, it became clear that the prosecution hung much hope on establishing more firmly an illicit romance between the accused prior to the death of Mr. Seale. When the defense objected to the attempt by Perley to introduce evidence of the same, a battle over the admissibility of the matter erupted between Perley, Booker and Dudley.[140] Perley prevailed, but was instructed to hold off on eliciting any testimony about any intimacy occurring after Seale's demise.[141] Little new, however, was disclosed. Some of the same witnesses who testified to the alleged paramours meeting on the street, walking arm-in-arm, and visiting each other in the home, took the stand and repeated what they had said months before in Mariposa. New witnesses confirmed and even enhanced the old accounts, including the tale of the two Defendants walking together in close conversation sharing a shawl. Perley's attempt to smear the Defendants and perhaps establish a motive for murdering Seale was met on cross-examination with testimony that while the two accused would often meet in public, such meetings "were not different from the ordinary meetings between ladies and gentlemen in Mariposa." Other men and

---

135 *Mariposa Gazette*, February 8, 1868.

136 *Daily Alta California*, February 13, 1868.

137 *Daily Alta California*, February 14, 1868; and *Marysville Daily Appeal*, February 15, 1868; *Sacramento Daily Union*, February 15, 1868; and *Red Bluff Independent*, February 19, 1868; *Mariposa Gazette*, February 22, 1868; and *Sonoma Democrat*, February 22, 1868.

138 *Sacramento Daily Union*, May 8, 1868.

139 Id.

140 *Sacramento Daily Union*, May 13, 1868.

141 Id.

women in town, it was conceded, "meet as frequently on the streets and talk."[142]

After planting or attempting to plant in the minds of the jurors the existence of a suspicious and unsavory relationship between the accused and the decedent's wife, the prosecution moved on to the testimony of Dr. Turner. Knowing it was crucial to establishing the presence of prussic acid in Swaney's body, and no doubt recalling the contrary testimony of others at the first trial, the defense strenuously objected to Turner offering any expert opinions. Perley rose and "made a long, eloquent and able argument and cited numerous authorities in reply to the objection made by the defense to the admission of the evidence of Dr. Turner, as an expert in the science of chemistry."[143] The District Attorney followed, with further citations, and was followed in turn by the exhaustive and equally eloquent argument of Judge Jones, which finally ended with an apology to the jury for the amount of time the issue consumed. Judge Cavis sided with Perley and allowed the testimony, which Perley elicited with thoroughness and skill—far more so than had been the case when Turner first testified back in December.

After the defense began its case-in-chief, and had proceeded day after day along course, Perley and his colleagues announced that they had acquired heretofore unknown evidence of the condition of the decedent three days prior to his death—a day that happened to correspond with the very day Swaney procured the prussic acid. The prosecution's presentation of its evidence not being complete, the defense declined to continue with its witness before the new evidence was introduced, hence the Court continued the matter to allow the prosecution's new witness time to arrive in town.[144] The witness, however, was not forthcoming despite the efforts of a deputy sheriff to locate him. More severe process was then used to obtain the witness' presence.[145]

When the testimony by witnesses for the prosecution and defense finally came to an end, the Court, mindful of the time already consumed, limited closing argument to two counsel from

---

[142] Id.

[143] *Mariposa Gazette*, May 15, 1868.

[144] *Sacramento Daily Union*, May 18, 1868.

[145] Id.

each side.[146] After arguments concluded and the instructions were given, the jury retired at 9 o'clock in the evening and deliberated all night and into the next afternoon. The jury again hung up, this time with only seven for conviction. A third trial was then ordered for the August term of the Court. After securing the pledge of "several of the most prominent citizens of Stockton" as his sureties, Swaney was released on bail amounting to $5,000.[147]

The third trial never occurred. A conference between Pillsbury and the Board of Supervisors concluded that the Board "knew of no newly-discovered evidence which would strengthen the case on the part of the prosecution; otherwise the enormous difficulty and expense of procuring the attendance of witnesses upon another trial...would be perfectly futile and of no avail on the part of the people."[148] The charges were dropped, the bond cancelled and the co-Defendant, Mrs. Seale, was never even tried. The end of what one paper called a "remarkable case," and another "a most important and interesting one, in fact one of the most interesting that has taken place in the Courts of California," turned out to be a dispute over the costs. Having been subject to an order to pay witness fees, the supervisors of San Joaquin County reacted poorly to the sheer magnitude of the bill and expressed reluctance to honor the obligation, and didn't actually do so until the Supreme Court ruled on the matter.[149] Meanwhile, the two accused of hatching a love-born murder plot, having bonded through the long ordeal of trial, took comfort in each other regardless of the scandal it might produce and entered into wedded matrimony in Stockton on February 7, 1869.[150]

In the wake of the Swaney-Seale trials, Perley's life and practice moved forward. Perley's and Volney Howard's case against Throckmorton for an accounting and an injunction at last came close to trial, yet was postponed until March of 1869.[151] Perley also

---

[146] *Mariposa Gazette*, May 29, 1868.

[147] *Shasta Courier*, May 30, 1868; and *Red Bluff Independent*, June 11, 1868.

[148] *Sacramento Daily Union*, August 8, 1868.

[149] *Marysville Daily Appeal*, August 9, 1868; *Red Bluff Independent*, June 4, 1868; *Mariposa Gazette*, May 29, 1868; and *Sargent v. Cavis* (1869) 36 Cal. 552.

[150] *Sacramento Daily Union*, February 13, 1869; *Daily Alta California*, February 16, 1869; and *Morning Union*, February 18, 1869.

[151] *Marin Journal*, November 21, 1868.

around this time handled his final appeal before leaving California for a second sojourn in Nevada. The case arose in the Fifth District Court, in Stockton.[152] Perley represented the Defendant, Thomas K. Hook, the Sheriff of San Joaquin County, a Republican no less, who won his office in the same election that propelled Perley's cousin into the Assembly. Hook's alleged wrongdoing came in the form of a trespass when seizing property from the Plaintiff under the belief it was owned by a debtor named Bogarts. Bogarts had arranged a fictitious sale of a team of horses to a Mr. Nichols in order to avoid the reach of his creditors. Nichols then took the team and sold it in Sacramento to Arthur Thornton. After Bogarts' creditors won a judgment against him, they presented an order to the Sheriff identifying the team as property of the debtor. At trial, the Plaintiff called a Mr. Borland, who provided testimony that Thornton had hidden the property on Borland's ranch. Perley cross-examined him, asking "if he knew where Thornton procured the possession of the property, and if he knew whether before the property was put in his possession by Thornton it had ever belonged to Bogart, or was ever in his possession." Any answer was precluded by an objection sustained by the Court, apparently because the questions posed by Perley fell outside the scope of direct examination. Perley certainly had a right to make this inquiry, but to do so he would have to have called Mr. Borland as a witness in his case-in-chief. Perley then introduced testimony upon the question of whether Thornton, when he purchased from Nichols, "knew of the fraud on the part of Bogarts and Nichols." The testimony was unclear due to being contradictory. At the close of his case, he asked the Court to provide an elaborate instruction that essentially provided that if Bogarts conveyed the property as part of a scheme to defraud creditors, and that Thornton was aware of this fact when taking the property, Thornton had no right to the property and couldn't sue when it was taken from him. The Court rejected the instruction, the jury considered the evidence, and a verdict against Perley's client was the result.

The matter was on the Supreme Court's calendar for January 8, 1868.[153] On that day, Perley appeared and presented his

[152] *Thornton v. Hook* (1868) 36 Cal. 223.

[153] *Sacramento Daily Union*, January 1, 1868.

argument.[154] The argument was two-fold: his cross-examination of Borland was improperly cut short; and the jury instruction he requested ought to have been read to the jury. Regarding the first point, Perley explained how exactly Thornton "obtained his possession, who from, what he paid for it, when it was delivered to him, under what circumstances, and if this property had ever belonged to Bogarts, or was ever in his possession—and if so, where he parted with, and upon what consideration."[155] "It is only," he said, "by allowing this reasonable latitude that any case of fraud can ever be unraveled."[156] As for the second point, the rejected jury instruction might have mitigated the prejudice caused by the curtailing of cross-examination, but obviously was never provided to the jury. The result likely would have been a defense verdict since Thornton had failed to present evidence of the bona fide nature of his title and possession.

In an opinion made public on April 14, Justice Sanderson conceded that it isn't "always easy to determine the precise point beyond which a cross examination should not be allowed to proceed."[157] The general rule seemed appropriately applied here: "a party who has not yet opened his own case cannot be allowed to introduce it by a cross examination of the witness of his adversary."[158] There are situations where this rule isn't applicable, as when the question at issue "may apply equally to new matter and to matter already stated or at least it may be difficult to decide whether it does or does not." Such a case was the one at bar, but Justice Sanderson thought it appropriate to trust the resolution of the matter strictly to the discretion of the trial judge. As for Perley's requested instruction, Justice Sanderson thought it would have been appropriate had there been some fraud in the inducement on the part of Nichols or Bogarts, but there was none. "Had Nichols become the purchaser from Bogarts through fraudulent representations, which would have vitiated the contract between them and rendered it null and void, and afterwards sold to the Plaintiff, the instruction would have been on point. No title would

154 *Sacramento Daily Union*, January 9, 1868.
155 *Thornton v. Hook*, supra, at 226.
156 Id.
157 Id., at 227-228; and *Sacramento Daily Union*, April 14, 1868.
158 *Thornton v. Hook*, supra, at 228.

have passed from Bogarts to Nichols by reason of the fraud, and the latter, therefore, could have conveyed no title to the Plaintiff." Here, however, the title passed was valid from one party to the next. The better argument, said Sanderson, was one based on the statute of frauds, but even that wouldn't have been satisfactory in this case; for he who would take advantage of the statute of frauds to annul a sale, necessarily must confess to fraud between himself and the seller. Hook wasn't the purchaser, and wasn't the victim of fraud; he was the administrator of the law, who seized property that belonged to someone other than the wrongdoer. Under the circumstances of the case, he was properly subject to the judgment of the jury, hence the decision of the lower court was affirmed. Perley had lost again.

It was close in time to the Seale and *Thornton* matters that began a short period during which a mystery yet unsolved unfolded. When Perley next appeared, in western Nevada, it was as the Honorable D. W. Perley, and frequent mention thereafter was made of his status as "judge" or former judge. What Court he presided over and for how long and when precisely is not known. One account from New York in 1875 had it that Perley had served as "one of the judges of the Supreme Court" of Nevada, but the account was obviously erroneous.[159] A reference to the proceedings for recovery of damages by the newspaper proprietors whose presses were destroyed in the riots following news of the assassination of President Lincoln suggests Perley played a special role of a quasi-judicial kind in overseeing the claims, either in court or in some form of alternative dispute resolution procedure, though it appears perhaps that the reference may be in error, and that Archibald Peachy, who appeared at the trial of the claim of Etienne Derbec with Frank Pixley and others, may have been the person the writer intended to designate.[160] Whatever the truth, and whatever the venue or forum over which Perley presided, it was apparently a temporary one—so short in fact that no record appears in the surviving journals, though further search through the archives of the various courts, such as they still exist, might one day turn up evidence sufficient to solve this lingering enigma. The transient

[159] *Hudson Weekly Star*, January 14, 1875.
[160] *Sacramento Daily Union*, November 19, 1868.

nature of his judicial appointment is all but evident in the fact that by December of 1868, Judge Perley was well established as a resident of the boom town of Hamilton in the latest region to enjoy a burst of overwhelming optimism over the riches to be extracted from its soil.

Chapter Ten

RESURRECTION AT TREASURE HILL

East of San Francisco, Stockton and the Sierras, east even of Virginia City and the Reese River, lies a vast territory appearing on first sight to be naught but a wasteland, unfit for habitation except by lizards, desiccate in Spring and miserably cold in Winter due to a high altitude, comprising a sizeable portion of the Great Basin and perhaps one of the least hospitable portions of that region dubbed "the great American desert." The sage brush and tumbleweed so common in the rock-scape of Western Nevada was far less common here, though some vegetation exhibited a remarkable degree of tenacity in taking hold in the limestone surface rock. A scrubby breed of Mountain Mahogany tended to flourish here, "harder than the devil's horns" it was said, but well suited for use as fire wood. Occasionally, grass would grow, but true pasture was a rarity, and any soil that accumulated through natural processes was quickly swept away by the prevailing winds.[1] Lacking anything that might have made it a choice habitation for humanity, the region that would come to be known as White Pine did possess one advantage, which was the presence of three luxurious mineral belts: one on the western slope of White Pine Mountain about five miles in length; a second on the eastern slope; and a third, larger than the others, crescent shaped and close to the summit of a geographic prominence called Treasure Hill.[2] The presence of fossils, coastal corals and the long-abandoned shells of deep sea creatures near the summit of the latter peak suggested an epoch when the land lay submerged beneath the waves, on account either of Noah's deluge or some working of massive forces beneath the earth that in time thrust what formerly was below far above nearly everything else save God Himself.

Hidden amidst geologic formations comprised of slate, granite and limestone, silicious conglomerate and quartzite rock highly

---

[1] *Gold Hill Daily News*, November 19, 1868.
[2] *Carson Daily Appeal*, July 30, 1868.

colored with iron, reposed a fortune in silver, the quantity of which many surmised might dwarf the Comstock.[3] "On the whole," said one contemporary observer in 1868, "White Pine District has more promising lodes than any other district I have seen," the true richness of which had yet to be determined, but was sufficiently evident "to justify a considerable expenditure to ascertain what is below."[4] Another commentator expressed far less hesitation in assessing the worth of the riches to be found when noting the extraordinary value of the ores, including one specimen of horn silver assaying for $20,000.[5] Such enthusiasm, published in the papers in the Western United States, only whetted the appetites of those already hungry for spontaneous wealth, and fueled what became the latest in a series of rushes on the American frontier, the rise of new boom towns, and dreams of the future existence of a prosperous humanity in defiance of what, in this inhospitable environment, could actually be sustained.

That White Pine was "indeed the promised land of enterprise from the accumulation of whose treasures the State of Nevada will achieve solvency and augmented prosperity" few seemed to question.[6] The more than 300-mile journey from Washoe over rough roads offered only the barest obstacle to men inspired by a most fervent anticipation of accumulating the wealth of Croesus. As early as the summer of 1868, two lines of stages were operating routes to White Pine, and those finding passage in that manner could remark in their dispatches home of the "scores of people at any hour of the day or night, some on foot, and some on horseback, all making for the new El Dorado."[7] By mid-autumn, as snows approached, the dessert paths remained clogged with wagon trains, some drawn by teams of eight or even twelve mules, loaded with prospectors and provisions.[8] The back-up, it was said, extended all the way to California.[9] The reports of daily discovery of new ledges, spurred this massive immigration onward, further provoking thoughts both

---

[3] Id.
[4] *Gold Hill Daily News*, June 12, 1868.
[5] *Gold Hill Daily News*, July 29, 1868.
[6] *Carson Daily Appeal*, December 8, 1868.
[7] *Gold Hill Daily News*, July 29, 1868.
[8] *Gold Hill Daily News*, November 12, 1868.
[9] *Carson Daily Appeal*, October 10, 1868.

"jubilant and sanguine of making a pile in a very short time."[10] Even Governor Blasdel joined in the headlong rush, anxious to make a claim or two before the ground was completely covered.[11] Few thought more than a week in advance, and it was only as the clouds darkened and the atmosphere chilled that residents of the make-shift mining communities considered that man cannot live by whiskey and dice alone, or that a saloon, even a well-stocked one, offered little in the way of shelter from the storms to come. Alarm went out that "the supply of provisions at White Pine is not half adequate to the support of the population for any length of time," and that "nobody is prepared for winter."[12] All at once, the calls for food stuffs and building materials exploded. Despite high demand, high prices and a supply insufficient to quickly satisfy all needs, tenements manufactured from cut lumber replaced the sea of tents in the new towns of Hamilton, Chloride Flat and the loftily perched and ambitiously named Treasure City.[13] Optimism nevertheless reigned supreme. The streets remained lively even as operations in the mines slowed on account of the uncooperative turn of the weather and the residents, particularly of Treasure City, atop "a bleak, cold mountain," realized that water was even scarcer than timber.[14]

When so many harbored such profound optimism for the future, inevitability marked the pathway to an era riddled with conflict, both legal and otherwise. That White Pine promised "to be a prolific source of litigation if not of bloodshed" few possessed any doubt.[15] Pitted against each other were the original locators, headed by the discoverer of the first ore on Treasure Hill, A. J. Leathers, and the latter arrivals, referred to by the former as mere "claim jumpers."[16] Enhancing the prospect for conflict was the crazed pattern of locating claims, with those on the surface lying directly

---

[10] *Gold Hill Daily News*, July 29, 1868.

[11] *Carson Daily Appeal*, September 25, 1868; and *Carson Daily Appeal*, December 5, 1868.

[12] *Gold Hill Daily News*, November 9, 1868; and *Gold Hill Daily News*, November 18, 1868.

[13] *Gold Hill Daily News*, October 22, 1868.

[14] *Gold Hill Daily News*, December 18, 1868.

[15] *Gold Hill Daily News*, September 4, 1868.

[16] Id.

over other claims three of four layers deep.[17] The intensity of feeling between the factions only seemed to increase as the operations in the mines went dormant. Lawyers to resolve the inevitable legal troubles, and lawmen to keep the peace, were in great demand, and having seen like phenomenon during the Gold Rush of 1849 and the Silver Rush of the early 1860s, Perley could not resist the opportunity presented. Though stouter than he had been in earlier years, he managed, with Thomas Fitch, to cram himself into a stage and head east in November of 1868 after concluding matters as best he could in California.[18] Others had similar ideas, some of whom Perley unquestionably welcomed, if not as friends, then as friendly competition. Blasdel was a former client, and William Campbell a friend. Better yet was word from David Terry that he would venture to White Pine as well. Having only recently returned from exile in Mexico following the mass pardons granted by President Johnson, Terry thought to make a new start in an environment similar to one where he and Perley had ventured out together so many years before, and with such great success. Thinking they might have gotten the jump on many potential competitors before winter closed in, Perley and his companions found on their arrival in White Pine that the few boarding houses in town could scarcely accommodate them. Blasdell and Campbell, being long and lank, could "be hung like nails" on the walls of the few inns in operation, while others, like Judge Perley "must be laid down as they won't hang on a nail."[19]

The absence of court rooms and the seasonal decline in mining operations translated into little business for the cadre of lawyers gathering in the new community. Fitch and Delong, in the company of Senator Stewart, found a ready audience amongst the idle denizens of the camps and rudimentary towns for their appeals for votes in the 1868 election—for General Grant and for themselves and their party.[20] Others, like Will Campbell, bided their time in the saloons, drinking scotch and trolling for future clients to serve when the as yet unorganized courts finally opened for business.[21] Perley

[17] *Gold Hill Daily News*, October 20, 1868.

[18] *Gold Hill Daily News*, November 18, 1868.

[19] *Gold Hill Daily News*, December 8, 1868.

[20] *Gold Hill Daily News*, September 24, 1868.

[21] *Gold Hill Daily News*, December 29, 1868

himself exuded energy in abundance as a speculator on the lookout for mining claims. After discovering a promising ledge, he nearly froze to death one night "waiting for it to get light enough in order to write the location notice" before anyone else could stake a claim.[22] Aiming to generate income sooner rather than later, he formed a start-up construction business, but suffered some impediments in the form of a scarcity of materials, including linen for the walls and rooves of temporary housing for the budding population at Hamilton.[23] His endeavor, nevertheless, was a success. In the first month alone, Perley was reported to have earned $25,000 in his housing and real estate ventures.[24] Understanding that the coming season would bring trouble as well as opportunity, he and Campbell entered into a law partnership, and then combined their influence with that of DeLong to call for and then preside over a meeting at Hamilton to organize a county separate from Nye and Lander, and the establishment of institutions to protect the people from "the desperadoes who will doubtless be flocking here next Spring."[25] On December 30, at a public meeting presided over by Campbell, Perley offered resolutions to be presented to the Legislature, recommending organization of a new county called White Pine, with temporary commissioners selected to administer the municipality until elections could be held.[26] With sufficient support behind the initiative, the Legislature rather promptly enacted a law creating the new county, to take effect on April 1, with the town of Hamilton to serve as the county seat, where the county trustees would meet and the District Court would preside over legal proceedings.[27] While county officials were named in the Act itself and continued in office until the general election of 1870, town leaders drafted their own charters and planned to hold elections in the spring.[28] Perley's preeminence as a lawyer and good

---

[22] Marvin Lewis, *Martha and the Doctor: A Frontier Family in Central Nevada* (Reno: University of Nevada Press, 1977), at p. 158.

[23] Id.

[24] Letter of W.W. Bishop, Esq., *San Francisco Examiner*, January 20, 1869.

[25] *Gold Hill Daily News*, December 23, 1868.

[26] *White Pine News*, January 2, 1869.

[27] Myron Angel, *History of the State of Nevada and Biographical Sketches of its Prominent Men and Pioneers* (Oakland: Thompson & West, 1881), at p. 650.

[28] Id.

acquaintance with the lounging population secured his election to the post of Hamilton's City Attorney.[29]

Before winter fully gave way to the succeeding season, rain turned the dirt streets of Hamilton into "an awful Golgotha of mud."[30] "The condition of Main St. in this city," said a correspondent, "is certainly terrifying to all pedestrians who are compelled to travel it." To many in town, Perley became a hero when he solved the dilemma facing pedestrians attempting to cross the sloppy thoroughfares by throwing earth generated by the excavation of his Main Street lot onto the roadway and creating make-shift pedestrian bridges.[31] His popular profile rose even higher when he became a chief organizer of the Hamilton Protective League, aiming to defend the rights of early claimants against the wave of claim jumpers who threatened the interests of those, like himself, who came before the advent of the new year.[32] His home became a showcase of rare flowers and the destination of interesting travelers seeking good company.[33] The improvement of the weather and the optimism of the people encouraged good will and mirth, and the belief that any occasion was an opportunity to celebrate. In April, Perley, former Governor Blasdel and others organized a grand ball as a fund raiser for victims of a mining disaster at Gold Hill.[34] A second ball, said to be the "first annual," was held in May in Rain's Hall on Main Street, sponsored by the White Pine Hook and Ladder Company, No. 1, with Perley again acting in an organizing capacity, aided by DeLong, Delos Ashley and Jesse Pitzer.[35] Yet another ball was held to celebrate Independence Day, again with Perley as a chief organizer, this time with the aid of Judge Terry.[36] And a fourth in August.[37] And a fifth and sixth and seventh, again with Perley taking a lead in the planning of

---

[29] *Gold Hill Daily News*, April 17, 1869; and *Sacramento Daily Union*, April 20, 1869

[30] *Daily Inland Empire*, March 30, 1869.

[31] Id.

[32] *Daily Inland Empire*, June 21, 1869

[33] *Daily Inland Empire*, April 10, 1869; and *Daily Inland Empire*, May 5, 1869.

[34] *Daily Inland Empire*, April 24, 1869.

[35] *Daily Inland Empire*, May 13, 1869.

[36] *Daily Inland Empire*, July 4, 1869

[37] *Daily Inland Empire*, August 14, 1869.

festivities: to honor a Mrs. Veuve and a Mrs. Brandon, and mark the arrival of a new fire truck.[38]

As the opening of the "law campaign" approached and parties prepared for business in the municipal and district courts, Perley and Campbell formally announced the consummation of their partnership, to operate out of Perley's building at 23 Main Street.[39] One of the first matters on the docket for the partners was an "estate imbroglio" involving a dispute between rival claimants to a 300 acre parcel in Hamilton, and pitting them against the District Attorney and two other lawyers.[40] Perley's client, a Mr. Vogelsdorff, was a claim jumper who'd suffered arrest after his rival, W. F. Walton, showed up on the premises with an armed party to halt the destruction of older monuments and fences. When Perley's client made bail, Walton swore out a second complaint in another court, but the Sheriff, observing the chicanery, refused to act. Instead, he secured the property for Vogelsdorff and arrested Walton on the very charge the latter alleged against the former. As that matter proceeded in the municipal court, Perley prosecuted and defended against other lawsuits in which he was a named party, obtaining a confession of judgment in the first and bowing to a $120 judgment in favor of a man named Martin in the second.[41]

On the eve of the commencement of the first term of the new court for the Eighth Judicial District, Perley and Campbell announced the dissolution of their partnership, effective May 31. The reasons for it remain unknown, though it might be that the high strung Perley and the relaxed good old boy manner of Campbell made for an awkward collaboration. The break hardly indicated a rupture in good will; for the two men remained co-counsel on a number of cases still needing resolution, and Campbell even opted to relieve Perley of the distracting duties as City Attorney.[42] Acrimony and ill will simply didn't pay with so many cases to litigate in Judge William H. Beatty's Court. Among the cases on the docket, was George Cadwalader's suit against Perley—probably for

---

[38] *Daily Inland Empire*, July 28, 1869; *Daily Inland Empire*, August 14, 1869; *Daily Inland Empire*, October 16, 1869; and *Daily Inland Empire*, November 20, 1869

[39] *Daily Inland Empire*, March 30, 1869.

[40] *Daily Inland Empire*, April 24, 1869.

[41] *Daily Inland Empire*, April 29, 1869.

[42] *Daily Inland Empire*, June 8, 1869; and *Gold Hill Daily News*, June 8, 1869.

payment for services connected with his losing effort in the appeal in the Birds' Nest matter—a motion for reconsideration by Perley of the $120 Martin judgment, and an action by Perley and Campbell to vacate an attachment obtained by a man named Willard.[43] The case of the Plaintiffs Mosier and Guptiel found its way to the District Court, as well, and with it their assertion, by and through attorney and ex-Confederate Henry I. Thornton, of a perpetual right to enjoy the benefits of a spring percolating upward from a subterranean source. In defense of the Defendants, Perley took the position that they were entitled to draw water from wells located on their own land, regardless of how this affected the water table on adjacent properties. The duration of enjoyment of the spring by the Plaintiffs prior to the Defendants' alleged interference was entirely preempted by the latters' right to appropriate water below the surface of land described on their deed. A restraining order issued at an earlier time was reconsidered and then dissolved even as the matter proceeded forward on the ultimate merits.[44] Perley and Campbell also associated in as counsel of record in the case of *Kelly v Hughes*, and Perley himself presented a defense in a suit brought against him by the Bank of California.[45]

Each of these cases and others moved into trial posture with the coming of the Fall, by which time the partnership with Campbell seems to truly have come to an end. In the effort to overturn the decision in *Martin v. Perley*, Perley ultimately settled for costs and the matter was dismissed.[46] Perley and Judge Terry attempted to prove the claim of the Truckee Mining Company against the rival Isabella, winning an injunction and forcing the Isabella to surrender its claim.[47] Judge Beatty set the *Mosier* case for trial to begin in late October, which proceeded as scheduled once the fateful date arrived. After submission of the evidence at trial, Perley moved for a non-suit on two grounds: that no case could be made for injury by adjacent landowners arising from the Defendants drawing water from their own land, and the failure of the Plaintiffs to established

43 *Daily Inland Empire*, June 20, 1869; and *Daily Inland Empire*, June 22, 1869.
44 *Daily Inland Empire*, July 4, 1869.
45 *Daily Inland Empire*, June 30, 1869; and *Daily Inland Empire*, July 27, 1869.
46 *Daily Inland Empire*, October 19, 1869.
47 *Daily Inland Empire*, November 11, 1869.

any "visible connection between the wells and the spring."[48] After "elaborate" arguments adorned with "very fine legal points," Perley's position carried the day.[49] As soon as the *Mosier* matter concluded, Perley set to work trying the case of *Brooklyn v. Merced* on behalf of the Defendant Merced, opposed by Henry I. Thornton and Perley's erstwhile partner, John Garber. At stake was title to disputed mining ground "situated a little west of the Rice grade, a short distance above the toll house between this City and Treasure."[50] Typical of such suits, the issues of priority of location and identity of the ledge in controversy consumed the attention of the attorneys and their witnesses, as well as the large crowd that assembled to observe.[51] In the end, the Plaintiff's failure to record its claim after publishing its notice proved fatal to its cause.

Perley's experience as a defender and a prosecutor of the criminally accused made him the natural choice of Judge Beatty to defend T. J. Hauskins against the charge that he murdered Reuben Cross. Pitted against him as prosecutor in the matter was his former law partner, Will Campbell. Assisted by his some-time opponent Jesse Pitzer, Perley attacked the 53-person jury pool with peremptory and other challenges so successfully that a second venire was necessary.[52] Once the matter was finally tried and the evidence was in, Campbell rose to deliver a closing argument loaded with "glittering generalities" and little else.[53] Perley followed with "one of the most eloquent and exhaustive law arguments…ever witnessed in our District Court," marked by "authority after authority, going to the point that a man was justified in acting on apparent danger to himself or his property, whether real or imaginary," and delivered "in language at once forcible and convincing."[54] After laying the groundwork for a self-defense exoneration, Perley was followed by Pitzer and what was called "one of the greatest efforts of his life," without notes and

[48] *Daily Inland Empire*, October 26, 1869; *Daily Inland Empire*, October 27, 1869; and *Gold Hill Daily News*, November 20, 1871.

[49] *Carson Daily Appeal*, October 30, 1869.

[50] *Daily Inland Empire*, November 2, 1869.

[51] *Daily Inland Empire*, November 3, 1869; and *Daily Inland Empire*, November 4, 1869.

[52] *Daily Inland Empire*, October 12, 1869.

[53] *Daily Inland Empire*, October 15, 1869.

[54] Id.

completely from memory, without a single error or lack of precision, all done in a style completely comprehensible to the layman.[55] The combined effort of Perley and Pitzer, complimenting one another so perfectly, left such an impression that a not-guilty verdict seemed inevitable, especially in the wake of Will Campbell's labored hour and a half long rebuttal.[56] Judge Beatty's especial focus in his instruction to the jury on the nuances of the doctrine of self-defense planted firmly in the jurors' minds its supreme importance and perhaps conditioned them to approach all of the evidence from a rather prejudiced point of view. In any event, after slightly more than an hour of deliberation, the jury returned to the court room with the expected not-guilty verdict. A second trial was scheduled over the charge of attempted murder of the dead man's brother, apparently arising out of the same incident, but given the jury's findings that Hauskins' conduct was justified under the circumstances, no confidence existed that a conviction would follow.[57]

Pitzer seemed in many ways a good fit with Perley as a replacement for Campbell. An Ohio native who immigrated to California overland in 1849, Pitzer gravitated, like Perley, to the southern wing of the Democrat Party.[58] When the Party split in 1855, he moved with Terry, Perley and so many others into the Know Nothing camp and even won election to be Judge of the Ninth District Court in Shasta and Trinity Counties on the Party's ticket. He moved to Washoe in 1864 and White Pine four years later. Though a gifted trial lawyer with a special knack for criminal defense, he shared Perley's hypersensitivity and excitableness, which likely made the relations between the two men explosive at times, and yet respect endured for the rest of their lives, as evidenced by their continued close association.

Two factors appeared to militate against any formal partnership between the two men. Unlike Perley, Pitzer never left the Democrat fold. His arrival in White Pine in fact resulted from his effort to win the County over to the Democrat cause in the fall of 1868 in opposition to DeLong and Fitch. Downcast after losing a debate

---

[55] Id.

[56] Id.

[57] *Daily Inland Empire*, October 16, 1869.

[58] *Pioche Daily Record*, January 27, 1877.

with Senator Stewart, his eyes noticed the ore-rich nature of the ground, and prompted him on his return to Virginia City to tout the financial promise of White Pine County. A greater deterrent to a partnership was the presence in Hamilton of David Terry and strong prospects that existed for a reformation of an historic collaboration. As noted, Perley and Terry appeared in court together as counsel for the Truckee Mining Company.[59] A formal partnership between the two, however, was not to be, though the men worked together in other capacities.

Being something of a knight errant, David Terry took up the cause of young Jennie Fitzpatrick, who sought the annulment of a marriage of recent vintage and short duration. Opposing him as counsel for the husband were Pitzer and Will Campbell. Desirous of avoiding the embarrassment of public revelations of their private affairs, the parties agreed to waive a jury trial and seek assignment of the matter to a special master.[60] As a former judge (albeit of very short tenure and unknown venue) with significant experience in family law, Perley was a natural as a referee in the contentious matter, and his close relations with the attorneys for both parties likely assured all that his mutual regard for opposing counsel would guarantee a lack of partiality in reaching a decision. Nevertheless, the case invited enormous public interest. The prominent airing of his own peccadillos in the press induced a high degree of empathy by Perley for the estranged spouses, and led, no doubt, in the face of high anticipation of "rich disclosures" of a personal nature, to Perley ordering a closure of the proceedings to all but witnesses and interested parties.[61] Among those allowed in, however, informants abounded, and they fed the media a stream of details of the goings on in the courtroom which were printed to the extent they were fit for public consumption. In the end, the revelations were rather tame, confined to a report that Judge Perley favored setting the marriage aside on the grounds of illegality for reasons related in part to "very intricate legal points" set forth in a formal report of findings said by Judge Beatty to have been "an able document."[62] No improprieties of a sexual nature were found.

[59] *Daily Inland Empire*, November 11, 1869.
[60] *Daily Inland Empire*, November 23, 1869.
[61] *Daily Inland Empire*, November 25, 1869.
[62] *Daily Inland Empire*, December 1, 1869.

Rather, the controversy was confined to the legal incapacity of the wife—a minor—and the questionable consent of her step-father, without her legal guardian's knowledge, to wed a man with whom she wasn't particularly enamored.[63]

Perley's findings favoring annulment was presented to the Court with a strong recommendation, but Judge Beatty disregarded it and ruled for the husband and preservation of the marriage.[64] Terry appealed the decision as a misreading of the facts and misapplication of the relevant law. On appeal, the Supreme Court expressed surprise over the failure of the wife to challenge the obvious "irregular point of practice" in the form of Judge Beatty's disregard of its own order referring the matter to Perley for determination as to the facts, and the forming by him of a special verdict the court was obligated to adopt as its own.[65] With no objection on this ground, which might have resulted in a reversal of the District Court's ruling, the Supreme Court reflected on the call of the statute governing marriages between parties under the age of consent. On Jennie's behalf, Terry argued that the law at issue, while setting the age of consent for marriage by girls at sixteen, comprised an exception when the minor was subject to the authority of a guardian—in this case, the girl's mother.[66] The Court disagreed with this rather tortured construction of the statute and focused instead on the facts appearing in Perley's report, which confirmed the consensual age of the wife and the binding nature of her contractual commitments. These findings of material fact, however, said the Court "seem to have been overlooked in [Perley's] legal conclusions."[67] Such findings "are conclusive of the case. The appellant being of lawful consenting age to make a marriage contract, and entering into the same 'without force or fraud,' and 'with her full and free consent,' did make a valid binding contract, which can only be avoided by her for some reason by law provided for such avoidance; and none such has been presented in this case."[68]

---

[63] *Fitzpatrick v. Fitzpatrick* (1870) 6 Nev. 63.
[64] *Daily Inland Empire*, December 12, 1869.
[65] *Fitzpatrick v. Fitzpatrick*, supra, at 65.
[66] Id., at 66.
[67] Id., at 68.
[68] Id.

With the end of the 1869 term of the District Court, a veritable exodus of lawyers occurred. John Garber and John McQuaid left on the Monday stage bound for California, followed the next day by Perley, H. I. Thornton, Thomas P. Hawley and J. R Kittrell.[69] When the new term commenced in January, Perley was back in White Pine, facing several suits against himself: one by a Mr. Sanderson that was held over from the previous term for the purpose of hearing a motion for a new trial, and another brought by the State of Nevada for delinquent taxes for numerous lots situated in Hamilton.[70] A similar suit for unpaid taxes would soon face him in Ormsby County.[71] No doubt the land was worthless, hence the taxes went delinquent, and Perley found escheat by the State far easier than selling the land himself and making payment. Perley certainly faced more pressing concerns than tying up loose ends with unprofitable investments for which the creditor possessed an easy and rather pro forma remedy. His skills as an attorney being well known, and his willingness to stand up against public disfavor being one of his strengths, he found himself a participant in three different criminal trials, either as the prosecutor or counsel for the defense.

The first was the S. P. Howard matter. In December of 1869, a few doors down from Perley's office on Main Street, in the Sample Room operated by Howard and a business partner, Howard entered what began as a friendly conversation with a customer, James Cartwright. The tipsy crowd hardly noticed a change in demeanor among the men prior to Howard rising in a state of intoxication to announce "I'll show you what I'll do," and then open fire on Cartwright with a derringer.[72] Charged with murder, he retained Perley and Jesse Pitzer for his defense. The trial came off quickly, and rather than a death sentence, Perley and Pitzer convinced judge and jury to show lenience. Sentenced to the State penitentiary for a term of twelve years, Howard was consigned to the county jail until transport could be arranged. Unable to pay his legal fees, he turned

---

[69] *Daily Inland Empire*, December 22, 1869; and *Sacramento Daily Union*, December 23, 1869.

[70] *Daily Inland Empire*, December 19, 1869; *White Pine News*, January 1, 1869; and *Daily Inland Empire*, February 2, 1870.

[71] *Carson Daily Appeal*, April 5, 1870.

[72] *Elko Independent*, January 1, 1870.

over a property in Reno to his attorneys and then sat morosely in jail awaiting his transit to prison, thinking perhaps of the dismal fate that awaited his wife. But Perley and Pitzer had plans apart from compensation. Realizing their client's wife would lack a provider for years to come, they discretely deeded the property to the woman. When Howard's former business partner informed the editor of *The Carson Daily Appeal* of this "unostentatious charity," the editor lauded the attorneys and declared that "the act was Godlike."[73]

The second case was that of Charles Jones. Though the crime occurred six months before, delay was attributable to escape by the accused on horseback and successful evasion of detection by his pursuers until a tip reached the Sherriff of Esmerelda County. Tracking Jones down to his hiding place, the Sheriff apprehended the fugitive and brought him back to White Pine to stand trial for the homicide of his former partner in a hauling business, Thomas Matthews, during a drunken brawl.[74] Jones was a likeable, cheerful young man, a native of Ohio, a Veteran of the Union Navy and masterful horseman, of medium height, dark complexion, and a rather boyish appearance.[75] The District Attorney aimed to try him for murder, but hesitated for a moment when the highly competent Delos Ashley and R. D. Ferguson stepped forward for the defense.[76] Faced with such legal firepower, the District Attorney contacted Perley and asked him to sign on to assist as he had in the Swaney-Seale matter and so many others. Perley agreed and formally associated in as co-counsel on February 16.[77] The trial commenced the same day in a courtroom packed with spectators, a jury was selected and sworn, and the prosecution began to present its case.[78] Resting after taking testimony from eight witnesses, Perley and the prosecution yielded to the defense. Ashley took a chance by putting the Defendant himself on the stand, no doubt to speak of the threat posed by his drunken associate and the absence on his own part of

---

[73] *Carson Daily Appeal*, April 3, 1870.

[74] *The Daily State Register*, October 7, 1871.

[75] Id; *Carson Daily Appeal*, February 20, 1870; and *White Pine News*, February 19, 1870.

[76] *Carson Daily Appeal*, February 20, 1870.

[77] *White Pine News*, February 18, 1870.

[78] Id.

any intent to kill.[79] As the trial concluded, many were impressed by the young man's good nature, how cheerful he acted in the face of his misfortune, and that he was "not a bad man."[80] The jury was impressed as well, and though it convicted him of homicide, it asked Judge Beatty to show mercy in the sentence.[81] After Perley and the District Attorney defeated Jones' motion for a new trial, the Judge heard Jones' tale of the destruction of his previously good character through life in the armed forces during the late and terrible war and the roughness of the frontier, and issued his sentence: ten years confinement in the State Prison in lieu of death.[82]

The last was not heard of Jones after his delivery to the State penitentiary in the company of the Sherriff and fellow convict S.P. Howard.[83] A year and a half later, he took part in a massive prison break with twenty-eight other inmates. A surprise assault on the captain of the guard during an inspection signaled a general rush among the prisoners against the guards. Guns wrestled from the some of the captors were soon deployed against the remainder, and pistol and shotgun fire resounded through the halls. Caught in the melee, the visiting Lieutenant Governor of the State fought alongside the guards, as well as a civilian, Mat Pixely. Eager to leave confinement, Jones took up a revolver, and when Pixley fired on him, he fired back, striking him in the head and killing him on the spot.[84] Reports were that Jones was subsequently murdered by his fellow inmates, incensed over his empty promise of support to be found in the countryside and his contribution to their arrival, outside of the prison walls, to a veritable hornets' nest of popular animosity.[85] The report, however, proved incorrect. In truth, he was still on the run weeks later when the indictments were handed down for the murders arising from the prison break.[86] He was finally brought down by a bounty hunter in a fierce gun battle in Bishop Creek that left both men dead.[87] Perley's thoughts on the

---

79 Id.

80 *White Pine News*, February 19, 1870.

81 Id.

82 *White Pine News*, March 1, 1870.

83 *Carson Daily Appeal*, March 12, 1870.

84 *The Daily State Register*, September 19, 1871.

85 *The Daily State Register*, October 7, 1871.

86 *Gold Hill Daily News*, November 10, 1871.

87 *Gold Hill Daily News*, December 19, 1871.

matter aren't known, though perhaps he considered the mercy of the Governor, in light of subsequent events, as far crueler to the people than kind to a man who eventually proved himself to be a two-time killer.

The final criminal matter consuming Perley's time was the prosecution of Dan Lynch for the theft of a very fine horse owned by A. C. Cleveland.[88] A former legislator from Washoe, and one of the founding fathers with Perley of the County of White Pine, Cleveland had taken pride in reclaiming a beautiful farm from the desert waste of the Great Basin, with "acres and acres under fence and growing hay, grain, fruit and, in fact, everything known to the temperate zone."[89] Incensed by the theft of his animal on February 18, he awaited the results of the criminal proceeding with confidence that justice would be done. In frustration of this outcome appeared Perley on March 5 to enter a plea of not guilty on behalf of the accused.[90] During the succeeding month, between entry of the plea and the trial, some negotiations apparently occurred. When next in Court, the not guilty plea was withdrawn and in its place Lynch pled guilty.[91] The possibility of the proverbial harsh sentences for horse thieves in frontier Nevada gave way, instead, to a three-year sentence to the State penitentiary.[92]

Turning from criminal matters, Perley managed a victory in his case against Willard in the form of a $600 judgment, and then set legal affairs aside to head the invitation committee with Pitzer, Thornton, John Garber and David Terry for yet another grand ball, though he seems to have departed town for San Francisco before the public announcement and even left his mail unclaimed at the post office in Treasure City.[93] His business on the coast included introducing a "client" named Leota Turner to the attorney John McQuaid. Ms. Turner was in need of representation in a matter involving an alleged breach of promise to marry by Don Ortiz—a

---

[88] *Daily Alta California*, February 20, 1870; and *White Pine News*, April 14, 1870.

[89] *Second Biennial Report of the Nevada Historical Society, 1909-1910* (Carson City: State Printing Office, 1911), at p. 77.

[90] *White Pine News*, March 7 1870.

[91] *White Pine News*, April 12, 1870.

[92] *White Pine News*, April 14, 1870.

[93] *White Pine News*, April 14, 1870; *White Pine News*, May 27, 1870; *Gold Hill Daily News*, May 13, 1870; and *White Pine News*, 1870.

matter that proved a sensation a year later, and segued from a mere contractual dispute into a fight for fees and a prosecution of the woman for perjury. Between Perley's departure and return, armed interlopers led by a disgruntled A. J. Leathers occupied the Perley & Niagra Company mine, claiming priority of location dating back to October of 1865 and the completion of sizeable labor since that time.[94] Upon his return, Perley brought a suit to eject the occupiers with the aid of Jesse Pitzer. The Defendants enlisted the services of Ashley and Hunt and a trial was had in Judge Atwood's Justice Court well into the late hours of the night early in June, where "a large amount of testimony was taken on both sides, and a number of nice legal points were raised, and ably handled by the counsel."[95] Within days, Judge Atwood rendered a judgment for Perley and ordered Leathers and his associates to "restore the mines to the Plaintiffs," but without any requirement to pay damages.[96]

In the summer, he and Campbell argued in opposition to an appeal before the Supreme Court in the matter of *Estes v. Richardson* against Perley's frequent adversary, Delos Ashley. Ashley contended that the trial court erred in excusing a witness who admitted he had "'heard something of the matter,' that it would require testimony to remove the existing impression on his mind, that he 'had no bias or prejudice in the matter,' that the impressions upon his mind were very vague, and that he had never had any conversation 'with either plaintiff or defendant in regard to the suit, nor with anyone who pretended to know the facts." The prospective juror's biases apparently favoring the plaintiff, Ashley challenged the juror for cause without specifying the precise statutory basis for the challenge. Losing both the objection and the case, Ashley appealed, but the Supreme Court could find nothing amiss in the trial judge's decision to overrule Ashley's challenge for cause, and instead criticized Ashley for failing to specify into which precise statutory category his challenge fell.[97] Perley, of course, could not have been happier with this result. Even an arrest by the constable of Shermantown for taking shelter from the rain atop his horse on a boarded sidewalk beneath a protective awning he accepted with

[94] *White Pine News*, June 9, 1870.
[95] Id.
[96] *White Pine News*, June 11, 1870.
[97] *Estes v. Richardson* (1870) 6 Nev. 128; and *Carson Daily Appeal*, July 21, 1870.

uncharacteristic good humor.[98] Rather than threaten the constable with dire consequence should he be hauled before the justice of the peace, he went along willingly, and even treated an amused crowd to a round of drinks afterward. The press hailed the good sense of the justice of the peace for exercising "sound judicial discretion" and saving the town "from a tedious and costly appeal case, which might have gone into the books alongside Jarndyce vs. Jarndyce."[99] Perley's former reputation for combativeness being well known, it was a relief to all that the matter ended so well.

The summer and fall were rather sedate. Nothing on the litigation-front generated public comment or interest, at least as far as Perley was concerned. His most noteworthy activities were partaking in the organization of yet another celebratory ball with Pitzer, Ashley, Judge Beatty and others, and aiding his former law partner, Thomas Fitch, in winning reelection to Congress.[100] With Perley present at a gathering on Main Street in front of the Stone Saloon, Fitch took the platform to the boisterous applause of fifteen hundred enthusiastic supporters, all expectant that "true to the old faith, that eloquent tongue would give forth no uncertain sound."[101] In a speech typical of his campaign performances, Fitch reviewed the achievements of the Republican Party in the late war, the management of Reconstruction in the South, the complex problems of labor and capital in the industrializing nation, and matters touching upon citizenship for the Chinese. It was, said one report, "a master effort, never surpassed by any one, never equaled by any other speaker in the State." The effort, however, was not sufficient to overcome a resurgent Democracy which had in its favor the typical complacency of the dominant party in a by-election year. The differences between the parties were stark. As one rather biased source noted, while the Republicans could stand proudly on their record of abolishing slavery, establishing universal manhood suffrage, enacting civil rights laws, ending disunion, defeating any effort to repudiate the Union War debt and the debt owed to veterans, building the Pacific Railroad, promoting pensions and homesteads for vets, and remarkably reducing both taxes and the

98 *White Pine News,* July 15, 1870.

99 Id.

100 *Daily Inland Empire,* October 12, 1870; and *White Pine News,* August 7, 1870.

101 *White Pine News,* August 7, 1870.

national debt, all the Democrats had to show for themselves was sympathy and outright support for rebellion, devotion to slavery, destruction of orphan asylums for African American children, hostility to voting rights, persecution of freedmen, opposition to civil liberties, expansion of the public debt, reduction of wages through introduction of cheap foreign labor and prejudice against the men who fought and won the Civil War.[102]

Whether the case for election objectively favored the Republicans or not in the end didn't matter. Notwithstanding a humiliating and crushing defeat of his rival in a series of debates, Fitch lost by a narrow margin in the Fall, as did William Campbell, who was running for Attorney General.[103] Among the victors was Democrat gubernatorial candidate L. R. Bradley, who Perley had run out of Fremont's El Pescadero years before.[104] Some hope that Fitch might retain his seat came when Utah laid claim to Pioche and threatened to annex it, with the result that Fitch's opponent's winning margin would disappear. The threat, however, proved illusory; the boundary held, as did the previously determined tally of the votes.[105] Perley's former partisans in the Democrat Party were largely unsuccessful in California and elsewhere in the country, but their fortunes were high in the State where he resided and in which he at last had become a full-fledged member of the opposing faction.

More meaningful to Perley was the restoration of his fortunes. The loss of Mina in 1864 presaged a period marked by defeat personally and in the courts. The riches accumulated on the Comstock vanished, as did his landed wealth in the City. Notoriety in the press wasn't positive in nature. Indeed, there appeared to be a morbid fascination in his declining prosperity, particularly among those who continued to resent him for his role in the death of Senator Broderick. The great discoveries at Treasure Hill came at a moment that could not have been better calculated to provide him with an opportunity to replenish his bank account and afford him

---

[102] See *Gold Hill Daily News*, November 7, 1870.

[103] *Elko Independent*, November 9, 1870.

[104] See Earle Williams, *Rancho El Pescadero*, Volume 1, p. 11-12, BANC. MSS 80/58c; and Edward Bosqui, *Memoirs* (San Francisco: Edward Bosqui, 1904). At p. 137.

[105] *Gold Hill Daily News*, November 29, 1870.

the prospect, in yet another community lacking any history or precedents, to remake himself anew. He seized the opportunity without hesitation, established himself in a town and county where he quickly became a leading citizen and returned to top form in the pursuit of victory in the courts. Perley was back, in great spirits, on the brink of the greatest battle of his life.

Chapter Eleven

THE GOD OF THIEVES

New mineral strikes in eastern Nevada convinced many in the west of the enduring and ambitious future of that part of the State and the propriety of continuing investment in the development of the mines. South of White Pine lay Lincoln County. With geology similar to that in the north, small mining locations dotted the terrain there in the mid and late 1860s. Modest operations yielded in time to far more elaborate establishments funded by San Francisco investors, led by Perley's former client François Pioche. A full-scale rush occurred in 1871, centered on the Pioche Lode, close to a town of the same name. As the deserts around Pioche were exuding the same promise Hamilton had but a year or two before, the population ebbed southward. "Where a weary undulating stretch of sagebrush had been but a few days before was now the site of a Western city with its few stores, numerous beer and dance halls;...its rough grizzled miners and their ever-near companions, gamblers and painted women; with reckless days and sleepless nights."[1] Those who ventured to this mining oasis were counseled to beware; for the place attracted more than its share of ruffians and outlaws, and their relations with one another generated bloody and lethal commotions on a regular basis.

Not deterred by violence and inspired by the bright prospects for professional practice and mining speculation in Pioche, Perley convinced his long-time rival and friend, Delos Ashley, to join him there in a law partnership. They added a junior partner to their ranks to flush out what likely they hoped would be a formidable firm.[2] Ashley, however, did not remain long in the fold. He took a post as counsel for Pioche's Meadow Valley Mining Company and partnered up with Henry I. Thornton. Consequently, the younger partner, Henry Rives, would assume a more prominent place in Perley's practice.

---

[1] "Judge Rives' Life Was Full of Adventure," *Eureka Sentinel*, March 3, 1906.

[2] *Daily State Register*, February 25, 1871.

Rives had far more in common with the men Perley associated with in California than those with whom he had grown close in Nevada. A native of Virginia, Rives hailed from one of the most prominent families in that State. His father was a member of the Missouri Legislature prior to the War and later fell in service to the Confederacy while holding the rank of General. Among his close kinsmen were Senator William Cabell Rives and Judge Alexander Rives, as well as numerous members of the Virginia Legislature. He read law in the office of his uncle, Algernon Sidney Buford, a former State Assemblyman and future railroad president, before migrating to Carson City. Rives had served as a soldier for the Confederacy throughout the war, and when it was over, found his State in ruins and the South as a whole missing its former attraction.[3] Upon arriving in Nevada, he worked and studied in the law office of A. C. Ellis and gained a quick entry to the bar. It was a windfall for the genial Rives, with a noted faculty for drawing friends to himself, to make Perley's acquaintance, and then to win his confidence. For the young lawyer, a Democrat sheep in a Republican country, a guide was indispensable, both in the practice of law and in the ways of politics. Perley, for all his faults, possessed expertise in both fields.

While Rives likely handled minor matters, Perley focused on the greater, including the long-delayed hearing of the appeal in the case of *Mosier & Guptel v. Caldwell & Wilson*. The appellants, Mosier and Guptel, with Thornton as their counsel, argued that Perley's clients could not lawfully dig wells upon their own lands within a few feet of and above the plaintiffs' spring, and thereby cut off from the spring its supply of water, "because the supply of water to the spring came through a well-defined subterranean gravel channel from the lands of defendants, and this channel was intersected" by the defendants' wells.[4] Unable to find authority either from Nevada or even California for this argument, Thornton cited to Washburn's treatise on Easements and Servitudes and various cases from the east coast. Perley dismissed the argument with reference to the settled rule in both England and much of the United States, including California, that a land owner was entitled to draw water

[3] "Judge Rives' Life Was Full of Adventure," *Eureka Sentinel*, March 3, 1906.
[4] *Mosier v. Caldwell* (1872) 7 Nev. 363, 365.

from his own ground regardless of the effect on his neighbors.[5] Contrary to Thornton's account, Washburn actually supported this alternative view. Speaking for the Court, Justice Whitman went straight to Washburn's treatise: "It may be stated, as a general principle of nearly universal application, that while one proprietor of land may not stop or divert the waters of a stream flowing in a surface channel through it, so as to deprive a landowner, whose estate lies upon the stream below that of the proprietor first-mentioned, of the use of the same or essentially impair or disturb the use thereof; if, without an intention to injure an adjacent owner, and while making use of his own land to any suitable and lawful purpose, he cuts off, diverts, or destroys the use of an under-ground spring, or current of water which has no known and defined course, but has been accustomed to penetrate and flow into the land of his neighbor, he is not thereby liable to any action for the diversion or stoppage of such water."[6] Such water, said Whitman, "is not, and cannot be distinguished from the estate itself, and of that the proprietor has the free and absolute use, so that he does not directly invade that of his neighbor, or consequently, injure his perceptible and clearly defined rights." As the case at bar came clearly within this rule, the judgment of the lower court was correct.[7] Not content with losing, Thornton asked for a re-hearing on the grounds that the original statement of facts was in error, but Judge Whitman was unimpressed with the argument and rejected it. So long was the delay due to this final tactic that it wasn't until late November that the Court's final opinion saw print.[8]

The greater expenditure of Perley's efforts in Pioche was on behalf of a new employer, the Raymond & Ely Mining Company. Founded in San Francisco only a few years before by John Ely, William Raymond and other investors, the company's initial purpose was to track down the early claimants to the so-called Panaca in the vicinity of Pioche dating back to 1864 who'd stumbled onto a promising bed of ore based on a tip provided by friendly natives. The Panaca claims had been recorded in rather vague contours in a larger district that was "very ambiguous, and if taken

---

[5] Id.

[6] Id., at 366.

[7] Id., at 367.

[8] *Gold Hill Daily News*, November 20, 1871.

literally would only mean to mathematical lines intersecting one another and inclosing no superficial area."[9] After expending a few hours work on their ground, the original claimants departed, most of whom never returned on account of native hostilities, the turbulence of the Civil War and the cares of everyday life. In the wake of the apparent abandonment of the original claims, John Ely and his friends from San Francisco arrived, adopted a formal code of laws for their new district, located claims atop the Panaca lines, and "went to work in earnest and developed the mines."[10] Calling its two new shafts the Burke and Creole, the Raymond & Ely extracted ore in the days leading up to May of 1871, paying minimal dividends, but generating $30,000 a month.[11]

The quieting of any of the claims antedating those of the Raymond & Ely being a priority, Perley set to work tracking down claimants and buying them off. Learning in July of the residence in Filmore, Utah of at least one of the claimants to ground known as Lot No. 3, Perley procured the services of Thomas Grieves to travel east to negotiate a purchase. For his own part, Perley set out with Judge Hardy to trace the whereabouts of several other claimants in Utah, some of whom were eventually convinced to come to Nevada to negotiate a conveyance. Perley's own task being done, he departed Utah from Ogden by train on August 11, disembarked in Oakland and took a ferry across the Bay to San Francisco.[12] Returning to Pioche on August 14, Greives discovered Perley's absence. Worried that his own out-of-pocket expenses were in need of reimbursement and suspicious that Perley aimed to undermine his own claims in the lode, Greives abandoned his intention to transfer Lot No. 3 to Perley and made a deal instead with the noted Indian fighter Charles Forman.[13] When he discovered this betrayal, Perley sent Rives with the purchase price and a demand to convey the property to him, but it was too late.

---

[9] Rossiter W. Raymond, *Statistics of Mines and Mining in the States and Territories West of the Rocky Mountains* (Washington, D.C.: Government Printing Office, 1874), at p. 516.

[10] Id., at p. 517.

[11] Id.

[12] Louis J. Rasmussen, *Railway Passenger Lists of Overland Trains to San Francisco and the West*, Vol. I (Colema: San Francisco Historic Records, 1966), at pp. 185-186.

[13] See Grieves' testimony in the *Raymond & Ely v. Hermes* case, reported in *The Pioche Daily Record*, April 10, 1873

Perley filed suit in the District Court situated in Pioche to recover possession of the land wrongfully withheld from him. Forman and Grieves denied any obligation to Perley and any conspiracy to defraud him, but were unable to prevent him from obtaining an ex parte injunction against the sale or pretended sale of the property pending resolution of the suit. Vainly, Grieves explained that he hadn't been paid beforehand by Perley the $100 he used to purchase the mining claim, hence the purchase was made in his own name, solely for his own benefit. In the wake of obtaining his injunction, Perley issued a public warning against purchasing from Forman "a pretended title to No. 3 of the Pioche Lode," and advising any and all prospective buyers of the "injunction granted by the District Court of Lincoln County, against selling his said pretended title, on the ground that he acquired it fraudulently from my agent."[14] Rather than await a trial of the matter, Forman directed his attorneys—Ashley, Thornton, Kelly and C. H. Belknap—to appeal. Relying exclusively on California law, Forman's legal team argued that denial of allegations set forth in a bill of equity defeats an injunction, and that the same should only have been issued upon affidavits or via testimony at a contested hearing. Perley and his legal team, consisting of Quint & Hardy and Ellis & King, argued in response that the trial court possessed absolute discretion in such matters. Stating that "this action was too clearly erroneous to admit of discussion," the Supreme Court almost summarily overruled the trial court. The evidence introduced in support of Perley's ex parte request "entirely failed to sustain any of the material allegations against appellant."[15]

The resolution of competing claims only made sense if the ground to which they related remained worth the investment. The exhausting of the Burke and the Creole mines had already prompted the Raymond & Ely's super-intendant, Charles W. Lightner, to sink what he dubbed the Lightner Shaft, just outside the Company's original ground, on terrain formerly located by the Mammoth Company. By June, diggers discovered a ledge of ore of immense quality located only 100 feet below the surface. Lightner's

---

[14] *Daily Alta California*, October 23, 1871.

[15] *Perley v. Forman* (1872) 7 Nev. 311, 311-312.

confusion over the precise boundaries of the new ledge led to discussion with Perley, who advised him and the Company to make a formal claim. When Lightner refused Perley's advice due to his concern that a secondary claim overlapping with the first might endanger the legitimacy of or supersede the older location, Perley volunteered to locate the ground himself, as "an extension." To avoid conflict with the Raymond & Ely, Lightner measured off the Company's boundaries, fixing the western limit slightly to the west of the starting point of the defunct Mammoth claim. Perley then erected a monument marking his ground and posted a notice of location dated August 1, 1871, declaring the locator to be the "Hermes Mining Company"—a rather idiosyncratic name some later theorized honored the deity to whom theft was sacred, but in truth derived that very morning from the chapter of the Bible Perley had devotedly read, containing reference to Hermas, the friend of the Apostle Paul. A typographical error by the Recorder produced much fodder on a later occasion when Perley's enterprise was condemned by many as a masterful piece of organized crime.[16]

Convincing Lightner to join him in the formal organization of the new mining concern, and hearing of purchases recently made on adjacent ground originally located for the Monitor Company by George Hearst, Perley sped off to San Francisco in September, met with Hearst, James Ben Ali Haggin, Lloyd Tevis and others to discuss the prospect of financial backing. Throughout August, September and October, a blur of conveyances and reconveyances of older titles from the original locators to Perley, Lightner and Hearst culminated in the vesting of a singular title with the new company.[17] Drafting a corporate plan, with Hearst, Haggin and others as trustees, and stating an intention to capitalize the venture through the sale of $3,000,000 in stock priced at $100 per share, Perley issued formal notice to the world that the Hermes was a going concern.[18] With the backing of Hearst and Haggin and San Francisco money in hand, Perley returned to Pioche, hired a crew of men and set to work without any indication of hostility from his employers. It wasn't long before the Hermes exhibited the results of

---

16 *Pioche Daily Record*, May 14, 1873.

17 *Daily Alta California*, April 7, 1873; and *Eureka Sentinel*, April 19, 1873.

18 *Sacramento Daily Union*, October 17, 1871

over $100,000 in improvements, including a hoisting-works and a shaft 600 feet deep.[19]

The location and development of the Hermes, in parallel with the operation of the mining company that simultaneously retained Perley's services, while appearing as a gross conflict of interest and a breach of enormous magnitude of the duty of loyalty an agent owes his principle, may at first have been but a ruse, designed to hide the monopolistic overreach of the Raymond & Ely and allow for eventual consolidation of the two concerns after a sufficient period of competition. Apprised of the Hermes' interests, W. H. Raymond considered an offer to join the new company and a gift of 5,000 shares of stock, which he declined on account of his worry that his commitments to the Raymond & Ely precluded investment in a rival.[20] Neither offended nor threatened by Perley's new venture, Raymond appears actually to have remained pleased with the attorney's conduct, retained his services on behalf of the company, and even awarded him an additional $5,000 above his ordinary allowance.[21] Perley certainly hadn't ceased his efforts on behalf of his employer, and it was expected, after his return from one of his many travels out-of-State, that he would take appropriate action against scavengers from rival mining companies attempting to prospect on Raymond & Ely ground.[22]

No better testament to the Raymond & Ely's confidence in Perley came when Charles F. McDermott, one of the earlier claimants to ground occupied by the Raymond & Ely, initiated an action in San Francisco in Judge McKinstry's Court for the Twelfth District to prove the validity of what some characterized as a "black mail title"—that is, a spurious claim pursued for the purpose of obtaining a settlement.[23] Local counsel Hall McAllister adopted a wait and see strategy, perhaps anticipating a large fee should the matter go to trial. Anxious that any attacks on the Company and his own interest in the ore-rich ground be defeated before they ever reached a jury, Perley preferred a knock-out challenge on technical

---

[19] Raymond, op. cit., at p. 518.

[20] *Eureka Sentinel*, April 19, 1873.

[21] Testimony of D. W. Perley, *Pioche Daily Record*, April 15, 1873.

[22] C.W. Lightner to W.H. Raymond, December 8, 1871, reported in *Daily Alta California*, April 10, 1873.

[23] *Daily Alta California*, January 17, 1873.

grounds. After convincing his employers that McAllister wasted an opportunity to demur to McDermott's Complaint, he secured authority to go to San Francisco, with Judge Hardy as his assistant, relieve his old friend McAllister of his duties and file any appropriate motion. The motion he brought was a challenge to the Court's jurisdiction to hear a matter involving claims to land in the State of Nevada. The Raymond & Ely might be a California Corporation, but the land in contention was subject to the sovereign authority of Nevada, and was thus an inappropriate subject to dispositive rulings by a foreign court. Though his motion, technically a demurrer, was overruled, Perley sought a rehearing.[24] A new hearing was granted, though McDermott countered with a request for a temporary order restraining the payment of a recently declared dividend or the transfer of any stock on the Company's books.[25] Inclined to grant the requested order, the Court nevertheless acceded to Perley's argument that any restraint on the rights of the Defendant ought to be dependent on the posting by the Plaintiff of a bond of no less than $40,000.[26] It was all to naught, however, as the Judge almost at once sustained Perley's jurisdictional challenge, effectively dissolving the nascent restraining order and nullifying the effort to obtain longer lasting relief in the form of a perpetual injunction. The Court's almost perfunctory granting of leave to amend the Complaint was but an empty gesture in light of the fact that no amendment could likely cure so fundamental a defect.[27] Not wishing to take chances with further litigation, Perley proposed a settlement. Once a price was agreed to, McDermott waived any further rights to the location in exchange for valuable consideration.[28] The matter was formally dismissed just before Christmas.[29] In the eyes of his employers, Perley's able and efficient management had "saved the case."[30]

---

[24] *Daily Alta California*, November 2, 1872.

[25] *Daily Alta California*, November 12, 1872.

[26] Id.

[27] *Marysville Daily Appeal*, November 14, 1872.

[28] *Sacramento Daily Union*, November 27, 1872; and *Daily Alta California*, November 28, 1872.

[29] *Daily Alta California*, December 18, 1872.

[30] Testimony of W. H. Raymond, *Pioche Daily Record*, April 11, 1873.

Perley's preoccupation with mining activities and his return to prominence as lead counsel in a mining suit involving large capital interests corresponded with a strange revival of the tales of his past improprieties and peccadillos. Forgotten for the moment was his role in the Broderick duel, but etched into memories now recalled for public edification was the image of the man running through the streets naked save for his shirt tails, with a jealous husband hot on his trail, pistol in hand and ready to fire.[31] Commencing a string of bad press was a bizarre reference to his reputation in the context of a fire that swept through Virginia City, forcing up to half the Legislature to take spontaneous and hasty refuge in a train car, where many legislators were observed to be "dressed in the height of nude fashion—even to the extent of having one stocking, a night shirt, a shirt-collar and a straw hat on—the cold weather not even being felt."[32] It was, said one observer, "some very striking and very energetic demonstrations of speed on the part of others besides Perley."[33] Elsewhere, at the trial of Laura Fair for the murder of Perley's long-time friend and occasional collaborator, A.P. Crittenden, there appeared references to Perley's tendency to "speak unfavorably of many women who [were known] to be virtuous" and how "he would talk about most any one."[34] Yet another comment at the time came in the context of a discussion of the absurd apprehension of Jefferson Davis some years before attired as a woman as a means of evading capture by his pursuers. The commentator likened the Confederate President's scandalous behavior to "the eccentric light of Mr. Perley, the eminent lawyer, in a single garment, and that of white linen, through the public streets, at noonday," and of Crittenden, "who was shot by an insane woman, who labored under the hallucination that he had been her paramour for years."[35] Such troubles, said the commentator—rather ironically to be sure—"are incident to greatness."[36] And then there were the explosive revelations in the James Fisk murder case in New York City. In the trial of Ed Stokes for the financier's murder,

[31] *Marysville Daily Appeal*, July 27, 1871.
[32] *Gold Hill Daily News*, February 1, 1871.
[33] Id.
[34] *Sacramento Daily Union*, April 13, 1871.
[35] *Marysville Daily Appeal*, July 27, 1871.
[36] Id.

Josie Mansfield recollected from the witness stand how her step-father pointed a pistol at Perley's head in her mother's home and how a check was extorted from her admirer. Feigning ignorance of any of the reasons why such remarkable events ever occurred, Josie pointedly denied any intimacy with Perley.[37] Frank Lawlor at least confirmed that he hadn't been involved in the affair, nor threatened Perley, nor extorted any money from him.[38] Capping off the negative press was the testimony in the trial of Leota Turner for perjury that it had been Perley who brought her from Nevada to pursue her dubious claim of marital promise, and the suit by a woman named Emily Smith seeking recovery from Perley of an unpaid debt in the amount $567.28.[39] That these matters involved women, allegations of deceit and the exchange of money could only have evoked the usual public titillation any stories featuring Perley tended to generate.

The sparseness of the record of Perley's activities in the year 1872 suggest that it was during this remarkable barrage of negative publicity that he returned east after so many years, to reestablish a personal contact with the family he left behind. The long New Brunswick winter being something to avoid, and the spring tending to be saturated with black flies and midges, the likelihood is that his return occurred in the late summer, or early fall. The disappointing re-trial of his and Volney Howard's claims against Samuel Throckmorton dating back more than a decade ending in July, Perley's departure most certainly must have occurred shortly afterward.[40] The advancement of the railroads made travel rather direct and rapid, while telegraphs permitted communication almost instantaneously should some dire legal noose begin to tighten around the throat of a client. Still living in far off Oromocto was his elderly mother, as well as his brother William and his sisters Adeline and Matilda, each of whom were now the parents of large families. His mother, no doubt, was delighted at last to behold her famous and successful son. He and brother William must surely have compared notes with regard to their various successes—Perley

---

[37] *Sacramento Daily Union*, December 7, 1871.

[38] *Gold Hill Daily News*, February 1, 1872; and *Sacramento Daily Union*, March 7, 1872.

[39] *Daily Alta California*, May 11, 1872; and *Daily Alta California*, June 12, 1872.

[40] *Daily Alta California*, July 9, 1872.

as a leading attorney and figure of some notoriety on the Western American Coast, his brother as a leading lumberman of the central St. John and now a member of the ruling coalition with a seat on the Province's Executive Council. Their old foes Scoullar and Partelow were long gone, as was beloved Uncle George Hayward. The family as a whole had prospered and many of the younger generation were now looking for opportunities that rural New Brunswick simply didn't afford. Among these was brother William's son, named for his uncle, and soon to go by the name Junior, as if he really were Perley's own child and natural heir. Also present with the extended family was his cousin Jane Foshay's daughter, Frederica McKinstry Hazen. A young lady of eighteen years of age, of loyal and unselfish nature, a "consistent Christian" as well as "just, kind and public spirited," she was someone whom Perley no doubt portrayed in positive light to his bachelor law partner following his return to Nevada.[41]

Perley's return west corresponded with legal arguments in the matter of *Leahigh v. White* before the Nevada Supreme Court. His client, E. A. White, had purchased a lot in the town of Pioche from a man named Bliss after Bliss had lent money to William P. Leahigh to purchase the same lot. Bliss in fact had lent money to Leahigh and accepted a deed from him, supposedly as a security interest to guarantee repayment. When Bliss conveyed the property to White after Leahigh failed to repay the loan, White believed he had made a purchase, not taken an assignment of a mortgage. When the matter was presented at trial, the jury rejected Leahigh's claim that White's only interest in the land was as a mortgager, and that Leahigh himself was entitled to redeem the property by tendering the mortgage debt. On appeal, Perley defended the outcome of the trial by noting that if Plaintiff truly believed he had mortgaged his property to Bliss, he would have attempted to redeem it by tendering the full amount in default, not merely a portion of it. Failure to do so implied a lack of belief that a mortgage existed. He thought it a monstrosity of equity that Leahigh essentially contended that the alleged mortgage was "a mortgage which plaintiff could redeem but not a mortgage which defendant or his

---

[41] *The Eureka Leader*, October 30, 1883.

vendor could foreclose."[42] That he was attempting to convert a deed into a mortgage through parole evidence was highly improper and nowhere supported in the law. In reviewing the record, Chief Justice Lewis and the Court disagreed with Perley due to the fact that the Jury concluded that White had notice of the contract between Leahigh and Bliss prior to his own agreement with the latter, and that the intent of Leahigh and Bliss was for the deed, however worded, to memorialize a mortgage not a conveyance.

Losing the case was of no great matter, for too many other concerns simultaneously competed for Perley's attention. He and Rives, for instance, commenced an action to enforce a judgment in the case of *J. E. Colburn v. Robert McCausland*.[43] Rushing off to San Francisco, he there succeeded in requiring the attorney Henry Highton to post a $10,000 bond as a condition of releasing land at issue in a suit between them in the City from Perley's attachment.[44] He also continued acting on opportunities on the mining front: forming with Rives, Lloyd Tevis and others the La Paz Mining Company in Pioche, and hiring labor to begin digging a shaft.[45] By far his grandest scheme was the purchase of the nearly 400-acre Nat Louisy Ranch in the Steptoe Valley, just to the east of Hamilton. This long corridor of lowlands, watered by an ephemeral stream, presented that rarity in the Great Basin: ground fit for pasture and agriculture. The purchase appears to have been made about the time he and John Garber came through White Pine on their way to Pioche.[46] He returned to the Valley just before Christmas to inspect the progress of his men in stocking the ranch "with the best breeds of animals" and raising salmon in a large fresh water pond on the premises.[47] With him was his brother William's son, his namesake and nephew, Duncan W. Perley, Jr.—fresh from New Brunswick and ready to assume the mantle of the ranch's on-site manager.[48]

In Perley's absence from the State and during his preoccupation with other endeavors during much of the year 1872, the interests of

---

42 *Leahigh v. White* (1872) 8 Nev. 147.
43 *Pioche Daily Record*, October 29, 1872.
44 *Daily Alta California*, November 30, 1872.
45 *Pioche Daily Record*, November 24, 1872.
46 *White Pine News*, November 9, 1872.
47 *Pioche Record*, December 22, 1872.
48 Id.

his employer, the Raymond & Ely and his own company, the Hermes, once apparently capable of advancing on parallel and amicable tracks, began to move into conflict. Realizing his relationship with his employer was no longer tenable, he resigned his post at the onset of December.[49] Contributing to the unsettled atmosphere between the mining outfits was the reaching and over-reaching of new rivals eager to seize any piece of the ground already occupied and prepared to litigate in order to retain it. Had the quality and quantity of the existing ore on the Raymond & Ely's traditional ground remained high, discord might well have been avoided, but dismay germinated in the minds of the Company's trustees that their best days were behind them.[50] Everyone anticipated friction in the courts, hence the various interests began exploring who might be friend and who foe, at least for the short-term. With his eye on the primary enemy, Perley, accompanied by co-counsel Hardy, met with Delos Lake to discuss the possibility of an accord between the Hermes and Lake's client, the Pioche Phenix Company.[51] Even the Raymond & Ely was approached with the prospect of a consolidation of the two mines, but the talks, at this time, produced nothing of substance.[52]

Predictably, the storm of litigation came. In its formal Complaint, the Raymond & Ely accused Perley and his cohorts of having entered into ground not their own, held in fee by the Raymond & Ely, ousted the true owner and afterward unlawfully retained and wrongfully barred access. Worse yet were the misdeeds of Lightner and Perley, the company's superintendent and counsel respectively, who competed with their employer in violation of their sacred obligations. Perley "was appointed to and accepted the...position of attorney for said Plaintiff, upon the agreement and understanding...that the said Perley should attend and supervise all the legal business of Plaintiff, and should act in concert with said Lightner therein, and that the said Lightner should to the extent of his ability assist said Perley in protecting, maintaining, perfecting and strengthening title of Plaintiff, and the claim of said Plaintiff to said mine; that said Lightner and Perley

[49] *Daily Alta California*, April 7, 1873.
[50] *Daily Alta California*, January 17, 1873.
[51] *Daily Alta California*, January 3, 1873.
[52] "Financial and Commercial," *Daily Alta California*, January 17, 1873.

obtained and accepted their said respective appointments and large salaries...upon the understanding that they would act and conduct aforesaid, and in consideration thereof agreed to carry out said understanding, and to fulfill the duties of said trust in good faith."[53] Their creation of the Hermes was but a scheme to blackmail their employer into paying them $600,000 for the stock of their spurious company, and when the employer failed to respond, they initiated their invasion of the employer's ground and commenced extracting ore to which only the employer was entitled.

The portrait of Perley drawn within the four quarters of the pleading was perhaps the most comprehensive and least flattering yet rendered in more than thirty years of controversy. The many altercations of his life could be attributed to the Hobbesian reality of frontier life; his role in the duel with Broderick but an unfortunate chapter in the existence of a nation hurtling inevitably toward Civil War; his flight through the streets nearly naked a comic incident involving no crime, but enormous personal embarrassment. The betrayal of a client's trust—*that* was a matter of the greatest sensitivity, and if Perley had ever been sensitive to slights against his honor, this one ought to have generated the greatest and most terrible reaction. There was none, however. He remained calm. Instead of challenging his accusers to battle, he would restrain his normal impulses, aided perhaps by his daily reading and contemplation of the Word of God, and vindicate his name in a court of law. Assisting him in the effort would be a legal team composed of some of the finest lawyers in the west.

Aside from himself, his legal team consisted of Jesse Pitzer, Judge Mesick and W. W. Bishop. Of these, Pitzer and Mesick had already figured prominently in Perley's life. Ever accompanied by his Newfoundland dog, sometimes into the courtroom itself, the eccentric Pitzer had emerged of late as one of the finest trial attorneys in Nevada. At the height of his powers, with no sign yet appearing of the violent mania that would overcome him during his final years, Pitzer posed a formidable obstacle to any opponent. Formerly a judicial officer in Storey County, Judge Mesick ended his tenure there back in 1867 in order to pursue wealth in private practice—to grab for himself a share of the riches he watched from

---

[53] *Daily Alta California*, April 7, 1873.

above move from private hands to the pockets of the lawyers on both sides of any given legal controversy. Due to "some human weaknesses," the state of his finances hardly reflected either his skills as an advocate or his record of courtroom triumphs.[54] The last of Perley's co-counsel, William W. Bishop, surely had been known to Perley for some time, and certainly since his drift into the Republican fold. The man was a native of Pennsylvania, who grew up in Southern Illinois, where he entered the legal profession and became quite familiar and friendly with Governor Richard Yates, Stephen Douglas and even Lincoln himself.[55] When the War came, he displayed a prodigious talent for organization by raising three regiments of soldiers, but failed to qualify himself for service in any one of them due to lack of vision in one of his eyes.[56] He came to Washoe while the War still raged and moved east where he became "something of a power" in Republican circles.[57] Following his death in 1890, he was remembered as "a man of great force of character."[58] Others remembered him somewhat differently. He was capable enough, recalled the journalist Rollin Daggett, but "not particularly scrupulous," and though energetic on the stump in every election of the era, he harbored a tremendous thirst for hard liquor, and "was an inveterate gambler...ready at all times to sacrifice everything to his appetite for gaming."[59]

Opposed to them were Thornton, Garber, Delos Lake, Thomas Wren and Perley's erstwhile collaborator Judge Hardy. Each of these men knew Perley well, his strengths and weaknesses, and all were masters of law and formidable in the courtroom. Hardy, of course, was a close friend, whose fate, like Perley's, had been entwined with the fortunes of David Terry years before. Thornton was a bona fide member of the Chivalry, a veteran of the Confederate service and kinsman of Perley's close friends A.P.

---

[54] Charles Carroll Goodwin, *As I Remember Them* (Salt Lake City: Salt Lake City Commercial Club, 1913), at p. 262.

[55] "Hon. W. W. Bishop: Death of a Leading Member of the Legal Profession," *Sacramento Daily Record-Union*, August 27, 1890.

[56] Id.; and *The Morning Call*, August 27, 1890.

[57] R. M. Daggett, "The Bar of the Comstock in the Early Sixties," *The Morning Call*, January 28, 1894.

[58] *Sacramento Daily Record-Union*, August 17, 1890.

[59] R. M. Daggett, "The Bar of the Comstock in the Early Sixties," *The Morning Call*, January 28, 1894.

Crittenden, James D. Thornton and Samuel H. Brooks. Since the onset of the White Pine bonanza, they had clashed often in the courtroom, though were cordial outside of it. Delos Lake offered a far more conventional profile. The New York native had practiced in San Francisco before coming to Nevada, served as District Attorney and a Judge in the City. His one great scandal occurred in the aftermath of the collapse of Adams & Company in 1854, when he appointed a receiver for the Company's assets who subsequently failed to account for a single doubloon. Of the team, Wren was the only one who had extensive experience as a miner, or who understood mining engineering. The man was an Ohio native, of Virginia stock, who came to California in 1850 and toiled in the mines of the Sierras for over a decade before relocating to the Reese River, and later to White Pine and Eureka. He was active in Republican Party politics and partnered with C. E. Delong for a number of years following the dissolution of DeLong's professional association with Perley. In 1873, he was already on his way to earning a reputation as "one of the best mining lawyers on the Pacific coast," whose experience as miner and mine operator informed him with a degree of "technical knowledge of mining which was invaluable in his legal profession."[60] At the time of his death in 1904, after service in the Legislature, in Congress and on the bench, he would be celebrated as "one of the strong men of the State," ranking with "Beatty, Stewart, DeLong, Crittenden, Fitch, Hawley, [and] Nye" as "one of the builders who carved this commonwealth from the bleak desert."[61] The last of the team, John Garber, it will be recalled, briefly practiced with Perley on the Comstock, but found the professional relationship not to his liking. By the late 1860s, esteem for him within the profession grew significantly through his partnership with Thornton, first in Austin and then White Pine, and served him well in pursuit of a seat on the Supreme Court to replace the recently deceased John Neely Johnson. He served only a short time before being lured off the bench by the promise of a five-figure annual salary by the Raymond & Ely Company.[62] His resignation was bemoaned by many as

[60] "Judge Wren Dead," *Elko Weekly Independent*, February 12, 1904.
[61] Id.
[62] *The Daily State Register*, November 15, 1872.

depriving the State "of the services of one of the ablest jurists that have ever practiced within its limits."[63] Others discerned within it a part of a larger conspiracy, wherein "the Raymond & Ely Company, who have an important case at law, have been enabled to so far exert an influence in their own behalf as to induce Garber to resign in order that he might accept a fee from the said company and also to enable Governor Bradley to name a successor to Garber who should be committed in favor of the side of the case which the ex-Judge represents."[64]

This compelling cast of legal talent would challenge any judge regardless of the strength of character or legal acumen he possessed. Every ruling, every utterance on any point in the proceedings, was sure to provoke powerful response, laced with irony, and subtle innuendo that perhaps his Honor was lacking in intelligence and understanding. The venue of the case determined who that Judge would be. Since 1871, Mortimer Fuller presided over the District. He could boast no great academic pedigree, nor a distinguished practice at the bar. He had come west from Kalamazoo, Michigan during the Gold Rush and become a lawyer, but hadn't ever tried a case at law. The extent of his legal knowledge appears to have been obtained as a lawmaker during the span of two terms in the California Assembly. For a time, he operated a livery stable with his brother, and then moved to the Comstock to try his hand at mining. When nearly all others shunned the desolate eastern deserts, Fuller could be found there prospecting in what would become the Panaca. When first organized, the Raymond & Ely retained his services, not as an attorney or even a miner, but as a carpenter to assist in the construction of their mining works. Involvement in Republican politics led to service on the State Party's Central Committee with C. E DeLong, and support within the Party for his unlikely candidacy for a judicial position. He was by all accounts a strong, steady and honest man, and likely was less impressed by legal arrogance and erudition than he was by integrity and common sense. "When corruption was quite as bold in the land as it is now; when hundreds of thousands of dollars were the sums paid for men's consciences; when it was fashionable and even popular to be

---

63 *Pioche Daily Record*, November 9, 1872.
64 *The New Daily Appeal*, December 11, 1872.

allied with thieves; when judicial purity meant a mere pittance and a sneer, he did his work, and he did it honestly and well."[65]

Perley's first formal response to the accusations against him came in his Answer to the Complaint, denying "that on the first day of January, 1873, or at any other time, the said Plaintiff was seized in fee, or in possession of any part or portion of the ledge struck in the Lightner Shaft, which lies west on a point of said ledge...."[66] He denied that the ledge at issue was ever known or called the Raymond & Ely Ledge, that the Plaintiff owned the contested ground and is the owner or otherwise entitled to possession, that the Hermes entered the premises unlawfully and ousted or ejected the Plaintiff, that either he or Lightner were agents entrusted with the entire business of their employer, that he had any duty to do anything other than file lawsuits on the Plaintiff's behalf, that he and Lightner intended to extort money from their employer by "selling" it a rival claim, that he used his employer's money to purchase the lot from Grieves, that his relations with Grieves were part of a scheme between the men to secure titles adverse to the interests of the Raymond & Ely, that he used knowledge obtained in the service of the Raymond & Ely to acquire titles to land he should have secured for his employer, and that any of the various purchases made by himself, Hearst and Rives were done on the Raymond & Ely's behalf. He denied that there was any obligation upon his or Lightner's part "to prevent the Hermes Company from working upon its own ground, or sinking a shaft thereon, or to take any steps whatever against said Hermes Company," or "that the Hermes' shaft was sunk through any connivance or encouragement of Perley and Lightner, but on the contrary...was openly and notoriously prosecuted, with a full knowledge of a claim by the Hermes Company to one thousand feet of the ledge struck in the Lightner Shaft, from almost the time of location, up to the time of the commencement of this action, and that the Raymond & Ely Mining Company and the individual officers and trustees of said Plaintiff had full, complete, and perfect knowledge of the location thereof and the claim of title thereto upon the part of...Hermes."

[65] *Pioche Weekly Record*, December 3, 1881.

[66] "Answer of the Hermes to the Raymond and Ely Complaint; Denial of Each Separate Specification," *Daily Alta California*, April 12, 1873.

The Plaintiff, he contended, "looked on and saw [the] work openly and publicly prosecuted, and made no claim of title thereto until the commencement of this action, and after the Hermes Company had spent a large amount of money in working, opening and developing said mine, and had sunk a shaft thereon to the depth of six hundred feet and struck the ledge in controversy."[67] The truth, said Perley, was that the Hermes was the owner and lawful possessor of the ground, that its title was rooted in older titles and had been held for two years prior to the commencement of the suit. If the Raymond & Ely had any rightful title, it was compromised by the perfection of the adverse occupation by the Hermes, that the Plaintiff forfeited any rights it had for failure to comply with local mining ordinances, and that either the Plaintiff or its predecessors had actually abandoned the ground. And as for being a co-conspirator with Grieves to obtain titles adverse to his employer, Perley was actually suing Grieves for breaching an agreement to convey Lot No. 3 to him on his own account—a suit that was being defended on Grieves' behalf by the same counsel who were pursuing the action against the Hermes.

When the District Court opened, Perley moved aggressively to obtain an injunction against the operation within the bounds of the Hermes claim by the Ingomar Mining Company.[68] Perley fought a similar request for an injunction by the Kentucky Gold & Silver Mining Company through its counsel Pitzer and Mesick. Though he failed to defeat a motion brought by counsel who were preparing to defend him in the Raymond & Ely suit, he succeeded in imposing upon their client an obligation to post a large bond.[69] The Kentucky prevailed on the merits, but at the cost of providing security to the Hermes in the amount of $15,000.[70] Within days, rumors spread that ore was being surreptitiously removed from the Hermes mine in order to evade detection by the Raymond & Ely. Instead of staying to fight over the issue, Perley blew out of town yet again, en route to San Francisco, no doubt to meet with Tevis, Haggin and Hearst, and

---

[67] Id.

[68] *Pioche Daily Record*, January 9, 1873.

[69] *Pioche Daily Record*, January 10, 1873.

[70] *Pioche Daily Record*, January 15, 1873; *Pioche Record*, January 16, 1873; and *Pioche Record*, January 17, 1873.

to consider with them the grim task of trial against their primary rival.[71]

Preparation for litigation of a scope not yet seen in Nevada undoubtedly took its toll on Perley's constitution. His fondness for food and drink and his aging metabolism contributed to obesity, while the stress of his existence, with endeavors all around him, each needing attention simultaneously, contributed to a break down in mid-February on his return to Pioche. In ailing health and already irritable, his ire was roused to a white-hot intensity upon discovery of a theft from his extensive library of Irving's Collected Works and Darwin's *Descent of Man*. "The purloined scoundrels who slip into my room and abstract books out of my private library during my absence are notified that all such books had better be returned forthwith," or he would hunt them down through the processes of law.[72] But even as he lay confined in his bed, sick, angry and perhaps depressed, he roared his intention "to inaugurate active hostilities against each and all the adverse claimants who have now or may hereafter enter the field," and that he would, if necessary, "carry the war into Africa."[73] He was "an able and accomplished advocate," said one observer, "and when he throws his heart, soul and brain into a cause, as he has done in the case of the Hermes, his adversaries must not expect an easy triumph."[74]

Judge Fuller announced the trial schedule for his Court in the middle of March. The *Raymond & Ely v. Hermes* matter would have priority, with a trial date of March 24, followed by the case of *Kentucky v. Pioche Phenix*.[75] Already, the flower of the legal talent of the Pacific Coast and the great capitalists of the West were in motion, converging on Pioche and prepared to ensure that "the fight would be a contest of giants, intellectual and financial."[76] Hardy and Garber arrived in the second week of March; Haggin, Delos Lake, and Mesick shortly thereafter.[77] An injunction was

---

[71] *Pioche Review*, January 22, 1873; and *White Pine News*, February 8, 1873

[72] *Pioche Daily Record*, March 4, 1873.

[73] *Pioche Daily Record*, February 13, 1873.

[74] Id.

[75] *Sacramento Daily Union*, March 18, 1873.

[76] Raymond, op. cit., p. 515.

[77] *White Pine News*, March 8, 1873; and *Pioche Daily Record*, March 11, 1873.

obtained even before the responsive pleading was filed to halt any further clandestine extraction of ore. A threshold fight over the adequacy of the Complaint resulted in a grant of leave to amend, with an expedited time for the filing of a further Answer.[78] Perley's demand for all documentary evidence the Plaintiff intended to produce at trial was placed on hold until after the pleadings were settled.[79] Desiring to control costs and keep issues as simple for the jury as possible, he asked for and obtained an order limiting the number of mining experts to six per party.[80] Meanwhile, the people of Pioche grew more excited with each passing day. The town was "rocked to its center, and men, openly or covertly, linked themselves with the fortunes of the one or the other party."[81] Armed watchmen on both sides of the controversy, employed by the opposing mining interests, fixed eyes on the courthouse for any sign of impropriety and increased their vigilance once the jury was selected and ordered to take up quarters in the jury room for the duration of the trial.[82] Seeing their interests served best by competition among mining operations, one group of miners openly remonstrated against the Raymond & Ely: a "powerful and grasping corporation...trying to gobble up this entire district," whose ambitions might only be thwarted by the aroused attention of the people.[83] Referred to merely as "the Great Mining suit," the case was predicted to be "one of the most stupendous lawsuits ever commenced on the Pacific Coast."[84] Mobs appeared at the courthouse to cram its limited space each day as the preliminaries were dealt with, and many hundreds more waited anxiously outside.[85]

Jury selection consumed the first day of trial, but resulted in the impaneling of seven jurors.[86] The following day, in a courtroom "crowded to suffocation" and cracking to the point nearly of collapse due to so much congestion, the parties and the Court

---

[78] *Pioche Daily Record*, March 11, 1873.

[79] *Pioche Daily Record*, March 18, 1873.

[80] *Pioche Daily Record*, March 20, 1873; and *Pioche Daily Record*, March 22, 1873.

[81] Raymond, op. cit., at p. 515.

[82] Id.

[83] *White Pine News*, March 11, 1873.

[84] *White Pine News*, March 15, 1873.

[85] *Pioche Daily Record*, March 25, 1873.

[86] "Raymond & Ely Suit," *Sacramento Daily Union*, March 24, 1873.

suffered a diversion as counsel for both sides indulged in addressing the objections to the desire by the Plaintiff to introduce a mere copy of the notice of location of the Panaca claim and other records of the defunct Meadow Valley Mining District as a means of proving the validity of its title, traceable to its purchase of the dubious Panaca. Judge Fuller sustained the objections due to the lack of sufficient foundation, but indicated that he might revise his ruling should the testimony of various percipient witnesses provide a plausible explanation for the absence of the originals.[87] When the custodian of the missing records was called and asked for an explanation, he claimed not to have them and was promptly placed in custody and informed that the key to his liberty lay in disclosure of the whereabouts of the documents.[88] Another witness was called and asked of his knowledge of the records. When he professed ignorance, Henry I. Thornton declared due diligence had been shown, hence the copies ought to be admitted in place of the originals. Before Perley could explain why the copies still lacked any foundation for admissibility, every other attorney in the court room chimed in with an opinion on the matter. When the Judge ruled in favor of admissibility, Thornton attested under oath as to the veracity of the copies based on personal familiarity with the same derived from his past employment by the Meadow Valley Mining Company.

The next series of witnesses were brought forward to establish that the original Panaca locators diligently pursued their claims and had only broken off from the work on account of the outbreak of hostilities with the native peoples.[89] There being a degree of impossibility to mining as arrows and gunfire filled the air, the Plaintiff obviously hoped to defeat the Defendant's contention that the claims which it inherited had been abandoned, hence never perfected. The witnesses testified, too, to the precise location of their claims, and were supported in their conclusions by the Plaintiff's expert, the geologist and mining engineer Nelson Wescoatt, all for the purpose of showing that those older claims truly were the

---

[87] *Sacramento Daily Union*, March 27, 1873.

[88] "The Great Mining Suit: Full Proceedings Yesterday," *Pioche Daily Record*, March 28, 1873.

[89] Id.; and "The Great Mining Suit: Full Proceedings Saturday," *Pioche Daily Record*, March 30, 1873

forebears of the Raymond & Ely's present estate.[90] One man was so bold as to assert that the copies of documents more than ten years old conformed to the originals and that the originals also included an agreement among the first claimants to organize a mining district, called the Meadow Valley, subject to a uniform set of regulations.[91] When Thornton attempted to introduce a copy of the alleged mining laws operative in the Meadow Valley District as a prelude to demonstrating that all relevant claims were made in conformity with the same, Mesick objected on a wide front, contending that the loss of the original hadn't been proven hence no foundation existed for secondary evidence, that the mere title of that document as a set of rules hardly established that rules had been enacted by bona fide miners residing within the district, that the book from which the document was draw was a mere copy, was inaccurate and unreliable and had been transcribed by someone who was himself not a citizen of the mining district, and that the claims at issue predated the alleged adoption of the rules, hence the rules were immaterial, and even if this wasn't true, the rules were purely ad hoc, rather than authorized by any statute or ordinance of the governing legal authority, the Congress of the United States, or the Territory or State of Nevada. In response, Thornton conceded there was some minor discrepancy between the testimony and the records themselves, but this was unimportant. What mattered was that the records were not contested by the witnesses, who appear to have acted honorably toward one another, and that they generally supported the existence of an actual appropriation that was the foundation for the Plaintiff's title. That no law supported the miner's organization of a mining district hardly defeated the district's legitimacy, for the entire Comstock had previously organized itself in similar fashion, and had ever afterward been acknowledged by the courts of the land as a legitimate source of rights.

---

[90] Perley knew Wescoatt well. In 1865 they and several others located the so-called Horseshoe Ledge in Plumas County, California. The partnership didn't last long. Perley quit claimed his interest to Wescoatt for $100. See Plumas County Deeds, Volume 3, Page 2.

[91] "The Great Mining Suit: Monday's Full Proceedings," *Pioche Daily Record*, April 1, 1873.

As the argument over the admissibility of the district regulations persisted into the following day, Thomas Wren asserted that "the copy we offer is a well-authenticated copy of the originals. Most complete and unbroken has been the evidence that the first rough draught of the Meadow Valley laws was correctly transcribed into the record book of the district."[92] He implied, too, that perhaps the need for secondary evidence in place of the original document was the result of the chicanery of the other party, whose interest lay in an absence of evidence of all that went before. Judge Lake eloquently explained how the law recognized the authority of miners when organizing their ad hoc communities, and treated their ordinances as operative positive law. Next in turn, Garber pointed out the effect of good faith reliance by third parties upon the ratification of otherwise invalid ad hoc laws. Judge Mesick responded to what he perceived would be the rejection of his objections as mere technicalities by reminding the Court that "technicality is the very essence of the law. Technicality means accuracy. In all branches of science the most technical man is the most reliable."[93] Here, the supposed technicality that the locations of the original claimants were made without the support of any operative law meant that the locations were invalid. When Mesick was done, Judge Fuller did indeed overrule his objections and allowed the evidence to come in. Silent throughout the exchange, Perley now rose and demanded, in accordance with the Practice Code, that the unlearned judge justify and explain his ruling in accordance with the law. The Judge hesitated, then refused to comply, for a reason supplied on the spur by Garber, that the section of the Practice Code relied on by Perley indicated that the decision required a judge's signature, and nothing more.[94]

When the proceedings commenced the next day, it was agreed among the parties that counsel would accompany their experts on an inspection of the contested ground.[95] When the inspection was complete, Plaintiff's expert, Nelson Wescoatt, testified that he had no doubt that the ledge being mined by the Hermes was the same

---

[92] "The Great Mining Suit: Tuesday's Full Proceedings," *Pioche Daily Record*, April 2, 1873.

[93] Id.

[94] Id.

[95] "The Hermes Case Yesterday," *Pioche Daily Record*, April 3, 1873.

being mined by the Raymond & Ely. When on cross he was asked how he could be so confident that the two disconnected excavations were sunk in the same ledge, he vaguely referred to his experience on the Comstock and his "observation of the facts."[96] A second expert, John James, reiterated Wescoatt's conclusions, saying "I have no doubt that the Lightner Shaft and the Panaca Shaft are on the same ledge; have not the least doubt in the world," though he admitted he was neither a geologist nor an engineer.[97] Additional experts were called, all for the Plaintiff, piling on cumulative testimony and increasing the silent irritation of Perley's team, until it could be suppressed no longer and squabbling erupted, first over the extraction of ore for examination and then over the way in which the questioning was presented.[98]

On April 7, a concerted effort was made by Plaintiff's counsel to establish the full admissibility of copies of documents the contents of which the Court had allowed to be read, and thereby prove that they accurately reflected real titles that had ultimately passed to the Raymond & Ely.[99] A prior failure to produce the records having landed him in jail, the custodian now returned to report that his effort, in the Sherriff's charge, to scour the town for the originals netted nothing in the way of positive results. The records indeed were lost, but he now recalled that at some point in the past he'd delivered them to Perley and Rives—a revelation which Perley staunchly denied. Called to the stand, both W. H. Raymond and J.N. Vandemark claimed under oath to have seen a copy of the original consolidation agreement, and when Garber attempted to admit the copy in his possession into evidence, defense counsel objected on the grounds that the alleged contract lacked the signatures of the original parties, was irrelevant and the actual loss of the original had not yet been established.[100] Garber again contended the testimony of the witnesses represented adequate foundation for the unavailability of the original document and the innocence of the Plaintiff in causing its absence. Judger Fuller declined to allow

---

[96] "The Great Mining Suit: Thursday's Full Proceedings," *Pioche Daily Record*, April 4, 1873.

[97] Id.

[98] "The Great Mining Suit," *Pioche Daily Record*, April 5, 1873.

[99] *Daily Alta California*, April 8, 1873; and *Pioche Daily Record*, April 8, 1873.

[100] *Pioche Daily Record*, April 8, 1873.

introduction of the document, but again agreed to let its contents be read into the record.

To overcome the remaining obstacle to admission of the documents necessary to establish Raymond & Ely's title, Plaintiff's counsel raised the issue of Perley's alleged fraud and conflict of interest in obtaining possession of what became the Hermes, sparking a day-long argument. Mesick curtly stated that witnesses who testified that Perley had used their names in locating the Hermes claim were certainly entitled to seek recovery for any harm done them, but the Raymond & Ely could not absorb these harms as their own and then seek a remedy. Judge Hardy expounded for two hours alone, contending that Perley's misconduct disqualified any objection, and the evidence of fraud or dishonesty in connection with obtaining the mine was relevant to the larger harm suffered by the Plaintiff. Perley and Lightner had committed a fraud, and were in no position to discredit the best evidence of the validity of a title their conduct had demeaned. From there, his rhetoric descended to a plea to the jury, stating principles of law governing the conduct of agents, but really accusing Perley and his cohorts of the grossest misdeeds. "How could Messrs. Perley & Rives, standing as the representatives of the Raymond & Ely property, as the judges of the sufficiency of its titles, become themselves invested with interests therein averse to their employers' interests?"[101] So worked up did Hardy become that his health, still tottering after a recent stint of forced bed rest, compelled him "to retire on account of exhaustion."[102]

In countering Hardy's argument, Judge Mesick noted the fundamental incongruity of the Plaintiff's desire to expose the fraudulence of the Defendant's title with the causes of action pled in their Complaint.[103] Plaintiff, he said, alleged ejectment by the defense, which entails the allegation that title belonged to the Plaintiff. The proper procedure to follow was to prove one's own title. Once one failed to do so on account of the competing title of the Defendant, only then could one bring an action in equity to reject the legality of the Defendant's ownership through application

[101] "The Great Mining Suit: Monday's Full Proceedings," *Pioche Daily Record*, April 8, 1873.

[102] Id.

[103] *Pioche Daily Record*, April 9, 1873.

of principles of fairness. The second cause of action muddled the matter more, and hardly permitted introduction of the type of evidence Plaintiff sought to expose to the jury. That second cause of action attempted to charge Lightner and Perley "with some sort of improper misconduct," leading to the deprivation of title properly belonging to Plaintiff and a remedy in the form of equitable relief.[104] This mongrel mixing of law and equity simply could not be permitted. Having faced a choice between one or the other, Plaintiff chose both, and now, in pursuit of both theories, wrongly would bring evidence to the bar admissible only with respect to one of them. "The Complaint," he argued, "must be one thing or the other; and if it is in the nature of ejectment, then…the evidence assailing the validity of our title [is] inadmissible."[105] Garber countered by chiding the defense for failing to allege misjoinder of the two causes of action via a properly timed demurrer. Having failed to do so, the Defendant was stuck with the Complaint as pled, and the Plaintiff is free to present evidence to prove its contentions.[106] But even had the Hermes been more timely in its challenge it would have failed; for as in New York and California, Nevada has embraced the merger of law and equity, and legal and equitable claims can be pursued simultaneously. With this, Judge Fuller agreed. The evidence of Perley's alleged fraud could come in.

With this, the flood gates of testimony and evidence regarding Perley's activity in accumulating titles to land on which he located the Hermes were widely opened. Numerous deeds were introduced, as was the testimony of John Cahill, the owner of the Monitor claim, who related the details surrounding the sale of that interest to George Hearst. When he informed Lightner of Hearst's interest, Lightner urged him to sell to Hearst, whom he suggested was acting as agent of the Raymond & Ely. Cahill did so, all on the assumption that the sale was in furtherance of the interests of the Plaintiff, and eased, no doubt, by Lightner's promise to direct his way work assaying the value of the extracted ore.[107] In cross-examination of the witness, Perley managed to instill a bit of doubt about the man's recollection of events, and prompted the

[104] Id.
[105] Id.
[106] Id.
[107] *Daily Alta California*, April 10, 1873; and *Pioche Daily Record*, April 10, 1873.

exclamation: "I don't know exactly how it is, but they (meaning Hearst and Lightner) were both mixed up in this transaction."[108] Cahill was followed by Louis Tardos, clerk for the Raymond & Ely, and B. F. Sides, agent for Wells Fargo & Company, who confirmed the issuance of money to pay Hearst for the Monitor claim. Then came the aggrieved Thomas Grieves, who spoke of his sale of Pioche West Lot No. 4 to Perley, and his journey to Filmore to obtain Lot No. 3. By the time he returned to Pioche, the thought had formed in his mind that Perley had tricked him into selling his land, so he deeded No. 3 to a competitor, Mr. Foreman, of the Meadow Valley Company.[109] On Cross-examination, he said that he had gone so far as to sign a deed to convey No. 3 to Perley, but when he denied a deed presented to him was the same one, Perley indignantly responded, "how dare you deny it?" The meaningless exchange presaged a more useful admission by the witness that he went to Fillmore on his own account, not Perley's. That was, after all, his position in his own case against Perley, hence it couldn't be contradicted, even to aid Perley's enemies, without placing the testifier in jeopardy of a perjury charge.[110]

Other witnesses presented evidence that the purchase of land in the Monitor by Perley and Hearst was ultimately paid for by the Raymond & Ely, meaning either that Perley and Hearst were acting as the Raymond & Ely's agents, or committing some kind of fraud. A series of letters was introduced, supposedly proving Lightner's machinations, but actually demonstrating that he, Perley and Hearst were not acting in the shadows, but were quite open with the Raymond & Ely about what they were doing, without a hint of impropriety nor an objection from their adversary.[111] After Mr. Raymond was called again, and provided further testimony about his recollection of his contacts with Hearst and others, Perley crossed-examined him at length about the statements Perley had placed into the Answer in the McDermott case, contrary to what the witness was alleging now. Raymond admitted that the Answer had been shared with him, yet denied he had ever instructed Perley to include the allegations. When Perley pointed out that perhaps his

---

108 "Yesterday's Testimony," *Daily Alta California*, April 10, 1873.
109 *Pioche Daily Record*, April 10, 1873.
110 "Yesterday's Testimony," *Daily Alta California*, April 10, 1873.
111 Id.

efforts to resolve the case ultimately saved the Raymond & Ely from having to deny the validity of the titles they were now relying on, he said the matter remained uncertain, though he acknowledged the general view at the time that Perley's labor on behalf of the Raymond & Ely was exceptional. A fit of some kind, perhaps of coughing, prevented Perley from following up, and when the session resumed in the afternoon, Perley remained silent as Mesick assumed responsibility for completing Raymond's cross-examination.[112]

Perley's intention appears to have been to introduce the Answer he'd prepared in the McDermott matter, but never filed due to the settlement of the case. The Answer, as noted, denied the validity of the title held by McDermott, derived from earlier claims subject to the Panaca consolidation agreement. That very agreement was now the basis for Raymond & Ely's claim to the Hermes ground. Perley's objective was to impeach the Plaintiff's theory of the case. Mesick now took up the cause and read portions of the unfiled pleading. Raymond professed lack of memory, as well as ignorance of the "proper mode of defeating the McDermott title." The primary strategy he recalled was to deny the jurisdiction of the California Court over a matter involving claims to land in Nevada. Gradually, however, his recollection improved, and he quite distinctly remembered that he "protested against committing the Panaca title in that way."

Perley returned to the courtroom as Raymond concluded his testimony. He listened to another of the Plaintiff's witnesses—a Mr. Wilkin—speak of how Perley had discouraged him from purchasing land that Hermes later obtained, insisting that the land was both worthless and subject to the superior claims of the Panaca title holders. He recalled Perley mentioning his purchase of what became the Hermes ground "in the interest of the Raymond & Ely Co., of which company he was the attorney." On cross, Perley asked him point blank if he'd been paid for his testimony by the Raymond & Ely, if he recalled inspecting the actual Hermes ground instead of the ground he testified about, and if he'd attempted to intrude on the Hermes' ground via his own company's tunneling. The witness denied everything, insisted that his interrogator had admitted the

[112] *Pioche Daily Record*, April 11, 1873.

Hermes' ground belonged to the Raymond & Ely, and had it not been for a recent fire in town, he would have been able to produce documents to prove the details of their conversation.[113]

With the conclusion of the Plaintiff's case, Mesick came forward in Perley's stead to explain what the defense expected the evidence would show. Perley had intended to make the opening statement, but the sudden onset of "some infirmity of his throat" deprived him of that pleasure, thus he had little choice but to defer to co-counsel.[114] After praising the skills of opposing counsel, whom he called his friends, Mesick rather deceptively denigrated his own pending efforts, noting "there is very little romance in my composition," and expressing his trust in the jurors to infer from the evidence to be presented the outcome he believed was indisputable. He then proceeded methodically to summarize the allegations in the Complaint and point out the facts that would be presented in contradiction to them. The so-called Panaca was never an actual location, had never been worked, conformed with no mining regulations, and had been abandoned by the time Raymond & Ely came onto the scene. "From July or the forepart of August, 1864, until in the year 1870, there was not a stroke of work done in that claim for nearly six years, and the laws of the land denounce that omission, and the law of the district denounce that omission a forfeiture of every right whatsoever, even if a right had been previously acquired to this claim." Moreover, many of the claims on which the Plaintiff based its title were not actually acquired until *after* Perley and the Defendant issued their notice and erected their monument. The Lightner Shaft itself, the heart of the Hermes operation, lay outside any of the land claimed by the Plaintiff. The Panaca title, he declared, would be revealed to be "a myth, a fraud a pretense and an outrage." Lacking any basis for ownership of the land in question, the Plaintiff rightfully sought a more viable theory, but failed when alleging that Perley and Lightner, as agents of the Raymond & Ely, were obligated to advance only its interests, and that the results of any efforts expended were rightfully the property of the principal. "We expect to show," he explained, "not only that

---

[113] "The Great Mining Suit: Wednesday's Proceedings," *Pioche Daily Record*, April 11, 1873.

[114] "The Raymond & Ely vs. Hermes: The Opening Remarks of Judge Mesick for the Defense," *Daily Alta California*, April 14, 1873.

the Defendant in this case is in possession here, but never was to be charged, as Trustee of the Raymond and Ely Mining Company, as to this ground; but that, instead of the Raymond and Ely Mining Company being defrauded by acts of its agents referred to, it would be a monstrous fraud on the Defendant and the Hermes stockholders if the Raymond and Ely Mining Company were to be allowed to set up any such pretense in a Court of Justice." Nothing the Defendant and its agents did was surreptitious. From the beginning, "the Raymond and Ely...by reputation, by its Trustees and by all of its agents and officers, knew that that location had been made; knew that the Hermes Corporation had been formed and stock had been issued, and was being scattered throughout the market and purchased by a large number in this community." All the while the Hermes was "sinking a shaft on this ground... building hoisting works and...expending large sums of money and...developing this mine..., the Raymond & Ely... never lifted up its voice to warn a single man in the community that it had a claim to this mine." Consequently, the Plaintiff is "in no such position on account of these acts, which they winked at, or...kept silent about," to come so late in the day and inform the Defendant: "You held this property in trust for us."

By presentation's end, there was time sufficient to call a single witness, Perley himself, and have him sworn and nothing more.[115] The following day, the defense's star witness retook the stand and related his account of the relevant events.[116] Names other than his own and Lightner's were used on the first locations that became the Hermes, yes, but only at Lightner's request. Without explaining Lightner's rationale, he noted the location as a whole wasn't of particular value at the time due to the great depth necessary to delve before hitting the ledge. No conspiracy with Hearst existed—he had already made his location before Hearst came to town. It was only after Hearst's arrival that they agreed to combine their properties under the awning of the new company. The men he subsequently employed commenced work within ten days, digging the shaft that became the Hermes, without interruption until it was six hundred feet deep and the ledge was reached. Throughout the

[115] *Pioche Daily Record,* April 13, 1873.
[116] *Pioche Daily Record,* April 15, 1873.

time when the mine expanded, Raymond and his colleagues couldn't be bothered. "We were sinking on the Hermes location; it was so understood by Col. Raymond himself, he knew it in 1871." Raymond, in fact, came by Perley's office in September of that year. They discussed Raymond's brother's purchase of some claims in the Hermes ground for $6,000. "I wanted no trouble; we had located in good faith and I proposed to repay the $6,000 and give him a full share in the location." Remarkably, Raymond never raised the issue of any conflict of interest between Perley and the Raymond & Ely. Perley remained counsel for the company until the eve of this lawsuit, and, incredibly, remained at this very moment one of Mr. Raymond's personal attorneys. Far from acrimonious, his departure was resisted by his employer. The claims of various parties were familiar to him, and his investigation throughout eastern Nevada and Utah, his interview with claimants and review of records, in addition to conversations with the Plaintiff's current counsel when they were serving the same master, convinced him of the worthlessness of any competing claims to the Hermes ground. That, he suggested, was probably what accounted for the indifference of Raymond and Ely until the Hermes shaft struck the ledge.

The next day, Lightner took the stand.[117] He recounted his experience with Hearst: that he had heard Hearst was inspecting some ground in the area and had actually managed to purchase the Monitor title after Lightner himself had failed. Knowing Hearst for some dozen years, he spotted him in Pioche and "upbraided him for purchasing the title with the intention of injuring the Raymond & Ely Company." His insistence that Hearst sell out to his employer being rejected on account of the profit Hearst might turn on his investment by developing a mine, Lightner then appealed to their friendship, noting how the loss of the Monitor would bode badly for his future prospects with the Raymond & Ely. After much supplication, Hearst finally relented and agreed to a sale of three of the sections of the claim for a mere $12,000. Hearst confirmed this account with his own testimony. He'd had no conversation with either Lightner or Perley about anything before making his purchase, and didn't meet with those men until afterward. It wasn't

117 "Raymond & Ely vs. Hermes- The Testimony for the Defense- C.W. Lightner on the Stand," *Daily Alta California*, April 17, 1873.

until September 17 that Perley and Lightner mentioned the Hermes title and discussed a joint venture. That there was no conspiracy was self-evident, though the more vital fact, he implied, was the absence of any evidence that the ledge beneath the Hermes and the one comprising the Panaca under the control of the Raymond & Ely were one and the same. There was, he said, a meeting with Raymond in San Francisco, and he did offer the man, as instructed by Perley and Lightner, 5,000 shares of Hermes stock. Raymond, he said, wasn't averse to the idea; he simply wanted twice what was offered.

The effect of the testimony of Lightner and Hearst was profound. Favored at first to lose, some were now speculating that "the Hermes has a least an even show to win, and this too in spite of the evident bias of the *Pioche Record*, and the very extraordinary rulings of his Honor Judge Fuller."[118] The Plaintiff's allegations of "a cunningly conceived plot, and a most diabolical conspiracy on the part of certain worthy gentlemen connected with the Hermes" now appeared to be "a very shallow dodge, concocted, no doubt, with the view of influencing public opinion, if not the jury."[119]

Having established the lack of any conspiracy aiming to injure the Raymond & Ely, the defense then brought in several of the original Panaca claimants. The Plaintiff had attempted to demonstrate that the Panaca was a unified claim and that it had purchased the individual interests, or most of them, and was the rightful successor-in-interest. Peter Shirts said otherwise. The original prospectors had at first intended to divide everything equally, but eventually opted to segregate each individual interest.[120] The claims were abandoned, he said, after his return to Utah due to pressure from the Mormon Church, which frowned on mining.

The trial proceeded another five days before the last of the witnesses left the stand. Leading in the presentation of closing arguments was Henry I. Thornton, who occupied six hours in what was characterized by one correspondent as "a masterpiece of blended logic, invective and impassioned oratory."[121] After lauding

---

[118] *Eureka Sentinel*, April 19, 1873.
[119] Id.
[120] *Sacramento Daily Union*, April 17, 1873.
[121] "Drawing to a Close," *Daily Alta California*, April 22, 1873.

the noble achievements of the Raymond & Ely, he spoke of Hearst's appearance in the Fall of 1871, and how he "concocted a scheme by which he, Perley, then attorney of plaintiff, and Lightner were to reap the reward of Raymond's perseverance and energy; that Perley and Lightner located the Hermes Company on the Panaca ground, even taking in part of the ground opened by Raymond and Ely in 1870, and then Perley, Hearst and Lightner, with the money of Plaintiff, bought up several adverse claims to the ground covered by the Hermes location, and went to work on the Panaca ground...." He "concluded with an eloquent peroration, denouncing the perfidy and ingratitude of the policy of Lightner toward the Company which had fostered and enriched him, and demanding a verdict which should establish for all time the doctrine that the agent and lawyers to whom mining corporations are compelled to entrust the protection of their rights, cannot betray them to the first strolling speculator who may tempt them to a violation of their duty."

What some praised as Thornton's "fine forensic effort," others said was merely a "wholesale abuse of Mr. Hearst, Judge Perley and Colonel Lightner," consistent with that awful practice "to defame, vilify, abuse, traduce and blast (if he can) the good name of any citizen who may be opposed to his clients."[122] Hearst, it was said, was "a well-known, straightforward and esteemed citizen, while Colonel Lightner...is a fair square and honorable gentleman who has earned a first-class reputation for truth, veracity and fair-dealing covering the years of his residence in this State."[123] Of Perley's character, no one vouched—whether inadvertently or due to long memories of many scandals, who can say.

In reply to Thornton came W. W. Bishop. He explained that the rights of the Plaintiff were based either on the conformity of the original locations with the operative law of the day, or on actual, sustained possession.[124] The locations predated any mining regulations and were made, in truth, in bad faith, by Mormons who wished to keep the gentiles at bay, were little worked at the time and ultimately abandoned, not because of any threat posed by the

---

122 "The Pioche Mining Suit," *Daily Alta California*, April 23, 1873.

123 Id.

124 "The Great Mining Suit: The Twenty-Sixth Day of Trial," *Pioche Daily Record*, April 23, 1873.

natives, but because the Church prohibited mining as an unfit vocation for the Saints. Wren was up next for the Plaintiff and focused primarily on the geology of the ground and attempted to show that the land occupied by the Hermes truly was a part of the ledge on which the Raymond & Ely was located. Little could he resist, however, the urge to condemn the "arch conspirator" Perley, whose competing enterprise was funded by the coffers of his employer. He mocked the defense's contention that the Plaintiff failed to show that the original locators whose claims the Raymond & Ely obtained were actually miners by asking: "Is Mr. Perley a miner? Did he ever stick a pick in the ground with the view of working as a miner?" No. Instead of engaging in work so honorable, he was "living off and enriching himself from the bounty of the employer whom he was, and has been, trying, through fraud, to dispossess of some of his most valuable property."[125] Pitzer then followed for the defense, with the promise to "prove that the position of the Plaintiffs in this case is utterly untenable. They come into Court without location, without work, and claim to be owners of our property."[126] In contrast, was the fine work of Perley and Lightner in enriching the Raymond & Ely.[127] As stock prices rose, Perley's salary increased, from $400 per month to more than twice that; and he received additional bonuses—all after the Hermes had been located. Lightner received a gold watch, presented "with almost tears of gratitude...as a reward for his faithfulness and intelligent management of the affairs of the company."[128] To this very day, Perley remained Mr. Raymond's personal attorney. And then there was Raymond's acquiescence in Perley's Answer in the McDermott matter, never filed due to Perley's success with the demurrer, but which denied with vehemence the validity of the Panaca title.[129] "The President of the Company himself positively swears...that the Panaca location is worthless. He says that he is

[125] "The Arguments in the Raymond-Hermes Case: Wednesday's Proceedings," *Pioche Daily Record*, April 24, 1873.

[126] Id.

[127] *Daily Alta California*, April 25, 1873.

[128] *Pioche Daily Record*, April 25, 1873.

[129] Id.

satisfied that the old Panaca titles are made invalid by lapse of time if they were worth anything in the first place."[130]

It is perhaps the nature of the role of an attorney, charged with zealously pursuing his client's interests, that explains Judge Hardy adopting perhaps the harshest tone of all the Plaintiff's counsel against his old friend, and yet the intensity of his attack during closing remains explicable only through resort to some personal slight experienced along the road to trial but undocumented in the historical record. Or perhaps he resented the fact that while he toiled away as a salaried lawyer in someone else's employ, Perley was reaching for the stars as a mining entrepreneur and seemed to be on the brink of the ultimate success. Whatever the reason for his remarkably hostile presentation, Hardy commenced it with mockery, and ended, rather dangerously, with a denial of Perley's honor. He found it incredible that "Perley, with all his learning…don't know how to read or construe a plain notice of a mining location."[131] Those notices were available, and yet he disregarded them and proceeded instead to hijack the property of others. He and his co-conspirators "first appropriate our property, and then they organize a company and develop it with our capital." He even took a shot at Perley's girth by stating that the man's business practices had allowed him to have "lived and flourished and grown fat." The verified Answer prepared but never filed by Perley in the McDermott litigation proved nothing but Perley's deviousness. "If Mr. Perley was so anxious to serve his employers, why did he, when there was no necessity of his doing so, ever frame the Answer in the McDermott case? Why does he parade before the jury that paper as the strongest weapon against his former client and old benefactor, when had he properly performed his duty as an attorney," it would never have even been written?[132] The implication was that Perley used the McDermott case to set up his own defense in what he must have anticipated would be an action between the Hermes and Raymond & Ely. A conscious intent to use his access to the property and assets of his employer to subvert his employer's interests extended even to Perley's alleged failure to

[130] "The Arguments in the Raymond-Hermes Case: Thursday's Proceedings," *Pioche Daily Record*, April 25, 1873.

[131] *Pioche Daily Record*, April 26, 1873.

[132] Id.

maintain the Raymond & Ely's monuments. As he demanded of Perley rhetorically why he didn't "keep up the stakes," Perley actually attempted to interject a response, but Hardy continued on as if his target weren't even present. "You were paid $10,000 a year to attend to this business," but couldn't keep greed in check. In contrast, the impeached former Judge presented himself as the model of an attorney's rectitude. He'd worked side-by-side with Perley for the Raymond & Ely, but unlike Perley, "I never took any of the Raymond & Ely Company's ground, and never tried to!" It was Perley's status as the company's agent, concluded Hardy, that ultimately condemned Perley and vindicated the company's rights.

When Delos Lake stood up to address the jury on the Defendant's behalf, he reminded all that the action was one simply for ejectment—which entailed a showing that the Plaintiff possessed title to land occupied by the Hermes. He thought the jury might have forgotten this crucial point due to the Plaintiff's effort to prove its case not by appeal to evidence of title but to "denunciations and assertions that Mr. Perley and Mr. Lightner and George Hearst were no longer fit to inhabit this earth, on account of the outrages and crimes which they had committed against the Raymond & Ely Company."[133] In contrast was the "unstinted eulogy" presented by Plaintiff's counsel in honor of Mr. Raymond, both extravagant and ridiculous in tone. "[I]f the characters in which he had been waited were true, he was no longer fit to remain on earth, but deserved immediate translation...from these mundane spheres and take a position in the celestial realms." Perhaps the worst slander during the course of the trial had been upon Mr. Rives, "a young gentleman of unblemished character, the partner of Mr. Perley, an attorney and citizen who, in all his acts concerning the claim which had been brought before the jury in this suit, had acted with the advice and counsel and under the responsibility of Mr. Perley." When Garber stood and expressed doubt that anyone had actually demeaned Rives, Lake attainted Thornton of the offense. Thornton intervened to explain that his intent in speaking of Rives had been to highlight the misdeeds of Perley, who was responsible for any misconduct attributable to his partner. A seething Perley, satiated to

133 "The Arguments in the Raymond-Hermes Case: Friday's Proceedings," *Pioche Daily Record*, April 27, 1873.

the full with smears, defamations and affronts to his honor, and having sat with uncharacteristic self-control throughout the proceedings, suddenly exclaimed that he was indeed responsible for his actions, both in and out of the courtroom. Grasping Perley's meaning, and taking mental transport back to the days when honor must have blood, Thornton replied that he was prepared to hear from Perley anytime. "You shall hear from me, sir," retorted Perley, "without fail!"[134] When Thornton tauntingly insisted that Perley not forget his present announcement and "back out of it," Perley assured him that there was no danger in that because Thornton would surely hear from him.[135] Perhaps amused at the outburst, but mindful of the jury's impatience, Lake interrupted the exchange and said that on the present occasion he "desired the jury to hear from him, not be distracted by outside Bar remarks of counsels, who had no business interrupting while he was addressing the jury." Resuming, he thought to end with a well-meaning but not entirely plausible defense of Perley, of whose professional character, if not personal, no aspersion had ever been cast "in any court of justice, and was not touched by the facts in this case."[136]

The final word came from Mesick and Garber, for the defense and Plaintiff respectively. Mesick focused on the issue of the trust relationship between Perley and his employer, and explained that Perley, as the law agent of the Raymond & Ely, was hardly precluded from entering into the mining location market, and was as much entitled as anyone else to purchase claims and pursue independent interest in the mines. The titles held by the Raymond & Ely were hardly in conflict with those Perley obtained and on which were founded the fortunes of the Hermes. "The only question before you is whether the Raymond & Ely Company had an unqualifiedly good title at the time the Hermes location was made. If they had not, then it would be monstrous to claim that Lightner and Perley had not as good a right as anyone on earth to make that location."[137] Garber followed in the afternoon, to a courtroom more

---

[134] *Carson Daily Appeal*, April 29, 1873.

[135] Id.

[136] "The Arguments in the Raymond-Hermes Case: Friday's Proceedings," *Pioche Daily Record*, April 27, 1873.

[137] "The Arguments in the Raymond-Hermes Case: Monday's Proceedings," *Pioche Daily Record*, April 29, 1873.

packed than ever since the commencement of the trial. Responding to Mesick's defense of Perley, Garber denounced Perley's contest of his late employer's title. The denunciation was based on "a principle of law recognized and applied as far as civilization extends; it is sanctioned alike by morality and policy; it is a universal principle and it is engravened by the hand of God on the heart of every created man." The principle was the duty of loyalty and confidentiality an agent owed its principal, an obligation to delve into the principal's secrets in order to best represent him, and to cut a sharp tact away from any conflict of interest. The evidence, which he recounted as he saw it, could leave no doubt of Perley's true motive. "From August 1, 1871, he was willfully, deliberately and in violation of the law and his sacred duty.... He was advising the Raymond & Ely Company against their best interests," uttering statements to his employer that were "prejudiced, jaundiced, diseased and poisoned by this conflict between interest and duty."[138] The Answer in the McDermott case, wielded so prominently by the defense as proof of the position contrary to the one asserted by the Plaintiff, was in fact a trap sprung by Perley in anticipation of his great theft. "Having hoodwinked every officer of the Company into signing it, he then carries it away as a treasure of great value, conceals it from human view, and, finally, brings it into Court here, where it is seen in its true character as a snare specially designed to entrap his generous employers." Could there be, he concluded, "a more striking illustration of the policy, the justice and the morality of the rule, that attorneys shall not reap the fruits of treachery to their clients than is afforded by Mr. Perley's case?"[139]

As the matter was taken up by the jury, excitement grew, as did trepidation by those who'd placed wagers on the outcome over the thought of betting wrong. The safest option seemed to be a Plaintiff's verdict, hence more than $20,000 was placed in bets in favor of the Raymond & Ely, or at least a hung jury.[140] Others of more deliberative and measured mind, contemplated the meaning of the proceedings in Judge Fuller's Court. One commentator wondered over the fact that the matter was now the "longest

---

138 "The Arguments in the Raymond-Hermes Case: Last Day's Argument," *Pioche Daily Record*, May 1, 1873.

139 Id.

140 *Sacramento Daily Union*, May 1, 1873.

mining suit ever recorded in Nevada."[141] Another commented that "so much of personal acrimony has distinguished this famous lawsuit that to an outside observer it seemed more an effort on the part of counsel to abuse individual character than to attend to the settlement of a great point of law."[142] The cynics of the world mulled over the enormity of the costs: "court-fees, attorneys' fees, witnesses' fees, together with the board, lodging, and traveling expenses of the last-named; also the sums necessarily in ditching, digging, delving, assaying," that might have been better dedicated toward the payment of "numerous dividends to the stockholders of either company."[143] Perley for his part passed the interlude between testimony and verdict arranging for the shipment to Steptoe Valley of a wagon load of turkeys, chickens and hogs.[144]

The public had little time to wait. The jury rapidly addressed the vital issues and announced it was ready to publish its verdict. Outside the courthouse, a large crowd congregated, waiting to enter the premises to hear the verdict with their own ears.[145] Of the jurors, only three favored the Plaintiff. At once the building emptied, with investors and journalists rushing to the telegraph office to place stock orders in San Francisco and stories in the press of the western States. Others, including the losers in the numerous wagers placed the night before or that morning, fought in the streets, and some even drew pistols and fired.[146] Only the Judge and the lawyers remained behind, and they at once set to hearing the motion of the Plaintiff to set the verdict aside and repeat the just-concluded ordeal.[147] By the end of the day, it cannot to be doubted that they had joined the rest of the population in the local saloons to partake in the biggest mass bender in eastern Nevada history.[148]

The informed opinion seemed to be that the defeat of the Raymond & Ely spelled decline for the Pioche Lode. Success of a

---

141 *White Pine News*, April 19, 1873.

142 *White Pine News*, May 3, 1873.

143 Raymond, op. cit., p. 515.

144 *Pioche Daily Record*, May 1, 1873.

145 "Verdict in the Raymond and Ely vs. Hermes Case," *Pioche Daily Record*, May 2, 1873.

146 "Hermes Victor," *Daily Alta California*, May 2, 1873.

147 Id.

148 "The Great Law Suit: How the News of the Verdict was Received," *Daily Alta California*, May 2, 1873.

challenger in breaking off a portion of the Raymond & Ely claim would only encourage others and so deplete the wealth of the Company that few would continue to see mining stocks as a good investment. The Parties and their attorneys generally agreed that further litigation boded ill for everyone involved. Counsel for the Raymond & Ely nevertheless went forward with a motion for a new trial on June 19, with Thornton and Perley handling the bulk of the arguments for their respective clients, followed by Mesick and Garber the next day.[149] Illness among the lawyers' ranks postponed further argument, which finally concluded several days later.[150] When Judge Fuller announced his decision to grant the motion, the Hermes men in the street, thinking the opposite had occurred, entered into a brief phase of rejoicing, that soon enough received a tonic of hard truth to induce a depressed calm.[151] Behind the scenes, however, negotiations continued. A promising sign appeared when an agreement was reached between the Raymond & Ely and Hermes to assist one another in the litigation against the rival Kentucky and Pioche-Phenix Companies.[152] When Perley was spotted sharing a stage with Jim Hardy, many observers likely concluded that the harsh words the latter showered on the former during the late trial were forgotten, and that the two were engaged in far more productive conversation on behalf of their clients.[153]

The general conversation between the Parties and their representatives did indeed prove more productive. By the end of August, a concordat between the Raymond & Ely, Hermes, Meadow Valley and Pioche-Phenix Companies to consolidate and issue a stock common to all took shape.[154] "We are glad of this circumstance," noted the ironic editor of the *White Pine News*, "as our neighbors would have suffered seriously from dull times had the quarrel longer continued."[155]

Perley's fees in the case surely rose to princely heights. His activity in building up his ranch attests to the income at his

149 *Pioche Daily Record*, June 19, 1873; and *Pioche Daily Record*, June 30, 1873.
150 *Pioche Daily Record*, June 22, 1873; and *Pioche Daily Record*, June 23, 1873.
151 *Pioche Daily Record*, July 1, 1873.
152 *Sacramento Daily Union*, May 6, 1873.
153 *White Pine News*, May 17, 1873.
154 *White Pine News*, August 23, 1873; and *Daily Alta California*, August 30, 1873.
155 *White Pine News*, August 23, 1873.

disposal, and now with the consolidation of the stock of the rival companies, he was in a position to cash out and make a further profit. There remained some legal matters to tend to: an action for an injunction against the Ingomar Company; two lawsuits in which he was a named defendant in San Francisco brought by former Chief Justice S. C. Hastings and Wells Fargo—no doubt for debts outstanding for money or services advanced—and the defense of an accused forger in Pioche in which he shared the duty to exonerate the defendant with Henry I. Thornton—an objective the two men achieved following a trial in September.[156]

That Perley could co-exist well enough to cooperate in a felony case with a man he had been prepared to put a bullet through a short time before was a measure of the posturing their harsh words might have reflected, as well the extent of the bridging of the differences between their embattled clients. The present accord between the men hadn't germinated either immediately or without effort. Violence among partisans of the great suit erupted, and many accepted rather fatalistically that given "the reiteration of criminations and the bandying of bitter, rhetorical flourishes of a personal sort…it would be remarkable if the trial…should be brought to a close without a clash of arms."[157] The ordinary bluster of attorneys in the course of a high stakes trial, and the ofttimes ill-thought out rejoinders presented at the spur of the moment, however, could not compare to words of a different sort implicating "rigid exactions of the code duello—which code is undoubtedly recognized by Col. Thornton and Mr. Perley, between whom there seems to be an intensity of dislike impossible of restraint or disguise."[158] In light of the personal histories of the two men—Thornton's fire breathing dedication to the South and Perley's long, notorious commitment to street brawling and more formalized combat—it was expected that "a resort to the dueling code for the satisfaction of the wounded honor of the aggrieved party" would result.[159] Reports came that Perley wrote out a demand for satisfaction to Thornton, and was even contemplating challenging

156 *Pioche Daily Record*, September 9, 1873.

157 "The Code Duello: Blue Blood Verses Blue Nose," *Carson Daily Appeal*, April 29, 1873.

158 Id.

159 Id.

Garber and the rest of the Raymond & Ely's legal bullpen, but the reputed refusal of David Terry to act as second in an affair of honor involving two of his friends and the interference of others much desirous to avoid a truly pointless shedding of blood, delayed the transmittal.[160] How vested the two men were in an actual fight is uncertain, though likely the knowledge of so much loss of life in the cause of honor both personal and partisan in recent years gave each man reason to pause. The general public, too, was doubtful about private settlement of the sort associated with an era now dead and gone, and some mocked the affray as one that ought to be conducted not with pistols but, given Perley's girth, with harpoons.[161] Perley's past notoriety in affairs of honor and the heart, as well as his wider physical dimensions, made him the most prominent target of ridicule. One especially condescending account was that Thornton declined to settle the matter in the way Perley proposed, "by the test of who can stand out door the longest in their shirt," due to Perley's superior experience.[162] Another noted that while Perley was a native of the ice bound north, "the chilly winds and icebergs of his native land have not cooled the heated ardor of his blood, and he is equal to the emergency of taking fight to a legal opponent or fleeing from the wrath of a wronged spouse, clad only in *puris natrualibus*."[163] No doubt it was in response to the intercession of friends, referred to as a "peace commission," and a dawning in his own mind that such challenges hardly resolve anything and might actually lead to a penalty in the form of loss of the right to practice law in the State of Nevada, that prompted Thornton to send an explanation of his statement in Court to Perley, which Perley apparently accepted as adequate to end the matter. The two men, it is said, "shook hands across the bloody chasm."[164]

Perley's interest in developing new mines continued with the La Paz. Its initial success owed much to the boom of 1872, and its fortunes remained high in 1873 after Perley and his colleagues obtained a competing title from the Prairie Queen Mining Company

---

[160] *Carson Daily Appeal*, May 13, 1873; and *Russian River Flag*, May 8, 1873.
[161] *Salt Lake Tribune*, May 7, 1873.
[162] *Carson Daily Appeal*, May 17, 1873.
[163] *Gold Hill Daily News*, May 2, 1873.
[164] "Pioche News," *Salt Lake Herald Republican*, May 8, 1873.

and expanded the depth of its shaft to 100 feet.[165] Its early promise, however, ebbed, and by the end of the year assessments were being levied and payments from shareholders (including Perley) were listed as delinquent.[166] Far more promising for Perley was the further development of his ranch in the Steptoe Valley. To his herds of live-stock he added "two short-horned Durham bulls and two heifers of the same high-strain of blood, and a stallion and three mares of famous pedigrees."[167] Cultivation of the ground proceeded forward as well, with the planting of 160 acres of barley, "large quantities of wheat and oats, and all kinds of vegetables." The best and most modern machinery was being employed in the operation, and five hundred fruit bearing trees were planted, some of rare varieties, "embracing apples, peaches, pears, quinces, plums, cherries and apricots." The inclusion also of timber-yielding forest trees—maple, walnut, locust and elm—and 150,000 trout to stock a large pond assured the world that Perley's would be a model farm, exceptional in its own right, and an example to others to follow. On a trip to California after the Hermes verdict, Perley spent $10,000 in gold coin to purchase another one hundred head of young and pure blood Durham cows in Santa Clara County, and procured the use of seven cattle cars for shipment east to his ranch.[168] A thousand acres was said to be the full scope of his territory, with much of it dedicated to present and future projects. So recently mocked for his ill-temper and his past exploits in shirttails, Perley now enjoyed praise for "such interest manifested in the agricultural development of south east Nevada," and the expression of hope that his example would "induce capitalists to embark in the same branch of enterprise."[169]

Ever restless, though, and on the look-out for a new world in which his longing for success on the grand scale might at last be manifest, Perley would not remain in Nevada to pursue the perfection of his vision. Having prevailed in the greatest mining case in American history to date, represented presidential

[165] *Pioche Daily Record*, January 5, 1873.

[166] *Pioche Daily Record*, December 31, 1873.

[167] *Pioche Daily Record*, February 25, 1873; and *Territorial Enterprise*, March 18, 1873.

[168] *Pioche Daily Record*, June 3, 1873.

[169] Id.

candidates and Senators in legal actions in a variety of venues, and become something of a celebrity for his many extra-legal antics, the Far West, where these many landmarks of a lifetime transpired, might have seemed in his mind to be ground best left fallow as new fields were planted. To the east his eyes turned, not the eastern seaboard or even the Great Plains or Mid-West, but to that other hub of mercantile and human activity on the western frontier, Salt Lake City. From the time Perley arrived in California, until his involvement in Pioche, he had regular dealings with Mormons, all of whom looked to the capital of Deseret as a Jew did Jerusalem—the true home of their hearts and the place they longed to be. Perley himself had begun travelling to the Great Salt Lake several years before in search of the locators of abandoned mining claims, and money perhaps for investment in his various schemes. Aware of the gain to be had from closer affiliation with the Mormon capital, Perley joined Harry Thornton and others to successfully lobby for connecting it via telegraph wire with Pioche and the rest of Nevada.[170] Fitch had gone there in 1871 in connection with mining litigation, and once there accepted the offer of Brigham Young to defend the Mormon Prophet and other high-ranking members of the Church of Jesus Christ of Latter Day Saints from criminal charges arising from their practice of polygamy. Fitch's success representing the Church and its leaders led to his settlement there, and likely would have translated into elevation to the United States Senate had the Congress not rejected the Territory's initial bid to enter the Union as a State. It also provided Perley with an influential friend in Salt Lake City, and an ally in his quest to establish himself as quickly as he could as a man of influence in an entirely new forum. Leaving his nephew in charge of his affairs in Nevada, Perley packed up his library and belongings and headed east, probably by train, to the principal locus of the last phase of his very eventful life.

[170] *The Deseret News*, November 1, 1871.

Chapter Twelve

THE DEAD SEA

On the eve of the construction of the Transcontinental Railroad, travelers along the six-hundred-mile route between the Sierras and the Rocky Mountains endured a journey, either by stage or on horseback or on foot, all the more dreary for the immense amount of time involved. "Nature," noted one observer, "seems to be incomplete here," unprepared for the reception of man, and unable to provide the means to sustain more than the barest of populations.[1] Travelling west to east, as Perley did in the fall of 1873, the traveler encountered one bare, brown and vacant set of hills and valleys after another, each marked by the same dry, volcanic soil, so exceptional in its ability to absorb water, yet so poor in yielding anything except grease plant, sage brush and bunch grass.[2] The noted explorer, Sir Richard Burton, observed that as a rule, such creeks that exist in this terrain "dwindle to rivulets and sink in the porous alluvium before they have run a mile from the hill-foot, and reappear in the arid plains at a level too low for navigation."[3] Rain clouds pass at times in mass overhead, but move ever eastward before unleashing the bulk of their inner waters on the far side of the Continental Divide. The near perpetual drought yielded an alkali-based dust, "thick and constant and penetrating beyond experience and comparison," filling the air upon the gusting of the wind or the disturbances caused by the tramp of oxen, horse and boot, rising to imposing altitudes and taking on the omnipresent attribute of the Lord Himself.[4] Periodically, without warning and sometimes after an absence of many years, there descended into this bleak and dusty scene a scourge said to be Asiatic in nature, appearing like a cross between an arachnid and a

---

1 Samuel Bowles, *Our New West: Records of Travel Between the Mississippi River and the Pacific Ocean* (Hartford: Hartford Publishing Co., 1869), at pp. 282-283.

2 Id., at p. 274.

3 Richard F. Burton, *The City of the Saints and Across the Rocky Mountains*, Volume I (New York: Harper & Brothers, Publishers, 1862), at p. 283.

4 Bowles, op. cit., at pp. 275-276.

buffalo, possessing multiple legs, lacking wings, and numbering in the millions, gnawing away at anything edible, leaving utter devastation in its wake, and suffering no check save for its short life span and the presence of nearly equally numerous flocks of misplaced sea birds.[5]

Burton compared the surface configuration of the territory to that of Equatorial Africa: "a great depression in a mountain land: a trough elevated 4,000 to 5,000 feet above sea level, subtended on all sides by mountains 8,000 to 10,000 feet high, and subdivided by transverse ridges."[6] The rim of the basin, he noted, was "formed by the broken chains of Oregon to the North, and to the south by the little known-sub-ranges of the Rocky Mountains," the latter comprising the eastern wall, "while the Sierra Nevada hems in the west."[7] The presence of bench formations and a system of water marks in every valley hinted at the rages of the waters of the firmament and from the depths of the earth, and the submersion of all before a recession of epic proportion left indelible scars in its wake. The modern aridity of the land juxtaposed oddly with the coldness of the temperature, as well as the wild swings between heat and frigidity. The altitude of the lowest points of the basin being 4,000 feet above the level of the sea, and the highest heights exceeding 10,000 feet, the air was thin, and only those acclimated over time were able to comfortably engage in the slightest of exertions, free of nausea, sickness and fainting.[8] Though marked by variation in the nature of the rock extruding from the eroded surface, the majority of the mountains in this desert region were of igneous origin, "entirely denuded of vegetation, and look in some instances as if they have been blasted by fire."[9] And though monotonous at times, and aggravating as any obstacle in one's path might be, the country was not lacking in any aesthetic value. Mountains," said one traveler, "are always beautiful; and here they are ever in sight, wearing every variety of shape, and even in their hard and bare surfaces presenting many a fascination of form,—

[5] Burton, op. cit., at p. 285.

[6] Id., at p. 273.

[7] Id.

[8] Id., at p. 275.

[9] J.H. Simpson, *Report of Explorations Across the Great Basin of the Territory of Utah* (Washington, D.C.: Government Printing Office, 1876), at p. 49.

running up into sharp peaks; rising up and rounding out into innumerable fat mammillas, exquisitely shapen, and inviting possibly to auriferous feasts; sloping down into faint foot-hills, and mingling with the plain to which they are all destined; and now and then offering the silvery streak of snow, that is the sign of water for man and the promise of grass for ox."[10]

The hills and valleys of the Great Basin so characteristic of Nevada terminate in what is now Utah, and give way to a vast dusty, whitish, plain, warted with sand heaps and "horrid patches of salt soil," bunch grasses, greasewood and artemisia—bright red, yellow and sometime green—intermixed with the occasional dwarf cedar, almost entirely black.[11] "All was desert" here, said Burton, the soil of which was marked by "a thin fine silt" that took to the air in the dry season and became a putty-like mud during the spring and autumnal rains.[12] Its breadth varied, and served in some places, he said, to deter any transit due to the lack of water.[13] Numerous native tribes—Pavant, Ute, and Panak—roamed this country, eating insects and whatever edible plants could be scavenged, but ever ready to make off with whatever stock happened to stray from passing herds. The most pathetic in American eyes were the Go-shoots—a reengage band of Utes—who wore tattered rabbit pelts, sported unkempt hair, and, in the case of many of their women folk, roamed naked to the waist.[14] In time, the soil turned a salty blue in color, "like a frozen pond when the water still underlies it." Brackish swamps dotted the land, posing hazards for the unwary traveler, and emitting the most infectious and foul odor.[15] The whole scene, said J. H. Simpson, "is that of a somber, dreary waste, and over which a bird is scarcely ever seen to fly, and took on the appearance further east of a vast mud-flat, which in some localities was covered with an incrustation of common salt."[16]

At the lowest point of the desert, and near the middle of what is now Utah, there comes into view through the mists of countless

---

[10] Bowles, op. cit., at p. 278.
[11] Burton, op. cit., at p. 460.
[12] Id., at p. 454.
[13] Id., at p. 455.
[14] J.H. Simpson, op. cit., at pp. 52-53.
[15] Burton, op. cit., at p. 459.
[16] J.H. Simpson, op. cit., at p. 48.

mirages, the image of a "still and solitary sea," roughly the size of Lake Chad during Burton's time, forty miles in length and twelve in breadth, 4,200 feet above sea level, fed by streams originating in the Wasatch Mountains to the east, flowing from the top of the divide and through numerous picturesque valleys that by the early 1870s were flush with human population and replete with the signs of human industry.[17] Its western shore, said Burton, comprised "a perfect desert—a salt and arid waste of clay and sand, with the consistency of mortar when wet."[18] Near its shores the atmosphere was "reeking, bluish, and hazy, from the effects of active evaporation, and forms a decided change from the purity and transparency of the air elsewhere."[19] The salinity of the water was fatal to most organic life. Fish who made their way from the mountain streams, by ill luck or error in navigation, perished at once in the concentrated brine. Only an odd variety of shrimp could endure the toxicity of the Lake, and a bizarre moss-like algae, which floated among the saline waves near the Lake's margins.[20]

The Great Salt Lake, this Dead Sea of North America, fittingly feeds from a River called the Jordan flowing from the south and leading, if one were to follow its course up stream, to the great metropolis of the Basin, named for the Lake itself and founded over twenty years before Perley's transit by the Mormon tribes wandering through the desert in flight from the fury of Pharaoh and the peoples of the eastern States. A maze of irrigation channels fanned out from the Jordan and other streams before they reached their terminus in the briny waters of the Lake, delivering fresh water to the fields of the Mormon homesteaders, making the valley a happy place for the settler, and a refuge from the white dust of the surrounding wastes. The City itself was observed by contemporaries to have been "regularly and handsomely laid out, with many fine buildings, and filled with thick gardens of trees and flowers, that gave it a fairy-land aspect."[21] With well cultivated fields, the vast and picturesque sea to the west and the towering mountains to the east, perpetually snow-capped and covered in forests, it was

---

[17] See Burton, op. cit., p. 325.

[18] Id.

[19] Id.

[20] Id., at p. 326.

[21] Bowles, op. cit., at p. 202.

said of Salt Lake City that "no internal city of the Continent lies in such a field of beauty, unites such rich and rare elements of nature's formations."[22] Difficult it was to conceive that the founders of the place discovered it largely uninhabited, "dry and unfruitful," baked by the summer sun and covered in snows in winter. A diet consisting of roots, coarse herbs and the meanest of game animals permitted the majority of original settlers to survive the first year, and bought time until the tilling of the fields and the reaping of the first harvest.[23] No ordinary people would have considered it a place worthy of permanent repose. Only the vision of a modern Moses, a leader of the tribes through many tribulations, could convince these wanderers that it was Providence itself that had led them there. The rapid success in reclaiming the place from desolation gave rise to wonder. It was, said Captain Stansbury, "a thing at variance with all our preconceived ideas of its probability," and truly "one of the most remarkable incidents of the present age."[24] For its first twenty years of existence, it was the only town between the Missouri and Sacramento, a thousand miles from either end, separated from the rest of humanity by alkali deserts, rugged mountains and barren flats, but appearing as a veritable Garden of Eden, outfitted with wide streets on a grid pattern, green and cool gardens and orchards, and hundreds of homes of single story and white washed adobe walls.[25]

In 1873, the City was still small, only two miles broad, running parallel with the right bank of the Jordan River, which formed its western limit.[26] At the west end of the City was the court house, capped by a tin Muscovian dome.[27] Nearby was the public square, reserved for the institutions of the Church, including the massive yet uncomely tabernacle, and next to it, the private compound of the Prophet, where lived his many wives and even more numerous children. Imperfection in the *civitas* remained unresolved at this

---

[22] Id., at p. 203.

[23] Id., at p. 210.

[24] Edward Wheelock Tullidge, *History of Salt Lake City* (Salt Lake City: Star Printing Company, 1886), at p. 107.

[25] John Hanson Beadle, *Life in Utah; Or the Mysteries and Crimes of Mormonism* (Philadelphia: National Publishing Company, 1871), at 247.

[26] Burton, op. cit., at p. 197.

[27] Id.

time. In summer, the streets couldn't avoid the accumulation of dust, nor viscous mud in winter.[28] The laying of pavement would be the only cure for these inevitable and characteristic defects of all cities of the American frontier. Small fields were many within the town's limits, but most were unkempt, with weeds growing throughout, as well as sunflowers that outnumbered and towered over the corn stalks.[29]

Perley undoubtedly avoided the vagaries of travel across the open desert and exposure "to the vertical rays of a burning summer's sun, or the pitiless storm that threatened to blow everything to shreds," through resort to the recently completed Transcontinental Railroad.[30] The route ran north-east from Pioche, across the salt desert along the northern shore of Great Salt Lake and south along the eastern shore until terminating at Ogden, just north of the Mormon metropolis. What drew Perley to this remarkable yet strange oasis in the desert were the riches beneath the bleak countryside surrounding it. The good Lord had fashioned the well-watered lands of the continent that men might cultivate the soil and extract all manner of nutrients from it, fruits and vegetables, nuts, berries, and a host of legumes, roots and tubers. He made the arid regions of the earth for other purposes, including the removal of silver and gold bearing ore, copper and other elements of great utility and much in demand. Both sides of the Sierras had yielded and were yielding many fortunes, and more still had been founded further east in the rocky deserts of Nevada. It was as if the greater the elevation, the further east one went, and the more desolate the county, the more likely the ground was filled with treasure. Burton noted the general belief "that gold exists upon the Wasatch Mountains, within sight of Great Salt Lake City."[31] Lumps of virgin silver, he recalled, were "said to have been discovered upon the White Mountains...," copper, zinc, and lead have been brought from Little Salt Lake Valley and sixty miles east of the Vegas de Santa Clara, and bituminous coal lay "in the softer limestones south of the city, in a country of various marls,

[28] Id., at p. 198.

[29] Id., at p. 200.

[30] T.B.H. Stenhouse, *Rocky Mountain Saints: A Full and Complete History of the Mormons* (New York: D. Appleton and Company, 1873), at p. 692.

[31] Burton, op. cit., at p. 281.

indurated clays, and earthy sandstones."[32] The Mormons, however, shunned the vocation of the miner, not because of a lack of interest in wealth, but due to the admonitions of Brigham Young, whose observation of the moral condition of the mining camps persuaded him of the imperative of directing the faithful toward more wholesome pursuits.[33]

That public policy might change in favor of an opening of the mining wealth of Utah was evident from the attitude of the Chief Justice of the Territory, who chided Mormon morality on this point, and lauded the fact that "this mineral wealth is just beginning to be developed."[34] Perley's familiarity with the Mormons being great due to his occasional representation of members of the faith, and his apparent lack of any prejudice against them, allowed for an unimpeded consideration of the merits of removing to Salt Lake to intervene where no member of the Church was willing or able, explore potential mining sites and then develop facilities for the extraction of valuable minerals or ore. The optimistic description of the current development and future prospects for mining in Utah in the pages of Stenhouse's *Rocky Mountain Saints*, of which Perley possessed a copy, would only have encouraged his ultimate decision to relocate.[35] He would make a living practicing law in the local courts, but he would pursue his next great fortune in the yet to be discovered mines of the great territory of Utah.

Perley's career was never entirely mercenary. His engagement of difficult and unpopular cases is sufficient indicia of his commitment to the higher purposes of the law and of lawyers. Utah at the time was not merely a place to invest in mining ventures, but a land in legal turmoil due to the recent controversies between the Mormons and the territorial judicial establishment. In a speech to a convention of persons hopeful of drafting a constitution for a new State, Perley's friend and former law partner Thomas Fitch raised the alarm over the disruption reigning throughout the Territory, and the alliance of a breed of ruffians with anti-polygamy reformers to undermine the Mormon moral order and thereby exploit the myriad sins of mankind. "Every interest of industry is disastrously

---

[32] Id.

[33] Bowles, op. cit., p. 228.

[34] Tullidge, op. cit., at p. 520.

[35] Stenhouse, op. cit., at pp. 711-734.

affected by this unholy alliance," he cried, "every right of the citizen is threatened if not assaulted by the existence of this combination. Your local magistrates are trampled into the mire, theft and murder walk through your streets, without detection, drunkards howl their orgies in the shadow of your altars, the glare and tumult of the drinking saloons, the glitter of gambling hells, and the painted flaunt of the bawd plying her trade, now vex the repose of streets, which beforetime heard no sound to disturb their quiet except the busy hum of industry, the clatter of trade and the musical tinkle of mountain streams."[36] Perley, thus, was entering a region in many ways as lawless as was California in 1849, and was likely as ready now as he was then to stand as a champion of those principles of order embodied in laws both positive and natural, and intended to apply whether legislative and executive bodies were present to draft or execute them or not.

Salt Lake City's legal establishment had not the glamour nor the volume of work evident in San Francisco and Nevada. The great lawyers and judges of the nation hardly made their home in this remote locale. The bar, said a correspondent for the *Cincinnati Commercial*, "consisted of what appeared to be a large keno party keeping tally on a long pine table."[37] It was a backward place for sure, much effected by the religious attitudes of the people, and their adherence less to the Constitution and laws of the United States than to the *Book of Mormon, The Pearl of Great Price* and *The Doctrine and Covenants* of Joseph Smith. For two decades, the Mormons had resisted the attempts of the federal government to bring the faithful to heal. Their attachment to their Prophet generated suspicions in Washington, D.C. of disloyalty, particularly in the fevered days leading up to and during the Civil War. The practice of the Asiatic abomination of polygamy inspired disdain if not disgust. Both sentiments—suspicion and disgust— propelled American officials toward a confrontation, with the goal, periodically at least, of eradicating what were considered to be the Faith's more noxious elements. At first, the weakness of the federal establishment, combined with the strength of the Mormon Church

[36] Tullidge, op. cit., at p. 565.

[37] *History of the Bench and Bar of Utah* (Salt Lake City: Interstate Press Association Publishers, 1913), at p. 37.

and the fact that President Pierce had seen fit to vest Brigham Young with the office of Territorial Governor, impeded the efforts of federal judges and other federal officials from gaining ascendancy in the Territory. In time, as the non-Mormon population grew and a small garrison of federals troops took up abode outside the City, the balance of power shifted. Abruptly, the same President who assumed he was powerless to halt the secession of the Southern States, ordered U.S. troops to march west to Salt Lake City to assist the new territorial regime in eradicating practices at odds with the code Congress approved, including prohibitions on the hated practice of polygamy. Heralds of the approaching army were met with the defiant promise to trap the enemy in the narrow canyons to the east of the City and destroy those who might invade the country and yet again persecute the chosen people.[38] The invasion was quelled, but additional federal soldiers were allowed to take up quarters in the Territory. Federal officials, including a new court, took office, but order remained uncertain as they attempted to impose their authority in defiance of popular will and local proclivities. Most remarkable was the announcement of Judge Cradlebaugh, after repeated frustration of his efforts to seek justice against Mormons, that he wouldn't be prepared to enforce the law for their protection until they came to their senses and manifested a disposition to punish their own high offenders.[39] Utah's loyalty during the Civil War relaxed the tension existing between the federal government and the Mormons, but as the war progressed, the tension resumed. President Lincoln signed a bill outlawing polygamy in the Territory; and Congress stonewalled on the efforts by the people of Utah to convert their Territory into a constituent member of the federal union. Lincoln's subsequent lenience in addressing Mormon practices, continued by his immediate successor, was reversed by President Grant, who harbored a tremendous prejudice against the Mormons and committed his administration to bringing the sins of Mormonism, both secular and spiritual, to a close.

The chief instrument of President Grant's policy was the man he appointed as the new Chief Justice of the Territory, James B.

---

[38] Tullidge, op. cit., at p. 164.
[39] Id., at p. 238.

McKean. Subsequently known as a "modern Jeffries," McKean hailed from New York, served as a Congressman, then as a Colonel in the 77th New York Volunteers, which he organized.[40] He won appointment to the Chief Justiceship of the Territory in 1870, in part on the strength of his war record. Though "a man of rare social and literary attainments, courteous to the superlative degree and an able writer," his inclination toward fanaticism and naturally imperious disposition and irritability, combined with his spiritual upbringing in the Methodist tradition to birth a policy in Mormon Utah that proved unfortunate, if not disastrous.[41] His horror over polygamy appeared to be sincere, and it fueled his commitment to what he called a "mission which God has called me to perform in Utah."[42] The laws of man he considered to be secondary and easily preempted by the law of Heaven. On assuming office, he vowed that should he "find the local or Federal laws obstructing or interfering therewith, by God's blessing I shall trample them under my feet."[43] When the Mormon dominated Territorial Legislature refused to appropriate money to fund the courts presided over by judges hostile to the people's faith, McKean dismissed all jurors from service due to lack of funds to pay the fees owed them, but nevertheless declared the courts to be creatures of Congress, subject to funding directly by the federal government, hence not dependent on Utah for their sustenance and survival. He likewise denied the Legislature the power to create and fund the office of Territorial Marshall to oversee security in the courts, and asserted instead that only Congress or the Court itself had authority over the workings of justice in the Territory.[44] Though ultimately overruled on these points by Chief Justice Chase and the U.S. Supreme Court, McKean operated with confidence, and proceeded forward with indictments procured from non-Mormon grand juries of Brigham Young, the Mayor of Salt Lake City and others, for violation not of the laws and Constitution of the United States, but of Sections 32 and 33 of the Territorial Code, enacted by the Territorial Legislature, prohibiting

---

[40] *History of the Bench and Bar of Utah*, op. cit., at p. 28.

[41] Id., at pp. 27-28.

[42] Leonard J. Arrington, *Brigham Young: American Moses* (Chicago: University of Illinois Press, 1986), at pp. 371-373.

[43] Id.

[44] Stenhouse, op. cit., at p. 687.

adultery.[45] Retaining the legal services of Fitch, the Mormon Prophet fought the indictment, first via formal objections, then through a Petition for a Writ of Habeas Corpus. As the Prophet awaited his fate, he found comfort and strength in the prayers of the faithful, as well as in well wishes from Perley, Charles W. Lightner, Harry I. Thornton and Charles Forman, ostensibly for his role in sponsoring the construction of a telegraph line between Pioche and the Mormon capital.[46] Freeing Young through his Petition, pausing for a time due to the continuance of all criminal trials for a term, and then winning what amounted to a termination of the prosecution by the decision of Chief Justice Chase reversing Judge McKean's rulings on procedural grounds, Fitch then took to the stump to advance his client's cause politically. Calling McKean "that most dangerous of all public functionaries—a judge with a mission to execute, a judge with a policy to carry out, a judge panoplied with a purpose as in complete steel," he condemned the jurist for having "steadily subordinated his judicial duties and his judicial character to the fulfilment of his mission and the execution of his policy."[47]

Perley's earliest known residence in Salt Lake City was the Walker House, on Main Street.[48] Built a year before by Utah's Liberal Party founders and mining investors—the Walker Brothers—it was one of the few hotels of note, and probably the only one up to Perley's standards. He hastily formed a partnership with local attorney Murray A. Carter and set up an office on the second floor of the First National Bank Building on East Temple Street.[49] It was to here he moved the trappings of his profession: several tables, lamps, ink stands, book shelves and 7 book cases to hold a rather large library of law books, collected over the course of the past quarter century.[50] The library included Joseph K. Angel's treatises on Watercourses, Tide Waters, Limitations, Carriers, and Corporations, Beccaria's famous monograph on crime and the law

---

45 Tullidge, op. cit., at p. 536.

46 Id., at p. 539.

47 Id., at p. 564; and *Clinton v. Englebrecht* (1871) 80 U.S. 434.

48 *Salt Lake Tribune*, December 18, 1873.

49 *Salt Lake Herald*, December 18, 1873.

50 See Catalogue of Law Library, *In re Estate of D. W. Perley*, Utah State Archives, Series 1621, Third District Court: Salt Lake County, Probate Case Files.

governing it, the Fourth and Sixth editions of Francis Wharton's treatise on Criminal Law, as well as J. P. Bishop's tome on the same subject. Also by Bishop were his treatises on Marriage and the Law of Married Women. Greenleaf's *Evidence*, Chitty's *Pleading*, Emory Washburn's volumes on Real Property, Easements and Servitudes, all of Story's works, Halleck's account of the law of war and Vattel's *Law of Nations* also had places on the shelves. His long engagement in mining litigation necessitated possession of Brainbridge's *On the Law of Mines*, Copp's aggregation of U.S. mining decisions, Collier's treatise on Mines, and various books on metal, metallurgy and geology. Also included were treatises on Suretyship, Assignment, Bankruptcy, Bailments, Receivers, Fire Insurance, Injunctions, Motions for New Trials, Torts, Real Property, Attorney-Client relations, Ejectment, Patents, Vendors, Mortgages, Fraud, and, as events would later prove, an underutilized account of the law of Wills. A good deal of space was occupied by the voluminous Reports of the States of Alabama, California, Idaho, Indiana, Massachusetts, Nevada, New York, Pennsylvania, Tennessee, the United States Supreme Court and the various Federal Circuits. In the English tradition could be found *Coke on Littleton*, Blackstone's *Commentaries*, and the Law Reports of England in the Common Law Courts, the Chancery and the Exchequer. General reference works included Broom's *Legal Maxims*, the *Corpus Juris Civilis*, Elliot's *Debates on the Constitution*, Lomax's *Digest*, Kent's *Commentaries*, and commentaries on the Constitution by Tucker and Smith. There were historical and philosophical works as well: Burke's writings; Prescott's *Conquest of Mexico, Conquest of Peru*, and *Ferdinand and Isabella*; Gibbon's *Decline and Fall of the Roman Empire*; De Tocqueville's *Democracy in America*; Smith's *Wealth of Nations*; and to inspire eloquence, Cicero's orations, Homer and Vergil, the poems of Byron, Cowper, Moore, Milton, and Scott, and the complete published works of the great advocate, Daniel Webster. Out of curiosity perhaps over how well the effort of the President's defenders compared to his own labors nearly two decades before on behalf of California's beleaguered Controller, he even possessed a published copy of the transcript of the impeachment trial of Andrew Johnson.

To facilitate good relations with persons of influence very soon after his arrival, Perley hosted "a grand dinner" next door at the

Woodcock Saloon and Dining Rooms, where "all the delicacies of the season, with Oysters from the Atlantic and Pacific, terrapin and games of all kinds" could be found both day and night.[51] Perley's fame as a lawyer in the Far West and the dearth of great advocates in Salt Lake City all but guaranteed that the party would be well attended. The guests at this "sociable affair" included the commander of federal troops at Camp Douglas and other military officers, and Chief Justice McKean.[52] It's likely that Fitch was present as well, despite his poor relations with the Chief Justice and his very public criticism of the man. Whether Perley thought well of the Chief Justice isn't known, though he wasn't one to pass up an opportunity to befriend a person in power and begin developing a relationship. Certainly, they had one great thing in common: a profound desire to advance the exploitation of Utah's mineral wealth.

Perley's establishment in Salt Lake City made news in California by mid-January, when a number of papers reported his relocation for the purpose of practicing his profession.[53] Among his first cases in the Territory was the defense, with George C. Bates, of the accused murderer William Lawless in a mining camp at a place called Ophir. With mining, it seems, came all the notorious sins that the Prophet warned against. It was no drunken gambling dispute, however, that gave rise to the matter, but an affair of the heart, engaged in by Lawless with respect to the sister of fellow miner George "Doc" Snively.[54] The day before the incident, Snively had driven Lawless from his home after finding him there. Instead of dedicating himself to the Lord's rest and contemplating the works of His hands, Lawless entered a saloon on a Sunday evening. Spying Snively warming himself beside a fire, Lawless cried "you son of a b---h, I've got you at last," drew a pistol and opened fire. The bullet struck as Snively simultaneously drew his own weapon and shouted "Don't shoot!" Thinking the pistol might fire at any moment, Lawless leapt at the mortally wounded man and fell to the ground with him. Lawless was arraigned in the probate court in

---

[51] Edward L. Sloan, *Gazeteer of Utah and Salt Lake City Director* (Salt Lake City: Salt Lake Herald Publishing Company, 1874), at p. 323.

[52] *Salt Lake Herald-Republican*, December 31, 1873.

[53] *Sacramento Daily Union*, January 12, 1874; and *Sentinel*, January 17, 1874.

[54] *Salt Lake Herald-Republican*, February 17, 1874.

Toole County, whereupon the two sides set to work subpoenaing twenty to thirty witnesses to appear at trial. Ultimately, Perley and Bates were able to convince the jury to convict on the lesser offense of manslaughter.[55] In the wake of the trial, neither the friends of Snively nor those of Lawless were satisfied with either the prosecutor or the defense.[56] The killer's own friends, it was said, believed he got off easy.[57]

The reliance on probate courts for the trial of civil and criminal matters was a consequence of the continuing disarray of the court system of the Territory of Utah. The virtual shutting down of the District Courts by Chief Justice McKean several years earlier stymied the resolution of disputes in mining and other fields, and deterred formation of a commitment to a culture of law and order. Every day additional actions were filed, only to join a growing backlog of unresolved and un-litigated matters. In meeting with fellow members of the Bar, Perley reached the conclusion that a petition directed to Congress for the purpose of urging that body to enact a law to organize the court system and allocate jurisdiction to this or that tribunal was imperative. "In the utter confusion and obstruction into which the administration of justice has fallen here," he and his fellow lawyers wrote, "on account of the vices and defects of local legislation, as well as on account of questions of jurisdiction, persons accused of crime cannot be brought to trial and civil causes involving property worth millions of dollars, are pending, with no means of bringing them to determination."[58] The probate courts had assumed general jurisdiction in the absence of any lawful grant of authority, but even where they managed to resolve legal disputes, the lack of any reliance on precedent rendered these determinations utterly worthless as guides through the growing and recorded body of common law. The publication of the petition generated criticism and a defense of the existing system.

---

[55] *Salt Lake Herald-Republican*, March 12, 1874; and *Salt Lake Herald-Republican*, March 21, 1874.

[56] *Salt Lake Herald-Republican*, March 21, 1874.

[57] Believing a better outcome was possible, his lawyers brought a writ of habeas corpus before chief Justice McKean. The Chief Justice discharged Lawless from the judgment of the probate, but ordered him to answer in the District Court. See *Salt Lake Herald-Republican*, November 24, 1874.

[58] *Deseret News*, March 11, 1874.

The probate courts, it was said, exercised jurisdiction in accordance with Territorial law; while the dormant District Courts might in fact be able to operate if only money were appropriated by the Legislature to pay petit and grand jurors.[59] Several attempts at reform had actually passed the Legislature by a wide margin, but met their end at the tip of the Governor's veto pen. "Most of these are professional gentlemen," said one critic of Perley and his fellow petitioners, "and I submit that they ought to be acquainted with these facts before making such assertions."[60]

To such criticism, Perley likely paid no heed on account of the press of business. His partnership with Carter, apparently a temporary measure to assist him in gaining a foothold in the region, ended after a short time, and he established a new office on First South Street, a few doors east of the headquarters of the *Herald-Republican*. The press spoke well of him at the time, referring to him as "an attorney of acknowledged ability," with "long experience as a mining lawyer in Nevada and California, where he gained an enviable reputation."[61] The advancement of cases through the life cycle of litigation, slow as it was at this time, necessitated his admission to the Territorial Supreme Court. This development must have pleased the Chief Justice, who surely had read the recent petition, signed by Perley, praising the jurist for his having "discharged the trust with such fidelity, boldness and impartiality as to inspire to see the supremacy of the law and its faithful execution in Utah," and calling for his reappointment by the President, lest there be "great rejoicing among those who oppose a faithful execution of the laws."[62] After much castigation from Fitch and the Mormons, a kind word was most welcome to the Honorable Mr. McKean, and likely wouldn't negatively prejudice Perley once any case of his came before the High Court.

Perley's mining interests also advanced. In Cottonwood, south of Salt Lake City, the tunnel of the Wellington Perley Mine, under the management of P. Page and Josiah Sampson, reached 500 feet in length, allowing access to "the token of wealth displayed by the

---

59 *Millennial Star*, April 14, 1874.

60 Id.

61 *Salt Lake Herald-Republican*, May 9, 1874.

62 *Deseret News*, May 13, 1874; and *Deseret News*, May 5, 1874.

immense bodies of ore."[63] A short distance from the mouth of the tunnel was sunk a discovery shaft forty feet in depth, and from it a level running along the ledge another 120 feet "showing a continuous body of ore the entire distance." The vein was said to have been well defined, with an average width of four feet, and from which a large amount of ore had been raised. That Perley had an interest in the operation seems apparent from the name of the mine, though it's possible, too, that the owners named it in honor of the famous lawyer, whose services perhaps they retained.

Perley's extended family appeared to be similarly flourishing. The children of his cousin James were marrying and having children of their own. His cousin Frederick continued in the cultivation of the grape. His nephew and namesake still managed the Steptoe Ranch, though he'd been brutally attacked by an enraged and severely drunken ranch hand.[64] Another man came to young Perley's aid and attempted to get the attacker outdoors. The attacker grabbed a large butcher knife and stabbed the man, causing death almost immediately. The tragedy did nothing to deter the fortunes of Perley's venture in the Valley, as the acreage cultivated "greatly exceeds former years, and a large yield is expected," while the cattle were doing well "despite the cold weather."[65] The best news of all was the arrival of Perley's cousin—referred to as his niece—Frederica McKinstry Hazen, for the purpose of joining his former law partner, Henry Rives, in matrimony. The two obviously made acquaintance with one another through Perley's agency. Either one had come to visit the locale of the other, or vice versa, and discovered during the sojourn a special form of chemistry not to be resisted. "To the worthy bridegroom, with whose friendship we have long been favored," announced the *Pioche Daily Record*, "we offer our sincere congratulations on his good fortune in winning so fair and sweet a bride, and to her on being united with so honorable and gallant a gentleman. To both we offer our most sincere and unaffected wishes for their unalloyed happiness, and that their married life may know but few of the sorrows with which

---

[63] "Our little Cottonwood Letter," *Salt Lake Herald-Republican*, June 6, 1874.
[64] *Gold Hill Daily News*, March 24, 1874.
[65] *Eureka Daily Sentinel*, May 19, 1874; and *Pioche Daily Record*, March 4, 1874.

this mortal life is checkered. To the bride and bride-groom we again say health and happiness."[66]

Some might have concluded that the sale by Perley to Rives of a portion of his stake in the Rancho Sausalito for a mere $5,000 was intended as a gift, though the reconveyance by Rives to James Ben Ali Haggin for the same amount not long afterward suggests a straw man transfer, possibly to repay a debt, possibly arising from the Hermes matter, and performed in a manner calculated to obscure the fact that Perley and Haggin were still in business together.[67] Some might have considered the conveyance worthless given how much litigation had occurred over the Rancho without a conclusive resolution. Perley may have sensed otherwise as the matter was at last before the Supreme Court and a decision was pending. The matter, it shall be recalled, had its origins in the mid-1850s, when William Richardson reached out to Volney Howard regarding the heavily encumbered Rancho Sausalito, comprising three square leagues in Southern Marin, and containing what is now Mill Valley, Sausalito and Lime Point. Richardson retained Howard to secure confirmation of his grants, as well as to devise a plan to manage the enormous estate. After Howard brought his then partner Perley into the case, the two men advised Richardson to convey the property "to some business man who had the capacity to manage it, in order to have the encumbrances paid off, and to save some portion of it."[68] The man they recommended was S. R. Throckmorton of San Francisco. In an agreement entered into in 1855, Throckmorton was to "sell so much of the land as he deemed necessary to pay all debts which were a lien on the property, and should sell the land [within] three years, and pay the grantors one-fifth of all proceeds over and above what was required to pay all debts and his own expenses and expenses of litigation."[69] In turn, Howard and Perley, as attorneys for the estate, were to conduct and manage the legal part of the business arising out of and connected with the property, and were "to commence and conduct all suits in law or equity, which may be necessary or proper, in order to set aside or remove any of the encumbrances now existing against

---

66 *Pioche Daily Record*, April 9, 1874.

67 *Marin Journal*, April 9, 1874; and *Marin Journal*, September 10, 1874.

68 *Howard & Perley v. Throckmorton et al.* (1874) 48 Cal. 482.

69 Id.

the...property, or any part thereof."[70] In around 1857, Howard and Perley conveyed an undivided half of their interest to E. L. Goold, and charged Goold with undertaking the lion's share of the legal duties on behalf of the estate.

In 1868, the litigation involving the estate appeared to be at an end and the estate remained largely intact. Throckmorton had begun to develop the massive property, and had even made money conveying portions of it to the U.S. Government, a land development company and a railroad entrepreneur. He'd received $400,000 through these sales, but still retained possession of another sixteen thousand acres. Aware that the estate's financial stability had been achieved, Howard and Perley literally confronted Throckmorton in the street and demanded payment of their share of the recent revenues. Stating initially that he considered the contract between them "dead long ago," Throckmorton soon recognized the deadly earnestness of the two attorneys and requested that they be patient until Goold returned to the West Coast from the nation's capital. Exasperated over the delay, the two men said they would forebear suing for the time being only if paid the small sum of $2,500. At this Throckmorton balked, though he did provide the financially strained Perley with $300 as a goodwill gesture. Bizarrely, instead of giving Perley the money directly, he asked him to draw a check on the Fireman's Fund Insurance Company, despite Perley having no account there.[71] As ridiculous as it was, he did it nevertheless, and the Fireman's Fund cashed it, apparently at Throckmorton's request.

After numerous promises to resolve the dispute went unfulfilled, the disgruntled lawyers sued in the District Court in Marin County to obtain an accounting and for an order for specific performance. The matter was continued to the March term of 1869, and, then, on stipulation, continued a second time to July.[72] Pushed out yet again to November, the Plaintiffs reconsidered the framing of their case and sought leave at this late date to amend the pleadings. When leave was granted, they stipulated with

---

[70] Id.

[71] *Howard & Perley v. Throckmorton*, California State Archives, Supreme Court Records, Supreme Court Civil Case Files, San Francisco Office, 1850-1960, Case No. 3637.

[72] *Marin Journal*, November 21, 1868; and *Marin Journal*, July 10, 1869.

Throckmorton to continue the matter even further.[73] The filing of the amended complaint evoked a demurrer that landed on the court's law and motion calendar in March of 1870.[74] Predictably, the hearing on the demurrer was continued, again on stipulation.[75] The issue was at last submitted on briefs in November for decision by Judge William Wallace, even as related matters proceeded apace, including one brought against Throckmorton by the Richardson heirs.[76] The matter still wasn't resolved in March of 1871, when it was yet again continued.[77] In the Fall, the case at last appeared on the brink of resolution, and the *Journal* declared its readiness to "publish a full report in our next…of the matter of *Perley & Howard v. Samuel R. Throckmorton,* in which the plaintiffs sue to recover a portion of the Sausalito property."[78] These intentions proved overly optimistic as the matter was continued a final time into December.

Overseen by Perley's old adversary Alexander Campbell, Throckmorton's defense was that Perley and Howard had abandoned their duties hence were owed nothing, that the amount received from the various sales was far less than $400,000, and was for lands that fell outside the bounds of the estate in which Perley and Howard alleged an interest. At the commencement of the trial, Perley testified that he and "General Howard" were partners operating as Howard & Perley in 1855 when they entered into a professional relationship with Mr. Richardson with respect to the Sausalito property. "It was," he said, "vastly incumbered with judgments and debt, liens and mortgages and claims of various kinds. We found it totally impossible for him to extricate the estate and deemed it advisable for his own interest to have some business-like man to manage it; some man of greater energy, greater capacity and talent to carry on such an estate."[79] From the time that Throckmorton came on board to exercise this role, until Perley's partnership with Howard ended in 1857 or 1858, he attested that "I

[73] *Marin Journal,* November 20, 1869.

[74] *Marin Journal,* March 5, 1870.

[75] *Marin Journal,* March 12, 1870.

[76] *Marin Journal,* November 26, 1870.

[77] *Marin Journal,* March 4, 1871; and *Marin Journal,* March 11, 1871.

[78] *Marin Journal,* November 25, 1871.

[79] *Howard & Perley v. Throckmorton,* California State Archives, Supreme Court Records, Supreme Court Civil Case Files, San Francisco Office, 1850-1960, Case No. 3637.

had attended personally with Mr. Howard to all the duties of every kind arising under this contract. I was over [frequently] to...San Rafael and other places, attending to everything that required my attention." What specifically he did for the estate, he couldn't recall with specificity after the passage of so many years, though he identified the Barton Ricketson suit as particularly memorable. What was far clearer to him was that "there was a great deal of litigation during these 3 or 4 years that I acted, requiring almost incessant attention at every term of the court," sometimes accompanied by Howard, sometimes not. When he wasn't in court, he was meeting with Richardson, or engaged in "methodical plottings and scheming [over] how to evade all the debts of the estate and to extricate it from the debts impending over it in order to perform our part of this contract. The whole fight was for delay and staving off judgment under mortgages and other things."

Even after he assigned certain of his rights to Goold, Perley continued to work on the case. When Goold complained "that a great deal of the work was falling on him, more than the proper amount of it, and that I ought to do something as compensation out of my part of this fee," Perley told him "that I was willing to divide the fee with him." Throckmorton, he said, was pleased with the arrangement given the quality of Goold's work and never denied Perley's enduring stake. Indeed, Throckmorton continued to consult with Perley on estate matters, to update him on the estate's affairs and the progress of the various litigations. These updates continued even after his removal to Virginia City in the fall of 1862, almost always during his many visits to San Francisco. He may have only appeared once in court for the estate during this time, but he was ever "ready and able and willing to perform services whenever asked."

During the next morning, in the moments before resumption of proceedings, Perley attempted to review a mass of papers brought into court by Throckmorton as potential exhibits. He found the documents in such disarray "that it would take a man a whole day to sort them out." From the chaotic mess he pulled a number of papers relating to the Barton Ricketson matter drafted by himself back in 1860 and recalled that he "did everything in [the case] that Mr. Throckmorton wished me to do personally." Other records, relating to other cases, were absent, particularly from the Jardin

Mathieson & Company case and another prosecuted in the U.S. Circuit Court. Lack of a complete file of cases available for his review repeatedly stymied his testimony. "It will," he reiterated, "be wholly impossible for me to go into the details of the services rendered during this long time. It is too long a time."

On cross-examination by Alexander Campbell, Perley admitted he didn't actually try the Ricketson case; rather, he only argued the demurrer before Judge McKinstry and drafted and filed the answer and amended answer. He repeatedly blanked when asked for the names of any other cases on which he worked, but expressed confidence that his recollection could be refreshed if only the case files could be found. Understanding that his testimony was not without holes, he finally lost his temper when Campbell waxed skeptical over his insistence that he met with Throckmorton on a regular basis at any time during the early 1860s. When asked where these meeting took place, Perley excitedly replied "in the street, everyplace. I can't specify any particular place." His discomfort was all the more obvious when asked how long he would stay whenever he supposedly came to the City to deal with estate matters. Exasperated, he finally said he was as anxious to "get away from this place" back then as he was now, hence not particularly mindful of details after the fact.

Both Howard and Goold were helpful in confirming Perley's account and filling in a number of the gaps his testimony exhibited. When Throckmorton followed them on the stand, his testimony all but confirmed the merits of the Plaintiffs' case. He credited Perley with resolving several outstanding mortgages in 1855 and 1856, enjoining a decree issued in favor of another creditor and protecting the homestead itself from liquidation. When auctions occurred to sell off foreclosed portions of the estate, Howard was there on one occasion to place the winning bid, and Perley on another. "Rapid moves" made by counsel, he said, won the day and forced a number of parties to compromise their claims. Perley and Howard might have pulled off the miraculous had not the President vetoed the bill authorizing the $200,000 payment for the Lime Point track. It was at that point, however, that Perley disappeared. From 1862 to 1868, Throckmorton saw and heard nothing of the man. Given what he characterized as Perley's open and obvious abandonment of the contract, he was quite surprised when Perley showed up again in

1868 demanding payment of his share of the proceeds of the recent sales.

Throckmorton's defense turned in part on Perley's alleged disappearance, hence unavailability as counsel during the estate's time of need in the early and mid-1860s. Perley, of course, was in Washoe for part of that time, but even in the midst of intensive mining litigation he managed to return frequently to the City to tend to his affairs, both legal and romantic. Examining Throckmorton himself, Perley went to the heart of the matter by asking how he could have considered the contract abandoned "when you knew I had given Mr. Goold a part of my fee, at your request, to carry on this business?" When Throckmorton characterized Goold as Perley's "substitute" rather than as his agent or partner, Perley chided the man for "quibbling" over the meaning of the term. To Throckmorton's contention that Perley was nowhere to be found during the key period of time, Perley pointed out that he kept an office on the corner of Kearney and Sacramento Streets, and that Throckmorton might have contacted him either there or in Virginia City, where his location was well known. To Throckmorton's explanation that he never talked to him on the street about his needs nor wrote to him in Virginia City, Perley expressed wonder that he didn't since they met so many times and he was at most a mere two days journey away whenever he happened to be in Nevada. A man who truly needed counsel wouldn't have thought twice about requesting it.

Once the testimony ended and both sides rested, Judge Wallace took the matter under advisement. On December 15, 1871, he issued his ruling in Perley's and Howard's favor and referred the matter to a special master to complete the accounting of what was due.[80] Once the judgment incorporated the precise debt owed and was entered into the record, what Perley and Howard had won became clear: "about $34,000 gold, and an undivided interest, amounting to 2,600 acres, in the unsold, or the western and northern part of the original rancho," including the heights of Mt. Tamalpais, containing "a large amount of rock and chaparral, attractive to the lover of wild nature, but not of much value to the grain farmer, nor even to the owner of

80 *Marin Journal*, December 16, 1871; and *Marin Journal*, December 23, 1871.

horses, neat cattle or sheep."[81] Perhaps seeing the potential the land had for future development, and of course resenting having to share the proceeds of the land with two do-nothing lawyers who'd let Goold do all the work, Throckmorton brought a motion requesting a new trial on the grounds of "irregularity in proceedings and abuse of discretion, accident and surprise which ordinary prudence could not guard against, newly discovered evidence [and] error in law."[82] Though argued and submitted in July of 1872, it wasn't until November that Judge Wallace issued a ruling denying the request.[83] Reasoning that the assignment of their obligations to Goold was hardly improper, noting that Goold had actually performed all of the duties originally assumed by Perley and Howard, and observing that Throckmorton had accepted and availed himself of those services, a decree in the Plaintiffs' favored seemed eminently just.[84]

The extended procedural history of the case hinted that the end of the matter was not really the end. The case appeared on the Supreme Court's February, 1873 calendar, and was to be argued in April by Doyle & Barber, Alexander Campbell and W. H. Patterson for the Appellant, and Perley and Howard in pro se.[85] A stipulated continuance moved it to a November 4 hearing date, with Joseph P. Hoge taking the absent Perley's place as co-counsel with Howard.[86] One last continuance pushed it one more day, from the 4th of November to the 5th.[87] When at last the arguments were presented, Campbell and Patterson contended that as a contract for personal service of the kind entered into by Perley and Howard cannot be compelled through an order of the Court, the principle of mutuality precluded a similar order being imposed on Throckmorton.[88] They acknowledged that with respect to this rule, as with so many others,

---

[81] *Daily Alta California*, August 16, 1874.

[82] *Howard & Perley v. Throckmorton*, Supreme Court Case File, Case No. 3637

[83] *Marin Journal*, July 13, 1872; and *Marin Journal*, November 30, 1872.

[84] *Howard & Perley v. Throckmorton et al.* (1874) 48 Cal. 482, 489.

[85] *Sacramento Daily Union*, February 11, 1873; and *Sacramento Daily Union*, April 8, 1873.

[86] "The Courts," *Sacramento Daily Union*, April 29, 1873; and *Sacramento Daily Journal*, November 4, 1873.

[87] *Sacramento Daily Union*, November 5, 1873; and *Marin Journal*, November 6, 1873.

[88] *Howard & Perley v. Throckmorton* (1874) 48 Cal. 482.

exceptions existed, including when strict performance on one side has occurred. Perley and Howard, however, hardly strictly performed on the contract as they had delegated their duties to Goold. On his and Perley's behalf, Howard countered with the argument that lack of mutuality was never raised in the Answer, hence was no defense now. Lack of complete performance by Perley and Howard also was not an effective defense, since courts sitting in equity were only admonished to withhold a decree of specific performance where no performance on the part of the aggrieved party had occurred. When performance by the party seeking the decree has been substantial, the equity of the situation was far stronger. "After thirteen years' services under a contract, it is too late to set up the want of mutuality, because it would be a fraud."[89]

It wasn't until August that the Supreme Court ruled by affirming the lower court's decision.[90] Justice Rhodes summarized Judge Wallace's findings of fact and concluded that there was evidence to sustain them.[91] The contract, it was true, had not been fully performed by Perley and Howard, but substantial performance had occurred, and this was sufficient to allow for a decree of specific performance to issue against the other party. Surely Throckmorton had testified at the trial that he considered the contract abandoned by Perley and Howard, "but it is," said Rhodes, "by no means clear that Howard and Perley so intended," and the facts from the record supported a conclusion that no abandonment had transpired.[92]

Wondering at the twenty-year history of the matter, the *Alta* noted that the final decision was "not without public interest in several respects," including the involvement of famous lawyers and the fact that its subject matter was the fabulous Richardson patrimony. The land itself, however, might not have been worth all the trouble in the wake of the purchase of the best portions by the U.S. Government, the Sausalito Company and the railroad builders, "leaving only a small iron-bound frontage on the Pacific" and the

---

89 Id.

90 *Daily Alta California*, August 11, 1874; and *Sacramento Daily Union*, August 11, 1874.

91 *Howard & Perley v. Throckmorton et al* (1874) 48 Cal. 482, 489.

92 Id., at 490.

bear and deer infested country around and including Mount Tamalpais.[93]

The apparent end of the litigation must surely have come as good news to Perley and promised a tremendous windfall for him in the nearly $20,000 in gold and future profits from a sizeable interest in the vast Richardson Estate. Illness likely dampened his ability to fully enjoy the outcome, distracted him from the development of his ranch in the Steptoe Valley and impaired his pursuit of his law practice in Utah. What his illness was isn't known. He'd been laid up several times in the past few years; once in the weeks preceding the commencement of the Hermes trial, and another while the trial itself was proceeding. Reports were many that it was "lingering" in nature, meaning it had been contracted at some past date and worsened over time, rather than being the result of recent inception in Salt Lake City, as was stated by the editor of the *Pioche Daily Record*.[94] A Salt Lake City paper revealed that "he was sick here prior to his leaving for the Bay, and his visit there, he thought, would soon revive his shattered health."[95] What the Bay Area offered with respect to amelioration of adverse health conditions depends, of course, on the nature of the disease. The attack he suffered during the Hermes trial while speaking, and his need to forego making closing arguments, suggests a respiratory or throat related ailment, or some form of what was called phthisis. For such ailments, the best medical advice of the era recommended long travel only for those whose health was still not severely compromised. "Cases of rapidly progressing disease, especially with diffused infiltration on both sides, and considerable fever, are…to be excluded," while those suffering "attacks of intercurrent pneumonia, bronchitis, or pleurisy, with notable rise of temperature, should be kept at home."[96] Perley obviously was intent on leaving, and being a man of tremendous will, even advanced ill health was no barrier. The one thing the Bay offered

---

[93] *Daily Alta California*, August 16, 1874.

[94] See *Los Angeles Daily Herald*, September 9, 1874; *Marysville Daily Appeal*, September 9, 1874; *Sacramento Daily Union*, September 9, 1874; *Weekly Nevada State Journal*, September 12, 1874; and *Pioche Daily Record*, September 9, 1874.

[95] *Salt Lake Herald Republican*, September 11, 1874.

[96] I. Burney Yeo, *A Manual of Medical Treatment or Clinical Therapeutics*, Fourth Edition, Volume II (London: Cassell and Company, Limited, 1895), at p. 110.

absent from the Great Basin was an illusion of the absolute purity of the air, blown in coolly and steadily throughout all seasons of the year from the seemingly illimitable sea. A pure atmosphere, whether humid or cool, was considered of great ameliorative effect for those suffering from respiratory diseases, and whether remission of symptoms was the goal, or modest arrest of the disease's progress, or mere maintenance of the status quo, it was recommended that the patient be "where the last years of the patient's life may be made as pleasant and comfortable to him as circumstances will permit."[97] And quite apart from the climate, there was the thought that a change of location might place the patient in closer proximity to superior hygienic conditions… and…the means of obtaining a generous nutritious, and varied dietary, and suitable medical supervision."[98]

A more serious ailment was also afoot, though the periodic coughing fits may have distracted Perley from the threat it posed his life. His tendency over the years to indulge in savory meals and strong drink did not accord well with the real needs of his body. The ailment was gastro-enteritis, or an "acute inflammation of the bowels," that was generally thought by medical people at the time to originate either in some morbid condition of the stomach or intestine, or from "some mechanical injury" such as "strangulated hernia, intussusception, the impaction of gall-stones and other foreign bodies, and intestinal stricture."[99] Its principal symptoms included something resembling dysentery, very often beginning "in the upper bowel, or stomach, and spreading thence downwards," until it "gradually traverses the whole length of the intestinal canal, causing in its progress uneasiness, aching, and griping—frequently attended with nausea and sickness while the inflammation is still high up, with diarrhea and expulsive pains and efforts when it reaches the large intestine."[100] The tongue often became "furred and dry, the breath offensive, and the appetite impaired." Vomiting,

---

[97] Id., at pp. 110-111.

[98] Id.

[99] John Syer Bristowe, *Treatise on the Theory and Practice of Medicine* (London: Smith, Elder, & Co., 1880), at pp. 617-618. That he suffered from this condition is evident from the record of his death, set forth in San Francisco Area Funeral Home Records, 1835-1979, which can be accessed at www.familysearch.org.

[100] Bristowe, op. cit., at p. 619.

abdominal pain, hiccoughing in the extreme, distension of the belly, flatus, rapid pulse and alternating heat and cold spells were also common. The general approach to managing the underlying ailment was to relieve pain by preventing movements of the bowels and avoidance of the urge to force the bowels by the administration of purgatives. The most valuable resource in treatment of the condition was said to be "opium in large and frequent doses, best administered by subcutaneous injection."[101] Enemata of warm water, applications of ice, hydrocyanic acid, bismuth, and hot and cold compresses and even the occasional blood-letting were thought to be of varying efficacy as well.

His properties long gone, including his beloved Bird's Nest, Perley checked into the luxurious Cosmopolitan Hotel on the corner of Sansome and Bush Streets. The City was one he'd not been too long absent from since his arrival in California a quarter century before, hence it wasn't an unfamiliar place, nor bereft of friends, nor memories of loved ones long gone. For all its attractions and meaningful associations, however, he would not long enjoy his time in the City; for death came rather suddenly in the early morning of the 7th of September. Upon the discovery of his passing, the news quickly spread. His death was reported in summary fashion in numerous papers, as if he were the most humble of souls, unknown to the vast majority of humanity.[102] Other papers reported his death in an even more threadbare manner.[103] The *San Francisco Evening Bulletin* recalled that he had been Judge Terry's law partner, and noted that death occurred at 2 o'clock that very morning.[104] The *Stockton Independent* reported the same information, but recalled that he "was one of the early lawyers of this State and was a man who possessed talent of a high order." He was, it believed, "in early days…a law partner of Judge Terry of this City."[105] The *Lyon County Times* in Nevada referred to him as "a noted lawyer."[106] The *Marin*

---

[101] Id., at p. 622.

[102] *Los Angeles Daily Herald*, September 9, 1874; *Marysville Daily Appeal*, September 9, 1874; *Sacramento Daily Union*, September 9, 1874; and *Weekly Nevada State Journal*, September 12, 1874.

[103] *Sacramento Bee*, September 10, 1874; *Elko Independent*, September 12, 1874; *Territorial Enterprise*, September 12, 1874.

[104] *San Francisco Evening Bulletin*, September 8, 1874.

[105] *Stockton Independent*, September 9, 1874.

[106] *Lyon County Times*, September 10, 1874.

Journal cited his death, and referred to him as "a somewhat noted lawyer," and added that "he was the cause of the Terry-Broderick duel."[107] A Marysville paper stated that Perley "has been notable in this State for many things, but principally for having been the apparent moving cause for the Broderick-Terry duel."[108] "He was the sole instigator, but let it pass. His error lies entombed with him."[109] With a smile no doubt on his face as he recalled the Fall and Josie Mansfield incidents, the editor of the *Golden Era* wrote "many amusing anecdotes might be related of this modern Don Juan, did not the sanctity of the grave forbid."[110] *The Red Bluff Independent*, which had followed Perley's more ridiculous antics over the years, conceded that he was well known, but incorrectly stated he was "the second of Terry in the Broderick duel," as did the *Russian River Flag*.[111] *The San Francisco Daily Post* repeated the tale that he was Judge Terry's second, and reminded the readers that the duel resulted in Senator Broderick's death.[112] The *Chronicle* also noticed Perley's demise, but corrected the other papers' report of his role as Terry's second. "Terry's seconds on that occasion were Dr. Aylette and Calhoun Benham," it announced, but added that "Perley had a great deal to do with inciting the duel." The paper then recounted how "some months before the fatal event, Perley took some defense at some remarks about Terry made by Sen. Broderick and sent a challenge, which Broderick declined on the ground that the challenger was beneath his station." As Broderick would not fight Perley, Terry determined to demand satisfaction himself. He resigned his post as a member of the Supreme Court and sent Broderick his challenge, which Broderick accepted, thus sealing his fate.[113] The *San Francisco Daily Examiner* went further, explaining that "Mr. Perley achieved a sudden notoriety many years ago on account of his connection with the Broderick-Terry duel, which had its immediate origins in an altercation in regard to Judge Terry, at

---

107 *Marin Journal*, September 10, 1874.

108 *Marysville Daily Appeal*, September 10, 1874.

109 Id.

110 *The Golden Era*, September 13, 1874.

111 *Red Bluff Independent*, September 12, 1874; and *Russian River Flag*, September 17, 1874.

112 *San Francisco Daily Post*, September 8, 1874.

113 *San Francisco Chronicle*, September 9, 1874.

the dinner-table of the old International on Jackson Street, between Senator Broderick and Perley."[114] The paper further noted his removal to Nevada and partnership with Ambassador DeLong, and that he "was always esteemed a good lawyer." A summary was given of the fortune he made in Washoe and lost elsewhere, his modest life in San Francisco, and then his crossing of the Sierras a second time to find success in White Pine and Pioche, reaping a great "harvest in the large field of litigation there resulting from the conflicting titles to the then rich mines of that treasure trove." He was, concluded the paper, "a singular man in many points of character and some of his eccentricities were the subject of much comment at various times, but he was, also, as his friends always insisted, possessed of good human traits, and also decided force of intellect."[115] Oddly, the *Alta*, which had taken a great interest in him from the time of his arrival in California, made the barest of references to his passing.[116] The next day, a slightly more elaborate notice appeared, with a rare reference to his New Brunswick nativity and the date, time and location of his funeral.[117]

In reporting his death, the *Salt Lake Herald-Republican* said the "deceased had an enviable reputation as a brilliant lawyer. He was engaged in nearly all of the great mining suits that have taken place on the Pacific slope, and became profoundly proficient in that branch of the law, having few equals and no superiors as a mining attorney. As a companion he was genial and versatile. His memory served as a storehouse for all things written or known of men. Liberal, kind and gentlemanly, he was perhaps alone, too negligent of his own prosperity. He will be missed at our bar, and we feel convinced the attorneys of our city, as well as his friends, will deplore his early death."[118]

His native New Brunswick, in time, learned of his passing. "California and Nevada papers have announced the death of Hon. D. W. Perley," reported the *Telegraph* in late November.[119] The *Telegraph* and the *Carlton Sentinel* ran the approbation and brevities

---

[114] *San Francisco Daily Examiner*, September 9, 1874.

[115] Id.

[116] *Daily Alta California*, September 9, 1874.

[117] *Daily Alta California*, September 10, 1874.

[118] *Salt Lake Herald-Republican*, September 11, 1874.

[119] *St. John Daily Telegraph*, November 30, 1874.

printed in Nevada papers, noted his relationship to provincial politicians William E. and Charles Perley, and recalled his visit to the Province a few years earlier.[120] Back in Nevada, *The Eureka Daily Sentinel* was most emotive in its comments on Perley's death. "Poor Perley!," its editor wrote, "a man of generous, quick impulses, learned in classic lore; ready, it is true, to anger, but withal possessing a heart as tender and sympathetic as a woman. He was clear and logical as an advocate; subtle in analysis, and with a noble brain. He had strong friends and bitter enemies, and none, even of the latter, will deny him the possession of pre-eminent abilities, which he ever exerted in the interest of his clients. He was well known throughout the whole of Nevada and particularly in the eastern portion of the State."[121] The editor recalled his recent "triumphant vindication at the hands of an intelligent jury, at Pioche, after the long, tedious and acrimonious Raymond & Ely-Hermes litigation," and how, in being "pursued as he was with all the venom of an overwhelming local power, he had the moral courage to brave it all, and, like a lion at bay, he turned upon his persecutors."[122] "Peace to his ashes," the paper concluded. "May the turf rest lightly upon all that was mortal of one whom his intimates know only to love, honor and respect, whilst his enemies knew that in him they had a 'foeman worthy of their steel.'"[123]

In Pioche, a simple notice appeared on page 2 of the local paper, repeating what other media had printed, but was followed on page 3 by a far more extensive obituary.

> We most sincerely, regret to have to announce the death of this distinguished gentleman, which occurred yesterday morning at San Francisco. For nearly twenty-five years, Mr. Perley occupied a prominent position in the very front rank of the legal profession on this coast. He was not only remarkable for his professional ability and legal attainments, but also for a vast fund of general information, conspicuous amidst which was his taste for and knowledge of literature. Possessed of a wonderful memory, keen perception and fastidious taste, he brought to his legal and literary studies

[120] *Carleton Sentinel*, December 5, 1874.
[121] *Eureka Daily Sentinel*, September 9, 1874.
[122] Id.
[123] Id.

> talents of no ordinary character. Being animated with a thirst for knowledge and determination to master all difficulties, he gathered vast stores of information, which he dispensed with much tact and conversational power, rendering his society most agreeable, much sought after and highly prized. His untimely and unlooked for death leaves a gap in the profession and society that will not easily be supplied. The deceased was a native of Nova Scotia. In 1840 he went to Texas from whence in 1849 he removed to California, where his brilliant talents and genial social qualities were soon acknowledged, and placed him on the high road to fame and fortune. Ever fond of change and adventure, in 1862, he went to Virginia City, where he also acquired a very lucrative practice. In 1868 he removed to White Pine, and in 1870 settled in Pioche, where he remained until 1873. He afterwards went to Salt Lake, where he contracted the illness from which he died in San Francisco. He was never married, but leaves several near relatives, who will deeply deplore the loss of so kind and affectionate a protector. In their grief a very large circle of friends and acquaintances will most unfeignedly participate. To his relatives and friends we wish to offer our most respectful sympathy, and with them mourn the loss of a sincere friend whose great talents and acquirements and kindly nature bound him to all with no ordinary ties.[124]

The following day, the paper corrected itself by noting "we were incorrect in saying that he was never married. He was, but his wife died many years since; also his only child, a daughter, who we are informed, was remarkable for her grace and beauty."[125] Utterly unremembered was his long-departed son, George; for so little a time had he spent on the earth, and so long ago, that no one still living recalled his former presence. The sensitive Perley undoubtedly remembered him throughout his life from the time of the baby boy's birth, and acutely so, no doubt, as the end of his own days on earth came closer and reunion with the departed neared.

---

[124] "D. W. Perley," *Pioche Daily Record*, September 9, 1874; and *Gold Hill Daily News*, September 12, 1874.

[125] *Pioche Daily Record*, September 10, 1874.

His funeral occurred on Thursday, the 10th of September, at 11 o'clock at the Church of the Advent on Howard Street.[126] His casket was then conveyed up into the hills and through the gates of Lone Mountain Cemetery. The casket was interred in Vault No. 3, Lot 85, along the so-called Thistle Path, where his wife and daughter had previously been laid to rest.[127] Their earthly remains would repose there together for another sixty years, until removed by order of the People of San Francisco and cast into a collective grave in Colma. In that great charnel heap, their bones mixed with those of David Broderick, William Gwin, E. D. Baker, William Stewart, James King of William, Hall McAllister, Joseph P. Hoge, A. P. Crittenden, and so many others whose stories have intersected with the one told in the pages of this volume.

In Stockton, the trial of *Watrous vs. Fancher* was unable to go forward as scheduled due to the fact that "D.S. Terry, Esq., was necessarily detained in San Francisco attending the funeral of D. W. Perley."[128] A continuance was granted, but only on condition that the Plaintiff pay the costs incurred by Defendant on account of the delay.[129]

Two weeks after Perley's death, when the District Court in Pioche convened, resolutions drafted by Jesse Pitzer, W. W. Bishop and J. C. Foster were presented as a tribute of respect to Perley's memory, and entered into the minutes of the proceedings before the Court adjourned early that day in honor of the late counsellor at law.

> Whereas, it has pleased an all wise Creator to lay the hand of death on our esteemed friend D.W. Perley, and
>
> Whereas, in death the bar of this State has lost one of its brightest ornaments, and its members have been deprived of the society of a genial spirit, a talented associate who, while living, was alike urbane to the most unsuccessful as well as the most favored of the profession. And

---

126 *Daily Alta California*, September 10, 1874.
127 San Francisco Area Funeral Home Records, 1835-1979, www.familysearch.org.
128 *Stockton Independent*, September 11, 1874.
129 Id.

Whereas, we recognize that by the death of D. W. Perley a vacancy exists that but few can fill. His brilliant talents, cultivated by a life of industry, matured by well-directed study; his mind stored with useful knowledge, fully entitled him to the position he held—that of one of the leaders of the bar on the Pacific Coast.

Now, therefore, be it resolved, that we the members of the Bar of Lincoln County, deeply deplore the death of D. W. Perley, that we extend to the family of the deceased our most sincere sympathy, and that a copy of the forgoing be given to his nearest relatives.[130]

***

Perley's rather abrupt death necessitated the allocation of his current case load to other attorneys. In Chief Justice McKean's Third District Court, C. W. Bennett and a Mr. Whitney took on the defense of the matters of *H. W. Guest v. F. W. Randall* and *Samuel Smith et al. v. J. M. Richardson et al*, as well as the prosecution on behalf of the Plaintiff in *David Sanderson v. J. H. Ely*.[131] The Chief Justice continued the case of *S. F. Nuckols v. Perley* for recovery of a $2,000 debt pending settlement of Perley's Estate.[132] Remarkably, the attorney had no will, hence no one was authorized to oversee the disposal of his property. The distance between Utah and Perley's closest kin made administration of the Estate rather awkward for either his nephew in Nevada, or his mother and siblings in New Brunswick. Seizing the opportunity to ensure payment of a $700 debt, Joseph Gordon petitioned the Probate Court in Salt Lake City as soon as the news of Perley's death was reported, requesting under the laws of the Territory that he be issued letters of administration so that he might dispose of Perley's worldly possessions and any real property within the Territory's boundaries.[133] The request was summarily granted, as was the

[130] *Pioche Daily Record*, September 23, 1874.

[131] *Salt Lake Herald-Republican*, October 9, 1874; and *Salt Lake Herald-Republican*, November 28, 1874.

[132] *Salt Lake Herald-Republican*, October 24, 1874.

[133] Petition of Joseph Gordon, Utah State Archives, Series 1621, Third District Court: Salt Lake County, Probate Case Files, Box 8, Folder 24, Probate Case No. 413, Estate of D.W. Perley.

request that Frank Tilford, A. J. Stevens and C. W. Bennett form a committee to conduct an inventory and assessment of the value of Perley's Estate.[134] The inventory proceeded rapidly and was concluded by the end of the month. His effects were such as to fill two rooms: a bed, looking glass, wash stand, bureau, foot bath, stool, table and chairs, stoves, lamps, his book cases and nearly 1,500 books, curtains, a sofa and two spittoons, not to mention his cloths and personal items and various "what not."[135] An interest in a 160-acre mining claim was discovered and conveyed back to the person from whom Perley had taken the interest as payment for law work never completed on account of his death.[136] The Estate as a whole was valued at about $2,500, and the Res was ordered sold at auction. R. N. Baskin purchased the law books and S. P. Wolfe the book cases and other items. George C. Bates bought a number of the furnishings, and Fred Cartner successfully bid on the looking glass, bureau, and wash stand.[137] Tantalizing for the biographer was the residue of effects of purely personal nature, which the Court ordered returned to Perley's nephew in Nevada: a "large family Bible"—likely the one he read from on a daily basis later in his life—three appointment books, three photo albums, various deeds and leases relating to land in California and Nevada, and a tin case full of "family photographs," papers and letters.[138]

The settlement of Perley's Utah Estate dragged on for several years. The administrator pocketed the money obtained at the auction and ran off to Europe. When it became clear that Gordon

---

[134] Order Appointing Appraisers, dated September 30, 1874, Utah State Archives, Series 1621, Third District Court: Salt Lake County, Probate Case Files, Box 8, Folder 24, Probate Case No. 413, Estate of D.W. Perley.

[135] Inventory and Appraisment, Utah State Archives, Series 1621, Third District Court: Salt Lake County, Probate Case Files, Box 8, Folder 24, Probate Case No. 413, Estate of D.W. Perley.

[136] Order to Administrator to Make Deed, dated May 6, 1875, Utah State Archives, Series 1621, Third District Court: Salt Lake County, Probate Case Files, Box 8, Folder 24, Probate Case No. 413, Estate of D.W. Perley.

[137] Return and Account of Sales, Personal Property, dated November 27, 1874, Utah State Archives, Series 1621, Third District Court: Salt Lake County, Probate Case Files, Box 8, Folder 24, Probate Case No. 413, Estate of D.W. Perley.

[138] Order Setting Apart Certain Personal Property, dated October 23, 1874, Utah State Archives, Series 1621, Third District Court: Salt Lake County, Probate Case Files, Box 8, Folder 24, Probate Case No. 413, Estate of D.W. Perley.

wasn't returning, the remaining creditor, Stephen Nuckols, petitioned the Court for an order appointing a new administrator, who might complete the task and perhaps even pay him the debt owed in the form of a $2,000 loan, plus interest.[139] As the money obtained by Gordon was likely never to return to Utah, the Court appointed C. W. Bennett as the new administrator and ordered Gordon to make an accounting. The high improbability that such an accounting would ever be completed rendered it likely that action against the surety's bond would commence.

Unrelated to the legal proceedings in Utah, the fate of Perley's interests in Nevada fell into the hands of his nephew, who applied for and obtained letters of administration. In September of 1875, young Perley secured an order permitting him to sell 320 acres of his uncle's land in Elko County along Maggie Creek, for the purpose of paying the Estate's debts and his own expenses of administration.[140] How he came into ownership of the Steptoe Valley Ranch isn't clear, since he was only one of his uncle's heirs, but the likelihood is that he borrowed money to make a complete purchase. Those other heirs, including his father, grandmother and siblings, remained very interested in Perley's California Estate, which at the time of his death seemed to be limited to a share in Richardson's Rancho Sausalito. To administer the California Estate, the probate division of the Court in Marin appointed James Ben Ali Haggin and James D. Thornton. Haggin had been a client, business associate, financier and friend of Perley from their early days in California. Thornton had been acquainted with Perley beginning in 1854, when he immigrated to the State in the wake of the arrival of his father-in-law and distant cousin, Harry Innis Thornton, Sr. He had served in San Francisco as a Court Commissioner, and as evident in earlier chapters of this book, formed with Perley and another kinsman, A. P. Crittenden, part of the legal team charged with freeing David Terry from imprisonment by the Vigilance Committee and had peripheral involvement in the Bird's Nest matter.

---

[139] Petition for Removal of Administrator and for Appointment of an Administrator, dated August 21, 1876, Utah State Archives, Series 1621, Third District Court: Salt Lake County, Probate Case Files, Box 8, Folder 24, Probate Case No. 413, Estate of D.W. Perley.

[140] *White Pine News*, September 25, 1875.

The task before the two administrators proved daunting. In May of 1875, U.S. Attorney Walter Van Dyke filed suit against Throckmorton, Howard, Edmund L. Goold, and Perley's Estate in order to recover 20,251 acres of land in Marin County, "comprised in what is generally known as the Sausalito Rancho, with other property."[141] Van Dyke charged that the land as far back as 1835 had been procured by fraud and then, by further fraudulent means, innocently confirmed to the grantee by the U.S. Government. With the aid of Mexican officials, Richardson had lied about the grant, and then Throckmorton continued the lie. Volney Howard was alleged to have learned of the truth about the fraud while serving as attorney for the Land Commission and then quit that body in order to aid in the advancement of the deception after receiving a promise that he would be vested with a share of the wrongly procured estate. Only the land previously deeded to the Sausalito Land and Ferry Company and the North Pacific Railroad was to be excepted from the action, due to a desire to avoid disturbing "those people who have purchased their homes in good faith and for a valuable consideration."[142]

Shortly after the filing of the federal government's action, the Rancho's litigation profile expanded. E. L. Goold filed suit, naming Throckmorton, Howard, James B. Haggin, the Hibernian Savings and Loan Society, Perley's Estate and Thornton himself (as the Estate's Administrator), in addition to Perley's heirs: his mother, brother William, nephew Duncan W. Perley, Jr., and several other relations. Also named were the Savings & Loan Society, Thomas E. Janes, Louis L. Janes, Mortimer Janes, Lucy H. Janes, Judge John W. Dwinelle, E. W. Burr and J. M. Shotwell.[143] Tired of Throckmorton's failure to pay him his portion of the rents and profits, Goold sought a partition of the Rancho and the allotment to him of two twenty-fifth parts. His action wasn't entirely hostile to Howard, Haggin and the Perley Estate. He actually requested in his Complaint that shares of the Rancho be allotted to them in the final decree.

The U.S. Attorney's effort to nullify the Richardson grant came before Justice Stephen Field and his colleagues on the Circuit Court

---

141 *Marin Journal*, June 8, 1876.
142 Id.
143 *Marin Journal*, August 10, 1876.

in the Fall. Howard and his co-Defendants demurred to the Complaint on account of various foundational considerations.[144] In sustaining the demurrer, Justice Field explained that "the allegation…that the defendant Howard had notice of the fabrication of the papers from the Claimant, given in other proceedings before the Board, and other allegations imputing guilty knowledge, to him and to the other Defendants, are too vague and general to merit consideration, made as they are in a bill not verified and only upon information and belief. The District Attorney should at least have stated the sources of his information and the grounds of his belief, that the Court might see that the former was something better than idle rumor, and the latter something more than unfounded credulity."[145] Rather than granting leave to amend, Field dismissed the matter outright, implying the conclusion that matters of proof so long delayed could never be undertaken either fairly or with any reasonable degree of confidence that the ultimate outcome would bear resemblance to the truth.

Other prosecutors might have let the matter go in the wake of Justice Field's conclusive pronouncement. Walter Van Dyke was not among such souls. His political involvement had over the years placed him in contact with Howard and Haggin, but not in a congenial way. His profound Republican affiliations naturally clashed with their commitment to the Democrats. The fortuitous election of Van Dyke and Howard as delegates to the State Constitutional Convention while the contest over the Richardson Ranch was pending probably rendered the clash all the more pronounced.[146] Politics alone might not explain Van Dyke's decision to appeal the matter beyond Field to his brethren on the United States Supreme Court, but whatever the reasons for it, the maneuver proved futile, and perhaps an embarrassment for Van Dyke in the eyes of the leading judicial figures in the land. Upon reviewing of the briefs submitted by Van Dyke on the one side and Howard's attorney Delos Lake on the other, Justice Miller commented on "the verbiage, repetition, and argumentative matter" in the prosecutor's brief, as well as the absence of any "allegation

144 *Daily Alta California*, September 11, 1876.

145 Id.

146 Van Dyke would later win a seat on the State Supreme Court, where he served alongside the Perley Estate's California administrator, James D. Thornton.

whatever that any of the attorneys, agents, or other officers of the government were false in their duty to it, or that they assisted or connived at the fraud, unless a single allegation on that subject...sufficiently makes such charge."[147] In Miller's view, all agreed that Richardson had been granted the land, and that he occupied and developed it, and yet had failed to receive a final signed instrument from the Mexican authorities, hence the lack of that item, alleged by Van Dyke to have been obtained after the fact by fraud, appeared to be a mere technicality. Richardson's production of the missing item in the midst of the proceedings in the 1850s, he thought, was striking enough at the time to have drawn the attention and close scrutiny "of all the parties and of the court," and ample time existed then "to make all necessary inquiries and produce the necessary proof, if it existed, of the fraud."[148] That the Land Commission, the District Court, and the Attorney General of the United States might have overlooked evidence of fraud when it counted, in the course of three distinct stages of a complex proceeding Miller found extremely doubtful. Assuming the allegations of fraud were true, despite being undetected in the past, the principle that "fraud vitiates the most solemn contracts, documents and even judgments," would apply, and yet "by lapse of time, by the difficulty of proving the fraud, and by the protection which the law throws around rights once established by formal judicial proceedings in tribunals established by law," many rights "originally founded in fraud become...no longer open to inquiry in the usual and ordinary methods."[149] If Richardson and his agents had prevented the United States by fraud or deception from fully exhibiting its case—say through "a false promise of a compromise; or where the defendant never had knowledge of the suit, being kept in ignorance by the acts of the plaintiff; or where an attorney fraudulently or without authority assumes to represent a party and connives at his defeat; or where the attorney regularly employed corruptly sells out his client's interests to the other side"—the ancient fraud might now be actionable, but nothing of this sort appears to have occurred here.[150] In truth, the United States had

[147] *United States v. Throckmorton* (1878) 98 U.S. 61, 62.
[148] Id., at 64.
[149] Id., at 65.
[150] Id., at 65-66.

every opportunity, and every obligation, to rigorously test the evidence of the claim presented to the tribunal prior to the issuance of a final judgment. Since the fundamental issue before the Land Commission and District Court twenty years before was the validity of the title claimed by Richardson, the time to challenge the claim for fraud was then. And even if the Court were incorrect on this point, the belated federal action was doomed anyway on account of the impropriety of the U.S. Attorney bringing the action himself, rather than deferring to the Attorney General, or at least stating on the face of his pleading that he was acting under a grant of authority expressly issued by his superior. Why such a statement was absent from the bill, Miller didn't directly discuss, but he suggested it had something to do with Van Dyke's personal animus with respect to the respondents. "It would," said Miller, "be a very dangerous doctrine, one threatening title to millions of acres of land held by patent from the government, if any man who has a grudge or a claim against his neighbor can…institute a suit in chancery in the United States to declare the patent void."[151]

Goold's action would not be resolved so quickly. Delay commenced when Howard and Perley's administrators filed their own action on October 30, 1877, demanding not a partition, but an accounting from Throckmorton for all the rents and profits subsequent to the operative date of the Supreme Court's 1874 decision.[152] The rights of the Plaintiffs having already been established, the Superior Court granted the demand.[153] After the actuarial process was complete and a hearing was held, the Court ruled that after deductions for taxes and other overhead paid by Throckmorton, Throckmorton owed $1,895.30, in addition to $225.10 in litigation costs.[154] Throckmorton, of course, sought a new trial on the grounds that the only proper remedy for the Plaintiffs was an action for partition, and that the rents received were actually profits generated by Throckmorton's enterprise, thus owing to him alone. In rejecting the motion, the trial court explained that "we are no longer under a system in which form is of more importance than

---

[151] Id., at 71.

[152] *Howard v. Throckmorton* (1881) 59 Cal. 79.

[153] *Marin Journal*, April 17, 1879.

[154] *Howard v. Throckmorton* (1881), supra, at 85.

substance."[155] If the rents are owed to the co-owner, "he ought to have them, and the present seems the most convenient, and, therefore the proper form of action."[156] That the moneys received by Throckmorton were rents the Court could not deny, since the land was opened to cattlemen who paid a grazing fee for the privilege of unloosing their animals there. Failing in his motion for a new trial, Throckmorton appealed. The matter was complicated by the fact that Thornton ascended the Superior Court bench in April of 1878, and then to a seat on the State's Supreme Court in 1880.[157] It wasn't fully resolved until November of 1881, when the Supreme Court, without Thornton's participation, affirmed the District Court's decision.[158]

In the Goold matter, the District Court appointed J. M. Brown, G. W. Stilwell and William Vanderbilt as a commission to partition the lands of Throckmorton, Howard and Goold.[159] The partition was made and certain portions of the Estate were sold in order to pay Goold the money owed to him pursuant to the various judgments issued in the past. An order of execution issued by the District Court on May 9, 1881 directed that Goold receive the proceeds of the sale.[160] Perley's interest and the interests of other owners were expressly excepted from the order.[161] Exception occurred due to the conveyance to James Ben Ali Haggin of Perley's share by the new Administrator of Perley's estate, Harry I. Thornton, in exchange for $9,023.13.[162]

***

Perley's own children did not survive childhood. He had no offspring to carry on his name. He did have a large extended family, in New Brunswick and in the West. His young cousin Frederica Hazen resided until her death in Eastern Nevada. For a time, her

---

155 Id., at p. 86.

156 Id.

157 *Sonoma Democrat*, April 20, 1878; and *San Diego Union and Daily Bee*, October 2, 1879.

158 *Marin Journal*, November 17, 1881; and *Howard v. Throckmorton*, supra.

159 *Marin Journal*, December 4, 1879.

160 *Marin Journal*, May 19, 1881.

161 *Marin Journal*, August 25, 1881.

162 *Petaluma Weekly Argus*, September 20, 1878.

cousin—Perley's niece, Elizabeth Perley—joined her, and even seems to have considered settling down before opting to return home.[163] Frederica's daughter Maud married a prominent physician and eventually settled in California, where her descendants remain to this day. Perley's brother William continued to play a prominent political role in New Brunswick politics until his death. His son Del attempted to enter the Provincial Assembly, but was defeated on at least one occasion. He knew greater good fortune in the far west of Canada, where he won a seat in the Dominion Senate. His branch of the family endured in the west and his place in the political establishment was passed on to his son, Ernest. Perley's young cousin Walter, the nephew of Assemblyman Charles Perley, sadly perished on the Reese River from Mountain Fever in September of 1864. Another cousin, Theodore Miles Clowes, labored on in the mines after Walter's death until 1866, when the dearth of chances in central Nevada convinced him to move on to Salt Lake City and then Montana. He built a ranch in Silver Bow, married a lady from Carleton County, New Brunswick, and raised a family. In time, at least four of his siblings joined him in Montana. A nephew, Thomas Miles Clowes II, completed the law program at the University of Michigan in 1904, entered the bar, and practiced law for many years in Montana, Alaska and the State of Washington.

Perley's nephew and namesake was the closest thing to an actual adult child Perley ever had. Sharing his uncle's name, he also took his uncle's place in eastern Nevada society, and appears to have appreciated it so much that even after his uncle passed away and his Utah administrator transmitted to him the family Bible, photographs and other personal affects, he opted to stay. Retaining his uncle's ranch, he soon ventured into the saloon business, opening in the town of Ward an establishment called "The Palace."[164] A man of good nature with a strong instinct for food and drink, he also possessed a very determined streak. After companions at a rodeo at Willow Creek dunked him in a small stream, he crept off with the group's cook while everyone was asleep and diverted the waterway so that with the removal of a

---

163 *Pioche Daily Record*, November 18, 1874.

164 *Eureka Daily Sentinel*, September 22, 1877.

temporary dam the entire camp and everyone in it was flooded.[165] In August of 1878, just months after the *Eureka Daily Sentinel* had noted the passing of many of the great lawyers of the previous decade, including the elder Perley, the same paper announced D.W. Perley, Jr. "as a Republican Candidate for the State Senate" to represent White Pine County.[166] A month later, the County Republican Convention nominated him to stand in the general election.[167] With the Republican ticket headed by his uncle's former business associate, John H. Kinkead, Perley's chances looked promising. When the canvas came, he won against his Democrat opponent by a mere 17 votes and took the oath of office from Chief Justice Beatty on January 6 of the new year.[168] After assuming his seat, he was said to have been "the best-looking man in the body…tall and proportionately built, fair complexion, chin whiskers and moustache," and his eyes "sparkling and full of intelligence."[169]

The younger Perley's emergence as a political figure was greeted with high hopes. Though a Republican, many on the Democrat side thought well of him and considered him a good bet to resist what they believed were the baser impulses of the opposition.[170] These baser impulses related to the attractions of railroads and the lure of railroad dollars. The first bills he sponsored were innocuous enough: an act to cover the debts of White Pine County, another to modify the law governing notary publics, and one to approve the sale by the State of Nevada of land to the federal government to serve as a building site. His independence from his Party's alliance with the railroad interests seemed assured upon his sponsorship of a cap on freight and passenger rates within the State, and another to bar the employment by the State's railroads or its contractors and subcontractors of "any Chinese or Mongolian in any

---

[165] *Carson Daily Appeal*, June 8, 1875.

[166] *Eureka Daily Sentinel*, March 30, 1878; and *Eureka Daily Sentinel*, August 20, 1878.

[167] *Eureka Daily Sentinel*, September 14, 1878.

[168] *Gold Hill Daily News*, November 6, 1878; and *Eureka Daily Sentinel*, January 7, 1879.

[169] Hugh J. Mohan, *Pen Pictures* (Virginia City: Daily Stage Steam Printing House, 1879), p. 49.

[170] See for instance, *Ward Weekly Reflex*, August 17, 1878, which tended to favor the Democrats and actually endorsed Perley's unsuccessful opponent.

capacity whatever, on or about any of the works or any such corporation or association in this state." The latter bill, while tainted by discriminatory attitudes respecting the Asian races, was largely calculated to prevent the railroads from hiring cheap immigrant labor at the expense of the native born. The impact of foreign labor on wages for citizens prompted Perley's successful push for a resolution directed to the Congress to ban emigration from China—the source of the railroads' preferred labor pool. In the wake of his legislative accomplishments, even Democrat firebrand, journalist Hugh Mohan, praised Perley's skills as a parliamentarian, backed by "a full supply of common sense, tempered with excellent judgment."[171]

By April, the appearance of Perley's independence from the railroad interests faded. Disappointed, the anti-railroad element said "he held out manfully for a time, but…only for the expected time."[172] With Perley in mind, Democrats gathered in Ward and denounced "men who failed to fulfill their promises made in public before a convention of their fellow citizens," who voted for and approved "of the various measures introduced by the corporations intended to impoverish the people…and enrich the various railroad companies doing business in this state."[173] Suspicions that Perley had entered the payroll of the newly formed Eureka and Palisade Railroad Company eased as the primary suspect was revealed to be his White Pine colleague, Senator Henry A. Comins.[174] When Comins was accused in the pages of the *Reflex* of outright bribery, he took an oath that he hadn't done anything untoward, then filed an action for libel that some likened to "the celebrated case of the *Raymond & Ely vs. Hermes*, where every juror summoned in the case had been previously interviewed by an agent of the companies, and selected on account of the peculiar quality commonly called 'purchasable.'"[175] Comins' term soon came to an end, leaving Perley the County's senior Senator.

When the 1881 session of the Nevada legislature opened, Perley moved more obviously into the orbit of big rail. Within the first two

---

171 Mohan, op. cit., p. 49.

172 *Ward Weekly Reflex*, April 5, 1879

173 Id.

174 *Ward Weekly Reflex*, May 3, 1879.

175 *Ward Weekly Reflex*, August 9, 1879.

weeks of the session, he introduced S.B. 21, "an act to encourage the construction of a railroad from Eureka to the Colorado River."[176] The bill called for a bond to raise $500,000 for a line of tracks running through White Pine and Lincoln Counties. One paper expressed surprise "to see that Sen. Perley has lent himself to any such scheme," and doubted the State had the means and inclination to give any company so large a sum to build one.[177] Perley further confirmed his new allegiance to the railroads when he refused to permit his Committee on Federal Relations to take any action on a resolution asking Congress to establish nation-wide regulatory control over rates.[178] As Perley's railroad bill moved through the legislature, supporters and opponents rallied to encourage either its passage or defeat. To Perley's side came his kinsman, Judge Rives, who campaigned throughout the region, winning support from many through his "loud and forceful manner" of exposition.[179] With Rives' help, and a few useful revisions, the bill to fund the Eureka and Colorado River Railroad passed both the Assembly and Senate and was signed into law by Governor Kinkead.[180]

Within a short-time, petitions approving of a bond initiative were being signed and a survey of the projected line was commenced.[181] That the line was to run through the Steptoe Valley was certainly advantageous to Perley, whose ranch and surrounding property would undoubtedly increase in value. Instead of seeking re-election in 1883, rumors spread that he desired the office of State Controller. In truth, he appeared far more interested in pursuing a career with the railroads than anything else. Reports circulated that he'd made a killing in railroad stocks in July and was, by the end of that month, firmly in the railroad's grip, attempting to organize a construction company modeled "something after the Credit Mobilier."[182] Armed with bond money generated by the Bill he had sponsored, Perley set about purchasing water rights and other franchises for the road, as well as preparing

---

[176] *Senate Journal*, p. 46; and *White Pine News*, January 22, 1881.
[177] *White Pine News*, January 22, 1881.
[178] *White Pine News*, February 5, 1881.
[179] *Ward Weekly Reflex*, February 5, 1881; and *White Pine News*, February 12, 1881.
[180] *Ward Weekly Reflex*, February 26, 1881; and *Ward Weekly Reflex*, March 5, 1881.
[181] *Ward Weekly Reflex*, March 19, 1881; and Ward Weekly Reflex, May 7, 1881.
[182] *White Pine News*, August 13, 1881.

to bid on contracts to build sections of the line between White Pine and destinations to the east.[183] That he won the bid indicated the trust placed in him by the company.[184] In November, he and the line's superintendent, accompanied by Judge Rives, were surveying the route. He gained control of a 25-mile tract of timber land to be used for rails and charcoal and then commenced hiring the labor necessary to complete the project. Progress stalled as conflict with Jay Gould's Union Pacific and the Eureka & Palisade Railroads grew. In time, the entire project was scraped and the company merged with the Denver & Rio Grand. Perley's good nature and energy won him a position with that company. The new professional affiliation mandated his removal from Nevada to Utah—a move that came with some ease due to the fact that he'd already disposed, back in 1881, of his uncle's ranch.[185] Efforts to win the post of U.S. Marshall for the Utah Territory failed, as did a go at mining in Helena, Montana. The former job might have been his had not Chief Justice Beatty withdrawn his endorsement in favor of another candidate.[186] Some consolation eventually appeared in the form of the hand of the fair Minnie Evangeline Wescoatt, the ex-wife of the Raymond & Ely's erstwhile mining expert and a talented and well-regarded ceramic artist in her own right.[187]

The younger Perley's life in Utah came to a close in 1892 or 1893. Railroad work having come to an end, the couple and Minnie's children with Wescoatt sought new opportunities in San Francisco. Perley remained in the contracting business, but hit a dry spell soon after the turn of the new century. Desperate for aid, he wrote on his wife's letterhead to Senator Stewart for a patronage appointment in the Commissary Department of the U.S. military establishment in the City. His employment there for years afterward indicates the success of his entreaty to the great Stewart. The family survived the earthquake, but not the aftermath. His star having descended while

---

183 *Ward Weekly Reflex*, August 20, 1881; and *Ward Weekly Reflex*, August 27, 1881.

184 *Ward Weekly Reflex*, November 1, 1881; and *White Pine News*, November 22, 1881.

185 White Pine County Registry Office, 28:17.

186 William Henry Beatty to D. W. Perley, February 9, 1889, Records Relating to the Appointment of Federal Judges, Attorneys, and Marshalls for the Territory and State of Utah, 1853-1901, Roll 7, National Archives and records Services, available at http://www.familysearch.org.

187 *Daily Nevada Tribune*, November 27, 1888.

his wife's artistic fame grew, she left him for Los Angeles, where she obtained a divorce.[188] Her sons, who had adopted Perley's name, soon resumed the Wescoatt patronymic. His last years appear to have been rather dismal. He continued in his job with the federal government until his death and boarded in a public house, first on Van Ness Avenue, later on Laguna. He sought to recover his early prosperity, initially through illegal games of chance and then by organization of a mining company, neither of which efforts resulted in anything but failure.[189] He died in San Francisco, aged 74 years, on December 8, 1922.[190] The press of his native New Brunswick reported the cause of death being "shock" experienced as a result of surgery "for an intestinal obstruction."[191]

D. W. Perley, Jr. was not the only Perley in California following the elder Perley's death. In San Joaquin County, cousin Frederick and the widow and most of the children of cousin James continued to abide. Frederick died in 1880—a confirmed bachelor to the end. James' widow lived until 1879. She passed away at roughly the same time as her unmarried daughter Anna Augusta, who'd accompanied her father on his fateful trip to New Brunswick. Eldest son Henry returned to the family homestead with his wife after many years travelling abroad in search of gold. He died childless in 1899 while serving as Stockton's Harbor Master, followed by his widow three years later in San Francisco.[192] Second son Solomon advanced with his father into politics and was an active member of the San Joaquin Republican Party. His end is uncertain, though the author of the Perley genealogy reports that he died around 1870 in Colorado. Son Charles actually joined his uncle in Hamilton in 1869 or 1870 and sought his fortune as a miner. He grew to prominence as a labor leader in the mines before returning to California. He settled first in Liberty—apparently taking over the old homestead—then moved to Modesto near his younger brother George, where he married George's sister-in-law and raised a family. He died in 1914, at the age of seventy-nine. James' daughter Frances married an

188 *Los Angeles Herald*, August 1, 1908.

189 *San Francisco Examiner*, April 11, 1897; *San Francisco Chronicle*, April 12, 1897; and *The Record-Union*, July 3, 1897.

190 *San Francisco Examiner*, December 10, 1922.

191 "Died in California," *Daily Gleaner*, December 21, 1922.

192 *Stockton Daily Evening Record*, February 11, 1899.

accountant named David Mitchell and moved to San Francisco. Both she and her husband appear to have died by 1880, but their two children lived on, as do numerous descendants throughout California. Son Allen Wilmot Perley moved from San Joaquin County to San Francisco, and then to Los Angeles. The work he did was rather non-descript until, at the end of his life, he found regular employ in the movie industry as an actor. He died in Los Angeles on June 14, 1926.[193] James' son James Frederick Perley married in 1872, but was dead four years later. He was survived by his wife and three children, whose descendants survive to this day. Senator James' youngest son George was perhaps the most successful of his children. George moved to San Francisco at some point in the 1860s, possibly working for his brother-in-law David Mitchell as a bookkeeper.[194] In February of 1868, he came to Stanislaus County, where he found employ as a clerk for a mercantile house. He made a go of it on his own in Modesto in 1871, where he started a mercantile business, and eventually expanded into real estate and title searching. He made a fine match with Maine native Caroline Pendleton Cookson and had three children, including daughter Mabel, who in later years became a leader in the title industry. George became Modesto's leading citizen: a member of the Board of Freeholders who framed the City Charter, a City Councilor, and the Commissioner of Public Works. He was the prime mover on the Board of Trade and in the Chamber of Commerce, and an activist who contributed much toward the passage of the Wright Act of 1887, which permitted the formation of irrigation districts in the Central Valley, to better coordinate the use of the region's water resources by farmers. He died on October 14, 1923, at the age of 74.[195] Though his descendants are not many, they continue to reside in the State.

***

[193] *Los Angeles Times*, June 16, 1926.

[194] See George H. Tinkham, *History of Stanislaus County, California* (Los Angeles: California Historic Record Company, 1921), at p. 348-349.

[195] "George Perley, Pioneer Modesto Business Man and Civil Worker, Dies at Daughter's Home Here," *Modesto Evening News*, October 15, 1923.

The fate of many of those whose lives Perley shared to an intimate degree has already been related. Of his various law partners, all but two survived him. Perley's idol, General Williams, succumbed, perhaps drunkenly, to the misfire of a pistol in his office on the southwest corner of Kearny and Sacramento Streets on January 4, 1867.[196] Any suspicion that the wound through the head was intentionally self-inflicted while suffering one of his periodic fits of madness, the dying man unequivocally disavowed.[197] When the news of his death came to Judge Dwinelle at the Court for the Fifteenth District of California, proceedings were temporarily stayed in tribute to a lawyer so profoundly respected.[198] Delos Ashley actually left an active partnership with Harry I. Thornton in Nevada due to ill health and returned to California, where his condition steadily declined. He died in San Francisco, on July 18, 1873.[199] William Campbell followed Perley and Ashley to the grave in 1876 while on a trip to Santa Barbara. As soon as the news of his death reached Virginia City, a dozen or so attorneys announced their candidacy to replace him as Storey County's District Attorney. One of the candidates was another of Perley's former law partners, C. E. DeLong, whose reputed promise if elected was to dedicate at least half his salary to his predecessor's widow.[200]

DeLong's defeats in his career were as impressive as his victories. After several terms in the California Senate in the late 1850s and early 1860s, he parlayed his winning personality and political skills into a seat at the Nevada Constitutional Convention, but then was defeated twice for the office of United States Senator. President Grant appreciated his services to the Party during the elections of 1868 and 1872, as did Senator William Stewart. His reward was nomination and confirmation as Ambassador to Japan. It was on his return from his diplomatic post of four years that he sought the Storey County position, but he lost that race, and then his life after contracting typhoid or some such ailment while giving a speech in the lead up to the November general election.[201] Shaking

---

[196] *Sacramento Daily Union*, January 7, 1867.

[197] Id.; and *Marysville Daily Appeal*, January 5, 1867.

[198] *Daily Alta California*, January 6, 1867.

[199] *Santa Cruz Weekly Sentinel*, August 2, 1873.

[200] *Morning Union*, February 6, 1876.

[201] *Marysville Daily Appeal*, October 28, 1876.

his hand before his death were many friends and prominent citizens; and at his death-bed, his wife and five children "bade him an agonizing farewell."[202] His death was said to have "cast a shadow over the entire community..., for he was a representative man of Nevada; one who from a humble boyhood had won his way step by step to the foremost place among his fellow men."[203] The editor of the *Alta* commented on his relatively young age, and the fact that had he "lived a few years longer he would probably have been called upon to fill other responsible positions."[204]

Perley's final law partner, Murray A. Carter, died two years later, in 1878, while serving as a special agent of the Interior Department, assigned to investigate trespasses on Federal land in Mississippi and other States in the South.[205] Outliving these men, and many of the others with whom Perley practiced, was Mansfield Compton, who had returned to New York after the furor over his horrendous crime and the Governor's pardon subsided. He practiced without a blemish on his name for many years in the State before settling for the last eight years of his life in Brooklyn. He succumbed to the effects of dropsy and an enlarged liver in January of 1902.[206]

Perley's law partner in the middle-1850s, Joseph Pendleton Hoge, lived many years after Perley's death. By the middle 1870s, the former Congressman's best chances for public greatness appeared to have passed him by. A perennial hopeful to return to Congress as a member of the Senate, his foremost opportunity eluded him in the canvas of 1869. And yet, in the last phase of his life, his greatest contributions to the soundness of the civil order were accomplished. The people of San Francisco, conscious of his experience and powers of advocacy, selected him as one of their representatives to the Convention to draft a new State Constitution, and his fellow delegates there selected him to serve that body as President. It was he who guided the process whereby the current Constitution of the State was drafted. Shortly afterward, he served as Chairman of the Board of Freeholders, and assisted in the

---

[202] Id.

[203] Id.

[204] *Daily Alta California*, October 27, 1876.

[205] *Salt Lake Herald Republican*, October 11, 1878.

[206] *Brooklyn Daily Eagle*, January 29, 1902.

drafting of a new charter for the City of San Francisco. Remarkably, at the age of 79, he won election to a position as Judge of the Superior Court in San Francisco, and served until his death three years later.[207]

His and Perley's long-time colleague in litigation, Volney Howard, experienced similar autumnal resurgence in his political fortunes. He was one of the many prominent men who had come to California to win a place in the Senate, and one of the many who knew disappointment in that pursuit. His role in the Vigilance disturbance tarnished his excellent reputation, as did his commitment to the Southern wing of the Democrat Party. His relocation to Southern California was necessitated by his desire to reduce exposure to such severe criticism and make a new beginning without actually leaving the State. His fame and unquestioned brilliance as an attorney recommended him for the office of District Attorney, which he held for 3 years, until 1867. With Hoge, he found that the people still valued his experience, and the two were reunited at the Constitutional Convention, where Howard played a leading role. And like Hoge, his success there led to a seat on the bench of the Superior Court—in his case in the County of Los Angeles. He served a single term, and then, in the year 1889, passed away. The *Los Angeles Herald* laudingly recounted his remarkable career, and the County itself ordained that his portrait would hang in the Superior Court in perpetuity.[208] "This country," the paper said, "has produced but few men with a more comprehensive or absorbing mind, and none stored with a wider or more judiciously selected range of literature."[209] He was, it concluded, "a statesman in the highest sense…true to the point of direction as the needle to the pole," with a "courageous nature…incapable of fear" and utterly unwilling, when sure of his rectitude, to divert from his purpose regardless of the danger.[210] "Had he been more politic, more suave and bending in his character, more flexible to his own personal interests, he might have left his children greater riches as

---

[207] *Los Angeles Herald*, August 17, 1891.

[208] "Death of Volney E. Howard," *Los Angeles Herald*, May 15, 1889; "Death of a Foremost Man," *Los Angeles Herald*, May 15, 1889; and *Los Angeles Herald*, January 10, 1884.

[209] "Death of a Foremost Man," *Los Angeles Herald*, May 15, 1889.

[210] Id.

the world goes, but he could not have left them a more lofty and honorable heritage than that which descends to them from his pure and unsullied name and his great and lasting fame."[211]

John Garber was only briefly Perley's partner, and their relations afterward, particularly during the Hermes trial, were not entirely amicable, and yet his willingness to share a shingle with Perley is indicative of the caliber of persons Perley habitually attracted. He had, of course, briefly been a member of the Nevada Supreme Court. He practiced with Thornton and Bishop for a time in the middle and late 1870s and was thus involved in innumerable mining suits, though none as celebrated as the Hermes litigation. He returned to California and became almost at once a leader of the State Bar, and was "prominently connected with many of the great legal battles in the civil courts of this state," including the action by the federal government to tax the family of Governor Leland Stanford.[212] Though formerly a Democrat, he leaned Republican in later years, and was a friend of Theodore Roosevelt, Senator Beverage and Mark Hanna. It was Roosevelt who offered him a spot on the Panama Canal Commission, which he declined due to his advanced age. Death came in December of 1908. Among his pall bearers was William H. Beatty, then in his nineteenth year and serving as Chief Justice of California.[213]

Thomas Fitch—the friend Perley assisted with a temporary collaboration while Fitch was detained in San Francisco in 1867—pursued a truly adventurous path during the rest of his long life. Disappointed in his effort to win a Senate seat representing Utah, Fitch returned for a time to California, and then relocated to Prescott, Arizona. While there, he came to the attention of the Territorial Governor, John C. Fremont, who retained him as legal advisor. He returned to government service in 1879 as a member of the Legislature of Arizona Territory, and then, after moving to Tombstone, rose to national fame for his successful defense of Wyatt Earp and Doc Holiday against charges of murder arising from the legendary gunfight at the O. K. Corral. After that, it was hard to pinpoint where Fitch hung his hat and shingle in any given

---

[211] Id.

[212] *Sacramento Union,* December 14, 1908.

[213] *San Francisco Call,* December 16, 1908.

year: San Diego, San Francisco, New York City, Utah (where again he tried and failed to win a place in the U.S. Senate), Phoenix, Honolulu, San Bernardino, and Los Angeles. He died in Decoto, California, on November 12, 1923.[214]

Henry Rives' life was nearly as adventurous as Fitch's. His partnership with Perley won him fame, as well as a bride from Perley's own extended family. His good fortune continued in Pioche as an advocate, and his Southern ways, his courtesy, politeness and consideration, combined with his willingness to indulge in wine and song, placed him in the front ranks of those seeking political advancement. His chance came in 1878, when the Republican Party nominated him to fill a vacancy on the bench in Eureka. His victory prompted his removal to that place with his wife and young daughter, and a judicial tenure lasting a dozen years. The loss of the lovely Frederica and an infant daughter in childbirth in 1883 was a blow difficult to overcome. Universally revered as "just, kind and public spirited," her passing was the occasion for much public anguish, and a funeral of uncommon solemnity. As the preacher hailed her "most impressive nature," and 80 members of the Knights of Pythias fell in line behind the hearse, Senator Wren and other luminaries lifted the casket and walked to the grave, followed by the local bar, the town officials, firemen and citizens, filling a total of 60 carriages.[215] In time, Rives overcame the loss, and even flourished. He remarried, not once but twice, fathered two more daughters, and transitioned in time from the bench to a role as personal and corporate counsel to the mining magnate, Captain J. R. Delamar. Ever recalling the experience in the Hermes matter, when the lawyers on either side proved the true victors, his preference was always to resolve matters before ever going to court. He remained a figure of much interest in Nevada even after he removed to Salt Lake City. He schemed constantly in pursuit of Perley's dream to develop the remote and untapped mining grounds of the Great Basin, and even devised plans for the long-distance delivery of water. His enthusiasm never dimming, his life-force proved less robust on account of a wasting illness, exacerbated by his love of liquor. When his third wife left him over

---

[214] *San Bernardino Sun*, November 13, 1923.
[215] *Eureka Leader*, November 1, 1883.

his habitual drunkenness, he denied the charge, saying it was a lie fueled by her own "fits of nervousness and irritability."[216] His daughter with Frederica managed to make a fine match with Dr. William T. Dalby. Flanked by her two half-sisters wearing white swiss over pink silk, she entered the church in a gown of "white organdy over white silk," complete with a tulle veil and a long train, carrying a large bouquet of bride's roses.[217] Rives' death in 1905 came as little surprise to those who knew him. His natural gifts, it was thought, ought to have propelled him to greater heights, and yet his weaknesses, arising some speculated from the lack of any discipline learned early in life, acted as a perpetual drag on his success. His many friends could not protect him from the one great enemy of his life: himself. One moment he would be the picture of steady judgment and prudence, diligent work and professionalism, the next "he would break away and burn life's candle at both ends and laugh as he saw it burn."[218] Of his final decline, Judge C. C. Goodwin observed that "of late years he has passed through that most sorrowful period of a proud man's life, wherein the admiration of friends turns at length into pity, and he has had to walk around for years, and feel that pity when he looked in familiar faces, and knew that for his own sake those friends would feel a relief when they knew that his battle of life was over."[219] He was gone, but his fame lingered, and much of it was rightfully Perley's; for of his exploits recalled by his eulogists, one of the chief was winning the Hermes litigation, which in truth had been engineered by the great barrister himself, while Rives sat passively at the counsel table when not a percipient witness in the matter.

Of all of Perley's law partners, none shared with him the firmness of the bond of friendship and comradery as did his first, David Terry. The two men came of age together in Texas, became lawyers there and resolved, with that legendary company of adventurers, to brave the desert and take California by storm. That they actually did no one can contest—California's early history reads in part as the collective biography of these men. The War separated the two law partners, but their friendship never waned.

216 *Eureka Sentinel*, October 18, 1902.

217 *Eureka Weekly Sentinel*, October 8, 1898.

218 *Goodwin's Weekly*, February 24, 1906.

219 *Pioche Weekly Record*, March 2, 1906.

They reunited in Hamilton in 1869 and practiced together from time-to-time. Terry's lack of faith in the wealth of the eastern Nevada mining country eventually precipitated his return to Stockton and resumption of his former status as a leader at the bar and in the community, notwithstanding his history as an active rebel. The wild course of railroad development and the dissatisfaction of consumers with the power exercised by the railroad interests in setting rates for use of facilities that oddly owed much to public subsidy, was but one of the many factors leading to the call for a new Constitution. Terry's skill as an advocate and his reputation for personal bravery and honor made him a front runner to represent the people of San Joaquin County at the Convention. His election confirmed his rehabilitation and marked his return to the role of statesman surrendered two decades before with the office of Chief Justice in the days leading up to the fateful duel with David Broderick. Taking charge of the radicals who sought the heaviest of regulatory burdens on industry and wealth, Terry placed a check on their ambitions and "avoided many of the monstrous and unwise provisions which otherwise would have been engrafted into the Constitution."[220] With them, however, he made common cause against the railroads, which he saw as beneficiaries of a public gift, wholly ungrateful for what had been received, and rudely willing to use the gift as a weapon against the benefactor.[221] The unholy alliance between the State and big business had shaken his faith in the free market and instilled a belief that regulation of the latter by the former, rather than a cutting of the ties altogether, was the best hope for a more equitable arrangement. His extended analysis from the Convention floor of the proposed regulatory provision ultimately won the day. He was equally successful in advocating for a ban on the extension of credit by State and local governments to individuals and corporations, limiting the legislative session to a mere 60 days, and preventing a curtailing of the due process rights of indigent litigants through imposition of a bond requirement in any appeal.[222] By the end of the Convention, Terry's conscientious efforts "clothed him with new

---

220 A.E. Wagstaff, *Life of David S. Terry* (San Francisco: Continental Publishing Company, 1892), at p. 244.

221 Id., at p. 247.

222 Id., at p. 263 and pp. 274-275.

life and brought to him thousands of friends and admirers who had stood aloof from him in years gone by, schooled as they had been in the belief that he was a monster whose garments were dyed in the blood of a martyr."[223] His refusal to accept a challenge to a duel issued by A. C. Peachy in response to Terry's opposition to Peachy assuming a prominent place in the Convention hierarchy on account of his long-standing meretricious relationship with a woman not his wife, confirmed that Terry was indeed a new man, worthy of Statewide respect.

Terry's return to California politics did not lead to further office. Many, however, sought his advice and support, including Stephen Field—a perennial hopeful to win the Democrat nomination for the presidency. In 1884, Terry actually refused to lend his former judicial colleague his endorsement due to what he considered to be Field's special love for corporate interests. Field might have chosen to let the slight go by given the truly hopeless condition of his campaign, but his enormous ego got the better of him and prevented the dissipation of resentment over Terry's repudiation of his grandest aspiration. As Terry knew Field well, he might reasonably have felt that this resentment guided Field's evaluation of the merits of the action by the heirs of William Sharon to preempt the ruling of the State Supreme Court in favor of Althea Hill's claim that she was entitled to alimony from Sharon, to whom she contended she had secretly wed. When her case was first pressed, the widower Terry represented her, and when she triumphed at trial, it was due largely to Terry's legal acumen and stamina in presenting her case over the course of seven months. So pleased was she with the outcome, and so taken was he with her charm and beauty, that the two entered a state of holy matrimony in 1886.

Raising an entirely new theory, the late Senator Sharon's heirs brought a new action in federal court. Though the case ought to have been dismissed as outside the court's subject matter jurisdiction, Justice Field, who ruled the western Circuit like a shogun, retained the case on his docket. In the end, he held that the marriage was a fraud and that the new Mrs. Terry wasn't entitled to a dime. When Althea exploded with threats to shoot the Judge and was taken hold of by the marshal, Terry impulsively came to her

[223] Id., at pp. 276-277.

aid. The result was Fields' consignment of the couple to jail for contempt. In August of 1889, the two men unfortunately ran into one another at a train depot in Lathrop, California. Terry reportedly slapped Field in the face as he passed by, and was promptly gunned down by a body guard provided to Field by the Attorney General. The killer was quickly detained by the County Sheriff, and Field, viewed as an accessory, was arrested upon his arrival in San Francisco. Ultimately, the bodyguard was vindicated and Field held utterly blameless. The press throughout the country, of course, covered the sensational story, with some papers taking the side of Terry and accusing the bodyguard of cold-blooded murder, and others siding with Field. In California, Terry's ancient nemesis, the *Alta California*, smugly attributed the tragedy to Terry's inability to conform himself to the advancing norms of civilization. He had, said the *Alta*, "the misfortune to carry into a ripened state of society the conditions which are tolerable only where social order is not fully established."[224] When asked to adjourn in honor of the former Chief Justice's memory, the State Supreme Court declined on the grounds that no respect was due a man who had resigned his judicial position to fight an illegal duel, and whose death came in the act of assaulting a member of the nation's highest court.[225]

Terry's sensational death opened a floodgate of reminiscing about the Judge's violent history, a prominent piece of which was the duel that Perley's intemperate response to Senator Broderick did so much to initiate. In the retelling of what had already entered into legend, Perley's role was inevitably recounted. Having recently published several renditions of the Perley-Broderick controversy and the subsequent duel in honor of the thirtieth anniversary of the incident, *The Sacramento Union*, in the wake of Terry's killing, noted how "it will be remembered how Senator Broderick declined to meet Perley on the 'field of honor' because the latter did not hold a high political position, as he did."[226] *The San Bernardino Daily Courier* stated that Perley, "a lawyer and friend of Terry, who had served for him as a second in a duel in 1850," overheard Broderick's comments on the Judge, challenged Broderick to a duel, but was

224 *Daily Alta California*, August 15, 1889.
225 *The Press*, August 22, 1889.
226 *Sacramento Union*, August 18, 1889.

rebuffed because his status as an alien rendered him immune to any loss of civil liberty for engaging in an illegal contest.[227] The following day, the same paper reported that Perley broke with decorum and verbally attacked Broderick in the presence of ladies, was called a "dirty dog" in response, and, after printing a formal challenge at a local clerk's office, handed it to Broderick even before breakfast was over.[228] *The Los Angeles Herald* related that "Perley flared up and declared he would not stand by and hear his friend so abused and went so far as to say he would hold Mr. Broderick personally responsible for his language." In response, it was written that Broderick merely "flipped his hand at Perley and told him he didn't recognize him as an equal, but said he could send his master to him and he would settle the matter with him."[229] *The Ohio Democrat*'s account was that Perley was rebuffed with the words, "Sir, I only fight with gentlemen of my own positions."[230] The far-off *Wheeling Daily Register* noted that when Broderick uttered his criticism of Terry, Perley was busy chatting up several women at the table.[231] A Vermont paper, in recounting the incident, explained that Perley was a friend of both Terry and Broderick.[232] *The National Tribune* referred to Perley's challenge as "a bid for notoriety."[233] It reported that when Broderick declined Perley's challenge, he hesitated in sending a man to deliver the message for fear that an unhinged Perley "would inevitably assault or challenge the carrier." Congressman Joseph McKibben, it continued, volunteered to undertake the task, explaining that "if there was any trouble with Perley and anybody left the scene alive it would not be Perley." Within a month of the last report, a man claiming to have known both Terry and Perley was charging people admission for the privilege of hearing his tales of the two men in former times.[234]

***

227 *San Bernardino Daily Courier*, August 15, 1889.
228 *San Bernardino Daily Courier*, August 16, 1889.
229 *Los Angeles Herald*, August 15, 1889.
230 *Ohio Democrat*, August 24, 1889.
231 *Wheeling Daily Register*, August 16, 1889.
232 *Bennington Banner*, August 22, 1889.
233 *National Tribune*, August 22, 1889.
234 *Sullivan's Republic*, September 20, 1889.

Perley was now a part of history, and his role was defined, for all time it would seem. He was but an appendage to the larger story of frontier violence and the failure of some men to grow beyond the older ways and adapt to new circumstances. Forgotten was Perley's courage as a lawyer seeking justice for his clients in corrupt courtrooms and standing in the face of mobs howling for the blood of the criminally accused without respect for due process of law. Forgotten, too, was his role in shaping California's common law as a pioneering advocate in the State's Supreme Court, his near single-handed creation of State impeachment precedents, and his epic exploits in and out of the courtrooms of Nevada. Terry's death, however, hardly is to blame for the fixing of Perley's place in the narrative of the Far West's past. From the moment Broderick fell, Perley was destined for infamy for his part in the death of a man who would shortly become a symbol of resistance to the twin evils that afflicted the early Republic—slavery and secession. The news accounts of 1859 in time gave way to the first histories, and from that time onward, his role as the man who instigated the fateful duel was repeated and repeated, so that the essence of his humanity was reduced merely to that small moment in his entire lifetime, with no regard for his status as one of the great lawyers of the American frontier.

The first substantial history of the State, published as Perley was returning from Nevada to San Francisco, recounted his confrontation with Broderick at the breakfast table.[235] As precipitous at it was, it hardly marked the first time the incident had appeared in hard cover form. Already, foreign journalists, enamored with the seeming romance of the American West, had related Perley's distemper at the International Hotel, in French and German.[236] A short reference to the confrontation also appeared in a biographical profile of David Broderick in the pages of Horatio Bateman's *Biographies and Portraits of 250 Distinguished National Men* and Oscar

---

[235] Franklin Tuthill, *The History of California* (San Francisco: H.H. Bancroft & Company, 1866), at p. 553.

[236] Emile Laurent, *Histoire Anecdoitque du Duel, Dan Tous Les Temps et Dans Tous Les Pays* (Leipzig, 1861), at p. 248; and Israel Joseph Benjamin, *Drei Jahre in Amerika, 1859-1862* (Hanover: Gelbftverlag des Berfall, 1862), at p. 276.

Shuck's similar work, *Representative and Leading Men of the Pacific*.[237] Later that decade came John S. Hittell's *A History of the City of San Francisco and Incidentally of the State of California*, which again told of Perley's dispute with Broderick.[238]

In the early 1880s, two classic works appeared, again recounting the breakfast table spat: James O'Meara's *Broderick and Gwin*, and Benjamin Cummings Truman's colorful history of dueling throughout the world, *The Field of Honor*.[239] In 1888, Shuck's *Bench and Bar of California* and Bancroft's *California Inter Pocula* and *History of California, 1848-1859* appeared, in which Perley was remembered primarily for the Broderick confrontation.[240] Shuck's subsequent revision of the first of these volumes included the original references to Perley, but also several new anecdotes, including the near shoot-out with Harry Logan.[241] A year later, Hittell again reminded the public of Perley's challenge to Broderick in the pages of the *Overland Monthly*, but this time in the context of a critical review of Bancroft's hagiographic account of Senator Broderick. He defended Perley as the victim of "senseless fury" by the Senator, "inviting just punishment."[242]

Wagstaff's authorized biography of David Terry ought to have treated Perley's role in the Judge's life more extensively, but virtually all that Wagstaff had to say of Perley revolved around the

---

[237] *Biographies and Portraits of 250 Distinguished National Men* (New York: H. Bateman, 1870), at p. 110; and Oscar Shuck, *Representative and Leading Men of the Pacific* (San Francisco: Bacon and Company, 1870), at p. 393.

[238] John S. Hittell, *A History of the City of San Francisco and Incidentally of the State of California* (San Francisco: A.L. Bancroft & Company, 1878), at pp. 307-308.

[239] James O'Meara's *Broderick and Gwin* (San Francisco: Bacon & Company, 1881), at p. 227; and Benjamin Cummings Truman, *The Field of Honor* (New York: Fords, Howard & Hulbert, 1884), at pp. 394-395.

[240] Oscar Tully Shuck, *Bench and Bar in California: History, Anecdotes, Reminiscences* (San Francisco: The Occident Printing House, 1888; Hubert Howe Bancroft, *California Inter Pocula* (San Francisco: The History Company, 1888; and Hubert Howe Bancroft, *History of California*, Volume VI, 1848-1859 (San Francisco: The History Company, 1888.

[241] Oscar Tully Shuck, *A History of the Bench and Bar of California* (Los Angeles: The Commercial Printing House, 1901.

[242] John S. Hittell, "The Character of David C. Broderick," *The Overland Monthly*, Volume XIII (1889), No. 73, p. 105.

Broderick controversy.[243] An extended account of the Terry-Broderick duel appeared in the pages of the *Illustrated American* magazine in 1895, and again Perley's role instigating the matter was recounted.[244] Two years later, John Hittell's brother Theodore published his ornate and multi-volume history of the State, providing a short account of the squabble at the breakfast table and suggesting, quite falsely, that Perley's interest in challenging the Senator was to gain for himself "a position of great prominence."[245] Historian James Miller Guinn squeezed in a reference to Perley as a bit player in the roiling politics leading up to the Civil War, but recounted nothing of any real substance.[246] An old man now, Senator Stewart published his reminiscences in 1904, including his take on Terry's duel with Broderick, in the course of which he recalled Perley's pugnacious quality and his dissatisfaction lest he "could start a personal difficulty."[247] Thomas Samuel Duke's *Celebrated Criminal Cases of America* also regurgitated the traditional account.[248] Another jab at Perley came with Jeremiah Lynch's hagiography of Broderick. In telling the story of the meeting at the breakfast table, Lynch ignorantly explained that Perley "was an old and intimate friend" of Terry, "though his professional and personal standing had somewhat lessened since Terry was no longer his associate."[249] The noted writer Gertrude Atherton similarly referred to "a man named Perley" in her coverage of the incident, and repeated the tale that his motivation was "to wing his

---

[243] Alexander E. Wagstaff, *Life of David S. Terry: Presenting an Authentic, Impartial and Vivid History of his Eventful Life and Tragic Death* (San Francisco: Continental Publishing Company, 1892).

[244] Henry Austin, "Famous American Duels: Senator Broderick and Judge Terry," *The Illustrated American*, Volume XVIII, No. 284, July 27, 1895), at pp. 121-222.

[245] Theodore Henry Hittell, *History of California*, Volume IV (San Francisco: N.J. Stone & Company, 1897), at p. 222.

[246] James Guinn Miller, *History of the State of California and Biographical Record of Coast Counties, California* (Chicago: The Chapman Publishing Company, 1904), at p. 208.

[247] William M. Stewart, *Reminiscences of Senator William M. Stewart of Nevada* (New York: The Neale Publishing Company, 1908).

[248] Thomas Samuel Duke, *Celebrated Criminal Cases of America* (San Francisco: The James H. Barry Company, 1910), at p. 55.

[249] Jeremiah Lynch, *A Senator of the Fifties: David C. Broderick of California* (San Francisco: A.M. Robertson, 1911), at p. 203.

little name before the public camera."[250] A year later, the Fourth Volume of Zoeth Skinner Eldridge's *History of California*, an article by Michael Williams in the pages of *Pearson's Magazine*, and George Tinkham's *California: Men and Events* told the same old tale and nothing more—a fact that is especially surprising in Tinkham's case since Perley and the author were actually acquainted.[251] General Anson Mills referred to the tale, too, but his memoir lacks any indication that he possessed any but second hand knowledge.[252]

In the mid-1920s came Bailey Millard's *History of the San Francisco Bay Region* and *California and Californians* by Rockwell Hunt and Nellie Van de Grift Sanchez, which regurgitated as if by rote the old familiar story.[253] Jill Cossley Batt's *The Last of the California Rangers* referred to Perley merely as a "young man" who overheard Broderick's tirade.[254] The now standard blurb about the incident was reproduced in Catherine Coffin Phillips' *Portsmouth Plaza: The Cradle of San Francisco* and, remarkably, in Carroll Douglas Hall's exhaustive account of the duel itself.[255] The best opportunity for introduction of a more complete view of Perley came with the Huntington Library's publication of Albert Russell Buchanan's *David S. Terry of California: Dueling Judge*, but other than a few new yet superficial mentions of Perley's law practice with Terry and his role in assisting Terry financially in the wake of the duel, Buchanan's book disappoints both in its narrative style and

---

250 Gertrude Atherton, *California: An Intimate History* (New York: Harper & Brothers Publishers, 1914).

251 Zoeth Skinner Eldridge's *History of California*, Volume IV (The Century History Company, 1915), at p. 160; Michael Williams, "A Romance of San Francisco," *Pearson's Magazine*, Volume 33, No. 2 (February 1915), at p. 156; and George Tinkham, *California: Men and Events* (Stockton: Record Publishing Company, 1915), at p. 170.

252 Anson Mills, *My Story* (Washington, D.C.: Press of Byron S. Adams, 1918), at p. 347.

253 Millard, History of the San Francisco Bay Region, Volume 1 (American Historical Society, 1925), at p. 193; and Rockwell Hunt and Nellie Van de Grift Sanchez, *California and Californians*, Volume 2 (Lewis Publishing Company, 1926), at p. 271.

254 Jill Cossley Batt, *The Last of the California Rangers* (Funk & Wagnalls Company, 1928), at p. 287.

255 Catherine Coffin Phillips' *Portsmouth Plaza: The Cradle of San Francisco* (J.H. Nash, 1932), p. 371; and Carroll Douglas Hall, *The Terry-Broderick Duel* (Colt Press, 1939).

scope.[256] In 1963, Hamilton Cochran recapitulated in less elegant form Truman's *Field of Honor*, complete with an entirely predictable pastiche of Perley at the breakfast table. In the same year, the official account by the State Bar of the lives of the State's Supreme Court Justices, rather than providing a more thorough and useful profile of Terry's law practice in conjunction with Perley and Perley's role in his career, did what everyone writing on the subject had done before: that is, to mention Perley's momentary squabble with the Senator and nothing more.[257] Pop historian Lately Thomas, who'd produced entertaining tales of the Aimee Semple McPherson kidnapping, Mayor Gaynor of New York and the lobbyist Sam Ward, managed to do nothing new with the Perley narrative in his otherwise fine biography of Senator William Gwin.[258]

The first truly original presentation of Perley since his own lifetime occurred in the pages of *American State Trials*. In the Fifteenth Volume of this niche series appeared a detailed account of the Vigilance Committee's prosecution of Terry and a mention of Perley's appearance on Terry's behalf.[259] More recently, historians have retold the same old stories, and with it, Perley's marginal role in the duel, though one of them, Leonard L. Richards, embellished a truly remarkable element—that Perley was "an effeminate shill for the rich and wellborn."[260] Only Roxanne-Louise Nilan in *Politics for the Elephant: Gold, Power, and American Political Culture in California's Southern Mines, 1848-1854* and Nancy J. Taniguchi's *Dirty Deeds: Land, Violence and the 1856 San Francisco Vigilance Committee* have

256 Albert Russell Buchanan, *David S. Terry of California: Dueling Judge* (San Marino: The Huntington Library, 1956).

257 See Hamilton Cochran, *Noted American Duels and Hostile Encounters* (Chilton Books, 1963), p. 142; and J. Edward Johnson, *History of the Supreme Court Justices of California* (Bender-Moss, 1963), at p. 1839.

258 Lately Thomas, *Between Two Empires: the Life Story of California's First Senator, William McKendree Gwin* (Boston: Houghton Mifflin Co., 1969).

259 John David Lawson, *American State Trials*, Volume XV (Scholarly Resources, Inc., 1974).

260 Milton S. Gould, *A Cast of Hawks: A Rowdy Tale of Greed, Violence, Scandal and Corruption in the Chaotic Early Days of San Francisco* (Copley Books, 1985); Arthur Quinn, *The Rivals: William Gwin, David Broderick and the Birth of California Politics* (New York: Crown Publishers, Inc.: 1994); Donald R. Burrill, *Servants of the Law: Judicial Politics on the California Frontier, 1849-1889* (Lanham: University Press of America, 2010); and Leonard L. Richards, *The California Gold Rush and the Coming of the Civil War* (New York: Alfred A. Knopf, 2007).

provided anything new: a brief reference to Perley's relations with Benjamin Moore in Stockton, a mention of Perley's journey to California with Terry from Texas, and Perley's housing of Cornelia Terry during Judge Terry's captivity.[261] A rare critique of Perley's legal acumen came in Peter L. Reich's 1998 law review article touching on what the author characterized as the judicial destruction of the government's ownership of mining rights, even after title to public lands passed to individual settlers.[262] The critique, however, was hardly complimentary. Perley was accused of "novel" and incorrect arguments about Hispanic law, a failure to cite to appropriate legal authorities, and the "nebulous" invoking of guarantees set forth in the Treaty of Guadalupe Hidalgo. He was said by Reich to have joined Stephen Field as an engineer of the loss of a massive public domain that might, if retained, have provided the federal government with stronger power to protect the environment.[263]

The only other incident of Perley's life reported periodically over the years, but hardly so frequently as the Broderick matter, is the scandal involving Josephine Mansfield. Even prior to his death, the incident had found its way from the tabloids to hardcover. In the wake of the murder of James Fisk, New York journalist R. W. McAlpine published an account of the famed financier's life and death, and happened, in passing, to mention Warren's blackmailing operation.[264] Some years passed before another account appeared, but it was rather tame.[265] Modern and Post-Modern historians have occasionally found in the tale a repudiation of Victorian morality and a revelation of historic sex and gender repression, while others

---

261 Roxanne-Louise Nilan, *Politics for the Elephant: Gold, Power, and American Political Culture in California's Southern Mines, 1848-1854* (Stanford University Press, 1999) and Nancy J. Taniguchi's *Dirty Deeds: Land, Violence and the 1856 San Francisco Vigilance Committee* (Norman: University of Oklahoma Press, 2016).

262 Peter L. Reich, "Western Courts and the Privatization of Hispanic Mineral Rights Since 1850: An Alchemy of Title," 23 Colum. J. Envtl. L. 57.

263 For a discussion of Reich's critique, see the Appendix following this chapter.

264 R.W. McApline, *The Life and Times of Col. James Fisk, Jr.* (New York: The New York Book Company, 1872).

265 Amelia Ransome Neville, *The Fantastic City: Memoirs of the Social and Romantic Life of Old San Francisco* (Boston: Houghton Mifflin, 1932).

have characterized Perley as "lecherous."[266] The most recent reference occurs in the pages of the popular historian H. W. Brands' tale of the mighty Fisk's downfall.[267]

To those who remember him at all, Perley is a stock character in several moderately well-known events in American history: he played the young, irate, wealthy and insecure lawyer anxious for a level of notoriety his own merit was incapable of securing, and a lecherous middle aged man with wealth to spare, aspiring to get his hooks into a pretty young thing who proved far more clever than he by making him the first victim of her many shake downs of rich older men. Forgotten to even the well-informed reader is Perley's adventurous spirit that brought him from one of the remotest corners of British North America to the American frontier during the Antebellum Era, the physical courage and intellectual brilliance that allowed him to become a preeminent attorney in a violent place where some of the brightest legal talent on the continent assembled at the prompting of the Gold Rush. Lost to memory, too, are the important cases he handled—the first capital case appealed to the California Supreme Court, the Roach matter, the Mariposas, the first defense in a State impeachment trial, his ingenious effort to free Judge Terry during the Vigilance disturbance, the sage of the Bird's Nest, the Swaney-Seale prosecution, and *Raymond & Ely vs. Hermes*, among others—the relations he built with great and influential people wherever he went, the caliber of men with whom he formally and informally practiced law—from Hall McAllister to Thomas Fitch—the grand geographic scope of his practice, requiring frequent resort to stage and rail to manage the legal interests of his clients, and, finally, his ambitions as a real estate magnate and mining developer. Perley never held high office like the great lawyers in the American tradition, hence his contributions, like those of so many other able and influential advocates, have fallen prey to oblivion. The law of California and the West, however, was not made merely by the great men who filled public

---

[266] J. North Conway, *The King of Heists: The Sensational Bank Robbery of 1878 that Shocked America* (Guilford: the Pequot Press, 2009; Barbara Goldsmith, *Other Powers: The Age of Suffrage, Spiritualism, and the Scandalous Victoria Woodhull* (New York: Knopf, 1998).

[267] H.W. Brands, *The Murder of Jim Fisk For the Love of Josie Mansfield: A Tragedy of the Gilded Age* (New York: Anchor Books, 2011).

offices in the early and middling years of the region's history. It was made by men like Perley: ambitious, courageous, perhaps temperamental and arrogant at times, yet supremely learned and prepared to fight for honor as quickly as they fought for their clients on matters of important fact or principle of law. In the West's unsettled early days, when the law was virtually non-existent, it was men like Perley who made the closing of the frontier possible and permitted a further elaboration that in time created a gulf between the law as it is and the law as it was at the beginning. We do well to remember those like Duncan Wellington Perley who contributed so much and whose lives were additionally so remarkable in incident, romance and color. The past is not mere bones, but the bones of men and women whose hearts beat and lungs exhaled, and who, when recalling the surviving historical record, can be said to have lived not merely a life from day to day until their demise, but a life worthy of the name.

***

In the early Twentieth Century, the California State Library in Sacramento began collecting data about pioneers as the last of that breed were nearing the end of their days. To facilitate the transfer of information, cards were issued allowing the respondents to provide basic information about a particular person. In 1916, the library received an interesting card about D. W. Perley, "a pioneer of '49 and one of California's most brilliant lawyers."[268] The card was supplied by his nephew, and noted that "he was attorney for the principle law cases in his day, and won fees as high as $30,000." Squeezed onto the back of the card was the comment provided to the correspondent by his uncle's sometime friend, frequent opponent, and the last man he challenged to a duel, Harry I. Thornton. The antagonisms of the past having faded, Thornton summed up Perley with the high compliment that he was, of all the great lawyers of the Far West, "the best versed man in law in California at his time."[269]

---

268 *News Notes of California Libraries*, Volume 11, No. 4, October 1916 (California: State Printing Office, 1916), at p. 1153.

269 "D.W. Perley," *Pioneer Index File: 1906-1934*, California History Room, California State Library, Sacramento, California.

Appendix

D.W. PERLEY AND THE DEMISE OF PUBLIC SUBSURFACE LAND "RIGHTS"

A 1998 law review article addressed the reputedly willful disregard by American lawyers and judges in the mid-Nineteenth Century of the Treaty of Guadalupe Hidalgo's guarantee of public rights to minerals in the soil, and specifically identified D. W. Perley while in the service of John C. Fremont as a primary culprit in the process that led to a shift of mineral rights from the public sector to the private. "This disregard for applicable precedent," said the article's author, the very learned Peter L. Reich, "promoted industrial entrepreneurship at the expense of public resource access and of the environment."[1] The critique by Professor Reich is consistent with the disdain for private enterprise and a burgeoning love for central planning harbored by an academic and legal class that so often finds itself in the service of the state. It is no wonder that these cadres tend to view the Judge who ruled in Fremont's favor in response to Perley's argument as among the worst justices who have occupied seats on the bench of the United States Supreme Court.[2] Perley was bad enough, but a sympathetic Stephen Field rendered his argument lethal to the modern-day longing for state control of natural resources and a drastic reduction of property rights.

Of Perley's brief in the *Biddle Boggs* case, Professor Reich said it presented the "entirely novel contention" that Civil or Roman law "had originally considered minerals within private grants to belong to the landowner," but that this changed when mines were "'seized under various pretenses by the sovereigns of Spain,' and Mexico," which Perley characterized as "despotic ordinances."[3] Perley, he explained, "went on to assert that 'these prerogative laws' were

---

[1] Peter L. Reich, "Western Courts and the Privatization of Hispanic Mineral Rights Since 1850: An Alchemy of Title," 23 Colum. J. Envtl. 57, 58.

[2] See, for instance, Ian Millhiser, "The Five Worst Supreme Court Justices in American History, Ranked," Think Progress [https://archive.thinkprogress.org], March 24, 2015.

[3] Reich, op. cit., at 71

inconsistent with U.S. policy, that they were annulled by the conquests,' and that 'the civil law became necessarily revived,' but cited no authority other than the supposedly obsolete Hispanic legal sources."[4]

Reich's criticism of Perley and of Field appears to be too one-sided to be the result of a truly critical evaluation of their handiwork, for it ignores most of Perley's argument in the case, including the chief portions of it, which centered on the incompatibility of Mexican law with the United States Constitution and the barrier the Constitution posed to rights and obligations utterly foreign to it. That the Treaty Power could surmount such a barrier no one can reasonably believe. It is well settled, said one expert on the federal government's foreign affairs power, "that treaties are subject to the constitutional limitation that apply to all exercises of federal power, principally the prohibitions of the Bill of Rights."[5] The limitation has been identified, among others, by Stephen Field himself, who observed that the treaty power as expressed in the Constitution was unlimited "except by those restraints which are found in that instrument against the action of the government or of its departments, and those arising from the nature of the government itself and of that of the States."[6] The question of whether Perley was incorrect in disdaining the effect of the Treaty of Guadalupe Hidalgo, thus, turns on whether the Treaty interfered with rights protected by the Constitution. Field, of course, opted to avoid that question in his decision in *Biddle Boggs*, perhaps in order to prevent the creation of a federal question which might have served as a jurisdictional basis for an appeal to the Supreme Court of the United States. Instead, his opinion rested on the far narrower grounds that allowing unrestricted access by miners to the subterranean public domain would wreck havoc on the rights of those possessing unquestioned title to the surface.

That Field was correct cannot be doubted. The regime endorsed by Professor Reich incorporating the traditional Hispanic view of mineral rights itself was unworkable from the outset. After the federal government's abandonment of claims to a portion of all gold

[4] Id., at 71-72.

[5] Louis Henkin, *Foreign Affairs and the Constitution* (New York: W.W. Norton & Company, 1975), p. 137.

[6] *Geofroy v. Riggs* (1890) 133 U.S. 258, 267.

and silver in the ground before the Gold Rush and the military administration's abolition of any Mexican law governing mines in California,[7] the former legal regime was recreated through enactment by the legislature of the Possessory Acts of 1850 and 1852. The two Acts barred settlement for agricultural purposes on lands where mines might be located, and permitted access by miners to settled land if minerals were discovered subsequent to settlement. As noted by Charles McCurdy, when miners began sinking shafts on planted land claimed by agricultural settlers, destroying crops and rendering the land unprofitable for any purpose other than mining, an uproar reached the ears of California courts in a myriad of suits filed during the 1850s. A law that permitted the destruction of the productive investment of lawful settlers simply couldn't withstand scrutiny guided by equity and rights at common law, especially when the settlers were utterly unaware of the presence of any mineral wealth beneath their feet at the time of their first location.[8] The first court decisions, Reich is correct, favored the mining interests, but did so without any weighing of competing rights, or any indication that those who destroyed what others built were obligated to reimburse their victims for the loss. A remedy came in the form of the Indemnification Act of 1855, but even this was considered by many settlers as inadequate to protect the value of their investments in the land. The Field Court was in part a reaction to the undue favor shown to mining interests by the State, and its decisions reflect an impulse to protect the prior rights of actual settlers from miners whose tendency was to disregard anything save the putative riches under the soil. The values guiding Field were constitutional: the takings prohibition and the Due Process Clause, in addition to principles of vested rights traceable to the jurisprudence of the Marshall Court. Criticizing the Field Court's shift in favor of surface owners as the "flouting" of Hispanic law, the English Common Law as championed by the High Tory William Blackstone and the Treaty

---

[7] Karen Clay & Gavin Wright, "Gold Rush Legacy: American Minerals and the Knowledge Economy," in *Property in Land and Resources* (Cambridge, Mass: Lincoln Institute of Land Policy, 2012), at p. 69.

[8] Charles W. McCurdy, "Stephen J. Field and Public Land Law Development in California, 1850-1866: A Case Study of Judicial Resource Allocation in Nineteenth-Century America," *Law & Society Review*, Vol. 10, No. 2 (1976), at p. 247.

of Guadalupe Hidalgo ignores the fundamental conflict between those sources and the rights of property owners in a real world organized for the benefit of free citizens governed by a written constitution. That Field was correct is less relevant perhaps than the fact he was never overruled, either by the California Supreme Court or the Supreme Court of the United States. The probability is that he was not overruled because the policy he wove from the contradictory and uncertain strands of Mexican, State and Federal Statutes, International Law, the Common Law and the Constitution was considered by the people and the courts to represent an appropriate balancing of the rights of competing users of the land and competing claimants to its resources.

What Field ultimately decided in the latter case of *Moore and Fremont v. Smaw* was in essence what Perley himself had argued in *Biddle Boggs*. That decision did indeed reject what Professor Reich correctly identifies as a Common Law reservation of subsurface ownership of gold and silver to the state. The English Common Law tradition, however, was a royalist one, rooted in the Middle Ages, designed to promote the state's war making ability, and hardly consistent with a government that expressly rejected royalism and royal prerogatives in order to promote the happiness of the sovereign people. The Common Law was the law of California, but only to the extent it was formally received by the legislature, and it remained ever subject to revision, either by the legislature itself, or by the actions of courts exercising their ancient common law prerogative of judicial review. In exercising that prerogative, the courts were obligated to obey the higher law, including acts of Congress, treaties and the Constitution. Where any mere act of Congress or even a treaty conflicted with the Constitution, there was no question of which took precedence over the other. With respect to treaties, they certainly were to be followed as the law of the land, but if they entailed a dispossession of fundamental rights protected by the Constitution they were void. This was the view of Justice Field himself when he assumed a seat on the United States Supreme Court, and it is the view of the Court to this day.

It was undoubtedly true that Spain and Mexico reserved mineral rights when granting title to land, but the reservation was for the state itself, not the people, hence the argument championed by Reich is one that Fremont's opponents themselves rejected. They contended that they had a general license to enter the public lands of the United States, whether granted to landowners or not, in order to extract mineral wealth from the soil. Neither Blackstone nor the jurists of New Spain would have agreed with this monstrosity, hence it is to be doubted that Fremont's opponents believed it either. What former U.S. Attorney S. W. Inge and the rest of Fremont's opponents seemed to believe was that while the king was dead, the king's prerogatives belonged to the people themselves as sovereign citizens. The disingenuous convenience of bolstering this point with reference to the Spanish imperial prerogative to exercise ownership over all mineral rights in the realm is evident when pondering some hypothetical effort by the People's representatives in Washington, D.C., as the sovereign successors of King George and the Spanish Main, to restrict access to mineral rights, say on behalf of the environment. In such a scenario it is not to be doubted that Inge and his clients would have protested vigorously.

The Treaty issue being one complicated by the Treaty's apparent conflict with the rights of surface owners of the land, and the competing arguments for control of the sub-surface layers being reflective in part of the tremendous uncertainty that existed in the law at the time, it is perhaps unnecessary to pursue the issue any further. However, even if Professor Reich is correct that the Treaty had to be respected, it does not follow that only those rights guaranteed by the Treaty were worthy of respect, or that the government could not extend protection beyond them. The rights the Professor preferred to have been guaranteed to landowners were those existing in the surface of the land alone. Because Spanish law did not vest rights to mines with surface owners, he attests that those rights were not included in the guarantee. The argument is plainly incorrect. The Treaty provision at issue was designed primarily to protect the former citizens of Mexico from being dispossessed of their properties by the new sovereign. While these landowners might have only owned the surface in accordance with Mexican law, there was nothing in the Treaty that barred either the State or the federal government, acting either legislatively or judicially, from providing protections beyond what the Treaty required. In a sense, Perley's argument and Field's decision favored an extension of rights beyond what the Treaty mandated, and in this there was no violation of the Treaty.

Of course, it might be argued that the guarantee of rights embodied in the Treaty extended to the government's exercise of ownership over the minerals in the ground. What this hypothetical argument assumes to be a right, however, isn't exactly a right, at least not in the sense that the term was understood during the first century of the Republic. Generally speaking, governments were not seen as capable of possessing rights. They possessed powers and prerogatives, yes, but not rights. Rights, at least legal and constitutional rights, are historically defined as limitations on government's sovereign authority. As rights deprive governments of power and prerogative, governments were not seen as able to exercise or enjoy them. Some scholars have pointed out the use of the term "right" from an early age to describe the lawful powers of the state, but such usage is rare and tended to arise in the context of conflicts between the state and its contracting parties and the exercise of sovereign authority by a government when operating against other governments.[9] That Justice Iredel in 1797 thought it fair to describe the enforcement of a promise made to the federal government by an individual as the enforcement of a "right," or that Chief Justice Marshall similarly characterized the sovereign authority of the federal government in a state of war "to tempt the navigators of enemy-vessels to bring them into the American ports," is no firm or reasonable foundation on which to base the contention that in making a treaty with Mexico to guarantee rights in the land possessed by former subjects of the Mexican government the drafters were actually intending to transfer an imperial prerogative that transformed private interests in property into but a thin veneer of fee. That wasn't what those who drafted the Treaty intended, nor was it the intent of the Senate when the Treaty was ratified. Any public right to ownership of the subsurface layers of private property would have to await, to use Perley's phrase, more modern "despotic ordinances."

[9] Eugene Volokh, "Government Rights: Yes, Governments Do Have Rights, Not Just Powers," https://reason.com/volokh/2018/01/11/government-rights.

ACKNOWLEDGMENT

The path followed in the creation of this work has been long and crooked. Commencing in Fredericton, at the Provincial Archives of New Brunswick (PANB), a scholarly road to Emmaus led this author first to California and the historical research room at the old San Diego Central Library on 820 E Street, and then to Northern California, where rich repositories of records were discovered at the San Bruno branch of the National Archives, the Bancroft Library (BANC) on the Berkeley campus of the University of California, the Sutro Library in San Francisco, the Superior Court of San Joaquin County, the Stockton Public Library, the California State Archives and the State Library in the City of Sacramento. From thence, the road forked, to Carson City on the one hand, and to Texas on the other. Whether in New Brunswick or California, or at the Nevada Historical Society in Reno, the Nevada State Library and State Archives (NSA) in Carson City, or at the Texas State Library in Austin, or at various record facilities in the Lone Star State, numerous professional librarians and archivists whose names were never known or have long been forgotten assisted me with my research and lent me aid that perhaps one day I can pass on to others, who may, in all justice, forget that it was I who aided them.

Equally helpful in the effort to recreate the life and law practice of my subject has been the remarkable and very recent emergence of the internet as a scholar's paradise. Google and archive.org, for instance, have provided a grand public archive of many historic newspapers, as well as a library of books long out of print on many relevant historical and legal topics. Numerous on-line repositories of digitalized newspapers have proven especially helpful and made up for the dearth of manuscript collections and letters touching upon the life of Duncan Perley. I note with special gratitude the California Digital Newspaper Collection operated by the University of California at Riverside, the Smithsonian Institute's Chronicling America on-line database of digital newspapers, Tom Tryniski's Old Fulton NY Post Cards site, and the massive collection of digitalized papers offered by newspapers.com. JSTOR's digital library of academic journal articles saved much time that might have been spent less productively combing the dusty stacks at university libraries. Ancestry.com and familysearch.org were especially helpful in providing the source material for reconstructing Duncan Perley's antecedents, the antecedents of his wife, and the precise kinship between Perley and his many relations, both in New Brunswick and the American West.

There are several people whose names are remembered who provided aid to me that I must acknowledge. My friend from decades ago, and my friend still, Michael Martino, helped find me a job in Northern California so I could be closer to my primary source material. My sister Kim hosted me on a research trip to Texas at a time when she was living in Houston. My friend, Eddie Vodrazka, generously housed me during many research trips to Sacramento and even obtained for me a ticket for a seat on a bus to Nevada known among devotees of games of chance as "The Gambler Express." Instead of attending the casinos with my fellow travelers, I made my way to the State Archives.

I must also thank my friends and fellow lawyers Jeff Scharfen, and Andrew Quinn. Jeff and Andrew both read drafts of the manuscript, offered criticism, as well as their aid as proof readers. Finally, there is the woman to whom I dedicate this book, Becky Beissmann. For the crucial months during which the chapters of the volume took shape after so long a period of gestation, she was there, providing assistance in the daily processes of life, encouragement to my efforts, and hopes for my ultimate success in the attainment of a goal long in the making and now, at last, fulfilled.

FAMILY OF D.W. PERLEY

With Reference to Political Offices Held and Lines of Living Descendants In the United States and Western Canada

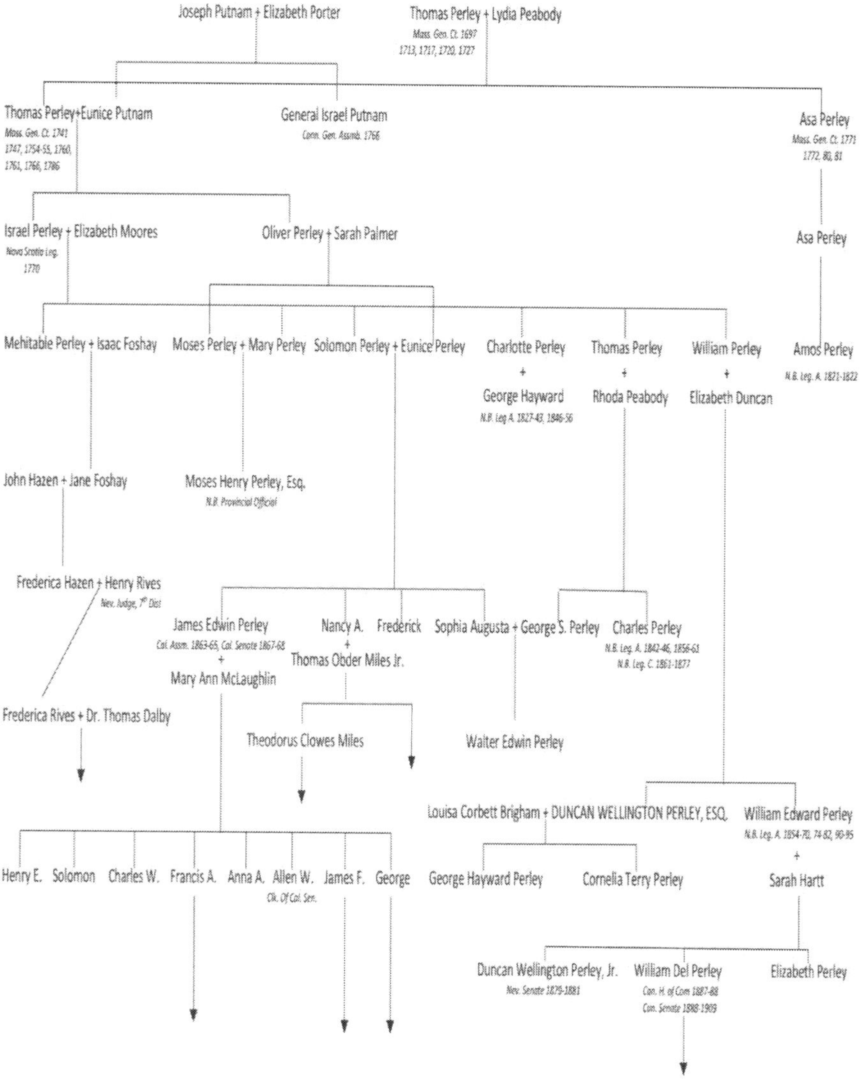

D.W. PERLEY'S RELATIONSHIP TO NEW BRUNSWICK'S RULING ELITE
Members of Provincial Supreme Court in Bold

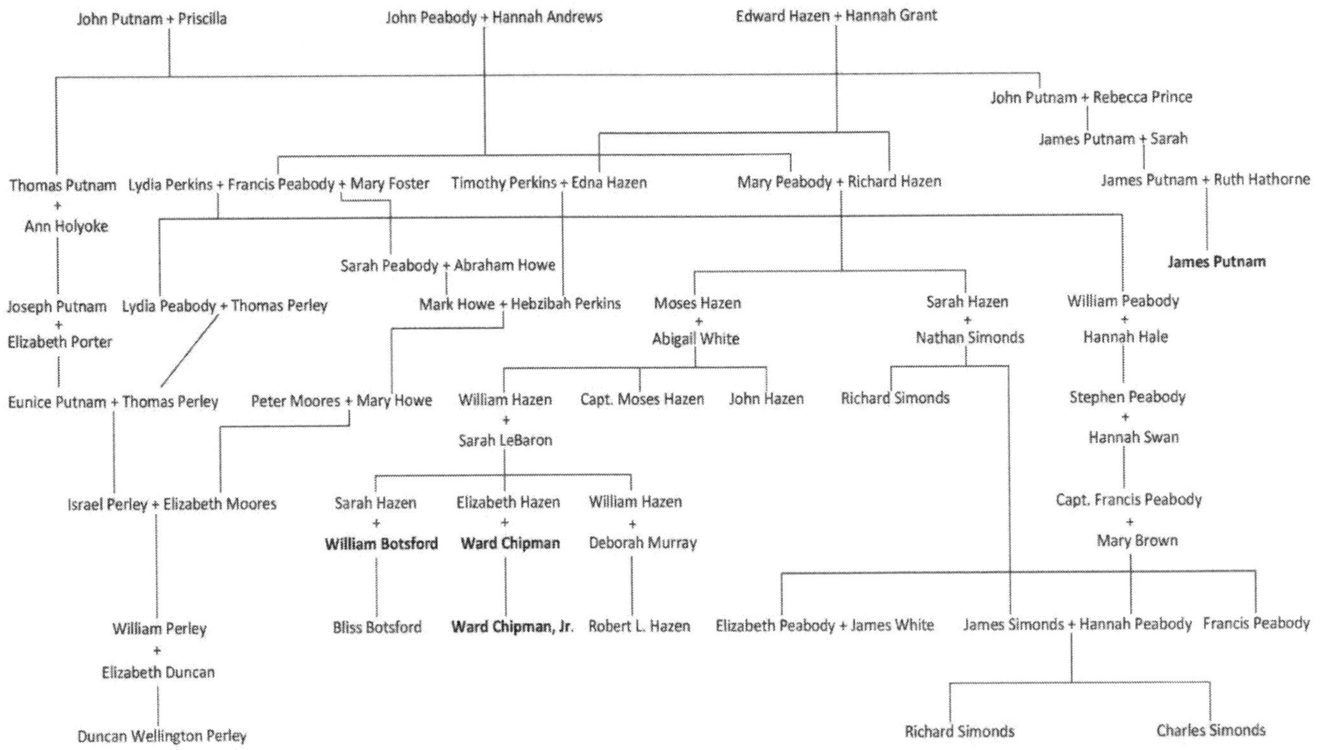

INDEX

ABOUT THE AUTHOR

Rex Grady is a native of California and a graduate of the University of California at San Diego, the University of New Brunswick (Canada), and Empire College School of Law in Santa Rosa, California. He possesses B.A., M.A., M.A. and J.D. degrees from those institutions. He is a trial lawyer and, since the year 2007, Professor of Constitutional Law and Legal History at Empire College. In addition to this book, he is the author of *Oromocto Adieu: Four Decades on the River and the Origins of North Lake Parish; Let Ocean Seethe and Terra Slide: A History of the Sonoma Coast and the State Park that Shares its Name*; the two volume *Cases & Controversies: A Student's Guide to Law School Exams in Constitutional Law; What is this Freedom?: Law, Faith and History in the Time of Trump*, and *Covid Days: A Further Chronicle of Law, Faith and History in the Time of Trump*. He lives in Santa Rosa, California with his wife and children.

Made in United States
Troutdale, OR
11/03/2026

56847586R00312